Divided Kingdom A History of Britain, 1900 to the Present

Divided Kingdom brings new clarity and breadth of treatment to the subject, integrating political, economic, social and cultural history alongside the international and imperial context. Highlighting changing living standards and expectations and inequalities of class, income, wealth, race, gender, sexuality, religion and place, this book analyses what has (and has not) changed in the United Kingdom since 1900, why, and how, helping the reader to understand how contemporary Britain, including its divisions and inequalities, was formed.

Exploring what has divided the United Kingdom and what has held it together, and challenging conventional interpretations, such as the 'dull' and culturally conservative 1950s and the 'swinging sixties', key themes include nationalisms, the rise and fall of the 'welfare state', economic success and failure, social movements challenging the status quo, the decline of colonialism and its impact, and relations with Europe.

PAT THANE is a Research Professor in Contemporary British History at King's College London. Previously Professor of Contemporary History at the University of Sussex and the Institute of Historical Research, University of London, she has been a Visiting Professor in New York, China, Australia, Japan, Taiwan and Chile. She is also a convenor of History and Policy and President of the Social History Society UK and a Fellow of the British Academy.

Divided Kingdom
A History of Britain, 1900 to the Present

Pat Thane
University of London

CAMBRIDGE
UNIVERSITY PRESS

CAMBRIDGE
UNIVERSITY PRESS

University Printing House, Cambridge CB2 8BS, United Kingdom

One Liberty Plaza, 20th Floor, New York, NY 10006, USA

477 Williamstown Road, Port Melbourne, VIC 3207, Australia

314–321, 3rd Floor, Plot 3, Splendor Forum, Jasola District Centre, New Delhi – 110025, India

79 Anson Road, #06–04/06, Singapore 079906

Cambridge University Press is part of the University of Cambridge.

It furthers the University's mission by disseminating knowledge in the pursuit of education, learning, and research at the highest international levels of excellence.

www.cambridge.org
Information on this title: www.cambridge.org/9781107040915
DOI: 10.1017/9781139644310

First published 2018

Printed in the United States of America by Sheridan Books, Inc.

A catalogue record for this publication is available from the British Library.

ISBN 978-1-107-04091-5 Hardback
ISBN 978-1-107-61250-1 Paperback

Contents

Abbreviations

AEGIS	Aid to the Elderly in Government Institutions
ALRA	Abortion Law Reform Association
ANC	African National Congress
ATS	Auxiliary Territorial Service
AWS	all-women shortlists
BIPO	British Institute of Public Opinion
BMA	British Medical Association
BME	or BAME (black and minority ethnic)
BP	British Petroleum
BSE	Bovine Spongiform Encephalopathy
BT	British Telecommunications
BUF	British Union of Fascists
CARD	Campaign Against Racial Discrimination
CHE	Campaign for Homosexual Equality
CEO	Chief Executive Officer
CPAG	Child Poverty Action Group
CRC	Community Relations Commission
CRE	Commission for Racial Equality
DEA	Department of Economic Affairs
DHSS	Department of Health and Social Security
DIG	Disablement Income Group
DLRU	Divorce Law Reform Union
DORA	Defence of the Realm Act
DP	displaced person
DSIR	Department of Industrial and Scientific Research
DSS	Department of Social Security
DUP	Democratic Unionist Party
ECHR	European Convention on Human Rights
ECtHR	European Court of Human Rights
EEC	European Economic Community
EMS	European Monetary System

EOC	Equal Opportunities Commission
EPCC	Equal Pay Campaign Committee
ERM	(European) Exchange Rate Mechanism
EU	European Union
FIS	Family Income Supplement
FOE	Friends of the Earth
GLC	Greater London Council
GLF	Gay Liberation Front
HP	hire purchase
HRA	Human Rights Act
IBA	Independent Broadcasting Authority
ILEA	Inner London Education Authority
ILO	International Labour Organization
ILP	Independent Labour Party
IMF	International Monetary Fund
IND	Immigration and Nationality Directorate
IRA	Irish Republican Army
JSA	Job Seekers Allowance
KC	King's Counsel
LCC	London County Council
LGB	Local Government Board
LNU	League of Nations Union
LRC	Labour Representation Committee
LSE	London School of Economics
MBA	Masters in Business Administration
MIG	Minimum Income Guarantee
MO	Mass Observation
MoD	Ministry of Defence
MOD	Ministry of Overseas Development
MOH	Medical Officer of Health
NAB	National Assistance Board
NALGO	National Association of Local Government Employees
NATO	North Atlantic Treaty Organization
NCB	National Coal Board
NCCL	National Council for Civil Liberties
NCEC	National Council for Equal Citizenship
NCUMC	National Council for the Unmarried Mother and her Child
NCW	National Council of Women
NHI	National Health Insurance

NHS	National Health Service
NRDC	National Research and Development Corporation
NUM	National Union of Mineworkers
NUPE	National Union of Public Employees
NUR	National Union of Railwaymen
NUSEC	National Union of Societies for Equal Citizenship
NUWSS	National Union of Women's Suffrage Societies
NVLA	National Viewers and Listeners Association
OPF	One-Parent Families
OPCS	Office of Population Census and Surveys
OWAAD	Organization of Women of Asian and African Descent
PAC	Public Assistance Committee
PAL	Paedophile Action for Liberation
PAYE	Pay As You Earn
PC	Pension Credit
PEP	Political and Economic Planning
PFI	Private Finance Initiative
POW	Prisoner of War
PR	proportional representation
QC	Queen's Counsel
RAR	Rock against Racism
RRA	Race Relations Act
RRB	Race Relations Board
RSPCA	Royal Society for the Prevention of Cruelty to Animals
RSPB	Royal Society for the Protection of Birds
RUC	Royal Ulster Constabulary
SBC	Supplementary Benefits Commission
SDF	Social Democratic Federation
SDLP	Social Democratic and Labour Party
SDP	Social Democratic Party
SERPS	State Earnings Related Pension Scheme
SHRG	Scottish Homosexual Reform Group
SNP	Scottish National Party
SPUC	Society for the Protection of Unborn Children
TGWU	Transport and General Workers' Union
TUC	Trades Union Congress
UAB	Unemployment Assistance Board
UCS	Upper Clyde Shipbuilders
UDA	Ulster Defence Association

UDC	Union of Democratic Control
UDI	unilateral declaration of independence
UN	United Nations
USSR	Union of Soviet Socialist Republics
VAD	Voluntary Aid Detachment
WAAC	Women's Army Auxiliary Corps
WAF	Women's Aid Foundation
WCA	Women Citizens' Association
WCG	Women's Co-operative Guild
WEA	Workers' Educational Association
WHO	World Health Organization
WI	Women's Institute
WLL	Women's Labour League
WLM	Women's Liberation Movement
WRAF	Women's Royal Air Force
WRNS	Women's Royal Naval Service
WSPU	Women's Social and Political Union
WVS	Women's Voluntary Service

Introduction

History helps us to understand the puzzles of the contemporary world by exploring how they came about. This book aims to convey the fascination of recent history for its own sake and to assist understanding of the present by offering a clear, reasonably comprehensive account of British history since around 1900 and its contribution to creating the present-day United Kingdom. It seeks to integrate the histories of politics, national and international, the economy, society, ideas, science, technology and culture, some more expertly than others. It is impossible to compartmentalize these or to neglect any of them if we wish to describe, analyse and understand as fully as possible the complex changes, continuities and discontinuities of this fast-moving period. They intersect and they have all mattered. The broadening of perspectives on history as, from the 1920s, economic history, then, from the 1960s, social then cultural history, became prominent alongside political history, has massively enriched our capacity to understand the past and the present. But history, especially recent history, is constantly revised as new sources come to light and perspectives change as events move on. Historical understanding, like understanding of the present, is always provisional and open to challenge. This book conveys how the recent past looked to one historian in 2017.

The starting point is 1900 because important issues and movements became prominent around that time and did not go away but survived to influence future events profoundly. In 1900, Britain was involved in a war to protect and extend her imperial authority in southern Africa, the Anglo-Boer War, in which the mighty British imperial army was in difficulties against relatively inexperienced opposition. It eventually won, but the experience was a warning of growing challenges to the Empire which continued and intensified, leading to intense debates and differences within Britain about the future of Empire and rapid decolonization after the Second World War, with considerable impact on Britain's status and influence in the world. Its relations with other European powers were tense in 1900, due mainly to competition for colonial control, but Britain soon judged it wise to ally with two leading European nations, France and Russia, as Germany emerged as a potential threat to them all, a threat realized with the coming of war in 1914. It also sought close relations with the United States, which was emerging as the strongest power in the international economy and politics, and reached an agreement with Japan, the first Asian country to become globally significant, militarily and economically, in the modern world. International economic growth, particularly in the United States and Germany, reinforced British fears of economic decline as the first industrial nation encountered successful competition.

Imperial confidence, and the very unity of the United Kingdom, was further challenged in these years by intensified demands by the Catholic majority of the population of Ireland for independence, resisted equally militantly by the Protestant minority in the north of Ireland. This led, from 1922, to the division of Ireland between an independent state in the south and the north which remained within the United Kingdom, though tensions between Nationalists and Unionists in Northern Ireland continued into the twenty-first century, especially explosively in the final quarter of the twentieth century. Around 1900 nationalism was also growing in Wales and Scotland, as the increasing centralization of power in Westminster threatened their cultural distinctiveness and capacities for self-determination. It led to, and survived, devolution of substantial domestic powers to elected governments in both countries from 1998, to some degree stimulating nationalist sentiments in England. The unity of the United Kingdom was even more in question in 2017 than in 1900.

Contemplating the beginning of the twentieth century from the standpoint of 2017, there are other striking similarities. Both major political parties, Conservatives and Liberals, opposed state 'intervention' in the economy on the grounds that it would undermine free enterprise and hamper economic growth, and resisted state action to improve social conditions because they believed it would threaten the assumed moral responsibility of all healthy individuals to work hard and provide for all the needs of themselves and their families, which was believed to be universally feasible. In the early twenty-first century, similar ideas – now labelled 'neoliberalism' – were again politically powerful, after being seriously challenged from the early twentieth century. In the early 1900s many Conservatives came to believe that Britain's economic power could be protected only by government intervening, as their successful rivals did, to impose taxes ('tariffs') on imports to raise their prices relative to British-produced goods in the home market. Tariffs, as proposed by Joseph Chamberlain, their leading advocate, would also preserve the Empire by including the colonies within a tariff wall. 'Tariff reform' became a major issue in early-twentieth-century politics, pitting the Conservatives against the Liberals who remained committed to free trade.

Another challenge to classic liberal ideology emerged when the Labour Party was formed in 1900, committed to creating a fair economy and a more equal society through increased state action in the interests of the mass of disadvantaged, hard-working people. At the same time, trade unions made more militant demands for better pay and conditions, leading some to fear imminent revolution, though the unions represented only a minority of skilled workers and had limited influence and no evident desire to overthrow the state. Rather, they helped to bring about the moderate, reforming, non-revolutionary Labour Party.

Classic liberalism was also seriously challenged by the shocking levels of poverty revealed by major poverty surveys conducted by Charles Booth and Seebohm Rowntree at the turn of the century, including among people in full-time work, in what was then the richest country in the world. Low pay in full-time work and underemployment, that is, the inability of people who wanted full-time work to find anything but precarious part-time jobs, were significant causes of poverty, especially for larger families, resulting in extensive child poverty that seriously limited children's life chances. Another out-come was a desperate shortage of decent housing for poorer families, who, if they could find a home, too often lived in overcrowded, insanitary 'slums' because they could not afford anything better. The revelations, together with pressure from the labour move-ment and from Liberals, philanthropists and the growing number of women activists troubled by what they saw and heard of social conditions, created demands for state action to support people whose poverty was clearly not their own fault. This led to the unintentional beginnings of a 'welfare state' when a Liberal government from 1906 introduced the first state pensions, together with national insurance and other reforms, including a more redistributive taxation system to fund the extension of state action.

State welfare expanded thereafter, especially after 1945, and was one of the major developments of the twentieth century, which partially survived into the twenty-first century, though it was much attenuated from the 1980s following the international surge of neoliberalism. This also led the state to withdraw as far as possible from regula-tion of the economy, which had also increased through the century. Successive further poverty surveys from the 1980s into the early twenty-first century showed poverty and income and wealth inequality returning to levels comparable with the 1900s following decades of decline. Again, a high proportion of poverty was among low-paid, full-time employees and insecure underemployed workers not guaranteed minimum weekly hours, often due to what are known, and widely criticized, as 'zero-hours' contracts. About 17 per cent of all children in Great Britain were found to be in poverty in 2015, and the number was rising. Homelessness and inadequate supply of affordable homes for people on low incomes were again major problems after receding from the 1920s to the 1970s. The size and influence of the unions, which had peaked to include more than half the workforce in the 1970s, so enabling them to gain improvements in wage and working conditions, dwindled following government restrictions and the decline of manufacturing and they could do little to help. The Labour Party became and remained one of the two major parties, with the Conservatives, after the decline of the Liberals from the First World War. It achieved real social and economic improvement while in government after 1945, but could not, as it hoped, gain consistent support from enough voters to sustain these achievements. Why it could not do so when so many benefited is a central question to be tackled below. In government again, under the neoliberal-inclined 'New Labour' from 1997 to 2010, it again temporarily reduced poverty and improved health and other state services, following cuts by its Conservative predecessors, but inequality between the richest and the poorest continued to expand, and it could not prevent a reversion to welfare cuts and further increases in poverty under its successors.

Income and wealth disparity and their outcomes were not the only inequalities challenged with new and lasting vigour from the first years of the twentieth century. Women campaigned for equality with men ever more outspokenly, especially demanding the vote, believing it would be the key to greater change. They gained the vote and change followed, but so gradually and incompletely that they are still campaigning in the twenty-first century against discrimination and for equal pay and work opportunities, equal legal rights and equal respect with men, among other inequities.

Public antagonism to immigrants was another lasting issue that was prominent around 1900, when it was directed at the largest immigrant group of the period, Jewish refugees fleeing persecution in the Russian Empire. Protests led in 1905 to the first official restrictions on immigration and access to British nationality. Racist intolerance and restrictions on immigration went on growing, especially from the 1960s as an increasingly diverse immigrant community expanded. Racist opposition persisted, as did organized support for tolerance and racial equality, leading to the first laws against racial discrimination in the 1960s. But racial tensions remain at least as powerful in the second decade of the twenty-first century as they were in 1900.

These strong similarities and continuities between the early twentieth and early twenty-first centuries demand analysis and explanation. They suggest profound, lasting divisions and inequalities within the United Kingdom. Exploring the reality and the experiences and perceptions of these and other inequalities, which always existed but emerged into public discourse only later in the century, examining what promoted and constrained them, and the origins and impact of campaigns to eliminate them, is a major theme of this book. The persistence or recurrence of certain inequalities is all the more striking because, as well as the significant similarities, there were also profound differences affecting all aspects of life in the United Kingdom between 1900 and 2017, major changes as well as continuities, progress in some areas followed by regression, and long-term improvement in others.

The United Kingdom declined as a world power, especially with the loss of Empire, though it remained internationally prominent, as ever more nations competed for influence in an increasingly complex, interconnected world. Tensions with other European countries recurred periodically. It ceased to be the world's wealthiest country, but was still the fifth richest in 2017. Manufacturing, on which its wealth was built in the nineteenth century, dwindled, but finance, in which it was also internationally dominant in 1900, flourished and expanded. Living standards rose for most people to levels unimaginable in 1900. Many were left behind, especially from the 1980s, but even their conditions were rarely as grim as those observed by Booth and Rowntree, though in relative terms their conditions and life chances lagged at least as far behind average standards. Most people lived longer, healthier lives, though the rich lived substantially longer, in better health, than poorer people. Many more people had access to more and better education, though, again, the poorest gained least.

Expanded educational opportunities contributed to the significant growth of research in science and technology, and the application of the resulting new techniques and findings changed many, ultimately perhaps most, aspects of life, with profound economic and cultural effects. It increased British military, naval then air force capabilities, including in both world wars, and brought major improvements in medicine, contributing to longer lives and better health. Communications of all kinds were transformed. The speed, modes and costs of travel over ever greater distances, with the development and steady improvement of sea, motor then air transport, transformed international trade and personal travel for work or leisure. Work was also changed by new technology from typewriters to computers and a mass of new techniques for speeding production. Leisure was transformed by films, radio, TV, recordings and the multiple products of the development of the internet from the later twentieth century, while older leisure pursuits survived, including sports, dance, theatre, literature, though all changing, influenced by new technology and often increasingly commercialized. Home care was revolutionized by a succession of new gadgets including vacuum cleaners, refrigerators and washing machines. So was personal communication as modern transport speeded postal services, then came telephones, first with fixed land-lines then, by the end of the twentieth century, mobile, versatile and omnipresent connections to the internet. Successive technological changes made an ever-widening, internationalizing, range of information accessible, of variable degrees of reliability, first through expanding print media and radio and television until it approached saturation on the internet in the early twenty-first century. Less positively, the internet opened up new opportunities for crime, including raids on bank accounts; scientific research delivered ever more lethal devices, making warfare increasingly destructive and terrifying, and technological change made a major contribution to global warming, the existence of which some deny, but most specialists see as the major threat of the twenty-first century.

The transformation of the methods, speed and costs of travel was one reason for increased movement between countries, both temporary and permanent, and increased migration to and from the United Kingdom. Immigration created an immensely more culturally diverse society, with the accompanying tensions paralleled by positive interactions and relationships between different ethnic and cultural groups.

Another profound cultural change, not predictable in 1900, concerned attitudes to sexuality and the family. British society slowly became more open, more tolerant of a wider range of behaviours and relationships, more willing to talk openly about issues long recognized but thought shameful and kept secret within families and communities, including mental illness, illegitimacy, transsexuality, and to support those affected. Similarly, rape and domestic violence had always existed and there had been periodic campaigns against them, but only determined campaigning by the women's movement in the 1970s brought them permanently into open public discourse, achieving changes in the law to punish perpetrators and support victims, though they failed to eliminate them and both crimes remained sadly pervasive in the early twenty-first century. It took still longer, until the early twenty-first century, for another ancient crime, child sexual abuse, to be openly acknowledged and punished.

In 1900, homosexuality was a criminal offence and homosexuals lived in secrecy. It was partially decriminalized in 1967 but not fully until the early 2000s. Meanwhile, it became widely acceptable to live openly as a homosexual, though homophobia did not go away. Unmarried couples, straight and gay, lived together openly from the 1970s for the first time, often with children – socially unacceptable in all classes and cultures in 1900 – and marriage declined, while divorce became easier and more frequent. There was continuing resistance to all these 'permissive' changes, especially in Northern Ireland where Christianity remained a force for cultural conservatism, more powerful than elsewhere in the United Kingdom, where religious observance declined over the century. Northern Ireland was the last country in the United Kingdom to extend homosexual rights. In 2017, it was the only country in the United Kingdom still prohibiting same-sex marriage and still has the harshest laws against abortion, which was legalized in England, Wales and Scotland in 1967. These differences further illustrate the divisions within the United Kingdom and inequalities in the experiences of its inhabitants throughout the century.

British history since 1900 cannot be presented as a simple story of progress or decline in any respect. This is illustrated particularly clearly by the complex trajectories of fundamental inequalities over the period. Demands for equality emerging in the early 1900s brought about the gradual extension of state action, both social and economic, especially after 1945 when full employment until the 1970s and a 'welfare state' narrowed income and wealth inequalities and raised average living standards. Women gained more political and legal rights and employment opportunities. Cultural shifts towards greater openness and tolerance, supported by laws against discrimination on grounds of sex, race, and later age, religion and disability – inequalities which were real but taken for granted and absent from public discourse in 1900, then identified and the subjects of active campaigns later in the century – carried on into the twenty-first century, though they were still incomplete and faced opposition. But progress in socio-economic equality went into reverse as neoliberalism became hegemonic from the 1980s, leading to inequalities comparable with those in 1900. The main aim of this book is to survey and analyse how these and other conflicting patterns of progress and decline came about, their effects and how individuals experienced them, seeking to describe and explain this complex picture of continuity and change, social cohesion and social division over time, to understand the origins of contemporary conditions and responses to them.

United Kingdom?

1900–1914

What is 'Britain'?

Inequality and diversity marked the economic, social and administrative structures of the districts and nations of the country in 1900. This perhaps explains widespread, and continuing, uncertainty even about its name. The official title was United Kingdom of Great Britain and Ireland, since the 1801 Act of Union united the United Kingdom of Great Britain with the Kingdom of Ireland. The kingdoms were increasingly disunited through the nineteenth century, as Irish nationalism challenged British control, especially in the mainly Catholic, mainly poor, rural South, which was also disunited from the mainly Protestant, more urbanized, North. 'Great Britain' included England, Wales and Scotland after the 1707 Act of Union joined the Kingdom of Scotland with that of England and Wales, which had been conjoined since 1542. It was and is generally called 'Britain' in everyday discourse, though the English, with the largest population, home of the Crown and the government, habitually spoke of 'England' and 'Britain' interchangeably, until chastened by assertive Scottish and Welsh nationalisms later in the century.

Nationalisms were alive in the countries of the United Kingdom in 1900, as elsewhere in the world. Most strongly in Ireland, but emerging in Scotland and Wales, which were anxious to defend their cultural distinctiveness against growing Westminster control. Welsh people, long controlled by England, wished to preserve their language and the cultural difference it signified; Scotland maintained separate legal and judicial systems and greater administrative independence. Its local government arrangements, including for education and Poor Relief, were never assimilated into those of England and Wales, requiring separate legislation; its established church was the Presbyterian Church of Scotland. Ireland retained similar control of certain internal affairs, while Wales had few independent powers.

Great Britain and Ireland were the largest 'British Isles', as they were described geographically (though Ireland resisted the label 'British'), which included the much smaller Channel Isles and the Isle of Man, neither integrated into the United Kingdom but constitutionally colonies within the Empire with a high degree of control over domestic affairs. The vast British Empire, consisting of countries on every continent, amassed under varying degrees of British control since the eighteenth century and said to cover one-quarter of the world's surface, gave the United Kingdom exceptional world economic and political power. But this never went unchallenged. There was recurrent resistance, most successfully by the United States which broke away in 1776. The century opened amid the Anglo-Boer War, 1899–1902, in which the mighty British imperial army experienced surprising difficulty in overcoming resistance by farmers of Dutch origin, known as Boers, to Britain's takeover of their territories in southern Africa containing the world's richest goldfields. Britain managed to defeat them and the Boer states of the Transvaal and the Orange Free State were incorporated into the Empire and granted self-government. They joined the Dominion of South Africa when it was inaugurated in 1910.

The Empire was never unquestioned within the United Kingdom and challenges grew following the shock of the weaknesses revealed by the war. Conservatives and Liberals were divided, especially the Liberals, though their leaders, including Asquith, Prime Minister 1908–16, and Edward Grey, Foreign Minister, 1905–15, were more committed Imperialists than many backbenchers. The Labour leader Ramsay MacDonald advocated 'Home Rule all round' and devolution to elected colonial governments. These differences persisted, within the United Kingdom and the Empire, through the first half of the century.

Who was British?

In law, since at least the seventeenth century, anyone born within the British Empire was a British subject of the Crown (not a 'citizen', a term reserved for republics, such as France), holding British nationality and identical rights to those of UK-born subjects. These included rights to reside and hold property in the United Kingdom, to work and vote (if suitably qualified, which females and men without property were not), to equality before the law, to free movement around the Empire and to equal rights everywhere within it – provided they had evidence of birth, a birth certificate or equivalent, which many poorer colonial people did not.[1] Wealthy colonials could be sure of equal rights throughout the Empire, poor seamen and others could not.[2]

The leaders of colonies with powerful white elites increasingly questioned this definition of nationality. As civil rights – particularly voting rights – were extended, faster in New Zealand (the first country in the world to enfranchise women in 1893) and Australia than in Britain, some excluded the indigenous people of their own countries and immigrants of different races or colour from other colonies. In response, the British Nationality and Status of Aliens Act 1914, for the first time enshrined in statute that 'a British subject anywhere is a British subject everywhere',[3] but made important concessions to the white-controlled Dominions, the status granted to Australia, Canada and New Zealand in 1907 and South Africa in 1910, conferring considerable devolved power. It allowed each Dominion 'to grant legal nationality in such terms as its legislature thinks fit'.[4] Australia could now exclude anyone not defined as 'white', and restrict the rights of indigenous Aboriginal people. All 'white' Australian adults, including women, had the vote from 1902; Aboriginal Australians not until 1967, when they were also included in the National Census for the first time. The official 'white Australia' immigration policy did not wholly disappear until 1973. Similarly, Canada defined nationality to exclude indigenous peoples, and South Africa excluded Asians and its black majority population. Unusually, in New Zealand the indigenous Maori gained a degree of formal equality in the Treaty of Waitangi, which established British sovereignty in 1840. They achieved parliamentary representation in 1867 and elected four MPs in 1868, better than elsewhere, though Maoris still felt marginalized both culturally and politically.

Even when it was established, British nationality was not always for life, especially for women. From 1870, any British-born woman was deemed on marriage to take the nationality of her husband and, if he was not British, she would lose her British nationality and all rights associated with it. Previously it had been impossible for men or women to renounce British nationality, even if they adopted that of another country. This caused increasing problems in international law for men, women and children in cross-national marriages, as married women gained more rights, unevenly across countries, including rights to own property and to custody of their children. The simplest solution, at a time when the only place in the world where women could vote

1 Ann Dummett and Andrew Nicol, *Subjects, Citizens, Aliens and Others: Nationality and Immigration Law* (Chicago, IL: Northwestern University Press, 1990).

2 Pat Thane, 'The British Imperial State and National Identities', in B. Melman (ed.), *Borderlines. Genders and Identities in War and Peace, 1870–1930* (London: Routledge, 1998), pp. 29–46; Laura Tabili, 'The Construction of Racial Difference in Twentieth Century Britain: the Special Restriction [Coloured Alien Seamen] Order, 1925', *Journal of British Studies* 33(1) (1994): 54–98.

3 *Hansard*, House of Commons, 1914, vol. LXII, col. 1201.

4 Ibid., col. 1199.

and oppose it was the American state of Wyoming (from 1869), was to require married women to take their husband's nationality. They could apply for re-naturalization as British five years after widowhood or divorce. In 1914, following protests, this was modified to apply immediately on widowhood, but not following stigmatized divorce. Once women could vote in many countries, after the First World War, this became an international campaigning issue until, gradually, most countries, including Britain from 1948, let them retain their nationalities on marriage.

Immigration

In 1900, immigrants from outside the Empire, 'aliens' as they were officially called, could buy British nationality for a payment of £3, without other conditions, though this was expensive for poor people. Migration was unrestricted, and passports were not required for crossing borders until the First World War. Previously how many people migrated to Britain, for how long, is uncertain. Around 1900, there were substantial numbers of Italians, Germans and others, mainly from Europe, in London and other cities, and well-established multi-racial communities in ports, including Liverpool, Bristol and Cardiff, where colonial and other seamen settled. Immigrants might be fleeing persecution or seeking work, including poor Italians and wealthy men of many countries attracted to the City of London, the world financial centre. However, the largest immigrant group in Great Britain came from impoverished Ireland.[5]

Despite persistent hostility to the Irish, immigration was not a significant issue until thousands of Jews fled from Russia from the 1880s, mostly escaping vicious pogroms but also severe poverty. Approximately 250,000 had reached Britain by 1914, often impoverished, they settled in particularly large numbers in East London. Like poor immigrants through the century, they were accused of taking jobs and homes from British people, disrupting their communities and culture, and lowering living standards. To avoid accusations that Jews were abusing public welfare services, including the Poor Law, causing intensified antisemitism, the established Jewish community, including wealthy businessmen and financiers, created institutions to support them, including Jewish schools and a Jewish Board of Guardians providing welfare aid. They helped immigrants to establish themselves in employment or small businesses, making a valuable contribution to the economy.

They received little thanks and protests led to Britain's first immigration restrictions in the Aliens Act 1905. Conservative Prime Minister Arthur Balfour told parliament: 'We have the right to keep out everybody who does not add to … the

---

5 David Butler and Gareth Butler, *Twentieth-Century British Political Facts 1990–2000* (London: Macmillan, 2000), p. 351.

industrial, social and intellectual strength of the community'.[6] To remain, immigrants must show that they could support themselves and their dependants 'decently' and could 'speak, read and write English reasonably well'. Criminals, the insane and those thought likely to apply for Poor Relief were excluded. No 'alien' could apply for naturalization before five years' residence. Following parliamentary pressure, the Act granted asylum to refugees who could prove they were escaping 'persecution involving danger of imprisonment or danger to life or limb on account of religious belief'.[7]

The advantages of British nationality grew as Britons gained more rights, including state old age pensions in 1908 and National Insurance in 1911.[8] 'Aliens', including colonials who could not prove their place of birth, and their British-born wives, were excluded from both. Following protests by the Jewish community, in 1911 the British-born widows, but not wives, of aliens could claim the pension, and non-naturalized aliens who had been resident for five years and were in regular work could contribute to National Insurance. Immigration, access to British nationality and associated rights were contentious through the century.

Emigration

Yet emigrants outnumbered immigrants. Over 1 million people emigrated from the United Kingdom to the United States and the colonies between 1903 and 1909; another 1 million emigrated before 1914, with about 10 per cent from Ireland, mostly poor people seeking better lives and mostly young men.[9] Smaller numbers of prosperous people travelled, not necessarily permanently or always to the formal Empire, seeking fortunes from gold-mining, banking, railway-building or other enterprises, often successfully. Others went as colonial administrators, agricultural advisers, education officers, police, doctors, missionaries and soldiers.[10]

Women made up a higher proportion of Irish than British emigrants, though the growing ambitions of British women for wider opportunities encouraged emigration. Women were a majority of the UK population due to their longer life expectancy and the higher male emigration rate, and some of these 'surplus women', as they were described, were attracted by the surplus of men seeking wives in the

---

6 David Feldman, *Englishmen and Jews. Social Relations and Political Culture, 1840–1914* (New Haven, CT: Yale University Press, 1994), p. 287.

7 Ibid., p. 290.

8 See p. 36.

9 Butler and Butler, *Twentieth-Century British Political Facts*, p. 351.

10 Bernard Porter, *The Lion's Share. A Short History of British Imperialism, 1850–2004*, 4th edn (Harlow: Pearson Longman, 2004), p. 199.

Dominions, while others sought greater equality, independence and work.[11] Many of the first female medical graduates of Glasgow University from the late nineteenth century worked in India, where the prohibition on male doctors treating women in purdah gave them opportunities unimaginable at home. In 1900, 63,909 women emigrated from Great Britain; in 1911, 156,606, mainly working-class women but also teachers, missionaries and aspiring businesswomen emigrated.[12] The most vulnerable émigrés were thousands of children from care homes, such as Barnardo's, who were sent to families and institutions in Australia, Canada, New Zealand and South Africa, unknown to their own families and often told that they were orphans when they were not, sometimes with happy outcomes, sometimes sadly not, a practice that continued in Canada until 1939 and in Australia into the 1960s.

Who Ruled Britain?

Constitutionally, the sovereign ruled the United Kingdom and the Empire: that is, Queen Victoria until her death in January 1901, aged 82; then her son, Edward VII, who died in 1910, when his son, George V, succeeded. The monarchy delegated power to a partially democratic House of Commons of 670 members and a wholly undemocratic House of Lords comprising twenty-six Anglican bishops and 561 hereditary peers,[13] mainly landowners plus growing numbers of businessmen and financiers – '500 men chosen accidentally from among the unemployed', as Liberal David Lloyd George described them – and holding substantial political and legal power. The Lords was the highest Court of Appeal, headed by the Lord Chancellor who presided over the House. For the Commons, 60 per cent of adult men, qualified by property holding, could vote, but no women. Most men without the vote were manual workers, but better-off men were also disfranchised if they were not independent householders paying local taxes (known as rates) but lived in family or other property, as many did before marriage.[14] Apart from the monarchy, all these constitutional inequalities were seriously challenged before 1914.

Politics in 1900 was dominated by the Liberal and Conservative parties. Both had clear social and ideological identities, while also providing space for moderately divergent views, increasingly so as the electorate and society became more diverse. The Conservative Party was identified with landed wealth, the Church of England,

---

11 A. James Hammerton, *Emigrant Gentlewomen. Genteel Poverty and Female Emigration, 1830–1914* (London: Croom Helm, 1979).
12 Hammerton, *Emigrant Gentlewomen*, p. 177.
13 Butler and Butler, *Twentieth-Century British Political Facts*, p. 225.
14 Duncan Tanner, *Political Change and the Labour Party, 1900–1918* (Cambridge University Press, 1990).

Empire and established institutions. The Liberals were identified with the urban middle classes, progressive landowners, Nonconformists and radical reformers. They were strong in the largely Nonconformist 'Celtic Fringe' of Scotland, Wales and southwest England, and among the skilled workers who gained the vote in 1867 and 1884 and elected Liberal MPs in constituencies they controlled, particularly mining districts – eleven in 1900. These distinctive, working-class, cloth-capped men, visibly different from other MPs, were labelled 'Lib-Labs' by their opponents and they adopted the title with pride.

The Conservatives decisively won the 1900 General Election, and 70-year-old Lord Salisbury, from an old aristocratic family, became the last premier to sit in the House of Lords. He was ailing and in 1902 was replaced by Arthur Balfour, his nephew – hereditary privilege flourished in both Houses. Signs of change included the newly formed Labour Representation Committee (LRC, later the Labour Party), which in its first election gained two seats and 63,304 votes; Irish Nationalists won eighty-two of the 103 seats in Ireland.

The LRC was founded in 1900 by trade unions and socialist societies, including the reforming intellectual Fabian Society, the rhetorically revolutionary Social Democratic Federation (SDF), both founded in 1884; the moderate socialist Independent Labour Party (ILP), founded 1892; and the Co-operative movement. The SDF left when the party committed to reform by parliamentary means rather than by revolutionary class war. The LRC was initiated by the unions following a series of legal decisions eroding their rights, which the leading parties showed no inclination to reverse, particularly following a strike on the Taff Vale railway in South Wales when the courts upheld the employers' claim that the union was liable for their losses from the strike, effectively making strikes impossible. The unions funded the LRC and paid their MPs, who were normally expected to serve unpaid on the, previously correct, assumption that all MPs had other incomes. The first Labour MPs were all working class, mostly former union officials. The LRC's first chair was James Keir Hardie, illegitimate son of a Scottish farm servant, a self-educated miner, founder of the ILP, its first MP, for West Ham 1892–5, then one of the LRC's first MPs, for Merthyr Tydfil from 1900.[15] The first secretary, who did most to develop and promote its ideas, was James Ramsay MacDonald, son of a poor, unmarried Scottish mother, a journalist and an MP from 1906. He presented Labour as the advanced wing of progressive Liberalism, dedicated to achieving 'British Socialism' by parliamentary means rather than the class war advocated by continental socialists, anticipating displacing Liberalism when all working people had the vote.[16]

15 K. O. Morgan, *Keir Hardie. Radical and Socialist* (London: Faber & Faber, [1975] 2011).
16 David Marquand, *Ramsay MacDonald* (London: Jonathan Cape, 1977).

Working-class voters did not always support Labour or the Liberals. Many voted Conservative, especially where nationalist, anti-immigrant sentiment was strong, as in east London against the Jews, in Lancashire against the Irish, though social deference or ideological conviction created working-class Conservatives everywhere. As landed wealth declined, the Conservatives attracted businessmen and financiers from Liberalism. The Liberals won the next election, in 1906, decisively, while the LRC gained thirty seats and adopted the name Labour Party. Liberal and Labour successes owed much to a secret pre-electoral pact not to compete where they would split anti-Conservative votes. The new government speedily paid its dues with the Trade Disputes Act 1906, reversing the Taff Vale judgment and increasing unions' immunity from prosecution. The first ever working-class Cabinet Minister, Lib-Lab John Burns, proud son of a washerwoman, was appointed President of the Local Government Board (LGB) responsible for the Poor Law. The Prime Minister was Sir Henry Campbell-Bannerman, son of a wholesale draper in Glasgow. In 1908, he resigned due to ill-health and was replaced by Herbert Henry Asquith, son of a Yorkshire wool merchant, a barrister who remained premier until 1916.

International Relations

Around 1900 Britain appeared isolated in Europe, mainly due to competition over colonization. There were tensions with France in North Africa, with Germany in southern Africa and with Germany and Russia in China. Russia was feared as a threat to its British-controlled southern neighbours, India and Afghanistan. The United States was emerging as an imperial power – much as it shunned the term – acquiring the Philippines, Hawaii, Cuba and other territories in the Pacific and Caribbean in the early 1900s, becoming a rival naval power along with France, Russia and, increasingly, Germany and Japan. Britain tried to maintain good relations with its rivals. It courted the United States and in 1902 signed a five-year treaty with Japan, both pledging not to compete in East Asia. In 1904, came an entente with France, essentially agreeing to share control of North Africa – Britain based in Egypt, France in Morocco. Japan fought and defeated Russia in 1905, the first modern example of an Asian state defeating a European one, challenging racial stereotypes. The weakness of the Russian state was underlined by the revolution of December 1905. Britain took advantage of this to reach an agreement with Russia in 1907, securing Afghanistan within its sphere of influence.

By 1907 Britain no longer seemed isolated and shared its European allies' apprehension about Germany and an anxiety to avoid a major war. They feared Germany's economic strength and evident desire to rival their international political and colonial powers. Demands grew in Britain for increased military and naval spending, despite resistance within both major parties.

The Economy

In 1900, Britain, the first industrial nation, was the world's leading trading nation and the centre of world finance. The City of London dominated investment in developing economies. City finance benefited from Britain's long-established free trade policy and consumers gained from resulting cheaper imports. But cheap food from Argentina, Australia, Canada and elsewhere disadvantaged home producers and agriculture declined. In the early years of the century manufacturing competition intensified, especially with America and Germany, whose home markets were protected by taxes on imports (known as tariffs). In 1900, Germany produced 13 per cent of world manufacturing and Britain almost 19 per cent; in 1913, this stood at 15 per cent and 14 per cent, respectively, while the United States produced 30 per cent of world output.[17] Hence the demand for protective tariffs – 'tariff reform' – was a major political issue in the 1900s, supported by the Conservatives against the Liberals and Labour who upheld free trade. Tariffs were strongly opposed in the City and by manufacturers still prospering in expanding overseas markets, including in textiles, mining and shipbuilding.

These industries peaked in output and employment in the 1900s, and while demand grew there was little incentive to diversify. At the same time, Germany and the United States developed new, less labour-intensive, industries using electrical power and new technology, producing road vehicles, advanced chemical products, electrical engineering and scientific instruments, which threatened the future of the British economy. Nevertheless, average UK living standards rose, signalled by expanding services, including transport, and growing consumption of such mass-produced goods as soap, chocolate, tobacco, newspapers and other printed publications, pharmaceuticals, ready-made clothing and footwear – signs that the economy could innovate and of an expanding home market.

Yet the largest occupation in 1914 was still domestic service, employing 1.7 million people, overwhelmingly female, another sign of profound social inequality. The economy was regionally concentrated, as it had been since industrialization. Mining dominated County Durham, south Wales, Derbyshire and the central and Fife regions of Scotland; textile production was concentrated in Tayside and the Borders, Lancashire and the West Riding of Yorkshire; steel manufacturing, shipbuilding and engineering were prominent in central Scotland and northern England. In these areas, average incomes were lower and premature death and illness higher than in southeast England, where employment was centred on government, finance and services. In 1913, the male death rate was 30 per cent above the national average in South Shields in northeast

17 Peter Clarke, *Hope and Glory. Britain 1900–2000*, 2nd edn (London: Penguin, 2004), p. 57.

England, while TB rates on Tyneside were 30 per cent above. In pit villages fresh water supplies and adequate drainage were exceptional: ash pits more common than flush toilets.

Wealth and Poverty

The human outcome of major inequalities of income and wealth as calculated by the radical Liberal economist Sir Leo Chiozza Money is shown in Table 1.1.

The sources of wealth and status were changing. Between 1870 and 1914 the value of shares grew fourfold, but landed wealth declined, with much rural land no longer in cultivation.[18] Many landed estates were sold, but wealthy landholders were not pauperized. Some invested in land abroad, often in the Empire; others profited from owning urban land, notably the dukes of Westminster who inherited what became the most prosperous districts of central London, including Belgravia, and remain one of the wealthiest families in Britain a century later. Or, like Lord Londonderry in north-east England, rich coal deposits under their land yielded fortunes; others transferred their assets into finance and business at home and abroad. Sons of landowners moved into the City and business increasingly intermarried with trade and finance. In 1896, a quarter of the peerage were company directors (up to a half by 1910), many of several companies. But still, in 1914, the greatest wealth was held by landowners, rivalled only by some leading City financiers.[19]

Increasingly, business wealth was concentrated in London rather than the industrial north and the Midlands. With the growth of public companies more people lived

Table 1.1 UK Income and Wealth, *c.* 1900

Total UK population 1901, 41,438,700
20% of employees earned above the income tax threshold of £150 pa.
0.5% earned above £5,000.
87% of private property was owned by 882,690 persons; 4,400,000 including families.
13% shared among 38,600,000.
17,000 property holders owned approx. two-thirds of private wealth.
90% of the population left no recorded property at death.

SOURCES: Leo Chiozza Money, *Riches and Poverty*, London, 1905, 1912; Harris, *Private Lives, Public Spirit*, p. 99.

---

18 Jose Harris, *Private Lives, Public Spirit* (Oxford University Press, 1993, repr. London: Penguin, 1994), pp. 97–8.
19 Harris, *Private Lives*, pp. 100–6.

wholly or partly on investment income. The middle classes continued their nine-teenth-century expansion in numbers and diversity, while the gap between middling and great wealth grew. In 1905, 861,150 people in the United Kingdom owned assets worth £500–£50,000. They can be assumed to constitute the middle class.[20] The lower middle class grew as clerical and lower-level managerial work increased with the expansion of central and local government and large business firms. Most of this new 'white-collar' class were upwardly mobile from the skilled working class, to whom they were perceived to be socially superior, signified by greater job security, though not always higher pay, 'respectable' dress (suits and ties for men), living in different neigh-bourhoods, following different leisure pursuits, though many kept in contact with their working-class families.

Poverty Surveys

The lower middle class and, to a lesser extent, skilled workers were certainly more secure than the much larger mass of unskilled workers and seriously poor people. Concern about people left behind by growing national prosperity prompted social research. From 1886 to 1902, Charles Booth, a businessman with a social conscience, organ-ized his survey of poverty, first in east London, known to be poverty-stricken, then throughout London. He did not conduct house-to-house surveys, but collected what he called 'a statistical record of *impressions* of degrees of poverty'[21] provided by school board visitors (who chased up truanting children), clergy and others in regular contact with poor people, supplemented by the observations of assistants living temporarily in low-income communities, such as the future Beatrice Webb (then Miss Potter) who reported on the Jewish population of east London. Reliable observation was possible when poverty was starkly visible in stunted growth, under-nourished bodies and rick-ety legs, clothing and household goods, or lack of them. On this basis Booth estimated that 30 per cent of all Londoners lived 'in poverty or in want', 8.4 per cent of these and 13.3 per cent of those in poverty in east London, were in the worst situation of being 'at all times more or less in want … ill-nourished and poorly clad'. He set no fixed income measure but defined poverty as 'having no surplus'.[22]

Booth stressed that these conditions were unacceptable in the wealthiest country in the world. It was suspected that they were peculiar to London, which attracted poor migrants seeking work and had a notoriously unstable labour market. In 1899, another philanthropic businessman, B. Seebohm Rowntree, tested this by surveying York, the

20 Ibid., pp. 106–10.
21 E. P. Hennock, 'The Measurement of Poverty: From the Metropolis to the Nation, 1880–1920', *Economic History Review* 40(2) (1987): 201–27.
22 Charles Booth, *Life and Labour of the People of London* 17 vols (London: Macmillan, 1902–3).

medium-sized, fairly representative, provincial town where his family chocolate factory was the largest employer at a time, as he put it, of 'average prosperity'. He sent investigators to every working-class household in York (11,560) to record income and expenditure and observations of living conditions, while gathering impressions from voluntary workers and clergy. Like Booth he did not try to establish an income-based poverty measure because household conditions were too variable, but sought to estimate the minimum income on which a family could survive in a state of 'physical efficiency', providing:

> a diet less generous as regards variety than that supplied to able-bodied paupers in workhouses. It further assumes that no clothing is purchased which is not absolutely necessary for health and … is of the plainest and most economical description … No expenditure of any kind is allowed beyond that which is absolutely necessary for the maintenance of merely physical efficiency.[23]

He built on the recent discovery that diet crucially affected health and on new techniques for measuring nutritional needs.

Typical were the Smith family, 'whose house is scrupulously clean and tidy. Mr Smith is in regular work and earns 20s a week. He keeps 2s a week for himself and hands over 18s to his wife'. When Mrs Smith was asked how she met 'any extraordinary expenditure, such as new dress or a pair of boots', she replied 'Well, as a rule, we 'ave to get it out of the food money and go short; but I never let Smith suffer – ' e 'as to go to work, and must be kept up, yer know!'[24] Rowntree concluded that 6.8 per cent of the working-class population of York (3.6 per cent of the whole) lived in this miserable condition, which he called 'primary poverty'. He recognized that few spent their incomes with maximum efficiency and many earning above the stringent minimum were 'obviously living in a state of poverty, i.e. obvious want and squalor' for no fault of their own. These – almost 18 per cent of the York population – he defined as living in 'secondary poverty'. Altogether, almost 25 per cent lived 'in poverty', a figure similar to that of London.

Rowntree and Booth concluded that most impoverished people were not idle 'shirkers'. They worked hard when they could, but suffered low pay (the majority), unemployment or underemployment. It was especially hard for large families. Rowntree found that 22 per cent in primary poverty were in families with four or more children, with only 2.3 per cent of primary poverty in York being due to unemployment, though it was a problem elsewhere and at other times. Important but lesser causes were sickness and old age, death of the chief wage-earner, almost always male, and the widow's inability to earn enough to support her children. Rowntree identified a 'cycle of poverty': low-income families were hardest hit when children were young, better-off when children

---

23 B. Seebohm Rowntree, *Poverty. A Study of Town Life* (London: Nelson, 1902), p. 352.
24 Ibid., pp. 85–6.

were old enough to work and left home, then impoverished again in later life due to ill-health and incapacity for work.

Poverty was not confined to towns, though this received most attention. It had always been endemic but less visible in the countryside, exacerbated by agricultural decline. Rowntree and others explored this also, finding similar conditions to the towns, without the debilitating pollution: low pay, miserable housing, widespread malnutrition causing sickness, especially among women and children, while prices were higher than in towns and there were concentrations of older people and widows as men fled to work in the towns or the colonies.[25] Rowntree did not try to measure rural poverty but described how:

> The be all and end all of life is physical efficiency … It means that a wise mother, when she is tempted to buy her children a penny worth of cheap oranges, will devote the penny to flour instead … It means that every natural longing for pleasure or variety should be ignored and set aside. It means, in short, a life without colour, space and atmosphere, that stifles and hems in the labourer's soul, as in too many cases his cottage does his body.[26]

Studies of urban poverty continued. Between 1912 and 1914, A. L. Bowley surveyed representative English towns. Bowley was a mathematician, concerned with precise measurement, who developed influential survey techniques. He rejected qualitative impressions and introduced the sample survey, examining systematically the earnings and outgoings of representative households. He confirmed that low pay, especially combined with large family size, was the main cause of poverty – as it was a century later.[27]

Qualitative surveys continued, including *At the Works. A Study of a Manufacturing Town* by Lady Bell (1907). This study of Middlesborough by the wife of a local ironmaster, drew on her experience of living there for over thirty years and working voluntarily, with other women, to improve conditions. It included statistics and details of budgets, but above all evokes Florence Bell's perception of the diverse realities of life at work, at home and at leisure for workers who created Britain's industrial prosperity. She wanted to inform those, like herself, who profited, commenting, 'If we see in a cottage one emaciated little child wasting away because it has not enough to eat, the sight will make more impression on us than many lists of infant mortality'.[28] She also showed that not all working-class households were so desolate 'that the needy and unhappy homes … [do not] … preponderate over the happy homes',[29] without downplaying the social deprivation she believed needed urgent remedy.

---

25 Mark Freeman, *Social Investigation and Rural England, 1870–1914* (Woodbridge: Boydell Press, 2000).

26 B. Seebohm Rowntree and May Kendall, *How the Labourer Lives: a Study of the Rural Labour Problem* (London: Nelson, 1913), pp. 312–13.

27 A. L. Bowley and A. R. Burnett-Hurst, *Livelihood and Poverty: a Study in the Economic Conditions of Working-class Households in Northampton, Warrington, Stanley and Reading* (London, 1915); see also p. 108.

28 Lady Florence Bell, *At the Works. A Study of a Manufacturing Town* (London: Arnold 1907, repr. London: Virago, 1985), p. xxxi.

29 Ibid., p. xxxii.

Many women campaigned for social reform. The belief that women would end the inequalities that male politicians had tolerated for too long was one motive for demanding the vote. They included the Fabian Women's Group, formed in 1908 to demand the vote and improved social and working conditions particularly for women. Led by Maud Pember Reeves, wife of the New Zealand High Commissioner, a successful campaigner for the vote in her home country and aware that New Zealand led Britain on social reform, they recorded the budgets and daily lives of families in Lambeth, south London, asking 'How does a working man's wife bring up a family on 20s a week?'[30] The report, *Round about a Pound a Week*, included details of incomes and budgets and described housing, diet, health and family life. It stressed how carefully most poor women managed inadequate, insecure incomes, contrary to the 'improvidence' perceived by critics ignorant of their lives.[31] The Fabians advocated a state-guaranteed national minimum income, sufficient to keep a family, which New Zealand had been the first to introduce in 1894, followed by Australia in 1896.

Most Lambeth wives were not in paid work. They had work enough at home, sometimes supplemented with employment as cleaners or by letting rooms to lodgers. The Fabians also campaigned for and with employed women, especially in the low-paid, largely non-unionized, appropriately labelled, 'sweated' trades, including tailoring, cardboard-box making, lacemaking, chain-making, carried on in small workshops or by female outworkers in their homes. In 1905, they organized a London exhibition displaying women's working conditions. The publicity, with pressure from labour organizations, persuaded the Liberal government to fix (low) minimum wages in these occupations through the Trade Boards Act 1909.

Leisure

Researchers also explored the brighter side of life. Booth and Rowntree stressed how those with adequate incomes could enjoy themselves and that one of the many deprivations of the very poor was the absence of pleasure. The favourite leisure activity of working-class men remained the pub and alcohol consumption rose in the 1900s. However, the range of leisure activities and their commercialization expanded as real wages rose and organized workers gained shorter working hours and Saturday afternoon off to watch football, while the better-off attended racecourses or watched or played tennis or golf. Improved transport provided day trips to the seaside or the country, or holidays for those who could afford it. The fastest growing towns between the censuses of 1901 and 1911 were seaside resorts. Working people went to Margate in the south or

30 Maud Pember Reeves, *Round about a Pound a Week* (London: Bell, 1913, repr. London: Virago 1979), pp. 146–58.
31 Ibid., p. 146.

Blackpool in the north (nearly 4 million in 1913[32]), the middle classes to Eastbourne or Southport and the rich to the French Riviera. Cycling was another popular way to escape the city, particularly for younger middle-class people. The rich still preferred fox-hunting and the grouse moors. Leisure, like everything else, was class divided. Working people could devote their leisure to self-improvement: the Workers Education Association (WEA) was founded in 1903 to provide evening classes with well-qualified tutors. Local authorities invested in public libraries, museums, galleries and music venues. For relaxation, music halls and, increasingly, cinemas attracted better-off working people. New, lasting, leisure opportunities and patterns were established.

In leisure, as in other ways, prosperous Britain in the 1900s was probably more unequal, socially and economically, than any other European country.[33] Despite some improvement, opportunities deteriorated due to rising prices in 1910–13, causing a wave of strikes among better-paid, unionized, skilled workers. In 1912, 40 million working days were lost in strikes, notably in mining. It was one of many challenges to the Liberal government and some feared revolution. Rather, workers were continuing the demands for better working conditions and greater equality which created the Labour Party.

Votes for Women

Women's campaigns were another challenge. They grew from the mid-nineteenth century, along with the numbers of educated, independent women demanding better education and employment, equal property, divorce and child custody rights, eliminating domestic violence and much else. Despite some gains, the law still subordinated women, especially married women, to men. By 1906, many women had lost patience and believed that only when they had the national vote could they gain the equalities and social improvements denied them by male politicians. Textile workers from Yorkshire and Lancashire, shop workers and the 30,000 members of the working-class Women's Co-operative Guild campaigned alongside middle- and upper-class women.[34]

Since 1869 the minority of independent female property-holders paying local rates (mainly better-off widows and unmarried women) had been able to vote in local elections. This passed easily through Parliament two years after it rejected John Stuart Mill's bid to extend the national vote to women in 1867. Parliament judged it acceptable for women to elect local authorities which dealt mainly with social conditions, such as public health and Poor Relief, which were believed to suit women's interests and

32 Geoffrey Searle, *A New England? Peace and War 1886–1918* (Oxford University Press, 2004), p. 554.

33 Harris, *Private Lives*, p. 100.

34 Jill Liddington and Jill Norris, *One Hand Tied Behind Us. The Rise of the Women's Suffrage Movement* (London: Virago, 1978).

capabilities when serious matters of state did not. Some women agreed. Women could be elected to school boards when they were established in 1870 to develop compulsory state education. After a struggle, they gained election to Poor Law Boards of Guardians, then to rural and urban district councils. Election to the more significant county and municipal councils was granted by the Liberals in 1907. In 1900, there were about 1 million female electors and 1,589 elected women; by 1914 this had risen to 2,488.[35]

Women were active in national politics not only on 'women's issues', but in pressure groups of all kinds and were indispensable as canvassers, fundraisers and organizers for the political parties that denied them the vote. The parties established women's branches: the Conservative Primrose League, founded 1884, in 1900 included 64,003 'Dames'; the Women's Liberal Federation, founded 1886, had about 70,000 members in 1910, 115,097 by 1914; the Women's Labour League (WLL) was formed in 1906, supporting the Labour Party, with a cross-class membership of 5,000 in 1914.[36] The more active women were in politics, the more absurd their disfranchisement appeared, especially when they gained the vote in New Zealand and Australia, then in Finland in 1906, even in the Isle of Man from 1881 female property-holders voted for their parliament, the Tynwald. The National Union of Women's Suffrage Societies (NUWSS) was formed in 1897, led by Millicent Garrett Fawcett, a Liberal, married to a radical Liberal politician. It was committed to peaceable lobbying and composed mainly of Liberal women disappointed by the party's failure to support women's suffrage. Initially, as a tactical first step, it demanded the vote on the same terms as men, which would have limited it, like the local vote, to better-off single and widowed women.

The Women's Social and Political Union (WSPU) was founded in 1903 by Emmeline Pankhurst, an ILP stalwart from Manchester, her daughters and friends. It also supported the limited franchise as an initial aim. It was committed to public campaigning, impatient with the NUWSS' quiet, apparently ineffective, lobbying. Horror at the WSPU's unfeminine behaviour drove the *Daily Mail* to endow them with a diminutive intended, with a striking lack of success, to be disparaging: 'suffragettes'.[37] Women's suffrage was not a prominent issue in the 1905 election, but from 1907 the WSPU, frustrated by politicians' lack of response, interrupted ministers' public speeches shouting 'Votes for Women'. By 1909, they felt driven to demonstrations, window-smashing and other actions which did not harm people but provoked arrest, fines and imprisonment. They responded with hunger strikes in prison and resistance to the forced feeding that followed. The behaviour of the women and the police and prison authorities shocked

35 Patricia Hollis, *Ladies Elect. Women in English Local Government 1865–1914* (Oxford University Press, 1987), p. 486.
36 Christine Collette, *For Labour and For Women. The Women's Labour League, 1906–18* (Manchester University Press, 1989).
37 Jad Adams, *Women and the Vote. A World History* (Oxford University Press, 2014), p. 204.

opponents and supporters and some women defected to the NUWSS, but the WSPU placed women's suffrage firmly on the public agenda. Quiet lobbying and noisy demonstrations were both essential to promoting 'the Cause'. In 1911, an unknown number of suffrage campaigners boycotted the National Census, arguing 'If women don't count, neither shall they be counted'. To evade it, groups of women joined all-night hikes or parties, some spent census night roller-skating in a rink in central London. Emily Wilding Davison hid overnight in a broom cupboard in Parliament.[38]

All three British political parties and the Irish Nationalists[39] included suffragists and 'antis', male and female. Most Liberal backbenchers appear to have supported women's suffrage, but did not prioritize it, and the Cabinet was less persuaded, but in 1912 the government was driven to introduce an Electoral Reform Bill proposing adult suffrage for men and women. This caused a hopeful lull in campaigning until the Speaker ruled woman suffrage out of order and militancy revived. Labour was the only party committed to full adult suffrage. From 1912, NUWSS shifted to supporting this option and supporting Labour. WSPU militancy mounted. Letter boxes were set on fire. Emily Wilding Davidson died after throwing herself at the king's horse in the 1913 Derby. Hunger-striking militants were punished with the Prisoners' Temporary Discharge for Ill-health Act, known as the Cat-and-Mouse Act because it discharged from prison women risking death only to recall them when they recovered. In 1914, Asquith at last promised to include women's suffrage in the government's next attempt at electoral reform, without indicating a date. This, and the whole movement, was overtaken by the war.

Marriage

Inequalities in marriage were one cause of women's protest. Not all women married, despite social expectations, mainly because they outnumbered men. In England and Wales there were 15.5 million males to 16.6 million females in 1900, and in 1914 this was 17.8 million males to 19 million females, with similar proportions in Scotland and Ireland.[40] Marriages did not always last, with their greatest destroyer being death. Of marriages in England and Wales in the 1880s, 13 per cent ended by death, most often of the husband, within ten years, with 37 per cent ending this way within twenty-five years.[41] Widowers were more likely than widows to remarry, seeking care

---

38 Jill Liddington, *Vanishing for the Vote. Suffrage, Citizenship and the Battle for the Census* (Manchester University Press, 2014).

39 Myrtle Hill, *Women in Ireland. A Century of Change* (Belfast: Blackstaff Press, 2003); Louise Ryan and Margaret Ward (eds), *Irish Women and the Vote. Becoming Citizens* (Dublin: Irish Academic Press, 2007).

40 B. R. Mitchell and P. Deane, *Abstract of British Historical Statistics* (Cambridge University Press, 1962), pp. 12–14.

41 Michael Anderson, 'The Social Implications of Demographic Change', in F. M. L. Thompson (ed.), *The Cambridge Social History of Britain. 1750–1950*, vol. 2 (Cambridge University Press, 1991), pp. 29–32.

for their children or themselves. Women often preferred the independence of widow-hood, even in poverty, including custody of their children, compared with the legally enforced dependence of wifehood, while men could be reluctant to support another man's children. Low pay and limited work opportunities made poverty almost una-voidable for single women without independent wealth. Impoverished single mothers were as numerous in the mid-nineteenth century as in the late twentieth, for different reasons.[42]

Some marriages failed. Divorce was legalized in England and Wales in 1857, having been, since the Reformation, available only to the few who could afford a private Act of Parliament. From 1857, a wife could be divorced for adultery, but to divorce her hus-band she had to prove adultery plus additional 'aggravation', such as cruelty, desertion or incest. The gender double standard of expected sexual behaviour pervaded the law. Also, divorce was expensive, prohibitively for most people. But one of many differences between Scotland and England and Wales was that, under Scots law since before the Reformation, men and women could divorce on equal terms, for desertion as well as for adultery. It was somewhat cheaper and costs might be met by the Poor Law, though the stigma was considerable, especially for women, and the administrative hurdles daunting. There was no divorce in Ireland, where it was anathema to all the dominant religious groups.

In England and Wales from 1878, wives could claim in magistrates' courts a sep-aration order and maintenance from husbands guilty of violence or desertion. This followed a feminist campaign against 'wife-torture', as they described domestic vio-lence,[43] but extracting payment could be difficult. In 1900, 494 divorces were granted in England and Wales and more than 5,000 separation orders. Legal separation did not permit remarriage. Some believed that the obstacles to divorce encouraged 'illicit unions', with couples cohabiting because they could not divorce and remarry, arous-ing disapproval in some quarters and demands for divorce reform in others. This was investigated by a Royal Commission on Divorce and Matrimonial Causes, appointed in 1910, which concluded in 1912 that, 'beyond all doubt', divorce was 'beyond the reach of the poor', led to 'irregular and illicit unions', and should become more accessible. It recommended extending and equalizing the grounds for divorce between men and women.[44] Nothing changed due to opposition from those who believed reform would destroy marriage and then the onset of the First World War.

---

42 See p. 459.
43 Frances Power Cobbe, 'Wife-Torture in England', *The Contemporary Review*, XXXII (April–July 1878): 55–87; Lori Williamson, *Power and Protest. Frances Power Cobbe and Victorian Society* (London: Rivers Oram, 2005).
44 Stephen Cretney, *Family Law in the Twentieth Century. A History* (Oxford University Press, 2003), pp. 161–318.

It is impossible to know how many couples lived together unmarried, perhaps parenting children, not necessarily because they did not want to marry but because they could not, often presenting themselves to the world, and being accepted, as married.[45] They were numerous enough to arouse the concern and sympathy of respectable members of the Royal Commission, including the Archbishop of York. In Scotland, the situation was, again, different. Couples could divorce more easily, but many churches would not remarry them and civil marriage did not exist until 1939, as it had in England and Wales since 1836. But 'irregular' stable partnerships could be officially registered as they could not in England and Wales, and they amounted to 12 per cent of all registered partnerships, including marriages, between 1855 and 1939,[46] similar to the figure for the whole of Great Britain in the late 1990s.[47]

Population Panic

There was greater anxiety about the size and physical fitness of the population. The birth rate began an unprecedented decline in the 1870s, a trend shared with other European countries, continuing to the 1930s. Births fell from 36 per 1,000 population in England and Wales in 1877 to 23.8 in 1914; in Scotland from 35.3 to 26.1; in Ireland from 26.2 to 22.7.[48] It was believed that births fell fastest among the middle classes, careful people who planned their lives, seeking to improve their families' living standards and their children's life chances, while the feckless masses had too many children who were malnourished and feeble, causing national 'physical degeneration' and potential economic and military decline. Similar fears were widespread in Europe.[49] Pessimism was stoked by eugenic theory, created in 1883 by the English mathematician, Francis Galton, who argued that poverty caused debilitating physical and mental conditions which were inherited and could be halted only by preventing reproduction of the 'unfit'. Eugenics gained adherents internationally, though in Britain it was always challenged by the belief that, even if physical weakness associated with poverty was inherited, it could be countered effectively by welfare and environmental reforms.

To discover which families were restricting their births and why, the 1911 Census asked every woman who had been married how many children she had borne and how

45 Pat Thane and Tanya Evans, *Sinners? Scroungers? Saints? Unmarried Motherhood in Twentieth-Century England* (Oxford University Press, 2012), pp. 8–13; Ginger S. Frost, *Living in Sin. Cohabiting as Husband and Wife in Nineteenth-Century England* (Manchester University Press, 2008).

46 I am grateful to Eleanor Gordon and Anne-Marie Hughes, University of Glasgow, for this information.

47 Jane Lewis, *The End of Marriage? Individualism and Intimate Relations* (Cheltenham: Edward Elgar, 2001), p. 34.

48 Mitchell and Deane, *Historical Statistics*, pp. 29–31.

49 Daniel Pick, *Faces of Degeneration. A European Disorder c. 1848–c. 1918* (Cambridge University Press, 1989).

many had died. To assist analysis of the census data, the Registrar-General, the official keeper of information about births, marriages and deaths, in charge of the Census, constructed the first official division of the population into social classes, defining six grades according to the occupation of the head of household (assumed to be male): Professional (class I), Managerial (class II), Skilled non-manual (class III Non-manual), Skilled Manual (III Manual), Semi-skilled (IV), Unskilled (V).[50] The classification did not succeed in explaining why the birth rate was falling, but it survived the century, influencing social research and perceptions of social class and status, though persistently debated and modified, not least to allow women class status independent of men.[51]

The Census was not fully analysed until the 1920s, due to the war. It revealed no clear class differences but significant local inequalities in births affecting all classes, probably related to economic, gender and age structures. Mining communities, with little women's employment, had the highest birth rates, though these also gradually declined, while in textile districts, where married women conventionally worked in factories, they were lower.[52] As more women in all classes sought freedom and equality, the less they tolerated repeated pregnancy, childbirth, miscarriage, child deaths or secret, illegal abortions, all causing long-term damage to their physical and mental health and lowering their children's life chances in large, poor families. But births were hard to control especially for poorer people and knowledge was limited. Condoms, caps and sponges were available, but disapproved of and costly. The commonest methods were the oldest, *coitus interruptus* and abstention from sex.[53]

Fears of degeneration and declining 'national efficiency' were multiplied by Britain's difficulties in the Anglo-Boer War.[54] Leading army men argued that the failure to sweep to quick victory over inexperienced Boer farmers owed more to the poor physical condition of British males than to poor leadership. It was reported that one-third of army volunteers were rejected due to physical inadequacy (too short, too thin or too weak) or poor health, though the evidence was conflicting. The Interdepartmental Committee on Physical Deterioration, appointed to investigate, concluded in 1904 that deterioration in overall physical standards was unproven (medical witnesses, in particular, were sceptical), but working-class health and nutrition were, and long had been, seriously poor. It found little evidence that such conditions were genetic and proposed remedies,

---

50 S. R. S. Szreter, 'The Genesis of the Registrar-General's Social Classification of Occupations', *British Journal of Sociology* 35 (1984): 285–317.
51 Michael Savage, *Social Class in the Twenty-First Century* (London: Penguin, 2015).
52 Eilidh Garrett, Alice Reid, Kevin Schürer and Simon Szreter, *Changing Family Size in England and Wales. Place, Class and Demography, 1891–1911* (Cambridge University Press, 2001).
53 S. Szreter and K. Fisher, *Sex Before the Sexual Revolution: Intimate Life in England, 1918–1963* (Cambridge University Press, 2010).
54 See p. 9.

including extending and enforcing controls on overcrowded homes and smoke pollution; improved food and milk distribution; more open spaces; better work conditions and shorter hours to prevent fatigue; medical inspection and state-sponsored meals in schools; instructing mothers about diet and child care and schoolgirls in cookery and nutrition; and encouraging physical exercise, including in schools.

Women took advantage of these fears to demand action against another severe problem, the high infant death rate, arguing that an obvious way to compensate for falling births was to prevent infant deaths and help the babies grow up fit and healthy. Infant mortality was high in all classes but highest among the poorest. On average in England and Wales 154 infants of every 1,000 born died in their first year in 1898–1902; in Scotland it was 128; and in Ireland it was 108.[55] In the poverty-stricken textile town of Batley, Yorkshire, almost one in six infants died. Women, including in the largest working-class women's organization, the Women's Co-operative Guild (WCG), argued for many of the same reforms as the Interdepartmental Committee: free medical attention and free, pure, milk for babies and their mothers; instruction and support for working-class mothers in feeding and nurturing their babies and themselves, ideally provided in local welfare centres.[56] Women's groups, including the WCG and the WLL, raised voluntary funds to establish such centres and a few local authorities followed their example.[57] The infant death rate fell, but remained high: in England and Wales it stood at 105 deaths per 1,000 in 1914; in Scotland at 111; and in Ireland at 87. It is unclear why improvement was greater in England, Wales and Ireland than in Scotland.

Conservative Social Reform

Existing institutions could not resolve the social inequalities revealed by surveys and campaigners. Public assistance was available only through the Poor Law, which refused support outside intentionally grim workhouses to anyone judged capable of work and gave minimal help to others, generally observing its basic legal obligation to prevent death from destitution. Growing recognition of the realities of involuntary unemployment,[58] poverty due to low pay and the near impossibility for many working people to save against sickness, unemployment and old age caused mounting criticism of the system and demands for change. Those who could, saved through the Post Office Savings Bank, or trade unions or non-profit friendly societies, run by and for working people

55 Mitchell and Deane, *Historical Statistics*, p. 37.

56 M. Llewellyn Smith (ed.), *Letters from Working Women, Collected by the Women's Co-operative Guild* (London: Bell, 1915, repr. London: Virago, 1978).

57 D. Dwork, *War is Good for Babies and Other Young Children. A History of the Infant and Child Welfare Movement in England, 1898–1918* (London: Routledge, 1987).

58 Jose Harris, *Unemployment and Politics 1886–1914* (Oxford University Press, 1977).

and providing sickness, old age and sometimes unemployment benefits in return for regular contributions. But these were accessible only to the regularly and better paid and few families could afford to cover wives and children as well as male wage earners. Friendly societies had about 5 million members in England and Wales in 1911, almost half of all working men and few women.[59]

Charity helped. It had a long history in Britain and grew through the nineteenth century. Married middle-class women were effectively barred from the labour market and charity gave them useful, fulfilling employment outside the home, which often convinced them that only the state had the resources to solve major social problems.[60] As pressure for state action grew, the Conservatives responded with the Midwifery Act 1902, which required midwives to be trained and registered in an effort to reduce infant and maternal deaths from inexpert handling of childbirth, which was believed to be all too common especially in poorer districts. It was good in principle, but reduced the supply of midwives and increased their cost, further burdening poor families, though untrained women continued to practice in their communities.

Also in 1902, Balfour introduced an Education Act to expand and improve state secondary education in England and Wales (with separate legislation for the different Scottish system) to improve the skills of the future workforce and enhance competitiveness. Secondary schools were funded to provide free places for able children from poor families and secondary school attendance grew – doubling in Wales between 1901 and 1911[61] – but many families could not afford to keep their children out of employment past the minimum leaving age of 13. Schools signified and reinforced social inequalities. About 10 per cent of children attended private schools, day or boarding, with small classes and superior facilities.

The 1902 Act also abolished separately elected school boards in England and Wales, transferring responsibility for education to county and municipal councils and improving coordination between local public health and education authorities. Many areas now appointed school medical officers to identify and treat ill-health among schoolchildren whose families could not afford medical care.[62] In 1905, the government permitted Poor Law guardians to provide free school meals for 'necessitous' schoolchildren, on the school's recommendation, but many parents rejected the stigmatizing association with the Poor Law. Over 300 charities provided free meals unevenly across the country.

---

59 Paul Johnson, *Saving and Spending. The Working Class Economy in Britain, 1870–1939* (Oxford University Press, 1983), pp. 49–54.
60 F. Prochaska, *Women and Philanthropy in Nineteenth-century England* (Oxford University Press, 1980).
61 George Smith, 'Schools', in A. H. Halsey and J. Webb (eds), *Twentieth-century British Social Trends* (London: Macmillan, 2000), p. 183.
62 B. Harris, *The Health of the Schoolchild. A History of the School Medical Service in England and Wales* (Buckingham: Open University Press, 1995), pp. 40–1.

Unemployment peaked in the winter of 1902–3. Unemployed workers demonstrated, demanding help other than the hated Poor Relief. At the worst times, the Lord Mayor of London opened funds for the 'relief of distress', but philanthropy could never cope with the need. Demonstrations grew so insistent that the Unemployed Workmen Act 1905 allowed local authorities to register unemployed people and provide paid work, mainly infrastructural such as road building, financed by a combination of local rates and voluntary funds, but it was difficult anywhere to provide enough work to meet the need. On 6 November 1905, 3,000 unemployed women marched silently to Westminster. Balfour urged more voluntary donations. Support for Labour and reforming Liberals grew.

In August 1905, Balfour announced a Royal Commission to investigate the 'Poor Laws and Relief of Distress'. Its members represented the range of viewpoints on the 'social question', including Charles Booth; Fabian Beatrice Webb; George Lansbury, Labour politician and activist on the Poplar Board of Guardians, east London; Octavia Hill, housing reformer; and representatives of the firmly moralistic supporters of self-help, the Charity Organization Society (COS). A trade unionist was added belatedly following protest. It reported in 1909.

Liberal Social Welfare

Demands for social reform contributed to the Liberal and Labour election successes in 1906 and substantial numbers of backbenchers entered Parliament committed to reform. Whether, or to what extent, the state should take on such welfare responsibilities and whether state action risked undermining personal responsibility had long been debated; the debate continued through the century, more prominent at some times than others. At this time, more people were persuaded that starkly visible social deprivation was generally not the fault of the individuals, as the Poor Law had always assumed, and only the state had the resources and the authority to help. More traditional Liberals were unconvinced and most Liberal leaders remained non-committal during the election, giving more prominence to free trade, yet, soon after, the Workman's Compensation Act 1897 was extended, making employers liable for accidents at work and obliging them to compensate employees. Other reforms followed.

Children and Young People

Also in 1906, a Labour backbencher introduced a Bill allowing (but not obliging) local authorities in England and Wales to provide free meals for needy schoolchildren, funded by charities when possible or from the rates. The Poor Law was not involved. This was the first publicly financed service, other than schooling, for deprived people, free of charge and punitive disabilities. It helped starving children, challenging those who believed the state was undermining parental responsibility by recognizing that, generally, parents were not culpable for child poverty and that many on low incomes needed help caring for their children. By 1911/12, 131 of the 322 education authorities in England and Wales provided free meals – ninety-five were funded by local rates, the rest by charity. About 100,000 children were fed in London, and 258,000 elsewhere in England and Wales. It was hard for councils in poor districts with limited incomes to meet all the need, and from 1914 the scheme became compulsory, subsidized by the Exchequer, feeding during school holidays was authorized and eligibility was determined by school medical officers who assessed need based on health rather than parental income. Further legislation in 1907 required local authorities to 'provide for the medical inspection of schoolchildren' in state elementary schools to maintain their 'health and physical condition'. This also was financed initially from the pressurized local rates, then by the Treasury from 1912, which also funded optical, dental and other treatment previously inaccessible to poorer children. The measures improved children's health and their capacity to learn.

The Probation Act 1907 established the modern probation service, a first resort for minor offenders, including children and young people, designed to prevent further offending with help and advice. The state took more responsibility for children in the Children Act 1908, which established separate juvenile courts, reformatories for under 16s for whom probation was thought to be inappropriate or had failed, and remand homes to keep them out of adult prisons, providing support and training. The Prevention of Crime Act 1908 established Borstals for training young offenders in work skills, while the Poor Prisoners' Defence Act provided legal aid for poor people indicted for criminal offences.

Under the Children Act, local authorities took responsibility for child victims of cruelty and abuse, a problem exposed by the National Society for the Prevention of Cruelty to Children (NSPCC) from the 1880s.[63] It worked to help children but, aware of its limitations, campaigned for state action, then cooperated in administering the law. The Act introduced penalties for child abuse and neglect and all children were removed from Poor Law to local authority care, where possible 'boarded-out' (fostered) or placed in charitable institutions, in both cases supervised by female local officials. From 1913, children aged 3–16 could not remain in workhouses for more than six weeks.

Reforming Taxes

The Liberals moved cautiously on social reform, though faster than their predecessors. This was partly due to the difficulty in getting reform past the Conservative-dominated Lords, who rejected or amended many proposals. Another obstacle was

---

63 George Behlmer, *Child Abuse and Moral Reform in England, 1870–1908* (Stanford University Press, 1982).

insufficient revenue to meet the growing demands on the state, including for defence. The first Liberal reforms cost the Exchequer little, devolving most of the costs to local authorities or charities. A major obstacle to increasing revenue was the government's commitment to free trade. Its refusal to raise revenue from tariffs on imports or taxes on consumption left only the unpopular option of raising direct taxes. Asquith, as Chancellor of the Exchequer, believed that increasing the flat rate income tax of 1s in the £ on incomes of £150 and above would harm those on lower taxable incomes. The alternative was an innovative graduated income tax, making higher earners pay more, which existed nowhere in Europe. It was supported by Labour and Liberal reformers. A Select Committee on Income Tax supported it in 1906, persuading a reluctant Treasury. Asquith proceeded cautiously, aware of opposition from traditional Liberals and in the Lords. In 1907, he took a first step by the least painful means of reducing the tax to 9d on earned income up to £2,000 pa. The revenue was compensated by raising inheritance tax on estates worth over £150,000.[64] When Asquith succeeded Campbell-Bannerman as Prime Minister in 1908, David Lloyd George became Chancellor and planned to go further. Meanwhile, he proceeded with another Asquith initiative: old age pensions.

Pensions

Campaigners demanded state pensions from the 1870s. The aged poor were widely seen as a major deserving group who experienced severe poverty when they could no longer support themselves after years of hard work and low pay. In 1901, people over 65 made up 5 per cent of the UK population. The only public support was minimal, stigmatizing Poor Relief, which many shunned, even at the cost of misery and starvation. Evidence of their plight accumulated from a series of official investigations and Charles Booth's first major poverty survey, *The Aged Poor in England and Wales* (1894), which led him to become a leading pension campaigner. Opponents invoked the accustomed rhetoric that families should take responsibility not the state. But Booth's work and Poor Law experience showed that many older people had no close relatives because they had never married or their children had died, also that families of very poor older people were often poor themselves, giving what help they could, often in the form of meals, housework and care in sickness, but it was limited. When Thomas Pitkin, a 64-year-old part-time rural labourer, was asked by the Royal Commission on the Aged Poor in 1894 whether his eleven children helped him, he replied 'No. I have had to help them when I can. They have got large families most of

64 Martin Daunton, *Trusting Leviathan. The Politics of Taxation in Britain, 1799–1914* (Cambridge University Press, 2001), pp. 330–74.

them … The daughter that I have lives about the length of this room, perhaps, from me and she looks after my house'.[65]

When Bismarck introduced the world's first state pensions in Germany in 1889, he stimulated and divided British campaigners. German pensions were funded through a pioneering national insurance scheme, requiring workers and employers to contribute, subsidized by the state. This restricted the pensions to better-paid, mainly skilled, mainly male, workers who could afford weekly contributions. This suited Bismarck's aims to stimulate economic growth through increasing the security of key workers and to undermine support for socialism by demonstrating the benevolence of the liberal state. Some British campaigners advocated insurance pensions, but the driving force behind the pension campaign was concern about poverty in old age, which most afflicted the low paid and irregularly employed who could not afford contributions, particularly women who were the majority of older people. Booth, with strong support from the Labour movement, advocated non-contributory, tax-funded pensions as introduced in Denmark, Australia and New Zealand in the 1890s. Asquith decided this was the most effective solution and prepared legislation before becoming premier.

Lloyd George introduced the Old Age Pensions Bill in June 1908. It was constrained by the revenue problem and the Treasury's reluctance to spend, then amended in Parliament. It was strongly opposed in the Lords, but they did not yet risk taking the unprecedented step of rejecting a Treasury measure. The outcome was a minimal, stringently means-tested, maximum weekly pension of 5s (25p) per week, 7s 6d (75p) for married couples (average full-time earnings for a male manual worker were 27s (£1.35)), paid at age 70, at the Treasury's insistence, to save money, though it was widely accepted that few poorer people could support themselves past 60 or 65. Claimants had to prove they had not been imprisoned for crime or convicted of drunkenness in the previous ten years and were not guilty of 'habitual failure to work according to his ability, opportunity or need for his own maintenance or that of his legal relatives'. Also excluded were 'aliens' and their wives.[66] The qualifications were scarcely less stringent than for Poor Relief, though the pension was not administered by the Poor Law and escaped its stigma. Lloyd George admitted the pension was too small to live on, but argued that it would encourage and supplement saving and family support. It was the first tax-funded cash payment to the poor outside the Poor Law and 490,000 people qualified for the first pensions on 1 January 1909, two-thirds of them female, who appeared delighted, praising 'that Lord George'.[67] Pension claims were assessed by local volunteer committees, state supervised, and paid through the Post Office. Like

65 Pat Thane, *Old Age in English Society. Past Experiences, Present Issues* (Oxford University Press, 2000), pp. 186–92.
66 See p. 12.
67 Thane, *Old Age in English Society*, pp. 216–35.

other Liberal reforms, administration was collaborative between statutory and voluntary bodies. This usefully cut costs, but was also a matter of principle for Liberals who believed in encouraging voluntary action and cooperation between charity and state welfare.

Poor Law Reform

Pensions, like the Children Act, reduced the number of paupers, although for aged people needing institutional care the workhouse remained the only public provision. The number of paupers in England and Wales fell from 916,377 in 1910 to 748,019 in 1914, from 2.6 per cent to 2 per cent of the population.[68] In February 1909, the Royal Commission on the Poor Laws reported. Its work was protracted by differences between the majority of commissioners and a radical minority (including Webb and Lansbury) who issued separate reports. Both were critical of the failure to prevent or ameliorate severe poverty and recommended abolishing the Poor Law, replacing it with specialized services for specific needs, including allowances enabling mothers of young children to stay home to rear healthy children, non-punitive cash support for the involuntarily unemployed and help to find work, along with rigorous investigation of individual circumstances to identify 'shirkers' who should receive compulsory work training. Both also proposed raising the school leaving age to 15; the minority added part-time education to age 18. The main differences were majority support for national insurance for sick or unemployed workers; the minority preferred non-contributory benefits providing 'a national minimum of civilized life' for low earners unable to afford contributions. Also the majority proposed the substantial involvement of charities in providing new services, cooperating with the state; the minority supported cooperation, but believed that, for efficiency, national uniformity and accountability, policy should be directed by the state. Reform was strongly opposed by the LGB, and the Poor Law survived fundamentally unchanged, for the present. Demands for change did not go away.

Housing and Town Planning

The Liberals also tackled the major problem of urban overcrowding. The Housing and Town Planning Act 1909 encouraged local authorities to condemn unfit dwellings and plan further development at low density, with gardens and open spaces, influenced by the pioneering planners Ebenezer Howard and Patrick Geddes. They inspired the building of Letchworth from 1903, the first 'Garden City', providing homes and work away from London, but only for those who could afford the rents, as the poorest could

---

68 M. E. Rose, *The Relief of Poverty, 1834–1914* (London: Macmillan, 1982), p. 50.

not. Owner-occupation was rare at this time except among the wealthiest. The garden city concept influenced the building of London County Council's (LCC) (and Britain's) first council housing estates from the turn of the century, and private ventures, including Hampstead Garden Suburb, started 1905, designed for workers by its philanthropic initiator, Henrietta Barnett, though rents and travel proved too costly. More successfully, Port Sunlight on Merseyside (opened in 1890) and Bournville in Birmingham (with 300 houses by 1900) were built for workers by Lever Brothers and Cadbury's, respectively. The 1909 Act was not mandatory and was mainly effective after the war.[69]

The 'People's Budget'

Lloyd George's first Budget, in April 1909, the 'People's Budget' he called it, progressed towards a graduated income tax. Earned incomes up to £2,000 pa continued to be taxed at 9d in the £, from £2,000–£3,000 at 1s, then at 1s 2d. Above £5,000 a super-tax of 6d in the £ was charged on all income above £3,000. Death duties rose on estates worth over £5,000 and a new tax took 20 per cent of the profit from land sales. Taxpayers earning up to £500 pa received an innovative £10 tax allowance for each child under 16, perhaps to encourage the 'respectable middle' to have more children. A £200,000 development fund was introduced to create rural employment through measures including afforestation and developing smallholdings.[70]

The land tax incensed the Lords even more than higher income taxes. They took the unprecedented step of rejecting the Budget by 375 votes to 75. The government held firm, made it an issue of public confidence in their policies and called an election in January 1910. They lost seats (from 400 to 275) and their overall majority, but the Conservatives won only 273. Labour rose to forty seats and, along with the Irish Nationalists, helped the Liberals hold on. Peers expressed their determination 'to die in the last ditch' to preserve their privileges. At Asquith's request, the new king, George V – Edward VII died in the midst of the crisis in May 1910 – agreed to appoint enough new peers to outvote the Tories if the Liberals won another election and the Lords remained intransigent. An election in December brought similar results. The Liberals carried on, still supported by Labour (forty-two seats) and Irish Nationalists (eighty-four). Labour's reward included the introduction of salaries for MPs of £400 pa.

The Parliament Act, 1911, limited the Lords' powers. To avoid a flood of Liberal peers, the Lords passed it by 131 votes to 114, with many abstentions. It established that finance Bills required approval by the Commons alone, allowed the Commons to overrule the Lords on any government measure after a maximum delay of two years,

69 William Ashworth, *The Genesis of Modern British Town Planning* (London: Routledge, 1954, repr. 1968).
70 Daunton, *Trusting Leviathan*, pp. 361–5.

and reduced the maximum period between elections from seven years to five. The powers of the Lords were significantly curbed and they were forced to pass the Budget. By 1914, direct taxes contributed 52 per cent of government revenue compared with 40 per cent in the 1890s.[71]

Balfour resigned in 1911 after losing three elections and failing to stop the Parliament Act. He was replaced by Andrew Bonar Law, a Glasgow businessman, born in Canada, son of a Presbyterian minister whose family had migrated from Ulster, a determined opponent of free trade and Irish independence.

National Insurance

Lloyd George returned his attention to social reform. After Parliament agreed the Pensions Act, he visited Germany to investigate national health insurance. He was frustrated by the limitations imposed on pensions and believed that national insurance would more successfully fund further innovations. In addition to sickness insurance, he proposed widows', orphans' and disability pensions to assist some of the poorest families, but the Treasury judged these to require higher contributions than many workers could afford and he was forced to drop them. National Health Insurance (NHI) passed calmly through Parliament in 1911, granting insured workers sickness benefits for twenty-six weeks (10s per week for men, 7s 6d for women – unequal compensation for unequal lost pay) and free access to a GP. They and their dependents received free hospital treatment only for the highly infectious scourge of TB. As in Germany, national insurance mainly covered regularly employed working men, leaving most working-class women and poorer, irregularly employed men without free healthcare except the inadequate services of the Poor Law. Severely disabled people received a long-term pension of 5s per week; the wives of insured men received Maternity Benefit of 30s (£1.50) to provide care in childbirth, not, as initially planned, paid to the man, following a campaign by the WCG who feared it would go to the pub not the wife. Contributions from workers aged 16–65 were 4d per week for men, 3d for women; employers paid 3d and the state paid a little under 2d per week per worker, 'nine pence for four pence', as Lloyd George put it. Contributions were collected and benefits paid and administered by organizations experienced in such work, mainly friendly societies and trade unions, defined as 'approved societies', supervised by a central National Insurance Commission. This further example of cooperation between the state and voluntary agencies soothed the latter's fears of state competition, while the state avoided a costly new bureaucracy.

The same structure was adopted for Part II of the National Insurance Act, the world's first experiment with unemployment insurance. In 1908, Winston Churchill, a Liberal

---

71 Daunton, *Trusting Leviathan*, p. 35.

at this time, became President of the Board of Trade, the department responsible for work conditions, amid high unemployment. He recruited William Beveridge, then working among the poor of east London at Toynbee Hall settlement house while completing an influential study of unemployment.[72] On Beveridge's recommendation, labour exchanges, nationwide offices providing information and advice on available work, were introduced in 1909. In the same year came the first attempt to control low pay. Following the campaign by Fabian women,[73] trade boards were established in four non-unionized trades covering 200,000 female workers, on which employer and worker representatives negotiated pay, but they were under-resourced and poorly regulated and female pay remained low.

Meanwhile, Beveridge, with civil servants, devised unemployment insurance. Insurance could not solve the greatest labour market problem: workers in irregular and low-paid jobs who could not afford sufficient contributions to cover their high risk of unemployment. The scheme covered 3 million workers in just three, exclusively male, trades, shipbuilding, engineering, building and construction, which normally experienced fluctuations but not high unemployment. Workers and employers contributed 2½d per week, providing 7s per week for fifteen weeks after the first week of involuntary unemployment, administered and paid by labour exchanges, where registration was compulsory to assist the search for work. Claimants were expected to seek work, but could refuse work in conditions inferior to the norm in their regular occupation. It passed easily through Parliament as Part II of the National Insurance Act, and by July 1914 covered 2.3 million workers, costing the state about £1 million. It did not solve the major problems of unemployment but it was an important start. Also in 1908, militant miners were granted an 8-hour day and in 1911, after a long campaign by female trade unionists, a Shops Act established half-day closing each week, reducing shop workers' very long hours.

The Liberals significantly expanded the social responsibilities of the state, unintentionally sowing the seeds of a 'welfare state' which grew through future decades, though profound inequalities persisted.

Irish and Colonial Nationalism

The government faced increasingly urgent Irish demands for independence. When the Liberals returned to power in 1905, nationalists hoped they would revive Gladstone's offer of 'Home Rule'. But this had split Liberals in the 1880s and party leaders hoped to avoid it. Campbell-Bannerman sought compromise, while support for radical nationalist Sinn Féin ('Ourselves Alone') and outright independence grew in the south of

---

72 William Beveridge, *Unemployment. A Problem of Industry* (London: Longmans, 1909); Jose Harris, *William Beveridge. A Biography*, 2nd edn (Oxford University Press, 1997), pp. 138–97.
73 See p. 21.

Ireland, along with demands for continued union with Great Britain concentrated in the Protestant northeast. The Nationalists gained from Liberal dependence on their votes from 1910, leading to a Home Rule Bill in 1912, giving an Irish parliament significant domestic authority while Westminster controlled defence and taxation. With a leader of Ulster Protestant descent in Bonar Law, Conservative opposition was stronger than ever. The Ulster Unionist opposition mobilized, with substantial Conservative support. In September 1912, half a million Protestants signed the Ulster Covenant, declaring resistance to Home Rule, drawn up by Belfast lawyer, Edward Carson. The paramilitary Ulster Volunteers were established and by 1913 numbered 100,000. The Nationalists also mobilized and both imported weapons. Ireland seemed close to civil war when world war intervened. The Bill was delayed by the Unionist Lords for the two years allowed by the Parliament Act and became law in 1914, after the outbreak of war, when it was decreed that it would be implemented when peace returned.

Irish Nationalism inspired independence movements in the Empire. They were stirring in the most prized colony, India – though the Liberals kept Indian nationalism at bay by admitting some Indians to influential positions[74] – and in Egypt – not formally a colony but under firm British control. There were riots in British Guiana, rebellion in northwest Nigeria in 1906 and recurrent resistance in Kenya, all forcefully resisted,[75] though the Liberals always sought ways to accommodate colonial aspirations. Like Irish nationalism and the many other challenges to the status quo before 1914, these were put on hold through the war, then revived more vigorously.

Conclusion

The first years of the twentieth century placed firmly in public discourse a series of issues which resonated through the century. These included the extent and causes of poverty and the relative responsibilities of the state, the individual and voluntary action for alleviating it; the Liberals so increased the state's role that they were later hailed as founding what became a 'welfare state', unintentionally, and future developments were by no means certain by 1914. There were tensions around immigration, foreshadowing worse in the future, leading to the first of many state controls. A vigorous women's movement challenging gender inequality had achieved little by 1914, but did not go away. Nor did an increasingly organized, more successful, labour movement fighting inequalities of income, wealth and opportunities. There were visible threats to Britain's international political and economic power, including to its imperial authority, about to become intense with the onset of a war of unprecedented horror.

---

74 Porter, *Lion's Share*, pp. 218–19.
75 Ibid., p. 199.

2 The 'Great' War

An Unwanted War

The government was poorly prepared for war. Few people wanted it and, to the last minute, government leaders hoped, even expected, to avoid it. In early 1914 international relations appeared calm. Then Ottoman rule in the Balkans collapsed, Slavic nationalism threatened the Austro-Hungarian Empire and Archduke Ferdinand, the Austrian heir-apparent, was assassinated at Sarajevo. On 28 July Austria declared war on Serbia, which was supported by a reluctant Russia when the tsar failed to negotiate peace. Conflict in central Europe did not necessarily involve Britain and Liberal Foreign Secretary, Sir Edward Grey, worked to negotiate détente. Then Austria's ally, Germany, invaded Belgium, en route to attack France, allied by treaty with Germany's bitterest enemy Russia. Britain was committed by the entente of 1904 to support France and politicians were anxious to contain Germany.[1] Protection of vulnerable Belgium justified war for many Liberal and Labour supporters who were otherwise opposed. Two Cabinet ministers resigned on the declaration of war: John Burns and the aged Liberal, John Morley.

Nationally, the full extent of opposition is uncertain. There was resistance on the left to this 'rich man's war'. Ramsay MacDonald resigned as Chairman of the Parliamentary Labour Party. Hardie, who supported him, had resigned in 1908 and died in 1915. Other Labour leaders believed there was no real option and supported the war. Thereafter, MacDonald worked with Liberal opponents of war and others in the Union

1 David Reynolds, *Britannia Overruled. British Policy and World Power in the Twentieth Century*, 2nd edn (London: Routledge, 2000), pp. 89–91.

of Democratic Control (UDC), aimed idealistically at securing future peace through democratic international cooperation, replacing the secret Great Power diplomacy that had failed to prevent war.

Financial Crisis

Wholly unexpectedly, the war opened amid an unprecedented, severe, largely forgotten international financial crisis. The fear, then reality, of war caused panic selling on the European exchanges in late July and the world's leading stock exchanges closed in desperation since everyone was selling and no one was buying. The centre of world finance, the London Stock Exchange, closed for the first time since its foundation in 1773, followed by that in New York. Financial transactions across national boundaries became impossible, other than in gold which was increasingly scarce. In London, there was a run on the banks and huge queues outside the Bank of England as people tried to exchange bank notes for the security of gold sovereigns.

The Bank's gold reserves fell perilously low. Like the Treasury, where Lloyd George remained Chancellor, it was taken by surprise. Both bought time by declaring an unprecedented extended Bank Holiday from 3 to 7 August; Britain declared war on Germany on 4 August. After days of intense discussion with officials and trusted advisers, Lloyd George took another unprecedented step by issuing bank notes directly from the Treasury rather than, as normal, from the Bank. These were new, hurriedly printed, notes for £1, later also 10s (50p). Previously the lowest denomination note was £5, worth over £400 at early twenty-first century rates, and too large for most everyday transactions. The value of notes and currency in circulation more than doubled. The Gold Standard, the internationally agreed valuation of the currency in relation to gold, was effectively, though not officially (until 1919), abandoned and the money supply inflated. When the banks reopened they were awash with small, shoddily printed notes, produced by the official printer of postage stamps and of similar size, which proved highly popular, becoming permanent features of the currency in enlarged format. Gold flowed back into the Bank. International debts were repaid, other than to Germany and Austria which were delayed until after the war. The financial system was restored; only one small British bank and a few stock exchange firms (of hundreds) failed. In January 1915 the London Stock Exchange reopened.[2]

This decisive action prevented catastrophe and established unprecedented Treasury control over the financial system; valuable in wartime. The banks bought quantities of bonds issued by the Treasury at generous interest rates to fund the war. Lloyd George preferred to pay for the war, as far as possible, through loans rather than by raising

---

2 Richard Roberts, *Saving the City. The Great Financial Crisis of 1914* (Oxford University Press, 2013).

taxes. He had prevented the failure of businesses essential to the war effort and interruption to essential supplies from abroad.

War

Lloyd George's assertion of control over a potentially disastrous crisis was matched only patchily by decisive government action in other spheres. The Defence of the Realm Act (DORA), passed on 8 August 1914 and amended several times during the war, gave the government sweeping powers to do whatever it thought necessary 'for securing the public safety and the defence of the realm'. It used them cautiously. The railways were brought under government control, while remaining privately owned, because they were essential for moving men and supplies. Planning was difficult because it was hard to foresee how the war would progress in a world transformed since the last major international war a century before. Following scientific and technological developments, especially in chemicals, metals and engineering, it was possible to produce high explosives and powerful weapons with greatly enhanced killing power. Railways mobilized and manoeuvred armies faster than in previous wars. The war speeded up the development of aircraft into significant fighting vehicles.[3] Newly developed radio massively benefited naval warfare, though radio equipment was too cumbersome to be widely useful on land. For war purposes, the government funded technological research and development. Physicists, chemists and engineers developed the tank (another innovation, also too cumbersome to be useful in this war), chemical weapons, synthetic fabrics and underwater apparatus. War injuries, physical and mental, stimulated advances in medical knowledge. In 1916, the government established the Department of Scientific and Industrial Research and the Medical Research Council to fund further research.[4]

Attitudes to War

Popular patriotism became more evident once war was inescapable, even among notorious critics of the government. The Irish Nationalist leader, John Redmond, joined the all-party campaign to encourage volunteering. Among suffrage campaigners, the WSPU suspended action, with many of its leaders supporting the war as militantly as they had previously challenged the government. Emmeline and Christabel Pankhurst believed loyalty would be rewarded with the vote. Christabel proclaimed, 'To win

---

3 David Edgerton, *England and the Aeroplane. Militarism Modernity and Machines* (London: Penguin, 2013).
4 Peter Dewey, 'The New Warfare and Economic Mobilization', in John Turner (ed.), *Britain and the First World War* (London: Unwin Hyman, 1988), pp. 70–4.

votes for women, national victory was needed for, as Mother said, "what would be the good of a vote without a country to vote in!".[5] Some WSPU members formed the first, initially unofficial, uniformed women's police corps, the Women's Police Service, primarily to maintain social, especially sexual, order in wartime, including protecting women from assault. They gained Home Office support, though not powers of arrest, and were a visible presence, along with a similar body formed by the National Union of Women Workers, patrolling nationwide.[6] Sylvia Pankhurst abandoned the politics of her mother and sister, as she moved left and they moved right. A close friend of strongly pacifist Keir Hardie, she opposed the war and became a founder member of the British Communist Party in 1920. Emmeline, formerly of the ILP, was later a Conservative Party candidate, persuading herself that the Conservatives were more likely than Labour to grant women the vote and raise working-class living standards.[7]

Leaders of the NUWSS opposed the war, gaining dissident refugees from the WSPU. Millicent Garrett Fawcett suspended suffrage activity, which was unlikely to be effective in wartime, while preserving the organization to provide services 'to give aid and succour to women and children brought face to face with destitution in consequence of the war',[8] ready to revive campaigning when possible. The NUWSS helped to equip and staff hospitals for soldiers at the front, assisted Belgian and Russian refugees, provided 'comforts', including warm clothing, for the troops, part of the substantial, mainly female, voluntary contribution to the war effort.[9]

The most unequivocal anti-war organization was the No-Conscription Fellowship, founded in 1914 by Clifford Allen of the ILP. Its secretary, Catherine Marshall, left the NUWSS when it rejected explicit pacifism; supporters included ILP members including Philip Snowden, radical intellectuals including Bertrand Russell, Quakers and other conscientious objectors. Peak membership was about 5,500, though it supported about 16,500 men who refused to fight for reasons of conscience, either political or religious. After conscription was introduced in 1915[10] most were granted exemption by special

---

5 Christabel Pankhurst, *Unshackled. The Story of How We Won the Vote* (London: Hutchinson, 1959), p. 288.

6 Louise Jackson, *Women Police. Gender, Welfare and Surveillance in the Twentieth Century* (Manchester University Press, 2006), pp. 18 ff; P. Levine, '"Walking the Streets in a Way no Decent Woman Should": Women Police in World War I', *Journal of Modern History* 66 (1994): 34–78; A. Woollacott, '"Khaki Fever" and its Control: Gender, Class, Age and Sexual Morality on the British Homefront in the First World War', *Journal of Contemporary History* 29 (1994): 325–47.

7 June Purvis, 'Emmeline Pankhurst in the Aftermath of Suffrage', in Julie V. Gottlieb and Richard Toye (eds), *The Aftermath of Suffrage. Women, Gender and Politics in Britain, 1918–1945* (London: Palgrave Macmillan, 2013), pp. 19–36.

8 Sandra Stanley Holton, *Feminism and Democracy. Women's Suffrage and Reform Politics in Britain, 1900–1918* (Cambridge University Press, 1986), p. 130.

9 Ibid., pp. 131 ff; Peter Grant, 'Voluntarism and the Impact of the First World War', in Matthew Hilton and James McKay (eds), *The Ages of Voluntarism. How We Got to the Big Society* (British Academy and Oxford University Press, 2011), pp. 27–46.

10 See pp. 45–6.

tribunals and 90 per cent accepted alternative forms of service, including ambulance driving. However, 1,298 rejected the tribunals' authority and were imprisoned, often in harsh conditions. Ten died or, like Allen, suffered serious health consequences. Russell replaced Allen as Chair, after losing his Fellowship of Trinity College, Cambridge over his opposition to the war, and was imprisoned. Britain and the United States were the only combatant nations to recognize conscientious objection. Outright opposition to the war was less than the government expected.[11]

Politics and the War

There was an electoral truce between the leading parties, initially until January 1915, since the war was widely expected and it was hoped, would be short. When it proved not to be, the truce was renewed monthly. Lord Kitchener, commander in the earlier war in South Africa whose length and effects had been underestimated, was appointed Secretary of State for War in August 1914, and, unusually, foresaw a three-year conflict. He directed military operations almost unchallenged.

The government's announced strategy was 'Business as Usual', coined in a speech in August 1914 by Churchill, now running the Admiralty, who welcomed 'this glorious, delicious war' as he described it to Margot Asquith, the premier's wife.[12] It aimed to play Britain's accustomed role in continental wars: let the allies fight on land, with British financial support, while the Royal Navy defeated enemies at sea and protected trade. But it quickly became apparent that British soldiers were needed to protect France and the Navy suffered reverses against the Germans. The paymaster this time was the United States as the balance of world power shifted further.

Recruitment and the War Economy

In 1914, Britain and its colonies were alone among combatant nations in having no conscription. It had been proposed in Britain but passionately resisted, especially by Liberals, as unacceptably intrusive on individual freedom. Due to the traditional reliance on the Royal Navy for defence, Britain had a relatively small permanent army of approximately 400,000, supplemented by the Territorial Army of part-time reservists created before the war. In the first month of the war 300,000 men volunteered, followed by a further 462,901 in September 1914.[13] They were reinforced by volunteers from

---

11 J. M. Bourne, *Britain and the Great War, 1914–18* (London: Hodder Arnold, 1989), p. 212; J. Rae, *Conscience and Politics* (Oxford University Press, 1970), pp. 226–7.
12 Searle, *A New England?* p. 663.
13 Ian Beckett, 'The British Army, 1914–18: The Illusion of Change', in John Turner (ed.), *Britain and the First World War* (London: Unwin Hyman, 1988), p. 101.

the Empire, including South African Boers. The indispensable Indian Army mobilized 827,000 Indians through the war and played a major role, especially in the Middle East.

The 'rush to the colours' in Britain has been attributed to patriotic frenzy. Volunteering was most intense between 25 August and 9 September 1914. Patriotism there certainly was. An unknown number of men were perhaps persuaded by women waving white feathers or otherwise urging enlistment. Another driver was the impact of the war on the economy. Many volunteers, as often in the past, were unemployed or insecure workers, and unemployment was high in the early months due to normal seasonal fluctuations exacerbated by war-related dislocation. Around 480,000 men may have lost their jobs by the end of August.[14] Again, some volunteers were rejected due to physical defects. Voluntary enlistment declined as large government contracts for clothing, boots, munitions and other wartime essentials created work.[15] Still, 136,811 enlisted in October 1914, 117,860 in December 1914, over 1 million by the end of the year and 2.5 million by the end of 1915.[16] Increasing numbers of white-collar workers volunteered, as rising prices hit non-unionized workers on fixed pay and hours or they faced pressure to defend their country. Inexperienced recruits took months to train and many volunteers suffered death, injury and disease as fighting intensified.

The government did not prevent enlistment by workers in occupations essential for war production and not all volunteers were unemployed or low-skilled. Too many abandoned jobs in key industries, including mining, metal-working and shipbuilding. Within a year, nearly a fifth of the UK's skilled engineers and a quarter of skilled explosives workers had enlisted, leaving a depleted workforce to cope with rapidly rising demand. Employers introduced bonuses and higher pay to induce the remaining workers to work longer hours and sought less-skilled workers to fill the gaps, even women, who gained higher pay and more regular work than usual, though still unequal with men.[17] This flouting of hard-won working conditions caused strikes in highly unionized industries: workers feared employers would take advantage of the war to undercut pay and conditions permanently. The government, mainly driven by Lloyd George, felt forced by war needs to overcome its reluctance to intervene in labour disputes. Negotiations with employers and unions led in March 1915 to a Treasury Agreement: union leaders would relax working practices and suspend strike action throughout the war if prewar practices resumed thereafter. This did not prevent strikes, notably in Clyde shipbuilding and the South Wales coalfields, and they intensified in the last

14 Beckett, 'British Army', p. 103.
15 Ibid.
16 Ibid., p. 101.
17 See pp. 58–9.

two years of war due mainly to rising prices. Unions had exceptional bargaining power when employers and government were anxious to maximize production in a situation of full employment.[18]

By early 1915 there was a serious munitions shortage. There had been no build-up of production before the unwanted war or preparation for rapid increase if needed. In March 1915, Lloyd George moved to the new Ministry of Munitions to resolve another crisis. In July, the Munitions of War Act permitted the ministry to enforce suspension of work practices and compulsory arbitration of disputes in war-related industries. The right to strike was abolished in these industries and could be extended to others. Workers could not leave a munitions trade without permission. Unions were conciliated by limiting business profits to 20 per cent above prewar rates. Rocketing profits – by 32 per cent in coal, shipbuilding, iron and steel and engineering,1914–16 – fuelled workers' resentment.[19] In 1916, minimum wages were established for munitions workers (of whom 340,844 were women in June 1916, rising to 947,000 by the end of the war[20]) and agricultural workers in 1917. Trade boards, later renamed Whitley Councils with greater powers, were extended to improve wages and conditions in a wider range of non-unionized industries.[21]

Lloyd George then announced another innovation, stating, hyperbolically: 'We are fighting Germany, Austria and drink; and as far as I can see, the greatest of these deadly foes is drink'. As war workers' earnings rose, so did alcohol consumption. The war provided space for actions likely to be highly controversial in peacetime and temperance supporters, including George V and Lloyd George, seized their chance. In 1915, for the first time, licensing hours were limited, in most places from 12 noon to 2.30 pm and 6.30 to 9.30 pm. All-day licensing returned only in 1988. The alcohol content of beer was reduced and tax on spirits shot up. By 1918, consumption of spirits was 40 per cent of its prewar level; the effect on productivity, if any, is unknown.

Increasingly, conscription seemed unavoidable as it became clear that British soldiers would have to go on fighting on several fronts and falling numbers of volunteers could not fulfil the need, especially as casualties grew. Lloyd George, having originally opposed it, realized the necessity. Kitchener, weakened by repeated, costly, strategic failures, also shifted his view, reluctantly. Conscription had strong Unionist support and still much Liberal opposition. It created tension in the Cabinet and Asquith delayed the decision as

18 Alastair Reid, *The Tide of Democracy. Shipyard Workers and Social Relations in Britain 1870–1950* (Manchester University Press, 2010), pp. 177–85; Noel Whiteside, 'The Population at War', in John Turner (ed.), *Britain and the First World War* (London: Unwin Hyman, 1988), pp. 94–5.

19 John Davis, *A History of Britain, 1885–1939* (London: Macmillan, 1999), p. 119.

20 Bourne, *Britain and the Great War*, pp. 185, 195; Deborah Thom, *Nice Girls and Rude Girls. Women Workers in World War One* (London: I. B. Tauris, 2000).

21 Rodney Lowe, *Adjusting to Democracy. The Ministry of Labour in British Politics, 1916–39* (Oxford University Press, 1986).

long as possible. In December 1915, Lloyd George threatened to resign and Asquith gave in. The Military Service Act, January 1916, compelled single men and widowers aged 18–41 to serve, unless they were clergy, conscientious objectors or workers in essential industries. Recruitment remained inadequate and from May 1916 married men were also conscripted. In 1918, the upper age was raised to 50, 55 for doctors. Ireland was excluded, the Nationalists having voted against conscription, with eleven Labour and twenty-two Liberal MPs. Sir John Simon resigned from the Cabinet over the issue. The army numbered 3.8 million in March 1918, 5.6 million including colonial troops.[22]

Servicewomen

Following manpower shortages and deaths, women volunteers were recruited to the armed services for the first time. The Women's Army Auxiliary Corps (WAAC) was formed in 1917 for non-combatant tasks behind the lines, to release men for the front. Its core was the voluntary Women's Legion, founded by the Marchioness of Londonderry and including former WSPU members, to provide cookery and transport for the services. The WAAC was strongly resisted by senior officers, who acquiesced only due to the acute shortage of men. About 80,000 women had enrolled by the end of the war. Later in 1917 the Women's Royal Naval Reserve (WRNS) was formed for the same purpose. In April 1918 the Royal Air Force (RAF) was founded from the Royal Flying Corps, formed in 1912 and attached to the army, and the Royal Naval Air Service, responding to the growth of German air power. From the start, its woman's branch, the Women's Royal Air Force (WRAF), provided support. Voluntary Aid Detachments (VADs), mainly engaged in nursing behind the lines, often in horrifying conditions, as one of the nurses, Vera Brittain, later described,[23] included 40,000 women in 1914 and 80,000 by 1918. Dr Flora Murray and Dr Louisa Garrett Anderson formed the Women's Hospital Corps in 1915, supplying female doctors.

Families at War

Many servicemen's families suffered poverty, often not for the first time, when the men went to war. Sylvia Pankhurst helped families in east London, horrified by their conditions, as she later described:

> poor wan, white-faced mothers, clasping their wasted babies, whose pain-filled eyes seem older than their own. Their breasts gone dry, they had no milk to give their infants, no food for the elder children, no money for the landlord.[24]

22 Dewey, 'The New Warfare', p. 74.
23 Vera Brittain, *Testament of Youth. An Autobiographical Study of the Years 1900–1925* (London: Gollancz, 1933).
24 Sylvia Pankhurst, *The Home Front* (London: Hutchinson, 1932, repr. London: Cresset Library, 1987), p. 19.

Initially, their only support was from charities, as in previous wars, mainly the Soldiers' and Sailors' Family Association (SSFA, founded in 1885) and the Soldiers and Sailors Help Society (SSHP). But charity could not cope with the unprecedented numbers serving in this war. From October 1914, the government, for the first time, paid allowances to families: for the ranks, 12s 6d per week to the wife, 2s to each child, more for officers' families.[25] Later, they even paid allowances to 'unmarried wives' when these emerged in unexpected numbers, but only when the relationship had preceded the serviceman's enlistment by at least six months, there was at least one child and 'evidence that a real home had been maintained'. The woman had to prove that the serviceman was her sole support and that she 'would otherwise be destitute'. It was paid even if the serviceman had a legal wife, if the conditions were satisfied.[26] It also emerged that many servicemen supported ageing parents and means-tested weekly allowances of up to 10s were paid to parents who were 'incapable of self-support and in pecuniary need'.[27]

From November 1915, widows and children of the war dead received state pensions at levels related to rank and pay, 21s maximum for the widows of non-commissioned servicemen. 'Unmarried wives' eligible for separation allowances received a maximum 10s per week, plus allowances for children, 'if and as long as she has children of the soldier in her charge'. Dependent parents received pensions but, if judged capable of work, just a gratuity equal to one year's service pay. By 1917, these rules were causing hardship as prices rose. The pension limit was raised to 15s and the gratuity was paid irrespective of capacity for self-support. From 4 August 1914 to 21 March 1919, 221,692 pensions were paid to non-commissioned servicemen's parents, 192,698 to widows and 2,645 to 'unmarried wives', suggesting how many servicemen were young, single and supporting impoverished parents.

Allowances and pensions were low compared even with unskilled wages.[28] They were often paid only after long delays for assessment and could expose wives (married and unmarried) to moral policing by administrators, since payments were withdrawn for 'immoral behaviour'.[29] But payments by charities had been even more strictly policed, Poor Relief still more so, and the payments could be more regular and sometimes higher than the man's prewar take-home pay. The government accepted that allowances should be at least minimally adequate for subsistence, and they improved the well-being of some families so visibly that feminist Eleanor Rathbone demanded their continuation as peacetime family allowances.[30]

25 Susan Pedersen, *Family, Dependence and the Origins of the Welfare State. Britain and France, 1914–1945* (Cambridge University Press, 1993), pp. 108–15.

26 Thane and Evans, *Sinners?* pp. 11–13.

27 Thane, *Old Age in English Society*, pp. 302–4.

28 J. M. Winter, *The Great War and the British People* (London: Macmillan, 1985), p. 236.

29 Pedersen, *Family Dependence*, p. 112.

30 Susan Pedersen, *Eleanor Rathbone and the Politics of Conscience* (Yale University Press, 2004).

The families of civilian workers generally fared better. After the first months, war production brought unprecedented full employment. After the first year, unemployment rarely rose above 1 per cent.[31] By mid-1918, wage rates in agriculture, mining, dock and railway work were 90 per cent above 1914 levels. Food prices and the overall cost of living doubled, but incomes rose faster due to regular work and longer hours. Many households had more earners, as women and young people found work. The shortage of teachers, as male teachers enlisted, led some local authorities tacitly to suspend compulsory education for older children. Older people returned to or remained in work if they were fit, eagerly forsaking meagre pensions. A. L. Bowley's survey of wartime living conditions concluded that wage earners in general gained, the unskilled and semi-skilled more than the skilled,[32] but white-collar workers often experienced relatively fixed hours and pay and suffered from rising prices.

Rent Strikes

Many families suffered hardship from rising rents in centres of war production, including Glasgow and London, due to increased demand from the influx of workers and the rapacity of some landlords. New construction, unless directly related to the war effort, almost ceased. Even before the war, there was a serious housing shortage, especially in the big cities, and Glasgow was believed to have the worst housing in Europe.[33] Some munitions manufacturers, shipbuilding firms and other employers in essential industries built homes to attract scarce labour, including Vickers Armaments in Barrow-in-Furness, where the population grew by 10,000 in two years. Clyde shipbuilders restricted rents on housing they owned, dealing with a fraction of the need. Rent strikes and demonstrations followed. In May 1915 in Govan, a district of Glasgow of mainly clerical, supervisory and skilled workers, women led the first rent strikes, supported by shopkeepers and tradesmen who were suffering because high rents reduced demand. As the Scottish socialist Willie Gallagher described:

> Mrs Barbour, a typical working-class housewife, became the leader of a movement such as had never been seen before … street meetings, backcourt meetings, drums, bells, trumpets – every method was used to bring women out and organize them for the struggle. Notices were printed by the thousand and put up in the windows … In street after street scarcely a window without one: WE ARE NOT PAYING INCREASED RENT.[34]

31 Mitchell and Deane, *Historical Statistics*, p. 65.
32 A. L. Bowley, *Prices and Wages in the UK, 1914–20* (Oxford University Press, 1921).
33 Joseph Melling, *Rent Strikes. People's Struggle for Housing in West Scotland 1890–1916* (Edinburgh: Polygon, 1983).
34 S. Damer, 'State, Class and Housing: Glasgow 1875–1919', in Joseph Melling (ed.), *Housing, Social Policy and the State* (London: Croom Helm, 1980), p. 93.

Strikes and demonstrations followed in London, Coventry and elsewhere. Again Lloyd George moved fast, introducing the Rent and Mortgage Interest (Rent Restriction) Act 1915, which limited rent and mortgage interest rates to 1914 levels. But there was initially no penalty if landlords broke the law and no means of enforcement, other than victims appealing to the magistrates' courts. Magistrates, often landlords themselves, were not always sympathetic. Rent rises continued along with housing shortages and overcrowding worsened in key centres. Restricted rents gave landlords less incentive to invest in improvements and conditions deteriorated further.[35]

Living Standards

Yet many families experienced real improvements. The clearest sign that average living standards rose, despite rising costs, was improved civilian health and longevity after the first year of war. In the first year, more malnourished children were reported in large towns.[36] Thereafter, poverty diminished, fewer infants died[37] and mortality fell among adult civilians. Digestive disorders, diarrhoea and degenerative diseases declined, probably due to improved nutrition.[38] Malnutrition in largely working-class Doncaster fell from 31 per cent in 1913 to 5 per cent in 1915.[39] These improvements occurred despite the absence at war of 13,000 of the 24,000 prewar doctors in the United Kingdom, but many working-class people, especially women, were not covered by NHI and had never been able to afford a doctor. Workers were helped by factory welfare facilities installed to help overcome labour shortages and increase productivity, encouraged by the government from 1916 through the Special Welfare Department of the Ministry of Munitions: canteens providing cheap, hot meals, health centres, improved sanitation and washrooms.

Like doctors, many nurses were recruited for war service. More were trained than before but too few for civilian needs, despite increased pay. Shortage of medical and nursing care in TB sanatoria, combined with greater risk of infection from overcrowding due to high rents and housing shortages, contributed to increased deaths from TB, and perhaps to deaths in the exceptionally virulent influenza epidemic of 1918–19, in which 151,446 people died in Britain, though the impact was similar throughout Europe, including in countries not involved in the war, and among rich and poor.

---

35 J. Melling, 'Clydeside Housing and the Evolution of State Rent Control', in Joseph Melling (ed.), *Housing, Social Policy and the State* (London: Croom Helm, 1980), p. 139–67; J. Melling, *Rent Strikes*; D. Englander, *Landlord and Tenant* (Oxford University Press, 1983), chs 10–12.

36 A. Marwick, *The Deluge. British Society and the First World War* (London: Pelican, 1967), p. 133.

37 See p. 57.

38 Winter, *Great War*, pp. 108–15.

39 B. Waites, *A Class Society at War. England, 1914–1918* (Leamington: Berg, 1987).

Civilian hospital services deteriorated as war casualties were prioritized, increasing inequalities between improved health for the majority and deprived minorities. Older people with low incomes were particularly vulnerable. Death rates among men aged 65–74 rose from 64.7 per 1,000 in 1914 to 70.7 in 1915, dropping to 67.5 in 1917; among women, deaths averaged 51.4, 56.2 and 52.2 respectively.

Families including adult workers fared better than those with small children, especially if headed by a single mother. Numbers in severe poverty probably fell, but the gap between the poorest and the rest grew with the cost of living. The government denied this, pointing to declining applications for Poor Relief from 1915, but applicants' incomes almost certainly slipped further behind those of employed workers. The income gap between workers who gained from war conditions and the mass of the middle classes may have narrowed slightly, though they all fell far behind the employers who profited from war production, especially before business profits were restricted and direct taxation increased in 1916. A minority of landed families were hard hit by death duties following the deaths of one or more heirs, and a number of landed estates were broken up, hastening a process visible before the war. But the war had little lasting effect on the distribution of wealth and income.[40]

The Board of Trade concluded in 1918 that there had been 'an almost unbelievable expenditure of effort on the war without this entailing any large amount of suffering to the civilian population'.[41] Privileged people commented on the improved behaviour of the masses, as, apart from a distressing tendency to strike, they appeared more regular in their habits and less prone to drunkenness and fighting. They looked less barbaric to refined eyes. The destitute 'residuum' seemed almost to have disappeared. This was widely attributed to restrictions on the sale of alcohol. More plausibly it was due to full employment, long hours of hard work and higher living standards for many, though not all, working people.

War Finance

The outpouring of paper currency, combined with a shortage of supplies, including food, caused prices to rise by 40 per cent in 1914–15. Inflation increased thereafter, fuelled by increased demand as incomes rose and by the weaker pound as Britain became increasingly dependent on supplies from the United States. Before the war, home food production had declined due to cheaper imports but these were disrupted by the war.[42]

---

40 Alan S. Milward, *The Economic Effects of the Two World Wars on Britain* (London: Macmillan, 1970, 2nd edn 1984), pp. 24–44.

41 Board of Trade, *Report on the State of Employment in the United Kingdom in July 1918* (London: HMSO, 1919), p. 14.

42 Avner Offer, *The First World War. An Agrarian Interpretation* (Oxford University Press, 1991).

The government encouraged home production, but this took time. Throughout the war Britain was heavily dependent for food on troublesome Ireland; Irish farmers had too much to gain to resist and the severe food shortages feared were avoided. Effective compulsory rationing was introduced only in the last year of war. Britain suffered less from food scarcity than most combatant countries.

The basic rate of income tax rose from 1s 2d to 6s in the £, becoming more graduated and redistributive, ranging by 1918 from 13 per cent on earned incomes above £500 pa to 43 per cent at £10,000 and above. Lloyd George initially increased taxes cautiously, partly due to political opposition from the Conservatives and some Liberals and because the likely costs of war were uncertain. He wanted to avoid burdening the population and causing resentment. But as time went on and costs rose it became unavoidable, and in a war emergency there was less resistance to tax rises than in peacetime.

When Reginald McKenna succeeded Lloyd George at the Treasury, the financial situation was urgent. In his first Budget, in 1916, he raised income tax and lowered the threshold from £160 to £130, while increasing children's allowances so that the increases fell mainly on single men and childless couples. The number of taxpayers increased by 350 per cent, including more working-class people, causing some resistance. Labour supported higher taxation of the rich, but McKenna and the Treasury held to the Gladstonian principle of 'equitable' taxes across the classes.[43] McKenna introduced taxes on imported motor cars and films and raised the excess profits duty. He did not believe the country could bear much more taxation, but Britain was committed to a costly land war and it rose further.[44] Tax revenue rose from £227 million in 1914, when it exceeded spending, to £889 million in 1918, but covered only about 30 per cent of war expenditure. In 1918, income and supertax accounted for 36 per cent of revenue compared with 29 per cent in 1913/14.[45] War costs were met by the sale of government bonds and loans, mainly from the United States on easy terms.[46]

The Politics of War

Financial and military crises in the first eighteen months of war intensified criticism of Asquith's government. Particularly spectacular was the failure of Churchill's strategy, as First Lord of the Admiralty, for the navy to control the Dardanelles, passageway to the capital of the Ottoman Empire, Istanbul, and knock the Ottomans out of the war, so protecting Egypt and the route to India. The resulting disaster, especially the slaughter

43 Martin Daunton, *Just Taxes. The Politics of Taxation in Britain, 1914–1979* (Cambridge University Press, 2002), pp. 47–9.
44 Ibid.
45 Mitchell and Deane, *Historical Statistics*, pp. 394, 398.
46 Daunton, *Just Taxes*, p. 36.

at Gallipoli in April 1915 of 2,000 Australian and New Zealand and about 2,000 other allied troops, lost Churchill the Admiralty and galvanized Australian and New Zealand nationalisms. With the munitions shortage it increased disaffection with the government, supported by a strident press campaign.

Asquith and Lloyd George decided the solution was coalition government, formed in May 1915. This deferred the election due in December 1915, which the Liberals would certainly have lost. Eight Unionists joined the Coalition Cabinet and Arthur Henderson – Labour leader after MacDonald's resignation – became Labour's first Cabinet minister, not in a key wartime role but as President of the Board of Education. Redmond refused to join the government until a timetable for Home Rule was implemented. From the other side of the Irish conflict, Sir Edward Carson became Attorney-General. The key positions remained in Liberal hands. Bonar Law took the Colonial Office.

The Easter Rising in Dublin in 1916 caused more complaints of government weakness and excessive eagerness to placate the Nationalists. It was fuelled by disenchantment with the war in Ireland, as in Britain, particularly following the heavy casualties at Gallipoli, since substantial numbers of Irishmen had volunteered, and also by fears of conscription being extended to Ireland. The Rising was staged by dissidents who refused to enlist in the British Army. The formation of the Coalition alarmed Nationalists by bringing Unionists, especially Carson, into the government. The repression following the Rising was excessive in relation to its limited scale: martial law was imposed, sixteen Sinn Féin leaders shot, 1,000 prisoners deported to the mainland. Sir Roger Casement, the former British diplomat and Irish nationalist, was executed for treason after seeking German military support for the Nationalists. These reprisals strengthened Sinn Féin, aided by Irish-American funds, against the moderate Nationalists. The repression alienated the Nationalists in Parliament and was opposed by backbench Liberals without appeasing the government's Unionist critics, while the Conservatives were also divided. The war continued to go badly. There were 400,000 casualties in the disastrous Somme offensive of July–November 1916, increasing concerns about the conduct of the war. Conscripts, like volunteers, took months to train. Not until 1917 was the British Army large and well-trained enough to impact decisively on the war, fortunate timing when other combatants, on both sides, were exhausted, other than the newly mobilized US forces who also took time to adapt. Not everyone in Britain restrained their alcohol consumption and Asquith's weakness for drink – 'old Squiffy' as he was known – was increasingly noted under the strains of war, deepened by the death of his eldest son on the Somme. The leaders of every parliamentary party suffered. Henderson also lost a son, Bonar Law lost two and Redmond's brother died.[47]

---

47 Clarke, *Hope and Glory*, p. 83.

In June 1916 Kitchener died at sea. Disillusion and pessimism about the war spread, increased by tales of German atrocities in Belgium. Germans, or those with German-sounding names, and their property, were attacked. Thirty-two thousand Germans of military age resident in Britain were interned and others repatriated; 200 were detained as suspected enemy agents, twelve were executed. In 1916, MI6 was formed to detect subversion. German-owned property was confiscated. Xenophobia spread to others of foreign origin. Jews were wrongly accused of evading military service. Wealthy Jews, including Edward VII's friend, financier Sir Ernest Cassell, born in the Rhineland but resident in Britain since 1869, felt obliged to write 'loyalty letters' to *The Times* and make large donations to war-related charities; in Cassell's case £400,000 for medical services and support for servicemen's families.[48] The royal family suppressed its German origins and changed its name from Saxe-Coburg-Gotha to Windsor in 1917, persuading their British relatives to follow: the Battenbergs became Mountbattens.

Air defences failed to repel Zeppelin raids over London and other cities from January 1915, killing one man in Great Yarmouth in the first raid. Systematic bombing began the following summer: 556 were killed, 1,357 injured. In 1917, Zeppelins were replaced by bombers as aircraft technology improved, in Germany as in Britain, creating a new lethal threat.[49] The failure of the 1916 harvest, plus the German U-boat blockade, brought food and fuel shortages, queues and rising prices.

Lloyd George, Prime Minister

By December 1916 the Coalition had virtually broken down amid discontent and poor progress in the war. The Cabinet Secretary, Maurice Hankey, proposed a small War Committee to relieve Asquith of primary responsibility. Asquith refused to preside over it and resigned. Bonar Law would not form a government without Asquith's support. Lloyd George agreed to become Prime Minister, with stronger backing from other leading Unionists, who dominated the new Cabinet, than from Liberals. Lloyd George probably did not intend to lead a coup, but he was convinced of the need for streamlined administration dedicated to all-out war and, following his decisive actions so far, he was widely believed to be the only man capable of achieving victory in reasonable time.

A five-member War Cabinet included Arthur Henderson and three Conservatives. Lloyd George tightened control of the economy and brought experts into government, including businessman Viscount Devonport, a wholesale grocer, at the new Ministry of Food. A Ministry of National Service was created under Neville Chamberlain, son

---

48 Pat Thane, 'Private Bankers and Philanthropy. The City of London, 1880s–1920s', in Y. Cassis and P. Cottrell (eds), *The World of Private Banking* (Farnham: Ashgate, 2009), pp. 247–62.
49 Edgerton, *England and the Aeroplane*.

of Joseph, to direct civilian manpower, and a Ministry of Shipping, under Glaswegian ship owner, Joseph Maclay. The Labour Department of the Board of Trade became the Ministry of Labour, led by trade unionist, John Hodge. Herbert (H. A. L.) Fisher, historian and Vice-Chancellor of the University of Sheffield, became President of the Board of Education. Devonport increased food supplies, introduced penalties for food hoarding, fixed food and coal prices and, in November 1917, introduced food rationing. Maclay requisitioned ocean-going merchant ships, reorganized the ports to speed up the turnaround of shipping and increased shipbuilding. As government activity grew, the civil service doubled in size.

War propaganda intensified. From the beginning of the war, a poster campaign – 'Women of Britain say Go!' and other memorable images – urged recruitment and there were uncoordinated efforts at censorship, news management, subversion of enemy morale and appeals to allies, neutrals and the Empire. From February 1917 they were coordinated in a new Department, later Ministry, of Information, under newspaper owner and friend of Lloyd George, Lord Beaverbrook. Poster campaigns continued. Postcards, stamps and pamphlets promoted support for the war, while news was strategically placed in newspapers. Pamphlets and leaflets were circulated in enemy countries. Newsreels and feature films, more new technology, were encouraged to spread news of the war, sometimes representing trench warfare with a realism likely to have ambiguous effects on audiences.

The news did not improve. An unprecedented mutiny broke out in September 1917 at Étaples, a reception unit in northern France devoted to 'hardening' British recruits. In 1917, 30 per cent of the British merchant fleet was sunk by German U-boats, another wartime innovation.[50] A convoy system cut losses thereafter. Major engineering strikes in May 1917, later in mining, were triggered by inflation, profiteering, direction of labour and attempts to control wages. Trade union membership rose from 4 million to 6.5 million between 1914 and 1918, with the proportion of women members rising from about 10 per cent to 20 per cent.[51] Discontent strengthened the Labour Party as the focus of opposition to the Coalition, with which many Labour supporters had little sympathy, still less when Henderson resigned in August 1917. A visit to Russia following the revolution of February 1917, which toppled the tsar, convinced him a Bolshevik coup and Russian surrender were likely and he advocated a negotiated peace. He aroused hostility in the Commons and Cabinet by supporting a conference in Stockholm of European socialists, including Germans and Russians, to discuss roads to peace. He was replaced as party leader and Cabinet member by the less prominent George Barnes. Events in Russia increased government determination to stop the

50 Clarke, *Hope and Glory*, p. 88.
51 Ibid., p. 97.

revolutionary contagion spreading to Britain. Rationing and fixing food prices defused the worst tensions and morale rose during 1918.

In April 1917, the United States finally entered the war, driven, reluctantly, by the sinking of American ships by German U-boats in the Atlantic. This greatly relieved the British government and helped to speed up the peace, as the United States brought in troops, supplies and finance, all of which were running short in Britain. Following his re-election as US President in November 1916, Woodrow Wilson tried to end the war by calling, hopelessly, for 'peace without victory'. He proposed averting future wars through a new, permanent, international forum, the League of Nations, and pushed for a liberal peace characterized by arms reduction, open trade and decolonization under its aegis.[52]

It was some months before the United States had forces and resources mobilized and made a real impact on the war. Meanwhile, Russia withdrew after the Bolshevik Revolution of November 1917, agreeing the Treaty of Brest-Litovsk with Germany, which favoured the Germans, leaving the allies weakened and spurring the Germans on to mount major offensives on the Western Front from March 1918, advancing to within almost 40 miles of Paris. There was sympathy in Britain with Wilson's desire for peace, but most politicians and leaders of the armed services saw no alternative to pressing on to victory. Germany was not the only enemy. This was a 'world' war, in which, for Lloyd George among others, opposition to the Austro-Hungarian Empire in central and South Eastern Europe, to the Ottomans in the Middle East and the protection of India were as important as defending Western Europe. Hence, the agreement with France in 1916 to divide between them control of the Arab territories of the Middle East after the war (the Sykes–Picot agreement) and the promise of a Jewish homeland in Palestine in the Balfour Declaration of 1917, designed to appeal to Jews in Europe and the United States and build a dependable client community in the region.[53]

Irish Nationalism remained troublesome. The Coalition, with its strong Unionist presence, favoured a hard line, but Lloyd George was anxious not to alienate the United States by increasing conflict in Ireland and tried unsuccessfully to negotiate compromise. In April 1918, a renewed German offensive led the Cabinet to approve conscription in Ireland, in return for committing to a negotiated Home Rule settlement. Sinn Féin coordinated an anti-conscription campaign. In May 1918, Sir John French, former, unsuccessful, commander of the British Expeditionary Force in France, was appointed Lord Lieutenant of Ireland to head a 'quasi-military government'.[54] It proved impossible to reach a Home Rule settlement acceptable to English and Irish Unionists and Irish conscription was abandoned, but too late to prevent further deterioration in civil order.

52 Reynolds, *Britannia Overruled*, p. 103.
53 Ibid., pp. 100–1.
54 Davis, *History of Britain*, p. 135.

In July 1918, Sinn Féin, the Irish Volunteers and the nationalist Gaelic League were proscribed and military rule reinforced.

Reconstruction

Demoralization at home and devastation abroad made it urgent to plan for the peace in order to convince people things could get better. The Asquith Coalition established a Reconstruction Committee in March 1916, mainly concerned with rebuilding the postwar economy. The Lloyd George Coalition pursued 'reconstruction' more determinedly, focusing on social policy. This was driven by continuing strikes and signs that the Labour Party would pose a serious challenge at the next election, especially since it was expected to be fought with an extended franchise. After the October Revolution in Russia, Lloyd George was convinced that reform was essential to avert a British revolution, despite the perilous condition of the nation's finances, proclaiming that Britain must choose between 'reaction' and 'reconstruction'. He preferred the latter, and it was much needed, but this aspiration was not universal. There was strong opposition to reform in the Conservative Party, likely to grow after the war.

He was influenced also by wartime campaigns, many of them supported by Labour and women's organizations, including raising the state pension as pensioners suffered from rising prices; it rose to a still inadequate 7s 6d per week in 1917.[55] At the other end of the age scale, campaigns about infant mortality continued, mainly by women but with greater male support as adults died in the war. The Bishop of Fulham announced: 'While nine soldiers die every hour in 1915, twelve babies die every hour, so that it was more dangerous to be a baby than a soldier'. A *Daily Telegraph* leader proclaimed: 'If we had been more careful for the last fifty years to prevent the unheeded wastage of infant life, we should now have had at least half a million more men available for the defence of the country'. Concern deepened when it was reported that of every nine men conscripted in 1917/18, three were 'perfectly fit and healthy; two were upon a definitely infirm plane of health and strength ... three could almost (in view of their age) be described with justice as physical wrecks; and the remaining man was a chronic invalid with a precarious hold on life'.[56]

Births declined even faster than before, deepening concerns for the future of the nation, especially because 'illegitimate' births rose from approximately 4 per cent to 9 per cent of all births during the war. This unleashed a moral panic about the deterioration of morals among young people in wartime. More probably, as was proven in the next world war,[57] it was due to the absence of young men at war delaying marriage

55 Thane, *Old Age in English Society*, pp. 309–11; Winter, *Great War*, pp. 189–203.
56 Winter, *Great War*, pp. 48–64.
57 See p. 182.

following pregnancy, as it delayed births in established marriages. Almost certainly in peacetime premarital pregnancy was more common than moralists cared to believe. But a serious cause for concern was that 'illegitimate' babies had higher death rates than others, often because their mothers were poorer and more isolated.[58]

Improvements in infant care began before the war. A government circular in 1914 encouraged local authorities to provide comprehensive ante- and postnatal care, as women's groups demanded. The LGB met 50 per cent of the cost of clinics, health visitors, hospital beds and skilled midwives. From 1915, local authorities could establish depots selling milk at cost price and the Board of Education funded childcare classes for mothers. In 1916, concern about war deaths impelled the LGB to fund the full costs of nurses, health visitors, doctors and midwives for poorer mothers and clinics and hospital treatment of infants in regions where provision remained poor. Full-time health visitors in England and Wales increased from 600 in 1914 to 1,355 in 1918.

The improvements owed much to women who saw campaigning and implementing change as their war service, paid or voluntary. A volume of heart-rending *Letters from Working Women*, recounting women's experiences of repeated childbearing and child death in poverty, published in 1915 by the Women's Co-operative Guild, expressed the need, typically:

> How I managed to get through my second confinement I cannot tell anyone. I had to work at laundry work from morning to night, nurse a sick husband and take care of my child three and a half years old. In addition I had to provide for my coming confinement, which meant I had to do without common necessaries to provide doctor's fees, which so undermined my health that when my baby was born I nearly lost my life, the doctor said through want of nourishment ...
>
> I had to depend on my neighbours for what help they could give during labour and the lying-in period. They did their best, but from the second day I had to have my other child with me, undress him and see to all his wants, and was often left six hours without a bite of food, the fire out and no light, the time January, and snow had lain on the ground two weeks.
>
> When I got up after ten days my life was a perfect burden to me. I lost my milk and ultimately lost my baby. My interest in life seemed lost ...[59]

Voluntary health centres for mothers and children increased and donations poured in, assisted by the charitable Infant Welfare Propaganda Fund which launched a week of publicity, National Baby Week, in July 1917. Infant deaths declined[60]: in deprived Wigan, for example, from 139 per 1,000 to 119 per 1,000 between 1914 and 1918.[61] How much this owed to local services or to rising family living standards, assisted by cheap milk, is uncertain. The improvements were not shared by other belligerent countries.

58 Thane and Evans, *Sinners?* pp. 13–18.
59 Margaret Llewelyn Davies (ed.), *Maternity. Letters from Working Women* (London: G. Bell 1915, repr. London: Virago), pp. 23–4.
60 Winter, *Great War*, p. 141.
61 Ibid., p. 148.

This was one example of the voluntary work that contributed substantially to the war effort, mostly carried out by women, supported by generous donations and royal patronage. Initially volunteers helped mainly servicemen's dependants and Belgian refugees. Later they mainly focused on providing bandages, dressings and medical care and sending 'comforts' for men at war, including tobacco, socks, blankets, warm clothes, especially necessary in the harsh winter of 1914–15, supplementing state efforts. The press criticized the government for leaving such support to charity.[62]

Women and War

Poorer women needed paid work, though many suffered unemployment early in the war, with many employers choosing to dismiss domestic servants when the war began. Later, as the war economy opened new opportunities, others eagerly left service for better pay, conditions and independence. The number of servants declined by 400,000 between 1914 and 1918.[63] In 1914 5,966,000 women were recorded as employed in the United Kingdom compared with 7,311,000 in 1918, including in the women's branches of the armed services.[64] Almost 1 million worked in the metal and chemical trades compared with 200,000 before the war, a quarter directly employed by the Ministry of Munitions. This brought greater freedom, independence and higher pay but, often, sickness and stress due to working long hours in poor conditions. About 300 'munitionettes' died and others were physically and/or mentally impaired due to chemical poisoning or explosions. Some 100,000 women were employed in transport. More women took over traditionally male jobs as the war progressed, most visibly as ticket collectors and conductresses on buses and railways, even driving trams and buses or ambulances, shocking some people. Much of the work was temporary because, like munitions, it was not needed in peacetime or, like bus conducting, was repossessed by men returning from war.

Medical training opened up for women as the absence of male doctors at war left a shortage at home. In London, eleven medical schools admitted no women in 1914; they were confined to the London (Royal Free) School of Medicine for Women. Most other UK university medical schools admitted a few women. By 1915, women were urged to respond to the national need and train as doctors. By 1918, seven London medical schools admitted women and other universities increased their intake, generally specifying that this was for the wartime emergency only. After the war, some schools excluded women again and everywhere places were severely cut.[65]

---

62 Grant, 'Voluntarism and the Impact of the First World War'.
63 Whiteside, 'Population at War', p. 92; see also p. 16.
64 See p. 46.
65 Carol Dyhouse, 'Women Students and the London Medical Schools, 1914–1939. The Anatomy of a Masculine Culture', in *Students. A Gendered History* (London: Routledge, 2006), pp. 137–55.

There was more lasting expansion of middle-class 'white-blouse' employment as clerks, secretaries and telephonists, speeding up a prewar trend as the scale of government and business grew permanently during and after the war. In wartime, about 400,000 more women were employed in banking, finance, commerce and public administration.[66] On average, women's pay rose from half to two-thirds that of men, though in no occupation was pay equal. Where women took men's industrial jobs, unions and employers agreed to 'dilute' the work, redesigning skilled work into semi- and unskilled tasks deemed suitable for unskilled women on lower pay. This aroused realistic fears among male trade unionists that employers would find it profitable to continue such arrangements after the war, hence many of the strikes. Some unions demanded equal pay where men and women did the same work, not necessarily from commitment to gender equality but to protect male pay.[67] Some women launched strikes for equal pay. In August 1918, bus and tram workers gained, not equality, but an additional 5s per week for women, 2s 6d for girls, followed by a similar deal for munitions workers. A strike on the London Underground produced an agreement for equal pay for the duration of the war. The tensions forced the government to consider the future of women's work and pay: the War Cabinet Committee on Women in Industry recommended in 1919 that women doing the same, or similar, work to men should receive equal pay in proportion to output. They believed, on slight evidence, that women were only two-thirds as productive as men, so should not receive equal hourly or weekly pay. Comparing pay for exclusively female work, such as nursing, with exclusively male work was rejected as impossible.[68]

Over half a million men were missing after the war, increasing the female majority in the population, though less dramatically than is sometimes thought: it rose from 107 women per 100 men to 110 women per 100 men between 1911 and 1921 in England and Wales; and from 106 to 108 women per 100 men in Scotland. The gap was widest among people in their twenties among whom women were an 11 per cent majority in 1911 and 19 per cent in 1921. Despite persistent myths of embittered spinsters left desolate by a 'lost generation' of men, the proportion of married women in this age group changed little, since previously many had never married. The 'surplus woman problem' probably affected the politics of the vote more than the lives of most women.

The Vote

The demand to extend the franchise for women and men continued during the war, initially more muted than before. Conscription made it especially difficult to refuse the vote to men compelled to risk their lives for their country. For some, the war

66 Helen Glew, *Gender, Rhetoric and Regulation. Women's Work in the Civil Service and the London County Council, 1900–55* (Manchester University Press, 2016), pp. 100–21.
67 Gail Braybon, *Women Workers in the First World War* (London: Routledge, 1989).
68 'Report of the War Cabinet Committee on Women in Industry', *Parliamentary Papers*, 1919, xiii, Cmd. 135.

was a further reason to reject votes for women, because they did not fight; others argued that women deserved the vote for their essential wartime work. In 1916, Asquith's Cabinet delegated the issue to a cross-party Speaker's Conference.[69] This encouraged the NUWSS to resume lobbying, together with the smaller Women's Freedom League and United Suffragists. They recognized they were unlikely to achieve equal adult suffrage at this stage because of the 'surplus' of women in the population: the prospect of women forming the majority of voters horrified many politicians. Suffragists proposed, as a first step, a higher age limit for women voters. When Henry Nevinson, journalist and devoted woman suffragist, returned from war reporting in July 1916, he found a 'suffrage crisis in full blaze, but really promising for the first time'.[70] The WSPU refused to renew campaigning, while Sylvia Pankhurst's left-wing Workers' Suffrage Association demanded full adult suffrage and no compromise.

In March 1917, a majority of the Speaker's Conference recommended votes for all men at age 21 and at 30 or 35 for women who were independent householders or wives of householders. They also recommended a reduction in the residence qualification for all voters from one year to six months, just one month for servicemen, and a version of proportional representation (PR) to replace the first-past-the-post voting system. Some suffragists objected that the age limit would exclude young women munitions workers and others who had contributed significantly to the war effort. Mrs Fawcett agreed, but thought it wise to compromise, then to campaign for a full democratic franchise, as the suffragists then did. The Labour Party agreed.[71] The Conference proposals, minus PR which Parliament rejected, were embodied in the Representation of the People Act, setting women's qualifying age at 30, which Parliament passed relatively easily in February 1918. All men who had served in the war, regardless of age, gained the vote, while conscientious objectors were excluded for five years after the war. The pauper disqualification, which previously disqualified all recipients of Poor Relief, was abolished. The electorate tripled, from 7 to 21 million. Later in 1918, more easily still, women were allowed to stand for Parliament before they could vote, at age 21. This seeming anomaly was quite logical since adult men disfranchised by the property qualification (e.g., if they lived in their parents' property, as wealthy men often did before marriage) had long stood for Parliament, as MPs who had benefited attested.[72]

---

69 So-called because it was chaired by the Speaker of the House of Commons.
70 Holton, *Feminism and Democracy*, p. 146.
71 Ibid., pp. 146–8.
72 Mari Takanayagi, 'Parliament and Women, c. 1900–1945', unpublished PhD thesis, King's College London, 2012.

Social Reform

Once franchise reform appeared unavoidable, winning new voters with social reform was more urgent for Lloyd George: 'The nation is now in a molten condition' he told the Reconstruction Committee in 1917.[73] This became the Ministry of Reconstruction in July 1917, headed by Liberal, Christopher Addison. The aim, according to the War Cabinet, was 'not so much a question of rebuilding society as it was before the war, but of moulding a better world out of the social and economic conditions which have come into being during the war'. It prioritized easing the transition from war to peace. Demobilization and the running down of war industries was predicted to create 3.3 million unemployed, with associated poverty and unrest. The Ministry of Labour, where Beveridge still advised on employment policy, recommended one year's unconditional unemployment relief for dislocated workers and ex-servicemen. The Ministry of Reconstruction recommended a housebuilding programme – much needed and capable of creating jobs. Committees were established to examine reform of the Poor Law, housing, education and health, mostly reporting after the war.

Armistice

The Germans were never defeated. A truce, the Armistice, was signed at 11 am on 11 November 1918 because the Hapsburg Empire, then Germany, abruptly collapsed. Germans and Austrians suffered severely from food and other shortages. In Germany the strong political left increasingly opposed the war and its leaders, with mutinies, strikes and proto-revolutions in October and November 1918, inspired by events in Russia. The Kaiser abdicated and a non-communist, socialist republic was proclaimed. Armistice negotiations were conducted between the new German government and representatives of the United States, excluding the allies. When they protested, they were told the alternative was to fight on alone. Europeans could not doubt that the United States was now a world power, both politically and economically. While the British economy focused on the war, the United States took over Latin American markets, while Japan, emerging as a major trading nation, entered those in India and East Asia. United States war loans further strengthened its position in international finance, while London weakened. Industrial production expanded in India (especially textiles) and Australia (shipping and steel) and both competed with Britain after the war. The Empire massively supported Britain in the war, supplying one-third of military manpower and causing at least 205,000 deaths among Indian, Canadian, Australian, New

---

73 Davis, *History of Britain*, p. 137.

Zealand and white (only) South African troops, while sharing food shortages and price inflation.[74] The experience boosted colonial confidence, fuelling nationalism and independence movements.

Within the United Kingdom, 723,000 service personnel were killed, 6.3 per cent of the male population aged 15–49, and 15,000 merchant seamen; 1,100 civilians died in air raids.[75] Death rates in battle were highest among the social elite, because officers led the attacks: almost 28 per cent of men entering Oxford and Cambridge universities 1910–14 died in the war.[76] The war changed much worldwide. In this sense it was indeed a 'world war', as it was known in Germany throughout the war and in the United States when they, China and Brazil joined in 1917. In Britain the term was not widespread until what quickly became known as the Second World War.[77] For Britain 1914–18 was the 'Great War'.

Conclusion

The war changed the world balance of power and Britain's place in it, politically and economically, including its relations with the colonies, many of which gained confidence and aspirations from their war experience. Domestically, there were small shifts in the inequalities between classes and between men and women. The experience of full employment, unknown in peacetime, and higher living standards, changed the expectations of many working people, putting pressure on politicians to prevent potentially dangerous deterioration after the war, especially now that so many working men and women had the vote, the Labour Party was stronger and the Russian Revolution had set a dangerous precedent. Decisive state action had visibly contributed to improved conditions, including freedom from the starvation ravaging other European belligerents by the end of the war, increasing pressure for further intervention. Labour was committed to state-led reform and hoped for electoral success after the war, especially with the Liberals deeply divided following the Asquith/Lloyd George split. Most women had gained the vote and were poised to make use of it, while some, especially younger middle-class, women experienced greater independence and work opportunities during the war on which they could build in peacetime. The United Kingdom was not transformed by the war, but there were changes, presaging future change.

---

74 Robert Holland, 'The British Empire and the Great War, 1914–18', in Judith M. Brown and William Roger Louis (eds), *The Oxford History of the British Empire, vol. IV: The Twentieth Century* (Oxford University Press, 1991), p. 117.

75 Reynolds, *Britannia Overruled*, p. 104.

76 Winter, *Great War*, pp. 75, 93.

77 David Reynolds, *The Long Shadow. The Great War and the Twentieth Century* (London: Simon & Schuster, 2013), pp. 278–80.

3

Reconstruction?

1918–1922

A New World Order

The Lloyd George-led Coalition won the December 1918 election. It faced vaster world-wide changes than had been created by any previous modern war, profoundly affecting Britain nationally and internationally. The United States and Japan were stronger, both politically and economically. One empire was transformed when Tsarist despotism was replaced by the Union of Soviet Socialist Republics (USSR) and, after further conflict, by independent states in former territories of the Russian Empire in Poland, Ukraine, Estonia, Latvia, Lithuania and Finland.[1] Two long-established empires collapsed, the Ottoman and Hapsburg, and the smaller, more recent German empire, mainly in Africa. Hapsburg decline gave independence to Hungary, Czechoslovakia and a king-dom of Serbs, Croats and Slovenes, later called Yugoslavia. The disintegration of the Ottoman Empire led to the creation of five new states on putatively national lines: Syria, Lebanon, Mesopotamia (later Iraq), Palestine and Transjordan (later Jordan). Two empires expanded: the French and the British.

A postwar settlement was debated at a lengthy conference at Versailles, then at meet-ings around Europe, leading to a treaty in 1919. A major, contentious, theme was how to deal with Germany; demands for reparations greater than Germany and its allies could afford created major problems. An important outcome was the foundation, final-ized in 1920, of the League of Nations, conceived by Woodrow Wilson primarily to mediate in international conflicts to prevent future war, but acquiring wider powers. It was crippled from the start by resentment among the defeated nations, suspicion in

1 Reynolds, *Long Shadow*, pp. 10–11.

the USSR of an organization conceived and dominated by capitalist countries and the refusal of the US Senate – Republican controlled from 1918 – to ratify the Versailles Treaty or the League. The United States was retreating again into isolationism, many of its lawmakers fearing, among other things, the spread of socialism in Europe. Wilson suffered a severe collapse in September 1919 and was disabled until his death in 1924.

In Britain the League had strong and growing support. The non-party League of Nations Union (LNU) was founded in November 1918, before the League itself, inspired by Wilson's ideals. Led by the moderate Conservative, Lord Robert Cecil, a Coalition minister, son of former Conservative leader, Lord Salisbury, it was a broader-based, more popular successor to the UDC, sharing its liberal, internationalist idealism which it promoted between the wars.[2] The League of Nations achieved some minor diplomatic successes before failing to prevent the next world war. It became a valuable meeting ground for international campaigners on many issues, including women demanding equalities for themselves and oppressed minorities.[3] Its most lasting successes were in areas distant from Big Power diplomacy, especially establishing the International Court of Justice in The Hague and the International Labour Organization (ILO), which achieved much improvement in working conditions internationally and which both survived into the twenty-first century. George Barnes, one of the few Labour members of the Cabinet, played a major role in the development of the ILO.[4]

The Versailles Treaty did not grant Middle Eastern countries the independence taken for granted for European states. Self-determination was much invoked at Versailles and elsewhere, but was not applied equally to all nations. Under a new institution, the 'Mandate',[5] controlled by the League, Britain was granted power in Mesopotamia, Transjordan and Palestine and France in Lebanon and Syria, until their inhabitants were judged fit for self-rule. France and Britain again carved up the Middle East but under new rules, fulfilling the secret Sykes–Picot agreement of April 1916 to partition the Ottoman Empire.[6] Britain's established 'protectorate' of Egypt was confirmed and Britain and France divided, also as Mandates, the former German colonies in Africa. The British and French empires grew larger though not necessarily stronger than before.

---

2 Helen McCarthy, *The British People and the League of Nations. Democracy, Citizenship and Internationalism c. 1918–45* (Manchester University Press, 2011).

3 Marilyn Lake, 'From Self-determination via Protection to Equality via Non-Discrimination. Defining Women's Rights at the League of Nations and the United Nations', in M. Lake, P. Grimshaw and K. Holmes (eds), *Women's Rights and Human Rights. International Historical Perspectives* (London: Palgrave, 2001), pp. 254–71.

4 Sandrine Kott and Joelle Droux (eds), *Globalizing Social Rights. The International Labour Organization and Beyond* (London: Palgrave Macmillan, 2011); R. Korbet, 'George N. Barnes and the Creation of the ILO, 1919', PhD research in progress, King's College London.

5 Susan Pedersen, *The Guardians. The League of Nations and the Crisis of Empire* (Oxford University Press, 2015).

6 See p. 55.

New Politics

Parliament was dissolved soon after the Armistice. The Coalition opted to hold together to fight the election of December 1918, still headed by Lloyd George, expecting to gain from victory in the war, though most Labour MPs withdrew. The Liberals remained divided. Most, but not all, Conservatives supported the Coalition, many of them uncertain of their party's future with the new electorate.

The turnout was low – 58.9 per cent – due to postwar disruption and the very recent extension of the franchise. Labour's vote more than tripled, from 371,772 in 1910 to 2.4 million, that is, from 7 per cent to 22 per cent, but its seats increased only from forty-two to sixty-three, due to one of the anomalies of the first-past-the-post voting system: it gained large majorities in relatively few, mainly working-class, districts. The effect was magnified by the boundary changes accompanying the franchise reform, the first since 1885, the first-ever attempt to equalize the size of constituencies, reflecting the rapid growth of suburbs, creating new suburban seats favouring the Conservatives. Labour also lost out because Coalition Liberals and Conservatives did not oppose each other and from the unpopularity of its candidates who opposed the war. MacDonald, Snowden and Henderson lost their seats.

Shortly before the election, Labour adopted a new constitution, drafted by Henderson and Sidney Webb, setting out the party's principles and establishing a constituency party structure, with specified roles for women, and allowing direct individual membership; previously membership was possible only through affiliated organizations, including trade unions and the Fabian Society. Clause 4 of the constitution stated that the party aimed:

> To secure for the producers by hand or by brain the full fruits of their industry and the most equitable distribution thereof that may be possible on the basis of the common ownership of the means of production (distribution and exchange).

This was intended to signal the party's support for white-collar ('producers by brain') as well as manual workers as much as commitment to nationalization, but it aroused lasting right-wing forebodings about socialist public ownership. Labour's election programme featured moderate 'state socialism', including a larger state role in running the economy, rather than comprehensive nationalization, with redistributive taxation and social reform, little different from Lloyd George's platform.

Labour made gains in the election and held together. The Liberal Party was in tatters. Asquith and many of his closest colleagues lost their seats. Their faction won only twenty-eight seats against the Coalition Liberals' 133. The Coalition were decisive winners with 478 seats out of 707. The Conservatives held 335 and dominated the new government. The composition of the Commons shifted: fewer landowners (only 15 per cent of Conservative MPs), about 30 per cent professionals and about

38 per cent of Conservative and Liberal MPs were businessmen. The Conservative MP, former businessman and future party leader, Stanley Baldwin, whose family iron foundry had prospered in the war, was said to have described them as 'a lot of hard-faced men … who look as if they had done very well out of the war'.[7] About 3.5 per cent of Liberal, 1 per cent of Conservative and 56 per cent of Labour MPs had working-class backgrounds, a decline from 89.5 per cent of Labour members before the war, but a larger working-class presence in Parliament than ever before.[8]

MPs could still pursue careers outside Parliament. Parliamentary work remained leisurely by later standards and few successful businessmen or professionals believed they could live on the newly instituted parliamentary salary of £400 pa (about £22,000 today). The Commons met more often than before the war, when in some years there had been no autumn session. MPs attended and participated in debates and committees more than before and constituency work became more demanding, with a larger electorate often with more problems, but it could still be considered part-time work and those who wished, and had a secure majority, could do very little.[9]

Expansion and Resistance in the Empire

The postwar government faced growing challenges in the Empire, including, in 1919, nationalist risings in India, Egypt and Mesopotamia. Prewar movements were invigorated by the belief that colonies deserved reward for their efforts, and deaths, in the war, and by the Western allies' assertion that they fought the war to defend the right to national self-determination. By 1918, of the 943,344 Indians who had entered wartime service, 64,449 had been killed and 69,214 wounded, and India paid £146 million towards the war.[10] But nationalist risings were violently suppressed. In India, in the Amritsar massacre of April 1919, British troops under General Dyer killed almost 400 unarmed demonstrators, wounding over 1,000 others. The violence was widely criticized in Britain, but Dyer was supported by Parliament and several newspapers. The right-wing *Morning Post* raised £26,000 to reward him for preserving India from the nationalists.[11] Mohandas Karamchand Gandhi, the nationalist leader, a lawyer trained in London, was arrested. Nationalists were infuriated and strengthened. Also in 1919 came the first serious Arab–Jewish clash in Palestine.[12]

---

7 Quoted in J. M. Keynes, *The Economic Consequences of the Peace* (London: Macmillan, 1919), p. 133.
8 Richard Toye, 'The House of Commons in the Aftermath of Suffrage', in Julie V. Gottlieb and Richard Toye (eds), *The Aftermath of Suffrage. Women, Gender and Politics in Britain, 1918-1945* (London: Palgrave Macmillan, 2013), pp. 72–3.
9 Ibid., pp. 72–5.
10 Holland, 'British Empire and the Great War', p. 117.
11 Porter, *Lion's Share*, p. 254.
12 Ibid., p. 252.

Negotiations followed, designed everywhere to achieve cooperation without under-mining British control – always Britain's preferred strategy. It was determined to hold Egypt and control of the Suez Canal, the route to India. Under a new constitution, Britain controlled foreign policy and retained free movement for its troops, leaving domestic affairs to Egyptians. Controlling India was even more vital. The loyal war service of so many Indians convinced some in Britain that they deserved reward, while others recognized, reluctantly, that compromise with the independence movement was essential to avert further conflict. The government committed to introducing self-governing institutions, and in 1919 transferred some powers to new, elected pro-vincial bodies run by Indians, beginning the process of Indianization of the military, police and civilian services and gradual limitation of the British presence. The new institutions gave Indians experience of political engagement and administration, the beginnings of a democratic political culture, which encouraged aspirations to inde-pendence, especially because their powers and funds for social and economic devel-opment were limited. They assisted Congress, the nationalist party led by Gandhi, to organize and expand a national party structure.[13]

In Palestine, the Balfour Declaration promising a Jewish homeland[14] deepened antagonism between Jews and Arabs. It was controlled by a British High Commissioner (in 1920–5 the Jewish Liberal, Herbert Samuel) backed by a military garrison. In Iraq, the RAF suppressed tribal insurgency in remote areas hard for ground troops to reach; a client king, Feisal, was installed and relative peace and access to oil, an increas-ingly vital source of power, were secured under close British supervision.[15] In 1919, Britain negotiated the Anglo-Persian agreement to prolong her presence in oil-rich Persia (now Iran). Britain now had a continuous belt of influence or control from the Mediterranean to India.

Irish Independence

The most successful challenge to the Empire came in Ireland, where a bitter strug-gle and martial law continued through 1920–1. In the General Election of December 1918, with the expanded electorate,[16] seventy-three Sinn Féiners were elected and seven moderate Nationalists. The Sinn Féin successes included the first woman to be elected to Westminster, feminist Countess Constance Markiewicz, imprisoned in Holloway at the time for her role in the Easter Rising – spared the death penalty because she was

13 Judith M. Brown, 'India', in Judith M. Brown and William Roger Louis (eds), *The Oxford History of the British Empire, vol. IV:. The Twentieth Century* (Oxford University Press, 1999), pp. 421–47.
14 See p. 55.
15 Reynolds, *Britannia Overruled*, pp. 106–11.
16 See pp. 59–60.

female. Sinn Féin, including Markiewicz, refused to take its seats in London and met in Dublin as an Irish parliament, the Dáil. It proclaimed independence in January 1919, appealing for support to the Versailles conference and the self-determination formula. After further fighting and repression, in July 1921 the Coalition opened talks with Sinn Féin, under pressure from America and from hostility in Britain to the repression and cost of maintaining over 25,000 soldiers in Ireland. Lloyd George overruled opposition by the Unionist majority in the Coalition to Irish independence and a treaty in December 1921 divided the island, granting Dominion status within the Empire and autonomy to what became the Irish Free State in the twenty-six counties of the south, while six largely Protestant counties in the northeast gained regional Home Rule within the United Kingdom. This was reluctantly accepted by Nationalists and Unionists mainly to prevent further destructive warfare, though it was followed by a bitter civil war in the south in 1922–3 between those who did and those who did not want to continue fighting for a united independent Ireland.[17]

'A Fit Country for Heroes'?

From January 1919 Lloyd George was absorbed with the peace conference with little time for Parliament or domestic issues. He supported expansion of the Empire and a just rather than a vindictive settlement with Germany. Domestically, he aspired 'to make Britain a fit country for heroes to live in'.[18] But he faced conflict within the government over the way forward, and was too preoccupied with international affairs and tired after years of hard work to pursue reform wholeheartedly. The success of wartime state controls increased support by Labour and some Liberals for continuing 'state socialism' to improve living standards and strengthen the economy. But many Conservatives and businesspeople wanted de-control and lower taxes, convinced that further appeasement of the working classes would encourage Bolshevism. There was deep division between those who believed the country would best recover from the war and repay the substantial war debt by continuing state control over key sectors of the economy, designed to maximize investment, efficiency and full employment, combined with improved health, welfare and education services to maximize the skills and efficiency of the workforce, and those committed to a private enterprise economy untrammelled by state controls, with low taxation, persistent themes of twentieth-century Conservative politics. This division deepened over time and continued through the century.

17 F. S. L. Lyons, *Ireland since the Famine* (London: Fontana, 1973), pp. 381–470; R. F. Foster, *Modern Ireland, 1600–1972* (London: Penguin, 1990); R. F. Foster, *Vivid Faces. The Revolutionary Generation in Ireland, 1890–1923* (London: Penguin, 2015).
18 Speech in Wolverhampton, 24 November 1918.

Before the Armistice, the Ministry of Reconstruction proposed a series of reforms. The Minister, Addison, a medical doctor, supported by civil servants, wanted a coordinated national health service, under a Ministry of Health, taking over and extending the health responsibilities of the Poor Law, the school medical authorities and the National Insurance Commission (NIC), designed to reduce health inequalities. This met fierce resistance from the LGB among others. A Ministry of Health was established in 1919 following the lethal influenza epidemic of 1918–19.[19] It absorbed the responsibilities of the NIC and replaced the LGB, which was otherwise unchanged, but had no power to deliver a transformed national health system.

The Poor Law remained unreformed, despite a report by a Ministry of Reconstruction subcommittee in January 1918 recommending comprehensive dismantling, proposed by Beatrice Webb, a member of the committee, pursuing the reforms she advocated in 1909,[20] particularly transferring the administration and institutions to local authorities. Poor Law administrators successfully resisted change, arguing, dubiously, that they had provided a safety-net against wartime starvation and protected Britain from the near-revolution afflicting much of Europe.[21] Another committee investigated old age pensions. It heard strong arguments that pensioner poverty required a substantial increase in pensions, but the Treasury insisted this was unaffordable. In 1919, the maximum pension rose to a still inadequate 10s weekly and the income limit was raised.[22] The Maternity and Child Welfare Act 1918 was a greater success for the long women's campaign.[23] The wartime deaths, the return of many damaged men and the continuing concern about 'national efficiency' made it urgent to nurture fit future generations of adults. It permitted, but did not oblige, local authorities to establish state-subsidized health and social care before, during and after childbirth for mothers and children. Women's groups worked hard to persuade local authorities to implement these powers.[24]

Managing the postwar labour market was more contentious. The government rejected Beveridge's proposals for planned demobilization to minimize dislocation at the end of the war, fearing resistance among servicemen.[25] When the war ended unexpectedly, it had no demobilization strategy and proposed to prioritize men with jobs waiting, often those most recently enlisted. This understandably antagonized men who had served for years and longed to return home. Britain was virtually alone among combatants in avoiding serious unrest in its forces during the war, but now mutinies

19 See p. 49.

20 See p. 34.

21 Pat Thane, *Foundations of the Welfare State*, 2nd edn (London: Longmans, 1996), pp. 130–2.

22 Thane, *Old Age in English Society*, pp. 311–18.

23 See pp. 28, 56–8.

24 Caitriona Beaumont, *Housewives and Citizens. Domesticity and the Women's Movement in England, 1928–64* (Manchester University Press, 2013).

25 Harris, *Beveridge*, pp. 246–56.

erupted at camps in northern France and Folkestone and 3,000 servicemen demonstrated in central London. It was all relatively peaceful but the government acted, fearing worse. Long-serving men were released first. A non-contributory Out-of-Work Donation was hastily introduced for ex-servicemen and civilians whose war-related work terminated. It was more generous than other benefits, with allowances for wives and children, to prevent servicemen returning home to destitution.

Education reform proceeded more smoothly, guided by H. A. L. Fisher at the Board of Education. The Education Act 1918 raised the school leaving age to 14, introduced compulsory part-time continuation schools for young people in employment aged 14–18, abolished elementary school fees and encouraged local authorities to establish day nurseries and schools for disabled children. Elementary schools were obliged to provide more advanced courses for older, more able children, beyond the basic current curricula. The earnings of elementary schoolteachers doubled and their pensions trebled. Later, a limited number of state scholarships to university were introduced for able, poorer students. Fisher aimed to improve opportunities for working-class children, who indeed benefited from more and better education, though fewer than he hoped.[26]

New groups needing support after the war were disabled servicemen, their families and those of the war dead. After providing allowances and pensions during the war, administered by a new Ministry of Pensions from 1917, the state could not abandon them in peacetime, especially when discharged, disabled servicemen protested about inadequate allowances and work training. They formed associations, including the National Federation of Discharged and Demobilized Sailors and Soldiers, one of the organizations that in 1921 formed the British Legion, which became their main campaigning and support institution. About 1.2 million men – one-quarter of all who had served in UK forces – qualified for disability pensions. The amount was determined by the degree of disability and the serviceman's rank and was subject to regular medical inspection and review. Two-thirds of disabilities were rated as minor, including loss of fingers or toes. About 40,000 were pensioned on the basis of total or near total disability, including total paralysis, loss of two limbs or severe psychological disorder. Psychological conditions risked being taken less seriously because they were less understood than obvious physical trauma, though the emerging specialisms of psychology and psychiatry developed due to servicemen's needs. Similarly, the need to treat physical injuries created new skills. Cosmetic surgery developed for the severe facial disfigurement that was all too common; orthopaedic surgery was transformed by the multitude of bone injuries and prosthetic limbs massively improved, becoming lighter, more flexible and cheaper. Servicemen who contracted TB or malaria on active

26 Thane, *Foundations of the Welfare State*, pp. 141–3.

service suffered lasting ill-effects which were not always recognized as war disabilities or compensated. The British Legion from its foundation worked to help them and aroused public and government awareness of neglected victims of the war.[27]

Adjusting to Democracy

Unlike parliamentary politics before 1915 and after 1945, which were characterized, until 2010–15, by alternating single-party government, this was true for only nine years, 1918–39, in three of which, 1924 and 1929–31, the governing party, Labour, held a minority of seats. At other times there were coalitions, mostly Conservative-dominated. The main parties, especially the Conservatives, adjusted slowly and cautiously to the unfamiliar, expanded electorate. There were signs of widespread scepticism about party politics despite quite high turnouts in elections after 1918, though Britain maintained striking political harmony compared with upheavals elsewhere in Europe.

Scepticism about political parties did not necessarily imply indifference to political issues. Another notable feature of the period was the large and growing number of non-party associations devoted to specific political and/or social goals, including the British Legion, the LNU, women's organizations demanding gender equality in many spheres, campaigns to improve almost every aspect of social conditions,[28] often urging supporters to use their votes, as 'active citizens', to achieve their aims, eager to encourage and educate new voters in political awareness, seeking to mobilize the new, more democratic system to improve British society. The term 'citizenship' – previously regarded as rather alien to 'subjects' of the British crown – had a new resonance through the 1920s and 1930s as more people gained full voting rights.[29]

Industrial Relations

Among the largest associations were trade unions, challenging the government after the war as before. They expanded from 16 per cent of the labour force in 1910 to 48 per cent by 1920, 6.5 million workers, of whom 1 million were women. The economy remained buoyant between 1918 and 1920, and unemployment, though rising, was much lower than feared. This increased union bargaining power, with the wartime constraints on industrial action gone. Early 1919 saw strikes in the mines, cotton textiles,

27 Winter, *Great War*, pp. 273–8.
28 Pat Thane and Helen McCarthy, 'The Politics of Association in Industrial Society', *Twentieth Century British History* 22(2) (2011): 217–29.
29 Pat Thane, 'The Impact of Mass Democracy on British Political Culture, 1918–1939', in Julie V. Gottlieb and Richard Toye (eds), *The Aftermath of Suffrage. Women, Gender and Politics in Britain, 1918-1945* (London: Palgrave Macmillan, 2013), pp. 54–69, and other essays in this collection.

among London ship-repairers, engineers in Glasgow and Belfast, on the London Underground and Southern Railway, sometimes accompanied by riots, as in Glasgow, where armoured cars and the cavalry were mobilized.[30] The police went on strike in London, Birmingham and Liverpool in 1918 and 1919, despite being forbidden to unionize. Their incomes had not kept up with wartime inflation, they resented poor promotion prospects and had other discontents with working conditions. They had a strong and popular case and achieved most of their demands.[31] In 1919, 35 million working days were lost to industrial disputes, 27 million in 1920, 86 million in 1921 when unemployment returned.[32] Most strikers sought to consolidate their wartime gains in living standards as the cost-of-living rose by a further 20% by 1920. They also fought to preserve the wartime reduction in the average working week from 56 to 48 hours. Workers often still worked longer hours but for higher overtime pay. The 'eight hour day' became a standard demand, increasingly effective though resisted by many employers because it increased costs.[33]

Worker militancy reinforced fears of 'bolshevism', though there is no sign they had substance. The Communist Party of Great Britain was established in 1920, but was, and remained, tiny, with limited influence. The Labour Party distanced itself by forbidding dual membership. Communism was strongest on 'Red Clydeside', and in 1919 the red flag flew over Glasgow City Chambers. Its leaders, including James Maxton and the young Emanuel Shinwell, both later Labour MPs, were briefly arrested.[34] They and other leftists showed few signs of seriously threatening the state, but the internal intelligence force (MI5), established during the war to detect treason, justified its continued existence by tracking and reporting on suspected subversives in peacetime.

Economic Policy

Some trade unionists supported maintaining wartime economic controls, particularly the 'triple alliance' of miners, railwaymen and transport workers who felt they and their industries had benefited from state control. This conflicted with the determination of many Conservatives to roll back the state and 'set business free'. Lloyd George and fellow Coalition Liberals wished to preserve the controls at least long enough to stabilize and hopefully expand the postwar economy, maintain full employment and

30 Alastair J. Reid, *United We Stand. A History of Britain's Trade Unions* (London: Allen Lane, 2004), pp. 182–5.
31 Joanne Klein, *Invisible Men. The Secret Lives of Police Constables in Liverpool, Manchester and Birmingham, 1900–1939* (Liverpool University Press, 2010).
32 Clarke, *Hope and Glory*, pp. 70, 107.
33 H. A. Clegg, *A History of British Trade Unions since 1889, vol. 2: 1911–1933* (Oxford University Press, 1985).
34 Gordon Brown, *Maxton. A Biography* (Mainstream, 2002); R. K. Middlemass, *The Clydesiders. A Left-wing Struggle for Parliamentary Power* (London: Hutchinson, 1965).

keep industrial peace, bolstered by social reform. Some Conservatives, in the party's paternalist tradition, sympathized.

Some Conservatives renewed pressure for tariffs to protect industry from competition. In 1921, a 33.5 per cent duty was imposed on manufactured imports, exempting the Empire. Coalition Liberals successfully resisted food tariffs. On other controls, anti-state Conservatives had their way; most were dismantled by 1922. Food rationing continued due to fears of unrest among demobilized men and the unions. By late 1920 world food prices were falling and the government halted subsidies, abolished rationing and closed the Ministry of Food. There was some public support for continued control of the coal industry, given its importance in domestic and business life and the notorious inefficiency of private control, divided among many owners. A committee was appointed under Mr Justice Sankey to consider its future, which reported in 1920 favouring some form of nationalization and increased pay for miners. Most of the Cabinet accepted the pay rise but not public ownership and the mines were decontrolled in 1921, with some tariff protection. Miners protested but gained little support at a time of rising unemployment. Sir Eric Geddes, Conservative Minister of Transport, a former railway director, in 1921 proposed nationalization of another key industry bedevilled by multiple competing owners, the railways, but withdrew following backbench hostility. He arranged amalgamation of existing companies into four large groups to improve efficiency.

Housing

Conservative Coalitionists successfully prevented continued state control of the economy. Lloyd George shared their fears of socialism, believing the answer was improved social conditions, so that workers had less reason to challenge the state. Supported by Addison, he persuaded the Cabinet to focus on two particularly pressing social issues, housing and unemployment. The major prewar housing problems were worsened by wartime conditions. In 1917, the Committee of Enquiry into Industrial Unrest argued that poor, overcrowded housing encouraged militancy which could be prevented only by building more affordable homes. The Ministry of Reconstruction investigated housing design. Too much working-class housing had no separate space for food preparation and storage or washing, lacked running water or an indoor toilet or washroom, all causing ill-health. In 1917, it appointed a Women's Housing Sub-Committee, representing the three main political parties, to recommend improved housing design. Their proposals for healthier, easier to manage housing included indoor toilets and washrooms, hot and cold running water, windows which provided ventilation, looked attractive, excluded draughts and were easy to clean, adequate work surfaces and cupboards at convenient heights. They influenced the conclusions of the Tudor Walters

Committee which had been commissioned by the Local Government Board, the ministry responsible for housing, to make recommendations on building standards and housing design, which also reported in 1918.[35] Intelligence reports in 1919 stressed that housing still caused severe discontent.

Addison's Housing and Town Planning Act 1919, obliged local authorities to survey housing need and create homes at rents workers could afford. They were to finance building by borrowing on the capital market, guaranteed by the Treasury, the first substantial subsidy to local authority housebuilding. As a result, by 1922, 170,000 new council homes had been built. Further legislation in 1919 subsidized private housebuilding, and 30,000 more homes resulted. In 1920, private landlords were assisted with a 15 per cent rise in rents, which remained controlled by government. Rent strikes erupted again on Clydeside, though with less support than before. Subsidized building boosted the economy by creating jobs and increasing demand for furnishing and other essentials. Between the wars, better designed council houses and semi-detached private housing became part of the landscape, generally laid out on 'garden suburb' lines on the edge of towns. But council house subsidies were never sufficient to fund rents affordable by those in greatest housing need whose problems of overcrowded, insanitary housing remained acute. Council houses were rented mainly by skilled workers, clerks, teachers and other lower paid white-collar workers, who needed better housing but were not the neediest.

Unemployment

Out-of-Work Donation cost £62 million when it was wound up in 1921, far beyond the initial £38 million estimate. The Treasury then agreed to a near-universal unemployment insurance (UI) scheme, which would be cheaper in the long-run. The relatively generous Donation had raised expectations that could not be undermined without risking unrest. In 1921, UI was extended to cover almost 12 million workers earning under £250 pa, but excluding agricultural and domestic workers and certain groups for whom unemployment was rare, including civil servants and teachers. It now included some more vulnerable workers but was less generous than Out-of-Work Donation: unemployed men received 15s per week, women 12s, for up to fifteen weeks each year. Allowances for wives and children were added in 1921. Those still unemployed after fifteen weeks could claim a lower, means-tested allowance, named 'extended benefit'.

Unemployment rose in autumn 1920 leading to demonstrations in London and elsewhere.[36] Still many lower paid, irregularly employed workers were not covered by UI and put pressure on the Poor Law, but districts with the greatest poverty had the lowest

---

35 Mark Swenarton, *Homes Fit for Heroes* (London: Heinemann, 1981).
36 P. A. Ryan, 'Poplarism 1894–1930', in Pat Thane (ed.), *The Origins of British Social Policy* (London: Croom Helm, 1978), pp. 71–2.

rate incomes and could least meet the need. A Labour-controlled borough council in Poplar, east London, held a much-publicized revolt, led by George Lansbury, local councillor, Poor Law Guardian, future leader of the Labour Party and editor of the left-wing *Daily Herald*. The paper ran a 'Go to the Guardians' campaign, encouraging unemployed workers to march to workhouses and demand relief, knowing there would not be space to accommodate them, exposing inadequate support for the involuntarily unemployed.[37] In 1921, Poplar councillors refused to pay their annual contribution to the LCC budget, arguing that richer districts should subsidize poorer ones. They were imprisoned, causing further demonstrations and a national crisis as unemployment continued to rise. The Ministry then introduced a 'rate equalization' system for London only, whereby richer boroughs subsidized poorer ones, and a slightly more generous Poor Relief scale. Protest continued, including in Poplar, against the stringent allowances and in poor districts of other cities the problem persisted.[38]

Slump

The economy benefited in the short run from demand from businesses in Britain and Europe re-equipping after the war, bringing rising real wages and high levels of employment. Then, in March 1919, against Treasury advice, Britain formally left the Gold Standard, the internationally agreed exchange rate between currencies and gold, effectively devaluing the pound. It had mattered only nominally since the financial crisis of August 1914 due to wartime disruption of financial transactions. Despite hopes that the change would boost British exports by reducing prices, it caused a speculative boom, inflation, high interest rates and falling exports. In mid-1920 the postwar bubble burst, markets contracted internationally and unemployment rose sharply. Britain's industrial output fell by 10 per cent in just over a year, particularly in the major export industries of coal, iron and steel, mechanical engineering, shipbuilding and textiles, all of which faced increased international competition. By 1921, 1.8 million insured workers were unemployed and receiving costly benefits. The total would not fall below 1 million until 1940. To boost employment, in December 1920 an Unemployment Grants Committee was established, with a £3 million annual budget to subsidize wages on local authority public works projects; by 1922 this had produced £26 million worth of schemes. In October 1921, £10 million was announced for relief works plus export credits and cheap loans for job creation schemes, but such measures could help only a minority of the unemployed.[39]

---

37 Ibid., p. 73.
38 Ibid., pp. 70–80.
39 W. R. Garside, *British Unemployment 1919–1939. A Study in Public Policy* (Cambridge University Press, 1990).

The crisis fuelled demands for cuts to public spending, promoted by a furious 'anti-waste' campaign mounted by the Harmsworth brothers, who between them owned *The Times*, the *Daily Mirror* and the *Daily Mail*. These papers pilloried 'squandermania', sponsoring an 'Anti-Waste League'. Their influence demonstrated the growing significance of the press in politics and society as the habit of daily newspaper reading grew,[40] creating the largest readership in the world. Daily circulation of the *Daily Mail* rose from 900,000 in 1910 to 1,968,000 in 1930, and that of the *Daily Express* from 400,000 to 1,603,000. Readership of more elite papers rose less dramatically: *The Times*, regarded as the reliable 'paper of record', rose from 45,000 to 187,000; the liberal *Manchester Guardian* from 40,000 to 47,000.[41] Two 'anti-waste' candidates won by-elections in June 1921, taking Coalition Conservative seats.

The Chancellor, Austen Chamberlain, responded to the crisis by cutting the basic rate of income tax from 6s to 4s in the £, then became Conservative Party leader in March 1921 when Bonar Law resigned due to ill-health. The Treasury called for 20 per cent cuts in all spending departments. The housing budget was slashed and Addison resigned. Lloyd George reluctantly submitted to 'anti-waste' pressures and appointed a committee of businessmen, including Stanley Baldwin, to propose economies. It was chaired by Sir Eric Geddes and worked closely with the Treasury before reporting in 1922. It was labelled the 'Geddes axe' for the savagery of the cuts that followed. They hit hardest the recent reforms in housing and education, but not unemployment benefit for fear of the consequences. The housing subsidy was withdrawn, saving £2 million pa, but sacrificing jobs in the building industry. Education was targeted for cuts of £16.5 million, which required the sacking of 43,000 teachers. Fisher's resistance, supported by teachers, reduced the cuts to £5.7 million, but grants for free places in secondary schools and the new university scholarships were abolished.

The End of the Coalition

Lloyd George looked increasingly weak and the Conservatives now dominated social and economic policy. He was undermined further by scandal. Since the 1890s parties had raised funds by selling peerages and other honours. Lloyd George, having no real party, built up a political fund for himself and his supporters. Revelations in the press that he had raised £1.5 million by creating twenty-seven peers and eighty-five baronets in 1920–21 strengthened his many opponents. A meeting of the parliamentary Conservative Party in October 1922 voted, against Chamberlain's will, to

---

40 Adrian Bingham, *Family Newspapers. Sex, Private Life and the Popular Press, 1918–1978* (Oxford University Press, 2009), p. 1.

41 Butler and Butler, *Twentieth-Century British Political Facts*, p. 538.

withdraw from the Coalition and fight the next election – which could not be long delayed – independently.

Lloyd George resigned. Bonar Law, apparently recovered, was re-elected party leader, formed a government and called a November election. The Conservatives won comfortably, with 345 seats out of 615 (the total reduced since Irish independence), after promoting a 'red scare' against Labour – not for the last time. In the election, the Liberals remained hopelessly divided, with declining support, with supporters of Asquith and Lloyd George still unreconciled. Labour did better, with 4.2 million votes to the Conservatives 5.5 million, but won only 142 seats. It had made fourteen by-election gains between 1919 and 1922 and lost just one, in Woolwich East – significant because Ramsay MacDonald stood, reluctantly, under pressure from Arthur Henderson, when veteran left-winger Will Crooks resigned due to ill-health. Woolwich had a Labour council and a Labour tradition, but was home to a large army barracks and the Woolwich Arsenal, a major centre of wartime munitions manufacture, was the largest local employer. MacDonald's anti-war record was unlikely to be helpful and the Conservatives played it to the full, fielding a working-class local hero promoted to captain in the war and awarded a VC. It was a nasty, highly personal campaign, and the Conservative beat MacDonald by 683 votes. He was elected in 1922 for Aberavon in South Wales for which he had been selected before the Woolwich episode, which had a strong anti-war tradition, and returned to the Labour leadership.[42]

Labour was successful enough elsewhere to fuel Coalition fears of advancing socialism. Its support grew as Coalition promises of reform flagged, with the Liberals still divided. It gained in local elections: local government still had considerable power and independence on issues of major importance to Labour voters, including housing and education. In 1919, Labour took control of three counties (Durham, Glamorgan and Monmouthshire) and greatly increased its representation on borough councils, including the biggest council in the country, the LCC. In the General Election it gained from the Liberals in mining and inner city areas and in Wales and Scotland. Prominent, progressive Liberals drifted to Labour,

Women and Politics

What role did the new women voters play in the still male-dominated political world? Six million gained the national vote; 5 million joined the local government electorate, along with 1.25 million men. Women aged 30 or above could vote nationally if they, or their husbands, were ratepayers qualifying for the local government vote. About 2 million women over 30 were disqualified from voting, nationally or

42 Marquand, *Ramsay MacDonald*, pp. 273–5.

locally, because they were not ratepayers or married to a ratepayer, that is, were lodgers, live-in domestic servants or shop assistants, daughters or sisters living in a parent's or sibling's home or mothers living with an adult child. A small number of women and many more men had two national votes if they were university graduates qualified to vote in one of the nine UK university seats. British-born wives of 'aliens' could not vote, while 'alien' women marrying British men became British with all the accompanying rights. Women increasingly protested, including to the League of Nations, that everywhere in the world they lost their original nationality on marriage.[43] The right of male businessmen to vote twice if their residence and business premises were in different constituencies did not apply to businesswomen. Equally irrationally, three single men 'jointly occupying' a rateable property each had the vote, whereas if three women did so, only two could vote. Such anomalies further stimulated the vigorous women's campaign of the 1920s for a universal equal franchise of age 21.[44]

How women voted is and was unknown, though there was no reason to expect 'women' *en masse*, any more than 'men', to show predictable, uniform voting preferences. Despite the belief of some historians and political scientists in a persistent preference of women to vote Conservative,[45] there is no good evidence of female or male preferences in the absence of reliable opinion polls before the Second World War. All parties tried to target female voters. Journalists between the wars were as curious as politicians and crowded around polling stations at elections, questioning women, generally concluding that, like men, they varied in their voting preferences among themselves and from election to election, depending on their evaluation of the issues, on class and other variables, as polls suggest they have done since 1945.[46] Class may have been a more important influence on voting than gender.

There is every sign that women, after the generally low turnout in the 1918 election, used their votes. It was once argued that, after gaining the vote, the women's movement believed it had won, then splintered and collapsed and women made little use of their new rights. But leading feminists, including Millicent Garrett Fawcett, Eleanor Rathbone and Sylvia Pankhurst, from their different perspectives, recognized that partially gaining the vote was not the end but the start of another battle, to use the vote to achieve gender equality, including equal voting rights, and social improvements

43 See pp. 10–11.

44 Cheryl Law, *Suffrage and Power. The Women's Movement, 1918–28* (London: I. B. Tauris, 1997).

45 J. Lovenduski, P. Norris, C. Burgess, 'The Party and Women', in A. Seldon and S. Ball (eds), *Conservative Century. The Conservative Party since 1900* (Oxford University Press, 1994), pp. 611–36.

46 Ibid.; Esther Breitenbach and Pat Thane (eds). *Women and Citizenship in Britain and Ireland in the Twentieth Century* (London: Bloomsbury, 2010).

long neglected by male-dominated parliaments.[47] They pursued this battle through the interwar years and after.

Women continued to be active in all political parties.[48] Labour-supporting women took advantage of the opportunity from 1918 to join constituency parties and gain recognized roles in the party structure. By 1927, at 300,000, they made up half the individual membership, a higher proportion in some constituencies. This did not give them equal influence with male members, since the block votes of the trade unions were still decisive at the party conferences, where key policies were approved.[49] The Conservative Party had about 1 million female members in the 1920s, who also officially gained a position in the party organization but no greater influence in party policy.[50] The Liberal Party, having alienated many women by failing to grant the vote before the war, and divided as it was after the war, had about 100,000 women members by 1928.[51] In all parties, women actively promoted the political education and political skills (e.g., public speaking) of other women, encouraging them to be active citizens by using their votes.

But women lacked noticeable influence in any party; they were still regarded by many men mainly as useful canvassers and fundraisers. For decades they found it hard to gain selection for winnable parliamentary seats; prejudice against women in politics ran deep. There was no shortage of women willing to stand for election: seventeen stood in 1918, but only Countess Markiewicz was elected.[52] Nancy Astor, Conservative, and American by birth, was the first woman elected, in 1919, for Plymouth, replacing her husband when he inherited his father's title and seat in the Lords. She retained the seat until she was defeated in the Labour landslide of 1945. She found the Commons a lonely and often hostile place until Liberal Margaret Wintringham took her husband's former seat in a by-election in 1920 following his death. Unlike Astor, she was a former suffragist, active in women's organizations as well as the Liberal Party, but they cooperated and Astor supported causes promoted by women's organizations. In 1922, they both won again, while thirty-one other women stood unsuccessfully.

47 Pat Thane, 'What Difference did the Vote Make? Women in Public and Private Life in Britain since 1918?' *Historical Research* 76(192) (2003): 268–85; Pat Thane, 'What Difference did the Vote Make?' in Amanda Vickery (ed.), *Women, Privilege and Power. British Politics, 1750 to the Present* (Stanford University Press, 2001), pp. 253–88.
48 Breitenbach and Thane, *Women and Citizenship*.
49 Pat Thane, 'The Women of the British Labour Party and Feminism', in H. L. Smith (ed.), *British Feminism in the Twentieth Century* (Aldershot: Edward Elgar, 1990), pp. 124–43.
50 Lovenduski et al., 'The Party and Women'.
51 Pat Thane, 'Women, Liberalism and Community, 1918–1930', in E. Biagini (ed.), *Citizenship and Community. Liberals, Radicals and Collective Identities in the British Isles, 1865–1931* (Cambridge University Press, 1996), pp. 66–92.
52 See pp. 67–8.

Women had more success in local government where they were already established.[53] Female local councillors increased from 259 to 754 between 1914 and 1923; female Poor Law Guardians from 1,536 to 2,323. They were fewest on county councils, most on small rural district councils.[54] Locally elected women, like men, were not necessarily affiliated to parties, since independents were active and successful in local government. Party members or not, elected or not, women could wield influence at this level. Preston, Lancashire, was transformed from a Conservative to a Labour stronghold in the 1920s when working women formed a strong Labour Women's Section and persuaded an initially unsympathetic local party to adopt and, following success in local elections, implement a programme of improvements in education, maternity and child welfare, healthcare, housing and public amenities such as baths and washhouses.[55] Women were similarly active elsewhere.[56]

Party membership and election to Parliament was not the only way women influenced national politics. Many activists realized that they could be effective through collective organization to achieve specific aims, as they had organized for the vote, and, that achieving comprehensive gender equality required a wide spread of activism. The WSPU did not revive after the war, but in 1918 the NUWSS was renamed the National Union of Societies for Equal Citizenship (NUSEC) and dedicated to helping women use the vote, informing them about political issues and procedures, and campaigning alone and with other organizations for reforms. Eleanor Rathbone formed the Women's Citizens Association (WCA) in Liverpool in 1913 with similar aims. She chaired the NUSEC from 1919 and the organizations worked closely together.[57] Both were determinedly independent of party politics in order to include women of diverse political views, though their members might join parties and they supported party candidates, male and female, who supported their causes in local and central government elections.[58]

Other organizations committed to similar aims included Women's Institutes (WIs), founded from 1915 by suffrage campaigners, including former militants, on a model founded in Canada, to give countrywomen opportunities for personal and political

53 Hollis, *Ladies Elect*. Lowri Newman, "'Providing an Opportunity to Exercise their Energies". The Role of the Labour Women's Sections in Shaping Political Identities, South Wales, 1918–1939', pp. 29–44; Thane, 'Women and Political Participation'; E. Breitenbach, 'Scottish Women's Organizations and the Exercise of Citizenship, c. 1900–c. 1970', pp. 65–7, all in Esther Breitenbach and Pat Thane (eds), *Women and Citizenship in Britain and Ireland in the Twentieth Century* (London: Bloomsbury, 2010).
54 Martin Pugh, *Women and the Women's Movement in Britain*, 2nd edn (London: Macmillan, 2000), p. 57.
55 Michael Savage, *The Dynamics of Working Class Politics. The Labour Movement in Preston, 1880–1940* (Cambridge University Press, 1987).
56 Beaumont, *Housewives and Citizens*.
57 In 'What Difference Did the Vote Make?', I mistakenly state that they merged in 1924. This happened only in Glasgow.
58 On extensive women's activism in Scotland, see Breitenbach, 'Scottish Women's Organizations', pp. 67–73.

development in spaces free from the traditional rural social hierarchy, dominated in Britain by the wives of squires and clergymen. WIs, like Labour Party women, encouraged women who worked in the home to value their domestic work and skills, and their important contributions to society and the economy in raising children and supporting working men, campaigning for recognition of this indispensable, hard work, while they also fought for improved conditions for women in paid work. They and other organizations cooperated in increasingly successful campaigns to improve often appalling rural housing and access to water and electricity supplies, still lacking in much of the countryside in the 1930s.[59]

Women's political awareness was promoted, alongside other goals, by the growing number of women's trade unions, professional, confessional and single-issue groups, including the National Union of Women Teachers, the Council of Women Civil Servants, the (Roman Catholic) St Joan's Social and Political Union, the Union of Jewish Women and the Women's Co-operative Guild. Among others, the League of the Church Militant (founded 1909 as the Church League for Women's Suffrage) campaigned for greater representation of women in the Church of England and, particularly, for the ordination of women (achieved in 1994). In 1919, women gained equal representation when the lay councils of the Church were reorganized. Women were admitted more readily to the ministry of Nonconformist churches: by the Congregationalists in 1917 and Baptists in 1926.[60] At least 130 women's organizations were active in the 1920s, almost certainly drawing into public life a larger number and a wider social range of women than ever before.[61]

An early parliamentary response to women's campaigns was the Sex Disqualification (Removal) Act 1919, which, in principle, abolished disqualification by sex or marriage for entry to or continued employment in the professions or the exercise of any public function. It was a compromise with Bills promoted by Labour and women's organizations which included the equal franchise and did not go as far as many campaigners wanted.[62] It did not eliminate major obstacles still facing women seeking to enter the professions or the higher levels of the civil service. They experienced prejudice, restricted entry (including limits on the numbers of women admitted to the minority of medical schools that accepted them after the war[63]), limited promotion prospects and lower pay than men for the same work. The marriage bar, prohibiting

59 Maggie Andrews, *The Acceptable Face of Feminism. The Women's Institute as a Social Movement*, 2nd edn (London: Lawrence & Wishart, 2015). On Scottish Women's Institutes, see Breitenbach, 'Scottish Women's Organizations', pp. 68–9.
60 I am grateful to the late Sue Innes for this information.
61 Law, *Suffrage and Power*, pp. 232–7.
62 Takanayagi, 'Parliament and Women'.
63 Carol Dyhouse, 'Women Students and the London Medical Schools, 1914–39: The Anatomy of a Masculine Culture', *Gender and History* 10(1) (1998): 110–32.

employment of married women and requiring them to resign on marriage, remained throughout the public and much of the private sector despite campaigns against these inequalities throughout the interwar years.[64] But the Act enabled women to become lawyers and magistrates and to sit on juries for the first time in their long history. In the early 1920s, the first women were called to the bar, though they faced prejudice and discrimination.[65] In 1920, 200 women were appointed as magistrates, presiding over the ancient, lowest, unpaid, but indispensable level of the judicial system. No longer were women involved in legal processes, including marital or family cases or concerning physical or sexual assault, always alone facing courts wholly composed of men. There were 1,600 female magistrates in England and Wales by 1927 out of a total of 25,000.[66]

Women gained and lost in the postwar labour market. They had to leave work that was primarily war-related, such as munitions, or to which men expected to return. The labour market again became strictly gender divided. It was difficult to find alternative work, especially when unemployment rose. Many women returned reluctantly to domestic service, where the numbers gradually climbed to close to prewar levels: in 1911 there were 1,662,511 live-in servants, in 1931 there were 1,600,017. White-collar work offered more opportunities, mainly for younger, more educated women. The numbers employed in the civil service, local government, teaching and nursing increased as the public sector expanded. Private businesses, such as banks, grew in number and size during and after the war, creating more secretarial and clerical posts for women, though in none of these occupations did they have anything approaching equal opportunities. Often they did identical work to men, but earned less, had more limited promotion prospects and were required to leave on marriage.[67] The BBC, founded in 1922, and the John Lewis (department store) Partnership, founded 1918, were unusual in having no marriage bar and providing equal pay and opportunities, at least in principle. In reality, gender inequality persisted even in these rare institutions which officially deemed it outdated in the modern world.[68] But young, unmarried, middle-class women gained new freedoms now that they could earn a living and live independently, enjoying new leisure activities and more relaxed dress codes, risking the disapproval of conventional moralists.

Before marriage, most working-class women had no choice but to enter the labour market, most from age 14, some at 12 or 13. Females aged 15–24 in employment increased from 47 per cent to 63 per cent between 1911 and 1921, mainly due to the

64 Law, *Suffrage and Power*, pp. 82–4; Glew, *Gender, Rhetoric and Regulation*.
65 Judith Bourne, *Helena Normanton and the Opening of the Bar to Women* (London: Waterside Press, 2016).
66 Anne Logan, *Feminism and Criminal Justice. A Historical Perspective* (London: Palgrave Macmillan, 2008).
67 Glew, *Gender, Rhetoric and Regulation*.
68 Kate Murphy, *Behind the Wireless. A History of Early Women at the BBC* (London: Palgrave Macmillan, 2016).

middle-class influx.[69] The largest occupation (23 per cent) was, still, domestic service, while 13 per cent worked in the textile industries, 12 per cent were clerks and typists and 9 per cent shop assistants, another occupation which expanded during and after the war. Women, like men, gained increased wages during and after the war until 1920, when they declined. Throughout, young women under 18, were the lowest paid sector of the workforce, regarded as cheap, disposable labour, though their incomes could be vital to their families as unemployment grew or if their mother was widowed or separated with younger children. The standard argument for unequal pay, that men supported families whereas women did not, overlooked such realities and the fact that unmarried men benefited from higher pay. In some occupations women were forced to retire at earlier ages than men, especially from public-facing occupations, such as receptionists or shop workers, for which post-menopausal women were deemed insufficiently decorative.[70]

Remembrance

The war did not cease to affect the lives of combatants and non-combatants on 11th November 1918. It lived on in the experience and visibility of disabled soldiers and the impact on the returners and their families. My grandfather screamed in his sleep with nightmares of battle until he died in the 1960s. It survived too in literature, art, the new medium of film and in the solid form of memorials to the war dead. Rarely has a war been so remembered. Never before in modern history had a war destroyed so many lives, and no past culture had such capacities for communicating and memorializing these realities.

The war did not officially end until the signing of the peace treaties in June 1919. This was followed by victory parades in Paris, then London. Triumphalism offended some ex-servicemen, who refused to participate, and the official and popular mood shifted to remembrance. The 11th November became Remembrance Day in the United Kingdom and elsewhere. In London, it was marked by a ceremony at which the king, leading politicians, military and other dignitaries laid wreaths in memory of the fallen, while the nation observed a two-minute silence at the 'eleventh hour of the eleventh day of the eleventh month' when the fighting had stopped. The first ceremony in 1919 was held in the gardens of Buckingham Palace. That of 1920 was more public and opened with the unveiling of a stone monument in Whitehall, the Cenotaph, Greek for the 'empty tomb' it represented, inscribed to 'the Glorious Dead'.

---

69 Selina Todd, *Young Women, Work and Family in England, 1918–1950* (Oxford University Press, 2005), pp. 20–3.

70 Thane, *Old Age in English Society*, pp. 283–6.

It was designed by the architect Edward Lutyens as a temporary structure for the 1919 victory parade. By popular demand it became permanent. From 1920, it was the regular site for the official Remembrance Day ceremony, with wreath-laying, march-pasts by people who had served in the war, watched by large crowds, while similar ceremonies were held at local memorials, often accompanied by reading the names of the local war dead.[71] After the BBC opened in 1922 it was broadcast to the nation. In 1921 and through the 1920s ex-servicemen protested at the ceremony that survivors should also be remembered, not abandoned to suffer unemployment and poor housing. The wreaths were made from artificial poppies from 1921, when they were introduced by the British Legion in memory of the flowers growing in the battlefields of Belgium and France. They were made by disabled ex-servicemen and sold each year to help war victims and their families. Poppies became indissolubly associated with remembrance and the annual Whitehall ceremony. From 1934, as another war loomed, the pacifist Peace Pledge Union sold white poppies to symbolize opposition to war.

From 1916, the government funded cemeteries for the UK and Empire dead in the war zones, which became memorials. At least 100,000 men had no known grave. From 1920 they were commemorated by the tomb of the Unknown Soldier in Westminster Abbey.[72] The Cabinet proposed a museum to keep alive memories of this exceptional war. India and the Dominions wanted it also to commemorate their substantial roles: it was named the Imperial War Museum and opened by King George V at Crystal Palace in 1920. From 1924 to 1935 it moved to South Kensington, then in 1936 settled in south London. It was designed to represent everyone who had participated in the war effort, women and civilian workers as well as fighters, with advice from a specially convened women's committee.[73]

In Britain, perhaps more than elsewhere, the war lived on in literature, especially poetry. This ranged from the romantic work of Rupert Brooke, written early in the war, before his death from sepsis in Gallipoli in 1915, before bitterness at the slaughter set in, to the deep regret of Wilfred Owen at the young lives sacrificed to the decisions of older men, until his own death in the final week of the war, aged 25, and the lasting bitterness of Siegfried Sassoon, a damaged survivor, like Owen haunted by the fact that he had killed Germans. Most works by eminent literary figures, including Robert Graves' autobiography *Goodbye to All That* (1929), conveyed a lasting sense of the futility of the war, though a lesser-known genre of lower-brow novels represented the war as an

---

71 J. M. Winter, *Sites of Memory, Sites of Mourning* (Cambridge University Press, 1995), pp. 103–5.

72 Winter, *Sites of Memory*, p. 27.

73 Alyson Mercer, 'Representations of Gender in British War Museums', unpublished PhD thesis, King's College London, 2015.

adventure, including exciting travel, of which at least some less celebrated soldiers were proud. The experience of the war inspired some who are not remembered as poets, including the future Labour premier, Clement Attlee, writing, among other verses, at Gallipoli:

> Stand to. The huddled sheeted figures creep
> From step and dugout, yawning from their dreams
> Of home and England.[74]

The literature was produced spontaneously over many years, while war artists were appointed by the government, an unprecedented initiative in state sponsorship of the arts. This originated in 1916 in the propaganda department, which sought eye witness images to illustrate its output. The artists included Paul Nash and Stanley Spencer, who served in the Royal Army Medical Corps (RAMC), whose most memorable war paintings were frescoes, *Resurrection of the Soldiers*, evoking the unheroic character of daily military life, commissioned in the early 1920s for a chapel in Berkshire built to commemorate a dead serviceman. Henry Tonks was another official artist, Principal of the Slade School of Art, a former surgeon who served in the RAMC then sketched, among other images, portraits of men severely facially disfigured in war and treated by the pioneering cosmetic surgeon, Harold Gillies.[75] Larger numbers of memorable paintings of the war and the survivors were produced in Germany by Dix, Beckmann and others.

Filmed responses to the war came mainly from France and America, where film production took off faster than in Britain, though they had large British audiences. First came Abel Gance's *J'Accuse* (1919), with haunting images of soldiers returning from the dead; later *All Quiet on the Western Front*, made in America in 1930 from the German veteran Erich Maria Remarque's 1929 novel about a group of school friends destroyed in the war. In these and other ways the war long haunted British and other societies, contributing to changes in culture and politics after the war.

Conclusion

Under the Coalition government the United Kingdom began slowly to adjust to a world and a country not wholly but substantially changed by the war, alongside efforts to turn back the clock. It had to face up to reduced international political and economic power,

74 Kenneth Harris, *Attlee* (London: Weidenfeld & Nicolson, 1984), p. 36.
75 Simon Millar, 'Rooksdown House and the Rooksdown Club: A Study into the rehabilitation of facially disfigured servicemen and civilians', unpublished PhD thesis, King's College London, 2015.

emerging colonial nationalisms, increased involvement of the state in directing economic and social change, with an incomplete but unprecedented democratic franchise producing challenges to deeply rooted inequalities from a stronger Labour Party and a trade union movement resisting serious unemployment, while enfranchised women claimed their rights as citizens. The adjustment continued until the next world war and was far from easy.

4 Democratic Britain?

1922–1931

Conservative Government, 1922–3

The difficulties of adjustment, especially for the traditional holders of power, were evident in the short-lived Conservative government which followed. Bonar Law became Prime Minister in 1922 without a clear strategy and still in poor health, lacking support from experienced Conservatives in a divided party, including Austen Chamberlain who refused to serve. He resigned in May 1923 suffering from throat cancer, and died in October. He was succeeded by Stanley Baldwin, Chancellor of the Exchequer, with limited ministerial experience and also without a clear strategy. He was chosen over more experienced Conservatives because he was untainted by association with the Coalition.

The big problem was persistent unemployment. Bonar Law opposed state intervention to fund public works, convinced that tariffs could protect and revive industry and trade, but did not implement them because they were so divisive. Baldwin had entered Parliament in 1906 as a tariff reformer, heir to a family iron foundry which expected to benefit from protection, and also believed tariffs were the best ammunition against unemployment. He suffered from a 'chronic inability to take decisions until they were forced on him',[1] but faced strong pressure from industrialists supported by most of the Cabinet, and a tariff plan was devised, excluding food imports because Labour and the Liberals gained votes from rising food prices.

But unemployment did not fall and the government achieved little. The only substantial legislation was the Housing Act 1923, a partial reversal by Minister of Health Neville Chamberlain of the cuts to subsidies many of his colleagues had

1 John Charmley, *A History of Conservative Politics, 1900–1996* (London: Macmillan, 1998), p. 70.

supported the previous year. Following an outcry, given the continuing housing cri-sis, Chamberlain introduced a subsidy of £6 per year for twenty years for each house built by local authorities or private enterprise, if the houses met certain standards, though these were below those established in 1919. True to Conservative prefer-ences, private enterprise was prioritized and council housing subsidized only where the minister ruled that private builders could not meet local needs. The Act also, for the first time, allowed local authorities to advance loans to potential owner-occupiers unable to afford a deposit. Owner-occupation was rare before 1918, perhaps no more than 10 per cent of all homes in the United Kingdom.[2] It grew between the wars to 32 per cent in 1938,[3] encouraged by the Conservatives. The leader of the Conservatives on Leeds City Council told his Labour opponents in 1926, 'It's a good thing for peo-ple to buy their houses. They turn Tory directly. We shall go on making Tories and you will be wiped out',[4] a widespread, long-lived belief in his party. Home ownership became a normal aspiration for the growing middle class and increasingly for skilled manual workers who prospered in the new industries of the 1930s.[5] Home buying was assisted by low interest rates, the growth of profit-making building societies and financial institutions supplying mortgages, encouraged by Conservative-led governments.

Baldwin's commitment to tariff reform was incendiary enough to draw together the warring wings of the Liberal Party – at least on the surface. In November 1923, Lloyd George shared a platform with Asquith for the first time since 1916, upholding free trade. Labour, led by MacDonald again, supported free trade and proposed raising rev-enue and paying off the war debt through a capital levy, a wealth tax aimed at those who had profited from the war. The divisions were so deep and the economic crisis apparently so intractable that Baldwin believed he could not avoid another election specifically over tariffs, which he called for December 1923. He perhaps underesti-mated popular hostility to tariffs and overestimated the appeal of his emollient 'one nation' public self-presentation. The Conservatives again won most seats, but lost eighty-seven. They had alienated free-trading Lancashire and the Liberals (fighting again as a single party) won half of all agricultural seats, apparently punishment for the Conservatives excluding food tariffs. Labour and the Liberals gained seats in southern England. Labour increased its dominance in the big conurbations, including London, and took the second largest number of seats, 191 and 30.5 per cent of the vote, to the Conservatives' 258 and 38.1 per cent. While still taking most working-class votes,

---

2 A. H. Halsey and J. Webb (eds), *Twentieth-century British Social Trends* (London: Macmillan, 2000), p. 488.
3 Ibid., p 487.
4 Melling, *Housing, Social Policy and the State*, p. 116.
5 See pp. 121–2.

Labour now attracted more white-collar public sector workers and middle-class radicals. Clement Attlee, public school and Oxford educated, social work lecturer, future Labour Prime Minister, was first elected in 1922.

The Conservatives had no overall majority but Baldwin tried to hold on, meeting the new Parliament. Liberals and Labour voted him down. Asquith, as Liberal leader, like many of his colleagues, had no desire for another Conservative-dominated Coalition and believed a progressive alliance with Labour held more hope for the future. As he told the parliamentary Liberal Party, a Labour government 'could hardly be tried under safer conditions' than a minority administration dependent on Liberal support.[6] The first Labour government was formed in January 1924, but it could not hope to pass legislation without support from other parties. The Conservatives had miscalculated, perhaps arrogantly, perhaps still baffled by the expanded electorate.

The First Labour Government

Labour formed its first government in 1924 in unpromising circumstances, with a minority of seats, a weak economy and rising unemployment. The other parties were unlikely to support radical interventions. Asquith faced criticism, especially from Liberal businesspeople, for 'putting in the Socialists' and some deserted to the Conservatives. More working-class voters moved decisively to Labour from the Liberals, who never regained the 29 per cent votes they achieved in 1923. Labour had to grasp the opportunity to govern, aiming for a responsible image and useful experience, which would be valuable in future elections. MacDonald became Prime Minister. For the first, and probably the last, time the Prime Minister's family groceries were delivered to Downing Street in a Co-op van.[7] MacDonald did not expect the government to last long but he intended no moves that might accelerate the end. He had long expected Labour to replace the Liberals as the party of radical reform, as it did.[8] He did not get on well with Asquith, whom he found patronizing, still less with Lloyd George.

Signalling Labour's moderation, MacDonald dropped the promised capital levy,[9] which upset left-wingers. Philip Snowden, a very orthodox Chancellor, opposed it, believing economic recovery required tax reductions, and Parliament would probably have rejected it. MacDonald also distanced himself from the unions, discouraging strikes. He had difficulty selecting ministers from his inexperienced party. He became

6 Marquand, *Ramsay MacDonald*, pp. 298–9.
7 Ibid., p. 307.
8 Pat Thane, 'Labour and Local Politics. Radicalism, Democracy and Social Reform, 1880–1914', in Eugenio Biagini and Alastair Reid (eds), *Currents of Radicalism. Popular Radicalism, Organized labour and Party Politics in Britain, 1850–1914* (Cambridge University Press, 1991), pp. 261–70.
9 See p. 88.

Foreign Secretary, foreign affairs being his main interest, and Henderson became Home Secretary, despite his election defeat. He speedily won a by-election in Burnley. Former Liberals were recruited, including Haldane as Lord Chancellor and Charles Trevelyan at Education, with a moderate Conservative, Lord Chelmsford, at the Admiralty.

Labour Social and Economic Policy

Despite potential parliamentary opposition, Labour promoted progressive social reform. John Wheatley, the left-wing 'Clydesider' Minister of Health, rescinded the 'Poplar Order' restricting Poor Relief payments,[10] then introduced the most radical Housing Act yet, increasing subsidies for building for rent, mostly by local authorities, while extending Chamberlain's subsidy to private construction. Housebuilding greatly increased, creating jobs and more council housing, though the poorest could still rarely afford it.

At the Ministry of Labour, Tom Shaw raised unemployment benefit to 27s for a family of four, and (opposed by the Treasury) abolished the unpopular means-test for 'extended benefit'.[11] Unemployed people who exhausted their insurance entitlement were now mostly removed from Poor Relief, though not to a notably generous system. Shaw retained and toughened the test introduced in 1921 requiring claimants to prove to a Local Employment Committee that they were 'genuinely seeking whole-time employment but unable to obtain such employment', providing evidence of searching for work. Some left-wingers opposed this but Parliament supported it, along with working-class voters with little sympathy for supposed 'scroungers'. Unemployment remained above 1 million, but falling.

Labour had long been committed to free education to university level, with maintenance grants for poorer families, strongly supported by R. H. Tawney, Professor of Economic History at the London School of Economics (LSE) and a leading Labour advocate of education as the road to social equality.[12] He believed the state education system undervalued the intellects of working-class children and joined a Labour-appointed committee chaired by Sir Henry Hadow, Vice-Chancellor of Sheffield University, to explore reform of secondary education. In 1926, the committee recommended raising the school leaving age to 15 (already Labour policy) and the reorganization of secondary schooling. Children would be selected by examination at age 11 to attend one of three types of school, judged appropriate to their abilities: academic, technical or a new type of 'modern' school in which 'the courses of instruction though

10 Ryan, 'Poplarism', pp. 75–6.
11 See p. 74.
12 Laurence Goldman, *The Life of R. H. Tawney. Socialism and History* (London: Bloomsbury Academic, 2014).

not merely vocational or utilitarian should be used to connect the school work with interests arising from the social and industrial environment of the pupils'.[13] The committee believed these distinctions were realistic, that the lifetime abilities of children could be identified by examination at age 11, and that the three types of school would be equally esteemed and would improve educational opportunities for most children, while Britain gained a more educated workforce and reduced juvenile crime. In 1926, the Conservative government was unwilling to promote this system, but the Board of Education encouraged local authorities to adopt it, especially while Labour was back in government in 1929–31. By 1931, it was available to one-third of children and became firmly established after 1945.[14] Labour was also committed to a free national health service for all and appointed a Royal Commission to investigate NHI, amid criticism of the variations in services provided by approved societies. This also reported to a less receptive government in 1926 and major reform of healthcare was deferred.

Snowden's April 1924 budget removed £14 million in direct and £29 million in indirect taxes, mainly on imports, a return towards free trade, designed to promote industrial efficiency and growth. MacDonald promised disarmament and the naval budget was severely cut. Snowden also increased pensions as promised in Labour's election manifesto. Following demands for improved support for retired people and civilian widows and orphans, the Conservatives had appointed a committee chaired by civil servant Sir John Anderson, which in 1924 recommended raising the means limit for old age pensions, which Snowden adopted. About 70 per cent of over-70s now qualified, suggesting the extent of poverty among older people since the means limit remained stringent. Snowden hoped improved pensions would stop older workers competing for the shrinking pool of jobs, though the Anderson committee found that unemployed people over age 60 had much less chance of re-employment than younger workers.[15] It also recommended contributory pensions for insured workers aged 65–70 and the wives of insured men, and widows' and orphans' pensions for their families, creating parity with war widows and removing another group from Poor Relief. Snowden approved the recommendations but the government fell before he could act.[16]

Labour introduced a minimum wage for miners and backed a private members' bill to nationalize the coal industry, but it also fell with the government along with the proposed subsidized construction of a national electricity grid, improved electrical supply to rural areas and work-creating afforestation and major road construction.

---

13 *Report of the Consultative Committee to the Board of Education on the Education of the Adolescent* (London: HMSO, 1927).

14 See pp. 131, 195.

15 Paul Johnson, 'The Employment and Retirement of Older Men in England and Wales, 1881–1981', *Economic History Review* 47(1) (1994): 106–28.

16 Thane, *Old Age in English Society*, pp. 318–23.

Foreign Policy

Throughout the summer, MacDonald was active in delicate and ultimately successful negotiations in London with German, Allied and US representatives for a final
peace treaty.[17] An international committee, chaired by the American General Dawes,
examined the proposed German reparations, which were widely criticized as being too
harsh. In April 1924, it recommended gradual payments, starting at a lower level than
proposed, plus a £40 million loan to help Germany rebuild its economy. MacDonald
worked hard to persuade the French to accept the Dawes Plan and withdraw from the
Ruhr and to convince the Belgians that an economically crippled Germany was dangerous. He then negotiated the loan with British and (mainly) US bankers. Agreement was
achieved in early August and the peace treaty finally signed. This was the government's
major, significant achievement.[18]

Then it faced a series of crises. In September, the *Daily Mail* revealed that a bar-
onetcy had been awarded, on MacDonald's recommendation, to his friend Alexander
Grant, a wealthy man of humble origins who had loaned him money and a Daimler
car. It was all the worse because MacDonald had been highly critical of Lloyd George
during his honours scandal. The next furore arose from MacDonald's decision to recognize, then seek a trade agreement with, the USSR, further convincing his enemies
that he was a crypto-Bolshevik. In fact, he was pursuing his overriding desire for lasting
peace by trying to normalize Soviet relations with other countries, while increasing
Britain's declining exports and settling the claims of British bondholders on the pre-
revolutionary government which the Bolsheviks had repudiated. Conservatives and
Liberals opposed the agreement and it was likely to be defeated in Parliament.

Then an article in the Communist Party's *Workers' Weekly* in July 1924, by its temporary editor J. R. Campbell, advised soldiers to refuse to fire on striking workers. The
politically inexperienced Attorney-General, Sir Patrick Hastings, ordered his prosecution for incitement to mutiny. MacDonald, with others in the Cabinet, fearing the tensions this would arouse in the party, ordered withdrawal of the prosecution and were
accused of bending to far-left pressure. The press savoured it to the full. A Conservative
censure motion was supported by the Liberals and passed by the Commons. MacDonald
took it as a vote of no confidence and resigned. He handled the domestic crises badly,
not least because he was exhausted by his successful international negotiations.

Given the major disadvantages it faced, Labour's first government had been quite
successful, particularly in international affairs, especially compared with its predecessor with its large majority. Labour had established its capacity to govern, though its
enemies would never admit it.

17 Marquand, *Ramsay MacDonald*, pp. 329–56.
18 Ibid., p. 378.

Conservative Government

The election followed in October. In the campaign, Baldwin abandoned unpopular tariffs but offered no solution to the economic problems. He took the easier route of an ostensible 'one-nation' strategy, disavowing any 'sectional, narrow, partisan or class policy', promoting a romantic, bucolic image of 'England' while vigorously attacking Labour's supposed Bolshevism, highlighting MacDonald's efforts to normalize relations with the USSR, despite the moderation of Labour's policies in office. He was greatly assisted four days before the election when the *Daily Mail* published the banner headlines, 'Civil War Plot by Socialists', 'Moscow Order to our Reds. Great Plot Disclosed Yesterday'. It had a copy of a letter allegedly written by Zinoviev, President of the Communist International in Moscow, to its British representative, urging revolution in Britain. It alleged that MacDonald and Henderson had received a copy some weeks before but had not responded or made it public, implying, it suggested, their collusion in the revolutionary plot. It was released by the Foreign Office together with its protest to the Soviet government (partly drafted by MacDonald, a fact not revealed by the *Daily Mail*). A weary MacDonald was convinced, rightly, that the letter was a forgery, though the Foreign Office took it seriously, but he was slow to defend himself, again handling the affair poorly. The *Daily Mail* and many Conservatives gleefully interpreted this as evidence of guilt. The episode probably did not decisively affect the election, but it further embittered the campaign and relations between the parties.

The Conservatives won a large majority, with 8 million votes and 419 seats. Labour increased its vote to 5.5 million on a higher turnout, 76.6 per cent, though it gained fewer seats, 151. The Liberals won only 17.6 per cent of votes and forty seats, mainly in north Wales, the Scottish Highlands and southwest England, though even there they were flagging. They had dominated Scotland and Wales before 1914, but now slumped to ten seats in Wales, eight in Scotland, losing mainly to Labour. Asquith again lost his seat in Paisley. He was ennobled as Earl of Oxford and remained party leader, while Lloyd George led the party in the Commons. More Liberals abandoned the party. It was crippled by the conflict among its leaders and appeared to have nothing distinctive to offer. Labour was now clearly the main opposition. Forty-one women stood, but just four were elected, three Conservatives and one Labour.

The result cheered financiers, who feared a secure Labour government, and sterling rose in value, temporarily. A sustained period of one-party government followed until 1929, the longest since 1915. Baldwin's Cabinet included all Conservative factions, even, surprisingly, welcoming Winston Churchill back to the party in the prominent position of Chancellor of the Exchequer, another Liberal defection. Neville Chamberlain turned down the Chancellorship, preferring the Ministry of Health since he had ambitious social reform plans, and, he commented, 'liked spending money far better than saving it'.[19] Churchill had left the party twenty years before over tariff reform and remained a free trader; his appointment further signalled Baldwin's resolve to abandon tariffs. In general, however, Baldwin was weak on strategic direction, especially on economic policy, leaving ministers much freedom while developing a public persona of avuncular moderation, making shrewd use of the new media of radio and cinema newsreels.

Churchill stepped straight into preparing the 1925 Budget. He faced intense pressure from the City, the Bank of England and the Treasury to return to the Gold Standard. This was strongly opposed by the influential Liberal economist, J. M. Keynes, a wartime Treasury adviser, who believed it would raise the prices of Britain's already weak exports and increase unemployment, as it did. The City was more concerned to re-establish its prewar position as the leading source of international loans, now overtaken by the United States, by restoring confidence in sterling than with reviving exports and manufacturing. Churchill, though initially sceptical, gave in and announced in his Budget the return to gold at the prewar rate. To appease voters other than City financiers he reduced income tax by 6d in the £. He told Neville Chamberlain he needed to balance this 'by doing something for the working class' in his Budget, so gained Chamberlain's permission to appropriate his plan to reform and extend pensions as previously proposed by Snowden.[20] Chamberlain later introduced old age pensions from age 65 for NHI contributors, widows' pension for their wives, still at 10s per week too small to live on, while orphans received 5s. The numbers receiving Poor Relief to supplement the old age pension rose from 8,600 in 1920 to 69,900 in 1928.[21]

General Strike

Many employers responded to the rise in export prices and falling overseas demand following the return to gold by reducing wages or imposing longer hours. Miners threatened to strike. To prevent this, Baldwin announced another Royal Commission on the coal industry, chaired by the Liberal Sir Herbert Samuel, and a nine-month subsidy to the industry until it reported. It proposed amalgamation of pits into larger combines, nationalization of mining royalties and the abolition of the recently introduced minimum wage for miners, so alienating both sides.

When the subsidy ended in April 1926, the employers proposed wage cuts. Baldwin attempted mediation, but the miners called a strike, expecting widespread sympathy action. The General Council of the Trades Union Congress (TUC) tried unsuccessfully to mediate and, reluctantly, called an unprecedented general strike supporting the miners from 3 May 1926. They did not aim to overthrow the state as their more

19 Davis, *History of Britain*, pp. 175–6.
20 See p. 91.
21 Thane, *Old Age in English Society*, pp. 323–7.

apocalyptic opponents believed. The response was impressive though incomplete. The docks, railways and trams were almost immobilized. The Seamen's Union refused to strike, keeping seaborne trade moving, the road haulage industry was lightly unionized and vulnerable to unemployment so responded patchily, while the TUC ruled out disrupting domestic electricity supplies. It ordered building workers to strike except those building homes and hospitals and forbade interference with health and sanitary services or food distribution. It was as anxious as the government to avoid conflict and alienating voters.

The government was prepared for a confrontation long anticipated against workers who were more reluctant strikers than right-wing stereotypes portrayed.[22] A Cabinet Supply and Transport Committee was established in 1919 in preparation. Through local Organizations for the Maintenance of Supplies (or Organizations of Mugs and Scabs as the strikers called them[23]) around 100,000 volunteers unloaded ships, distributed provisions by road and preserved law and order. Ex-army officers drove trains, students stoked power stations and some desperate unemployed workers replaced strikers. Success at maintaining services was patchy but it became clear the government could withstand a long strike, whereas strike pay crippled the unions despite help from street collections.[24] The miners rejected attempted mediation by Herbert Samuel and, on 12 May, with no settlement in sight, the TUC terminated the strike. The miners struggled on for a further six months to ultimate defeat.

The Trade Disputes Act 1927, outlawed the general sympathy strike. This did not arouse massive opposition in the labour movement since the tactic was unpopular and had failed. Baldwin avoided too punitive a response for fear of further conflict and to preserve his 'one-nation' image. This enraged some in his party, but they wisely avoided prolonged antagonism. He resisted the more extreme curbs on unions proposed on the backbenches, including compulsory strike ballots. However, the Act obliged union members positively to opt-in to paying subscriptions to the Labour Party, rather than contracting out if they chose, as about one-quarter of members did. Baldwin was happy to antagonize Labour, though it had sought to remain neutral in the strike since MacDonald always opposed militancy. Labour's income fell by 18 per cent, less than expected, or hoped by some, because the Act strengthened Labour support and stimulated members to ensure that that maximum numbers of unionists opted-in. The strike split the Liberals again. Asquith loyalists supported the government, Lloyd George opposed, along with left Liberals including Keynes. Asquith resigned, and died in 1928; Lloyd George became party leader.

22 Stuart Ball, 'Baldwin, Stanley (1867–1947)', *Oxford Dictionary of National Biography*, online edition, January 2011, available at: www.oxforddnb.com.
23 J. Skelley (ed.), *1926 The General Strike* (London: Lawrence & Wishart, 1976), p. 363; Gordon Phillips, *The General Strike. The Politics of Industrial Conflict* (London: Lawrence & Wishart, 1976).
24 Skelley, *1926*, p. 366.

The General Strike delivered a warning to employers, who had also lost out in the twelve days. There were some reprisals but no big counterattack and wage cuts became less frequent. A revival of the world economy helped: commodity, including food, prices fell internationally, reducing the cost of living and discontent among workers, but exports remained lower than before the war and unemployment remained above 1 million.

Breaking Up the Poor Law

The government's main response to the gloomy economic situation was to cut spending, 'austerity' as similar moves came to be known decades later. It was reluctant to risk protest by cutting unemployment benefit, despite the cost, but in 1925, harried by a press campaign against 'dole scroungers', appointed an investigation under Lord Blanesborough, a former judge, which reported in 1927.

The last resort of unemployed workers who did not qualify for or had exhausted insurance benefits was Poor Relief. The Ministry of Health reminded Guardians in 1921, during the Poplar crisis,[25] that, even amid mass unemployment, relief 'should of necessity be calculated on a lower scale than the earnings of the independent labourer who is maintaining himself by his labour' to incentivize the search for work,[26] nor should they pay cash relief long term. But as involuntary unemployment grew, more Guardians were reluctant to deposit claimants in workhouses, even if workhouses could accommodate the numbers. They became mainly depositories for the sick, mentally and physically disabled and aged poor.[27] But areas with the greatest poverty could least afford out-relief and some relieved unemployed claimants only in kind – mainly food – in return for unpaid work.

Strikes presented further problems. A Court of Appeal judgment of 1900 (the *Merthyr Tydfil* judgment) established that Poor Relief could not be paid to anyone refusing available work, as strikers did, until destitution reduced them to a condition no longer definable as 'able-bodied'. Their families could be supported. Local practice, as ever, varied. The Ministry of Health greeted the General Strike by lowering relief scales and reminding Guardians to obey the strict letter of the law. The miners' unions had minimal strike funds. Paupers in England and Wales doubled from 1.2 million to 2.4 million during the strike. In most mining districts more than 50 per cent of families were on relief. Strikers and unemployed people were encouraged by strike committees and political organizations to press Guardians to increase payments to those qualified

25 See p. 75.
26 Thane, *Foundations of the Welfare State*, p. 174.
27 M. A. Crowther, *The Workhouse System 1834–1929* (London: Batsford, 1981), pp. 88–112.

for relief. Guardians in areas of high unemployment treated strikers more generously than elsewhere, if they could afford it, but in more prosperous parts of the Midlands, miners were almost literally starved back to work. Some Guardians went too far even for the Ministry. When Lichfield Union (Staffordshire) threatened to withdraw all relief to miners' dependants on the grounds that 'the miners had work to go to and it was the guardians' duty to see that they went back', they were reminded of their duty to relieve destitution, whatever the cause. The Ministry also tried to restrain the more generous boards. Under the Board of Guardians (Default) Act, July 1926, it could suspend and replace with an appointed board any Guardians persistently raising loans above the permitted limit. The Boards of West Ham in east London and Chester-le-Street, a mining area in Derbyshire, were suspended in August 1926, and others followed. Challenges to official policy grew with the number of Labour-controlled boards through the 1920s.

Chamberlain responded by at last reforming the Poor Law. The Local Government Act 1929 abolished Boards of Guardians and their Scottish equivalents, Parochial Boards, transferring their powers to county and borough councils in England and Wales, burghs in Scotland, integrating the administration and funding of what was now called 'Public Assistance' with other local responsibilities under Public Assistance Committees (PACs), often using the same officials and buildings as before. Local authorities in areas of greatest need were assisted by carefully regulated government grants. Labour Guardians, especially, opposed the reform, believing, rightly, that it was designed to tighten central control over Poor Relief, reducing scope for democratic action, to the disadvantage of many unemployed people and, especially, strikers and their families.[28]

When the Blanesborough committee reported in 1927, unemployment and the costs of relief had risen further, despite tighter administration of the 'genuinely seeking work' test which trebled the claims rejected, mainly by taking less account of whether there was, realistically, work available to seek. Unemployed married women found it harder to obtain benefits if their husbands were, or in theory could be, working. The committee found no significant evidence of 'scrounging' and optimistically assumed that unemployment would soon decline. It recommended, following recovery, return to a fixed ratio between contributions and benefits and retention of the means- and 'genuinely seeking work' tests, which were embodied in the Unemployment Insurance Act 1927. Since unemployment did not decline, indeed worsened from 1929, extended benefit, now renamed 'transitional benefit', continued for a further seven years, while stringent administration of the work test threw many people on to Public Assistance.[29]

---

28 Crowther, *Workhouse System*.
29 Anne Crowther, *British Social Policy 1914–1939* (London: Macmillan, 1988), pp. 40–6.

Healthcare

Chamberlain did little to improve health services, despite continuing concern particularly because unemployment and poverty increased ill-health at a time when medical knowledge and the capacity of medicine to cure was undergoing unprecedented expansion. The Royal Commission on National Health Insurance established by Labour produced two conflicting reports in 1926. Both recommended that it should cover sickness benefits for dependents of insured workers, also medical care in childbirth and dental and optical treatment. Both criticized the lack of coordination among health services and the unequal provision of services by approved societies. The minority recommended abolition of approved societies, with their functions transferred to local authorities. The majority opted for pooling and redistributing the societies' funds to equalize services between those with mainly older and/or lower paid members and limited funds and societies with younger, fully employed members and higher incomes which provided more services, including dental and optical care. The government was more concerned with cutting public spending than reform; its only response was substantially reduced state national insurance contributions, which worsened the inequalities.[30] Wheatley's generous housing subsidies were cut.

Conservatives were persistently divided over economic and social policy and public spending, many opposing Chamberlain's reforms, attacking Baldwin as a 'semi-socialist' for tolerating them and demanding fiercer cuts.

Towards a Democratic Franchise

They were divided also over women's campaigns for greater equality. In 1919, the NUSEC resolved to focus initially on certain causes: equal pay for equal work; reform of the laws on divorce and prostitution, to establish 'an equal moral standard'; pensions for civilian widows; equal parental rights to custody of children; and opening the legal profession to women.[31] Following dedicated activism, by 1928 there was decisive movement towards all the objectives except equal pay. It was easier to gain changes in the law at little cost to the state than to persuade government – still less private employers – to raise women's pay.

Activists campaigned on behalf of women working in and outside the home. Some embraced the term 'feminism', which has been divisive since its invention in France in the late nineteenth century. Others, equally committed to gender equality, resisted or evaded it for fear of alienating potential support, not least because the conservative

30 Crowther, *British Social Policy*, pp. 52–6.
31 See pp. 81–2.

press, particularly the *Daily Mail*, insistently promoted stereotypes of 'embittered' 'hysterical' feminists.[32] Labour Party women, who were as divided as any about the feminist label, some regarding it as too middle class,[33] insisted that domestic work should be regarded as work, like that in the formal labour market, since supporting working men and raising children was equally vital to society and the economy. They argued that domestic work conditions should be improved by well-designed housing and that hard-working 'housewives', like male employees, deserved an 8-hour day – 'eight hours work, eight hours sleep, eight hours leisure' – not their normal relentless labour. Also women workers in or out of the home deserved the support of social services, including day-care for children, enabling them genuinely to choose whether or not to take paid employment. The choice would be more realistic if work at home was paid, the aim of the campaign for family allowances, promoted by Eleanor Rathbone. Rathbone did not share the conventional belief that married women should stay at home, but argued that those who did so deserved payment by the state for their work, just as service families had received wartime allowances.[34]

Campaigners also demanded protection of women and children from sexual and physical abuse, within and outside the family, through tighter laws and the appointment of policewomen to support victims.[35] Local authorities could appoint women to permanent police posts from 1920, though by 1939 only forty-three of 183 authorities did so and there were just 174 women among 65,000 police in England and Wales. A new occupation opened slowly to women.[36] As further protection, the Criminal Law Amendment Act 1922, for which the NUSEC and others campaigned, raised the age of (heterosexual) consent from thirteen to sixteen. The Infanticide Act 1922 removed another grievance long highlighted by women by eliminating the charge of murder for women who killed their infants where they were proven to be suffering from what would now be described as postnatal depression.[37] Also in 1922, the maximum maintenance for women and their children under separation orders was increased, easing escape from intolerable marriages. In 1925, the grounds on which either partner could obtain separation were extended to include cruelty and drunkenness, and women were no longer required to leave the marital home before applying for a separation order. The

32 Adrian Bingham, *Gender, Modernity and the Popular Press in Inter-War Britain* (Oxford University Press, 2004).

33 Thane, 'Women of the British Labour Party'.

34 Pedersen, *Eleanor Rathbone*.

35 Roger Davidson, '"This Pernicious Delusion". Law, Medicine and Child Sexual Abuse in Early Twentieth-century Scotland', *Journal of the History of Sexuality*, 10(1) (2001): 62–77; Breitenbach 'Scottish Women's Organizations', pp. 69–70.

36 Jackson, *Women Police*.

37 Daniel Grey, 'Women's Policy Networks and the Infanticide Act 1922', *Twentieth Century British History* 21(4) (20011): 441–63.

Matrimonial Causes Act 1923, initially drafted by the NUSEC, equalized the divorce law in England and Wales with that in Scotland,[38] enabling wives as well as husbands to gain divorce for adultery alone. No divorce was possible in Northern Ireland, except by the expensive process of private Act of Parliament, until 1939 when limited procedures were introduced. Further legislation in 1937 extended the grounds for divorce in England and Wales, but it remained expensive for many people and some still resorted to secret cohabitation with new partners.[39] In 1924, mothers acquired equal rights with fathers to claim custody of children over age 7 following marriage break up. Lack of custody rights also trapped women in unhappy marriages, though, again, the costs of legal proceedings were prohibitive for many and the law courts were still inclined to support fathers over mothers.

The Bastardy Act 1923 legalized legitimation of children following the subsequent marriage of their parents, improved procedures whereby unmarried mothers claimed maintenance from the fathers of their children and doubled to £1 the maximum weekly maintenance. It was promoted by the National Council for the Unmarried Mother and her Child (NCUMC), supported by the NUSEC and other groups, and introduced in Parliament by Neville Chamberlain, Vice-President and later President of the NCUMC. This was founded in 1918 to support stigmatized unmarried mothers and their children, whose numbers grew during the war, and to promote such changes. It was committed to helping mother and child stay together, resisting the adoption of 'illegitimate' children enforced in Ireland, Australia, Canada and parts of the United States, causing intense pain to many unmarried mothers. In Britain, mothers often returned to their parents' home, where the children grew up sometimes believing their grandparents were their parents, to hide the shame of illegitimacy. Others were assisted to live in hostels, to take live-in domestic work where their children could join them or to place their children in foster care while they worked.[40]

Most of these legal changes, and more, initiated and often drafted by women's groups, were guided through Parliament by a dedicated body of male MPs, since women MPs were so few. Notably, Major John Hills, a Conservative social reformer, who fought in the war and married Stella, step-sister of Virginia Woolf, with whom he remained on cordial terms after Stella's early death, introduced and supported several reforms.[41] The outcome was not gender equality, but it edged closer. Through such campaigns, women became a stronger, more assertive political presence after 1918, while fighting on for the equal franchise.

---

38 Cretney, *Family Law*, pp. 196–318.
39 Ibid.; Thane and Evans, *Sinners?* pp. 34–5.
40 Thane and Evans, *Sinners?* pp. 29–53.
41 Hermione Lee, *Virginia Woolf* (London: Vintage, 1997), pp. 134–41. E. H. H. Green, 'Hills, John Waller (1867–1938)', *Oxford Dictionary of National Biography*, 2004, online edn, January 2008, available at: www .oxforddnb.com; Glew, *Gender, Rhetoric and Regulation*, pp. 45, 134, 144, 183.

Baldwin announced in the 1924 election campaign that, 'The Unionist Party is in favour of equal political rights for men and women,'[42] and that, if the Conservatives won, it would be referred to an all-party committee. MacDonald had supported a Labour backbencher's Equal Franchise Bill, but lost office before it could proceed. The Liberals also officially supported equality. After the election it was not mentioned. Baldwin was perhaps deterred by hostility on the Conservative backbenches to enfranchising 'irresponsible' young women, creating a majority female electorate and by the predictions of the incorrigible *Daily Mail* that:

> If the women come to use their power (and they may gradually come to do so) they can dominate the state and control all its departments. They will almost certainly claim in the immediate future a much larger proportion of appointments, so that men will be steadily dislodged.[43]

This was more than most ardent feminists dared aspire to. The strident opposition of the *Daily Mail* and its sister paper the *Daily Mirror* to the 'Flapper Vote' was unusual. It was not driven just by crude sexism – the two papers normally appeared quite supportive of aspiring young women, not least because they needed their readership – but by the extreme anti-socialism of their proprietor, Lord Rothermere. He was convinced that the new voters were likely to be employed and therefore susceptible to trade union and socialist influence and would keep Labour in power. When the equal franchise finally went through Parliament, the *Daily Mail* warned that it 'may bring down the British Empire in ruins'.[44]

Women repeatedly reminded Baldwin of his pledge. Early in the new government, Labour MPs William Whiteley and Ellen Wilkinson introduced another Equal Franchise Bill, one of several since 1919. The government rejected it but felt obliged to promise an all-party conference on the issue, perhaps in 1926. The NUSEC and other associations organized demonstrations, meetings and deputations to ministers, hinting at a return to militancy if Baldwin broke his promise. Another Labour Bill was introduced in March 1926. The campaign, with press publicity, crescendoed at a July demonstration, when 3,500 women, of all parties and backgrounds, marched to Hyde Park, including Emmeline Pankhurst, Millicent Fawcett and other veteran suffrage campaigners, wearing their prison badges. Activism continued into 1927, courting maximum publicity and support – without response from the government.

In March 1927, Baldwin met a deputation introduced by Nancy Astor, including Eleanor Rathbone and Lady Rhondda, editor and founder of the feminist journal *Time*

42 Law, *Suffrage and Power*, p. 202.
43 Adrian Bingham, 'Enfranchisement, Feminism and the Modern Woman. Debates in the British Popular Press, 1918–1939', in Julie V. Gottlieb and Richard Toye (eds), *The Aftermath of Suffrage. Women, Gender and Politics in Britain, 1918–1945* (London: Palgrave Macmillan, 2013), p. 96.
44 Bingham, *Gender, Modernity*, p. 136. Adrian Bingham, '"Stop the Flapper Vote Folly": Lord Rothermere, the *Daily Mail* and the Equalization of the Franchise, 1927–8', *Twentieth Century British History* 13(1) (2002): 17–37.

and Tide among other activities.[45] He excused his inaction on the grounds that he had been preoccupied by the General Strike, the miners' strike and war in China, and promised a statement soon. Lobbying continued until, in April, Baldwin announced the introduction of a Bill in the next session of Parliament extending the franchise to women at age 21, not 25 as some Conservatives demanded to keep women voters a minority. After so many broken promises, the campaign continued, more intensely when the next session was delayed until February 1928. On the day of the State Opening of Parliament, suffragists delivered a petition to the Prime Minister's house and a letter to the king at Buckingham Palace, while cars, driven by women, festooned with plac-ards demanding equal votes, circled Parliament Square to the sound of whistles and car horns. The King's Speech did not mention the franchise, but, that evening, Baldwin informed Parliament that an Equal Franchise Bill would be introduced, enabling newly enfranchised women to vote in the election due in 1929. Introduced in March, it passed easily through Parliament, though 218 MPs stayed away from the second reading, when there were just ten votes against.[46] Women were at last allowed to vote at age 21 on the same terms as men, enfranchising 5,221,902 women. The electorate became 53 per cent female.

Foreign and Colonial Affairs

Conservatives were divided also over foreign and colonial policy. Like MacDonald, Baldwin wanted international peace, but contributed less to achieving it. He supported the League of Nations and disarmament, but not actively enough for British supporters of the League, and clashed with the United States over naval disarmament, which they opposed. He appointed Lord Robert Cecil[47] to the Cabinet, responsible for relations with the League but with little power. Government compromises and foot-dragging over League policies, especially disarmament, caused his resignation in 1927. Austen Chamberlain won more acclaim as Foreign Secretary through his role in negotiating the Locarno Treaty of 1925. This essentially completed earlier work by Lloyd George to normalize relations with Germany by allowing it to participate in constructing an international agreement on recognition of national frontiers, safeguarding against invasion. In 1927, new tensions emerged when British forces joined allies to protect Shanghai, Asia's greatest port, where Britain had substantial investments, at the start of a long civil war between nationalists and communists in China.

Tensions continued in Palestine and Egypt and, above all, in India. There was seri-ous communal rioting between 1924 and 1928, and Gandhi was again imprisoned.

45 Angela V. John, *Turning the Tide. The Life of Lady Rhondda* (Cardigan: Parthian, 2013).
46 Law, *Suffrage and Power*, pp. 208–18.
47 See p. 64.

India caused the deepest tensions between anti- and pro-imperialists (pre-eminently Churchill) in the Conservative Party. In 1927, a Commission was appointed under Sir John Simon to investigate the effects of the constitutional reforms of 1919.[48] It was seen in India, rightly, as an anti-independence gesture and, as it travelled around India in 1928–9, attracted boycotts, demonstrations and riots. An all-party committee under Motilal Nehru drew up a constitution for an independent India which was presented to Baldwin's government shortly before the 1929 election. It was left to his successor to deal with.

General Election, 1929

Whether, or to what extent, the new female voters fulfilled Lord Rothermere's nightmares and swung the election in Labour's favour in 1929 is impossible to judge, though some Conservatives blamed them.[49] More women stood than ever before: thirty Labour, ten Conservative, twenty-five Liberals and four Independents, including Eleanor Rathbone for the 'Combined English Universities' (all but Oxford, Cambridge and London). More were elected than ever before: nine Labour, three Conservatives, one Liberal and Rathbone.

The big issue was the economy. The Liberals had the clearest policies. Briefed by Keynes, their manifesto, *We Can Conquer Unemployment*, proposed, without hope of implementation, a loan-financed £250 million (6 per cent of GDP) public works programme employing 600,000 people per year. Labour had no clear alternative. Nor did Baldwin, whose government's record was not an asset. Its achievements were few and mainly due to the Chamberlains, though Neville Chamberlain's reforms were among the issues that divided the party. Baldwin chose the unadventurous slogan, 'Safety First', borrowed from road safety propaganda. He hoped, again, to counter what he represented as the wild plans of his opponents with a reassuring, fatherly, authentically 'English', image.

Labour won most seats, 288, to the Conservatives' 260, but the Liberals rose to fifty-nine and Labour again lacked an overall majority. It gained 8.3 million votes, 37 per cent, the Conservatives 8.6 million, 38 per cent. Many middle-class voters had suffered the effects of the return to gold and tight monetary policies, did not benefit from cuts to taxes on business and agriculture, and resented Baldwin's rejection of tariffs. Robert Cecil urged voters to ignore party politics and vote for supporters of the League of Nations to secure peace, underlining Baldwin's weakness in foreign policy. Baldwin resigned and a Labour government returned, again in unpromising circumstances.

48 See p. 67.
49 Stuart Ball, *Portrait of a Party. The Conservative Party in Britain, 1918–45* (Oxford University Press, 2013), p. 82.

Divided Britain

The 1924–9 government exposed severe divisions in British society, most visibly between militant workers and employers, militant women and opponents of gender equality, employed and unemployed, rich and poor. Strikers, suffrage campaigners and unemployed workers periodically erupted onto the streets, but they did not cause violent confrontation or a serious threat to social or political stability, especially compared with events elsewhere in Europe. Baldwin's government, like its immediate predecessors, avoided conflict with the unemployed by providing cash benefits adequate – just – for survival, and somewhat expanding other areas of social welfare provision despite the depression. UK public expenditure on social services rose from £365 million in 1924 (35.5 per cent of total expenditure) to £438 million (39.6 per cent) in 1929.[50] Successive British governments since the nineteenth century had avoided severe conflict by timely compromise. The tradition was upheld by all political parties through the interwar years.

The United Kingdom was divided regionally, even more than before. The troubled export industries were geographically concentrated, mainly on Clydeside (shipbuilding and engineering), Tyneside and northeast England (shipbuilding, mining), Lancashire (cotton textiles and engineering) and the coalfields of South Wales. In these areas there was little alternative employment and they suffered disproportionately from poverty, ill-health and high infant mortality. Meanwhile, the economy diversified, developing new industries supplying electricity, motor vehicles, cycles, chemicals, aircraft, consumer, including electrical, goods, products generally depending on home rather than export demand. These concentrated in the Midlands and South (e.g., motor manufacture in Coventry and Oxford, electrical goods in west London, Bristol and the southwest) where prosperity expanded. Unemployed workers in the depressed regions could not easily move to the new industries, though their children might. Employers could find labour closer at hand, were reluctant to employ potential militants from highly unionized industries and preferred younger to older men, and, especially in new light industries, lower paid women.

Through the 1920s the income share of the top 1 per cent fell fractionally from 20 per cent to approximately 18 per cent of total incomes, and the share of total wealth of the top 1 per cent of wealth-holders fell from 40 per cent to approximately 38 per cent.[51] Incomes, of course, differed between occupational groups and men and women (see Table 4.1).

50 Crowther, *British Social Policy*, p. 15.

51 A. B. Atkinson and S. Morelli, *The New Chartbook of Economic Inequality*, 2014, available at: www.chartbookofeconomicinequality. See p. 411.

Table 4.1 Average Net Earnings by Occupational Class

	1922–4 (£)	1935–6 (£)
Men		
1 Professional		
A: Higher	582	634
B: Lower	320	308
2 Managers etc.	480	440
3 Clerks	182	192
4 Foreman	268	273
5 Skilled manual	180	195
6 Semi-skilled	126	134
7 Unskilled	128	129
Women		
1 Professional		
A: Higher	–.	–
B: Lower	214	211
2 Managers etc.	160	168
3 Clerks	106	99
4 Forewoman	154	156
5 Skilled manual	87	86
6 Semi-skilled	98	100
7 Unskilled	73	73

SOURCE: Guy Routh, *Occupation and Pay in Great Britain, 1906–79* (London: Macmillan,1980), pp. 120–1.

The Upper Class

The greatest inequality, as ever, was between rich and poor, the miserably unemployed and successful businessmen and, on another cloud, the elite 'fast set' enjoying the 'roaring twenties'. The contrast was especially visible in the increasingly outspoken, intrusive popular press[52] and cinema newsreels, both fascinated by the exotic behaviour of this 'glamorous' world, including their entertaining divorces. This social scene was headed by the Prince of Wales, inhabited by members of the traditional upper class, including

52 Deborah Cohen, *Family Secrets. Living with Shame from the Victorians to the Present Day* (London: Viking, 2013), pp. 181–211.

Lord and Lady Mountbatten, increasingly also by film stars –Chaplin, Olivier, Vivien Leigh – sportsmen, actors and actresses and occasional politicians. A focus was the presentation to the king each year of 'debutantes', young women from wealthy families launched into the marriage market in a London 'season' of dances, parties, cocktails and fashionable sporting events, including horse racing at Royal Ascot and, a new arrival, tennis at Wimbledon, with the blessing of the monarchy whose status this annual ritual reinforced. It became more hectic and self-conscious as media scrutiny grew, with freer mixing of the sexes and more activities.[53]

Increased taxation since the war slightly narrowed the income gap between rich and poor, and some landed wealth was depleted by death duties following the wartime deaths of heirs, but the wealth of the richest 5 per cent declined only slightly. Its composition shifted as wealth from land declined somewhat and commerce, manufacturing and brewing prospered, assisted by an expanding advertising industry. Signifying shifts in popular consumption, two of the largest fortunes were left at death by the First Earl of Iveagh, of the Guinness brewing family, who left £13.5 million in 1927, and Bernhard Barron, inventor of the cigarette slot machine and founder of Carreras cigarettes (from a humble background and a major benefactor to the Labour Party), who left £4 million in 1930.[54]

Schools still perpetuated and reinforced class and gender divisions. The most elite, male public schools, Eton, Harrow, Westminster and Winchester, trained and built networks among upper-class men, while many of their sisters were still educated at home. Other boarding schools provided for the upper middle classes of both sexes, separately, including Charterhouse for boys, Roedean and Cheltenham Ladies College for girls.

The Middle Classes

Between the 'upper' and 'lower' orders, the middle classes grew further in size and diversity with the continued expansion of central and local government, banking and insurance, publishing, the professions, including architecture and surveying, accountancy, engineering, science and technology and new areas of business, creating more occupations, from senior management to the lowest strata of clerks, sales and service workers. Professional, managerial and clerical workers increased from 2.4 million to 3.4 million between 1911 and 1931.[55] Upward mobility from working-class backgrounds became a more realistic aspiration than ever before as educational opportunities grew

53 Ross McKibbin, *Classes and Cultures. England 1918-51* (Oxford University Press, 1998), pp. 22–37.
54 Ibid., pp. 37–40.
55 Noreen Branson, *Britain in the Nineteen Twenties* (London: Weidenfeld & Nicolson, 1975), p. 92.

and 'white-collar' jobs expanded. As Table 4.1 shows, they differed from skilled manual work less in pay than security of employment, often with pensions, less physically
demanding work, wearing a suit and tie or the female equivalent, though the 'marriage
bar' generally required women to leave on marriage, with a 'marriage gratuity' replacing a pension. Gender inequality in pay and promotion was still taken for granted,
with a few exceptions, at least in principle, in new organizations striving to be 'modern',
including the BBC, John Lewis stores and the LSE under Beveridge's directorship from
1919 to 1937.[56]

By 1939, almost 60 per cent of middle-class families owned or were buying their
home, while working-class people owned a smaller proportion of the housing stock
than in 1915.[57] The spatial and cultural class divide was more visible than ever between
the inner cities and the growing suburbs of semi-detached houses, with three or more
bedrooms and gardens. The size – smaller than older middle-class housing – was
determined by falling family size, as the birth rate continued to drop, and declining
numbers of live-in servants, replaced by daily servants. The owner-occupied suburbs
grew alongside, generally regarded as socially superior to, council estates, though,
due to relatively high rents, council tenants were still mostly lower middle class or
better-paid skilled workers. Council houses were generally smaller, more often ter-
raced, but with gardens, bathrooms, indoor WCs, a huge improvement on previous
lower-income housing.[58]

The new suburbs and estates divided the residents from the inner cities and contact
with the poorer working class, often from their own families, though many workers commuted back to work on improving public transport. Initially, they included
few amenities, even shops or pubs, and were lonely for women at home with children, often grateful for the company of the increasingly ubiquitous radio. In the BBC's
first year, 1922, there were 5.8 BBC licences per 1,000 families, by 1930, 37, by 1936
68.3, 7 million in total.[59] The BBC developed programmes appealing to this captive
female audience and appointed and promoted women to provide them.[60] The suburbs
encouraged more privatized family lives. Telephones remained a rare, but growing,
form of contact except among the rich. In 1922, there were 176,000 personal telephones, by 1930 551,000, by 1938 1.14 million, while the distinctive, red public phone
boxes spread from the first in London in 1926 to over 20,000 nationwide by the later
1930s.

---

56 Murphy, *Behind the Wireless*.
57 McKibbin, *Classes and Cultures*, p. 73.
58 See pp. 73–4.
59 Sue Bowden, 'The New Consumerism', in Paul Johnson (ed.), *Twentieth-Century Britain. Economic, Social and Cultural Change* (London: Longman, 1994), p. 246.
60 Murphy, *Behind the Wireless*, pp. 189–220.

The Poor

Surveys of poverty increased as the social sciences expanded in universities. They revealed less desperate destitution than before the war, but it had not disappeared. In 1924, Bowley and Hogg repeated their five towns' study of 1913, asking *Has Poverty Diminished?* They adopted the same stringent poverty measure, with adjustments for changing expectations and standards (the diet now included 2 lbs of meat per week). They calculated that the minimum weekly wage required by a family of five was 37s 6d and found 6.5 per cent of working-class people on lower incomes in the five towns, Reading, Northampton, Warrington, Bolton and Stanley, Co. Durham. They found alarming levels of child poverty, mainly caused by low pay or the absence, death or disability of a male earner. Bowley concluded that the lowest wages had risen, leaving only large families and those without a regular male income vulnerable to severe poverty.

The Social Survey of Merseyside, conducted in 1929–30 by researchers at Liverpool University, used a similar but more stringent poverty measure. It found 16 per cent in poverty, only 2 per cent of whom received Public Assistance. Again, inadequate earnings were the main cause though unemployment was increasingly significant. On Merseyside, 10.9 per cent of the people lived below the Registrar-General's overcrowding standard of more than two persons per room. In inner Liverpool only 7.6 per cent of families had access to a garden, 9.8 per cent to a fixed bath and 30 per cent had shared access only.[61]

In 1929–31, H. Llewellyn Smith, retired Ministry of Labour civil servant and former researcher on Booth's London survey, headed a team at the LSE, advised by Bowley and using a similar poverty measure, aiming to repeat Booth's survey in selected areas. They concluded that 14 per cent of the population of east London were 'subject to conditions of privation which, if long continued, would deny them all but the barest necessities and cut them off from access to many of the incidental and cultural benefits of modern progress'. In the whole LCC area 9.6 per cent were in poverty (in contentious Poplar it was 24 per cent) compared with 44.6 per cent in the 1890s; 16 per cent of children in east London were in poverty. Inadequate wages caused 38.5 per cent of London poverty, lack of a male earner 37 per cent and old age caused 16.5 per cent.[62]

---

61 D. Caradog Jones (ed.), *The Social Survey of Merseyside* (Liverpool/London: Liverpool University Press/ Hodder & Stoughton, 1934).
62 Ian Gazeley, *Poverty in Britain, 1900–1965* (London: Palgrave, Macmillan, 2003), p. 82.

Race

Racial inequality also persisted. Discrimination against Jews continued at all social levels. Many Jewish people contributed to society and the economy, especially in business, though for some this reinforced the stereotype of malevolent profiteers. There had long been small black and Asian populations and visitors from British colonies, including members of colonial elites, students, servants and illegitimate children of colonial administrators. An Indian from a prosperous family, Shapurji Saklatvala, arrived in 1905 to work for the motor car business of his relative, J. N. Tata, owner of India's largest commercial and industrial empire. He was elected Labour MP for North Battersea in 1922, not the first brown-skinned MP but rare. In 1924, he was re-elected as the only Communist MP. During the General Strike he was imprisoned for a seditious speech in Hyde Park and did not stand for Parliament again.[63]

During the war, apart from colonial servicemen, substantial numbers of Asians and Africans were recruited to the merchant navy, who after the war continued to work on the ships and often settle in ports, including the docklands of east London with the largest multi-racial community, Liverpool, Cardiff and Bristol. While their labour was in high demand during the war they were readily accepted as Empire-born Britons. As unemployment rose they were accused of taking the jobs of British-born workers and their nationality was questioned by police, port and immigration officials, especially if they claimed unemployment benefits or improvement in their normally atrocious pay and working conditions. Since poor people from the colonies rarely carried evidence of their birthplace it was difficult to prove they were British and entitled to benefits. Harder still when in 1925 the Home Office introduced the Coloured Aliens Seamen's Order defining all 'coloured' seamen as 'aliens' unless they could prove otherwise, as few could. These and other racial tensions simmered through the interwar years.[64]

Nation

Another source of division was emerging nationalism in Scotland and Wales. These were minority movements, mainly of intellectuals inspired by the Irish and the League of Nations' commitment to self-determination. They were reactions also to the growing

63 Michael Squires, *Saklatvala. A Political Biography* (London: Lawrence & Wishart, 1990).
64 Laura Tabili, *Global Migrants, Local Culture. Natives and Newcomers in Provincial England, 1841–1939* (London: Palgrave Macmillan, 2011); Tabili, 'The Construction of Racial Difference in Twentieth Century Britain', pp. 54–98.

power of the Westminster government and of English institutions. Plaid Cymru, the 'Party of Wales', was formed in 1925 mainly to preserve and promote the Welsh language, which was declining as children attended English-speaking schools and the English-speaking BBC reached more homes. They campaigned for Welsh-language teaching in schools and Welsh-language broadcasts. Support was limited. Plaid fought all parliamentary elections from 1929, when its single candidate gained no votes. Two candidates gained 0.1 per cent of the Welsh vote in 1931. It won its first seat in Carmarthen in 1966.[65]

Scottish nationalism owed more to the desire to preserve and extend distinctive Scottish institutions against the power of Westminster. Several Bills proposing varying degrees of self-government failed in Parliament between 1919 and 1928. The National Party of Scotland, founded in 1928, advocated independence and promoted Gaelic culture. With other groups it formed the Scottish National Party (SNP) in 1934. More moderately, this advocated devolution within the Empire, but also lacked mass support. Nationalists ran two candidates in 1929, three in 1931, without success until the Motherwell by-election in 1945.[66]

Leisure

Leisure activities were also class, race and gender divided, but increasingly significant and diverse features of everyday life. Many manual workers had more leisure as working hours continued to fall, while unemployed people had too much but could not afford costly pursuits. Salaried workers had one or two weeks' paid holiday each year from the late nineteenth century, rare for manual workers, who campaigned for paid holidays along with shorter hours. In 1925, about 1.5 million manual workers were covered by paid holiday agreements of some kind, but holiday time could be as little as three days per year, often one week, rarely more. Those who could holidayed in the growing seaside resorts, themselves still class divided, or they took day trips, increasingly organized and advertised by expanding coach and rail companies. A better-off minority travelled by car: about 474,000 were licensed in 1920, 1,760,533 in 1930.[67] The rich travelled abroad.

Playing and watching sports increased for those with time and cash to spare, mainly men. Cricket was popular, crossing boundaries of class, town and country, mainly in England, though the classes rarely played together. In county and national

65 K. O. Morgan, *Rebirth of a Nation. Wales, 1880–1980* (Oxford University Press, 1981).

66 Christopher Harvie, *Scotland and Nationalism. Scottish Society and Politics, 1707 to the Present*, 4th edn (London: Routledge, 2004).

67 Butler and Butler, *Twentieth-Century British Political Facts*, p. 372.

teams 'gentlemen' amateurs were distinguished from paid 'players' until the distinction was abolished in 1962. Cricket was less popular in Wales, even less in Scotland and Northern Ireland. Women sometimes played, but not in public, and rarely shared the mass working-class male devotion to watching and playing football, or the less popular variant, rugby, in either its upper-class version of rugby union or the mainly northern, working-class, rugby league. Mainly female sports – netball, hockey, lacrosse – were not public spectator sports and were practised mostly in independent schools; elementary schools rarely had space for sports. Also middle and upper class, increasingly popular, and unusual in including both sexes, though in separate tournaments, was tennis. In Scotland, golf was popular across classes, though its elite clubs excluded women into the twenty-first century; in England, it was male, middle and upper class, notorious for its social, gender and racial exclusiveness. Horse racing also became more popular with the better-off who could afford to attend and working men who placed bets off-course, not always legally. Hunting and shooting remained upper-class pastimes, while dog racing expanded to entertain the workers.

New technology shaped other pursuits. Apart from radio, cinema-going expanded, especially among young, unmarried workers, male and female, and married women attending in the afternoon, since seats were cheap (most no more than 6d).[68] Film-going too was class divided: despised by many intellectuals and better-off people as too Americanized, encouraging passive consumption rather than creative involvement. But cultural creativity was far from dead. In particular 1922 emerged as an *annus mirabilis* in which modernist literature became irreversibly established. It saw the publication of two pinnacles of the genre, James Joyce's *Ulysses* and T. S. Eliot's outstanding poem, *The Waste Land*. Also the first volume of Marcel Proust's *À la Recherche du temps perdu* was translated into English and the fourth volume published in France. Virginia Woolf published *Jacob's Room* and, inspired by Proust, began work on *Mrs Dalloway* (published 1925), and E. M. Forster started to complete *A Passage to India* (1924) having published nothing since *Howard's End* in 1910. All these authors, like very many other people, were agonized and mentally stressed about the state of the world following the destruction of war. Their responses reshaped literature and helped to reshape the world, along with the other remarkable developments of the time, including the opening of the BBC, also in 1922, Louis Armstrong's development of modern jazz, film and the birth of modernist architecture.[69]

68 Claire Langhamer, *Women's Leisure in England, 1920–1960* (Manchester University Press, 2000).

69 Kevin Jackson, *Constellation of Genius..1922, Modernism and all that Jazz* (London: Hutchinson, 2012); Bill Goldstein, *The World Broke in Two. Virginia Woolf, T. S. Eliot, D. H. Lawrence, E. M. Forster and the Year that Changed Literature* (London: Bloomsbury, 2017).

The Second Labour Government

That something was profoundly changing in this class-divided society was suggested by the election, again, of a Labour government, though still in a minority. MacDonald returned to the premiership, anxious, again, not to alienate the Liberals on whom the government depended in Parliament, or the voters, with extreme policies. Lloyd George agreed to support a moderate Labour government but warned that 'the very hour the Ministry becomes a Socialist administration its career ends',[70] though he knew the Liberals could not afford another election soon. They were still very divided, with many backbenchers reluctant to cooperate with Labour; they repeatedly split on parliamentary votes. Lloyd George wanted electoral reform, that is PR, pointing out that Liberals had gained 23 per cent of the vote but only 9 per cent of seats. MacDonald gave this some encouragement, though he opposed most forms of PR because they broke the link between MPs and constituencies, and it divided Labour.[71]

The Crash

Labour soon faced an even worse economic crisis than before. In October the New York Stock Exchange crashed and world trade collapsed, mainly due to speculative mania on Wall Street following long-term depression in the United States. In 1930, UK unemployment rose to 2.5 million.[72] To make things worse, the Conservatives bequeathed a deficit of government expenditure over revenue (carefully disguised by Churchill) which grew to £14.5 million by spring 1930 as tax revenues fell and the costs of unemployment benefit rose. Labour could not easily resolve a world crisis originating outside Britain, which did not stop Conservatives blaming them. Labour aimed to manage it by creating work, protecting the living standards of the unemployed and increasing taxes on higher incomes. In 1929–1931 it funded public works costing £100 million, creating about 300,000 jobs while contributing, as Keynes advocated, to necessary modernization of infrastructure, including roads and bridges. Benefits for juveniles and dependants increased and the 'genuinely seeking work' clause was abolished; unemployment benefit could now be refused only if a claimant rejected suitable work. Income tax, surtax and estate duty rose.

Labour attempted other social improvements despite the crisis. By 1929, the more manageable end of the housing problem, affecting many skilled and white-collar workers, had largely been solved. The glaring remaining problem was overcrowded,

70 Davis, *History of Britain*, p. 187.
71 Thane, 'Labour and Local Politics', pp. 265–6.
72 Mitchell and Deane, *Historical Statistics*, p. 66.

often insanitary and bug-ridden, privately rented 'slums'. Labour policy shifted from housebuilding to 'slum clearance', clearing and releasing land for building low-cost replacement homes near city centre workplaces. The Housing Act 1930 subsidized local authorities according to the number of families re-housed from cleared slums. They were instructed to survey their housing stock and produce five-year plans for clearance and replacement. The greatest housing need began to be tackled, slowly in the economic circumstances.

In 1929, widows' pensions were extended to include wives of insured men who had died or were over 70 when they were introduced in 1925. In 1931, Labour responded to the demands of Labour women, and many others, to make birth control more easily and cheaply available. The birth rate was still declining in all classes, but concern persisted about the effects on the health especially of poor women, and on family living standards, of repeated pregnancy and childbirth and about the risk of illegal abortion. Aware of hostility from their substantial Catholic vote, Labour cautiously allowed local authority health and welfare clinics in England and Wales to give free birth control advice to married women (only) whose health was at risk from pregnancy. It did not risk a parliamentary vote on this contentious issue, but issued a Ministry of Health memorandum. Four years later 224 councils (of 474 in England, Wales and Scotland) provided birth control clinics, sometimes interpreting their role more flexibly than the strict letter of the memorandum.[73]

But there was strong resistance in Parliament to any reform. Combined Liberal and Conservative votes defeated attempts to amend the Trades Disputes Act and abolish the university seats which gave graduates two votes. A move in 1931 to raise the school-leaving age to fifteen was crushed in the Lords. Under pressure, a Royal Commission on Unemployment Insurance was appointed to investigate potential savings, also a committee to investigate further spending cuts, chaired by Sir George May, former chairman of the Prudential Assurance Company.

The government became bitterly divided over unemployment benefits, the largest item of public spending. MacDonald, Snowden, again a cautious Chancellor, and Margaret Bondfield, Minister of Labour, the first woman Cabinet minister, proposed 15 per cent cuts. Most of the Cabinet opposed this unless it was matched by equivalent sacrifice by the better-off. Opponents included Arthur Henderson, George Lansbury and a junior minister outside the Cabinet, the wealthy former Conservative MP turned Independent then Labour MP, Oswald Mosley. Mosley proposed a large scheme of loan-financed public works, fewer planning controls, raising the school-leaving age and lowering the pension age to reduce competition for work, and tariffs, with special

---

73 Claire Debenham, *Birth Control and the Rights of Women. Post-suffrage Feminism in the Early Twentieth Century* (London: I. B. Tauris, 2014).

arrangements for imperial trade. This was rejected and Mosley resigned from the government in May 1930 to campaign for his programme within the party. He won support from Keynes among others, and at the party conference in October 1930 he came close to winning the vote, but his package was unlikely to get through Parliament given continuing Liberal and much Labour opposition to tariffs and the proposed increase in government spending. Also Mosley's domineering personality aroused suspicion. So, even more, did the New Party he then launched, initially to promote his economic ideas, though it soon lurched into right-wing nationalism.[74]

The Agricultural Marketing Act 1931 – the work of Christopher Addison, now a Labour MP and Minister for Agriculture – controlled agricultural prices.[75] In June 1931, the first report of the Commission on Unemployment Insurance concluded that there were more jobseekers than jobs, but recommended an 11.5 per cent cut in benefits. This was again rejected by the Cabinet. The international crisis deepened. Banks collapsed in Austria and Germany, they withdrew their funds from London and the Bank of England's gold reserves shrank. In July, the May Committee increased panic with a dramatic report, blaming the financial crisis on the profligacy it claimed was inherent in democracy which encouraged public spending. It projected an unrealistically high deficit of £120 million for 1932–3 and recommended equally unrealistic cuts of £96.5 million pa, £66 million from unemployment benefits alone, through cuts to payments, higher contributions and more means-testing, severe 'austerity'. It proposed no sacrifices by higher earners. Keynes described the report as 'a most gross perversion of social justice'.[76] The Cabinet would only accept higher contributions by workers if taxes also rose. It was one more episode in an ongoing battle through the twentieth century between proponents and opponents of state social and economic intervention, always acute at times of economic crisis. As Keynes suggested, it was not obvious that severe cuts to public spending would assist rather than retard recovery.

At this point government finances could escape bankruptcy only with a large overseas loan, for which bankers chose to require all-party approval since the financial markets had little confidence in a Labour government. The Conservative and Liberal leaderships refused. On 21 August, with the government deadlocked, the Governor of the Bank informed MacDonald that gold was draining away and national bankruptcy was imminent. Nine of twenty Cabinet members still refused expenditure cuts, threatening resignation. The government could not continue and on 23 August MacDonald informed the king that the Cabinet was resigning and proposed a meeting of party leaders to discuss the way forward. This recommended a cross-party National

74 See pp. 141–2.

75 K. O. Morgan, 'Addison, Christopher First Viscount Addison, 1869–1951', *Oxford Dictionary of National Biography*, 2004, online edn, January 2011, available at: www.oxforddnb.com.

76 Marquand, *Ramsay MacDonald*, p. 610.

Government, already proposed by the king, a passionate anti-socialist with no desire to keep Labour in office. A ten-member Cabinet was formed, including MacDonald, Snowden and J. H. Thomas from Labour, Baldwin and Neville Chamberlain and the Liberal Herbert Samuel (Lloyd George was ill and out of action). Baldwin had little incentive to demand an election and no ideas for resolving the financial crisis. His party was much divided and he was seen, inside the party and out, as a weak leader with few decisive policies, while those he had – moderate imperial preference and Dominion status for India – deepened the divisions.[77] The Labour government, like other governments exposed to the international crisis they could not control, lost office, constrained by the limitations of its minority position, party divisions and opposition in Parliament.[78]

Labour's Foreign Policy

As in 1924, MacDonald was distracted from economic problems by pressing foreign and colonial affairs. Reluctantly, he appointed Henderson Foreign Secretary, when he made it his price for serving in the government, further worsening their relationship since MacDonald could not resist intervening in foreign policy. He was determined to improve relations with the United States, which Baldwin had undermined, hoping, as always, to increase international harmony and the potential for lasting peace, and to increase Anglo-American trade. He was the first British Prime Minister to pay a, successful, official visit to the United States in September–October 1929. He led international naval disarmament negotiations in January 1930, when increasingly militaristic Japan, Britain and the United States, but not France and Italy, agreed cuts. He believed passionately that disarmament was the route to peace. A strong supporter of the League of Nations, he appointed Robert Cecil British delegate to the League, with a room in the Foreign Office, which Baldwin had denied him, and greater influence.[79]

Henderson completed MacDonald's work of 1924 by achieving full diplomatic relations, then a commercial treaty, with the USSR. He was involved in negotiations achieving the withdrawal of occupation forces from the Rhineland and ensured that Britain signed the Young Plan of August 1929 which further revised German reparations, increasing the payments to Britain. In May 1931, he encouraged the League of Nations to agree to a world disarmament conference, at which he presided in February 1932.

77 Ball, *Conservative Party*, pp. 83–5.
78 Andrew Thorpe, *A History of the British Labour Party* (London: Macmillan, 1997), pp. 67–78.
79 Martin Ceadel, 'Cecil (Edgar Algernon) Robert Gascoyne [known as Lord Robert Cecil], Viscount Cecil of Chelwood, 1864–1958', *Oxford Dictionary of National Biography*, 2004, online edn January 2011, available at: www.oxforddnb.com.

Empire to Commonwealth

Colonial affairs remained relatively quiescent until in 1929, following an Arab uprising against growing Jewish immigration to Palestine, Lord Passfield (Sidney Webb), Under-Secretary for the Colonies, drafted a White Paper proposing restrictions on Jewish immigration and the sale of Palestinian lands to Jews. A furore followed among Zionists internationally, Conservative imperialists and some Labour MPs and Passfield retreated. The Jewish population of Palestine continued to grow steadily.

There was little investment in colonial welfare through the 1920s, though it was much needed. Labour's Colonial Development and Welfare Act 1929 provided grants, but, in the difficult economic circumstances, allocated only £1 million for the first three years and little more thereafter. Still in 1938 Uganda had only 1,300 hospital beds for a population of 3 million, fewer than 5 per cent of Ugandan children and only 10–15 per cent of Nigerian children attended school. Conditions were little better in other African colonies.[80]

The new government raised nationalist hopes in India since Labour, including MacDonald, had long been committed to greater colonial independence. MacDonald proposed a conference and the viceroy, Lord Irwin (a moderate Conservative, later Earl of Halifax), sought to reassure nationalists of the government's commitment to granting Dominion status. But Congress refused to join the conference unless it was committed to a self-governing constitution for India. In March 1930, it called a major civil disobedience protest; 60,000 resisters were imprisoned, including Gandhi and Nehru. In November 1930 the conference met, without Congress, but included seventy-four Indians. MacDonald proposed a route to self-government, but there were major differences among Muslims, Hindus and Sikhs over their relative levels of representation. Attempting to reconcile the differences took much of MacDonald's time until, in January 1931, there was broad agreement to an all-India federation with an elected legislature. This was welcomed by Baldwin and fiercely opposed by Churchill. Gandhi was released and in September joined the second conference. By this time Labour had been replaced by the National Government. Completing satisfactory arrangements for India was a major reason why MacDonald was determined to remain Prime Minister, but neither he nor Baldwin could restrain the Conservative imperialists in the new government. A less conciliatory viceroy was appointed, attempts at conciliation ended, civil disobedience revived, its leaders were arrested yet again and the conflict continued.[81]

While Labour remained in power it achieved an important step towards colonial independence with the Statute of Westminster 1931. This confirmed the shift from

---

80 Porter, *Lion's Share*, p. 270.
81 Ibid., pp. 296–9.

British Empire to 'British Commonwealth' following resolutions of the Imperial Conferences (meetings of Dominion prime ministers) in 1926 and 1930, which sought to clarify the status of the Dominions. It defined them as 'autonomous communities within the British Empire, equal in status … united by a common allegiance to the Crown and freely associated as members of the British Commonwealth of Nations'. The Statute ended the automatic superiority of the Westminster Parliament over all Dominion parliaments, increased their autonomy and established a mechanism for achieving Dominion status. It signalled greater equality between at least the white-controlled colonies and Britain.

Conclusion

The United Kingdom adjusted quite calmly to the huge expansion and diversification of the electorate as it finally became democratic, contrary to the apprehensions of generations of politicians and despite the severe Depression. This was partly due to the cautious response by leading politicians of all persuasions, averting major conflict by compromising with demands by labour and by women for greater equality, while preventing severe unrest among the unemployed by ensuring that, for the first time, they had guaranteed, if basic, support, helped by falling international prices especially for food. The Conservative leadership restrained the confrontational instincts of some supporters and demands for extreme spending cuts, while Labour had its first opportunities to govern, though as a minority on both occasions, in the second in exceptionally difficult financial circumstances. On both occasions it had real, often underestimated, achievements in foreign, colonial and domestic policies, including extending democracy in what was now the Commonwealth, rather greater than those of its Conservative predecessors, despite internal divisions similar to those of the other leading parties. The economy did not collapse, indeed remained more stable than many of its competitors. In 1931, the United Kingdom remained deeply divided and unequal, in multiple ways, but the inequalities did not lead to conflicts comparable with those emerging elsewhere in Europe, which became increasingly evident and threatening as the 1930s progressed.

5 The Thirties

1931–1939

Spending Cuts and Party Splits

The change of government did not lessen the crisis. The coalition was not expected to last. Following the initial meeting, Herbert Samuel, Liberal leader in Lloyd George's absence due to illness and now Home Secretary, drafted an agreement that 'the Parties will return to their original positions' when the financial emergency ended. It was an exceptional response to an exceptional crisis and urgent measures followed. The supporters of spending cuts had won. Snowden remained Chancellor, delivering an emergency budget making the 10 per cent cut to unemployment benefit the Labour Cabinet had rejected, raising contributions, reducing the benefit period and introducing a means-test for 'transitional' payments to the long-term unemployed who had exhausted their insurance allowances. The Anomalies Act 1931 withdrew recognition as 'unemployed' from married women who were uninsured or whose entitlement to insurance benefit had expired, on the grounds that their husbands should support them and there were always vacancies for domestic servants – suitable work for women whatever their skills and former employment. This caused particular hardship and resentment in the Lancashire textile districts, hard-hit by unemployment, where married women normally worked in factories and their families depended on their incomes.

Snowden balanced the cuts by reducing public sector salaries, including those of ministers, increasing income tax from 4s 6d to 5s in the £, modestly increasing surtax and reducing exemptions and children's allowances. A further 1,250,000 people now paid income tax, overwhelmingly lower middle class. Between 1920 and 1932, the tax rate rose by 11 per cent on incomes over £50,000, by 380 per cent on £500 earned by married men with three children.[1] These measures passed easily through Parliament, but caused an unprecedented mutiny at the Invergordon naval base because seamen faced wage cuts of up to 25 per cent but admirals only 7 per cent. The government then limited all pay cuts to 10 per cent. The mutiny triggered another run on sterling and the Gold Standard was abandoned on 21 September. Within three months the pound had fallen by almost 30 per cent against the dollar and foreign exchange flowed back into London.

But there was no chance of a speedy return to previous political certainties. The Liberal Party split again: Sir John Simon formed the Liberal National Party, supporting the National Government, indicating that the party would fight the next election independently of the Lloyd George Liberals who would not commit long term to the Coalition. Labour was less profoundly divided because MacDonald took only a handful of followers into the National Government, but the belief that he and Snowden had betrayed the party and the neediest in society in surrender to financial interests was bitter and long-lasting. Labour's National Executive Committee expelled supporters of the National Government from the party.

MacDonald believed, with some reason, that he must remain premier to maintain confidence at home and abroad. He was still deeply concerned with foreign and imperial politics, especially Indian independence. He went on to convene three conferences, supported by Baldwin, assisted by Lord Irwin, while courting and conciliating Gandhi. This achieved the Government of India Act 1935, establishing an All-India Federation with increased self-government. Churchill and about 100 Conservatives opposed it in the Commons.[2]

General Election, 1931

Baldwin and his colleagues were unenthusiastic about coalition, but George V persuaded them that MacDonald should remain Prime Minister to provide stability through the crisis. They demanded an election, which they felt confident of winning, despite their divisions and fears that an election campaign might further weaken sterling. When it weakened dangerously anyway and the Gold Standard was abandoned it was argued that an election would produce a government with a clear mandate, strengthening confidence and the currency. It was called for October 1931.

It was strident and unpleasant. The components of the National Government – MacDonald's Labour followers, Simonite Liberals, Samuelite Liberals, Conservatives – campaigned separately, disagreeing particularly on tariffs, but agreeing to cooperate if they secured a collective majority. The Conservatives won 473 seats and 55.2 per

1 Daunton, *Just Taxes*, p. 159.
2 Porter, *Lion's Share*, pp. 285–7.

cent of the vote. They courted votes by unfairly blaming the ideology and incompetence of the 'socialists' for the international financial crisis. National Labour won thirteen seats and 1.6 per cent of votes, the Labour Party 6.6 million votes (33 per cent) but only fifty-two seats, holding support in old industrial areas and among public sector workers who feared Conservative cuts. It was led by Henderson, who declared capitalism had broken down, demanding industrial planning, import controls and nationalization of banking and credit, which Snowden, who did not stand in the election, and the Conservatives denounced as 'Bolshevism gone mad'. The ILP thought it not radical enough and disaffiliated in 1932, though it quickly lost members and did not fulfil its dream of becoming a successful, truly left-wing party. Henderson again lost his seat and was succeeded as leader by George Lansbury.[3]

The Liberals split three ways: National Liberals won thirty-five seats and 3.5 per cent of the vote with Conservative assistance, Samuelite Liberals 6.5 per cent but only thirty-three seats, and Independent Liberals, who rejected the coalition, won four seats and 0.5 per cent. The pro-National Government parties had 554 seats, a massive, Conservative-dominated, majority, though still, in principle, a coalition. Sixty-two women stood, including thirty-six Labour, sixteen Conservative and six Liberals; fifteen were elected: thirteen Conservatives, one Liberal and Independent Eleanor Rathbone again. MacDonald remained Prime Minister, while Snowden accepted a peerage and became Lord Privy Seal. Neville Chamberlain succeeded him as Chancellor.

The Economy

There was no financial collapse in Britain in 1929–31 and output and employment fell less than among its closest competitors, the United States, Germany and France, though exports were hit by the international slowdown. It was the world's largest importer of food and raw materials, which fell in price, increasing purchasing power. The relative mildness of the depression in Britain helps to explain why extreme politics were less attractive than elsewhere. The new government immediately abandoned free trade. Tariffs were prominent in the election manifestoes of most successful Conservatives, despite Baldwin's caution. Popular opposition diminished as food prices fell. Even the Liberals were divided on this, as on much else. The Cabinet approved a 10 per cent duty on all imports except basic food and raw materials and established a committee to propose further duties where appropriate.

Colonial imports were exempt. In late 1931, at a conference of Dominion leaders in Ottawa, the UK delegation, led by Baldwin and Neville Chamberlain, aimed to fulfil Jo Chamberlain's dream of imperial economic integration, to 'vindicate

---

3 F. M. Leventhal, *Arthur Henderson* (Manchester University Press, 1989).

my father's ghost' as Neville Chamberlain put it.[4] But the Dominions were economically stronger now and Britain weaker. They already gave some preference to UK goods and were unwilling to give more while their own farmers, businesses and workers suffered from the world depression. Aiming to reduce their dependence on food and raw material exports and develop manufacturing, they sought protection from competing UK exports and drove a harder bargain than expected, raising duties on non-UK imports but giving no further favours. The negotiations were often fractious, not the harmonious Commonwealth of its supporters' dreams, and the Dominions won. Snowden and the free trade Liberal ministers, including Samuel, resigned from the government. Exports to the Commonwealth fell in value by 22 per cent between 1929 and 1938, but the Ottawa agreement prevented them falling even faster. A steeper decline in Britain's share of world trade was prevented by agreeing with countries in and outside the Commonwealth which traded in sterling, including Scandinavia, the Baltic States, Portugal and Argentina, to manage the exchange rate, which kept the cost of imports from the sterling area stable until 1939.[5]

By 1932 the depression in the United Kingdom bottomed out and output recovered its 1929 levels by 1934, with new industries continuing to expand. This owed little to government policy. Tariffs probably slowed recovery as they protected companies facing competing imports, but raised the cost of raw materials, including steel.[6] The government refused to try to manage the economy, even if it had known how, other than by cutting public spending. Exports did not recover but interest rates fell, reducing repayments on the national debt among other advantages. Unemployment rose until January 1932, when almost 3 million were registered unemployed in Great Britain. By March 1935, it had fallen to 2.03 million, and to 1.8 million by April 1938. Cautiously, the government guaranteed loans for essential enterprises, including railways, shipping and expansion of London transport. Low interest rates enabled industries to invest cheaply and encouraged housebuilding and purchase, creating employment. Investment flowed into building as the crash of 1929–31 reduced confidence in other forms of investment. New prefabricated building methods reduced costs, but the private homes were not always of high quality: the later 1930s saw a wave of mortgage strikes by home-buyers unwilling to pay for hastily constructed houses with leaking roofs and warped window frames.[7]

4 P. Williamson, *National Crisis and National Government* (Cambridge University Press, 1992), p. 507.
5 Davis, *History of Britain*, pp. 9–12.
6 Dudley Baines, 'Recovery from Depression', in Paul Johnson (ed.), *Twentieth-Century Britain. Economic, Social and Cultural Change* (London: Longman, 1994), p. 195; F. Capie, *Depression and Protectionism in Britain Between the Wars* (London: Routledge, 1983, repr. 2013).
7 N. Branson and M. Heinemann, *Britain in the Nineteen Thirties* (London: Weidenfeld & Nicolson, 1971), pp. 187–9.

House sales increased demand for household goods, including such new inventions as vacuum cleaners, electric irons, cookers, refrigerators, all often home-manufactured. Demand was boosted by the new, flourishing hire-purchase (HP) method of weekly deferred payment. Prices fell, while incomes generally did not, increasing purchasing power. Falling family size also reduced costs for many families. The birth rate continued to fall, reaching its lowest level in 1933. The two-child family was increasingly the norm in all classes. Until 1938 the economy recovered as domestic demand grew, yet the numbers unemployed remained high as old industries continued to decline. From 1938, when there was renewed depression in the international economy, Britain was protected by rearmament, which had not been a significant part of the economy since 1918, though unemployment remained at 1.4 million in January 1940.[8]

New Technology, New Lifestyles

Neon signs in city centres and mass-produced gadgets signalled new technology underpinning economic expansion, transforming everyday life and creating work in favoured areas. Motor vehicles, especially buses and coaches, enabled more people to travel further for work, on day trips and holidays, while car ownership grew.[9] A lucky minority could afford appliances to lessen the drudgery of domestic work. Leisure was transformed by radio, cinema and the gramophone, providing unprecedented mass access to a range of cultural forms. This alarmed some on the left who feared that films, in particular, were a new opium of the people, diverting their attention from serious social concerns. George Orwell believed they were one reason why Britain escaped revolution in the 1930s:

> You may have only three halfpence in your pocket and not a prospect in the world, and only the corner of a leaky bedroom to go home to; but in your new clothes you can stand on the street corner, indulging in a private daydream of yourself as Clark Gable or Greta Garbo, which compensates you for a great deal.[10]

Cultural pessimists feared the machines would supplant live performance, shrink theatre and concert audiences, and replace participation in music, reading and amateur drama with passive watching and listening. They demanded government subsidies to keep the arts live, without success before the Second World War, though local authorities subsidized theatre and music, especially in larger cities.[11]

In reality, amateur performance and attendance at live events increased, along with reading. The determinedly educational BBC was directed from its foundation by John Reith who believed its central mission was to build an informed, cultured democracy. It

8 Butler and Butler, *Twentieth-Century British Political Facts*, p. 400.
9 Ibid., p. 372.
10 George Orwell, *The Road to Wigan Pier* (Harmondsworth: Penguin, [1937], 1962), pp. 79–81.
11 Howard Webber, ' Before the Arts Council', PhD in progress, King's College London.

opened drama, music and literature to a mass audience. Seventy-one per cent of British households had radio licences by 1939. Public libraries issued 85,668 books in 1924, 247,335 in 1939.[12] Chain stores, including Boots Pure Drug Company, ran popular libraries with low weekly subscriptions, while book sales rocketed. Publishing benefited from technological change and books were cheaper, particularly the new paperbacks. Penguin Books seized this market from its foundation in 1935, offering cheap reprints of classics, new novels and non-fiction studies of science and the arts, while Penguin Specials fed the widespread interest in current affairs, national and international, generally with a leftish slant. Penguin sought to appeal to all tastes, 'high', 'low' and 'middlebrow', selling books at 6d, while the cheapest hardbacks cost between 2s 6d and 5s, too expensive for many people. Its first publications sold in editions of 20,000; within three years the minimum was 50,000.[13] But cheap books could not match the market for proliferating periodicals catering for interests from fishing and golf to fashion and home furnishing, most successfully women's magazines, using new printing techniques generating eye-catching illustrations and attracting the expanding advertising industry.

A substantial appetite for low-cost books on social and political issues was also fed by the Left Book Club, founded in 1936 by publisher Victor Gollancz. He found that hardbacks on these topics, generally priced at 12s 6d or 18s, sold poorly. The club offered subscribers a book each month for 2s 6d. They helped to fix the image of unemployment as the dominant feature of the 1930s, through such works as Allen Hutt, *The Condition of the Working Class* (1933); Ellen Wilkinson, *The Town that was Murdered* (1939), about Jarrow, her constituency; and Wal Hannington, *The Problem of the Distressed Areas* (1937). On national and international politics its publications included Edgar Snow's report on the communist guerrillas in China, *Red Star over China* (1937); R. Palme Dutt, *India Today* (1940); and Clement Attlee, *The Labour Party in Perspective* (1937), surveying the past and present of the party. The club soon had 50,000 members and 500 local groups and, due to its left-wing slant, was closely observed by Special Branch, the arm of the police charged since the 1880s with investigating potential subversives.[14]

New leisure activities appealed to the independence and regular incomes of increasing numbers of young people, particularly dance halls promoting modern styles of music especially from America. Cinema audiences grew to about 23 million per week in 1939, mainly working-class, young people and married women. The *Social Survey of Merseyside* (1934)[15] estimated that 40 per cent of the local population attended cinemas weekly, with young people, there and elsewhere, going up to four times a week. More and grander cinemas opened, designed to create an atmosphere of luxury and

12 Butler and Butler, *Twentieth-Century British Political Facts*, p. 367.
13 Branson and Heinemann, *Britain in the Nineteen Thirties*, p. 255.
14 Ibid., pp. 275–8.
15 See p. 108.

fantasy, especially after 'talkies' replaced silent films from the late 1920s, though cheap local 'fleapits' survived. The middle-class film audience grew, fastest among younger people, as the middle class itself grew, though some intellectuals remained snobbish about the popular medium. A high proportion of films were American, stimulating moves to protect the British film industry and British culture from 'Americanization'.[16] Hollywood influenced fashion, for young men and women, and language; American slang became familiar. Potential cultural subversion was controlled by the British Board of Film Censors (BBFC) (established in 1912), which firmly policed portrayals of sex and crime and political or religious themes deemed to be dangerous. In 1936, it rejected a proposed film version of Walter Greenwood's *Love on the Dole*, a vivid account of the impact of unemployment which was a successful novel and stage play, but judged by the BBFC to contain 'too much of the tragic and sordid side of poverty' to be suitable for the cinema-going public, not least for depicting a clash between unemployed demonstrators and the police.[17] It had no problem approving *Sing as We Go*, starring the popular British actress Gracie Fields, as an unemployed millworker coping resiliently, finding alternative work in Blackpool until the mill miraculously, and improbably, re-opened.[18] The cinema was a refuge from reality and probably few who experienced unemployment and poverty were fooled. A survey of cinema-going among working-class youths in Manchester in the early 1930s found them critical of the films they watched, unconvinced they depicted life realistically.[19]

Spectator sports flourished, with attendance at football league matches reaching 14 million in 1937–8, mainly working-class men, compared with 6 million in 1908–9.[20] Other sports grew in popularity with participants and spectators, their class divisions unchanged.[21] Despite increased leisure time and higher pay for more people, one declining leisure activity was drink. The wartime restrictions on sales and pub opening hours remained and the amount spent on alcohol fell from £426.5 million to £306.4 million between 1920 and 1938.

The holiday industry grew substantially. Blackpool, Britain's most popular holiday resort, drew 7 million, mainly working-class, visitors each year in the 1930s, many on day trips. The first holiday camp was opened by Butlin's at Skegness in 1937, a new type of low-cost holiday venue providing the first cheap package holidays, with accommodation in wooden chalets set in green environments on the outskirts of resorts,

---

16 Mark Gardner, 'The British and French Advertising Industries, 1945–65', unpublished PhD thesis, King's College London, 2010.

17 Andrew Davies, 'Cinema and Broadcasting', in Paul Johnson (ed.), *Twentieth-Century Britain. Economic, Social and Cultural Change* (London: Longman, 1994), p. 275.

18 Ibid., p. 277.

19 Ibid., p. 278.

20 Ibid.

21 See pp. 110–11.

providing three meals a day, laundry and childcare facilities, entertainment for all ages, from swimming, snooker and physical exercise to dancing, beauty and fancy dress contests, with shops, bars, first aid centres and church services, after strict Sabbatarians expressed disapproval of holiday entertainment on Sundays.[22]

The camps catered for a growing working- and lower middle-class market, increasingly able to take holidays with pay, even for some manual workers following trade union demands, supported by the ILO and inspired by successful strikes for paid leave in France and Belgium. By 1938, 7.75 million workers in a total employed population of 18.5 million had paid holidays. About one-third of Britain's population took a holiday away from home of a week or more, more than ever before, but reflecting profound continuing inequalities. The closest many poorer families came to a holiday was hop-picking in Kent, which provided fresh air and additional income but was hard work in poor conditions. Many low-paid workers still received no pay even for public holidays, making them dread Christmas, Easter and other holidays when they had to restrict the family diet and/or fall into debt. As one woman wrote to the *Daily Herald* in 1937, holidays meant 'making one week's wages go the way of two'.[23] Campaigners stressed workers' need for a break from the physical and mental demands of continuous work and that paid holidays would improve productivity. Employers argued, predictably, that their businesses could not bear the additional costs, though more agreed paid holidays as the campaign mounted in the late 1930s. The *Daily Herald* vigorously supported the campaign as, more surprisingly, did the *Daily Express*. It criticized the inequality between waged and salaried workers and pointed to twenty-four countries that had legislated for annual paid holidays for all workers, including Chile, Venezuela, France, Finland, Norway and the USSR. It stressed the burden on 'the poor British housewife' of managing a reduced family budget due to holidays, also that her need for holidays, as respite from the daily grind, was as great as her husband's. The *Daily Express* was keen to attract women readers,[24] but the sentiments had substance. Even when low-paid families could afford time away, it was usually camping, caravanning or in self-catering accommodation, where women carried on cooking, cleaning and washing.[25]

Women took up the cause. Labour Party women organized a 'Seaside Campaign' in resorts in summer 1937, distributing leaflets and posters and organizing meetings to persuade those who could afford a holiday to support those who could not. They were supported by poverty researchers and doctors because public holidays without pay increased deprivation, malnutrition and poor health. The National Government

22 Sandra Dawson, 'Working-class Consumers and the Campaign for Holidays with Pay', *Twentieth Century British History* 18(3) (2007): 280.

23 Ibid., p. 287.

24 Bingham, *Gender, Modernity*, pp. 40–1.

25 Langhamer, *Women's Leisure*, pp. 36–9.

resisted, but in 1937 a Holidays with Pay Bill, the fourth introduced by a Labour MP since 1912, reached the Committee stage supported by the Conservative press and the leisure industry, with Butlin's promoting 'Holidays with Pay, Holidays with Play'. The government appointed a committee, chaired by medical specialist, Lord Amulree, which in 1938 recommended that all full-time workers should have at least one week's paid holiday each year, to improve their health and productivity and enable wives to 'enjoy rest and recuperation and freedom so far as possible from arduous household duties'. It proposed government encouragement of holiday camps to provide affordable holidays and employment. The Holidays with Pay Act, 1938, recommended, but did not enforce, at least one week's paid holiday each year for all full-time workers, not including public holidays – a slight gain for the poorest workers. Implementation was delayed by the war.

Unemployment

Unemployed people gained least from expanding leisure opportunities and new gadgets. Economic expansion focused on west London (east London remained depressed; there were never fewer than 100,000 unemployed Londoners through the 1930s), the West Midlands and the south of England, while the old industrial centres grew more depressed. In 1929, 4.6 per cent of unemployed people had been out of work for a year or more, by 1935 this reached 26 per cent and in northern England in February 1938 the figure was 35 per cent. Long-term unemployment was concentrated in coal, shipbuilding, iron and steel and textiles: 71 per cent of the workforce of Crook in the Durham coalfield had been unemployed for five years by 1936.[26]

Despite cuts, all unemployed people, other than married women, qualified for means-tested 'transitional payments'. Still, some local offices doled out government money more generously than others: in depressed Rotherham and Merthyr Tydfil, 98 per cent of claimants were paid the full rate, against a national average of 50.8 per cent.[27] Again, Neville Chamberlain, this time as Chancellor, faced protests against cuts. In 1934, he introduced a reformed insurance system administered by an Unemployment Insurance Statutory Committee, headed by Sir (as he now was) William Beveridge, providing payments for one year to those with sufficient contributions. A safety-net – administered by an Unemployment Assistance Board (UAB) – supported people who had exhausted or lacked cover, with minimal standard payments, lower than those paid by PACs in many districts, based on rigorous assessment of the income and possessions of

---

26 Davis, *History of Britain*, pp. 213–14; Pilgrim Trust, *Men Without Work* (Cambridge University Press, 1938).
27 Davis, *History of Britain*, p. 215; Garside, *British Unemployment*, pp. 66–87.

all members of the claimant's household. This new 'household means-test' caused mass protests in January 1935. The government, with an election looming, hastily decreed that no one should suffer reduced payments. But new claimants faced harsh treatment, giving the 'dole' of the 1930s its lasting, dismal reputation. The test was rigorously enforced; possessions were intrusively inspected to assess saleability, including anything beyond basic necessities, even 'excess' chairs. It was hated for its treatment of people who had worked hard and done their best but now could not find work, and for breaking up families, as working teenagers left home because their incomes reduced their parents' benefits.

Following further protests, higher payments were introduced in 1936, but they remained below Rowntree's stringent 'human needs' minimum, driven by the determination of administrators, including Beveridge, to keep benefits below wages as an incentive to work, despite the lack of work and very low pay in many occupations. In 1937 average insurance payments were about two-fifths of the median wage, that is, 24s 6d against 55s 6d.[28] In the later 1930s, the Ministry of Labour established 'training centres' where men cleared forests, dug ditches, made roads, levelled land or broke stones and women were trained in domestic skills in return for allowances. Attendance was voluntary though sometimes 'encouraged'. It effectively became compulsory for young, long-term unemployed men, but rarely led to regular, still less desirable, employment.

A minority previously on very low or irregular pay could feel better off on unemployment benefit, particularly those with large families receiving dependants' allowances, because the payments were regular and predictable and they could plan their outgoings, whereas previously they could not.[29] But, whatever system they experienced, most unemployed people resented treatment they thought mean and intrusive, especially skilled workers accustomed to working hard for a decent wage, proud of avoiding Poor Relief and knowing their plight was due to economic shifts beyond their control. They protested. Hunger marches of unemployed workers to London and other cities accompanied demonstrations outside Poor Law offices, labour exchanges and town halls. They were generally organized by branches of trade unions and unemployed workers themselves, some by the National Unemployed Workers Movement (NUWM), established by the Communist Party in 1921, which often claimed more credit than it deserved. The Labour Party officially kept its distance, though local parties were often supportive.

Police confronted marches and demonstrations fiercely. In October 1932, they banned a march in Belfast. When the marchers disobeyed, armoured cars were deployed, provoking stone-throwing by marchers shouting 'We must have bread'.

28 Thane, *Foundations of the Welfare State*, p. 171.
29 A. Deacon, *In Search of the Scrounger. The Administration of Unemployment Insurance in Britain, 1920–31* (London: Bell, 1976); Garside, *British Unemployment*, pp. 74–83.

The police responded with gunfire, killing one man and seriously wounding others. Another death, injuries and arrests followed. These were the most violent unemployment protests in the United Kingdom, fuelled by the deep antagonism between the (largely Protestant) police and, especially, the Catholics of Northern Ireland. The police were armed, whereas they were not elsewhere in the United Kingdom. These events were largely ignored in mainland Britain; the Home Secretary refused requests by MPs to discuss them.[30]

It was harder to ignore large protests on Merseyside. These also were prolonged by police resistance, using only batons but causing injuries and hostility. Disturbances followed from West Ham in east London to Croydon in the south London suburbs to North Shields in industrial northeast England. They culminated in October 1932 in the Great Hunger March against the Means Test from various centres to present Parliament with a petition with a million signatures. The marchers, on this and other occasions, were exclusively male. They met police resistance as they headed towards London. Special Branch officers, joining the march in disguise, sent alarming reports of their violent intentions.[31] As 2,000 marchers approached central London, almost 2,000 police were mobilized. Many more protesters joined rallies in Hyde Park and Trafalgar Square. They faced baton charges, injuries, arrests and were prevented from presenting the petition.

This spurred the foundation of another long-lasting association, the National Council of Civil Liberties (NCCL, now Liberty). Its founder, Ronald Kidd, a journalist, was shocked by the police violence he observed in Trafalgar Square, where seventy-five protesters were badly injured, especially because he noted police *agent provocateurs*, dressed as workmen, inciting violence among peaceful protesters. When another Hunger March was planned for February 1934, Kidd feared similar conflicts. He appealed to prominent liberals to express alarm at the threat to peaceful protest and the NCCL was formed. Its first president was the writer E. M. Forster. A letter by leading supporters, including Clement Attlee, Vera Brittain, A. P. Herbert, Harold Laski and H. G. Wells was published in the *Manchester Guardian*. They complained that hints by the Attorney-General that bloodshed could occur and police advice to shopkeepers to barricade their windows, encouraged by the Home Secretary warning Parliament of potential 'grave disorder and public disturbance',[32] could only cause tensions that were unjustified by the disciplined behaviour of the marchers.[33] When the march arrived in London, they were welcomed by Labour and Liberal MPs, including Attlee and Samuel,

---

30 J. Stevenson and C. Cook, *Britain in the Depression. Society and Politics 1929–39*, 2nd edn (London: Longman, 1994), pp. 189–90.

31 Ibid., pp. 194–5.

32 Ibid., p. 203; C. Moores, *Civil Liberties and Human Rights in Twentieth-Century Britain* (Cambridge University Press, 2017).

33 *Manchester Guardian*, 24 February 1934.

though MacDonald refused. Thousands gathered in Hyde Park with a heavy police presence. The NCCL again noted the presence of police *provocateurs*, but there was no conflict. Both sides were anxious to avoid accusations of provoking violence for fear of the consequences: the marchers of arrest, the government of further disorder and voter dissatisfaction.

Then came the 300-mile Jarrow March in 1936, one of the smaller marches but with big impact. Cinema newsreels and the press won sympathy throughout the country for 'The Town that Was Murdered'[34]: 77 per cent of its workforce were unemployed after its main shipyard closed in 1932. Ellen Wilkinson's book described vividly the reality of long-term unemployment and poverty. She was an organizer of the march and negotiated with the police, stressing the peaceful intentions and political neutrality of the marchers, but she was reproved by the Labour Party conference for potentially inciting conflict.[35] Baldwin announced that ministers would not receive marchers. The march took over a month, and was well received along the way with marchers sleeping in church halls and other community institutions, closely observed by Special Branch. Despite Baldwin, they presented their petition to Parliament, pleading for more jobs in Jarrow, and their leaders took tea with MPs. But the government did nothing for the town and the marchers' unemployment pay was stopped because they were deemed to be unavailable for work while marching. Marches and protests tailed off. They involved a minority of unemployed men, mainly in areas with traditions of protest and achieved no tangible gains, though they perhaps prevented government policy becoming even more punitive.

Perhaps their main achievement was to inform the more comfortable sections of the population of their plight and arouse sympathy. The sight of thin, poorly clad men marching determinedly, day after day, brought the impact of unemployment home more starkly than newsreels. When they marched through Windsor in 1934, royal servants threw them money. The media helped. Apart from the newsreels, in 1934 BBC radio ran a series of talks by unemployed men, called *Time to Spare*, and *The Times* published articles on the plight of mining communities. New and older media conveyed the reality of poverty and unemployment to the whole country as never before.

A New Deal?

Resentment among unemployed people and awareness of their conditions among sympathizers stimulated criticism of the government's failure to revive the economy, though not dangerously. Lloyd George, echoing Roosevelt's plans from 1933, talked

34 See p. 123.
35 Laura Beers, *Red Ellen. The Life of Ellen Wilkinson, Socialist, Feminist, Internationalist* (Cambridge, MA: Harvard University Press, 2016), pp. 337–44.

of a British New Deal; Keynes advocated increased spending through counter-cyclical public investment; Labour supported newly fashionable economic planning. Political and Economic Planning (PEP) was founded in 1931 as an independent think-tank (although this is not a term that would have been used at the time) of businessmen, academics and professionals devoted to impartial analysis of social and economic issues, on which they published reports through the 1930s and beyond. In 1933, the young Conservative MP for the depressed northeastern constituency of Stockton, Harold Macmillan, published *Reconstruction: a Plan for a National Policy*, followed in 1938 by *The Middle Way*, arguing that poverty must be eliminated to preserve freedom and all parties should plan for reconstruction. In 1934, a young, Labour- supporting, economist, Barbara Wootton, published *Plan or No Plan*, contrasting the economy of the USSR, which almost alone escaped the crisis of 1929–31 due to its isolation, favourably and idealistically with unplanned capitalism.[36] She was not alone among left-wing intellectuals in romanticizing communism compared with the problems of capitalism. The Webbs published *Soviet Communism: A New Civilization?* in 1935 following a trip to the USSR carefully managed by the Soviet authorities. Others, including R. H. Tawney, G. D. H. Cole, Harold Laski and Beveridge favoured planning with democratic participation. Some employers supported a moderate national economic strategy.

In cautious response, in 1934, with an election ahead, the government introduced the Depressed Areas (Development and Improvement) Bill, renamed more positively as it went through Parliament as the Special Areas Act, granting £2 million for industrial development in four areas suffering long-term depression. Trading estates were developed, unhampered by planning regulations, but the areas received too little funding for non-economic needs, including health, sanitary and social services to keep people fit for work and there were few inducements to business to move to places regarded as distant (from London), unattractive and full of trade unionists. They attracted only thirty-four of 2,000 new factories in England and Wales between 1934 and 1937.[37]

The government still preferred spending cuts to development plans. Education was severely cut; teachers' salaries fell by 15 per cent and reduced subsidies to local education authorities held back school building. In 1932, free secondary school places were replaced by means-tested fees. Progressive local authorities set the means limit high enough to protect free places for poorer children. Lower middle-class families with moderate incomes lost out when they could not easily afford fees. Opportunities for working-class children shrank in places where they had been improving, including areas of high unemployment in Wales and County Durham where local authorities could not afford to compensate for the cuts. Total local education spending rose,

36 Ann Oakley, *A Critical Woman. Barbara Wootton, Social Science and Public Policy in the Twentieth Century* (London: Bloomsbury, 2010), pp. 103–7, 113–15.
37 Davis, *History of Britain*, p. 219.

but improvements were uneven, greatest in some Labour- and progressive Liberal-controlled cities including Bradford, Manchester and the LCC.

Overall, secondary schools expanded, admitting more children on the basis of the selective examination at age 11,[38] but all-age, almost exclusively working-class, elementary schools deteriorated. In 1939, more than 2,000 children were in classes of over fifty pupils, 2 million in classes of over forty, many in old, ill-equipped, sometimes insanitary, buildings. Nursery education grew hardly at all. In 1938, 47 per cent of secondary school pupils paid no fees, but only 19 per cent of the 14–17 age group were in school. Poorer families often could not afford to keep children on past the minimum leaving age of 14. In 1936, Parliament raised the school-leaving age to 15, from 1 September 1939, the day Hitler invaded Poland. It was postponed until after the war. It was opposed by employers unwilling to lose cheap juvenile labour and children were exempted from staying on past 14 if they could secure 'beneficial employment'; beneficial to whom was unclear.

The only improvements to social security payments under the National Government were insurance-based and largely funded by contributors. In 1936, agricultural labourers were at last included in unemployment insurance. From 1937, lower middle-class workers earning above the national insurance limit, who could rarely afford private pensions insurance, could become voluntary insurers; 759,683 people had applied to join the scheme by the end of 1938.[39]

Other social provision contracted. Council house building dwindled, with the economy drive of 1931–3 terminating Wheatley's subsidies. The Rent Act 1933 decontrolled the rents of 500,000 more expensive private homes. The government, rather sluggishly, encouraged slum clearance and subsidized local authority rebuilding, under strong pressure: the Church of England issued a national slum clearance appeal; the BBC and leading newspapers published horrifying revelations about slum living;[40] the Prince of Wales was mobilized to make powerful speeches against slums and made well-publicized visits to a selected few. The Housing Act, 1935, defined 'slums' by an inadequate standard of overcrowding, defined as two persons per room or more, including all living- and bedrooms, allowing for segregation of the sexes. By this measure, 3.3 per cent of housing in England and Wales was overcrowded. A more stringent definition, applied in Leeds, including only rooms used for sleeping, found 21 per cent of households overcrowded. The official measure took no account of inadequate sanitation, damp or poor construction and maintenance, which were widespread. By 1939, 472,000 homes officially defined as slums were scheduled for demolition and 272,000 had been cleared.

---

38 See pp. 90–91.
39 Thane, *Old Age in English Society*, p. 331.
40 J. Stevenson, *Social Conditions in Britain between the Wars* (London: Penguin, 1977), pp. 173–222.

The 1935 Act also specified that council rents should not fall below local market rents for similar property. This aimed to support the private sector by deterring people able to rent or buy privately, but also deterred the poorest who most needed council housing but could not afford market rents. A solution, introduced in Leeds in 1933, when it was briefly Labour-controlled, was differential rents: tenants rather than houses were subsidized, according to income. Below a certain income, they paid no rent, creating resentment among tenants paying higher rents for similar housing. Leeds Conservatives accused Labour of establishing a 'socialist city state' and returned to power in 1934. They modified the scheme, so that all tenants paid some rent, but did not abolish it. Some subsidy was essential if the poorest were to have decent housing and councils fulfil their legal obligations. Many Labour supporters were dubious about differential rents because they were means-tested and redistributed from better-off working- and lower middle-class tenants, whose higher rents subsidized their poorer neighbours, rather than from rich to poor through taxation.[41] But it was the best option available and, by 1939, 110 local authorities of all political colours had adopted it in some form.

In the 1930s more poorer people gained council housing, though not all who needed it and not all who did so benefited. The impact of high council rents on poor families was revealed by a survey in Stockton-upon-Tees in 1927–8 of the diets of fifty-five working-class families on similar incomes, some of whom had been re-housed after slum clearance. Death rates in the re-housed families rose, despite better housing, fastest among the unemployed. This was attributed to poor diet, because the families had less to spend on food after paying rent.[42] This persuaded the British Medical Association (BMA), in 1933, to set standards for 'the minimum weekly expenditure on foodstuffs … if health and working capacity [were] to be maintained'. They estimated that, at 1933 prices, between 5s and 6s per week was needed for an adequate male diet,[43] but this was no immediate help to low-income families.

Housing at the lower end of the private rental market remained appalling, causing protests and rent strikes. Between 1931 and 1939, 2.5 million new homes were built in Great Britain, fewer than 600,000 of these by local authorities, not helped by further cuts to subsidies in 1938. Three-quarters of new private housing was in the South and Midlands, most council houses in London, Scotland and northern England; the housing stock embodied the differences between the 'two nations'. Much rural housing remained poor, though Women's Institutes still campaigned with some successes for improved housing, water and electricity supplies.[44] City centre rebuilding increasingly took the form of high-density flats on the continental European model. These

41 Melling, *Housing, Social Policy and the State*, pp. 127–33.
42 Gazeley, *Poverty in Britain*. p. 74.
43 Ibid., pp. 74–5.
44 Andrews, *Respectable Face of Feminism*, pp. 125–47.

were unpopular in England, though not in Scotland where flats were traditional, but larger English cities felt they had little option given the cost and limited availability of land. A model example was the Quarry Hill development in Leeds, begun in 1934, occupied from 1938 replacing some of the worst slums, designed by the City Architect on European modernist lines and including 938 well-equipped flats, with communal laundries, gardens and playgrounds. In most cities, the sprawl of suburban public and private development continued unrestrained from 1932 when local authorities were no longer obliged to prepare town-planning schemes, as the government sought to cut 'red tape' and assist private building. Satellite communities, with factories providing work, were built by Manchester council in Wythenshawe and Liverpool at Speke, but the absence of planning was increasingly problematic as the proliferation of suburbs increased demand for public transport and car ownership grew.

The National Health

National Health Insurance still provided uneven services. In 1939, it covered fewer than half the population, mainly men. GPs providing free services under the scheme were scarcer in poorer areas: in Manchester each GP might have over 1,000 patients, in Gloucestershire fewer than 700. The National Government cut its contribution to NHI in 1932. The families of insured workers and the uninsured still had no access to free health-care outside the Poor Law/Public Assistance, apart from local clinics for mothers and babies and the school medical service, also unevenly provided. Many GPs offered services in return for small weekly payments, which had at least 650,000 contributors by 1939.

The NHI, outside the most prosperous approved societies, still did not provide hospital treatment, except for TB. Traditionally, voluntary hospitals provided free care for poor patients with acute conditions, but they were poorly distributed around the country, most in big cities, especially London, and they were under growing financial pressure. The capacity of medicine to cure more conditions grew, increasing demand for hospital services from those able to pay, but essential new technology, drugs and staff were costly. Voluntary hospitals became more dependent on fee-paying patients. Some local authorities subsidized low-income patients and hospitals ran contributory schemes, means-tested patients and sought voluntary donations more vigorously.[45] Those who could afford it still often preferred treatment by doctors in their own homes whenever possible.

Local authorities took over the former Poor Law hospitals. They remained generally poorly equipped, providing lower standards of care than voluntary hospitals while carrying the burden of much chronic care, including of older people. In one such hospital, in West Middlesex, Dr Marjorie Warren was so appalled by the neglect of older patients

45 George Campbell Gosling, *Payment and Philanthropy in British Healthcare, 1918–48* (Manchester University Press, 2017).

she encountered that she revolutionized the regime, brightening the environment and encouraging activity and rehabilitation in place of permanent bed-rest, enabling some patients to leave hospital and inaugurating modern geriatric medicine in Britain.[46] This was rare. Provision was worst in the depressed areas despite some investment by the Special Areas Commission. By the later 1930s neither private nor public sectors provided adequately for the national need or demand for healthcare.

Unemployment did not always worsen health, since the heavy industries, where it was concentrated, had long caused sickness and disability. But it did not improve health, especially after 1932 when sickness and disability benefits for the unemployed were reduced. Cuts would have been greater but for opposition from a parliamentary alliance of Labour members and female MPs of all parties, led by Lady Astor. In 1939, the BMA voted narrowly for the extension of national insurance to dependants and the subsidized coordination of health services, but the details remained contentious and many doctors feared state control.

Local authorities were the main providers of healthcare for working-class women and their families. Maternity and child welfare and school medical services improved gradually and unevenly. By the later 1930s, all 409 local authorities in England and Wales supplied milk to expectant and nursing mothers, free or at cost price, and 97 per cent of babies received at least one visit from health visitors. About 50 per cent of mothers received antenatal care; more than 50 per cent of babies attended local health and welfare centres staffed by doctors and health visitors. They treated only minor ailments and were often overcrowded and under pressure, but they dispensed free or subsidized food and milk. Those who benefited welcomed them, while women's organizations campaigned for more.[47]

A survey of the health of 1,250 working-class women by the feminist Women's Health Enquiry Committee in 1933 found that 404 had received no professional advice on healthcare; 591 learned all they knew from district nurses and antenatal clinics, 245 from a health visitor and only sixty-seven from a GP. Their report, *Working Class Wives*, described how women put the needs of their families first and were more anxious to learn how to care for their children than themselves.[48] It gave a devastating account of women's ill-health and the inadequacy of services, though it was positive about welfare centres and health visitors in all but their numbers. Women's ill-health was often the result of repeated pregnancies, miscarriage, sometimes illegal abortions without qualified medical care, all worsened by poverty and bad housing. One example was the wife of an employed miner in Durham:

46 Thane, *Old Age in English Society*, pp. 436–8.
47 Thane, *Foundations of the Welfare State*, pp. 178–82.
48 Margery Spring Rice, *Working Class Wives. Their Health and Conditions* (London: Penguin, 1939, repr. London: Virago, 1981).

She is only 32, has been married fifteen years and has seven children the eldest of whom is 14. She lives in a colliery house; it has an open ash-privy at the back; the back bedroom is damp and the rain comes in; the kitchen ceiling is unsafe; there is no sink under the tap; the coal-house and ash-pit are at the end of a long garden and coal and ashes have to be carried through the sitting room which is used as a bedroom ... She gets up at 4 am and goes to bed at any time between 10pm and midnight ... She does her own baking and the diet given is miraculous. She drinks a lot of water and gets a lot of green vegetables from their own garden including lettuce daily in summer ... these are her own ailments, (1) Neuritis: from which she has suffered for two years owing, in her opinion, to getting wet, the heavy work of mangling etc. She rubs her shoulder with oils and puts on hot flannels with the advice of the colliery doctor; (2) Pyorrhoea: on the advice of the colliery doctor she has had all her teeth extracted; (3) Kidney trouble due to Bright's disease at 5 years; she takes medicine for this; (4) headaches and biliousness: lifelong due to the kidney trouble; she takes medicine for this; (5) Cystitis during her last pregnancy due to getting wet and heavy work; for this she rested in bed and kept warm; (6) Pain in right side during menstrual periods, due to ovarian trouble; the colliery doctor gives medicine for this by which 'he hopes to avoid an operation'.[49]

She was fortunate to have access to the colliery doctor.

To limit the effects of repeated pregnancies, women's organizations campaigned for, and when possible provided, birth control assistance.[50] Provision for poorer women came overwhelmingly from the voluntary sector, whereas better-off women paid doctors. Marie Stopes, a leading birth control campaigner since the early 1920s, converted two horse-drawn caravans into mobile clinics which travelled the country. In 1938, several voluntary organizations merged to form the Family Planning Association, developing a national network of clinics.[51] Births continued to decline in all classes, apparently achieved mostly by the cheapest methods, abstention from sex or *coitus interruptus*, that is, men 'being careful' or 'getting off the bus early' as it was commonly known, though nothing is certain about something few people discussed openly and about which there was still much ignorance.[52] The reasons for limiting families are equally uncertain, though the desire for higher living standards, with fewer mouths to feed, and the growing realization that social mobility was now possible for children whose parents could afford to keep them at school were important, together with the growing desire of women for control over their lives and bodies.[53]

With better services and improved living standards, infant mortality continued to decline in England and Wales from 64 to 55 per 1,000 live births from 1930–2 to 1940–2. It remained somewhat higher in Scotland and above average in the depressed areas, though it did not rise significantly. Another reason to have fewer babies was that they were more likely to survive. In contrast, maternal mortality rose from 3.09 to 5.94 per

49 Spring Rice, *Working Class Wives*, p. 86.
50 See p. 113; Debenham, *Birth Control*.
51 Ibid.; Beaumont, *Housewives and Citizens*, pp. 81–7.
52 Szreter and Fisher, *Sex before the Sexual Revolution*; Hera Cook, *The Long Sexual Revolution. English Women, Sex and Contraception, 1800–1975* (Oxford University Press, 2004).
53 Mass Observation, *Britain and Her Birth Rate* (London: John Murray, 1945).

1,000 births between 1921–5 and 1934.[54] It affected all classes, especially for first births, due mainly to sepsis. The rise may have been partly due to fewer births and the corresponding high proportion of first births, though poor diet in pregnancy left poorer women especially vulnerable. Most confinements, in all classes, still occurred at home, in highly variable circumstances, though more were in hospital. The numbers, qualifications and state regulation of midwives improved, though many poorer women by 1939 still gave birth with unqualified assistance, unable to afford a doctor or medication if things went wrong. Maternal deaths declined permanently from the later 1930s following the discovery of penicillin to counter infection.

It was suspected that abortion was a significant cause of maternal death and was increasing. In 1930, 10.5 per cent of maternal deaths were attributed to abortion, by 1934 the figure was 20 per cent,[55] when the Ministry of Health estimated that about 68,000 illegal abortions were carried out, though only seventy-three were reported to the authorities.[56] It was believed to be most common among older, married, working-class women. The Women's Co-operative Guild and the National Council of Women (NCW), among others, campaigned for the legalization of abortion. In 1936, the Abortion Law Reform Association (ALRA) was established by feminists, calling for safe, legal abortion for all women. They succeeded at last in 1967.[57] In 1937, the Birkett Committee was appointed to investigate abortion, in response to these pressures and the Ministry's concerns. Women's organizations submitted evidence. In 1939, it recommended against legalization but affirmed that abortion was allowable if pregnancy threatened a woman's life. This followed the judgment in the *Bourne* case, in 1938, involving a doctor accused of performing an abortion following the gang rape of an underage girl by members of the King's Guard in London. This set a precedent by ruling the abortion lawful because it was intended to save the mother's life by preserving her psychological health.[58]

The poor physical condition of military recruits was still invoked as evidence of low general standards,[59] along with eugenic 'explanations' of physical and mental weakness, but they were less influential in Britain than demands for positive action to remedy poor health whatever the cause. This was all the more important as panic mounted in Britain and elsewhere in Europe about the declining birth rate combined with rising life expectancy, creating the spectre of an ageing population, burdening a shrinking younger

---

54 I. Loudon, *Death in Childbirth. An International Study of Maternal Care and Maternal Mortality, 1800–1950* (Oxford University Press, 1994), pp. 240–6.

55 Barbara Brookes, *Abortion in England, 1900–1967* (London: Routledge, 1988), p. 43.

56 Ibid., p. 27.

57 See pp. 283–4.

58 Brookes, *Abortion in England*, p. 51.

59 C. L. Mowat, *Britain Between the Wars* (London: Methuen, 1972), pp. 512–13.

generation with the costs of their pensions and healthcare. This caused anguished debate involving such figures as Beveridge and Keynes, but no solutions since there was no known way to increase births.[60] Hitler's and Mussolini's attempts to reward mothers of numerous children did not increase their national birth rates and the British government was not inclined to follow them.

A government National Fitness Campaign aimed to raise physical standards, sponsored by King George V and his two successors, especially George VI. The flourishing Women's League for Health and Beauty was a largely middle-class branch of a wider physical exercise movement helping to improve health and raise expectations of 'normal' health.[61] *Working Class Wives* suggested that the ideas reached some working-class women, who exercised when they could.[62] The royal family encouraged sport and other outdoor pursuits, including walking in the countryside, known as 'rambling'. The Ramblers Association formed in 1935 to encourage this and to preserve access to footpaths threatened by landowners hostile to intrusion on their land. It was popular among middle-class people with rising incomes and time to spare.

There were growing demands for good healthcare for all and for the state to take responsibility. The reports of Malcolm Campbell, the Commissioner for Special Areas, repeatedly stressed that the poor quality of 'human capital' hindered economic development. The increasingly influential PEP reported in 1937 that the cost of sickness to the nation was £300 million pa: £120 million from working days lost through illness, the remainder being the costs of treatment and prevention, both of which, it argued, were inadequate. It was an early advocate of a tax-funded, National Health Service.[63]

Poverty and Social Conditions

Extensive poor health suggests the degree of continuing deprivation. More poverty surveys were conducted, by university and independent researchers using increasingly refined methods, generally aiming to influence government policy and popular perceptions and improve social conditions. In 1936, Rowntree repeated his study of York.[64] He used a more generous measure of poverty than in 1899, allowing for higher food expenditure and a small margin above necessities for such items as newspapers and radio, which had become part of normal life, but emphasized, as before, that 'the

60 Pat Thane, 'The Debate on the Declining Birth Rate in Britain. The "Menace" of an Ageing Population, 1920s–1950s', *Continuity and Change* 5(2) (1990): 283–305.

61 Ina Zweiniger-Bargielowska, *Managing the Body. Beauty, Health and Fitness in Britain, 1880–1939* (Oxford University Press, 2011).

62 Spring Rice, *Working Class Wives*, pp. 90, 112–13.

63 Thane, *Foundations of the Welfare State*, p. 177.

64 See pp. 18–20.

standards adopted … err on the side of stringency rather than of extravagance'. He set 43s 6d per week for a family of two parents and three children as 'a measuring rod by which to gauge the standards of social well-being actually possible for working-class families in York'.[65] Average male manual earnings at the time were 56s 9d per week.[66] He suggested that between 7 per cent and 10 per cent of working-class people 'are living below the poverty standard … because money is spent on non-essentials', meaning 'drink, cigarettes, gambling or any other purely personal expenditure', though he admitted he 'had no basis of ascertained fact' for this estimate and he was 'not here concerned to either to condone or condemn' such choices.[67] He concluded 'we shall not, I imagine, be very far wrong if we assume that about 40% of the working-class population of York are living below the minimum standard, in secondary poverty, 31% (20% of the whole population of York) through lack of means and 9% because of expenditure on non-essentials'.[68] Fifty per cent of working-class children were in poverty by this measure; 7 per cent of working-class people were in 'primary poverty', with insufficient income for necessities, compared with 16 per cent in 1899. Unemployment was the major cause (44.53 per cent), while low pay for regular work caused 9 per cent of primary poverty and old age 18 per cent.[69]

Surveys in relatively prosperous southern Southampton in 1931,[70] depressed northern Sheffield in 1931–2 and Bristol, a successful centre of new manufacturing, in 1937, using similar measures found 21 per cent, 15.4 per cent and 10.7 per cent, respectively, of working-class families in poverty. In all three the main cause was unemployment, following by inadequate pay, old age, sickness or incapacity and the absence of a male breadwinner.[71] There was serious deprivation even in quite prosperous areas. Professor John Hilton estimated in 1938 that 17 per cent of all families had no margin for saving, so any crisis plunged them into poverty. A study by nutritionist Sir John Orr in 1936, based on 1,152 family budgets, found that 10 per cent of the population (and 20 per cent of children) were seriously undernourished and up to 50 per cent were 'poorly' nourished, judged by 'a diet that will keep people in health; and the standard of health adopted is a state of well-being such that no improvement could be effected by a change in diet. The standard may be regarded therefore as the minimum for maximum health'.[72]

65 B. Seebohm Rowntree, *Poverty and Progress. A Second Social Survey of York* (London: Longmans Green, 1941), pp. 29–30.

66 Gazeley, *Poverty in Britain*, p. 67.

67 Rowntree, *Poverty and Progress*, p. 124.

68 Ibid., p 126.

69 Gazeley, *Poverty in Britain*, p. 94.

70 Ibid., pp. 86–7; P. Ford, *Work and Wealth in a Modern Port. An Economic Survey of Southampton* (Southampton University, 1934).

71 Gazeley, *Poverty in Britain*, pp. 89–97; H. Tout, *The Standard of Living in Bristol* (Bristol University Press, 1937).

72 John Boyd Orr, *Food, Health and Income* (London: Macmillan 1937), p. 7.

Other studies suggested that cleanliness and general health improved with better housing and water supplies. In London, in 1912, school medical inspectors found that 39.5 per cent of state school children were verminous; in 1937 that figure had fallen to 8 per cent. In Northampton, the average height of 12-year-old boys rose from 55.4 inches in 1910–13 to 57.3 inches in 1933, their weight from 74.3 lb to 79.9 lb. However, Boyd Orr found the average heights of boys of 14 at a public school, at Christ's Hospital (a charitable boarding school) and an elementary school to be 63.7, 61.1, and 58 inches, respectively; class inequalities had changed little since 1883.[73]

From 1920 to 1938 average real earnings grew modestly, by around 15 per cent, due more to falling prices than rising pay.[74] The falling birth rate enabled more families to avoid poverty due to having too many mouths to feed on low incomes. The narrowness of the margin is suggested by the numbers in poverty with more than two dependent children. Redistribution slowly increased.[75] In 1913, manual workers paid more in indirect taxes than they received in social services and benefits. In 1925, they paid 85 per cent of the costs, including through national insurance contributions, receiving £55 million more than they contributed. By 1937, they received between £200 and £250 million more. Total UK central and local government expenditure on social services rose to £5,969.3 million (11.3 per cent of GNP) in 1938,[76] but the distribution of earnings across income groups changed little[77] and wealth remained concentrated among the wealthiest: in 1938 the top 0.1 per cent of wealth-holders in Great Britain owned 27 per cent of personal wealth, the top 5 per cent owned 78 per cent.[78]

Gender Inequalities

The equal franchise did not remove other gender inequalities and women's organizations fought on to improve the rights and status of women. Women's trade unions expanded, including in teaching and the civil service, demanding wider work opportunities, equal pay and the abolition of the marriage bar.[79] Little changed, indeed, the marriage bar spread to the BBC in 1932, now sufficiently established and successful for ambitious men to overcome their doubts about joining this new institution, increasingly marginalizing women from top positions, though the bar was less strictly enforced

73 Mowat, *Britain Between the Wars*, p. 461.

74 Gazeley, *Poverty in Britain*, p. 67.

75 A. L. Bowley (ed.), *Studies in the National Income 1924–1938* (Cambridge University Press, 1944).

76 Thane, *Foundations of the Welfare State*, p. 204.

77 Ian Gazeley, 'Income and Living Standards', in Roderick Floud, Jane Humphries and Paul Johnson (eds), *The Cambridge Economic History of Modern Britain, vol. 2: 1870 to the Present* (Cambridge University Press, 2014), pp. 154–7.

78 A. B. Atkinson, *The Economics of Inequality* (Oxford University Press, 1975), p. 134.

79 Glew, *Gender, Rhetoric and Regulation*, pp. 122–45, 178–215.

than elsewhere; well-regarded married women remained and progressed. Women still had a better deal at the BBC than in most institutions, though they were not thought authoritative enough to be radio announcers or newsreaders until another war brought another shortage of men. When it was suggested, the *London Evening News* expressed horror at 'a Hobb's century [at cricket] being announced in a pleasant soprano, or the details of a heavyweight fight related by a girlish voice'.[80]

Women's associations still cooperated on many causes, disagreeing on others. In 1932, the NUSEC changed its name to the National Council for Equal Citizenship (NCEC), still encouraging women to vote and participate in local and national politics, promoting democratic citizenship and aiming to get more women elected. They encouraged local campaigning for social and health services, housing, contributing to real improvements.[81] Divorce reform was still a major, divisive issue, opposed by Anglican and Catholic women's organizations. The NCW, NCEC and the Women's Co-operative Guild, with others, supported the 1937 Matrimonial Causes Act, introduced by A. P. Herbert, the novelist and Independent MP. This broadened the possible grounds for divorce in England and Wales, allowing husbands or wives to seek divorce after three years' desertion or for adultery, cruelty or being of 'unsound mind and continuously under care and treatment' for at least five years, while a wife could sue for rape or sodomy. According to its preamble, it amended the law 'for the true support of marriage, the protection of children, the removal of hardship, the reduction of illicit unions and unseemly litigation, the relief of conscience among the clergy and the restoration of due respect for the law'.[82] In England and Wales divorce petitions rose from 23,921 to 37,674, 1931–5 to 1936–40,[83] though divorce remained expensive, impossible if one partner refused, and stigmatized, especially for women, and the campaign for further reform continued. In Scotland many of these provisions had long existed, the remainder were introduced in 1938. In Northern Ireland, in 1939, divorce became possible for the first time, other than by private Act of Parliament, on more limited grounds than elsewhere in the United Kingdom.

In 1935, unmarried working women formed the National Spinsters' Pensions Association (NPSA) to demand state pensions at age 55 on the grounds that unmarried women were often forced to retire at earlier ages than men. Led by Florence White, owner of a small confectionary business in Bradford, they claimed this was due to the poorer health of many women, that unemployed older women found it even harder than men to find work, employers discriminated against post-menopausal women and many middle-aged women gave up work to care for ageing parents then were left

---

80 Murphy, *Behind the Wireless*, pp. 83–114, 242.
81 Thane, 'What Difference Did the Vote Make?' pp. 253–88.
82 Cretney, *Family Law*, p. 236.
83 Halsey and Webb, *Twentieth-century British Social Trends*, p. 62.

destitute as they grew older. A government committee in 1938 largely agreed with these points, but feared that pensions at 55 would encourage employers to retire women early and married women would resent special treatment of 'spinsters'. They recommended no change, but in 1940 the pension age for women was reduced to 60 for insured women and wives of insured men, almost certainly influenced by the 'spinsters' campaign.[84]

Race

A new wave of Jewish immigration followed the rise of fascism in Europe, especially after Hitler came to power in 1933, totalling at least 50,000 by 1939. Many refugees were prosperous professionals and businesspeople, assisted in the United Kingdom by organizations founded to challenge Nazi antisemitism. They and the established Jewish community also encountered British fascism. Oswald Mosley's British Union of Fascists (BUF), as his New Party[85] was re-named in 1932, was increasingly active from 1933, more threatening than previous, tiny, British fascist organizations who mostly joined the new movement. It was modelled on Mussolini's activities in Italy, adopted a similar black-shirt uniform, holding rallies and parades throughout the country and supported by the Rothermere press: 'Hurrah for the Blackshirts' headlined the *Daily Mail* in January 1934. Rothermere thought it a bulwark against Communism.[86] Its violent treatment of opponents and increasingly vocal antisemitism discredited it as awareness grew of the nature of Nazism, alienating Conservatives and Rothermere, and membership declined. By 1936 it focused on east London, with its large Jewish population, holding rallies and marches, encouraging attacks on Jews and Jewish property. It appealed to some working-class people who believed Jews displaced local people from jobs, housing and services, though BUF activists were mainly middle class, male and female, and young (under 40) and local workers also joined their opponents.[87] Elsewhere their appeals to unemployed people were unsuccessful.

In October 1936, the Blackshirts planned a big march through east London. A counter-march and demonstration by Jewish, Communist, socialist, Liberal, Labour and Christian anti-fascists clashed with them in what is remembered as the Battle of Cable St, the peak of British fascism and resistance to it, in which seventy people were injured. The government responded with the Public Order Act banning political uniforms and paramilitary organizations, empowering the Home Secretary to regulate public

---

84 Thane, *Old Age in English Society*, pp. 284–6.
85 See pp. 113–14.
86 John Stevenson and Chris Cook, *The Slump. Britain in the Great Depression* (London: Routledge, 2009), p. 203.
87 Ibid., pp. 212–13; Julie V. Gottlieb, *Feminine Fascism. Women in Britain's Fascist Movement, 1923–1945* (London: I. B. Tauris, 2000); Julie V. Gottlieb and T. P. Linehan (eds), *The Culture of Fascism. Visions of the Far Right in Britain* (London: I. B. Tauris, 2003).

processions. Processions were banned in the East End and the BUF found it difficult to hold meetings. Elsewhere, rallies and demonstrations and opposition continued, while Mosley took care to avoid violence. His support dwindled. As the ferocity of Nazi anti-semitism became clearer, in 1938–9 restrictions on the entry of refugees was eased and immigration increased. Jews, including the new immigrants, still faced discrimination in employment, including in the professions, and antisemitism survived at all levels of society. The many earlier migrants who prospered and moved from east London and other inner city areas to the suburbs could be barred from clubs, restaurants, golf clubs and other venues.

Black and Asian residents also organized to resist discrimination and provide mutual support. The League of Coloured Peoples was founded in London in 1931 by Harold Moody, a Jamaican doctor appalled by the prejudice he encountered when trying to find a home and work in his profession and the racism that refused service to 'coloured' people in restaurants and hotels. The League aimed to improve relations between the races and challenge racism, supported by white radicals,[88] including campaigning to restore British citizenship to seamen in Cardiff when it was refused because they could not prove their birth within the Empire. The Indian Workers Association formed in Coventry in 1938 also initially to protect workers from racism and improve their living conditions. It quickly formed branches in London and elsewhere, including among the growing population of Indian professionals, businessmen and students actively supporting Indian independence.

The Second National Government

The National Government served a full four-year term. In June 1935, MacDonald's health declined and Baldwin replaced him. MacDonald was increasingly isolated, heading a 'national' government which was essentially Conservative, with minimal Labour support, indeed fierce and growing opposition within the party. He died in 1937.[89] In the election of November 1935, the Conservative vote fell slightly from 55.2 per cent to 53.7 per cent, and its share of seats from 472 to 432.

Labour, fighting as a united party again, led by Lansbury, gained 38 per cent, more than in 1929, but only 154 seats. Lansbury resigned and his deputy, Clement Attlee, narrowly and surprisingly defeated the more experienced Herbert Morrison, leader of the LCC, to succeed him. Attlee, the seventh of eight children of a solicitor in Putney, south London, was Labour's first middle-class leader, educated at Haileybury public

88 Anne Spry Rush, 'Imperial Identity in Colonial Minds: Harold Moody and the League of Coloured Peoples, 1931–5', *Twentieth Century British History* 13(4) (2002): 356–83.
89 Marquand, *Ramsay MacDonald*, pp. 671 ff.

school and Oxford. After graduating, he reluctantly followed his father into the law, then found his real vocation living in a settlement house and working with a boys club in Stepney, east London. For the first time he encountered working-class life and socialism and joined the Stepney branch of the ILP. In 1912, he became a lecturer in social work at LSE, then fought in the war. After the war he became the first Labour mayor of Stepney, then in 1922 MP for Limehouse. He was firmly on the left of the party. This and his support for the unemployed won him the leadership.[90]

The Liberal decline continued, with only 6.4 per cent of votes and twenty seats. The Conservatives were again dominant, though not in Wales where they had only eleven seats to Labour's eighteen and eight Liberals, though they had a clear majority in Scotland. Sixty-seven women stood: six Conservatives were successful out of nineteen candidates, one from thirty-five Labour candidates, one Liberal from six and Eleanor Rathbone again. However, Labour was reviving. Party membership rose from 1932, notably in suburban south-eastern constituencies such as Twickenham, Putney and Harrow. It won all ten by-elections between 1931 and 1935. After a disastrous performance in the municipal elections of November 1931 (of 709 candidates only 149 were successful and 206 seats were lost[91]), it recovered in 1932 (836 candidates, 458 successful[92]). In 1933, Labour controlled Glasgow for the first time, plus Sheffield, Norwich, Leeds, Bootle, Swansea and Barnsley. In 1934, it won decisive control of the LCC for the first time, plus Burnley and Oldham, and regained Derby, Stoke and Hull. These were important gains at a time when municipal government was still powerful and independent.

Labour gained from Liberal failures, but the successes owed much to serious promotion in the media, employing well-designed advertising and publicity, despite the doubts of some supporters about 'selling out' to commerce. Labour suffered from caricatures and exaggerated accusations of 'Bolshevism' in the Conservative press and aimed to hit back as newspaper readership, radio and newsreel audiences grew and attendance at political meetings declined. Like the monarchy and the Conservative Party, Labour grew aware that the media could help them win support and first used it effectively in the 1929 election. In 1931, it was helpless and divided but thereafter the media strategy revived. The party and the TUC established press offices to communicate with newspapers, newsreels and the BBC. Herbert Morrison before the 1935 election placed an article, 'The Case for Labour' in the *Daily Mail*. It countered with an editorial attacking 'our reckless socialists'.[93]

90 K. Harris, *Attlee*; John Bew, *Citizen Clem. A Biography of Attlee* (London: riverrun, 2016).
91 Stevenson and Cook, *Britain in the Depression*, p. 130.
92 Ibid., p. 132.
93 *Daily Mail*, 8 November 1935.

From 1926 the *Daily Herald* was revamped, with illustrations, better paper and presentation and a wider range of articles designed to broaden its appeal and revive its flagging circulation, so successfully that in 1933 it was the first newspaper in the world to reach a circulation of 2 million and seriously worried Beaverbrook. Labour pressed the reluctant BBC to allow more political broadcasts, with equal air time for opposition and government in place of what it perceived as the previously unbalanced output. The BBC was cautious because the National Government and the *Daily Mail* accused it of left-wing bias, as they long continued to do, but Labour's broadcasting increased. It strove to emphasize the party's respectability and constitutionality against opponents' representation of them as reckless revolutionaries, aiming to extend their appeal to clerks, professionals and women at home as democratic socialists dedicated to social welfare and a mixed economy, as indeed they were; presenting Labour rather than Baldwin's Conservatism as representative of the British nation, pitting 'all who work ... by hand or brain' against 'the small minority (less than 10% of the population) who own that great part of the land, the plant and the equipment without access to which their fellow-countrymen can neither work nor live'.[94]

As premier again, Baldwin faced unemployment again, no more effectively than before. Many Conservatives and the Treasury still resisted state intervention, but Chamberlain as Chancellor announced a road-building programme and the government continued limited aid to 'special areas'. But in 1937 the Commissioner for Special Areas, Sir Malcolm Campbell, resigned, critical of inadequate funding to attract business or to improve health and social services, and the excessive concentration of development in London, which he believed was already too large and congested. The government then reduced rents, rates and tax for five years for firms setting up in Special Areas. Trading estates were established in South Wales, Scotland and the northeast, but they chiefly attracted light industries producing consumer goods for the home market, including clothing and ice-cream, employing mainly low-paid women. There was no attempt to stop larger businesses expanding in London and the south.[95]

International Crises

Baldwin did most to boost the economy, or to stop it failing further, indirectly through rearmament, as international events became more ominous following

---

94 Laura Beers, *Your Britain. Media and the Making of the Labour Party* (Cambridge, MA: Harvard University Press, 2010), p. 143. Much of this discussion of Labour and the media is drawn from this book.
95 Davis, *History of Britain*, pp. 212–22.

Mussolini's invasion of Abyssinia in 1935 and the League of Nations' failure to prevent it. International tensions had been building for some time. In 1931, Japan (whose economy had collapsed in the 1929–31 crisis, followed by a military takeover of government) invaded the Chinese province of Manchuria, then attacked Shanghai, Asia's greatest port where there was still significant British investment.

There was still conflict in Palestine where the Jewish population more than doubled, from 172,000 to 384,000 between 1931 and 1936, mainly by those fleeing from Hitler. Arab opposition intensified when a British commission in 1937 proposed partition between Jews and Arabs, requiring mass relocation of Arabs. Two years' revolt followed and the proposals were withdrawn. By 1939, as war against Germany loomed, the British government was anxious not to alienate the Arabs of the Middle East lest they supported Hitler. A White Paper declared it 'no part of British policy that Palestine should become a Jewish state'. Palestinian Jews protested violently. Tensions continued also with Afghanistan and in Iraq. Relations with Egypt improved when the 1936 Anglo-Egyptian Treaty guaranteed Egyptian control over internal affairs, enabling it to be represented at the League of Nations. The British Army withdrew to the Suez Canal zone and Britain promised to protect Egypt against potential aggression from Italy following the invasion of Abyssinia.

Baldwin pledged to do 'what is necessary to repair the gaps in our defences',[96] but 'there will be no great armaments'.[97] Defence spending, about 2.5 per cent of GNP before 1935, rose to 3.8 per cent by 1937, about one-third of German expenditure.[98] Increased UK spending went disproportionately on air power, to match that of Germany. The hope, not shared by the armed services, was that, if war came, Britain could conduct it in the air without committing soldiers on the ground. The Admiralty stressed the need for naval defence against Japan.

The government pledged support for League of Nations sanctions against Mussolini, influenced perhaps by the results of the Peace Ballot organized by the LNU in 1934–5. This aimed to gauge public opinion on the League, international control of armaments and sanctions against aggressor nations. Ballot forms were delivered to every household, and 12 million were returned, representing one-third of the adult UK population: 95.9 per cent voted that the United Kingdom should remain in the League; 90.6 per cent supported all-round reduction of armaments by international agreement; 90.1 per cent supported the prohibition of the manufacture and sale of arms for private profit; 86.8 per cent supported economic sanctions against aggressor nations; and 58.7 per cent supported 'if necessary military

96 K. Middlemas and J. Barnes, *Baldwin. A Biography* (London: Macmillan, 1969), p. 866.
97 H. Montgomery Hyde, *Baldwin. The Unexpected Prime Minister* (London: Hart-Davis, 1973), p. 398.
98 Clarke, *Hope and Glory*, p. 187; Reynolds, *Britannia Overruled*, p. 124.

measures',[99] The ballot angered many Conservatives, the *Daily Express* and other right-wing papers, which always opposed the League, but the numbers were too large for politicians to ignore with an election coming.

After the election, Baldwin resisted challenging Italy over Abyssinia with sanctions or any other means. Instead, Sir Samuel Hoare, Foreign Secretary, devised a plan with the French Foreign Minister, Laval, to appease Mussolini, agreeing to his partitioning Abyssinia with the Abyssinians. The plan was leaked to the press before it could be put to the Cabinet or to Mussolini. Appeasement of an aggressor aroused fierce criticism, especially because Baldwin had reneged on his election pledge. Hoare was forced to resign. He was replaced by Anthony Eden, Britain's youngest Foreign Secretary to date, with considerable experience of foreign affairs in junior posts and a strong supporter of the League.

In January 1936 George V died. Baldwin's moving broadcast tribute helped to restore his public standing. Then, in March 1936, Hitler remilitarized the Rhineland, contrary to the Versailles agreement. The French proposed sanctions against Germany, but Baldwin refused for fear the crisis could escalate before Britain was prepared for war. He preferred to negotiate improved relations with Germany, but left this to Eden. Then in July 1936 the Spanish Civil War erupted. Sixty-seven-year-old Baldwin was exhausted and through the summer of 1936 took long periods of rest, leaving the government with little direction.

The Spanish Civil War roused many on the left, Labour, Liberals and Communists, to fight to support a democratically elected government challenged, ultimately successfully, by General Franco's militaristic nationalism. They included George Orwell, who described the war and left-wing factionalism among the fighters in *Homage to Catalonia* (1938). Some British volunteers were killed, including the poets John Cornford and Julian Bell (son of Vanessa) and lesser known working men. Spanish refugees, including children, joined Jewish migrants to Britain and were generally well cared for by British families.

The Communist Party was small, claiming 18,000 members in 1939, influential in a few trade unions, on radical Clydeside and attracting some distinguished intellectuals including the scientist J. B. S. Haldane and young literary figures including Stephen Spender and W. H. Auden. It attracted some students disillusioned with the political parties and with capitalism, but most members were working-class. By 1938, the BUF was more marginal still. Support for fascism did not disappear in Britain but it became politically insignificant after its brief outburst. The broad ideological range and relative

99 Martin Ceadel, *Semi-Detached Idealists. The British Peace Movement and International Relations* (Oxford University Press, 2000), p. 237; H. McCarthy, 'Democratizing Foreign Policy. Rethinking the Peace Ballot 1934–5', *Journal of British Studies* 49 (2010): 358–87.

flexibility of the main political parties, the relative security of most middle-class and many working-class people, and protection of the unemployed from extreme destitution created fewer sources of serious discontent or support for extremes of left and right than in some other European countries.

The Abdication

A different crisis followed the death of George V. He was a popular enough monarch, though hardly charismatic. Though diffident, he had a strong sense of social duty and worked at winning popular support, especially due to the need to overcome the family's German associations and his and his family's hatred of socialism, bolstered by the rise of the Labour Party and trade union activism, the overthrow and death of his relatives in the Russian Revolution, then the deposition by socialists of those in Germany.[100] Britain was now the only major European power with a monarchy. Royal visits to deprived areas, factories and mines were designed to win over the masses; increasingly frequent tours of the Empire to hold it together. The royal family, like their subjects, became aware of the power of the media and in 1918 appointed their first full-time press secretary, helping to create an image of a domesticated monarch and his family, devoted to the people, much as George hated such exposure.[101]

He revived traditions and created new ones now that royal events were visible to a vast public through new media. He reinstituted wearing the crown at the State Opening of Parliament, abandoned by Victoria and Edward VII. He attended the proletarian Football Association Cup Final, though his favourite sport was shooting on royal estates. Every year from 1932 he broadcast a Christmas Day message to Britain and the Empire, reluctantly but establishing a lasting tradition. The first consisted of just 251 words, written by Rudyard Kipling, but was so successful that he had to continue the ordeal annually.[102] His jubilee celebrations in 1935 and his funeral the following year were opportunities for national festivals to enhance the popular image of the crown.[103]

The royals demonstrated their care for their subjects through patronage of charities, with due publicity. It was also a means to keep state welfare at bay, another of George's bugbears. His heir, the future Edward VIII, was instructed to lend his name to charities and made not entirely enthusiastic visits to South Wales and other potentially troublesome areas to spare his father a hated task. Edward's less obviously engaging,

---

100 Frank Prochaska, *Royal Bounty. The Making of a Welfare Monarchy* (New Haven, CT: Yale University Press, 1995), p. 185.

101 McKibbin, *Classes and Cultures*, pp. 3–14.

102 Ibid., p. 9.

103 Ibid., p. 11.

stammering brother, the Duke of York, later King George VI, was a more enthusiastic patron of sports and boys' clubs, including the Duke of York's camp which brought together teenage boys from factories and public schools, to foster inter-class harmony and 'tame young bolshevists' among the former.[104]

Edward VIII was very different from the gruff, dutiful, exacting family man who was his father, except in his political views. He was a bachelor of 41, popular in the news-reels not just for visiting the deprived but as a member of the smart set, with a string of girlfriends. Unfortunately, his latest was an American commoner, Wallis Simpson, and, even worse, she had divorced once and awaited her second. He informed Baldwin that, when the divorce was through, he planned to marry her. Popular though the king was with a media avid for gossip, particularly about the divorces of fashionable people, no hint of this became public, in Britain at least. The European and American press had no reason to be reticent and the cuttings came to Downing Street and no doubt elsewhere. It was accidentally revealed in Britain in December 1936 by the Bishop of Bradford commenting in public that the new king needed God's grace in his calling, but seemed insufficiently committed to religious belief. This rather obscure statement gave the press the excuse to splash the revelations they found increasingly hard to suppress. There was agonized debate among the powerful. It was a problem for the Church because the king was its Supreme Head and members of the Church were forbidden to marry divorced partners. The Australian and Canadian governments warned they would not recognize Mrs Simpson as queen. Edward won support from Beaverbrook, Rothermere, Churchill and Mosley. Virginia Woolf noted in her diary signs of popular sympathy in a culture becoming more open about human relationships and critical of the 'Victorianism' of politicians and clerics who denied Edward the right to marry the woman he loved. This appears to have been Edward's own view. His determination to marry Wallis Simpson rather than keep her as his semi-secret mistress, in the long royal tradition, was another sign of the cultural shift. It is impossible to know how widely it was shared. Edward appears to have believed that he had popular support, and the Cabinet initially refused his request to broadcast his views to the nation on the ground that it was 'unconstitutional', perhaps fearing the popular response.[105] Curiosity about popular attitudes, and the belief that politicians and the press were out of touch with the people, influenced the creation in 1937 of a unique, long-lasting institution, Mass Observation (MO), initiated by the anthropologist Tom Harrisson, documentary filmmaker Humphrey Jennings and journalist Charles Madge, to research and report

104 Prochaska, *Royal Bounty*, pp. 169–212; Zweiniger-Bargielowska, *Managing the Body*, pp. 281–2.
105 Frank Mort, 'Love in a Cold Climate. Letters, Public Opinion and Monarchy in the 1936 Abdication Crisis', *Twentieth Century British History* 25(1) (2014): 30–63; Anne Oliver Bell (ed.), *Diaries of Virginia Woolf, vol. 5: 1936–41* (London: Hogarth Press, 1984), pp. 39, 40, 42, 43–4.

beliefs and attitudes by interviewing, overhearing and observing people in their every-day lives. They found that attitudes to the abdication were diverse but that Woolf was largely right.[106]

Baldwin asked Edward to persuade Mrs Simpson not to divorce, to avoid any question of re-marriage, implying that an unmarried liaison could be overlooked, in accordance with tradition.[107] When Edward refused, Baldwin insisted that he must abandon any idea of marrying her or abdicate. Attlee supported him. Within days Edward abdicated and his brother succeeded. His 7-minute farewell broadcast, which he was finally permitted to make, at 10 pm, belatedly won him further support. Baldwin terminated the crisis with another broadcast. King George VI's coronation, in May 1937, was another opportunity for orchestrated national celebration, reaffirming the role of the monarchy which survived unscathed a crisis some feared would destroy it, another sign of the relative calm of British politics at a time of international turbulence. It was carefully observed by MO.[108] The abdication also signified the monarchy's limited freedom of action. As Edward wrote in his autobiography, 'How lonely is a Monarch in a struggle with a shrewd Prime Minister backed by all the apparatus of the modern State'.[109]

After the coronation Baldwin retired from the premiership and from the Commons aged 70. He was exhausted and intermittently in poor health. He went to the Lords as Earl Baldwin of Bewdley. He was succeeded by 68-year-old Neville Chamberlain. The other possible candidate, Churchill, was too divisive in the party, and unacceptable to Baldwin after their many battles, particularly over Indian independence.

Chamberlain as premier had the opposite problem to MacDonald: he had always been absorbed by domestic politics. His brother Austen told him, 'Neville, you must remember you don't know anything about foreign affairs'.[110] This was especially unfortunate in 1937 as tensions grew in Europe.

Conclusion

The 1930s is remembered as the decade of the 'Slump', of long-term, degrading unemployment for many people. This was not so for all working-class people as new industries developed, but the regional inequalities between the 'Depressed Areas' and

106 Mort, ibid.; David Hall *Work Town. The Astonishing Story of the Project that Launched Mass Observation* (London: Weidenfeld & Nicolson, 2015).
107 Vernon Bogdanor, *The Monarchy and the Constitution* (Oxford University Press, 1995), p. 137/
108 *May 12 1937. Mass Observation Day-Survey*, eds Humphrey Jennings and Charles Madge (1937).
109 Edward Windsor. *A King's Story. The Memoirs of HRH the Duke of Windsor* (London: Cassell, 1951), p. 359.
110 Clarke, *Hope and Glory*, p. 184.

those of growth increased. The National Government prevented unprecedented inequality leading to serious political disruption, but seemed unable to narrow the gap between those who were and were not benefiting from growth, leading to growing demands for decisive action to achieve long-term change. But in the background to domestic concerns was the growing danger of another war, which still in 1937 many, probably most, in the United Kingdom hoped to avoid, still remembering the horrors of the 'Great' War.

6 The People's War

Appeasement

International relations looked threatening, especially in Europe. Neville Chamberlain became premier in 1937 convinced that Britain's defence capability did not match that of its potential opponents and doubtful that it could afford another war or increase defence spending without damaging the economy. The service chiefs shared his caution and overestimation of the opposition, since Britain's defences were relatively strong, especially the navy and air force.[1] Limited rearmament initiated by Baldwin stimulated employment just as the economy was faltering again, though this was not immediately clear.

Chamberlain was determined to avoid what he believed was Baldwin's foreign policy drift. Despite his inexperience, he took control of foreign affairs, driven by a determination to avoid war. He was convinced (correctly) that war would undermine the Empire which was so important to the Chamberlain family and (incorrectly) that German bombing would quickly destroy Britain. He knew he had strong support, as the Peace Ballot suggested,[2] especially among women.[3] An Imperial Conference indicated that the Dominions might not fight with Britain again. They supported appeasement of enemies in faraway Europe when Britain was not directly threatened, though Australia was less keen to appease nearby Japan. Chamberlain and his advisers sought to restrain

1 David Edgerton, *Warfare State. Britain 1920–1970* (Cambridge University Press, 2006), pp. 15–58.
2 See pp. 145–6.
3 Julie. V. Gottlieb, *'Guilty Women', Foreign Policy, and Appeasement in Inter-War Britain* (London: Palgrave, 2015).

France from military action while trying to build a relationship with Mussolini, who formally allied with Hitler from late 1936, accepting his control of Abyssinia despite Eden's intense disagreement. Chamberlain ignored Foreign Office advice, believing the dictators were rational men who would respond to negotiation, while his obvious reluctance to fight made them more ambitious. He hoped moderate Germans would topple Hitler, especially if they feared resistance from Britain if accommodation failed.

Germany, then Italy, allied with Japan in 1936. It was increasingly likely that Britain would have to fight in Asia to protect her interests. Chamberlain attempted, with little Foreign Office support, to agree with Japan not to compete commercially in China, but Japan showed no interest and in 1937 invaded China, with extreme violence, attacking British and US ships on the Yangtse River. Britain gave limited military supplies and moral support to China while trying to avoid conflict with Japan, risking alienating both. Chamberlain and his advisers did not believe Britain had any trustworthy allies. They mistrusted the French, and the United States was increasingly isolationist; whatever support Roosevelt wished to offer was likely to be constrained by Congress.[4] The Treasury rightly doubted Britain's capacity to withstand a long war without American economic support.[5]

The dispatch of emissaries to negotiate with Hitler caused Eden's resignation in February 1938, when his advice was again disregarded. He was replaced by Lord Halifax, former Viceroy of India and conciliator of the independence movement, skills Chamberlain believed invaluable in the present crisis. Then Hitler annexed Austria in March 1938 and threatened Czechoslovakia. Trenches were dug and gas masks issued in London. Despite official appeasement policies, civil servants sought to be better prepared than for the last unwanted war. New government departments were planned to administer wartime controls. Scientific and technological research capability, already strong, was expanded.[6]

Chamberlain, still desperate to maintain peace, fruitlessly flew twice to meet Hitler in 1938, when shuttle diplomacy was unusual (he had never flown before). In September 1938, Hitler invited him again, to Munich, with the French Prime Minister, to meet himself and Mussolini. Hitler stated that unless German-speaking Sudetenland, incorporated into Czechoslovakia at Versailles, was ceded to Germany, he would invade and war would follow. Chamberlain agreed, leaving the French no option, and returned home, notoriously declaring he had achieved 'peace in our time'. This convinced Roosevelt and Stalin, as well as Hitler and Mussolini, that Britain would not fight. Almost immediately this became less likely. In December 1938, attacks on

---

4 David Reynolds, *The Creation of the Anglo-American Alliance, 1937–1941. A Study in Competitive Cooperation* (Durham, NC: University of North Carolina Press, 1982), p. 22.
5 Ibid., p. 73.
6 Edgerton, *Warfare State*, pp. 21–46.

Jews and their property in Germany on *Kristallnacht* brutally exposed Nazi antisemitism and swung much British support behind war. In March 1939, Hitler abandoned his agreement, invaded the remainder of non-German-speaking Czechoslovakia and threatened Poland. Halifax abandoned appeasement and demands for war mounted. In early 1939, 669 Czech Jewish children travelled by train to Britain (the first *Kindertransport*) to the care of British foster parents, arranged by a British stockbroker, Nicholas Winton.[7] Many of their families perished in extermination camps and they never saw them again. It was one of many British efforts to rescue and support Jews, the other side of persistent antisemitism.

In April a Bill authorizing conscription in case of war passed easily through Parliament, to ensure that, this time, British fighting forces would be adequate when needed, despite doubts in the military who feared training conscripts would hinder mobilization. The build-up, especially of air defences, continued, capitalizing on technological advances including the development of fast fighters, Hurricanes and Spitfires, and Britain's unique advantage as the pioneer of radar.[8] The French were assured that Britain would fight with them if necessary. Chamberlain wavered at last and offered to guarantee Polish independence, confident that Russian opposition would deter the Germans from invasion. Few doubted that war was coming. In April, Italy invaded Albania and threatened Greece. On 1 September Hitler agreed a pact with Stalin despite his antagonism to communists, shocking the British government, then invaded Poland. Chamberlain still desired a deal, but was pushed by the Cabinet, Parliament, the public and the press into declaring war, along with France, on 3 September 1939.

The 'Phoney' War

Labour would not join a war coalition with Chamberlain. With the exception of some pacifists and left-wing dissidents, they were united in believing that Hitler had to be resisted and opposed appeasement. The National Government continued, drawing in more Conservatives including Churchill. Chamberlain convinced himself that the war would be over 'by the Spring',[9] not following military victory by Britain, of which he had little hope, but believing the German economy would collapse along with popular morale, causing Hitler's overthrow. The government kept contact with the German opposition, many of whom fled to Britain, as did leading politicians and others from occupied countries including Poland and, later, France.

British officials learned from the mistakes of the last war and were better prepared. Conscription began immediately and armament production rapidly increased.

7 Barbara Winton, *If It's Not Impossible … The Life of Sir Nicholas Winton* (London: Matador, 2014).
8 Edgerton, *Warfare State*, p. 141.
9 Reynolds, *Britannia Overruled*, p. 140.

Bewildered children were summarily evacuated from the cities to live with strangers, separated from their parents, except those under age 5 whose mothers accompanied them, though many returned home in the next months when the anticipated bombing did not materialize. The war seemed distant as Germany overran Poland and Russia defeated Finland. Britain did not engage in any significant military action until the failed attempt in April 1940 to oust the Germans from Narvik following their invasion of Norway. This awoke many people to the reality of war. The failure was primarily Churchill's at the Admiralty, but it enabled Chamberlain's growing body of critics, many in his own party, to challenge him. Labour moved a censure motion in the Commons. Chamberlain's long-time Conservative critic, Leo Amery, dramatically echoed Cromwell:

> You have sat too long here for any good you have been doing. Depart, I say, and let us have done with you. In the name of God, go![10]

The motion failed but the government majority fell from 250 to 80 because Conservatives abstained or supported the motion. Chamberlain resigned and Churchill replaced him as premier in a coalition government – cheered by Labour, who believed the United Kingdom now had a decisive war leader, but by few Conservatives. Chamberlain remained party leader and, as Lord President of the Council, a member of the five-member War Cabinet, with Halifax. Labour joined the coalition, prepared to support Churchill as an outright supporter of the war. Attlee and Arthur Greenwood joined the Cabinet.

In autumn 1940, Chamberlain resigned, suffering from cancer, and died shortly after. Churchill became party leader and his allies were rewarded. Eden returned to the Foreign Office. Beaverbrook took the important new post of Minister of Aircraft Production, successfully boosting production. Duff Cooper, who had resigned over Munich, replaced John Reith who Chamberlain had appointed Minister of Information, heading wartime propaganda. His removal was said to be Churchill's revenge for excluding him from broadcasting his opposition to Indian independence when he directed the BBC. Disappointed, Reith became Minister of Transport, later Minister of Works. The businessman, Lord Woolton, took the new Ministry of Food, quickly developing a successful system of rationing food, clothes and other essentials, including furniture, providing a basic range of sound, plainly designed goods under the 'Utility' label. A few items were unrationed, including lipstick, deemed essential to female morale. As new ministries were established and old ones expanded, the civil service grew and outside experts were recruited, including, again, Keynes and Beveridge.

10 House of Commons, *Debates*, 7 May 1940.

Attlee, officially Lord Privy Seal, efficiently controlled domestic policy. Churchill appointed himself Minister of Defence, controlling the armed services, to the frequent exasperation of the service chiefs, and became the charismatic war leader. Another leading Labour figure in the War Cabinet was Ernest Bevin, General Secretary of the Transport and General Workers Union, in the key role of Minister of Labour and National Service, briefed to avoid the problems of labour supply and industrial disputes of the previous war. Bevin had never sat in Parliament. The holder of a safe Labour seat was elevated to the peerage and Bevin was elected unopposed.[11] Herbert Morrison ran the Home Office and Home Security, another key post.

Labour controlled the main domestic ministries, giving them an opportunity to demonstrate their fitness to rule. There was an electoral truce through the war. The Conservative Party suspended annual conferences, but Labour did not and kept its party machinery operational. There was no General Election and the coalition parties did not (officially) fight each other in by-elections. The Conservatives faced a series of officially independent left-wing challengers who took six seats from them between 1942 and 1945. In the last two years of war the Common Wealth Party, established by the former Liberal, Sir Richard Acland and writer J. B. Priestley in 1942, won three seats from the Conservatives. Common Wealth comprised Labour supporters opposed to the party truce, disillusioned Liberals and intellectuals seeking a better postwar world, committed to land nationalization, greater democracy and morality in politics, equal opportunity, colonial freedom and world unity – idealistic and attractive to many voters.

The armed forces were quickly mobilized. In 1938 they totalled under 400,000, by 1940 over 2 million. An unprecedented extension of the conscription law in June 1940 made all persons and property liable for service. Railings outside houses were requisitioned for essential metals. It empowered Bevin to prevent enlistment of workers in occupations essential to the war effort and to retrain workers for essential tasks. By the end of 1941, more than 90 per cent of men aged 14–64 were in the services or essential occupations and there was a labour shortage. In December 1941, for the first time, unmarried women aged 18–50 became liable for mandatory service in the armed services, the Land Army, teaching, nursing, the civil service or other essential services and industries. Married women without children under 14 or unavoidable household (mainly caring) duties were required to register for war work and prosecuted if they failed to take work to which they were directed; 2,067 were prosecuted during the war.[12]

11 Alan Bullock, *The Life and Times of Ernest Bevin, vol. 1: Trade Union Leader, 1881–1940; vol. 2: Minister of Labour 1940–45* (London: Heinemann, 1960).
12 H. L. Smith, 'The Effect of the War on the Status of Women', in H. L. Smith (ed.), *War and Social Change. British Society in the Second World War* (Manchester University Press, 1986), p. 213.

The Auxiliary Territorial Service (ATS) was founded in 1938, during the Munich crisis and became the largest women's service, with 214,420 members by June 1943, working as cooks, waitresses,clerks, gaining skills including shorthand, switchboard operation or motor mechanics. The Women's Auxiliary Air Force (WAAF) and the Women's Royal Naval Reserve (WRNS) continued as non-combatant support units. Women were forbidden to use weapons in any service, no matter how vulnerable their situation. They went on guard duty bearing sticks, while male colleagues carried fire-arms.[13] Their role was to support the men, as recruitment posters made clear, appealing to women to join the WRNS to 'free a man for the fleet'; the WRAF 'to serve with the men who fly'.[14] By 1944, 494,000 women were in the auxiliary services.[15] The Women's Land Army was re-launched in June 1939, to help maximize food production as in the last war. Again, some farmers were reluctant to employ women in normally male work as tractor drivers, field- and plough-workers and shepherds, but they had little choice as men were conscripted. By 1943, there were 43,000 'Land Girls', plus 4,900 in the Timber Corps, cutting trees and managing forests.[16]

More men and women were recruited to the services than in the First World War and more survived; 360,000 British nationals were killed in war service, fewer than civilians killed by bombing. The services enabled some to gain an education and skills – conscription revealed much poor literacy – though some female graduates found their already limited opportunities constrained by conscription. If they dreamed of 'non-essential' careers, like architecture or filmmaking, it was forbidden until after the war, when they might be judged too old to train.[17] There was less opposition to this war, since few could object to resisting fascism. There were conscientious objectors to fighting and killing, including Quakers, but they were treated with greater sensitivity than in the previous war by tribunals controlled by the Ministry of Labour; most then supported the war effort in non-combatant roles, including as ambulance drivers.

The Commonwealth at War

Most Dominions fought with Britain, with varying degrees of commitment, which Hitler had apparently not expected, given their reluctance before the war. Ireland remained neutral, though its economy was weak and many Irish people moved to work in British factories and hospitals, relieving the labour shortage, and 43,000 joined the

13 Lucy Noakes, 'War and Peace', in Ina Zweiniger-Bargielowska (ed.), *Women in Twentieth Century Britain* (London: Pearson, 2001), p. 310.
14 Ibid., p. 314.
15 Ibid., p. 307.
16 Lucy Noakes, *War and the British. Gender and National Identity, 1939–1990* (London: I. B. Tauris, 1997).
17 Pat Thane, 'Girton Graduates. Earning and Learning, 1920s–1950s'. *Women's History Review* 13(3) (2004): 347–86.

UK armed services.[18] South Africa was divided but its parliament voted narrowly to support the war. There were difficulties in India where the Viceroy, Lord Linlithgow, announced that India would fully support the war, without consulting Indians. Congress resigned from the government. Attempted negotiations failed, not helped by Churchill becoming premier, given his determined opposition to independence or any form of self-government. Gandhi and Nehru led opposition to Indian involvement in the war. They were not pro-German but argued that India could not fight with Britain to preserve democracy when Britain denied India democracy. This argument was echoed in other colonies, particularly when the Atlantic Charter, a statement of fundamental principles for the postwar world, a democratic challenge to the Nazi 'New Order', issued by Churchill and Roosevelt in August 1941, upheld the 'rights of all peoples to choose the form of government under which they will live'.

In early 1941, 14,000 Congress supporters, including Nehru, were arrested. They were released later in 1941 following protests in Britain by the pro-independence India League, supported by trade unionists and Labour supporters. In August 1942, Gandhi was arrested again, for preaching non-violent protest unless Britain withdrew from India. Violent protest then caused 900 deaths.[19] In late 1942, Sir Stafford Cripps, a pro-Independence Labour member of the War Cabinet, went to India to conciliate as the Japanese approached its borders. He promised freedom and self-government after the war, but Congress refused to trust a government led by Churchill and protest continued. Gandhi was released in May 1944, due to poor health, after pressure in Britain and India, but other Congress prisoners remained in jail until Labour won the election of 1945.

Yet 2.5 million Indians fought with Britain, mostly successfully defending India's borders against the Japanese. About 42,000 defectors joined the Indian National Army, fighting with the Japanese. India became a supply base for Allied operations in the Middle East and Asia, developing Indian industry and the prosperity of many middle-class Indians. But about 3 million people died in the Bengal famine in 1943, partly due to a British scorched-earth policy intended to hamper a Japanese invasion, partly to Churchill's refusal to supply India's food needs. British control of India, indeed of the Empire, looked precarious, particularly following successful Japanese challenges. Burma was granted limited independence after occupation by the Japanese in 1943. Its National Army then had little choice but to support Japan, but defected to the allies when it seemed safe.[20]

---

18 Keith Jeffrey, 'The Second World War', Judith M. Brown and William Roger Louis (eds), *The Oxford History of the British Empire, vol. IV: The Twentieth Century* (Oxford University Press, 1999), p. 310.

19 Porter, *Lion's Share*, p. 306.

20 Jeffery, 'Second World War', p. 324.

Two and a half million troops, mostly volunteers, came from other colonies. More British troops were mobilized to defend the Empire/Commonwealth than colonial troops to fight in Europe in what was even more a 'world' war than the last.[21] About 374,000 Africans served, of whom almost 7,000 died. In October 1939, the UK armed services abandoned their traditional prohibition of non-white officers. By 1943, shortage of men led the RAF to recruit about 6,400 West Indians.[22] About 15,000 colonial seamen served in the merchant navy.[23] Many colonial servicemen gained a wider knowledge of the world and higher expectations, returning home wanting better lives, fuelling independence movements. The economies of some colonies, like India, gained from supplying the war: African countries supplied minerals, Malaya rubber, until it fell to the Japanese, East Africa, cotton and sisal. A Colonial Development and Welfare Act 1940 rewarded the colonies with promises of up to £20 million, though only £3 million was spent by 1945. In 1943, the Conservative Colonial Secretary, Oliver Stanley, pledged the government 'to guide colonial people along the road to self-government within the British Empire'. Ceylon was promised internal self-government and by 1945 had an approved constitution, along with Malta, Britain's vital base in the Mediterranean. Jamaica gained full adult franchise in 1944 and Trinidad and British Guiana received new constitutions, responses to growing demands for greater independence, following serious prewar riots over unemployment and poverty.[24]

The Real War

Meanwhile, the reality of war came home. In May 1940, German forces occupied the Netherlands and Belgium and moved into northern France, threatening the 250,000-strong British force, which retreated to Dunkirk. They and 100,000 other troops, mainly French, were rescued and returned to Britain by the Royal Navy, supplemented by a flotilla of volunteers in small boats. An outpouring of Churchill's rhetoric and Ministry of Information propaganda turned this retreat, leading to the surrender of France, into a myth of national triumph. Prominent in the newsreels were the 'plucky' small boats, represented as manifesting popular determination to fight and win after a setback threatened morale.

Chamberlain and Halifax favoured negotiated peace: Churchill and Labour leaders were determined to 'fight on'. German airplanes attacked and the war moved into the air. The RAF fought the Luftwaffe in the skies over Kent, in the 'Battle of Britain' as Churchill named it, preventing invasion, invaluably supported by radar stations placed

---

21 Porter, *Lion's Share*, p. 303.
22 Jeffery, 'Second World War', p. 313.
23 Ibid., p. 312.
24 Porter, *Lion's Share*, p. 310.

along the coast to detect enemy aircraft. Also invaluable were the many Polish refugee airmen. Initially, the RAF was dubious, then recognized their skills, which were needed as British airmen were killed, injured or exhausted. For the rest of the war Poles fought and died in the RAF and their own squadrons. Many stayed after the war, forming a community mainly in west London.

Serious warfare bred a certain paranoia. All Italians, Germans and Austrians in Britain faced internment as potential spies. 'Collar the lot!' Churchill ordered. Internment camps were established in British colonies, including Jamaica, often with poor conditions. In July 1940, 800 internees drowned when the *Arandora Star* was torpedoed *en route* for Canada. About 50,000 were interned in Britain, some in requisitioned holiday camps, many in basic conditions in the Isle of Man where 80 per cent of internees were Jewish refugees (unlikely Nazi spies). They did their best to use the time positively, creating music and intellectual activities. After much public and parliamentary criticism, internees were gradually released from 1941 and many joined the armed services.[25] In May 1940, Oswald Mosley and his leading lieutenants were arrested as security risks and imprisoned, Mosley initially in Brixton, then joining his wife and fellow fascist Diana, neé Mitford (they married in Berlin with Hitler in attendance), in Holloway, the only male inmate in the history of this women's prison. They were unusually privileged, with a cottage in the prison grounds and prisoners as servants, allowed to order luxuries from Harrods. This caused an outcry; Churchill was suspected of indulging them. They were released in November 1943 due to Mosley's ill-health.[26] During the war, adult refugees from Nazism were admitted reluctantly to Britain or Palestine. Herbert Morrison, as Home Secretary, refused to increase the number of visas for fear of stimulating antisemitism in Britain and Arab hostility in Palestine. He argued that Britain was too small an island to admit too many immigrants. Some passport officials turned a blind eye, admitting desperate refugees.[27]

Radar and the fighter planes could not stop all the bombers, which came in force in September 1940, hitting the ports of Plymouth and Portsmouth first. From 7 September London experienced fifty-eight consecutive nights of bombing, the 'Blitz'. From the beginning of the war, everyone was issued with gas masks and advice on constructing shelters. There were public shelters and London Underground stations were refuges throughout the war, disastrously when panic about a coming raid caused a rush into the newly built station at Bethnal Green in March 1943 in which 173 people, including sixty-two children, were crushed to death. Antisemites blamed pusillanimous Jews

25 Peter Gillman and Leni Gillman, *'Collar the Lot! How Britain Interned and Expelled its Wartime Refugees* (London: Quartet, 1980).
26 Robert Skidelsky, *Oswald Mosley*, rev. edn (London: Macmillan, 1990).
27 Lesley Urbach, 'Herbert Morrison's Changing Attitude to the Plight of the Jews, 1930–1945', M.Res., University of Southampton, 2015.

in an area with a large Jewish population, though the government exonerated them. About 42,000 people were killed by bombs in London through the war and about 50,000 seriously wounded; many lost their homes and businesses, schools and hospitals were destroyed or severely damaged. But it did not cause the demoralization the Germans hoped – 'London (Liverpool, Glasgow, Plymouth, etc.) can take it' was the response, encouraged by the Ministry of Information. In July 1940, an opinion poll showed popular support for Churchill at 88 per cent; it never fell below 78 per cent through the war. London did not suffer as badly again, though other towns and cities were hit, including the devastation of Coventry in November 1940. Britain retaliated by bombing Germany. Up to the devastation of Dresden in 1945 this caused more death and destruction than German bombs inflicted on Britain but no clear strategic gain.

The United States still held back. Roosevelt, re-elected president in November 1940, offered sympathy but no more, despite Churchill's efforts at persuasion. Again, Britain had financial problems. By the end of 1940, gold and dollar reserves were almost exhausted. By March 1941, the German naval blockade was so effective that British shipping losses reached half a million tons a month. Again, the only realistic source of help was the United States. In March 1941, Congress passed the Lend-Lease Act, enabling the president to lend or lease equipment to any nation 'whose defense the President deems vital to the defense of the United States'. It permitted the immediate supply of arms, warships and other goods to the United Kingdom, worth £27 million in the first instance, on condition that Britain terminated imperial preference and sterling exchange controls. The government reluctantly agreed and America gained comprehensively. The value of UK imports from the United States rose from £118 million in 1938 to £532 million in 1944,[28] while the United States moved into markets where Britain could not trade in wartime.

From mid-1941 the war took new turns. In June, Hitler, making no headway in Western Europe, turned east and invaded Russia, inflicting enormous losses on his former ally. Twenty million Russians died in combat or through starvation, as in the German siege of Leningrad in 1941–4 where up to 1 million people died, the heaviest casualties of any nation; only China came close. In December, the Japanese unexpectedly attacked Pearl Harbor, Hawaii, the main US naval base, leaving the United States little option but to declare war. Japan's allies, Hitler and Mussolini, declared war on the United States, and Britain on Japan, which aimed to displace it as the dominant imperial power in Asia. Britain underestimated this threat until, also in December 1941, the Japanese took Hong Kong, then Malaya, apparently with little opposition, then, most shocking, in February 1942, Singapore, Britain's key port east of Suez. They invaded from the north through Malaya, while Singapore's British and Australian defenders

28 Milward, *The Economic Effects of the Two World Wars on Britain*, p. 67.

faced south, causing shock and shame in Britain. Japanese forces moved on to Burma, imprisoning British and allied servicemen and civilians often in brutal conditions, later vividly evoked in the popular film *Bridge on the River Kwai* (1957). This was the lowest point of the war for Britain. Thereafter they were helped by the United States taking the main burden in the Pacific.[29]

The Germans advanced through North Africa, supporting the Italians. The Middle East caused problems for Britain throughout the war. Servicemen were stationed there to defend British possessions, and the oil, from the Germans, and were often resented locally. The Iraqi army rebelled in May 1941. The main British base was Egypt whose loyalty was always in doubt. German antisemitism aroused no opposition in much of the region. In Palestine violent conflict between Arabs and Jews and of both against the British continued, the Jews further alienated by British restrictions on Jewish refugees entering Palestine. Then, in October 1942, the allied Eighth Army commanded by the British General Bernard Montgomery defeated the Germans at El Alamein, removing a major source of conflict in the region.

The 'End of the Beginning'

Churchill proclaimed this was 'not the beginning of the end but it may be the end of the beginning'. Next came the allied assault on Italy and the fall of Mussolini. In June 1944, the allies, led by American commander, Eisenhower, opened a new front in Western Europe with the 'D-Day' landings in Normandy, surprising the Germans who had been deceived by false messages apparently planning landings elsewhere. The allied fight-back was immeasurably assisted by British access to coded German, Italian and Japanese radio communications by the expert code-breakers based at Bletchley Park, assisted by an early computer and the pioneering computer expertise especially of Alan Turing, unknown to the enemy or most British people until decades later.[30]

Most of the D-Day troops were Americans, based in Britain from 1942. There were over 1.65 million in the United Kingdom by 1944, about 10 per cent of whom were black. British attitudes were mixed: there were riots in East Anglia against the US Army practice of racial segregation in cinemas – black troops at the back, white at the front – and criticism of segregation elsewhere. However, black Britons, including colonial servicemen and war workers, experienced prejudice from both Americans and other Britons. Officially, the British government opposed discriminatory regulations in the US forces but refused to raise the issue with the US government, at first because they

29 Porter, *Lion's Share*, pp. 304–5.
30 R. Erskine and M. Smith (eds), *The Bletchley Park Codebreakers* (London: Biteback, 2011).

were trying to persuade them to support the war, then because they feared alienating them.

Learie Constantine, famous as a member of the West Indies cricket team, had moved with his family to Lancashire in 1928, frustrated at the lack of opportunities for black people in Trinidad, playing for a Lancashire team while continuing to tour with the West Indies. He was much admired in Britain and during the war and after used his position to publicize discrimination against himself and others. The Ministry of Labour appointed him to support the substantial numbers of West Indian technicians recruited to meet wartime needs. In towns without white Americans, they seemed content. Liverpool, where Constantine was based, had US bases nearby and frequent, sometimes violent, racial friction. He was abused by an American while eating in a restaurant with a white female colleague. In 1943, he was refused a room at a London hotel because US residents would object. He sued the hotel successfully. This was widely publicized, amid much sympathy and protest. Mass Observation surveys testified to popular appreciation of the black war effort, though refusal of hotel rooms to black and Asian people was not unknown before the war and this was not the last slight experienced by Constantine and others from British and Americans.[31] Some women fell in love with Americans, black and white, though they too experienced prejudice for dating and dancing with black servicemen, further fuelling the belief, widespread in this war as in the last, of rampant moral laxity among young people liberated by war conditions. Meanwhile, others snarled that 'Yanks' of all colours were 'overpaid, oversexed and over here', or grumbled they had 'come in late to two world wars'.

Two million troops, mostly 'Yanks', landed in northern France by the end of June 1944, followed by a long, slow advance against German resistance. By February 1945 the outcome was clear, though Germany still resisted. Stalin, Roosevelt (shortly before his death in April 1945) and Churchill met at Yalta, in the Crimea, to divide the world into spheres of influence as the victors had done in 1919, despite the official hostility of the United States and the USSR to colonialism. Britain was now the weakest ally, expecting, and receiving, least. Stalin already dominated Eastern Europe, having driven out the Germans. They discussed forming a new international organization to succeed the League of Nations, the United Nations Organization,[32] which was founded soon after in San Francisco. Meanwhile, the Western allies advanced on Germany from the west, the Red Army from the east, until in May 1945 Germany surrendered and Hitler committed suicide. The troops discovered the horrors of the concentration camps, whose existence had been rumoured, but the full extent of the incarceration and, above

31 Sonya O. Rose, *Which People's War? National Identity and Citizenship in Wartime Britain, 1939–1945* (Oxford University Press, 2003), pp 239–84.
32 Mark Mazower, *No Enchanted Palace. The End of Empire and the Ideological Origins of the United Nations* (Princeton University Press, 2009).

all, extermination, of at least six million Jews, and smaller numbers of communists, homosexuals, Roma and resisters, was beyond imagining.

The war against Japan continued until new US President Harry S. Truman consulted newly elected British Prime Minister Clement Attlee about ending it with the device the two countries (mainly the United States, with British expertise) had secretly developed in the New Mexico desert: the atomic bomb. On 6 August, the first bomb fell on the southern Japanese port of Hiroshima, followed a few days later by another on Nagasaki, both with devastating effects. Japan surrendered and the war ended.

The People's War?

The Ministry of Information and Churchill's rhetoric worked hard to foster the perception that the shared stresses of war drew British people together in new, sometimes unexpected, ways, softening old social divisions and conflicts, strengthening collective patriotic resistance. People were urged to 'Keep smiling through' in one of several popular songs by wartime star Vera Lynn. The Ministry employed MO to report on popular responses to the war to assist their targeting of morale-boosting propaganda.[33]

Conscription was a partial leveller, though the better-off, as ever, were defined as the natural officer class. Shared fear of bombing and invasion early in the war, then the experience of bombing, rationing and queuing, brought together people who might not otherwise meet. So did the rushed evacuation of children, at a time when the potential psychological damage from suddenly taking children from their families into wholly strange environments was not understood. The transition sometimes from very poor homes to those of better-off, or less deprived, families, could exacerbate social divisions. Some hosts blamed mothers for the impoverished appearance, lice-ridden heads and poor table manners of underweight children from desperate homes, who wet their beds due to what was not recognized as trauma. Others felt compassion for depths of poverty they had never encountered and demanded reforms to end such conditions. Some evacuees were generously received and benefited for the rest of their lives from better education, food and environment than they had known. Others suffered undetected abuse. Much was learned from the experience of evacuation, including about the psychological impact on children, though at some cost.[34]

Evacuation could be stressful for women who were expected to look after sometimes more than one, unknown, bewildered child. Billeting officers assessed who had

33 Paul Addison and Jeremy A. Crang (eds), *Listening to Britain. Home Intelligence Reports on Britain's Finest Hour, May to September 1940* (London: Bodley Head, 2010).
34 R. M. Titmuss, *Problems of Social Policy. History of the Second World War*, UK Civil Series (London: HMSO and Longmans, Green, 1950); John Welshman, *Churchill's Children. The Evacuation Experience in Wartime Britain* (Oxford University Press, 2010).

bedroom space and evacuees were allocated according to standard overcrowding rules, though some richer families probably escaped. Women caring for evacuees were exempted from conscription. Hosts received payments of 10s 6d per week for the first child, 8s 6d for others; this was more than the maximum service allowances of 5s for the first child, but insufficient to cover the costs, especially when growing children needed shoes and clothing their families could not afford. Relatives caring for evacuees were unpaid. Reluctantly, against Treasury opposition, the Ministry of Health sanctioned small clothing grants. Following protests there were small increases for children over 14 in 1940.[35]

Rich people retreated to country homes from the dangers of the cities, including encountering other classes. They suffered some deprivations: the London social season was suspended, but they could enjoy luxury foods in smart restaurants since all restaurants were 'off-ration'. They also evaded rationing with trophies from the grouse moors, since shooting and hunting with hounds continued. If their children were evacuated it was often to relatives in the Dominions, the long separation often causing distress. As in the last war, one of the worst deprivations suffered by many better-off families was the flight of servants to more appealing work, this time permanently. The royal family, including the young princesses, Elizabeth and Margaret, thought it their duty to reinforce the spirit of collective sacrifice by remaining in Buckingham Palace until it was bombed. They visited bombed-out families in the East End and made much of owning ration books like everyone else.

Women in all classes again supported the war effort through voluntary action. In 1938, the Home Secretary established the Women's Voluntary Service (WVS), initially to help with evacuation and the effects of the anticipated bombing. It fulfilled these and other functions throughout the war, invaluably supplementing stretched official services. It was a cross-class organization, with elite leadership, directed by Lady Stella Reading, widow of a former Viceroy of India, experienced in public and voluntary service.[36]

As in the last war, social conditions for most manual workers and their families improved and there was some narrowing of socio-economic inequalities due to full employment from 1940 and government policies. Allowances for service families, again including 'unmarried wives',[37] were provided from the start, more efficiently than before, though still not generous. A soldier's wife with two children received 32s weekly in 1939, 33s in 1940, 38s in 1941 and 43s in 1942. Average weekly male manual

---

35 Titmuss, *Problems of Social Policy*, pp. 142–82.
36 James Hinton, *Women, Social Leadership and the Second World War. Continuities of Class* (Oxford University Press, 2002), pp. 20–2.
37 See p. 47.

earnings in 1939 were 56s 9d. These payments were hard to live on. Public concern at poverty among servicemen's families led to an increase to 60s by 1945. Officers' wives also received low payments by the standards of their class and service personnel themselves were relatively low paid.[38]

From 1941, Woolton's rationing prioritized healthy foods at controlled prices, improving the diets of many low-income families, and local authorities could, and most did, establish British Restaurants, as Churchill insisted they were called, providing low-cost, nutritious, off-ration meals. By September 1943, 2,160 British Restaurants served about 630,000 meals daily.[39] The Food Policy Committee, chaired by Attlee, from 1940 approved grants of subsidized milk to mothers with children under 5 and daily milk and meals for schoolchildren. By February 1945, 1,650,000 children received meals, 14 per cent free, the remainder paying 4d–6d per meal; 73 per cent of schoolchildren received free milk.[40] Free vaccination of children against diphtheria eliminated a major prewar killer. Prewar efforts to reduce the child death rate and improve health progressed, benefiting the poorest most. The government intervened to improve social conditions more vigorously than in the last war, following its greater activity between the wars.

Unusually, the Chancellor of the Exchequer, Kingsley Wood (Conservative) was not in the War Cabinet until 1942 and had limited power to curb spending. Keynes served as unpaid economic adviser to the government, responsible to the War Cabinet rather than the Treasury, and advocated progressive taxation and controls on prices, wages and supplies to avoid inflation while financing the war. The tax changes further eroded inequalities. Purchase tax, to restrain consumption, and 100 per cent excess profits tax were introduced at the beginning of the war, continuing throughout. In 1939, the standard rate of income tax was 29 per cent, with surtax at 41 per cent on incomes over £2,000. Ten million people were liable for tax and the sum raised was £400 million. The standard rate rose to 50 per cent in 1941, surtax to 48 per cent, and tax allowances were reduced. By 1944–5, there were 14 million taxpayers paying almost £1,400 million pa. Tax collection became easier and cheaper in 1943 with the introduction of Pay As You Earn (PAYE) which placed the onus of collection on employers through deduction from pay in place of the long-established system of individual assessment by government officials and payment once or twice each year.[41] Between 1938 and 1948 the purchasing power

38 Penny Summerfield, 'The "Levelling of Class"', in H. L. Smith (ed.), *War and Social Change. British Society in the Second World War* (Manchester University Press, 1986), pp. 196–8.

39 Anne Hardy, *Health and Social Medicine in Britain since 1860* (London: Palgrave, 2001), p. 124.

40 P. Hall, H. Land, R. Parker and A. Webb (eds), *Change, Choice and Conflict in Social Policy* (London: Heinemann, 1975), p. 155.

41 Daunton, *Just Taxes*, pp. 179–80.

of the top one-sixth of income earners fell by about 30 per cent while that of the remainder increased by about 25 per cent, though tax avoidance appears to have grown on an unprecedented scale; among the lasting gainers from the war were accountants.

Price controls helped to stabilize the cost of living at 30 per cent above its prewar level, avoiding the inflation of the last war. Wages rose, but higher earnings made more manual workers liable for income tax. In 1938, the average adult male wage was £175 pa; a married man did not pay tax until he earned £225 or, if he had one child, £300. From 1941, a married man with one child paid tax on earnings of £161 pa, with two children £265. Average male pay was then £288 pa. National Insurance contributions rose. The tax structure became more regressive at lower levels and more progressive from middle incomes upwards. This aroused resentment, but insufficient to spark serious conflict since most workers enjoyed higher real incomes. Despite criticism in Parliament and the press, the government, urged by Bevin, avoided wage controls to prevent industrial conflict, without total success as days lost through strikes were fewer than in the last war but similar to the later 1930s, peaking at 3.7 million in 1944.

Tax rises were softened by the introduction in 1941 of 'postwar credits' inspired by Keynes. These represented additional taxes as temporary contributions to the war effort. The additional sum paid due to reduced allowances was recorded on certificates returned to the taxpayer, with the promise they would be repaid at 38 per cent interest by 1973 at latest. At least initially this was popular. Businesses were promised a 20 per cent refund of Excess Profits tax, which was paid soon after the war to boost reconstruction. Ordinary taxpayers waited much longer. Credits were repaid very gradually to slowly expanding categories of creditors. In 1972, the Conservative Financial Secretary to the Treasury announced that all remaining credits would be repaid by April 1973. He admitted that 'progress has been painfully slow' and 'a source of increasing irritation and disappointment'. Of the £740 million originally owed, £130 million was still outstanding to approximately 5 million people,[42] not all of whom survived or retained proof of payment.

The war did not evidently draw the nations of the United Kingdom closer. 'People's War' imagery in the press, government propaganda, politicians' rhetoric and film, including Humphrey Jennings' *Listen to Britain* (1942, funded by the Crown Film Unit of the Ministry of Information), which opened with a field of wheat blowing gently in the wind, evoked idyllic representations of the English countryside to evoke what 'Britain' was fighting to defend. The weekly magazine *Picture Post*, in the midst of the

---

42 *Hansard*, 9 March 1972, House of Commons, *Debates*, cols. 1793–4.

Battle of Britain, described what the 'British' would lose if Germany won, depicting sheep walking through an unmistakeably English village past the parish church, contrasted with an image of soldiers marching through a German town. The language of patriotism as before and long after the war, too often invoked 'England'. This caused resentment and strengthened Welsh and Scottish nationalism without weakening their support for the war. Welsh, Scottish and Northern Irish papers celebrated the heroism of their soldiers. Official sources began to display sensitivity. Early in the war, the War Office banned Scottish regiments on active service from wearing kilts, but quickly withdrew the ban.[43] In October 1939, the Ministry of Information warned the *British* Broadcasting Corporation to avoid the English/British error. Thereafter it produced programmes praising the war effort in Wales and Scotland and offered more programmes in Welsh and Gaelic.

Towards a New Jerusalem?

The belief that plans for 'reconstruction', designed to create a more equal and united society, had largely failed after the previous war made some determined to do better this time. The idea that the experience of this war promoted social solidarity and a determination to reduce inequalities and support redistributive state welfare was developed influentially by Richard Titmuss, Professor of Social Policy at LSE, in his official history of wartime social policy, *Problems of Social Policy* (1950). He argued that bombing and evacuation, in particular, revealed poverty, malnutrition and ill-health to people previously unaware of their reality. He concluded that the war increased government awareness of the value of creating, in peace and war, a fully employed, well-fed, fit, contented and socially cohesive population and increased popular support for extended state welfare. His analysis of the causes has been challenged,[44] but the government, far more than in the previous war, worked to improve wartime social conditions and a flow of influential reports proposed postwar reforms.[45] On 18 June 1940, the day after the fall of France, the Director-General of the Ministry of Information urged the government to promise social reform to boost civilian morale.[46] The War Aims Committee was established in August 1940 to plan postwar reconstruction, though it did little until 1942 when the war looked winnable. Meanwhile, reform proposals emerged from Whitehall, Parliament and elsewhere.

43 Rose, *Which People's War?* pp 220–31.
44 See pp. 194–5.
45 Paul Addison, *The Road to 1945* (London: Jonathan Cape, 1975, rev. edn London: Pimlico, 1994).
46 Ibid., p. 167.

Education

Education was affected by teacher shortages due to enlistment, bombing of school buildings and the evacuation of children and schools. Revelations of illiteracy among conscripts, while not a surprise, increased demands to improve schooling. In 1941, R. A. Butler became President of the Board of Education. He was a Conservative reformer, chair of the party committee on 'postwar problems', a title which avoided committing the party to radical change. Churchill was reluctant to devote government time to social issues amid wartime crises, but he was too preoccupied with the war to pay attention to discussions in the home departments. The Board supported the tripartite system of secondary education already developing and the concepts of 'parity of esteem' and 'equality of opportunity' between children of different backgrounds and aptitudes.[47] The TUC, Labour Party, LCC and some Welsh county councils advocated non-selective, multilateral (later known as 'comprehensive') secondary schools for all children. The concern to raise standards, in whatever system, was widely shared. In 1943, a report by a Board of Education committee chaired by Sir Cyril Norwood, head of independent Harrow School, rephrased the Hadow report's assertions,[48] still based on no clear evidence, that children divided into three 'rough groupings' with 'different types of mind' requiring different education from age 11: those 'interested in learning for its own sake, who can grasp an argument or follow a piece of connected reasoning'; those 'whose interests and abilities lie markedly in the field of applied science and applied art'; and those 'who deal more easily with concrete things than with ideas … abstractions mean little to him (sic) … his horizon is near and within a limited area his movement is generally slow'. The report was criticized by educationists and psychologists for unscientific assertions and, more widely, for its pejorative description of the third 'type', contrary to the language of 'parity of esteem'.

It impressed Butler who was anxious to reform secondary education before party politics revived after the war. He believed this would improve the Conservatives' electoral chances and pre-empt Labour moves to reform or abolish private schools and right-wing Conservative pressure to minimize spending on poorer children. Butler introduced the only major wartime social legislation: the Education Act 1944, which raised the school leaving age to 15 (implemented 1947), to rise to 16 as soon as practicable. It abolished all-age elementary schools, dividing state education at age 11 into 'primary' and 'secondary' sectors. The Board was renamed the Ministry of Education. It put its influence behind the tripartite secondary system, though this was not specified in the Act, nor any method of selection. It did not insist that all local authorities adopt

47 See pp. 90–91, 130–4.
48 See pp. 90–91.

it, indeed it could not given the established principle of local autonomy, but specified that within one year all local authorities must submit plans for the reorganization of secondary education. The LCC immediately proposed reorganizing London schools, many of them destroyed by bombing, on a 'multilateral' basis. Most authorities proposed tri- or bipartite structures suiting their school stock.

The Act abolished secondary school fees and increased grants to universities and students. Religious conflict was avoided with increased grants to faith schools and, for the first time, all state-funded schools were required to provide daily religious (it was assumed Christian) instruction following pressure from Anglicans and Nonconformists, to compensate for the declining number of Protestant schools. It passed smoothly through Parliament until women MPs introduced an amendment granting equal pay to teachers. Moved by Conservative Thelma Cazalet Keir, this passed the Commons by 117 to 116 votes. The following day, Churchill diverted his attention from the war to insist that this was a matter of confidence in the government and the amendment must be withdrawn. In 1936, Baldwin had similarly forced reversal of a vote for equal pay in the civil service, to the fury of the staff associations.[49] Protesting that the amendment hardly threatened the war effort, the House gave in, but Churchill, under pressure, appointed a Royal Commission on Equal Pay which reported in 1946. The women MPs won another amendment abolishing the marriage bar in teaching, which the Board of Education accepted because it anticipated a teacher shortage in the reformed postwar system. The Education Act owed little to wartime conditions but progressed prewar changes in the education system, owing much to Butler's efforts.

Health

Reorganization of health services to meet war needs featured in the careful prewar planning. An Emergency Medical Service (EMS) was established immediately, a centralized state system initially designed to treat victims of the expected bombing. Doctors and nurses were directly employed and paid by the government, often at higher rates than before. The EMS took over voluntary and public hospitals and established new ones in buildings of variable suitability. Access to non-war-related civilian health care was curtailed by the recruitment of doctors for war service, and long-stay patients, including many older people, were decanted from city centre to rural and suburban hospitals. The reorganization alerted the Ministry and the BMA to deficiencies in existing services. Healthcare reform was constantly discussed in the *Lancet* and the *British Medical Journal*.

---

49 Glew, *Gender, Rhetoric and Regulation*, p. 137.

Ministry officials became convinced of the need for a comprehensive health service for the whole population. Again, the poor physical condition of many recruits to the services and fear of the loss of young men at war, together with the condition of children evacuated from poor neighbourhoods, stimulated the demand for a healthier nation. In October 1941, the Minister of Health, Liberal Ernest Brown, announced that immediate reorganization was impossible but a comprehensive hospital service would be introduced after the war. He established a survey of hospitals, proposing that, following reform, patients 'would be called on to make a reasonable payment towards the cost whether through contributory schemes or otherwise'. Local authority Medical Officers of Health (MOHs) and GPs working with poorer people supported change enthusiastically. MOHs favoured requiring, rather than the present system of allowing, local authorities to provide services including for maternal and child welfare; these expanded further during the war partly due to demand from mothers and children evacuated to rural areas and small towns where services were sparse. Many additional health and welfare centres, maternity homes and nurseries were staffed by volunteers, often from WVS.[50]

In 1943, an MO survey for the Ministry of Information found widespread enthusiasm for a free national service, though some fears of bureaucratized, impersonal care. Many Conservatives opposed a state-managed service. In February 1944, a Ministry of Health White Paper proposed a compromise. It stressed the need for adequate healthcare for all and early treatment. On Labour insistence it included free health centres with salaried GPs, alongside fee-charging GP services. The voluntary hospitals would keep their independence but would be encouraged to cooperate with public hospitals and paid to perform certain functions for the national service. All medical services would be regularly inspected and medical education expanded. Churchill initially opposed its publication but the issue was too popular to ignore. The BMA, representing the elite of well-paid consultants, benefiting from private practice, opposed a universal state-run service, but, when it polled the profession, it found 60 per cent of doctors favoured a universal free service and 62 per cent a wholly or partially salaried service. The war gave ammunition to those already committed to reform and made converts, but the shape of reform remained uncertain in 1945.[51]

As in the last war, the health of most people not directly affected by bombing and war service improved. This was partly due to improved access to health services, also to full employment, better diets due to higher incomes and adequate supplies and rationing of unhealthy foods, including sugar. Between 1939 and 1945 the infant mortality rate fell by 20 per cent as more mothers received expert antenatal care and delivery, then

50 Hardy, *Health and Medicine*, pp. 110–38.
51 Brian Abel-Smith, *The Hospitals, 1800–1948* (London: Heinemann, 1964), pp 424–71.

support from local health centres and access to cheap milk, orange juice and other supplements.[52] Deaths among older children also fell, mainly due to prevention of infectious diseases. Deaths from TB, which mainly killed adults, and other respiratory diseases, including bronchitis, influenza and pneumonia, fell significantly following the development and more extensive use of effective drugs plus improved living standards.[53] For similar reasons, maternal mortality declined between 1938 and 1945 from 4.22 deaths per 1,000 births in England and Wales to 2.33, with similar falls in Scotland and Northern Ireland. The development of blood transfusion services during the war helped to reduce deaths following haemorrhage.

Housing

Housing was another focus of postwar planning, especially following bombing. Planners and architects seized the opportunity to generate plans, building on their growing prewar influence and international status. They were encouraged by the Ministry of Works, under John Reith, 1940–2, which ensured efficient repair of damaged housing, though new housebuilding and repairs to property unaffected by bombing virtually ceased. Evacuation, fear of bombing and bombing itself depleted the populations of large cities – that of east London fell by half. The drift of population from prewar 'depressed areas' continued, while the location of war industries away from big cities increased overcrowding in smaller towns, such as Reading, though not to the crisis proportions of the last war.

Following interwar demands for planning, the Barlow Commission on the Distribution of the Industrial Population was appointed in 1937 and reported in January 1940, recommending central planning of the location of housing, jobs and transport, and control of industrial and urban growth, especially in southeast England. Reith and his officials, including the town and country planning department recently transferred from the Ministry of Health, supported the proposals. A Green Belt Act introduced in 1938, to encircle London with a rural barrier against sprawl, was implemented after the war.

In 1941, Reith persuaded the Cabinet to establish a national planning authority. He appointed the Scott Committee to consider the future of the countryside, the Uthwatt Committee on compensation for redevelopment of land and set planner Patrick Abercrombie and LCC architect, J. H. Forshaw, to plan postwar rebuilding throughout London. Plans were developed for the postwar reconstruction of other cities,

---

52 J. M. Winter, 'The Demographic Consequences of the War', in H. L. Smith (ed.), *War and Social Change. British Society in the Second World War* (Manchester University Press, 1986), pp. 154–6.
53 Ibid., pp. 168–7.

including Glasgow, Sheffield, Exeter, Hull and Coventry. Such initiatives ended when Churchill dismissed Reith, again, in 1942 and, embittered, he left the government, but proposals continued. In September 1942, the Uthwatt Committee recommended nationalization of the rights in land suitable for development. Conservatives could not accept this blow to property rights, but it became Labour policy. Plans for urban expansion alarmed supporters of the countryside who before the war felt threatened by increasing numbers of out-of-town estates, transport developments, day trippers, ramblers, cyclists and picnickers. In 1942, the Scott Committee recommended a planning system for the countryside as well as towns, to protect good agricultural land from urban development, and enabling public access to unspoiled countryside by establishing National Parks where development was prohibited. The government committed to creating National Parks after the war. The Town and Country Planning Act 1944 provided the machinery for comprehensive redevelopment as envisaged by the more ambitious planners.[54]

Women's organizations still campaigned for improved housing. In May 1942, a Women's Housing and Planning conference was organized at the Royal Institute of British Architects in London by prominent women's associations, determined that plans for postwar housing should take account of women's views and needs.[55] The Ministry of Health established the Design of Dwellings Committee to improve home design and the layout of suburban estates. It included seven women, including three from the WIs and two from the WCG. The Women's Advisory Housing Council, formed by campaigners, issued a detailed questionnaire. More than 40,000 women of all classes responded, as summarized in a report to the Committee. Most wanted houses with sufficient living space and a garden, an upstairs, tiled bathroom and hot and cold running water; large, bright, soundproof rooms with rounded corners for easy cleaning; kitchens with conveniently placed, built-in cupboards and work surfaces, gas and electric cooking appliances and ventilated larders. In 1944, the Committee endorsed many of their recommendations, proposing national minimum standards which were introduced after the war.[56]

Planning for a better future was extensive, but in wartime emergency measures came first. In 1944, local authority building of prefabricated houses was subsidized to cover the shortage. They were cheap (c. £1,000 per house), quickly constructed and intended to be temporary, but the speed with which they caught the national imagination suggests the prevalence of poor housing. Affectionately called 'prefabs', for many tenants they were unimaginably better than their previous homes: unpretentious in appearance,

54 Addison, *The Road to 1945*, pp. 174–8; Ashworth, *Genesis of Modern British Town Planning*, pp. 191–237.
55 Beaumont, *Housewives and Citizens*, p. 171.
56 Ibid., pp. 173–4.

two bedroom bungalows with gardens, fitted kitchens, even refrigerators, water heaters and indoor bathrooms and WCs. Many survived for thirty years and more, some into the twenty-first century.

Beveridge and Social Insurance

Planning was proposed also for national economic and social reconstruction, notably by William Beveridge. He was not, this time, immediately recruited to assist the war effort. His limited diplomatic skills made him unpopular with Chamberlain and his colleagues and in the civil service, especially when he publicly criticized what he believed, sometimes wrongly, was inadequate planning for the war. He wanted to return to planning civilian labour and in July 1940 Bevin appointed him an adviser. But Beveridge underestimated Bevin and bombarded him with unwanted advice on the direction of labour and criticism when he was ignored. To escape, Bevin had him appointed chair of an interdepartmental committee on the coordination of social insurance, composed otherwise of civil servants. This was intended as a low-key committee, making no important recommendations. Beveridge was deeply disappointed, 'tears stood in his eyes when the new appointment was offered to him'.[57]

The committee arose from trade union pressure to revise the workmen's compensation scheme and wider demands to improve National Health Insurance, and there was a need, which Beveridge had long recognized,[58] to coordinate the various social insurance and income support schemes that had developed since the beginning of the century. The need for reform was clear early in the war. The old age pension had never been enough to live on. In 1940, responsibility for the welfare of older people was transferred from local Public Assistance committees to the former Unemployment Assistance Board, now the Assistance Board, and means-tested supplementary pensions of up to 5s per week were introduced for impoverished pensioners. Applications soared to 1,275,000 in the first months, double the number anticipated. It was, commented *The Times* 'a remarkable discovery of secret need'.[59] A government survey in 1942 revealed the wretchedness of many pensioners, unable to afford medical care, adequate food or heating.[60]

The terms of reference of Beveridge's committee were vague. The civil service members were too busy to give it much attention. Little was expected, but Beveridge grasped the opportunity to promote some long-cherished ideas; it became a one-man enterprise. Beveridge was determined to propose 'a comprehensive policy of

57 Harris, *Beveridge*, p. 363.
58 W. Beveridge, *Insurance for All and Everything* (London, 1924); Thane, *Old Age in English Society*, pp. 318–23.
59 Thane, *Old Age in English Society*, pp. 356–63.
60 Ibid.

social progress' to abolish 'want' (he rarely referred to 'poverty'). Its components were full employment, good education, adequate housing, a national health service and children's allowances to improve the health and life chances of children, in addition to improved social security benefits. As he wrote in his final report of November 1942:

> Social Insurance fully developed may provide income security; it is an attack upon Want. But Want is one only of five giants on the road of reconstruction and in some ways the easiest to attack. The others are Disease, Ignorance, Squalor and Idleness.[61]

The details of policies to attack the other four 'giants' were outside his brief, but, he argued, they were vital for the elimination of Want, by preventing it, whereas social insurance only provided for periods of crisis.

Beveridge's proposals embodied some of the enduring themes of his long career: dislike of means-tests, for their inefficiency in relieving need, of commercial bodies profiting from need, of 'police supervision' of claimants and the 'Santa Claus state', encouraging dependency not independence. Still politically Liberal, he believed in the psychological value of contributory insurance for encouraging self-sufficiency and thrift and providing cash allowances as rights that had been paid for rather than handouts from the taxpayer. The report also expressed his commitment to voluntary action and encouraging the 'haves' to help the 'have-nots'. He wanted the state to ensure that every need 'from the cradle to the grave' was covered to a genuinely adequate subsistence level, but no more. Those desiring a higher standard of living when they could not work should save for it, preferably through non-profit institutions like friendly societies.

Old age and widows' pensions, unemployment, sickness, disability, maternity and other benefits would be funded by contributions (paid by employee, employer and the state), both flat-rate, not income-related as in Germany and elsewhere in Europe, which Beveridge, supported by the Treasury, rejected because he did not believe the state should subsidize above-subsistence benefits. The whole working population would be covered, in all classes, hopefully encouraging universal support for the system, social cohesion and elimination of the stigma and inefficiencies associated with selective, means-tested benefits. He realized that some would fall through this 'safety net' because they could not work or contribute, including long-term disabled people and unmarried women who gave up work to care for ageing parents. He concluded, with regret, that they could not be fitted into contributory insurance and could be helped only by a means-tested public assistance scheme, an attenuated, he hoped less stigmatized, version of Public Assistance.

---

61 *Social Insurance and Allied Services*. report by Sir William Beveridge, Cmd. 6404 (London: HMSO, 1942), para. 8.

Married women not employed outside the home also presented difficulties because they could not contribute yet needed pensions and other benefits. Beveridge believed they should receive these by right, funded by their husbands' contributions, as partners, not dependants, of their husbands, because they 'must be regarded as occupied on work which is vital though unpaid, without which their husbands could not do their paid work and without which the nation could not continue'.[62] They should be assisted with domestic help to cover their essential work when sick. These views echoed those of Eleanor Rathbone, a friend of Beveridge, and many women's organizations.[63] Beveridge did not, as is sometimes suggested, believe that married women should stay at home, subordinated to their husbands in a 'male breadwinner welfare state',[64] but, realistically, that many of them did so, given the difficulties of combining work inside and outside the home and the inadequacy of affordable childcare. Also the marriage bar excluded married women from work in many occupations. This mostly died out during the war, but this was not evident in 1942. Beveridge feared, presciently, that if wives' benefits were funded directly by the state rather than by their husbands' contributions they would be denigrated as dependent upon hard-working taxpayers.

Married women in paid work would contribute and receive benefits, both at lower rates than their husbands because, being normally better paid, he should bear the housing costs. Beveridge also proposed insurance benefits for divorced and separated wives, funeral allowances and universal, state-funded children's allowances. Old age pensions for the first time should be paid on condition of retirement, from age 65 for men, 60 for women, but with higher payments for each year worked beyond the minimum, to encourage older people to keep working to combat the costs of the ageing society with which Beveridge was still much concerned.[65]

Experts and interest groups generally supported the proposals. Employers complained of the costs and of growing state power, though some recognized the potential gains to the economy of a more secure, healthy workforce. Keynes declared himself 'in a state of wild enthusiasm about the proposals', though concerned that the Treasury would resist the costs. He persuaded Beveridge to propose a gradual transition to full implementation of the scheme, over twenty years, to enable the insurance fund to grow and reduce the burden on the revenue. Some proposals met such strong opposition they had to be abandoned. Allowances for the stigmatized groups of deserted and divorced wives met fierce resistance for 'subsidizing sin'. The Treasury dismissed support for sick housewives as too difficult to administer.

---

62 Cmd. 6404, para. 107.
63 Thane, 'Women of the British Labour Party', pp. 128–31; Pedersen, *Eleanor Rathbone*.
64 Kathleen Kiernan, Hilary Land and Jane Lewis, *Lone Motherhood in Twentieth-Century Britain* (Oxford University Press, 1999), pp. 179–80.
65 See pp. 136–7.

Beveridge alone drafted and signed the report. He wrote in the Introduction, 'A revolutionary moment in the world's history is a time for revolutions, not for patching',[66] and worked hard to publicize his attempted revolution in the press and newsreels. The Conservative Minister of Information, Brendan Bracken, Churchill's ally, tried to delay publication, on the grounds that it was too socialistic, then realized its morale-building potential, but was restrained from promoting it too enthusiastically by Churchill and party colleagues who feared that it would raise excessive hopes and boost Labour's electoral chances. It sold 600,000 copies, unprecedented for an official document. Within two weeks of publication a Gallup Poll found nineteen out of twenty people had heard of it and 90 per cent, even in higher income groups, believed it should be implemented, though many feared it would not.[67] Churchill opposed issuing a summary to the armed forces, but had to retreat. A civil service scrutiny committee was highly critical of most of its key points. Churchill and other leading Conservatives refused to commit to reconstruction plans until after the war, but Attlee welcomed it as did backbenchers in all parties. Popular enthusiasm killed Conservative hopes that the report could be quietly shelved. In February 1943, backbenchers won the largest anti-government vote of the war for a commitment to implementation.[68]

Beveridge continued his publicity drive. He had revealed, and stimulated, a widespread desire for state action to create an improved, more equal, socially just society. He was disappointed not to be involved in government planning to implement his proposals, especially the most ambitious, full employment, at least for men. He did not oppose women's employment but did not think it so essential or that full female employment was realistically attainable. Full male employment had never been achieved in peacetime, but he was convinced greater equality was impossible without it and that the free market had irretrievably broken down, whereas full employment had been achieved in wartime, with an enormous extension of state planning and control and no breakdown of democracy. He believed similar practices could continue after the war.

To promote this ambition, in 1943 he formed a committee of young economists, mostly to his left, including Nicolas Kaldor from Cambridge, adviser to Labour governments in the 1960s, Barbara Wootton and Joan Robinson, a Cambridge economist and Keynesian who was shifting towards Marxism. Their report, published in November 1944 as *Full Employment in a Free Society*, recommended state investment in key industries, especially transport and power; increased state spending on essential services, including roads, hospitals, schools and defence; state subsidies to housing, medical services, food and fuel; state regulation of private investment and consumer demand

66 Cmd. 6404, para. 8.
67 Angus Calder, *The People's War. Britain 1939–1945*, 2nd edn (London: Panther, [1969] 1971; repr. London: Pimlico, 1996), p. 609.
68 Harris, *Beveridge*, pp. 365–432.

through control of interest rates, taxes and income distribution; planned location of industry and labour mobility, all managed by a Ministry of National Finance, relegating the Treasury to supervising departmental expenditure. It spurred the government to rush the publication of a *Full Employment* White Paper. This proposed greater management of the economy than before the war, but much less than Keynes or Beveridge envisaged, with little planning or close control.[69]

Work

Bevin managed and mobilized full employment in the wartime labour force highly successfully. Until a big dispute in the Kent coalfield in 1944, two-thirds fewer days were lost in disputes than in the last war,[70] while trade union membership grew by 50 per cent to 9 million. All strikes were technically illegal, following an agreement between the TUC and the government that disputes would be resolved through negotiation, but Bevin did not enforce this. Another important difference from the previous war was more strikes by women demanding equal pay, especially in previously male-dominated industries, including engineering, where one in three workers were female by 1943. Some were successful.[71] They were supported by the unions, due less to enthusiasm for gender equality than because, as in the last war, they feared employers would re-designate as less skilled the jobs taken by women, with permanently lower pay, as many employers indeed tried to do. A British Institute of Public Opinion (BIPO) poll in 1940 found that 68 per cent of respondents favoured 'equal pay for the same work'. But real change was slight: women's average weekly wages in manual work were 47 per cent of men's in 1938, 52 per cent in 1945, though the averages disguised greater variations by 1945. There were similar differentials among male workers, with those in 'essential' occupations faring best.[72]

Leisure

War disrupted leisure as well as work. Fewer holidays were possible. The most popular sport among working-class men, football, was hit by conscription of players and spectators, though some clubs carried on with amateur players and fewer matches. Longer working hours reduced leisure time, while the 'black-out' every night extinguished lights that could guide the bombers, making town and city centres inhospitable

69 Harris, *Beveridge*, pp. 432–43.
70 Butler and Butler, *Twentieth-Century British Political Facts*, p. 400.
71 Quoted in R. Croucher, *Engineers at War* (London: Merlin, 1982), p. 29.
72 Penny Summerfield, *Women Workers in the Second World War. Production and Patriarchy in Conflict*, 2nd edn (London: Routledge, 2012), p. 200; Summerfield, 'The "Levelling of Class"', pp. 187–8.

and sometimes dangerous, keeping people away from cinemas, pubs, dance halls and other leisure centres, though they flourished in quieter places. The BBC did much to compensate. Churchill made regular, rousing, evening broadcasts, heard by half the adult population in 1941. J. B. Priestley was another successful broadcaster, vigorously promoting populist patriotic rhetoric to the left of Churchill, to the alarm of many in the BBC and the government. The BBC gained an international audience for war reporting and transmitted coded communication with agents abroad and government propaganda, though it probably came as close to impartiality as possible in a major war. It also did its best to keep people happy. The post-Reith BBC instituted a second major radio service, the popular Forces (later Light) Programme, featuring and promoting, among others, singer Vera Lynn, 'the Forces Sweetheart', with resonant songs, including 'There'll be bluebirds over the white cliffs of Dover … tomorrow when the world is free'. It launched the first, enormously popular, radio comedy series, 'It's That Man Again' (ITMA), featuring Tommy Handley and characters including Mrs Mopp, an undeferential charlady. Also 'Music While You Work', broadcast from different factories daily, with popular music chosen by the workers. These innovations had to overcome the misgivings of the still Reithian Board of Governors – 'How can men fit themselves for battle with these debilitating tunes in their ears?' asked one – but they cheered many people through the war.[73]

The BBC audience for classical music and drama doubled, partly because the war reduced evening live performances. In London, the National Gallery, among other venues, in the absence of paintings which had been transported to caves in North Wales to escape bombing, compensated with live music at lunchtime, notably the pianist Dame Myra Hess. The Gallery's Director, Kenneth Clark, brought back one great picture each month to reward the audience who crowded to the concerts. Clark also developed and directed the official War Artists' Advisory Committee from November 1939, sponsoring artists, including Henry Moore, Laura Knight and John Piper, to record the human experience of war and buildings at risk of bombing and obliteration. Piper painted the devastation of London and Coventry; Henry Moore sketched people sheltering in the underground and miners, like his father, at the coal face; Laura Knight painted women's war work before being commissioned to record the war trials.[74]

War conditions reinforced prewar concerns about the decline of live performance with the progress of radio, gramophones and film.[75] This led to the establishment of the Council for the Encouragement of Music and the Arts (CEMA) in late 1939 when theatres and concert halls closed for fear of bombing and actors and musicians

73 Clarke, *Hope and Glory*, pp. 211–12.
74 Alan Ross, *The Colours of War. War Art 1939–1945*, Introduction Kenneth Clark (London: Jonathan Cape, 1983).
75 See pp. 122–3; Webber, PhD in progress.

were conscripted. CEMA was funded by the Pilgrim Trust, supported by the Board of Education, to encourage amateur performance, assist unemployed performers and boost morale. It funded tours by professional actors and concerts in canteens as well as halls. In the London blitz it sent 'flying squads' of musicians to air raid shelters, rest centres for the homeless and munitions factories. The Treasury gradually took over the funding. From 1942, CEMA was chaired by Keynes and shifted from mainly supporting amateur performance to maintaining professional productions, planning the restoration of Covent Garden as the home of national opera and ballet after the war and lobbying for a permanent body to maintain and supervise state patronage of the arts. The outcome was the foundation of the Arts Council in 1946.[76]

Reading flourished, less hampered by war conditions than other leisure pursuits, helped by public libraries, though the paper shortage reduced the output of most publishers, while newspapers and magazines shrank. Penguin escaped the worst wartime restrictions by negotiating to circulate its publications to the armed forces through the Army Bureau of Current Affairs, which worked to stimulate knowledge and debate in the services.[77]

Women at War

A higher proportion of British women were mobilized than in the previous war or than in other belligerent countries, with the possible exception of Russia, and more women experienced the war at close quarters. Of 130,000 civilian adults killed or wounded by bombing, 63,000 were women. More British women were employed than before the war. At the peak in 1943, approximately 7,250,000 were in civilian work, the services or civil defence, that is, 46 per cent of all women aged 14–56, 90 per cent of able-bodied single women aged 18–40 and 80 per cent of married women in the same age group without children under 14. There were 8,770,000 women who were full-time 'housewives'. Due to labour shortages, the marriage bar was lifted in most occupations and generally did not return after the war.[78] Married middle-class women were more likely to serve as volunteers, as the conscription laws allowed. Female civil servants increased 1,214 per cent between 1939 and 1945, from 14 per cent to 54 per cent of all government workers. Insured women in industry increased by 128 per cent, the proportion rising from 28 per cent to 39 per cent. In commerce, banking, insurance and finance

76 F. M. Leventhal, '"The Best for the Most". CEMA and State Sponsorship of the Arts in Wartime, 1939–1945', *Twentieth Century British History* 1 (1990): 289–317.

77 Nicolas Joicey, 'A Paperback Guide to Progress. Penguin Books, 1935–51', *Twentieth Century British History* 4 (1993): 25–56.

78 H. L. Smith, 'The Effect of the War on the Status of Women', in H. L. Smith (ed.), *War and Social Change. British Society in the Second World War* (Manchester University Press, 1986), pp. 210–11.

the proportion of women rose from 31 per cent to 63 per cent. A minority continued in all these occupations after the war.

As labour became increasingly scarce, in September 1941 the Ministry of Labour held a conference of women to discover how to encourage more women into the workforce. They were told that married women, especially, were concerned about low wages, work conditions, hours and childcare. Limited improvements followed: reduction of women's daily working hours in industry to ten and encouragement of employers to provide part-time work and childcare.[79] In 1938, only about 10 per cent of under 5s in England, Wales and Scotland, generally the poorest, attended publicly funded day-care.[80] From April 1941 the Ministry of Health established and funded nurseries and registered child-minders. Training courses were created for staff, opening further work opportunities to women. Nurseries opened and some employers provided day-care.[81] Mothers of young children were not conscripted, but the absence of a male breadwinner and the small service allowances forced many into employment despite the difficulties. By April 1943, the labour shortage was so acute that women previously exempt because of domestic responsibilities were directed into part-time work, often in shops, where staff shortages added to queues and the stress of wartime life.

Recruitment of women for war work intensified the equal pay campaign. Feminism did not die in wartime. It was invigorated by the indispensability of women to the war effort and by continuing rebuffs. Early in the war, Conservative MP, Irene Ward formed the Woman Power Committee of women MPs to urge government to employ more women in skilled work. It campaigned against the Personal Injuries Act 1939, which allowed unmarried male civilians 7s per week more in compensation (total 21s) for war-related injuries than unmarried woman, on the grounds that it was compensation for pay, which was normally unequal. Mavis Tate, Conservative MP, and Labour's Edith Summerskill protested in the Commons that the cost of living was equal for men and women, and demanded equal compensation. When this failed, they and leading women's associations organized rallies and deputations, which, in 1942, forced the government to establish a Select Committee which recommended equal compensation. In 1943, the government complied. Also in 1943 it invited leading women's associations to a National Conference of Women, raising campaigners' hopes. Bevin and the Chancellor lavished praise on women for their war effort, but refused equal pay. The response was the establishment of the energetic Equal Pay Campaign Committee

---

79 Beaumont, *Housewives and Citizens*, p. 145.

80 Sheila Ferguson and Hilde Fitzgerald, *Studies in the Social Services. History of the Second World War* (London: HMSO and Longman Green, 1954), p. 178 n. 1.

81 Ibid., pp. 190–1.

(EPCC) in January 1944, uniting women's groups, putting further pressure behind the establishment of the Royal Commission on Equal Pay in 1944.[82]

Prewar women's organizations remained active, though membership dropped due to evacuation, war work and other war circumstances. Some women transferred their energies to the WVS.[83] In September 1939, women's associations established the Women's Group on Public Welfare, which, chaired by Labour MP Margaret Bondfield, recruited women to inform people, especially women at home, of their rights to welfare, health and other services and to press government and official bodies to extend those rights. They investigated the circumstances of children and mothers whose problems had been exposed by evacuation and in 1943 published *Our Towns: A Close-Up*, advocating, among other things, better housing, nursery schools for all children from age 2 and domestic training for schoolgirls, as part of the long campaign by women's organizations to improve social conditions and increase opportunities.[84]

Population Panic

The war, of course, affected family life. Marriages surged from 17.6 per 1,000 of the population in England and Wales, 16.5 in Scotland and 13.4 in Northern Ireland in 1938 to 22.5, 21.2 and 15.1, respectively, in 1940. In all three countries the highest rates since official records began, surely driven by impending separation. They fell in 1943–4, then, not surprisingly, rose again in 1945–8, as the men returned.[85] The early surge of marriages did not lead to an equivalent rise in births. The birth rate fell early in the war, reaching the lowest levels since official records began, 13.9 per 1,000 population in England and Wales in 1941, 17.1 in Scotland in 1940. Births in Northern Ireland stayed close to low prewar levels. Then they rose in all three regions, reaching 17.7 in England and Wales, 18.5 in Scotland and 22.8 in Northern Ireland in 1944.[86] This was the beginning of a sustained rise – the so-called 'baby boom' – confounding prewar projections of indefinite decline. During the war, the rise was attributed to wartime conditions; decline and population ageing were expected to return postwar.[87] In 1942, a White Paper, *The Current Population Trend*, sought to calm population panic, and in

---

82 Beaumont, *Women and Domesticity*, pp. 146–53.
83 Ibid., pp. 136–7.
84 Beaumont, *Housewives and Citizens*, pp. 138–41.
85 Mitchell and Deane, *Historical Statistics*, table 16, p. 46; B. R. Mitchell and H. G. Jones, *Second Abstract of British Historical Statistics* (Cambridge University Press, 1971), table 14, p. 30.
86 Mitchell and Deane, *Historical Statistics*, table 10, pp. 30–3; Mitchell and Jones, *Historical Statistics II*, table 8, pp. 21–2.
87 Thane, 'The Debate on the Declining Birth Rate'; Eva M. Hubback, *The Population of Britain* (Harmondsworth: Penguin, 1947).

1944 the government appointed a Royal Commission on Population to clarify what was changing and why and propose policy responses. It reported in 1949.

Again, births to unmarried women increased, from 4.2 per cent to 9.14 per cent of live births in England between 1939 and 1945, in Wales from 3.7 to 7.9 per cent, in Scotland from 6 to 8.6 per cent and in Northern Ireland from 4.7 to 5.4 per cent.[88] From 1940 to 1945 almost 300,000 more 'illegitimate' children were born in England, Wales and Scotland than in the six years before the war.[89] As in the last war, this sparked moralizing about young women liberated from parental control, 'running wild', 'going out for a good time', especially with overseas, especially American, even black, servicemen. Married women with husbands absent at war aroused suspicion too. The Bishop of Norwich chastised 'women and especially young girls in town and village alike' for their casual relationships with soldiers.

But in this war, statistics challenged the moralizers. From 1938, parents were obliged to record their date of marriage on birth certificates and in 1939 the Registrar General published a *Statistical Review of England and Wales* which estimated, to great surprise and shock, that almost 30 per cent of first children born in 1938–9 were conceived out of wedlock, based on births within eight and a half-months of the parents' marriage. Some births might have been premature, but the Registrar-General believed these were balanced by parents who misrepresented their marriage date to hide premarital conception. Later *Statistical Reviews* showed that premarital pregnancies fell between 1939 and 1945 from 60,346 to 38,176, while 'illegitimate' births rose by a similar amount, from 26,569 to 64,743. It is unknown how many were legitimated by the parents' marriage when the father returned from war.

The wartime statistics showed that younger women were less prone to sexual irregularities leading to childbirth than their seniors. The number of premarital conceptions plus births to unmarried mothers among women under 20 in England and Wales declined from 12.1 to 10.7 per 1,000 between 1939 and 1943, returning to prewar levels by 1945. Among those aged 25–30 they rose from 26.6 to 46.5 in 1945, at ages 30–35 from 15.8 to 33.2.[90] The Registrar General concluded that the wartime rise in unmarried motherhood was not due to lax morals, but

> is almost unquestionably to be found in the enforced degree of physical separation of the sexes imposed by the progressive recruitment of young males into the Armed Forces … rendering immediate marriage with their brides increasingly difficult – and in the case of many quite impossible …
>
> Taking the six war years as a whole the average increase of 6% in the total number of irregularly conceived births will hardly be regarded as inordinate, having regard to the wholesale

88 Virginia Wimperis, *The Unmarried Mother and her Child* (London: Allen and Unwin, 1960), app. table 2a.
89 Ferguson and Fitzgerald, *Studies in the Social Services*, p. 103.
90 Ibid., pp. 93–4.

disturbance to customary habits and living conditions in conjunction with the temporary accession to the population of large numbers of young and virile men in the Armed Forces of our Dominions and Allies.[91]

A notably more sober – and convincing – assessment than some contemporary polemic.[92] As ever, women received most of the blame for perceived moral laxity, despite evidence that the black-out increased their risk of harassment and sexual assault.[93] As ever, some unmarried motherhood was due to rape, still generally under-reported and under-punished, and the women blamed. It is unlikely there was significant change in sexual behaviour during the war, rather some behaviours became more visible.

Clearer evidence emerged of who the unmarried mothers were and the realities of their lives. The official historians of the wartime social services, Sheila Ferguson and Hilde Fitzgerald reported:

> it would appear that the women who bore illegitimate children during the war belonged to all classes, types and age groups. Some were adolescent girls who had drifted away from homes which offered neither guidance nor warmth and security. Still others were married women with husbands on war service who were unable to bear the loneliness of separation. There were decent and serious, superficial and flighty, irresponsible and incorrigible girls among them. There were some who had formed serious attachments and had hoped to marry. There were others who had had a single lapse, often under the influence of drink. There were, too, the 'good time girls' who thrived on the presence of well-paid servicemen from overseas and the semi-prostitutes with little moral restraint … Some of the unmarried mothers of the war were of a 'new type' and surprised the moral welfare workers to whom they were referred. Their spirit of independence was considerable and there was little of the sinner or penitent among them.[94]

Pregnant wives of husbands absent at war could be particularly desperate. They could not disguise the fact that their absent husband was not the father. They could not have the child adopted legally because any child born to a married woman was legally the child of her husband and his permission was required. The Forces' Welfare Services gave sympathetic help to husbands and wives,[95] and the National Council for the Unmarried Mother and her Child (NCUMC) helped many women.[96] Unmarried mothers of 'coloured' children faced particular hostility and difficulty in finding lodgings and foster care, while white British women who married black Americans faced even greater discrimination in the United States. Officially, the government opposed

---

91 *Registrar General's Statistical Review of England and Wales for the Six Years 1940–1945*, Text, vol. 11, Civil, p. 144.
92 Rose, *Which People's War?* p. 74.
93 G. Braybon and P. Summerfield, *Out of the Cage. Women's Experiences in Two World Wars* (London: Pandora, 1987), pp. 206–7.
94 Ibid., p. 95.
95 Ibid.
96 Thane and Evans, *Sinners?* pp. 54–81.

discrimination or singling out mixed-race children for support in case it encouraged discrimination, but without positive action it was hard to achieve equal treatment.[97]

Wartime conditions made life even harder for unmarried mothers who did not have family support or an adequate income. There were fewer foster mothers, as women could find better-paid work, and fewer voluntary and local authority welfare workers, who were diverted to urgent war work.[98] The outcome was, as the founder of the NCUMC wrote, a 'fever of adoptions' by desperate women 'often arranged with the minimum of care and the maximum of irresponsibility'.[99] Babies were offered in newspaper advertisements, until legal regulation of adoption was tightened in 1943, though lurid press reports of sales of babies continued. In 1944, George Orwell and his wife adopted a baby straight from hospital, arranged by Orwell's sister-in-law, a doctor, though his wife was sick and died of cancer nine months later. The boy was brought up by Orwell's sister.[100]

Public sympathy for the mothers and children grew, alongside the opprobrium. In 1943, the Bishop of Derby asked the government to take responsibility because local services could not cope, supported by letters to *The Times* from public figures.[101] The Ministry of Health urged local authorities to help but provided no funding and little changed. It gave minimal financial help to just thirty-six unmarried pregnant workers in essential industries. Pregnant servicewomen might receive advice from officers about social services and/or adoption before being dismissed without pay. Due to concern for the reputation of the armed services, amid excited press comment, the government appointed a committee chaired by Violet Markham, long active in voluntary and government work and support for women's rights.[102] In the First World War she was secretary to an official investigation into reports of immorality among the Women's Auxiliary Army Corps stationed in France, which it concluded had no foundation.[103] Her report in 1942 on *Amenities and Welfare Conditions in the Women's Services* rejected the latest outcry equally firmly:

> Rumours that illegitimate pregnancy was both common and on the increase in the Services have been rife. This is the kind of rumour that starts in every war … We can … with certainty say that the illegitimate birth rate in the services is lower than the illegitimate birth rate among the comparable civilian population.[104]

---

97 Ibid., pp. 76–8; Ferguson and Fitzgerald, *Studies in the Social Services*, pp. 131–2.

98 Ibid.; Fitzgerald and Fitzgerald, ibid., p. 104.

99 Thane and Evans, *Sinners?* pp. 79–81.

100 Bernard Crick, *George Orwell. A Life* (London: Secker & Warburg, 1980), pp. 463–4.

101 Ferguson and Fitzgerald, *Studies in Social Services*, pp. 126–7.

102 Helen Jones (ed.), *Duty and Citizenship. The Correspondence and Papers of Violet Markham, 1896–1953* (London: Historians' Press, 1994).

103 Helen Jones, 'Markham, Violet Rosa (1872–1959)', *Oxford Dictionary of National Biography*, 2004, online edition, available at: www.oxforddnb.com.

104 *Report of the Committee on Amenities and Welfare, Conditions in the Three Women's Services*, 1942, Cmd. 6384, 31, 50.

The Ministry of Health then funded servicewomen who could not return to their families to live in voluntary homes or government hostels before and after confinement, giving more generous support than to civilians, providing care and advice, including on future work and training. This was kept secret during the war. The birth rate among unmarried servicewomen was never revealed and all records were destroyed after the war. For the first time, a government department was closely involved with helping unmarried mothers and their children, providing more than the bare necessities of food, shelter and maternity care. The wartime experience contributed to the postwar reform of services whose inadequacy was clearly revealed.

Conclusion

How far war conditions encouraged greater social cohesion, lessening inequalities, is uncertain, but there were some changes and hopes grew of more profound postwar transformation.[105] The war again improved the living standards of many people and, more than the last war, exposed to the government and many of the public unacceptable conditions that should and could be improved, generating blueprints for change, shaping politics and change after the war.

105 Jose Harris, 'Political Ideas and the Debate on State Welfare', in H. L. Smith (ed.), *War and Social Change. British Society in the Second World War* (Manchester University Press, 1986), pp. 233–43.

7

Facing the Future

Labour Britain, 1945–1951

Victory

With Germany defeated, Churchill wanted the Coalition to continue to the end of war with Japan. In August 1945, Japan surrendered after the devastation of Hiroshima and Nagasaki by the world's first atomic bombing by US aircraft, but advisers pressured Churchill to call an earlier election, believing victory over Germany would bring victory at the polls. The Coalition ended in May. Churchill formed a caretaker, largely Conservative, government with no Labour members and open party politics resumed, preparing for the first General Election for ten years. Labour campaigned on a programme of social and economic reconstruction and no return to prewar depression: *Let Us Face the Future* its manifesto proclaimed.

Labour gained from continuing resentment against the 'Guilty Men' of the Conservative Party who supported appeasement, while many who admired Churchill as wartime leader doubted his peacetime capabilities, given his past record. Labour also gained from its commitment to wartime proposals for social and economic reform, including those of Beveridge, amid the widespread desire not to return to prewar conditions, while Churchill equivocated. Individual membership of the Labour Party climbed after publication of the Beveridge report to a record 487,047 in 1945.[1] Labour ministers, including Attlee, had performed well in highly visible domestic roles. Labour had maintained its local organization better than the Conservatives and fought a well-organized campaign. There was little sign of the 'consensus' between the major

1 Butler and Butler, *Twentieth-Century British Political Facts*, p. 158.

parties some historians have perceived.[2] The Conservatives, consistent with their past and future inclinations, supported free enterprise, de-control, reduced state action and lower taxation, without which, claimed their manifesto, full employment was unsustainable. The manifesto, *Mr Churchill's Declaration of Policy to the Electors*, was, as the title implied, Churchill's personal statement, hurriedly drafted, stressing the national victory and attacking the 'socialism' of his former coalition partners. This, he claimed in a radio broadcast, 'is abhorrent to the British ideas of freedom ... There is to be one State to which all are to be obedient in every act of their lives ... I declare to you from the bottom of my heart, that no Socialist system can be established without a political police ... They will have to fall back on some form of Gestapo'.[3]

This equation of Labour with Nazism shocked many voters. Labour gained further support by responding calmly. Their manifesto stated, 'The Labour Party is a Socialist Party and proud of it', while seeking to appeal to the middle ground and middle-class voters. It was drafted mainly by Michael Young, head of the party's research department from 1945 to 1951, later a prominent civil society innovator.[4] He was another former Toynbee Hall resident and wartime Director of PEP. The manifesto stressed that, after 1918, 'the people lost that peace' to the 'hard-faced men who did well out of the war'. This time, Labour ministers had taken 'the profit out of war' with the 100 per cent Profits Tax, and continued controls would ensure 'Peace for the People'. Central to Labour's programme was economic planning and 'Jobs for All' at fair wages, to be achieved by increased production, especially in export industries, controlled location of industry, encouragement of science and technology to assist competitiveness as it had helped win the war, regulation of banking, nationalization of the Bank of England, of fuel and power (including mining), inland transport (including railways) and iron and steel, with 'fair compensation' to owners. Labour did not plan to nationalize manufacturing industry, a National Investment Board would direct its development and modernization using public funds where necessary. There would be controlled development of agriculture and supervision of monopolies and cartels, complemented by reformed social services, including a national health service providing excellent healthcare for all, family allowances, universal comprehensive social insurance, a vigorous housing and planning programme, rent and price controls, implementation of the 1944 Education Act and 'taxation which bears less heavily on lower income groups'.

2 H. Jones and M. Kandiah (eds), *The Myth of Consensus. New Views on British History, 1945–64* (London: Macmillan, 1990); R. Lowe, 'The Second World War, Consensus and the Foundation of the Welfare State', *Twentieth Century British History* 2 (1990): 152–82.

3 *The Times*, 5 June 1945.

4 Asa Briggs, *Michael Young. Social Entrepreneur* (London: Palgrave, 2001); M. Hilton (ed.), 'Michael Young in Retrospect', *Contemporary British History* 19(3) (2005): 277–320.

Economic reconstruction would take priority. Labour had argued since its foundation that the best route, to 'welfare' for most people was work with decent pay, with social assistance when they could not work for good reasons including age, sickness and unemployment.[5] The term 'Welfare State' appeared nowhere in the manifesto, nor in Beveridge's publications or statements. He, with Michael Young, disliked what they believed was its implied dependency of individuals on the state.[6] Young wrote in a report to the Labour Party:

> 'The very name … is against it. It must have been invented by a diabolical copywriter who knew that if the nation was not poisoned by the first cold word [welfare], recalling the smell of carbolic acid and the tough brown paper of ration books, it could be done to death by the second cold word [state] suggesting the Law Court, the Sanitary Inspector and the Recruiting Officer.[7]

Beveridge preferred the term 'social service state', implying the mutual responsibilities of citizens and the state rather than dependency. Associated though it has become with the post-1945 Labour government, the term 'welfare state' did not come into common use until the 1950s, initially as a term of right-wing Conservative abuse.[8]

International affairs appeared only briefly in the manifesto. Labour pledged to maintain peace by supporting the United Nations (UN), currently being established. Its first General Assembly, at which fifty-one nations were represented, met at Central Hall, Westminster, on 10 January 1946. The manifesto also pledged that 'The Labour Party will seek to promote mutual understanding and cordial cooperation between the Dominions of the British Commonwealth and the advancement of India to responsible self-government and the planned progress of our Colonial Dependencies'.

One Labour promise was anticipated when the brief caretaker government introduced the Family Allowances Act 1945. This instituted non-contributory weekly allowances for the second and subsequent children of all families, without stating when or the amount. It was one of the few Beveridge proposals on which the coalition could agree. Some thought it was designed to relieve poverty, others to boost the birth rate, others a victory for feminism. Feminists, supported by Labour and Beveridge, fought to amend the Bill, which initially paid the allowances to fathers, led by Eleanor Rathbone, still an Independent MP, who had long fought for family allowances as independent income for mothers. She lived just long enough to succeed.[9]

---

5 Pat Thane, 'Labour and Welfare', in D. Tanner, N. Tiratsoo and P. Thane (eds), *Labour's First Century* (Cambridge University Press, 2000), pp. 81–3.

6 Harris, *Beveridge*, p. 452.

7 Michael Young, 'For Richer for Poorer', Report to Labour Party Research Department (1951), quoted in Briggs, *Michael Young*, p. 201; Pat Thane, 'Michael Young and Welfare', in Michael Young in Retrospect', *Contemporary British History* 19(3) (2005): 293.

8 Harris, *Beveridge*, p. 452.

9 Pedersen, *Eleanor Rathbone*, pp. 359–68.

The caretaker government also continued the CEMA's wartime encouragement of the arts by establishing a government-funded Arts Council of Great Britain, chaired by Keynes.[10] From 1946, with a separate Arts Council for Northern Ireland, it worked to develop knowledge and practice of the arts and increase their accessibility. Council members included specialists in all branches of the arts. Labour increased its funding, aiming to raise the cultural standards of the nation and democratize access to the arts.

General Election, 1945

Voting started on 5 July, but results were not declared until 26 July because, unlike in 1918, those serving abroad were included, polling stations were established around the world and results took time to collect. The turnout was 72.7 per cent despite the outdated voting register. For the first time, Labour won a clear majority, by 146 seats with almost 48 per cent of votes to the Conservatives' 40 per cent. According to opinion polls, Labour won a majority of female[11] and younger voters and unprecedented middle-class support. It probably (it was never certain) won a large majority of service votes. It performed well not only in its traditional seats but in previously inhospitable areas like the east and west Midlands and southern towns like Taunton, Dover and Wycombe. It gained twenty-five of thirty-five seats in Wales and thirty-seven of seventy-one in Scotland. Labour had never run in Northern Ireland where the Conservatives held nine of the twelve seats. The Liberals slumped to twelve seats. Even Beveridge failed to win traditionally Liberal Berwick which swung to the Conservatives, having spent the campaign attempting to lend his charisma to promoting Liberalism around the country. The Communists had their last election successes of the century: Willie Gallacher won West Fife for the second time and Phil Piratin won Stepney, east London.

Labour in Parliament was changed, not only in numbers. Trade union-sponsored MPs were fewer than one-third, there was an influx of middle-class men and twenty-one women were elected, the largest number of female Labour MPs so far. A single Conservative woman was elected from fourteen candidates (Viscountess Davidson, who succeeded her husband in Hemel Hempstead in 1937 and was largely inactive in Parliament), one Liberal (Megan Lloyd George, daughter of the Liberal leader who died in 1945; she worked closely with Labour) and Eleanor

10 See pp. 178–9.
11 Monica Charlot, 'Women and Elections in Britain', in H. R. Penniman (ed.), *Britain at the Polls, 1979. A Study of the General Election* (Washington, DC: AEI Press, 1981), p. 244; James Hinton, 'Women and the Labour Vote 1945–50', *Labour History Review* 57(3) (1992): 59–66.

Rathbone was elected again but died in 1946. It was the largest number of women MPs so far: twenty-four of 640. Most Labour women gained seats thought unwinnable, hence unattractive to men, due to Labour's overall success rather than any determination by the party to increase female representation, despite continuing demands by Labour women. A report to the Conservative Party also expressed disappointment at 'the reluctance of Selection Committees to consider women' and the women's conference in 1947 urged branches to return more women to Parliament at the next election.[12]

Labour in Power

Attlee took characteristically calm control of his Cabinet. Morrison, his relentless critic always hoping to replace him as party leader, became Lord President of the Council, effectively deputy prime minister and coordinator of domestic policy; Bevin was Foreign Secretary; Hugh Dalton, an old Etonian economist, became Chancellor; Stafford Cripps, a wealthy, ex-public school barrister, on the far left of the party, was President of the Board of Trade, responsible for industrial and production policy. The only woman Cabinet minister was Ellen Wilkinson at Education. She died in 1947 and the Cabinet became exclusively male. Left-wingers Aneurin Bevan and Emanuel Shinwell were Ministers of Health and Fuel and Power, respectively, both areas in which Labour promised major reforms.

Constitutional Reform

Labour introduced significant constitutional changes designed to promote democracy. In 1948, it abolished university seats, which gave graduates two votes, and the business vote which allowed businessmen (but not businesswomen)[13] votes at both their home and business addresses. It reduced the number of MPs from 640 to 625 and undertook the first major redistribution of constituencies since 1918 to equalize them in terms of population shifts, establishing a permanent commission to review constituency boundaries periodically. The local government vote, previously restricted to ratepayers and their spouses, was extended to all adults. In 1949, the delaying power of the House of Lords was reduced from two years to one. The Lords was otherwise unchanged despite Labour's fears that it would overturn some of its proposed reforms, as it did, but there was no strong popular demand for Lords' reform. A few Labour peers were appointed.

---

12 Lovenduski et al., 'The Party and Women'. p. 627.
13 See p. 78.

Economic Policy

Labour implemented many of its election promises, but the legacy of the prewar decline of traditional industries, the costs of war and the high costs of continuing defence commitments prevented full implementation. The British and US governments were committed to rebuilding the German economy to avoid the crises caused by its weakness following the First World War. British occupation of part of northwest Germany until 1949 was another major cost.[14] Labour could not plan the economy or expand the welfare system as comprehensively as it hoped in its six years in office. It did not reject the liberal market economy but aimed to control and reform it, practising a modified Keynesianism acceptable to the Treasury. About 20 per cent of the economy became publicly owned, against less parliamentary opposition than some future Conservatives cared to remember. Churchill himself said that nationalization of the Bank of England in 1946 did not raise any issue of principle. There was little opposition to nationalization of the coal industry, which was vital but notoriously inefficient, nor to that of the seriously unprofitable but indispensable railways and canals, all in 1947, though the inclusion of profitable road haulage was controversial. The nationalization of cable and wireless companies in 1947, the establishment of public corporations to run British European Airways (BEA) and the British Overseas Airways Corporation (BOAC) in 1946, and the formation of the British Electricity Authority in 1948 and the Gas Council in 1949 to manage these two essential public utilities, took existing controls further. The promised nationalization of the profitable, complex and quite efficient iron and steel industry was most controversial, including within the Labour Party. The steelworkers' union opposed it, and it was incomplete by the 1950 election. Nationalized undertakings were run, like the BBC, as public corporations, with boards appointed by ministers but not answerable to them. They included previous owners and managers for their expertise, but no trade union representation as some had hoped. Nationalization substantially improved the industries' performance. It proved harder to regulate and improve the private sector. Harold Wilson, the young President of the Board of Trade from 1947, tried unsuccessfully to persuade colleagues to appoint government directors to the boards of private companies, to increase controls and nationalize uncooperative, inefficient companies.

Rationing and price controls continued, to restrain consumption, maximize exports and real earnings and improve the balance of trade. Income tax was more steeply graduated and the threshold raised, exempting most manual workers. Budgets in October 1945 and April 1946 increased surtax on incomes above £10,000 and death duties on larger estates, to 75 per cent on those worth over £21,500, raised to 80 per cent in 1950.

14 Christopher Knowles, *Winning the Peace. The British in Occupied Germany* (London: Bloomsbury, 2017).

Consumption was further restrained by increasing purchase tax, with punitive rates on luxuries (like champagne) while wartime Utility goods continued and were exempt. The standard rate of tax fell from 50 to 45 per cent and remained unchanged, while personal allowances and earned income relief increased. Average wages after tax rose in real terms by 21 per cent between 1938 and 1949, while salaries fell by 16 per cent, causing some middle-class disenchantment with Labour despite their gains from the health, social security and education reforms their additional taxes helped to fund.[15] By 1947–8 income tax was payable by 14.5 million people compared with 6 million in 1937–8, largely due to full employment and increased population. Six and a half million lower earners, mainly manual workers, still paid no direct tax.[16] Interest rates remained low to encourage borrowing for investment.[17] By 1951 the percentage of total personal wealth held by the top 0.1 per cent in Great Britain had fallen to 18 per cent, that of the top 5 per cent to 68 per cent.[18]

Measures to modernize and increase the efficiency of British industry included the creation of development councils; Board of Trade working parties to propose modernization strategies for specific industries; creation of the British Institute for Management to raise management standards; and the encouragement of joint production committees to involve workers in decision-making. The effects were limited. Businesses were reluctant to change while they experienced buoyant overseas demand and industries in competitor countries, especially Germany and Japan, were devastated and needed British products to aid reconstruction. Short-term gains hindered necessary long-term reconstruction. The unions accepted wage restraint in return for price controls to achieve full employment. Labour repealed the 1927 Trade Disputes Act, removing the restrictions on general strikes and public sector unions. It reverted from contracting-in to contracting-out of party membership in affiliated unions, which increased by 25 per cent. Union membership grew to almost 10 million by the early 1950s.[19]

Managing the economy became even harder when the US government, now led by Harry Truman, suddenly cancelled lend-lease when the war with Japan ended instead of the staged termination expected. The United States demanded that Britain pay for commodities already ordered under the agreement, worth £161 million, while the costs of further imports rose when they were no longer protected by the agreement. Keynes negotiated a large dollar loan from the United States and Canada on stringent terms, requiring sterling to become fully convertible against the dollar. US imports rose in price and fell. Bread was rationed for the first time to limit wheat imports. The *Daily*

---

15 David Kynaston, *Austerity Britain, 1945–51* (London: Bloomsbury, 2007), p. 173.
16 Daunton, *Just Taxes*, p. 180.
17 Ibid., pp. 194–228.
18 Compared with 1938, see Atkinson, *Economics of Inequality*, p. 134.
19 Butler and Butler, *Twentieth-Century British Political Facts*, p. 400.

Mail called it 'the most hated measure ever to have been presented to the people of this country',[20] screaming 'Britain's Women Unite in Revolt Against Food Cuts ... Say "Feed Us First"'.[21] though the restrictions were moderate, had little effect on consumption and ended in 1948.[22] Following this and other outbursts, Labour's concern about what it perceived as a biased press, with excessively concentrated ownership restricting democratic debate, led to the appointment of a Royal Commission on the Press in October 1946. It reported in 1949, ineffectually proposing better training of journalists.[23]

The loan gave the government a breathing space but convertibility, introduced in July 1947, caused the pound to collapse. Dalton, shaken by the crisis, inadvertently broke parliamentary rules by disclosing his proposed emergency budget to a journalist and Cripps replaced him as Chancellor. This followed the worst winter of the century so far, with a prolonged freeze in January–March 1947 followed by severe flooding. Potatoes were rationed for the first time because the weather had ruined the crop. Energy supplies could not cope and manufacturing, transport and trade were severely disrupted. From early February, for three weeks, electricity was cut off from much of industry and domestic supplies were cut for 5 hours each day. Restoring the balance of trade became even more urgent, leading to further increases in taxation, reduced clothes rations and the suspension of foreign currency for pleasure travel. Food imports from dollar economies were cut further, including meat.[24] Conservatives and their supporters in the press blamed the failures of socialism for these privations. A doctor argued, under the headline 'Dying England', that Britain was suffering from 'prolonged chronic malnutrition' due to rationing.[25] Nutritionists, including Sir Jack Drummond, pointed to the reduction in malnutrition since the 1930s and much improved health especially among poorer children. The rationed diet was certainly monotonous, but that of poorer working-class people always had been. It was now more nutritious and full employment enabled more people to eat better.

In 1947, defence costs still took almost 18 per cent of GNP. This was controversial in the Labour Party and some (including Keynes before his death in 1946) accused the government of seeking to maintain an unsustainable 'great power' role. Attlee agreed the costs were excessive (Bevin did not) and they fell gradually until the outbreak of the Korean War in 1950. Britain could not easily or quickly reduce its role in the reconstruction of Germany, including helping to feed the population of the British zone.

20 *Daily Mail*, 3 July 1946.
21 Ina Zweiniger-Bargielowska, *Austerity Britain. Rationing, Controls and Consumption, 1939–55* (Oxford University Press, 2000), p. 214.
22 Ibid., pp. 83–4, 215–18.
23 Bingham, *Family Newspapers*, p. 22.
24 Zweiniger-Bargielowska, *Austerity Britain*, pp. 214–26.
25 Quoted in ibid., p. 221.

Then, as Russian control of eastern Germany hardened, it seemed essential to keep an army presence in Germany to protect Western Europe against the onward march of another totalitarian regime, which no other European country could do. Also, Britain could not withdraw from commitments in the Middle East and Commonwealth.

The emerging Cold War, as it became known, led the United States in 1948 to seek to strengthen Western Europe against Communism with funds, described as Marshall Aid after their initiator, US General George Marshall. Aid was granted to European countries with credible economic recovery plans. Britain received the largest share, around $2,700,000 to the end of 1950, when it needed no further assistance. This helped the economy to stabilize and in February 1948 Harold Wilson announced a 'bonfire of controls', removing some restrictions on industrial production and supply of items including perambulators, toys, cutlery, linoleum and cosmetics, and relaxing others. Clothes were de-rationed in May 1949. Women could now experiment with fashion, including the 'New Look', with long, swirling skirts, rejecting wartime constraints and uniformity, launched by designer Christian Dior in his first Paris collection in 1947. Paris fashion was expensive, but women made copies, despite humourless disapproval: Cripps complained about wasted cloth; 'the ridiculous whim of idle people' sniffed Liverpool Labour MP Bessie Braddock.[26]

One purpose of controls was to prevent, or limit, the 'black market', evasion of rationing, often small-scale and hard to track, including retailers' 'under-the-counter' sales of rationed goods, sales of home-grown goods or surplus, stolen, sometimes forged, coupons especially for clothing. There were 20–24,000 prosecutions for transgressions each year between 1946 and 1950, but much went undetected.[27] Petrol rationing ended in 1950 having been progressively relaxed amid protests by motorists. De-rationing could increase demand uncontrollably. When sweets and chocolate were de-rationed in April 1949 demand so outstripped supply that they vanished into a flourishing black market and rationing was reintroduced in August.

Creating a 'Welfare State'

Labour was committed to expanding and improving social services, but its prioritization of economic reconstruction, plus relentless Treasury pressure to cut costs, constrained reforms. Far from recklessly diverting funds from economic development, as some have suggested,[28] 'the "welfare state" of the 1940s was an austerity

---

26 Kynaston, *Austerity Britain*, p. 257.

27 Zweiniger-Bargielowska, *Austerity Britain*, p. 163.

28 Corelli Barnett, *The Audit of War. The Illusion and Reality of Britain as a Great Nation*, 2nd edn (London: PaperMac, 1987); Jose Harris, 'Enterprise and the Welfare State', in T. Gourvish and A. O' Day (eds), *Britain since 1945* (London: Macmillan, 1991), pp. 39–58.

product of an age of austerity', designed to assist economic expansion.[29] An early indicator came in 1946 when Labour implemented family allowances under the 1945 Act, at 5s per week, not 8s as Beveridge believed necessary to dispel family poverty.

Education

The 1944 Education Act was implemented quickly, introducing selection by examination at age 11 to grammar, technical or secondary modern schools.[30] Labour did not promote 'multilateral'/comprehensive schools, believing that '11+' selection would promote equality of opportunity once all state secondary schools were free, though some local authorities continued to establish them. Independent schools were not reformed or abolished as some hoped. More teachers were trained, including many ex-service personnel who received special funding; 10,000 were in training in 1937–8, 21,000 in 1949–50.[31] The school-leaving age rose to 15 in 1947. There were more state scholarships to universities and increased university funding, especially for science and technology to assist economic development. But there was little school building unless forced by war damage and few of the promised technical schools materialized. They required buildings, equipment and teachers with the skills needed for the urgent task of modernizing the economy. Not until 1950 did education expenditure exceed prewar levels, but only by 4 per cent. Most wartime nursery schools closed and new ones opened only 'where exporting industries need the services of working mothers'. Publicly funded childcare remained limited.

More children received more and better education, continuing prewar trends, but working-class pupils overwhelmingly left secondary modern schools (which educated almost two-thirds of secondary pupils) at 15 without qualifications, and the selective grammar schools for the 'academically able' were disproportionately male and middle-class. There were fewer grammar school places for girls, since most of these schools had traditionally been built for boys, most remained single sex and no new schools were built: girls had to achieve higher grades in the 11+ exam in most districts to gain a place. This went largely unnoticed at a time when girls were still generally expected to aspire to marriage rather than education and careers and most left school at 15.

---

29 J. Tomlinson, 'Welfare and the Economy. The Economic Impact of the Welfare State, 1945–1951', *Twentieth Century British History* 6 (1995): 219–20.
30 See pp. 90–91, 168–9.
31 Halsey and Webb, *Twentieth-century British Social Trends*, p. 224.

Housing

Housing was a major issue for voters in 1945 and Labour's promised housing drive was more convincing than Churchill's vague statements. The Town and Country Planning Act 1947 built on wartime proposals, making all new development subject to planning permission and allowing local authorities to plan 'green belts' around towns to check sprawl, as already introduced around London. The New Towns Act 1946 inaugurated a succession of New Towns, publicly financed to encourage construction of factories and housing away from conurbations and develop declining areas. Stevenage (Essex) was designated first in 1946. Twelve followed by 1950, six in southern counties to take London overspill, two in Scotland, two in northeast England and Cwmbran in South Wales, while Corby (Northants) became a major steel-producing centre. Each was controlled by a government-appointed development corporation. Beveridge, elevated to the Lords where he was Liberal leader, chaired those of Newton Aycliffe and Peterlee, County Durham. Corporations purchased land compulsorily, antagonizing many farmers and landowners. They were expected to attract businesses and build housing mainly for affordable renting. New Towns were intended to be socially mixed, self-sufficient communities, including some owner-occupiers, but mainly providing work and good homes at reasonable rents for working-class people.

Nationally, private housebuilding was limited to 20 per cent of the total. Labour's priority was resolving the working-class housing crisis, and rents were frozen at 1939 levels. But only in 1948 did Labour meet its target of 240,000 new homes each year. In the crisis year, 1947, only 189,000 were completed. By 1951, 1,192,000 had been built, 189,000 for owner-occupation. The shortage was estimated at up to 2 million and housing was again a major issue in the elections of 1950 and 1951. Numbers were held back partly by the insistence of the minister, Aneurin Bevan, that council houses met high standards: cottage style, with adequate space, indoor toilets, bathrooms and gardens, which raised costs. Also the Treasury imposed strict expenditure controls and Labour prioritized building directly related to economic development, including factories and housing for essential workers, especially in export industries. Hence, also the failure to build schools and hospitals and constraints on the rebuilding of towns devastated by severe bombing, including Coventry. Reconstruction began but plans were scaled back and rebuilding was more conventional than planners had hoped.[32] Still, in 1951 in England and Wales, 1.8 million households shared a dwelling compared with

32 N. Tiratsoo, *Reconstruction, Affluence and Labour Politics. Coventry, 1945–1960* (London: Routledge, 1990); Junichi Hasigawa, *Replanning the Blitzed City Centre* (Buckingham: Open University Press, 1992).

1.9 million in 1931[33]; 37 per cent lacked access to a fixed bath; 8 per cent shared with another household; 8 per cent lacked a WC, 13 per cent shared.[34]

Health

Bevan's, arguably Labour's, greatest achievement was the National Health Service (NHS). He was a surprising appointment, lacking experience of health administration, though, growing up in South Wales, he had experienced ill-health and poor services in working-class communities. The NHS became law in 1946 and was implemented in 1948. It reorganized and improved coordination of existing services, nationalizing the voluntary hospitals and dental, optical and other ancillary services. All services became 'free at the point of delivery' for everyone, following long, often fraught, negotiations with the BMA. Bevan overcame the resistance of many senior consultants by 'stuffing their mouths with gold', as he put it, responding to their hostility to a salaried public service by agreeing to payment by fees based on numbers of patients and allowing continued lucrative private practice within NHS hospitals. Younger doctors were generally more supportive. There was also opposition, including from Herbert Morrison, who had headed the successful public health programme of the LCC, to the centralized structure which reduced the health powers of local government. Bevan wanted a national service ideally providing equal standards of care across the United Kingdom.[35]

The NHS transformed the lives of many people, especially working-class women who previously had least access to good medical care, providing universal free access to hospitals and GPs. Free access to undramatic but essential optical care and spectacles, dentistry and chiropody was transformative, especially for many older people. One doctor described a woman who was bed-ridden, apparently deaf and thought to be suffering from mild dementia. Once her corns were treated, impacted wax removed from her ears and her severe constipation cured she was active again.[36] It was no longer common for working-class people to have all their teeth extracted as a twenty-first birthday present to prevent future agony. The need for such services was underestimated and in the early years costs rose faster than anticipated. Despite impressive improvements in staffing and treatment, no new hospitals were built until the late 1950s, though repairs and reconstruction were unavoidable. Few promised health centres materialized because they required new building. The stigmatized area of mental healthcare lagged

33 A. H. Halsey (ed.), *Trends in British Society since 1900* (London: Macmillan, 1972), p. 302.

34 Ibid., p. 305.

35 John Campbell, *Nye Bevan. A Biography* (London: Hodder & Stoughton, 1987); Charles Webster, *The National Health Service. A Political History*, 2nd rev. edn (Oxford University Press, 2002).

36 Thane, *Old Age in English Society*, p. 446.

behind services for physical health, though 50 per cent of NHS beds in 1948 were occupied by mentally ill people.

National Insurance

The National Insurance Act 1946 transformed the social security system based, broadly, on Beveridge's recommendations. National Insurance was universalized to cover the whole employed population and the wives of insured men, providing flat-rate old age and widows' pensions, maternity and funeral benefits. Sickness and unemployment allowances were provided for those normally in paid work, as compensation for lost pay, plus payments for wives and children. Payments were funded by flat-rate contributions from workers and employers, subsidized by taxation. Labour, like Beveridge, stressed that benefits were a right, purchased through contributions, not 'hand-outs' from the state, but they were lower than Beveridge proposed. He recommended their introduction gradually over twenty years, to build up a sufficient fund to cover full subsistence-level payments and payment of unemployment and sickness allowances for the whole period of need. Labour was anxious to deliver its promises to voters. Higher pensions were paid immediately to mainly working-class contributors to the existing National Insurance scheme. New, generally better-off, entrants to the insurance system had to build up contributions for ten years. Unemployment benefits rose by 2s per week, sickness benefits by 8s, pensions by 16s, but, on Treasury insistence, to cut costs, they did not provide full subsistence.[37] In 1948, 495,000 pensioners needed means-tested supplements to their pension in order to survive, by 1951 this had risen to 767,000,[38] as Beveridge had never intended. For the first time the pension was conditional on retirement. Beveridge's proposal to pay higher pensions for each year of deferred retirement, to encourage longer working lives, was implemented minimally, with additional payments too small to encourage continued work. A proposal by James Griffiths, Minister for National Insurance, to link payments to an index of prices or wages was rejected by the Treasury. UK state pensions have never provided enough to live on. Sickness and unemployment payments were restricted to fixed time periods, then those still in need had also to apply for means-tested benefits. The maternity grant was raised from £4 to £12 10s and fourteen weeks' maternity benefit of 36s per week was payable to all mothers, including, for the first time, unmarried mothers.

Means-tested supplementary benefits were paid by the National Assistance Board (NAB), under the National Assistance Act 1948. This at last formally abolished the

37 Hugh Pemberton, 'Politics and Pensions in Post-War Britain', in H. Pemberton, P. Thane and N. Whiteside, *Britain's Pensions Crisis. History and Policy* (Oxford University Press/The British Academy, 2006), pp. 43–6.
38 Rodney Lowe, *The Welfare State in Britain since 1945* (London: Palgrave, 2005), p. 157.

Poor Law, replacing Public Assistance with a theoretically less stigmatizing, somewhat more generous, 'safety-net' for those whose insurance payments were inadequate or who could not fit into national insurance because they had not worked. These included single mothers who were now, minimally, supported at home, and not required to seek work while they had children at school. They and others on NAB benefits could receive additional payments, for example, for clothing or household equipment, when needed. Such support was basic but better than before.[39]

Postwar social insurance covered more people with higher benefits than before, but these soon slipped behind those of other west European countries. The system was rigid, regressive, since flat-rate contributions took more from the incomes of the lower- than the higher-paid, and only partially redistributive due to taxpayer contributions. Beveridge was disappointed and critical of the outcome, including the continued salience of means-testing.[40]

Social Services

Local authority social services expanded. A furore over the death in January 1945, due to neglect and cruelty, of a 12-year-old boy, Dennis O'Neill, placed in foster care by a Welsh local authority, influenced the 1946 report of the Curtis Committee on the Care of Children. This revealed the inadequacy of childcare arrangements, awkwardly divided between local authorities and the voluntary sector, unevenly across the country. The Children Act 1948 radically restructured children's services, bringing all childcare under local authority control. Authorities were obliged, and funded, to take into care all orphans and children under 17 whose parents were judged unfit to care for them, and to supervise adoption procedures, prohibiting informal adoption. They were required to supervise children in foster care and support them to age 17, through the transition to work.[41] Also in 1948 corporal punishment was abolished in the criminal justice system.

Local authorities were required to support unmarried mothers and their children, assisting them to stay together when possible. They might fund voluntary organizations for this and other care work, including for older and disabled people, but must supervise and control them. But, again, there was no new building and people needing institutional care, whom authorities were obliged to shelter, were housed in former workhouses, the only available buildings, if there were no places in voluntary institutions. Residential and domiciliary 'social' care, provided by voluntary organizations

39 Thane and Evans, *Sinners?* pp. 106–9.
40 Harris, *Beveridge*, pp. 451–3.
41 J. Keating, *A Child for Keeps. A History of Adoption in England, 1918–45* (London: Palgrave, 2009), pp. 190–4.

or local authorities required means-tested payments, unlike free healthcare, creating confusion, especially for older and disabled people for whom the dividing line between 'health' and 'social' needs was often unclear, a problem still unresolved in the twenty-first century.

Voluntary action remained a vital source of social services. Voluntary organizations faltered initially, uncertain of their roles as state welfare expanded and, partly as a result, donations declined. Many Labour supporters were hostile to 'patronizing', 'demeaning' charity, from past experience, but Attlee, a former lecturer in social work at LSE with experience of East End voluntary work, was not. Also he and his colleagues realized that public funds could not meet all needs in the current economic circumstances and encouraged collaboration between statutory and voluntary services, especially at local level.[42] Existing voluntary organizations found new roles, including advising clients on negotiating new statutory services, and new organizations emerged as gaps were revealed in the welfare system. Among others, the National Association for Mental Health (now MIND) formed in 1946 to campaign for improved services for mentally ill people.[43]

Legal Aid

An important new service, legal aid, assisted poorer people to access the law. The Legal Aid and Advice Act 1949 was described by the Attorney-General as 'the charter of the little man to the British courts of justice without question of their wealth or ability to pay',[44] but it, too, was introduced slowly to limit costs. Aid, means-tested (by the NAB) to finance court proceedings, including for divorce, was introduced in October 1950, but not until the 1960s was it available for representation in magistrates' courts, including for childcare proceedings. Legal advice was not state-funded until 1959, and then was limited. Free advice was widely available from voluntary Citizens' Advice Bureaux and from law centres established by some local authorities and voluntary bodies.[45]

42 N. Deakin and J. Davis Smith, 'Labour, Charity and Voluntary Action. The Myth of Hostility', in Matthew Hilton and James McKay (eds), *The Ages of Voluntarism. How We Got to the Big Society* (Oxford University Press/ The British Academy, 2011), pp. 69–93.

43 Tanya Evans, 'Stopping the Poor Getting Poorer. The Establishment and Professionalization of Poverty NGOs, 1945–95', in N. Crowson, M. Hilton and J. MacKay (eds), *NGOs in Contemporary Britain. Non-State Actors in Society and Politics since 1945* (London: Palgrave, 2009), pp. 147–63; Pat Thane, 'Voluntary Action in Britain since Beveridge', in M. Oppenheimer and N. Deakin (eds), *Beveridge and Voluntary Action in Britain and the Wider British World* (Manchester University Press, 2011), pp. 121–34.

44 Cretney, *Family Law*, p. 316; *Hansard*, House of Commons, *Debates*, 15 December 1948, vol. 459, col .1221.

45 Cretney, *Family Law*, pp. 314–18; R. I. Morgan, 'The Introduction of Civil Legal Aid in England and Wales, 1914–1949', *Twentieth Century British History* 5(1) (1994): pp. 38–76.

Disability

Labour implemented another wartime measure, the Disabled Persons' Employment Act, 1944. Disabled adults had been neglected by the state, apart from small payments to contributors to National Health Insurance and the means-tested pension provided in 1920 for blind people from age 50. The 1944 Act arose from Bevin's attempts to maximize the workforce by including people disabled in the war, beginning in 1941 with retraining schemes. The Act required employers of more than twenty workers to take, at normal pay, at least 3 per cent from a new, voluntary, Disabled Persons Register for those fit to work as effectively as non-disabled people, not in treatment under the Mental Health Act or of 'habitual bad character'. Employers did not comply enthusiastically and it was not rigorously enforced. After the war, Labour established rehabilitation centres and vocational training for disabled people, overwhelmingly male, and workshops for those unfit for regular work. From 1946, state-subsidized Remploy factories employed only disabled people, producing a variety of goods, some continuing until privatization in 2013. The needs of people too disabled to work were met by the NHS, social services and the NAB. The 1944 Act was presented as equalizing opportunities and protecting disabled people from stigma. It greatly helped a minority of moderately disabled people, but did little to improve opportunities for others.[46]

Outcomes

For all their limitations, Labour's social policies provided greater security for most people, at last a 'national minimum', a real if inadequate 'safety net' preventing the poorest falling too far behind the rising living standards of the majority. Poverty and inequality declined but were not eliminated. The reforms were only minimally redistributive and greatly benefited many middle-class people, especially the lower middle classes on limited incomes who could not easily afford private education, healthcare or other benefits. They tended to use health services more than poorer people and their children stayed in education longer. This was not an unintended consequence of universalism but conscious Labour strategy to win better-off voters while improving conditions for poorer people, recognizing that taxpayers would more willingly fund services benefiting themselves than support the poorest. Labour hoped to remain in government long enough to expand social welfare as the economy recovered, as the Swedish Social Democrats constructed a comprehensive welfare state during their

---

46 Helen Bolderson, 'The Origins of the Disabled Persons Employment Quota and its Symbolic Significance', *Journal of Social Policy* 9(2) (1980): 160–86; Jameel Hampton, *Disability and the Welfare State in Britain. Changes in Perceptions and Policy, 1948–1979* (Bristol: Policy Press, 2016).

long rule from 1931 to 1976. Labour's social policies of 1945–51 were intended as a beginning not an end.

Full Employment

National 'welfare' gained most from the achievement of full employment, certainly fuller employment for longer than at any time in modern British history. Unemployment hardly rose above 500,000 before 1951, mostly due to normal turnover, except in the crisis of 1947 when it reached 1,916,000 at the height of the freeze in February.[47] Beveridge defined full employment as allowing for 3 per cent 'frictional' unemployment due to turnover.[48] Pockets of above average unemployment survived, particularly on Merseyside and Clydeside, along with labour shortages in some areas and occupations. With work more readily available, workers fled poor conditions in dangerous industries, including mining. Given its importance, the government tried to attract workers by reducing the standard working week from six days to five and sanctioning housebuilding in mining districts. Miners' meat ration was doubled in 1946.[49]

Full employment and labour shortages drew attention to productivity, which was comparatively low, creating pressure to work more intensively which workers did not always welcome. The ageing dock labour force resisted de-casualization and longer hours.[50] Married women who were the traditional backbone of cotton textile production needed extra pay less urgently when their husbands had regular work. Both industries were short of labour. The labour market shrank when the school-leaving age rose and National Service was introduced in 1947. Eighteen-year-old males were conscripted into the armed services in peacetime – unprecedented in British history – for eighteen months, extended to two years in 1950 and continuing until 1961,[51] to maintain the size of the British army and its capacity to respond to crises, including colonial independence movements, at minimum cost. Many workers fled austerity and cold, particularly to Australia, encouraged by the 'ten pound Poms' scheme: from 1947 ex-servicemen migrated free, other British adults for £10, children £5. Between 1945 and 1950, 175,138 UK citizens settled in Australia, considerably more than in any other country. Australia encouraged migration in order to remain 'white', preferably of

---

47 Butler and Butler, *Twentieth-Century British Political Facts*, p. 400.
48 William Beveridge, *Full Employment in a Free Society* (London: Allen & Unwin, 1944), p. 21.
49 Zweiniger-Bargielowska, *Austerity Britain*, p. 25.
50 N. Whiteside, 'Towards a Modern Labour Market? State Policy and the Transformation of Employment', in B. Conekin, F. Mort and C. Waters (eds), *Moments of Modernity. Reconstructing Britain, 1945–1964* (London: Rivers Oram, 1999), pp. 76–95; G. Phillips and N. Whiteside, *Casual Labour and the Unemployment Question in the Port Transport Industry, 1880–1970* (Oxford University Press, 1985).
51 Richard Vinen, *National Service. Conscription in Britain, 1945–63* (London: Allen Lane, 2014).

'British stock', and it was concerned about its low birth rate.[52] The Ministry of Labour tried to encourage older workers to delay retirement and employers to keep them on, with little success. Few employers were persuaded that older workers were efficient and capable of learning new skills, despite strong evidence to the contrary.[53]

Women's Work

When Beveridge, Keynes and the politicians discussed 'full employment' they meant male employment. They did not necessarily oppose women working, but did not think it realistic to expect most women to work full-time all their adult lives. During the war, the government forecast a postwar labour shortage and planned to keep as many women at work as possible.[54] In 1943, 7.75 million women were employed, by 1947, 6 million. Many younger women gave up work after the war to start families, which the government encouraged in order to raise the birth rate. Mothers of young children experienced strong social pressure against taking employment and childcare was scarce. The Ministry of Labour encouraged older women to remain in or return to employment and many did, though rarely in conventionally male work. A strict gender division of labour revived. The expansion of social, health and education services created work judged suitable for women. The abolition of the marriage bar in most occupations – though it survived in banking until the 1960s and the diplomatic service until 1973 – increased opportunities. The social prohibition against middle-class married women's employment declined, while more working-class women chose to stay at home, at least while their children were small, as male employment and family incomes improved, often relieved to escape the double burden of work in and out of the home. A new, cross-class, pattern emerged of women employed until the birth of their first child, taking a break for child-rearing, returning later, often part-time.[55] This was easier to combine with domestic responsibilities and suited employers who were not required to give part-timers paid holidays or other benefits. Employed women increased by 300,000 each year between 1947 and 1950, 11.5 per cent worked part-time in 1951, mostly 'returners' aged over 40.[56]

Equal pay remained rare despite continuous campaigns. The Royal Commission on Equal Pay in 1946[57] provided the most comprehensive official description and analysis

---

52 A. J. Hammerton and A. Thomson, *Ten Pound Poms. Australia's Invisible Migrants* (Manchester University Press, repr. 2012).

53 Thane, 'The Debate on the Declining Birth Rate', p. 301.

54 Pat Thane, 'Towards Equal Opportunities? Women in Britain since 1945', in T. Gourvish and A. O' Day (eds), *Britain since 1945* (London: Macmillan, 1991), pp. 191–5.

55 Ibid.

56 V. Beechey and T. Perkins, *A Matter of Hours* (Minneapolis, MN: University of Minnesota Press, 1987), p. 16.

57 See p. 169.

in the whole century of women's unequal position in the labour market and the attitudes of the major interest groups. It acknowledged the problem of defining 'equal pay': 'equal pay for equal work' evaded the problem that most of the labour market was gender-divided and work defined as 'male' was normally higher paid than that labelled 'female'. It proved difficult to judge whether 'male' work genuinely required more skill or carried greater responsibility, since workers, employers and unions were reluctant to clarify such points. There were clear differences between the public and private sectors. In the former men and women commonly did identical work for different pay and skills and levels of responsibility were transparent, women campaigned more actively for equal pay (especially now their other bugbear, the marriage bar, was removed), were a large part of its expanding workforce, strongly unionized and generally supported by their unions, even those with majority male membership.[58]

Pay inequality varied across occupations and from place to place with no clear rationale. Again, it was clearer in the public sector, where the pay gap averaged 50 per cent at lower levels, 10 per cent at higher levels, but in 1950 women held only 7 per cent of higher, administrative grade, civil service posts.[59] The Treasury insisted that equal pay in the public sector was unaffordable. The Council of Women Civil Servants, representing women in the higher grades, wondered why the Treasury did not economize by employing more women, since they were so much cheaper.[60] Recruitment and promotion were as unequal as pay. In most professions, including university teaching, architecture, medicine and in Parliament, equal pay formally existed but few women were appointed and even fewer promoted to the highest levels. In 1946, of 44,341 doctors, 7,198 were female; 325 of 9,375 architects; about 164 among 17,100 solicitors.[61]

Most women worked in the private sector, where the gender division of labour was normally strict, pay and grading systems often obscure and women less unionized. On average, women in industry earned 47 per cent less than men. The Commission concluded that this was partly because women were often younger than male workers, but other differences were hard to explain.[62] Representatives of private sector employers claimed to favour equal pay – where men and women did precisely equal work, which was unfortunately rare because, they believed, men were more skilled, efficient, flexible, reliable, committed, physically stronger and had family responsibilities. They argued that raising female pay would raise prices and undermine exports and evaded suggestions from Commissioners that in wartime women had proved as productive as men in the same work.

58 Glew, *Gender, Rhetoric and Regulation*, pp. 150–9.
59 Ibid.
60 Ibid.
61 *Report of the Royal Commission on Equal Pay* (London: HMSO, 1946), p. 43.
62 Ibid., p. 163.

The TUC supported equal pay for 'equivalent' work and advocated greater access to training for women. Unions no longer defended male claims to a 'family wage' after family allowances were introduced, but they opposed legislation for equal pay and government intervention in wage bargaining, preferring collective bargaining and job evaluation to establish equivalence between male and female work. Women's organizations, including the Fawcett Society, the National Council of Women, WIs and the Fabian Women's Group unequivocally criticized inequalities at work.

After extensively surveying pay inequality, the Commission concluded that it was generally based on unproven assumptions about women workers and the oversupply of women for the limited work open to them. It made a strong argument for 'equal pay for work of equal value', but concluded that implementation in the near future could harm the economy. Three of the four female members (the Principal of Somerville College, Oxford, a trade unionist and a company director – the fourth, the Countess of Limerick, was a Conservative who rarely attended; there were four male members plus a male chair, the judge Sir Cyril Asquith) signed a minority report stressing the clear evidence of unjustifiable inequality revealed by the Commission and supporting mandatory equal pay.

Labour was supposedly committed by a vote of its annual conference in 1944 to equal pay for equivalent work, and in 1947 the conference supported equal pay throughout the public service by a large majority. In Parliament, members of all parties supported this but, repeatedly until 1951, Labour spokesmen stated they supported the principle but, until the economy strengthened, implementation would delay recovery. The Equal Pay Campaign Committee was reinvigorated and with other organizations held large public meetings and wrote to MPs urging equal pay in the public sector.[63] Thelma Cazalet Keir, who lost her seat in 1945, led a march to Parliament chanting 'we want equal pay now'.[64] The government was unmoved and demands continued until the Conservatives conceded equal pay in the public sector in 1955.[65]

Immigration

The labour shortage forced employers, including the government, to look abroad. The first resort was always Ireland, still poorer than Britain. Irish immigration was particularly encouraged by the UK government from 1944, especially of women, always a high proportion of Irish immigrants, to fill shortages of nurses, other hospital workers and teachers. From 1946, 50,000–60,000 Irish women and men entered Britain to work

63 Glew, *Gender, Rhetoric and Regulation*, pp. 149–58.
64 Beaumont, *Housewives and Citizens*, pp. 151–2.
65 See p. 227; Thane, 'Towards Equal Opportunities?' pp. 184–91.

each year,[66] but they could not fill all the vacancies. About 120,000 Polish ex-servicemen stayed and worked in Britain after the war, and some Italian former POWs.[67]

The next option was continental Europe. At the end of the war in Europe over 6 million people were homeless refugees in the allied zones, having fled invasion or been transported by the Nazis to concentration camps or for forced labour, living in 'Displaced Persons' (DPs) camps mainly in Austria and Germany. Offering employment in Britain reduced the costs of supporting them in camps and, since they were not British nationals, the Ministry of Labour could control their terms and places of employment, directing their labour as it could not British or Irish workers in peacetime. From 1946, female DPs were brought to Britain initially mainly for domestic work in the health services. From 1947, men were encouraged especially to work in mining. They were known officially as 'European Volunteer Workers' and were recruited in the camps by Ministry of Labour officials. They often came reluctantly, feeling they had no option, hoping to return to their home countries, though many settled permanently.[68]

The scheme ended in January 1949, largely because DPs returned home or settled elsewhere and the supply dried up. By then, 57,000 men and 20,000 women had worked in Britain, about 40 per cent of the women in domestic work in public institutions, 50 per cent in textile factories, and around 50 per cent of the men in agriculture, 20 per cent in mining. The largest group (16,210 men, 4,720 women) were Ukrainian.[69] They were generally housed in hostels or other supervised dwellings, allocated to specific employment, often well below their skill levels and paid less than British co-workers, expected to stay for three years, register with the police as aliens and report regularly.[70]

Next, about 10,000 women were recruited from former enemy countries, Germany and Austria, where work was scarce. This aroused particular resentment in the West Indies, where unemployment and poverty continued. The government was criticized, vociferously, for recruiting workers from former enemy countries rather than British people from colonies that had fought with Britain in the war. The Ministry of Labour was reluctant to recruit West Indians, due, they said, to the costs of transportation and doubts about their 'suitability'. They were concerned that, as British citizens, West Indians could not be controlled as the Europeans were, though nor could they be prevented from entering Britain if they chose. Officials also expressed concern about racism, though this lurked within their own assumptions. It had not declined. In 1948,

66 Linda McDowell, *Working Lives. Gender, Migration and Employment in Britain, 1945–2007* (Oxford: Wiley-Blackwell, 2013), p. 79.

67 Ibid., pp. 83–94.

68 Ibid., pp. 71–94. Linda McDowell, *Migrant Women's Voices. Talking about Life and Work in the UK since 1945* (London: Bloomsbury, 2016).

69 McDowell, *Working Lives*, p. 78.

70 D. Kay and R. Miles, *Refugees or Migrant Workers? European Volunteer Workers in Britain, 1946–1951* (London: Routledge, 1992).

in Liverpool with its established black and Asian population, an Indian restaurant was violently attacked, after which the police arrested a black seaman, followed by further demonstrations and attacks on hostels and cafes frequented by black people, while the police claimed 'there isn't any colour question in Liverpool'.[71]

Unemployment at home drove West Indians abroad, many to the United States. In June 1948, 492 Jamaican men and two women reached Britain in HMS *Windrush*, heralding major colonial immigration. The labour shortage drove the Ministry of Labour eventually to recruit from the West Indies, first, in 1950, women from Barbados to work as hospital domestics, then men to staff public transport. From its foundation, the NHS depended upon immigrant, mainly colonial, labour and expertise, including doctors, generally recruited into lower status areas of medicine, including geriatrics and mental health. About 1,000 men and women arrived from the Caribbean in 1951. If not recruited by British officials for specific occupations, they found work, often at lower levels than their qualifications and experience merited, men mainly in construction, manufacturing, public transport, labouring or street cleaning. Women worked in manufacturing, especially textiles and clothing, transport, many as nurses or aides in the NHS, though they were discouraged from training as higher-status State Registered Nurses.[72] They supplied essential labour but often had difficulty finding accommodation and experienced racism, for which some were prepared by their wartime experience in Britain.[73]

The Family and Population

The population was changing in other ways. Before the Second World War, for centuries significant numbers of people had never married.[74] In the 1931 Census 9 per cent of adult men had never been married and 15 per cent of women. The reasons are uncertain. Women were still a majority of the population but this cannot wholly explain non-marriage among women, still less among men. After the war there was a more even gender balance due to rising male life expectancy and fewer men emigrating alone, and marriage became almost universal. Ages at first marriage fell to historically low levels from a norm over the previous 300 years of 27 for men, 25 for women, to 22.6 for women, 24.6 for men in 1971.[75] Probably, full employment and rising living

71 Kynaston, *Austerity Britain*, p. 292.

72 McDowell, *Migrant Women's Voices*, pp. 109–28.

73 Colin Holmes, 'Immigration', in T. Gourvish and A. O' Day (eds), *Britain since 1945* (London: Macmillan, 1991), pp. 209–18; M. Phillips and T. Phillips, *Windrush. The Irresistible Rise of Multi-Cultural Britain* (London: HarperCollins, 1998).

74 E. A. Wrigley and R. Schofield, *The Population History of England, 1541–1871. A Reconstruction* (Cambridge University Press, 1989), pp. 424–8.

75 Lewis, *The End of Marriage?* p. 30.

standards enabled more people to marry at earlier ages. Marriages also lasted longer because they started earlier, life expectancy rose and divorce was still difficult. This has been recalled, nostalgically, as a golden age of 'traditional' long, stable marriages. In fact, it was historically new and unusual in number and length of marriages.

Expectations of 'happy' marriage perhaps rose also, perhaps unrealistically, with higher living standards and exposure to media portrayals of idealized homes and relationships, though not all marriages were contented or lasting.[76] Divorces in England and Wales rose from 16,075 in 1941–5 to 38,382 in 1951; in Scotland from 7,065 in 1940–5 to 12,175 in 1946–50.[77] Divorces were still few and harder to obtain in Northern Ireland. In England and Wales legal aid enabled more people to divorce,[78] but the consent of both partners was required, not always forthcoming, and the acceptable grounds remained restrictive. There were 26,835 applications for separation orders in England and Wales from 1950 to 1954 compared with 14,382 between 1930 and 1934.[79] The numbers of unmarried, cohabiting couples remained unknown, but enough were suspected for such 'illicit unions' to remain a prominent argument for divorce reform.[80]

Births, unexpectedly, continued to rise in the so-called 'baby boom'. Average family size remained stable, at around two children. More births were due to more marriages not larger families. In 1951, 14 per cent of all births within marriage were premaritally conceived,[81] more than before the war, suggesting that postwar Britain was less sexually repressed than is sometimes believed. Younger marriage ages owed something to 'shotgun marriages' precipitated by pregnancy, while births registered as 'illegitimate' in England and Wales fell from 6.6 per cent in 1946 to 4.8 per cent in 1951.[82] Infant mortality remained low. But pessimism about the birth rate continued.[83] In 1945 an MO survey concluded that there was danger of further decline – in the wrong families:

> Have we to rely on the improvident and wishful-thinking for the perpetuation of the race? …
> For the eugenic future something … is needed which will make the thoughtful breed as much
> as the thoughtless …[84]

News of Nazi experiments had not suppressed eugenic thinking in Britain. In 1948, PEP produced the dramatic, strongly eugenist, *Population Policy in Great Britain*, making similar points and advocating higher family allowances to boost the birth rate,

---

76 C. Langhamer, *The English in Love. The Intimate Story of an Emotional Revolution* (Oxford University Press, 2013).

77 Halsey and Webb, *British Social Trends*, p. 62.

78 See p. 200.

79 Kiernan et al., *Lone Motherhood*, p. 47.

80 See pp. 25, 100.

81 Kiernan et al., *Lone Motherhood*, p. 35.

82 Wimperis, *The Unmarried Mother*, table 4.

83 See pp. 136–7.

84 Mass Observation, *Britain and her Birth Rate*, pp. 206–7.

especially of 'quality' babies. This was supported by Eva Hubback, feminist and long-time campaigner for family allowances, in *The Population of Britain* (1947) a successful Pelican paperback. She recognized that the threatened population decline could be offset by immigration, but argued that this would be 'a counsel of despair, as it is a sign that we have failed to maintain the vitality and spirit to keep our community alive'.[85]

The Royal Commission on Population, appointed in 1944, reported in 1949. It sought to calm panic but expressed concern about future births. It accepted that an important reason for fewer prewar births was the 'emancipation of women': 'the more independent status and wider interests of women today, which are part of the ideals of the community as a whole, are not compatible with repeated and excessive child-bearing'.[86] It recommended higher family allowances and improved social services to help women combine childcare with greater freedom. It also warned of the risk that 'a disproportionately small number of the nation's children come from the higher income groups', creating a 'tendency towards lowering the average level of intelligence of the nation'.[87] It pointed to the labour shortage and the likelihood that a low birth rate would necessitate extensive immigration from outside Europe, while 'the rate of increase of some Oriental peoples has undergone a marked acceleration' as that of Europe and the United States fell:

> the sources of supply of suitable immigrants to Great Britain are limited, as is also the capacity of a fully established society like ours to absorb immigrants of alien race and religion.[88]

The postwar New Jerusalem would be no cultural melting-pot. The Commission opposed restricting emigration of 'people of British stock' for this 'has done much to maintain the strength and solidarity of the Commonwealth and our many ties of sympathy with the USA', and 'the consequence for Britain's economic future and for her place in the world might be serious'.[89] It recommended further study of migration, stressing that demography 'might be decisive in its effects on the prestige and influence of the West ... [and] ... the maintenance and extension of western values, ideas and culture'.[90] The Commission expressed some lasting fears but offered no solutions.

Olympics

More cheerfully, Britain hosted the 1948 Olympic Games, the first since 1936 in Nazi Germany. The International Olympic Committee wanted another Games as soon after

---

85 Hubback, *Population of Britain*, p. 246.
86 *Report of the Royal Commission on Population*, Cmd. 7695 (London: HMSO, 1948–9), p. 41.
87 Ibid., p. 4.
88 Ibid., pp. 124–6.
89 Ibid., p. 125.
90 Ibid., p. 134.

the war as possible to signal a return to peacetime normality and international cooperation. London was invited to host it as the least damaged major European city. Following
the financial crisis of 1947, it was labelled the 'Austerity Olympics'. The government
supported it but provided little funding and asked other nations to contribute food
and equipment. No new stadia were built: Wembley football stadium was converted
for athletics, and the king and queen opened the Games there in July. Male athletes
were housed in barracks around London, females in colleges. Their food supplies were
rationed, though at the more generous level for workers in heavy industries, supplemented with unrationed, readily available, whale meat. Bedding was provided but competitors had to bring their own towels and many brought food.

The weather was good: an unpredictable heatwave followed the frozen winter. The
British team trained at Butlin's, not very successfully, winning only three gold medals
and coming twelfth in the medals table. But the Games were judged a success in the circumstances. Japan and Germany were excluded and the USSR stayed away, but a record
fifty-nine nations participated, crowds turned out, and the Games made a small profit,
created employment and a positive atmosphere. It was the first Olympics shown on TV,
though with few viewers: in June 1948, there were 50,000 TV licences and 100,000 by
March 1949.[91]

Foreign Affairs

This successful international event failed to dispel concern about Britain's place in the
world. There were hopes, particularly in the Foreign Office, that wartime cooperation
between the USSR, the United States and the United Kingdom would continue, with
the United Kingdom unavoidably the junior partner but still a major international
player. Attlee and, particularly, Bevin were strongly anti-communist, as were most of
the Labour Party, but did not want an open breach with the USSR. This was hard to
avoid as Soviet ambitions became clear and the Cold War dominated international
relations.

Bevin was a prime mover in creating the North Atlantic Treaty Organization (NATO)
in 1949, binding the United Kingdom, the United States, Canada and European allies
against aggression towards any member state. Its construction required considerable
diplomatic skill, especially to overcome the reluctance of the United States, which
threatened to retreat again into isolation. Also, pro-Jewish forces in the United States
were highly critical of Britain's role in Palestine and there was continuing US hostility to
British colonialism. These tensions led Labour, secretly, from 1947 to develop an independent nuclear 'deterrent', for which Britain had the expertise since British scientists

91 Kynaston, *Austerity Britain*, p. 305; Janie Hampton, *Austerity Olympics* (London: Aurum, updated edn. 2012).

had contributed considerably to developing the atomic bomb. Britain was within range of a Soviet nuclear attack as the United States was not. The extension of Communist control of Eastern Europe, with the takeover of Czechoslovakia in February 1948 and a blockade of Berlin in June, shifted US policy, assisted by Britain's withdrawal from Palestine and Indian independence. Britain and the United States flew supplies into Berlin until the blockade ended in May 1949. The North Atlantic Treaty was signed in April 1949.[92]

The US alliance was not popular throughout the Labour Party, particularly among the small pro-Russian faction and the larger number, strong in the parliamentary party, who preferred an international 'third force', independent of the United States or the USSR, led by Britain.[93] But as an 'iron curtain … descended across the Continent', as Churchill memorably put it in March 1946, then, in 1949, the Communists proclaimed victory in China and the USSR announced its development of atomic weapons, hopes dwindled of an alternative to an ideologically bifurcated world. When communist North Korea invaded non-communist, but undemocratic, South Korea in June 1950, fear of the onward march of communism impelled Western intervention, formally a UN operation, but US led. British troops landed in Korea in August 1950 and remained for the three years of the Korean War. Other West European countries, especially France, saw closer European cooperation as the key to future peace. Bevin seemed supportive but the government prioritized its links with the United States and the Commonwealth. The Cabinet unanimously refused to join the European Coal and Steel Community – the precursor to the European Union – when invited in 1950.

Indian Independence and Beyond

In the Commonwealth the Indian independence movement continued. A mission led by Cripps in 1946 to discuss limited independence got nowhere, while resistance to British rule grew along with tensions between the Muslim and Hindu communities, causing riots in northern India in 1946 with hundreds of thousands of deaths. Muslims had grown politically stronger during the war and had supported Britain, while Congress had been alienated by the incarceration of its supporters. Attlee quickly announced support for full independence, with which he had long sympathized, and agreed partition between predominantly Hindu (India) and Muslim (Pakistan) states. A new viceroy was appointed, Admiral Lord Mountbatten, former allied commander in South East Asia, socialite member of the royal family, who persuaded London that speedy British departure was essential to avoid chaos and more deaths. He hurried

92 Alan Bullock, *Ernest Bevin. Foreign Secretary 1945–51* (Oxford University Press, 1985).
93 Jonathan Schneer, *Labour's Conscience. The Labour Left, 1945–51* (London: Routledge, 1988).

Indian politicians into agreeing partition, which Muslims supported far more than Hindus. Independence in August 1947 was accompanied by bloody ethnic conflict, about a million deaths, many more refugees and much personal anguish as the subcontinent was divided. India and Pakistan became independent republics and Dominions within the Commonwealth.[94]

Burmese nationalism also remained strong. In December 1946, it was offered independence. This drew the predictable wrath of Churchill who thundered in Parliament, '"Scuttle" is the only word that can be applied'.[95] In July 1947, the moderate nationalist leader, Aung Sang, and most of the cabinet were assassinated. Under their anti-British successors, in January 1948 Burma left the Commonwealth. In 1948, Ceylon, anxious to avoid domination by India, became a Dominion. Communism surfaced in Malaya, mainly among the large Chinese population. Britain imposed a 'state of emergency' in June 1948, which continued for five years, requiring substantial commitments of troops and expenditure; Malaya's rubber and tin resources were too important to lose.[96]

In Ireland, in 1948, Éamon de Valera was defeated by a coalition dominated by republicans hostile to Britain. In September 1948, the new Taoiseach, John Costello of Fine Gael, announced, unexpectedly, that Ireland would leave the Commonwealth. The other Dominions decided the Irish decision must be respected, but that links between Ireland, the United Kingdom and the Commonwealth should remain. An unusual compromise was agreed: in April 1949, Ireland left the Commonwealth, but Irish citizens retained full nationality, including voting, rights in Britain and trade privileges in the Commonwealth.

Labour worked hard to hold the Commonwealth together as a unique international, multi-racial, group of independent nations, a focus of resistance to Communism, especially as it spread in Asia. It ceased to be the 'British' Commonwealth and the Dominions Office became the Commonwealth Relations Office. From 1947, the government sought planned progress of remaining colonies towards orderly transfers of power to stable, pro-British governments. The British Nationality Act 1948 enabled each Dominion to determine who qualified for its citizenship, all colonial citizens remaining automatically British, but as 'Commonwealth citizens' escaping subjection to the crown. Australia could now exclude 'non-white' Commonwealth citizens. To assist transitions to independence, the Colonial Development and Welfare Act, 1945, aimed to reassure restive colonies and improve their economic and social conditions in preparation for self-rule, providing £120 million for ten years of planned development.

94 Brown, 'India', pp. 421–46.
95 William Roger Louis, 'The Dissolution of the British Empire', in Judith M. Brown and William Roger Louis (eds), *The Oxford History of the British Empire, vol. IV:. The Twentieth Century* (Oxford University Press, 1999), pp. 337–8.
96 Ibid., pp. 329–56.

Roads, houses, hospitals and universities were constructed amid Conservative criticisms of government 'waste', though still too few to meet the need. Development Acts in 1949 and 1950 went further. The poorest colonies gained least and too many of their economies remained dependent on a narrow range of products, but there was some reduction in international inequalities despite tight UK finances.

In 1948, Britain withdrew from Palestine, in a bloodbath, as the Arab–Israeli struggle intensified. Britain was attacked for refusing entry to Jewish refugees for fear of Arab hostility. Revelations about the extermination camps increased Jewish demands for an independent homeland, with strong international support especially from the United States. A Jewish rebellion erupted in October 1945, with bombings, sabotage and assassinations, seeking Arab–Jewish partition, rejecting the British aim of a bi-national state. Attlee was eager to withdraw, amid antisemitic riots in Manchester and Liverpool in April 1947 following the hanging of two British servicemen in Palestine, and a revival of antisemitism in east London. The UN supported partition, arousing further violence. Britain could see no route to a peaceable solution, so relinquished the mandate and withdrew from Palestine in May 1948. A separate state of Israel was immediately declared. Arabs refused to recognize it and a 'War of Independence' continued until 1949 when ceasefires were followed by Israel extending its territory, evicting Arab residents, and long-continuing tension.[97]

In the other Middle East mandates Britain sought partnerships, offering investment, development aid and technical assistance in return for treaties guaranteeing its interests, mainly defensive, particularly against the USSR, and protecting its access to oil. By 1950, British companies were prominent controllers of this increasingly important resource. Britain dominated Iran until 1951, when the Iranian government nationalized its oil resources, partly owned by the UK government. In 1953, a US- and UK-inspired coup toppled the nationalist Iranian premier, Mohammed Mussadeq, and restored Western control of oil, with ownership of the Anglo-Iranian Oil Company now shared between the United States and the United Kingdom. The Shah of Iran, who connived in the coup, began a period of personal rule and repression which continued until he was overthrown in 1979.

General Election, 1950

The election due in 1950 took place in February. Labour stood on its record, making few new promises. Its leaders were ageing and weary and few younger people had been brought into prominent roles. The party manifesto, *Labour Believes in Britain*,

97 Anthony Clayton, 'Imperial Defence and Security, 1900–1968', Judith M. Brown and William Roger Louis (eds), *The Oxford History of the British Empire, vol. IV: The Twentieth Century* (Oxford University Press, 1999), pp. 298–9.

was largely drafted by Morrison, promising nationalization of sugar, cement and water supply. A swing against Labour was expected as continued rationing, controls and high taxes alienated many middle-class voters, most vociferously members of the British Housewives' League, but it was a smaller, less representative organization than its promoters in the popular press suggested.[98] An MO survey in 1949 concluded that most middle-class women thought continued rationing necessary for economic growth.[99] The Conservatives encouraged anti-austerity sentiment, though they too ran a low-key campaign promising no dramatic changes, not even ending rationing. To win women voters, they promised equal pay in the public sector, more housebuilding and higher living standards. Labour stressed the benefits to women and their families of the NHS, better education, full employment and price controls.

Labour was well organized. Individual party membership rose to 729,000 in 1949 while union affiliated membership almost doubled. The Conservative Party did not reveal membership but it probably also rose. Labour's introduction of boundary changes to reflect population change disadvantaged it by increasing the number of suburban seats. Local election results were ominous: Labour lost control of Birmingham, Glasgow and Manchester in 1947, and in 1949 of the LCC, Bristol, Leicester, Newcastle and Wolverhampton. Labour's General Election vote rose to 13.26 million, but it held only 315 seats; the Conservatives gained 12.5 million votes and 298 seats, giving Labour an overall majority of five.[100] The turnout was 84 per cent, the highest of the century, though the press noted the lack of excitement, or even interest, in the election up to polling day.[101] The outcome suggested that electors were engaged and evenly divided. Labour held its working-class vote, among women more firmly than men,[102] while losing middle-class voters, male and female.[103] An unprecedented 126 women stood, including twenty-eight Conservatives, forty-two Labour, forty-five Liberals. As ever, most were in unwinnable seats and even fewer were elected than in 1945: six Conservatives, fourteen Labour, one Liberal. The overall swing from Labour was 3.3 per cent, but in Wales it was only 0.3 per cent and in parts of rural England under 1 per cent.

Labour continued to govern, in a weak position, though the economy looked strong. Cripps had built up budget and balance of payments surpluses. Exports rose in value from £920 million in 1946 to £2,752 million in 1951, though imports rose faster, from

98 James Hinton, 'Militant Housewives. The British Housewives' League and the Attlee Government', *History Workshop Journal* 38 (1994): 129–56.
99 Mass Observation archive, File Report, September 1949.
100 Butler and Butler, *Twentieth-Century British Political Facts*, p. 236.
101 S. Fielding, P. Thompson and N. Tiratsoo, *England Arise! The Labour Party and Popular Politics in 1940s Britain* (Manchester University Press, 1995), pp. 193–4.
102 Hinton, 'Women and the Labour Vote', pp. 59–66.
103 Thorpe, *A History of the British Labour Party*, p. 131.

£1,082 million to £3,501 million. Britain's share of world trade grew.[104] But the Korean War from June 1950 increased defence costs. In October 1950, the fatally ill Cripps was replaced as Chancellor by 44-year-old Hugh Gaitskell, bringing some younger blood into the Cabinet, to the chagrin of the still younger Harold Wilson, also an economist. Gaitskell was previously Minister for Fuel and Power, ex-public school (Winchester, like Cripps) and Oxford, an academic economist who entered Parliament in 1945. A strong egalitarian, in his first budget in April 1951 he raised the standard rate of tax to 9s 6d in the £; the top rate was now 97.5 per cent. But he caused a crisis by introducing charges for false teeth and spectacles supplied through the NHS. Bevan – already opposed to increased defence spending and the close association with the United States – resigned, with two junior ministers, Harold Wilson, future Prime Minister, and John Freeman, Parliamentary Secretary at the Ministry of Supply and future TV personality. The crisis was poorly handled. Attlee was in hospital, Bevin had just died: the generation of wartime Labour ministers was fading, literally dying out.[105]

The Conservatives took advantage of the small majority to force votes which Labour MPs had to attend, however weary or sick, for fear of defeat, sapping morale. When Bevin became seriously ill, Attlee reluctantly promoted Morrison to the Foreign Office to appease the centre and right of the party. Morrison was inexperienced in foreign policy, past his best and handled poorly the Korean War, a series of spy scandals and the Iranian oil crisis. Labour could not risk new or contentious policies. Nationalization of iron and steel was implemented in February 1951 as arranged before the election. Labour did not nationalize sugar, faced by the industry's campaign featuring 'Mr Cube', brandishing the 'sword of free enterprise', on thousands of packets of sugar. Rationing and controls were gradually abolished while prices rose.

Celebrating Britain

Herbert Morrison gained more credit for the Festival of Britain. It was held in May–September 1951, and was his brainchild and major preoccupation, planned from 1947 as an international celebration of recovery from war and the beginning of a vibrant future, held on the centenary of the first Great Exhibition, modelled on that and subsequent international exhibitions. For financial reasons, it was scaled back to a national representation of Britain's past, present and future achievements. It was uncertain to the end whether it would be ready in time and forebodings that, if so, it would waste money and be very dull – doubts enthusiastically encouraged by the Beaverbrook press, silenced when it opened to popular acclaim. The most notable events were in London

104 Clarke, *Hope and Glory*, pp. 227–31.
105 Thorpe, *History of the British Labour Party*, pp. 132–4.

but there were eight official, government-funded exhibitions elsewhere in United Kingdom and arts festivals around the country. Two thousand towns and villages organized local history pageants, concerts, floral displays, sport, refurbished ancient buildings or developed recreation centres.

All forms of recreation were reviving, despite austerity. With little to buy in the shops, people sought solace in entertainment. West End theatres were packed and dance halls heaved. Cinema attendances hit an all-time peak of 1,635,000 in 1946. The major football clubs returned, the FA Cup resumed in 1945–6 and the Football League in 1946–7. BBC radio continued to offer entertainment, including comedy, as well as cultural education. That such education was needed, not just by 'the masses', was suggested by responses to an exhibition at the Victoria and Albert Museum in December 1945 of works by Picasso and Matisse. The novelist, Evelyn Waugh, announced that Picasso had as little artistic merit as an American crooner and art critics and other intellectuals were disparaging.[106]

The Festival celebrated the revival of leisure, pleasure, the arts and the economy, seeking to improve the 'quality of life', opening the best of culture to all, assisted by the Arts Council. This played a prominent role, sponsoring a two-month London Season of the Arts, focusing on British music, theatre, painting and literature, including 200 classical concerts, newly commissioned operas and ballets, and classic British plays. It financed twenty-three arts festivals, including established events at Stratford, Edinburgh and Aldeburgh and new ones in Liverpool, York, Norwich, Oxford, Cambridge and other towns. The Festival also aimed to show how industry could modernize its methods and output and encourage demand for modern products. The centrepiece was a large exhibition in a group of, often temporary (for reasons of economy), buildings in modern architectural style on the south bank of the Thames in central London. Most dramatic was the Dome of Discovery, displaying, under a huge aluminium saucer structure, innovations in science, technology and design. Scaled-down versions of the South Bank exhibits were transported around the country by a mobile Land Travelling Exhibition and to seaports by the festival ship, *Campania*. The one permanent structure on the South Bank was the Royal Festival Hall, created to bring music – jazz and popular music as well as classical, though the latter predominated – to a wide audience in a grand, modernist building. The Festival also offered more popular pleasures at the funfair and pleasure garden (modelled on eighteenth-century Vauxhall) in Battersea Park, London. This proved to be problematic: plagued by strikes it opened three weeks late, was mired in mud after heavy rain and lost money.

The Festival represented a vision of the new, modern Britain to which Labour aspired, promoting the expertise of architects, industrial designers, engineers, scientists, town

106 Kynaston, *Austerity Britain*, p. 96.

planners, all involved in its planning. It displayed what was judged to be fine design of everyday household goods, public buildings, neighbourhoods and homes, all in modernist style assisted by the Council of Industrial Design, established by Hugh Dalton as President of the Board of Trade in 1944 to democratize good design while rejuvenating British manufacturing. The Council arranged the 'Britain Can Make It' exhibition at the Victoria and Albert Museum in 1946 – renamed 'Britain Can't Have It' in the press, since so many of the goods were unobtainable, still in preparation or for export only. The British Industries Fair at Earl's Court from May 1951 carried this mission forward, in parallel with the Festival, since the goods were now more accessible, though rarely cheap.

Exhibitions displayed scientific achievements, including that in Glasgow celebrating the development of industrial power, culminating with atomic power. Another was held at the enlarged Science Museum in London. The Belfast exhibition showed how modern technology could transform agriculture. Another in poor, severely bombed Poplar, east London, presented modern, 'scientifically' built homes, schools, church and shopping centre, in a new estate named after local Labour hero, George Lansbury. Everywhere, the modern, scientific future was contrasted to a miserable past of old techniques and poorly built, ill-equipped buildings.[107]

Churchill and other Conservatives opposed the Festival as another example of socialist waste, and some intellectuals, including, again, Evelyn Waugh, disparaged its populism. 'Don't Let's Make Fun of the Fair' sang Noel Coward condescendingly. The conductor, Sir Thomas Beecham, called it a 'monumental piece of imbecility and iniquity'.[108] But the royal family remained eager to court popularity, and George VI opened the Festival at a service in St Paul's, followed by the inaugural concert in the Festival Hall, despite his failing health. Princesses Elizabeth and Margaret attended concerts and other events. Almost 8.5 million people visited the South Bank, attracted by the flowers, illuminations along the riverfront, fireworks, cafes and nightly entertainment as well as the official exhibition, escaping austerity gloom. The writer Michael Frayn sneered that 'the chips-and-peas type food provided by the catering firms failed signally to rise to the occasion',[109] though it may have been just what many visitors wanted.

Eight million visited Battersea Pleasure Gardens, but it produced a serious deficit, not helped by the decision, urged by the Churches and endorsed by Parliament, to close the Festival on Sundays, when most people were free to attend. Attendances were poor

107 B. Conekin, '"Here is the Modern World Itself". The Festival of Britain's Representations of the Future', in B. Conekin, F. Mort and C. Waters (eds), *Moments of Modernity. Reconstructing Britain, 1945–1964* (London: Rivers Oram, 1999), pp. 228–46.

108 Michael Frayn, 'Festival', in M. Sissons and P. French (eds), *Age of Austerity, 1945–1951* (Harmondsworth: Penguin, 1964), p. 340.

109 Ibid., p. 348.

in Edinburgh and disappointing in Glasgow. The total cost of the Festival was £10 million, within the estimate and at around 3s per head of population it was not excessive. Foreign visitors were attracted and spent money. A dense crowd, but not the dying king, attended the open-air closing concert on the South Bank, starring Gracie Fields. For many it was a welcome, well-deserved celebration.

General Election, 1951

Attlee hoped the Festival would build support for Labour when another election could not be long delayed. He chose October 1951. Labour claimed credit for the Festival's success and the improvements it celebrated. They stood on their record since 1945, contrasting it to Conservatism in the 1930s, arguing that it could best be trusted to maintain peace and full employment, reduce the cost of living, increase production and 'build a just society'. With good reason, given its achievement of full employment without serious inflation and bringing the economy close to balance despite the unavoidable crises of the years of transition from the war, while developing an exceptional if imperfect range of welfare measures.[110]

Labour's manifesto listed no further nationalizations but promised, vaguely, to take over businesses 'which fail the nation' and to 'associate the workers more closely with the administration of public industries and services'. A major issue again was housing. Labour promised to build more council homes, but its past failures lost working-class votes. The Conservatives were committed by a resolution of their party conference to build 300,000 houses a year. They promised to reverse Labour nationalization, rationing, controls and high taxes, claiming that they prevented economic growth, increased bureaucracy and eroded civil liberties. They jeered that shortages forced people to eat horse meat.

Labour's vote rose to just under 14 million and 49.2 per cent; the Conservatives' to 13.7 million and 48.68 per cent, but Labour won only 295 seats, the Conservatives 321, Liberals 6, having, for financial reasons, run 366 fewer candidates than in 1950. Again, the turnout was unusually high, 82.5 per cent, and the electorate was deeply, closely divided, though, again, journalists commented on the apparent lack of public interest.[111] Labour lost further middle-class support but took a higher share of the working-class vote than in 1950. Again, it was a victim of the first-past-the-post effect, winning a majority of votes but concentrated in too few seats. Among women voters it almost returned to the high 1945 level. Women MPs fell to seventeen: eleven Labour, six Conservatives. The Conservatives gained an overall majority of seventeen

110 Alec Cairncross, *Years of Recovery. British Economic Policy 1945–51* (London: Methuen, 1985).
111 Fielding et al., *England Arise!*, p. 200.

and formed a government. In an evenly divided society, split primarily by class, Labour above all lost much middle-class support it had gained in 1945, due mainly to continuing high taxation and restrictions on consumption.

Britain in 1951

Despite the setback of the Korean War, the economy had substantially recovered. This was not wholly due to Labour policies, but also to worldwide demand and the creation of international institutions to prevent recurrence of the interwar crises. The Bretton Woods agreement of 1944, much influenced by Keynes, introduced almost thirty years of financial stability in the world economy when nations agreed to hold their currencies at stable exchange rates against the US dollar, while the United States kept the dollar stable against gold, reinforcing US hegemony. Following Bretton Woods, the International Monetary Fund (IMF) was established to facilitate international economic cooperation and assist nations through financial difficulties.

Labour's commitment to full employment and economic development contributed substantially to the recovery. The increased efficiency of key industries and improved supply of resources, including coal and electricity, assisted profitability, while improvements in healthcare, education and social security enhanced the quality and efficiency of 'human capital', while improving everyday life and diminishing inequality. By 1951, investment had grown, output expanded, the balance of payments was restored, productivity improved and the private sector more closely regulated.[112] Labour's regional policy improved the prospects of regions which suffered before the war.[113] Average real earnings rose to 1951, raising living standards amid full employment, especially as controls and rationing were relaxed.

But Labour did not create the planned economy envisaged before and during the war, 80 per cent of business remained in private hands and business leaders resisted what they saw as government 'interference', especially when they appeared to be doing well with unchanged methods. The gap between richest and poorest narrowed only slightly,[114] and much manufacturing still required modernization to remain competitive. Labour achieved much in six difficult years but much remained to be done.

112 J. Tomlinson, 'Labour and the Economy', in D. Tanner, N. Tiratsoo and P. Thane (eds), *Labour's First Century* (Cambridge University Press, 2000), pp. 57–60.
113 Cairncross, *Years of Recovery*, pp. 507–9
114 Gazeley. *Poverty in Britain*, p. 161.

8

An Affluent Society?

1951–1964

Divided Britain

In 1951, Britain was still deeply divided and unequal, as the election result indicated unusually clearly. Labour had started but not completed substantial social and economic change. The future was wide open for the Conservatives to take this further in the same or different directions. 1950s Britain has a reputation for dull cultural conservatism, dominated by 'family values' and sexual repression, when a 'male bread-winner' culture confined women to the home in 'the nadir of British feminism'[1] and other forms of protest amid unprecedented 'affluence'. Equally questionably, it has been described as 'a golden time; a more innocent age before … illusion after illusion was … painfully shattered'[2] in the 'swinging sixties'. History does not divide neatly by decades and through the 1950s to the mid-1960s Britain experienced a more complex reality of gradual, cultural change, less than some people hoped, sparking intense resistance from others, presaging greater changes to follow.

Politically, historians have described this as a period of 'consensus' between Labour and Conservatives on economic and social policies, as the Conservatives confronted the challenge of sustaining Britain's successful recovery from depression and war in a revived, increasingly competitive world economy. Differences between the parties were indeed less acute than in earlier and later decades, not least because the Conservatives knew they must attract more of the majority working-class electorate following their

1 Pugh, *Women and the Women's Movement in Britain*, pp. 284–311. He does suggest that this 'conventional description 'is a considerable exaggeration', p. 284.
2 Peter Hennessy *Having it So Good. Britain in the Fifties* (London: Penguin, 2007), p. xvii.

narrow victory in 1951. But profound differences remained between the parties, and among Conservatives, especially on state responsibility for economic planning and control and on public versus private provision of welfare. Differences in economic policy became increasingly important as the British economy appeared to be slipping behind its competitors through the 1950s. The welfare state survived thirteen years of Conservative rule, to the regret of some government supporters, because it was popular, but it did not expand as Labour hoped and much innovation was delegated to the private sector. Domestically, the parties had very different visions, seeking to shape society and the economy and deal with major inequalities in very different ways. One thing they had in common was supporting the peaceable advance of independence within the Commonwealth while retaining this unique international network, aiming to maintain Britain's status in international politics, another major area of insecurity in the uncertain 1950s.

Churchill Returns

Churchill returned to Downing Street, aged 77, in poor health, promising, with no hint of 'consensus' to 'set the people free' from 'socialist controls'. In reality, his government and 'the people' benefited from economic revival which owed much to Labour's controls, above all full employment and evident improvements to everyday life. Beneath the rhetoric, Conservative election promises were cautious, as, due to their small majority, were their actions. In this unmistakably class-divided society they needed to win working-class votes. They were constrained too by fluctuating world trade and the large defence budget (30 per cent of expenditure) boosted by the Korean War, the costs of conflict in Commonwealth countries seeking independence,[3] and development of the atom bomb, which was now public knowledge. The first A-bomb test took place, safely distant in the Australian desert, in 1952, with damaging effects on those in fallout range, including British soldiers and unknown numbers of aboriginal people, unacknowledged for decades.

The Cabinet was also cautiously constructed, mainly from Churchill's trusted wartime associates, favouring conciliatory reformers: Anthony Eden as Foreign Secretary, R. A. Butler as Chancellor of the Exchequer, Harold Macmillan placed, disappointed, at a new Ministry of Housing to fulfil the commitment to build more homes. Like Labour, the Conservatives were slow to encourage new talent, until Iain Macleod, age 39, was appointed Minister of Health, after impressing Churchill with his parliamentary attack on Bevan's handling of the NHS.

3 See pp. 233–6.

'Stop–Go'

The Conservatives immediately faced a worsening balance of payments deficit and pressure on sterling in an international downturn. Butler – a less consensual Chancellor than expected – blamed excessive Labour spending and, obeying Treasury orthodoxy, cut social spending. Prices and unemployment rose and protests induced the withdrawal of some cuts. The economy faced recurrent problems through the 1950s and the government responded with alternating cuts and expansion – 'stop–go' as it became known – but no clear strategy other than, whenever possible, cutting taxes and reducing public ownership and controls. The economy actually grew exceptionally fast by UK standards, averaging 2.42 per cent per year from 1950 to 1973, but competitors grew faster, including Germany and France. UK productivity particularly lagged behind. Its main European competitors successfully implemented policies to which Labour aspired but Conservatives shunned: central planning and cooperation between management and unions, achieving wage restraint in return for investment in technology, growth and job creation.[4] Labour successfully encouraged such cooperation in Germany during the occupation, but failed to persuade British business and unions to follow suit. Initiatives including development councils to guide modernization and the British Institute of Management to improve the perceived poor quality of British management[5] were discontinued by the Conservatives and they had no alternative plans to modernize industry.

Instead, like previous Conservative governments, they sought cuts to social spending to reduce taxes. Their manifestoes in 1951 and later elections significantly referred to the 'Health Service', dropping 'National'. In June 1952, prescription charges of 1s (10p) were introduced and further dental charges. Treasury officials and some Conservative backbenchers proposed other charges, including 'hotel' fees for hospital stays, but the Ministry of Health and Cabinet resisted, fearing popular hostility.[6] NHS staffing was frozen; Macleod as Minister of Health from 1952, and the Treasury, wanted more cuts. An inquiry into NHS finances was appointed, chaired by Cambridge economist Claude Guillebaud.

Supporters of shrinking the welfare state welcomed Rowntree's third and final survey of poverty in York, published in 1951.[7] More superficial, less thorough, than the earlier surveys, by 80-year-old Rowntree with an assistant, using a slightly more generous poverty measure, it concluded that poverty was almost eliminated: only 2.77 per cent

4 Nicolas Crafts, 'Economic Growth during the Long Twentieth Century', in
Roderick Floud, Jane Humphries and Paul Johnson (eds), *The Cambridge Economic History of Modern Britain, vol. 2: 1870 to the Present* (Cambridge University Press, 2014), pp. 45–9.
5 Tomlinson, 'Labour and the Economy', pp. 57–60.
6 Howard Glennerster, *British Social Policy since 1945*, 3rd edn (Oxford: Blackwell, [1995],2007), p. 86; Helen Jones, *Health and Society in Twentieth-Century Britain* (London: Longman, 1994), pp. 117–47.
7 B. Seebohm Rowntree and G. S. Lavers, *Poverty and the Welfare State. A Third Social Survey of York Dealing only with Economic Questions* (London: Longman, Green, 1951).

of individuals, 4.64 per cent of working-class households, two-thirds retired, were now in primary poverty in York, still held to be a typical provincial town. They attributed the decline to postwar social legislation and price controls, describing lives 'below the minimum', typically:

> Two rooms and kitchen [i.e., no bathroom] ... Widow aged 76 lives alone. Old age pension £1.6s. Supplementary pension [means-tested from NAB] 8s. Value of home-grown vegetables, 2s. 6d. Total income £1.16s.6d. Deficit [below poverty line] 5s.2d. Widow says she concentrates her spending on food, even though she sometimes has to go without a fire in consequence. Shoe repairs are a big problem, but she has a good stock of clothes and hopes she won't live long enough to wear them out.[8]

Such experiences were real, but the methods of sampling and calculating living costs were faulty. Later reworking revealed that approximately 12 per cent was a more accurate estimate, including more younger people.[9] Poverty had diminished, though by less than Rowntree suggested; his report entrenched the belief that poverty was now minimal and concentrated among older people.

In 1952, Iain Macleod and another young Conservative MP, Enoch Powell, published *The Social Services: Needs and Means*, attacking the 'welfare state', as they called it pejoratively, arguing, as Beveridge had feared,[10] that it encouraged dependency on the taxpayer and reduced incentives to work. The NHS, in particular, was too costly and should be financed by private insurance. Social services and payments should be targeted on the neediest: 'the question ... is not should a means test be applied to a social service, but why should any service be provided without a test of need?'[11] A long assault on universal services began, guiding Conservative social policy for the remainder of the century and beyond. The desire to cut public spending did not prevent the government commissioning in 1951 a costly north–south motorway. Labour aimed to overhaul the road network and develop motorways – in which Britain lagged behind continental rivals – to assist economic growth, but decided it was too expensive. The Conservatives responded to pressure from business and increasing car ownership, but progress was slow: the first section of the M1 opened in 1959.

A New Age?

In February 1952, King George VI died and a young, female sovereign, Elizabeth II, was represented as symbolizing positive change, a 'New Elizabethan age', romanticizing past national greatness. Then, less romantically, in December 1952, London vanished into

8 Ibid., p. 62.
9 Gazeley, *Poverty in Britain*, pp. 168–73.
10 See pp. 174–5, 188, 198.
11 Conservative Political Centre, London, 1952, p. 5.

the Great Smog, a fog so thick and polluted that about 4,000 people died, many more suffered breathing problems, and travel and business were disrupted. Over decades, fogs had worsened as more steam trains belched smoke, domestic coal fires increased, steam-driven industry grew and three large, coal-fired power stations opened along the Thames. London was divided between inner areas inhabited by poorer people in overcrowded, polluted districts and smarter, more expensive districts, beyond the recognized 'smog line'.

It was one of Britain's worst public health catastrophes, but the government and media were slow to respond. Then prize animals died at London's Smithfield Show. The press sounded the alarm, Labour MPs asked questions in the Commons and the National Smoke Abatement Society campaigned. The Conservatives resisted intervention, but in May 1953 appointed a committee of enquiry, which in 1954 recommended designated smokeless zones and smoke-controlled areas, with government subsidies for householders to convert to smokeless fuel. These were implemented in the Clean Air Act 1956, the first significant attempt to control environmental pollution, though with exclusion clauses for industrial emissions following pressure from industry. These limited its effectiveness and were much criticized, but pollution diminished in London and elsewhere, improving the quality of life until in the next century vehicle and other emissions caused new health hazards.[12]

In 1953, Butler took advantage of an upturn in world trade to switch policy to 'Go' with a series of cuts to direct and indirect taxes, aiming to increase investment and consumption. Road haulage and steel were de-nationalized and controls on supplies reduced while price controls remained. In another boost to private enterprise, in 1954 legislation permitted the establishment of commercial TV stations, financed by advertising, to rival the BBC, though regulated by a government-appointed Independent Television Authority (ITA), which established regional commercial TV companies. Its first chair was Sir Kenneth Clark, perhaps to win over resistant intellectuals who, fearing 'Americanization' of TV and lower standards, initially refused to view the commercial channels.

300,000 Houses

One area of public spending was too important to cut. The continuing shortage and poor quality of housing was a big issue in the recent elections and the Conservatives promised to build 300,000 houses each year. In 1952, 248,000 were completed, 212,000 in the public sector, 37,000 privately owned. In 1953, 327,000 were completed, 262,000

12 Roy Parker, 'The Struggle for Clean Air', in P. Hall, H. Land, R. Parker and A. Webb (eds), *Change, Choice and Conflict in Social Policy* (London, Heinemann, 1975), pp. 371–409.

council homes, 65,000 private, the largest number of council homes built in any year of the twentieth century, except 1954, which matched it. Macmillan celebrated by opening the 300,000th house. The target was achieved annually until 1957; private building grew to 178,000 in 1963 while the public sector shrank to 130,000, despite continuing need among low-income households.[13] Achieving the target was impressive, though it was partly due to reducing the size of the standard 'people's house' and cutting the proportion of council homes with three or more bedrooms from four- to two-fifths. Councils were encouraged to build high-rise flats: the Housing Subsidies Act 1957 increased subsidies for blocks above five storeys, despite their unpopularity especially among families with children. Fewer amenities were provided for council estates or New Towns. In 1951, 53 per cent of housing was privately rented and rents were still controlled. Landlords still protested that controlled rents left no margin for repairs. The Repairs and Rents Act 1954 allowed them to raise rents if their properties were in good repair. Private rentals fell to 32 per cent by 1960, while owner-occupation rose from 29 per cent to 42 per cent.[14]

Coronation Year

Elizabeth II's coronation in June 1953 was an occasion for partying and consuming in a society in which more people felt better off. Keen as ever to secure their status, which faced little challenge, the monarchy launched an unprecedented spectacle: the new queen rode through London in a golden coach, wearing cloth of gold, leading a procession of royals and leaders from around the world before an audience of unprecedented size. She later toured the country. Most British people watched the coronation live on their own or another TV. The number of TV licences increased from 344,000 in 1950 to 4.5 million in 1955.[15] Meanwhile cinema attendances slipped by a third and football crowds declined when matches could be watched for free on the small black-and-white screen.

The coronation appeared to unite and celebrate the Commonwealth, as more member nations gained independence. Commonwealth leaders attended the ceremony and joined the procession, including an unexpected star, the buxom, beaming, much photographed Queen Salote of the Pacific island of Tonga. When, on Coronation Day, New Zealander Edmund Hillary and Nepalese Tenzing Norgay reached the summit of Everest for the first time ever, flying the Union Flag at the summit, it was publicized as one more sign of a new, triumphant era. Less uplifting, a few weeks later John Christie

13 Butler and Butler, *Twentieth-Century British Political Facts*, pp. 356–7.
14 Ibid., p. 357.
15 Ibid., p. 547.

was tried for multiple murders of prostitutes and his wife. Sensational press coverage exposed tensions, miserable living conditions and a degraded environment in run-down, multi-racial Notting Hill. Christie's lawyers tried to defend him on grounds of insanity caused by the pressures of trying to maintain respectability in the face of the alien culture of his Jamaican landlord and neighbours. They failed and he was hanged, but the attempt suggested the persistence of racist and other divisions in a society sup-posedly united by the coronation.

The year 1953 was also eventful internationally. In July, the Korean War ended. This and a change of president in the United States, from Truman to Eisenhower, and the death of Stalin brought hopes that international tensions would subside. At home, in coronation month, Churchill suffered his second major stroke. Its seriousness was hidden, including by the press, pressured by his allies. He never fully recovered but was unwilling to resign, though no longer fit for the job. Butler deputized, while Eden underwent major surgery from which he also never quite recovered. Churchill at last gave into pressure and resigned in April 1955. The far from robust Eden succeeded him, Macmillan became Foreign Secretary and an election was called for May 1955.

General Election, 1955

World prices fell when the Korean War ended, enabling the end of food rationing in mid-1954, which of course was popular, though it stimulated imports, threatening the balance of payments and leading to further controls on spending. In the election campaign, the Conservatives claimed credit for maintaining full employment, ending rationing, cutting bureaucracy and increasing consumption. Butler announced:

> We have burned our identity cards, torn up our ration books, halved the number of snoopers, decimated the number of forms and said good riddance to nearly two-thirds of the remaining wartime regulations. This is the march to freedom on which we are bound.[16]

It was still not a march to a clear economic strategy, despite increasing evidence that Britain lagged behind faster-growing rival economies. The 1955 Budget, a month before the election, further reduced the standard rate of tax to 8s 6d in the £ and increased personal allowances, removing over 2 million people from direct taxation. Doubts were expressed about the wisdom of increasing purchasing power and, probably, prices, but the likely political advantage was irresistible. As well as TVs, ownership of cars and motor cycles grew. The value of HP and other instalment purchases grew from £208 million to £461 million between 1951 and 1955.[17]

---

16 R. A. Butler, *Art of the Possible* (London: Hamish Hamilton, 1971), p. 173.
17 Butler and Butler, *Twentieth-Century British Political Facts*, p. 427.

The Conservatives were keen to win women voters and probably succeeded, including working-class women. This was partly because they built more houses and ended rationing while full employment continued, raising living standards. The campaign for equal pay continued. Campaigners, including the EPCC, helped to fund the film, *To Be a Woman*, directed by Jill Craigie, wife of Labour MP Michael Foot, describing the working lives of women, in and out of the home, and the unfairness of pay inequality. It was widely shown in 1951–2, supported by demonstrations and petitions to Parliament, encouraged by the Labour-controlled LCC granting equal pay in 1952.[18] The Treasury remained hostile and the government prevaricated, despite promising equal pay in the public sector in 1951. Then, before the election, Butler announced the introduction of equal pay in the civil service, local government and teaching, where demands had been most insistent, gradually over six years.[19] The EPCC disbanded, its aim achieved, but urged women to organize in the private sector. In November 1955, women at the Hillington engineering works near Glasgow struck for restoration of the near equal pay they had achieved through strikes during the war; their pay gap had widened again to 24 per cent. Protests over private sector pay inequality continued in the unions and among Labour women, supported by other women's organizations, through the 1950s and 1960s.[20]

They had little support from Labour leaders who showed scant interest in the issues concerning many women, who were alienated also by conflicts in the party and appreciated the improvements in living standards and opportunities for their children, for which Conservatives took credit, while some leading Labour men, who also deserved credit, sneered at aspirations for more comfortable lives. The failure of some Labour supporters to come to terms with what was soon called the 'affluent society' (after the US economist J. K. Galbraith's book of that name, published 1958[21]), caused resentment. A party publication condemned 'the lifeless time-wasting of so many ... people who find in TV almost their only pleasure'. The female editor of *Labour Woman* in 1959 deplored the Tories' 'crude materialistic appeal to the purely self-regarding interests of the electors ... How many more refrigerators, washing machines, TV sets, vacuum cleaners and motor cars under the Tories?'[22] Reiterated hostility to the washing machine, in particular, may have alienated working-class women by presenting it as a manifestation of selfish, individualistic consumerism, rather than the liberation from the exhausting hours of the weekly wash it actually was. The Conservatives published

18 Glew, *Gender, Rhetoric and Regulation*, pp. 157–67.
19 Ibid., pp. 165–6.
20 Elizabeth M. Meehan, *Women's Rights at Work. Campaigns and Policy in Britain and the United States* (London: Macmillan, 1985), pp. 35–55.
21 J. K. Galbraith, *The Affluent Society* (London: Pelican, 1962, repr. 1962, 1963).
22 *Labour Woman*, 1959.

pamphlets addressed to women, stressing the advantages of consumer goods and warning of controls and rationing should Labour win.

They gained also from Labour feuds. The left grew stronger in the unions. Bevan resigned from the Shadow Cabinet in 1954 in opposition to nuclear arms. In March 1955, the Commons agreed the manufacture of a hydrogen bomb, with official Labour support. Bevan and sixty-two Labour MPs abstained and he lost the party whip. Labour, led by a weary Attlee, unable to hold together his squabbling party but reluctant to retire, offered no new policies, arguing again that full employment, stable prices and progress to greater equality required planning, controls and increased taxes on higher incomes. The Conservatives were helped further by a newspaper strike lasting almost a month, a dock strike and threatened rail strike, offering opportunities to attack the unions.

They secured a clear majority, gaining 13,286,569 votes, 49.7 per cent, and 345 seats; Labour won 12,404,970 votes, 46.4 per cent and 277 seats on a turnout of 76.8 per cent. Voters remained quite evenly divided but constituencies still were not. Labour's share of the non-manual vote and male voters increased slightly, while its share of female votes fell from 46 per cent to 42.5 per cent.[23] The swing to the Conservatives, 1.8 per cent, was fairly uniform across the country, less in Scotland, where unemployment was high, and more in the prosperous Midlands.

1955–1959: Decline?

Dalton resigned from the Shadow Cabinet, calling on his 'fellow veterans' to follow. Most obeyed, except Morrison, aged 67, who still hoped to succeed Attlee. More, younger, men – and Bevan – were elected to the all-male Shadow Cabinet. In December, Attlee, aged 72, resigned the leadership after twenty years. Hugh Gaitskell, leader of Labour's right-wing against the Bevanite left, defeated Morrison and Bevan for the leadership.

Eden appointed an all-male Cabinet, all privately educated, most at Eton. In an autumn Budget Butler reverted to 'Stop', clawing back double the revenue given away before the election as the balance of payments plunged to a deficit of over £450 million due to predictably increased imports, reinforcing the view that the Conservatives had no consistent economic strategy. Local authority building was severely cut, purchase tax increased, two-thirds of the tax reliefs announced in April were withdrawn. Gaitskell accused Butler of deceiving the nation. The reaction in the opinion polls (ever more influential as they proliferated in the 1950s) was so negative that in December 1955 Butler was replaced as Chancellor by Macmillan, infuriating both.

23 Thorpe, *History of the British Labour Party*, p. 141.

As Foreign Secretary, in June 1955, Macmillan refused an offer by the six members of the successful European Iron and Steel Community to join a wider economic union. He shared the Foreign Office view, popular in the Conservative Party, that 'The Empire must always have first preference, Europe must come second',[24] strongly opposed by the United States, which wanted Britain to integrate with Europe and abandon colonialism. However, 47.8 per cent of Britain's trade was with the Commonwealth and only 13 per cent with the six powers of the proposed European Economic Community (EEC),[25] and the government wished to preserve the sterling area. As Chancellor, Macmillan was alarmed by the financial situation and in February 1956, after wrangles with Eden, announced more emergency measures: reduced bread subsidies to be followed by abolition, increased bank rate and hire purchase deposits and further cuts to public spending.

Hopes of savings from cuts to the NHS were dashed when the Guillebaud Committee reported in 1956. It concluded that costs had not soared as critics suggested, but had fallen since 1948 from 3.75 per cent to 3.25 per cent of GNP. Capital spending on hospitals was only one-third the prewar level; they ran with remarkable efficiency given that 45 per cent were built before 1891, 21 per cent before 1861. It recommended more spending on renovation. Rather than evidence of waste, it found that the NHS was highly cost-effective compared with healthcare in comparable countries, while charges for dental treatment and spectacles deterred people who needed them. This was not what the government or the Treasury wanted to hear and did not stop calls for cuts from the backbenches, but it did stop the government rushing to implement them.[26]

On another major social policy issue, the government claimed to want to improve education and skills in view of Britain's poor performance in technological innovation in business compared with rivals. Local authorities were encouraged to open technical colleges to enable younger workers to learn skills. In 1957, eight technical colleges became Colleges of Advanced Technology providing degree-level training financed by central government. The advisory committee of the Ministry of Education produced a succession of reports proposing improvements. In 1954, *Early Leaving* stressed the numbers of able children leaving school at 15 without qualifications, recommending generous grants to help them stay on, which was not implemented. In 1959, the Crowther Report on 15–18 education proposed expansion of post-school education and raising the leaving age to 16, which also was ignored. Equally fruitlessly, in 1963, the Newsom Report, *Half Our Future*, reinforced the message of *Early Leaving*, suggesting improvements to secondary modern schools, especially in deprived areas. In the

24 Clarke, *Hope and Glory*, p. 258.

25 James Ellison, 'Why has Europe been such a Difficult Subject for Britain?' *Britain and the European Union. Lessons from History* (London: Mile End Institute, Queen Mary University of London, 2016), p. 7.

26 Sally Sheard, *The Passionate Economist. How Brian Abel-Smith shaped Global Health and Social Welfare* (Bristol: Policy Press, 2014), pp. 84–8.

same year, the Robbins Report recommended expanding the universities, which still educated only 4 per cent of 18–21 year olds, overwhelmingly upper- and middle-class and male, compared with 8 per cent in France and 20 per cent in the United States.[27] The Treasury slightly increased university funding. Some new universities were already planned, with philanthropic and local funds. Sussex opened in 1961, East Anglia in 1963, others soon after, despite pessimists, notably novelist and university lecturer, Kingsley Amis, warning, notoriously, 'more will mean worse'.[28] The Conservatives did little to improve the education system.

Suez

The inexperienced Selwyn Lloyd replaced Macmillan at the Foreign Office and could be trusted to do as Eden and his officials wished. This was soon put to the test. In summer 1956, Gamal Abdel Nasser, Egypt's leader since an officers' coup in 1952 against the client regime in place since the First World War, nationalized the Suez Canal, legally, compensating the shareholders. Britain, under pressure from Nasser, had recently withdrawn from bases in Egypt, other than one in the canal-zone. Eden hoped withdrawal would conciliate Nasser, against opposition in the party, including from Churchill.[29] But in 1956 Nasser felt threatened by negotiations for the pro-Western Baghdad Pact of Middle Eastern countries with Britain and the United States, centred upon his main regional rival, Iraq. He was also threatened by raids from Israel, which saw him as a dangerous ally of Palestinian Arabs. He turned to the USSR for support, reinforcing Western fears of growing Soviet power in the Middle East. These were tempered by a resounding speech denouncing Stalin at a party congress earlier in 1956 by Nikita Khrushchev, First Secretary of the Communist Party. Seeking rapprochement, Eden invited Khrushchev and Nikolai Bulganin, Soviet Prime Minister, to Britain for a successful ten-day visit in April.

Eden had recently been awarded the Nobel Peace Prize, but he became more intemperate following a botched gall bladder operation. The United States sought a negotiated settlement with Nasser, but Eden was determined to show that Britain could act independently of Washington and prepared an invasion force. The French were equally concerned to protect the canal link to their colonies and about oil supplies, and believed Egypt was supporting Algeria in its bitter war for independence from France from 1954. Guy Mollet, the socialist premier of France proposed invading Egypt together with Israel. Eden agreed, without informing Foreign Office officials. Israeli troops invaded in October, then France and Britain announced their support, ostensibly to protect the canal, though Egypt

27 Glennerster, *British Social Policy*, pp. 92–3.

28 *Encounter Magazine*, July 1960.

29 Reynolds, *Britannia Overruled*, p. 191.

was running it efficiently. An outcry erupted in Britain, including from a small group of moderate Conservative MPs and the Labour Party, uniting Bevan and Gaitskell against what they believed was unnecessary use of force. The United States led overwhelming opposition in the UN. Sterling collapsed. Britain immediately, on 6 November, agreed a ceasefire, then withdrawal, enforced by the United States in return for supporting sterling. France felt betrayed. A UN peacekeeping force moved in. On 4 November, with world attention focused on Suez, Russia seized the opportunity to crush brutally a movement for independence in Hungary. This was stimulated by Khrushchev's denunciation of Stalin, but the USSR had changed less than Hungarians and many in the West hoped.[30]

Britain now appeared weaker internationally, the United States even stronger, summed up in a much-quoted comment in 1962 by US Secretary of State, Dean Acheson: 'Great Britain has lost an Empire but has not yet found a role'. Following Suez, Eden's health collapsed and he withdrew to recuperate at the holiday home of James Bond creator, Ian Fleming, in Jamaica. Two junior ministers resigned and Butler took temporary control. He had serious doubts about the Suez venture and tried to be conciliatory, while overseeing the humiliating retreat. Petrol prices rose following the crisis. Eden returned in January 1957, apparently fit and expecting to continue as Prime Minister. He met scathing newspaper headlines, widespread unpopularity of the Conservative Party and a cold reception in the Commons. His health deteriorated, doctors advised he was unlikely to recover and he resigned. Butler was expected to succeed, but the Cabinet and still influential Churchill preferred the more decisive Macmillan.

'Supermac'

Macmillan appointed younger men to his still all-male Cabinet and sidelined Butler's supporters, though Butler himself became Home Secretary. Peter Thorneycroft became Chancellor. Macmillan's calm control of the Cabinet, his soon famously 'unflappable' style, won respect in Parliament, though it took longer to win over voters antagonized by Suez. He was well aware of the economic as well as international difficulties. He stated in a speech in Bedford in July 1957:

> Let's be frank about it; most of our people have never had it so good. Go around the country, go to the industrial towns, go to the farms, and you will see a state of prosperity such as we have never had in my lifetime – nor indeed ever in the history of this country. What is beginning to worry some of us is 'Is it too good to be true?' or perhaps I should say 'Is it too good to last?' For amidst all this prosperity, there is one problem that has troubled us … ever since the war. It's the problem of rising prices. Our constant concern is – can prices be steadied while at the same time we maintain full employment in an expanding economy? Can we control inflation? That is the problem of our time.[31]

---

30 Keith Kyle, *Suez. Britain's End of Empire in the Middle East* (London: I. B. Tauris, repr. 2011).
31 *The Times*, 22 July 1957, quoted in Kevin Jefferys, *Retreat from New Jerusalem. British Politics, 1951–64* (London: Macmillan, 1997), p. 65.

Macmillan's much quoted, accurate, claim that most British people had 'never had it so good' was delivered as a warning about the state of the economy, not the triumphal message since remembered. It resonated with many people who were better off than before but felt insecure. But the government still had no clear economic policy and alternating cuts to taxes and public spending continued.

As promised, the Rent Act, 1957, decontrolled rents on higher value property, on all properties when tenants left and allowed controlled rents to rise to twice the property's rateable value. This aroused strong opposition. There were about 6 million private tenants, mostly on low incomes.[32] Controlled rents in London rose on average from 14s per week to 22s 4d in 1957–9, outside London from 9s 4d to 13s 1d. One result, especially in London, was unscrupulous landlords forcing out controlled tenants by making their lives intolerable, sometimes with loud music and all-night parties. This became a major scandal, labelled 'Rachmanism' after the most notorious perpetrator, Peter Rachman, when his tenants in deprived, multi-racial Notting Hill complained of intimidation and extortionate rents for slum housing. Rachman, himself a Ukrainian immigrant who became very wealthy from his property dealings, later from owning fashionable nightclubs, died, unpenalized, in 1962.[33]

Labour Revisionism

Labour attacked the Conservative handling of economic and social policy, led by Shadow Chancellor Harold Wilson, while Gaitskell appeared to achieve consensus in the party. Bevan, now Shadow Foreign Secretary, reluctantly retreated from unilateralism, claiming he 'would not go naked into the conference chamber' without the bargaining power of nuclear arms, realizing that factionalism harmed Labour. Others proposed new approaches. Future Labour minister, Anthony Crosland's *The Future of Socialism* (1956) argued that nationalization was outdated in the modern world of large multinational businesses. The way forward was acceptance of the mixed economy, controlled by Keynesian-style demand management, with social reforms promoting equality. Crosland believed that Labour should applaud the improved living standards of most working people, encourage pleasure, not grim devotion to duty, ceasing to condemn materialism:

> We need not only higher exports and old age pensions, but more open-air cafes, brighter and gayer streets at night, later closing hours for public houses, more local repertory theatres … it is not only dark Satanic things and people that now bar the road to a new Jerusalem, but also, if not mainly, hygienic, respectable, virtuous things and people, lacking only in grace and gaiety.[34]

---

32 Glennerster, *British Social Policy*, pp. 82–5.
33 Ibid., p. 84.
34 C. A. R. Crosland, *The Future of Socialism* (London: Jonathan Cape, 1956), p. 355.

Labour must also tackle 'the more serious question of socially imposed restrictions on the individual's private life and liberty ... the divorce laws, licensing laws, prehistoric (and flagrantly unfair) abortion laws, obsolete penalties for sexual abnormality, the illiterate censorship of books and plays, the remaining restrictions on the equal rights of women'.[35] Many party members disagreed with him, but he perceived major cultural changes in progress, presaging future Labour reforms.

By the end of 1957, Labour was ahead in the opinion polls and Macmillan's approval ratings were the lowest of any premier since the war.[36] Thorneycroft became increasingly alarmed about the state of the economy, debt and defence spending, and proposed severe cuts to social spending. Macmillan, thinking of the next election and fearing industrial disputes, refused. Thorneycroft and his junior ministers, Nigel Birch and Enoch Powell, resigned. Derick Heathcoat Amory became Chancellor. In public Macmillan dismissed these 'little local difficulties' with more nonchalance than he felt and left to tour the Commonwealth. Amory cautiously implemented some cuts and the government fared badly in polls and by-elections into 1958. Then the international economy and the government's ratings revived. Modest tax reductions and reduced controls followed. An *Evening Standard* cartoon of a caped, bespectacled figure soaring into the sky – 'Supermac' – signalled the revival.

Decolonization

Preserving the Commonwealth while Britain's colonial authority dwindled was a major theme of the Conservative years, essential to their aim of preserving Britain's international status. The 'Emergency' in Malaya continued until 1960, a front in the Cold War, a costly confrontation with mainly Chinese-origin communist guerrillas.[37] It became less intense after 1955 as Britain built good relations with the Muslim majority and non-communist Chinese in Malaya, helping them build representative institutions, while wearing down the communist resistance. Malaya became internally self-governing under non-communist leadership and increasingly prosperous as the value of rubber rose on world markets. It became independent within the Commonwealth in 1957, with Britain still responsible for defence and retaining access to invaluable supplies of rubber and tin.

Strong national consciousness also emerged in the Caribbean, though less violent than elsewhere. When British Guiana was allowed to elect its own government in 1953, it chose the People's Progressive Party, led by Dr Cheddi Jagan, which promised radical political and economic reforms likely to limit the profits of foreign-owned (often

35 Ibid.
36 Butler and Butler, *Twentieth-Century British Political Facts*, pp. 266–8.
37 See p. 212.

British) companies. Britain decided this was communism, invaded and overthrew the government. Jagan compromised and British troops remained. Tensions followed for another decade until the conflict subsided and the country became independent, as Guyana, in 1966.

Cyprus was increasingly important as British control in the Middle East declined, as a military and naval base safeguarding access to oil and Britain's remaining interests in the eastern Mediterranean and east of Suez. The majority Greek community demanded union with Greece, which the Turkish minority resisted. From 1955, the demands of the pro-Greek movement (EOKA) became violent and armed forces, including many conscripts, and police were mobilized. Following US and NATO intervention and diplomacy by the Governor, Sir Hugh Foot, Cyprus became an independent republic within the Commonwealth in 1960, though tensions between Greeks and Turks continued and British bases remained.

The other centre of serious conflict in the 1950s was Kenya, where violent racial disturbances, arson and killings began in 1952, organized by the militant Mau Mau movement of mainly landless men, disowned by the peaceable independence movement led by Jomo Kenyatta, who had lived and studied for many years in Britain. Nevertheless, when British troops mobilized against Mau Mau, the British authorities imprisoned Kenyatta in 1953 for allegedly controlling them. This strengthened the independence movement. The Colonial Secretary, Oliver Lyttleton insisted Mau Mau were not a politically inspired independence movement but an 'anti-European, anti-Christian force' committing the worst crimes 'you can imagine',[38] a view widely echoed in the press. Many Mau Mau activists were imprisoned and, as they claimed then and proved decades later when survivors were at last compensated, suffered appalling conditions causing many deaths while the conflict continued. About 9,600 Africans were killed and seventy Europeans. An outcry when eleven Mau Mau were beaten to death by British guards in the Hola prison camp in March 1959 made the government change tack, encourage peasant land settlement and prepare Kenya for independence with majority African rule, though the constitution initially allowed 50,000 European settlers the same number of elected representatives as 5 million Africans. Kenya gained self-government in 1963 and became a republic in 1964, with Kenyatta as president after being freed only in 1961.

Macmillan, like Attlee, supported peaceful transitions to independence under suitably cooperative leaders wherever possible. He was committed to the Commonwealth, led by Britain. Peaceful independence was easier to achieve in countries without Kenya's high density of white settlement and resulting tensions. Ghana, in 1957, became the first black African republic in the Commonwealth, led by Kwame Nkrumah, peacefully,

---

38 'Mr Lyttleton's Return', *The Times*, 7 November 1952, p. 6.

though Nkrumah had been imprisoned for supporting independence. Macmillan appointed the liberal Ian Macleod as Colonial Secretary in 1959, briefed to speed up decolonization. A rush of mostly peaceable independence followed. By 1960, the violent 'emergencies' were over, the defence budget was cut and conscription ended in 1961.[39]

Independence within the Commonwealth, 1957–68
1957 Malaya
1960 Nigeria, Somaliland, Cyprus
1961 Sierra Leone, Tanganyika
1962 Jamaica, Trinidad and Tobago, Uganda
1963 Kenya, Malaysia formed of Malaya, North Borneo, Sarawak and Singapore (which broke away in 1965)
1964 Malawi, Malta, Zambia
1965 Gambia
1966 British Guiana (Guyana), Bechuanaland (Botswana), Basutoland (Lesotho), Barbados
1967 Leeward Islands, Windward Islands, Aden (People's Republic of South Yemen)
1968 Swaziland

There was certainly 'a wind of change blowing through Africa', and elsewhere, as Macmillan stated in another much quoted speech in 1960 to the parliament of South Africa. He continued, 'whether we like it or not, this growth of national consciousness is a political fact', a warning to a white government determined to refuse equality to the majority black population, which it ignored. In the same year, a demonstration by black activists at Sharpeville, in Transvaal, was brutally suppressed, leaving sixty-nine dead and 180 injured, stimulating anti-apartheid activism in Britain. The leading opposition organizations in South Africa, the African National Congress and Pan-African Congress, were banned and thousands were imprisoned or went into exile. South Africa was ejected from the Commonwealth, no longer dominated by Britain and the white Dominions, in 1961, because it would not abandon, or modify, apartheid.[40]

South Africa was not the only problem in southern Africa. In 1953, the Central African Federation was formed from Nyasaland and Northern Rhodesia, both overwhelmingly black, and (Southern) Rhodesia, with a white government on the South African model. Theoretically, the Federation created a multi-racial society respecting all races equally – a model for neighbouring South Africa. But the black population still felt subordinate and by 1960 there were nationalist risings in Nyasaland and Northern Rhodesia which continued despite, or because of, violent repression, until they seceded and became independent as Malawi and Zambia, respectively, in 1963. Rhodesia remained unchanged causing problems for future British governments.[41] White settlers

39 Porter, *Lion's Share*, pp. 310–15; Vinen, *Conscription*.

40 Shula Marks, 'Southern Africa', in Judith M. Brown and William Roger Louis (eds), *The Oxford History of the British Empire, vol. IV: The Twentieth Century* (Oxford University Press, 1999), pp. 565–9.

41 Ibid., pp. 563–71.

relinquished power reluctantly. The white Dominions still prohibited immigration by Africans, Asians and anyone non-white, with rare exceptions. This discrimination was abolished by Canada only in 1962, by 'white Australia' in 1973, New Zealand in 1987 and South Africa with the fall of apartheid in 1994.

Immigration

The right of Commonwealth citizens, regardless of colour, to migrate to Britain, with equal rights with everyone of British nationality, had never been restricted.[42] Immigration grew, from a growing range of countries, though emigrants, mainly to the white Dominions, still outnumbered immigrants. Most immigrants, still, were Irish. By 1958, there were about 900,000 Irish-born residents, the largest number since the nineteenth century, with about 125,000 West Indians and 55,000 Indians and Pakistanis. Immigration from the Caribbean and south Asia was not encouraged by the government which feared racial conflict, though official recruitment schemes continued due to labour shortages. When the United States restricted immigration from the Caribbean in 1952, the United Kingdom became a greater magnet for West Indians fleeing poverty and unemployment at home. Most came independently, aiming to better themselves, though they were regularly shocked by the restricted opportunities and racism they encountered. Smaller numbers came from Cyprus and Hong Kong, with an influx of refugees from Hungary following the Russian invasion of 1956. Italians were the fifth largest immigrant group; the community established mainly in London in the nineteenth century expanded numerically and geographically from 1945. There was significant immigration of white Commonwealth citizens and substantial internal migration. Around 2 million moved from insecurity in Scotland, Wales and northern England to the Midlands and the South between 1951 and 1962.[43]

Black and Asian immigrants clustered in occupations short of labour. Asians in northern textiles and engineering and foundry work in the Midlands; West Indians in the public sector, especially transport (mainly men) and the NHS (mainly women), which also relied on south Asian doctors. Chinese, Cypriot, Asian and Italian restaurants transformed the variety and quality of eating-out across Britain, a lasting cultural change in a country not famed for its cuisine. Asians also became small shopkeepers. Immigrants tended to cluster together, often severely overcrowded, for security and because discrimination by white landlords left them little choice. One such district was run-down, overcrowded Notting Hill, where serious race riots erupted in 1958. Like east London at the beginning of the century, racism emerged in a deprived community

42 See pp. 9–10, 212.
43 D. Butler and A. King, *The British General Election of 1964* (London: Macmillan, repr. 2008), p. 40.

encountering significant immigration. A year later an Antiguan youth, Kelso Cochrane, was brutally murdered there, it was believed by white attackers, the worst of a string of white on black attacks in London, Nottingham and elsewhere. Also in the late 1950s, Cypriot café owners were attacked in north London, where Cypriots congregated, sparked by attacks on British servicemen in Cyprus by EOKA nationalists, the violence from which many Cypriots had fled. Oswald Mosley marched again, through Notting Hill, leading what he now called a 'one nation' movement, demanding 'Keep Britain White'; in the 1959 election he stood in North Kensington.

That Mosley lost his deposit suggests that extreme racists were a minority. This was the view of Lord Justice Salmon when sentencing nine youths, aged 17–20, for assault in the 1958 Notting Hill riots:

> You are a minute and insignificant section of the population who have brought shame on the district in which you lived, and have filled the whole nation with horror, indignation and disgust. Everyone, irrespective of the colour of their skin, is entitled to walk through our streets with heads erect and free from fear. This is a right which these courts will always unfailingly uphold.[44]

They were sentenced to four years' imprisonment, to widespread approval. Following the riots, white residents protected black youths, and the Inter-racial Friendship Co-ordinating Council was founded. The evening after Kelso Cochrane's murder, 500 black and white people attended a 'We mourn Cochrane' meeting in St Pancras town hall and a thousand people of all backgrounds attended his funeral.[45] A Gallup poll asking who caused the riots found that 27 per cent suggested white people, only 9 per cent suggesting black. Also, 70 per cent would not move home 'if coloured people came to live next door', 9 per cent would move, though 26 per cent would do so 'if coloured people came to live in great numbers in your district', 39 per cent would not, and 35 per cent 'might do'. But only 13 per cent approved of inter-racial marriages and 71 per cent were opposed.[46] The Communist Party led counter-demonstrations in Notting Hill and anti-racist graffiti appeared. Immigrants formed defensive organizations, including the West Indian Standing Conference, founded in 1958. The Indian Workers Association, formed in 1938,[47] revived and expanded, supporting immigrants and campaigning against racism. The Movement for Colonial Freedom, founded 1954, campaigned for laws against race discrimination and for colonial independence. Led by white activists, it included black trade unionists and colonial students.

---

44 Ann Dummett, *A Portrait of English Racism* (Harmondsworth: Pelican, 1973), p. 11.
45 Mica Nava, 'Sometimes Antagonistic, Sometimes Ardently Sympathetic. Contradictory Responses to Migrants in Post-war Britain', *Ethnicities* (2013): 1–19; Mica Nava, *Visceral Cosmopolitanism. Gender, Culture and the Normalization of Difference* (Oxford: Berg, 2007).
46 *News Chronicle*, 8 September 1958.
47 See p. 142.

Claudia Jones, a Brixton-based activist and editor of the first black weekly paper in Britain, the *West Indian Gazette*, proposed a carnival, as in her native Trinidad, to build unity and showcase Caribbean arts and culture. The first carnival was held in January 1959 in St Pancras Town Hall – indoors because it was planned to coincide with the Trinidadian carnival and January is less clement in London than in Trinidad – in a district with fewer racial tensions than Notting Hill. The BBC televised it and it was widely acclaimed. Successful indoor events continued until the first outdoor carnival, held peaceably in Notting Hill in relatively warm August 1966, establishing an annual tradition celebrated into the twenty-first century.

Nevertheless, the government faced pressures to restrict non-white Commonwealth immigration. It feared alienating Commonwealth countries, whose nationals still had full rights as British citizens, but tried to reduce immigration by negotiation with the countries concerned. While by no means all-pervasive, racial intolerance and inequality persisted and showed no sign of disappearing. Labour MP, Fenner Brockway, introduced unsuccessful Private Members Bills to outlaw discrimination – another demand that did not go away.

Youth Culture and 'Delinquency'

Other expressions of intolerance help to explain the 1950s' reputation for cultural conservatism. Conservative backbenchers and others complained of national moral decline especially among young people, increasingly defined and perceived as a troublesome social group, called 'teenagers' as the term coined in America in the 1940s came into common use in Britain. Growing convictions of young men and other signs of misbehaviour created panic about soaring 'juvenile delinquency', though in any year of the 1950s only 2 per cent of boys aged 14–21 were convicted and 0.2 per cent of girls, while the numbers aged under 20 rose from about 3 million to 4 million between 1951 and 1966 due to more births.[48] Fashionable psychologists encouraged the belief that mothers who abandoned their homes and children for paid work created 'delinquency' among neglected children, and that schools no longer inculcated the 'traditional' values that allegedly prevented transgressions. Others blamed the decline of religion or the influence of television.[49]

In general, recorded crime, especially violent and sexual crime, increased[50]: violent crimes in England and Wales rose from 6,249 in 1950 to 25,549 in 1965, sexual offences from 13,185 in 1950 to 20,155 in 1965. It was, and is, unknown whether this was due

---

48 Louise A. Jackson, with Angela Bartie, *Policing Youth. Britain 1945–70* (Manchester University Press, 2014).
49 Ibid., p. 25.
50 Mark Jarvis, *Conservative Governments, Morality and Social Change in Affluent Britain* (Manchester University Press, 2005), p. 44.

to increased reporting of crime, greater police diligence in recording crime or more offences. Butler established a research unit at the Home Office in 1956 to investigate. The White Paper, *Penal Practice in a Changing Society*, 1959, proposed a £20 million building programme to reduce overcrowding in jails and improve the rehabilitation of offenders, mental health treatment and improved processes of discharge and after-care to prevent re-offending, also providing detention and training centres to keep young people out of prison. The Criminal Justice Act, 1961, incorporated many of these proposals. Some Conservatives, including the Lord Chancellor, Lord Dilhorne, believed the penal system should be more severe to deter crime. There were demands for restoration of corporal punishment of young offenders (abolished by Labour in 1948). The 1958 conference of Conservative women supported beating with the 'cat- o' nine-tails' for sexual crime.

'Affluence' was blamed for deviance among young men who could afford to patronize proliferating coffee bars and new clothing fashions, including Edwardian-style ('Teddy boy') draped jackets, which peaked in the mid-1950s, and later, in the early 1960s, smoothly tailored Italian modernist ('Mod') fashion, often along with newly invented motor-scooters, also Italian. Another group of young 'Rockers' challenged what they saw as the effeminacy of Mods, aggressively masculine in leather clothing, roaring on motor bikes past quieter scooters. 'Rockers' skirmished with 'Mods' on weekend trips to seaside resorts, generating more excitement in the popular media than real trouble. More serious was the violence of young men in the Notting Hill and other race riots, though, as we have seen, these were minority activities which were justly punished.

Young women also enjoyed wider work opportunities in expanding service and consumer businesses, lower paid than men but enough to afford stiletto heels and paper-nylon petticoats under swirling skirts, promoted in popular new weekly magazines – *Marilyn* ('The great all-picture, love-story weekly', founded 1955), *Valentine* (1957) and *Boy Friend* (1959). The market for affordable female fashion boomed and its creators hit the headlines, especially Mary Quant from the mid-1950s and Biba from 1963. Young men and women danced together to 'pop' music pouring out on vinyl records (73 million sold in Britain in 1963[51]), film and TV, first from American rock 'n' rollers (including Bill Haley, Chuck Berry and Elvis Presley) then British talent including Cliff Richard and Tommy Steele, then the Beatles. Much of the press believed youthful energy was enlivening dull British culture, but it was disparaged by cultural conservatives as creating American-style degeneration. Academic Richard Hoggart was not alone among intellectuals in criticizing 'the juke box boys' with their 'drape suits, picture ties and American slouch', who spent their evenings in 'harshly lighted milk bars', putting 'copper after copper into the mechanical record player', representing 'a peculiarly thin and pallid

---

51 Butler and King, *British General Election of 1964*, p. 39.

form of dissipation'.[52] There was panic, as during the war, about the sexual behaviour of liberated youth and, as before and as in other age groups, no sign that it had previously been as constrained as convention believed or become as rampant as moralists feared.

The changing youth culture grew out of the greater economic independence of young people as more of them found decently paid work more easily than before, despite most leaving school without qualifications. Amid full employment, parents needed less support than before; young people could afford to enjoy themselves and the market responded. But youth, like adult, affluence was by no means universal: there were real inequalities between regions of continuing unemployment, such as Merseyside and Clydeside, and the rest. Young men also now faced an awkward time between leaving school at 15 and call-up for conscription at 18, years of uncertainty when it was hard to settle into a career. Nevertheless, a new, distinctive, youth culture emerged which disturbed cultural conservatives but did no obvious harm and brought lasting change.

Critics and Counter-Cultures

Changes in British culture through the 1950s and early 1960s aroused alarm and criticism from traditionalists and from those who thought it was not changing fast enough. A growing tide of public social criticism from the later 1950s, unparalleled earlier in the century, itself signified change. It too was a product of 'affluence', gaining audiences from the new mass medium of TV, from more people with time and cash to attend theatres and clubs and buy magazines and books and a popular press eager for controversy.

In the slowly expanding universities growing social science and cultural studies departments analysed social conditions and change, exposing multiple inequalities. Paperback publishers, still led by Penguin, mass produced their commentaries. One highly successful publication in Penguin's popular, blue, Pelican imprint was *The Uses of Literacy*, published in 1957 and re-printed four times between 1958 and 1962, by the upwardly mobile, once working-class, academic, Richard Hoggart (born 1918), founder in 1964 of the influential Centre for Contemporary Cultural Studies at Birmingham University. It was a passionate diatribe against the 'candy floss world' of contemporary mass culture, arguing that popular music, magazines, newspapers, film, TV, radio and advertising exploited affluence, creating 'a mean form of materialism', through their 'thin bonhomie' encouraging 'an effete attitude to life' and 'rootless and shallow lives'. Hoggart believed these media should encourage the self-improvement that had once characterized working-class patrons of the WEA and Working Men's Clubs. The 'emerging common man' (he said little about women) was being formed

---

52 Richard Hoggart, *The Uses of Literacy* (London: Penguin, 1969), pp. 248–50; Bill Osgerby, 'Youth Culture', in P. Addison and H. Jones (eds), *A Companion to Contemporary Britain, 1939–2000* (Oxford: Blackwell, 2005), pp. 128–32; Bill Osgerby, *Youth in Britain since 1945* (Oxford: Blackwell, 1998).

by 'mass entertainments [which] are in the end what DH Lawrence described as "anti-life"', in place of the materially poorer but, he believed, socially richer, more cohesive, working-class community he remembered in Leeds between the wars: 'They are full of a corrupt brightness, of improper appeals and moral evasions ... [belonging] ... to a vicarious spectators' world, they offer nothing which can really grip the brain or heart'.[53]

Hoggart's message that affluence and new technology did not necessarily create a better society was echoed in another Pelican by the American economist, J. K. Galbraith, *The Affluent Society* (1958), warning that America had already taken this path, of 'private affluence and public squalor', which Europe should avoid. Other critics, including Anthony Crosland,[54] argued that cultural change was too slow and prosperity had good as well as bad effects. Michael Young left his Labour Party post in 1951, becoming an independent social researcher and gadfly, critical of the centralized state socialism he believed Labour had sponsored and seeking ways to enable everyone to enrich and control their own lives materially and culturally.[55] In 1952 he founded the Institute of Community Studies in Bethnal Green, east London, for research into everyday life. One of its first publications was *Family and Kinship in East London* by Young and Peter Willmott (1957, Pelican 1962), which revealed their surprise that, contrary to Hoggart's lament for the death of working-class community, it was flourishing in Bethnal Green. They challenged commonplace sociological assertions that formerly cohesive families were falling apart in the modern, affluent, mobile world, discovering in east London strong, supportive extended families. The chief threat to working-class community and family they identified was public housing policy, demolishing east London 'slums' and moving tenants to distant estates, far from kin and familiar neighbourhoods. Another Institute of Community Studies publication, *The Family Life of Old People* (1957, Pelican 1963) by sociologist Peter Townsend, challenged another commonplace assumption, that families no longer cared for their older relatives. He demonstrated that family care was often more effective now that families had social service support, were better off and had more time, hard and impoverished though many older people's lives were in other respects.

Women's situation was scrutinized, including by two female social scientists, Alva Myrdal and Viola Klein in *Women's Two Roles. Home and Work*.[56] They challenged the widespread belief that mothers of young children should be their full-time carers, creating delinquents if they chose selfishly to work outside the home, promoted by the influential 'maternal deprivation' theory of psychologist John Bowlby (also published by Pelican).[57] Myrdal and Klein described this as 'a new and subtle form of

---

53 Hoggart,*The Uses of Literacy*, pp 318–46.
54 See pp. 232–3.
55 Thane, 'Michael Young', pp. 293–9.
56 Alva Myrdal and Viola Klein, *Women's Two Roles. Home and Work* (London: Routledge, 1956).
57 John Bowlby, *Child Care and the Growth of Love* (Harmondsworth: Pelican, 1953).

anti-feminism' which imposed 'new and exacting standards of motherhood'. Like many others, including social workers concerned with children,[58] they accepted that young children needed supportive care but not necessarily full-time care by the natural mother. Rather, like feminists for decades before them, they argued that women's work inside and outside the home should be equally valued,[59] that women should be helped to choose when and whether to work in or out of the home with maternity leave of one to two years, access to training before returning to work, better designed housing, day nurseries and shorter working hours for men and women, enabling couples to share domestic responsibilities. But one-third of men interviewed disapproved of married women working and most disapproved of mothers of young children 'going out to work'. Few gave much help around the home. Employers were unwilling to adapt to the needs of married women.[60] British feminism was alive in the 1950s, assisted by the translation, for Penguin, of Simone de Beauvoir's *The Second Sex*, in 1953.

It was needed. A survey for the Ministry of Labour in 1959 revealed the limited prospects of unmarried women. Among women who graduated in science and engineering in Britain in 1954–6 (only 708), 74 per cent were employed in teaching or other public services, such as the NHS, because they despaired of their prospects in industry or scientific research. Employers confirmed their reluctance to employ women, pay them equally (because men had families to support), or promote them because they expected difficulties if women managed men. Another study by female academics at LSE found schoolgirls interested in careers in science and technology were discouraged by teachers and employers who did not believe women performed well in these fields. The 1961 Census showed that of 249,000 people active in science and technology only 18,300 were female, despite shortages of suitably trained workers.[61] A survey of young mothers at home in north London in the early 1960s found many feeling isolated and bored, keen to work as soon as possible, even if their husbands disapproved (as 27 per cent did), but no childcare was available and they were pessimistic about finding fulfilling work. Thirty-five per cent of the working-class wives and 21 per cent from the middle-class regretted marrying too young, generally to escape their families or monotonous low-paid work.[62]

Sociologists also analysed and criticized secondary school selection. About 25 per cent of 11-year-olds attended grammar schools, 30 per cent in Wales; fewer than 5 per cent entered the few technical schools; two-thirds attended secondary moderns.

58 Thane and Evans, *Sinners?* pp. 92–4.
59 See p. 99.
60 V. Klein, *Britain's Married Women Workers* (London: Routledge, 1957).
61 N. Seear, V. Roberts and J. Brick, *A Career for Women in Industry* (London and Edinburgh, 1964); Thane, 'Towards Equal Opportunities?' pp. 200–2.
62 Hannah Gavron, *The Captive Wife. Conflict of Housebound Mothers* (London: Routledge, 1966; repr. Harmondsworth: Pelican, 1970).

Selection was intended to grant equal opportunities to all regardless of background, yet research revealed that in England and Wales (more in England than Wales) three out of five children from professional and managerial backgrounds attended grammar schools, only one in ten children of unskilled manual workers. Middle-class children were more likely to stay on past 15. Secondary modern schools prepared most working-class children to leave at 15, without qualifications, for manual work. The system did not promote social mobility. The proportion staying to 18 and progressing to higher education in Wales was double that in England. Scotland had long had a more inclusive school system. Demand grew for comprehensive schools. By 1964, there were 200 in Britain including in parts of Wales and the Labour-controlled LCC.[63]

Five per cent of UK children attended independent schools in the 1950s compared with 9 per cent in the 1930s, with some parents now preferring free grammar schools. One in eight middle-class children gained university places, while fewer than one in a hundred working-class children did so. Adequate means-tested maintenance grants were available for university students from low-income families who performed well in national examinations and no-one paid fees. But by 1960 still only 4 per cent of 18–21 year olds attended university, only 25 per cent of whom were female, 15 per cent at Oxford and Cambridge. Females overwhelmingly studied arts subjects. A much higher proportion of females attended two-year teacher training colleges, to enter a traditionally female occupation.[64]

Angry Young Men (and Women)

Inequalities in 1950s Britain were challenged also on the stage and in literature by a disparate group of writers bundled together by the media as 'Angry Young Men'. John Osborne's play, *Look Back in Anger* (1956) attacked the continuing hegemony of the upper middle-classes. Class inequalities were a major focus of the anger, as in Colin Wilson's widely cited essay, *The Outsider* (1956). John Braine's novel, *Room at the Top* (1957), expressed the limits and tensions as well as satisfactions of upward social mobility for a northern working-class man. The highly successful film of Braine's book (1959) treated sex more frankly than previous British films. Alan Sillitoe's novel, *Saturday Night and Sunday Morning* (1958), also a successful film in 1960, about a factory worker in Nottingham, showed how grim and alienating such work still was, only relieved by wild weekends of drink and sex. Yet even more popular than the 'angry' outpourings were Ian Fleming's exciting, less socially challenging, adventures of one of the social elite, James Bond, also successful films, the first one being *Dr No* in 1960.

---

63 Clarke, *Hope and Glory*, pp. 284–6.
64 Halsey and Webb, *Twentieth-century British Social Trends*, pp. 225–6.

A rare female contribution to theatrical social critique was Shelagh Delaney's *A Taste of Honey*, first staged 1958, filmed in 1961, both immediately successful. Delaney was only 19 when she wrote it, reacting to boredom with a play by well-established Terence Rattigan, about, as usual, repressed upper middle-class people, the opposite of the emotional explicitness of the Angry Young Men. The play was set in a desolate flat overlooking a gas-works and slaughterhouse in Salford, where 16-year-old Jo lived with her feckless, drunken mother. When mother went off with a salesman, Jo had a brief affair with a black sailor, became pregnant and was abandoned. She was rescued and supported with her child by a gentle young homosexual, until her mother drove him away. Jo challenged racism, homophobia and the stigma of unmarried motherhood, much that radicals hated in 1950s Britain, but with no happy ending – a complete contrast to Rattigan's world.

Another female contribution was Nell Dunn's ambiguously titled novel, *Up the Junction* (1963), about working-class life and sex near Clapham Junction in south London. Unlike many writers challenging convention in the 1950s and early 1960s, Dunn was a Chelsea heiress whose marriage was celebrated at the Ritz Hotel. In 1959, she and her husband moved to working-class Battersea. She worked in a chocolate factory while her husband, Jeremy Sandford, studied the plight of homeless families, creating a radio documentary which inspired Ken Loach's TV film, *Cathy Come Home* (1966) and serious concern about homelessness.[65] *Up the Junction* portrayed working-class women, mostly in their early twenties, who Dunn worked with and befriended. Like Delaney and the 'angries', Dunn showed that 'affluence' had not eliminated class divisions, class identity or insecurity, nor did she romanticize working-class life past or present in one of the less glittering sectors of London, with shabby terraces, outdoor toilets, railways and smoky air. But it was not miserable. Work was plentiful. If a job or an employer did not suit it was easy to leave and find another. Young working-class women could afford the fashions for piled up 'beehive' hairdos, pointed 'winkle-picker' shoes and American pop music, consumption represented as fun, not as symptoms of moral decay, while living in familiar environments with their families. Women of all ages were sexually active and certainly not deferential to men, deriding them, well aware of the violent tendencies and unreliability of too many of them, suggesting that little had changed in relations between the sexes. The sexual awareness of older women portrayed by Dunn challenged assertions of unprecedented moral decay among the young; and she showed the downside of sex, describing an illegal abortion. She found life in Battersea a release from Rattigan-style repression in Chelsea.[66]

65 See p. 269.
66 Stephen Brooke, 'Slumming in Swinging London. Class, Gender and the Post-War City in Nell Dunn's *Up the Junction* (1963)', *Cultural and Social History* 9 (2012): 429–44; Stephen Brooke, *Sexual Politics. Sexuality, Family Planning and the British Left from the 1880s to the Present Day* (Oxford University Press, 2011), pp 156–8.

Criticism of the limitations imposed upon British life and social and economic progress by a dominant, interlocking elite was not confined to the arts. In 1962, Anthony Sampson, an *Observer* journalist who had worked for some years in South Africa published *Anatomy of Britain*, blaming the 'white tribes' of the ruling class for creating a 'living museum', holding Britain back from political and economic modernization. Economic journalist Michael Shanks made similar arguments in his Penguin *The Stagnant Society* (1961), and they were echoed by, among others, a collection of essays edited by Arthur Koestler, dramatically titled *Suicide of a Nation?*[67]

Another, newer, genre of social critique, with similar targets, was the fashion for satirical comedy. In 1960, a group of recent Oxbridge graduates, of differing social backgrounds (middle-class Peter Cook and Jonathan Miller, working-class Alan Bennett and Dudley Moore) launched *Beyond the Fringe* at the Edinburgh Festival, satirizing social class differences, politicians, the Church and established conventions. When they opened in London they were a lasting hit. In 1961, Cook opened The Establishment Club in Soho, which, until 1964, provided nightly satirical cabarets. The club took its name from an article by journalist, Henry Fairlie, in the right-wing *Spectator* magazine in 1955. He noted a curious aspect of the notorious defection to Russia of diplomats Burgess and Maclean in 1951 – the highly placed social acquaintances who rushed to defend the traitors. He concluded, sympathetically, that this was how power worked in Britain, through a matrix of loyalties forged through family connections, elite schools and universities, which he labelled the 'Establishment' – the structure Sampson later anatomized. The term was embraced by social critics as representing all they opposed. Fairlie was among those who declared their pleasure that the Establishment existed to keep worse at bay, like those crowding The Establishment Club and the other critics. Awareness of class remained strong at all levels of society.

The fortnightly magazine, *Private Eye*, founded in 1961, still flourishes in the twenty-first century. It was produced by public school and Oxbridge men, satirizing politicians and the social elite, determinedly exposing dishonesty and sleaze. The instantly popular weekly BBC TV show, *That Was the Week That Was*, in 1962–3 satirized politicians and even the monarchy, jovially with song, dance and pointed comment. Following complaints from politicians and other 'Establishment' figures the BBC withdrew it in 1964, lest its impartiality was compromised in election year. It never returned.

Concern that Britain was falling behind other countries, failing to modernize socially, economically and politically, due above all to its rigid class structure, dominated by an inward-looking, traditional elite which limited opportunities for others, was widespread and growing by the later 1950s. But it was by no means universal and the Conservatives had to decide how far they could go with it, anxious to appear 'modern' but aware of deep social divisions and the opposition of many of their supporters to change.

---

67 Arthur Koestler (ed.), *Suicide of a Nation? An Enquiry into the State of Britain Today* (London: Hutchinson, 1963).

Conservativism and Cultural Change

Cultural change and growing demands for reform alongside assertive traditionalist opposition presented Conservative leaders with a series of delicate decisions. In 1956, Labour MP Sydney Silverman introduced a Bill to abolish hanging which passed all stages in the Commons but, like another in 1948, was defeated in the Lords, perhaps not helped by high-profile murder cases such as that of Christie in 1953 and Ruth Ellis' conviction for murdering her violent lover in 1955 – the last woman to be hanged in Britain. 'Hangers and floggers' did not dominate the Conservative Party or the wider culture, but party leaders could not ignore them. Butler opposed them – one reason why he was an unacceptable party leader, though Macmillan and other leading ministers quietly agreed with him. Macmillan feared the 'hanging and flogging' image alienated liberal-minded voters and Butler felt encouraged to compromise, introducing the Homicide Act 1957, which established separate categories of capital and non-capital murder and a defence of 'diminished responsibility'. It was a first step, difficult to implement but fewer people were hanged.[68]

Affluence was accused of encouraging excessive drink and gambling – among the masses, not in gentlemen's clubs or at Ascot. In 1956, Macmillan, as Chancellor, introduced Premium Bonds to encourage Post Office savings by giving savers regular cash prizes by lottery, criticized for encouraging gambling. A committee was appointed to investigate illegal off-course betting on horse racing. This was extensive because betting was not legally available to the many, mainly working-class, people unable to attend racecourses and without bank accounts required for betting by phone. In 1956, it recommended legalized betting offices. Conservative opposition was so strong that Macmillan did nothing, though it emerged in the 1959 election manifesto, encouraged by younger Conservative modernizers in the party's radical Bow Group advocating reform of 'outdated remnants of Victorianism', including the gambling, licensing, Sunday Observance and censorship laws. Following the election, the government introduced the Betting, Gaming and Lotteries Act 1960, permitting licensed betting shops and legalized gaming. Unintentionally, it triggered a bingo boom, mainly among older people, and, more worrying, gaming machines, 'one-armed bandits', in pubs and cafes. By 1964, there were over 24,000, making £10 million per year profit. Butler also introduced changes in the licensing laws, again prodded by the Bow Group, despite opposition in the party and the Churches. The 1961 Licensing Act extended evening pub closing hours from 9.30 to 11 pm, but the restricted Sunday hours (normally 12–2.30 pm, 6.30–9.30 pm, while in parts of Wales pubs were closed all day) were unchanged to appease 'temperance and non-conformist opinion'.[69]

68 Jarvis, *Conservative Governments*, pp. 50–64.
69 Ibid., pp. 65–85.

The Wolfenden Report

Adult sexual behaviour also caused controversy. Female prostitution was legal, though soliciting, judged to be a public nuisance, could attract the maximum fine of £2. Prosecutions rose from 2,966 in 1938 to 9,756 in 1962 and complaints grew. Sir David Maxwell-Fyfe, as Home Secretary, decided that the law should be reviewed, together with homosexual law since offences had also increased. All forms of sexual activity between men (not women) in public or private were criminal offences. In 1938, there were 134 recorded cases of sodomy and bestiality in England and Wales, in 1954 there were 1,043; of 'gross indecency', 316 in 1938 and 2,322 in 1955.[70] By the mid-1950s about 4 per cent of the male prison population was convicted of homosexual offences. Issues around homosexuality were publicized following the defection of the spies Guy Burgess and Donald Maclean in 1951, whose homosexuality was held to explain their treason by making them vulnerable to blackmail. In 1952, the mathematician Alan Turing, awarded the OBE for cracking the Enigma code at Bletchley and helping win the war, was arrested for homosexual offences. He accepted a hormone treatment 'cure' in place of prison. He became impotent, grew breasts, suffered depression and committed suicide in 1954. In 1953, the prominent actor, John Gielgud, was arrested and fined £10 for importuning in a public lavatory, unleashing press criticism of the leniency of the penalty. At his next appearance on stage he was greeted with standing applause, suggesting a certain public support for homosexual rights. In 1954, came the sensational trial of Lord Montagu of Beaulieu and Peter Wildeblood, Diplomatic Correspondent of the *Daily Mail*, imprisoned for inciting two RAF men to commit 'unnatural acts' in private.

Prejudice against homosexuals was deep, but there were hints of change and more open discussion of sexual issues. The American Alfred Kinsey's *Sexual Behavior in the Human Male* was published with much publicity in Britain in 1948, followed by *Sexual Behavior in the Human Female* in 1953. Kinsey revealed that 37 per cent of his sample of white, middle-class American males had experienced sex with another man. Quiet campaigning for reform was led by the Sex Education Society, revived by medical practitioner Norman Haire in 1947 until his death in 1952 when the organization flagged. In 1954, the Moral Welfare Council of the Church of England published a report by clergy and doctors, *The Problem of Homosexuality*, which asserted it was indeed a sin, but sins were not necessarily crimes and reform should be considered. Butler, in 1954, appointed a committee chaired by Sir John Wolfenden, Vice-Chancellor of Reading University, to examine the legal treatment of homosexuality and prostitution.

70 Jeffrey Weeks, *Sex, Politics and Society. The Regulation of Sexuality since 1800* (London: Longman, 1989), pp. 238–40.

The Wolfenden Report on Homosexual Offences and Prostitution was published in 1957. It concluded that, despite the official numbers, there was little sign that these activities were increasing. Prostitution was possibly more visible – though less so in many areas than a hundred years earlier – but the main cause of more convictions was police zeal in pursuing offenders, especially in London and other cities, particularly following the appointment of an ardent Roman Catholic, Sir Theobald Mathew, as Director of Public Prosecutions in 1944, then a zealous Metropolitan Police Commissioner, Sir John Nott-Bowes, in 1953.[71] The report echoed contemporary conventions in regretting 'the general loosening of former moral standards' and 'the emotional insecurity, community instability and weakening of the family'.[72] Less conventionally, it recommended decriminalization of male homosexual behaviour in private (only), arguing for a distinction between sin and crime, public and private morality, as there was with regard to adultery and lesbianism. Criminal penalties should apply only when male and female sexual behaviour caused a public nuisance. It denied that homosexuality was a disease, but recommended further research into its causes and the possibility of effective 'treatment' to be offered to perpetrators of homosexual offences.

Most of the popular press reacted to the proposals on homosexual law reform with horror. The *News of the World* claimed they would lead to 'the most dreadful corruption and pollution', though the left-leaning *Daily Mirror* and the liberal *New Chronicle* supported decriminalization.[73] Butler inclined to agree with the proposals, but believed they were too far ahead of public and Conservative opinion and the Cabinet opposed them. The Homosexual Law Reform Society and the Albany Trust, a research and counselling service for homosexuals, were formed in 1958 to campaign for implementation. The Street Offences Act,1959, implemented Wolfenden's recommendations on prostitution, criminalizing soliciting in public and increasing the maximum penalties. This was strongly supported by responses to opinion polls and by most of the press. 'Tarts will no longer cling to every lamp-post', commented the *Daily Mirror*.[74] Many women opposed it because, like past legislation controlling prostitution, male customers went free. Butler agreed but was overruled by the Cabinet. The Wolfenden Report justified this because 'the simple fact is that prostitutes do parade themselves more habitually and openly than their prospective customers, and do by their continual presence affront the sense of decency of the ordinary citizen'.[75] Prostitutes moved off the streets and risked greater exploitation by male pimps. There was little public sympathy for women whom even the *News Chronicle* described as 'hardened professionals not driven to it by want,

71 Weeks, *Sex, Politics and Society*, p. 240.
72 Ibid., p. 239.
73 Bingham, *Family Newspapers*, pp. 188–90.
74 Ibid., p. 169.
75 Weeks, *Sex, Politics and Society*, p. 243.

but choosing it for gain'.[76] Convictions for prostitution declined to 2,726 by 1960, but prostitution did not. Strip clubs and cafes associated with vice and organized crime grew as alternative locations.[77] This brought condemnation but no government action.

Divorce

Divorce law reform was still contested between liberals and conservatives.[78] It remained difficult to divorce unless an 'offence', normally adultery, had been committed and both partners consented. In 1951, Labour MP Eirene White introduced a Private Member's Bill to add seven years' separation as grounds for divorce, introducing the concept of no-fault divorce. It also required husbands to make adequate provision for their families' maintenance, to meet concerns that women and children were often poorer after divorce. It gained an easy majority (131 votes to 60) in the Commons on its second reading. To avoid controversy, the government persuaded Eirene White to withdraw the Bill by establishing a Royal Commission on Marriage and Divorce. Chaired by Fergus Morton, a Chancery judge known as a safe pair of hands, it reported in 1956. Eirene White and others put the case for reform familiar since the beginning of the century,[79] that many marriages broke down but the partners could not divorce, leading often to unmarried cohabitation which was generally thought undesirable, including by many cohabitees. Divorces that did occur were often collusive between the partners, based on pretended adultery, notoriously organized by fixers acting as witnesses to pretended assignations. Partners might extort favourable financial terms in return for agreement to divorce. The opposition argued, as they always had, that divorce was already too easy. In fact, after a peak following wartime disruption, divorce petitions fell from 206,678 in 1946–50 to 146,353 in 1956–60 in England, Wales and Scotland, though still very substantially above prewar levels.[80]

The Commissioners expressed widespread divisions on divorce and the family. Nine of the eighteen opposed change because 'it is obvious that life-long marriage is the basis of a secure family life and that to secure their well-being children must have that background'. They felt 'grave anxiety' that marriages were breaking up which in the past would have survived because:

> Greater demands are now made of marriage, consequent on the spread of education, higher standards of living and the social and economic emancipation of women. The last is probably the most important. Women are no longer content to endure the treatment which in past

76 Bingham, *Family Newspapers*, p. 168.
77 Jarvis, *Conservative Governments*, p. 101.
78 See pp. 25, 100, 208.
79 See p. 25.
80 Halsey and Webb, *Twentieth-century British Social Trends*, p. 62.

time their inferior position obliged them to suffer. They expect of marriage that it shall be an equal partnership and rightly so. But the working out of this ideal exposes marriage to new strains. Some husbands find it difficult to accept the changed position of women: some wives do not appreciate that their new rights do not release them from the obligations arising out of marriage itself and, indeed, bring in their train new responsibilities.[81]

They recognized the reality of cultural change but resisted it, suggesting that it might 'become necessary to consider whether the community as a whole would not be happier and more stable if it abolished divorce altogether'.[82]

This was the most negative judgment on divorce reform of any report of the century, but nine other members, including Morton, were more moderate. They recommended marriage counselling, influenced by psychology and the emergence of the Marriage Guidance Council (founded 1938, now Relate). They believed modern psychological techniques could achieve reconciliation, but suggested divorce could be available after seven years' separation proved breakdown, though most would still refuse it if either party objected.

The Bow Group supported liberalization but most Conservatives did not. The government avoided commitment, but several of the Commission's less controversial recommendations were embodied in legislation which extended the courts' powers to act on failure to pay due maintenance following divorce, to ensure children were well supported and simplified divorce of a mentally ill partner.[83] The Report exposed particularly clearly the deep continuing cultural divide concerning the family and sexuality: traditional ideas were strongly challenged but still dominated the law.

The Royal Commission also disagreed about the legitimation of children whose parents subsequently married when one or both parents was married to another at the time of birth. The majority objected that legitimation would remove 'A powerful deterrent to illicit relationships ... with disastrous results for the status of marriage as at present understood'.[84] The minority argued 'there was no evidence that the law did deter couples from forming illicit unions ... [and] ... the hypothetical risk of promoting immorality had to be weighted against the real benefits which legitimation conferred on a child'.[85] At the time, at least one-third of 'illegitimate' children were living stably with unmarried parents, many of whom were unable to divorce.[86] In 1959, Labour MP John Parker introduced a Private Member's Bill which passed easily through the Commons, but was rejected by the Lords. The government overrode the Lords and the Legitimacy Act 1959 enabled 6,506

81 *Report of Royal Commission on Marriage and Divorce, 1951–5* (London: HMSO, 1955), Cmd. 9678, para. 45; Cretney, *Family Law*, p. 335.

82 *Report of the Royal Commission*, para. 54; Cretney, *Family Law*, p. 336.

83 Cretney, *Family Law*, pp. 455–8.

84 Ibid., p. 552; *Report of the Royal Commission*, para. 1180.

85 *Report of the Royal Commission*, para. 1182; Cretney, *Family Law*, p. 552; Thane and Evans, *Sinners?* pp. 95–6.

86 Thane and Evans, *Sinners?* pp. 88–91.

births to be re-registered as legitimate in 1960, in 1967 13,043. The easy passage through the Commons was a liberal challenge to prevailing moral panics about assumed increases in illicit cohabitation and illegitimacy, especially among 'schoolgirl mothers'. The number of births to unmarried mothers under 20 had indeed risen since the war, but more slowly than the numbers of teenage females.[87] Cultural conservatism did not always win.

Censorship

There were also successful challenges to the Lord Chamberlain's power to censor publications and theatre judged 'obscene', defined in the nineteenth century as likely 'to deprave and corrupt'. The Labour government took a relaxed approach to censorship, but Maxwell-Fyfe reverted to a hard line. The Society of Authors, with Roy Jenkins, a backbench Labour MP, lobbied the government until it appointed a Select Committee on Obscene Publications. This concluded in 1958 that, as the Society advocated, artistic merit should be a defence against prosecution, while controls on hard-core pornography should be strengthened. Under continuing pressure, the government introduced the Obscene Publications Act 1959, which allowed the vague defence of 'publication for the public good' and increased police powers to seize hard porn.[88]

Penguin books put it to the test in 1960 by announcing publication of the banned *Lady Chatterley's Lover* by D. H. Lawrence – at 3s 6d it was widely affordable, which appears to have strengthened the Attorney-General's decision to prosecute. A much publicized trial followed, notorious for the prosecution barrister's preferred test of suitability for publication: 'Would you approve of your young sons, young daughters – because girls can read as well as boys – reading this book? … Is it a book you would ever wish your wife or your servant to read?'[89] Thirty-six writers, scholars, including Richard Hoggart, and the radical Bishop of Woolwich– who proclaimed it 'A book all Christians should read' – spoke for the defence. They succeeded and 3 million copies sold within three months. The flood of real pornography continued until the Obscene Publications Act 1964 introduced more effective controls.[90]

Out of the growing tensions between cultural conservatism and its growing range of critics in the 1950s came a succession of proposals for liberal reforms. None were new and the results were limited, but they signified on-going cultural change leading on to more profound changes a decade later.

---

87 Ibid., pp. 83–4.
88 Jarvis, *Conservative Governments*, pp. 113–16.
89 Alan Travis, *Bound and Gagged. A Secret History of Obscenity in Britain* (London: Profile, 2000), pp. 128–65.
90 Jarvis, *Conservative Governments*, pp. 116–19; Andrew Holden, *Makers and Manners. Politics and Morality in Post-War Britain* (London: Politico's, 2004), pp 87–93; Travis, *Bound and Gagged*, pp. 92–127.

Less controversial was the Life Peerages Act 1958, introduced in the Lords by the Earl of Home, a Conservative MP until he inherited his title in 1951, then Leader of the Lords. It enabled political parties to nominate lifetime as well as hereditary peers and, at last after forty years of women's pressure, life, but not hereditary, peeresses to serve in the Lords. It was the first serious reform of the Lords, after a long succession of unsuccessful Private Members' Bills, justified by the serious decline in hereditary peers' attendance. In 1959–60 there were 859 hereditaries, plus the Law Lords and Anglican bishops, with an average daily attendance of 136. The Conservatives also still sought to appease female voters. An amendment deleting the clause admitting women was supported in the Lords by Nancy Astor's son, Viscount Astor, but defeated by 134 votes to thirty. Labour opposed the whole reform, with Gaitskell demanding either total dismantling of the Lords or a wholly elected chamber, but it drew wider expertise into the Lords and peers became more active in parliamentary business.[91]

General Election, 1959

Macmillan prepared for an election in October 1959. In February, he made a high-profile visit to Moscow. Khrushchev, now premier, was still believed to be someone the West could work with, and the visit boosted Macmillan's image as a world statesman. Back home, he persuaded the Chancellor to deliver another generous pre-election Budget, including bigger tax cuts than before the 1955 election, costing £360 million. Labour and some economists argued this would harm economic recovery, but the Conservatives promoted them as signs of economic success, with enthusiastic press support. They launched an expensive poster campaign featuring families enjoying affluent consumption under the slogan 'Life's Better with the Conservatives. Don't Let Labour Ruin It'. Macmillan took advantage of a visit by President Eisenhower, with whom he had good relations, to display US–UK reconciliation after Suez and his own world statesman credentials in a joint TV programme.

Labour disparaged such features of consumer society as advertising and PR. Gaitskell said 'The whole thing is somehow fake'. Nor could they afford the almost £500,000 the Conservatives spent on promotion; Labour spent about £103,000.[92] They did run effective TV broadcasts assisted by a rising young MP with TV experience, Anthony Wedgwood Benn. It was the most televised election so far and both parties were increasingly concerned with media presentation. For the first time both held daily press conferences. Labour was now less visibly divided and Gaitskell made a good impression as he toured the country. It focused on increasing economic growth

91 *The House of Lords Reform*, Cmd. 7027 (London: The Stationery Office, 2007).
92 David Butler and Richard Rose, *The British General Election of 1959* (London: Macmillan, 1960), pp. 20, 27.

through planned investment and expansion of education, including development of comprehensive schools to improve opportunities for working-class children, stressing continuing inequality between rich and poor. It proposed ambitious pensions reforms to assist the largest group known to be poor.[93]

Labour also promised re-nationalization of road haulage and iron and steel, and further public ownership if necessary. The Conservatives, with no apparent sense of shame, accused Labour of bribing the electorate with unaffordable promises while remaining the party of rationing, controls and nationalization. On other themes, they tried to steer delicately between cultural liberals and conservatives, emphasizing Conservative commitment to upholding moral standards and the family and strengthening the 'national character', while Butler represented the party as 'modern', adapting to change, highlighting the recent reforms concerning personal life. The manifesto promised further liberalization, loosening statutes 'laced in Victorian corsetry' as Butler put it.[94]

The Conservatives won an unprecedented third successive victory, increasing their majority to 100 seats with 49.4 per cent of votes, to Labour's 43.8 per cent, from a 78.8 per cent turnout. The Liberals won six seats. The swing to the Conservatives was greatest in the prosperous West Midlands and Greater London, while areas of high unemployment, including Clydeside and Manchester, swung to Labour. Conservatives started a long decline in Scotland and remained a minority in Wales. They had a strong hold on middle-class voters, better-off workers and, probably, women in all classes, though Labour gained slightly among women while losing among voters under 30. Macmillan claimed that class war was obsolete. Some Labour leaders feared affluence had so undermined its traditional support that it had no future. *Must Labour Lose?* in the new materialistic world, asked a sociological analysis of its performance, starting an anguished debate in the party.[95] The victory was widely attributed to 'Supermac's' leadership and the economic revival.

1959–1963: Crises

Continued Conservative success required sustained economic revival. The boom peaked in 1959–60 with growth of 4–5 per cent, but Heathcoat Amory's pre-election measures stimulated consumption and imports grew almost twice as fast as exports. He wanted to reduce spending and raise taxes, but Macmillan feared justified criticism of the government's pre-election tactics and refused. Heathcoat Amory resigned. Macmillan replaced him with the trusty Selwyn Lloyd. The little known Earl of Home

93 Thane, *Old Age in English Society*, pp. 373–6.

94 Jarvis, *Conservative Governments*, p. 65

95 M. Abrams and R. Rose, *Must Labour Lose?* (Harmondsworth: Penguin, 1960); Thorpe, *History of the British Labour Party*, pp. 145–51.

became Foreign Secretary. Lloyd was reluctant to puncture the spending boom but the weakening of sterling, exacerbated by a dock workers' strike which helped to widen the trade gap, forced the bank rate back to 7 per cent in July 1961. Lloyd froze public sector pay, exhorting restraint in the private sector, noting that average incomes had risen 8 per cent in the previous year, but productivity by only 3 per cent. He cut spending and raised prescription charges despite the conclusion, in 1959, of a committee on prescription costs that 'the present charge is a tax which ... is resented by patients and doctors as a tax on illness ... [and] ... has proved disappointing financially'.[96] An important reason was that Enoch Powell, Minister of Health from 1960, planned to redevelop the hospitals. Civil servants in the Ministry, backed by the Guillebaud Report and a Labour campaign, persuaded the Cabinet of the need for a major hospital-building programme. In 1962 the Hospital Plan proposed ambitiously to build ninety new hospitals, drastically redevelop 134 and extend 360 at a cost of £500 million over several years.[97] It was unclear how, or whether, funds could be raised and the Plan was not fulfilled when it was abandoned in 1973 amid economic crisis. But it protected hospitals from cuts and much needed new hospitals were built, fewer than hoped but a significant improvement. There was much criticism of the government's see-sawing fiscal policies in the Commons and the press.

There was further conflict in the Labour Party. At the 1959 conference Gaitskell failed to persuade the party to abandon Clause 4 of the 1918 constitution committing it to public ownership.[98] He supported some nationalization but believed the party must lose its class-war image in a changing society. This exacerbated divisions in the party with no obvious gain, raising doubts about his leadership. Morale was low. After Bevan's death in 1960 the conference voted narrowly for unilateral disarmament, following a leftward shift among trade union leaders. Gaitskell pledged to 'fight and fight and fight again' against the decision. The left backed Harold Wilson in a challenge to Gaitskell's leadership and what they saw as his divisive tactics. Gaitskell won easily and reversed the unilateralism resolution in 1961, restoring his image as a strong leader.[99]

Macmillan also sought to change the government's image. Iain Macleod was appointed Party Chairman and Leader of the House, in the hope that a younger, forceful voice would inject a sense of purpose and progress into the party. Increasingly concerned about Britain's flagging competitiveness, the Conservatives sought a strategy

96 Glennerster, *British Social Policy*, p. 88.
97 Ibid.; Nicolas Timmins, *The Five Giants. A Biography of the Welfare State* (London: Fontana, 1996; rev. edn London: HarperCollins, 2001), pp. 209–11.
98 See p. 65.
99 Thorpe, *History of the British Labour Party*, pp. 149–52; Phillip Williams, *Hugh Gaitskell. A Political Biography* (London: Jonathan Cape, 1979).

for economic development. In 1960, they organized the European Free Trade Area (EFTA), with Denmark, Austria, Norway, Portugal, Sweden and Switzerland, to foster trade and growth with less regulation than the EEC (formed 1958) and without its political goals, but it was less successful. British trade increasingly focused on the EEC as its colonial and world trading declined. In 1953, it provided 10 per cent of imports, by 1960 it was 15 per cent, while imports from Australia and New Zealand dropped from 14 to 8 per cent. Britain's share of world trade in manufactures fell from 16 per cent in the mid-1950s to under 13 per cent in 1960. While rival European economies expanded, Britain failed to keep up. In 1961, Macmillan persuaded the Cabinet that Britain must apply to join the EEC. Edward Heath, a committed Europhile, was recruited to the Cabinet to negotiate entry. The party was, and remains, divided over EEC membership and some backbench opponents began to contemplate 'Supermac's' retirement. In a further move to rescue the economy, in 1962 the National Economic Development Council (NEDC) was established to bring together employers, unions and the government to pursue planning techniques successfully employed by competitors in the EEC and advocated by Labour.

The government's popularity plummeted. In March 1962 the Liberals were overjoyed to win Orpington, in suburban Kent, from the Conservatives in a by-election, the biggest by-election upset since the war and a rare Liberal success. Macmillan decided to sacrifice Lloyd, the most unpopular member of an unpopular government, but sought to disguise it by sacking six more Cabinet members in July 1962, on what the press labelled the 'night of the long knives'. The speed and brutality of the sackings, some quite unexpected, further damaged Macmillan's reputation within the party and out. He was no longer 'unflappable'. Labour won three Conservative seats in by-elections. Macmillan tried to refresh the party's image by promoting younger men (only), including Reginald Maudling as Chancellor; half the Cabinet were still old Etonians. But in 1962–3 unemployment rose to the highest level since 1947, 878,000 in February. It was an exceptionally hard winter, bringing power cuts, and the government was blamed for not safeguarding energy reserves.[100]

Racial tensions continued. The election brought new Conservative MPs from the West Midlands into the Commons, demanding immigration control. The government was less concerned about Commonwealth sentiment as it courted the EEC. In 1962, it introduced the Commonwealth Immigration Act, restricting immigration to those with 'special skills' or guaranteed employment, the first formal restrictions on immigration of Commonwealth citizens. It did not apply to Irish immigrants, who were not members of the Commonwealth. Gaitskell attacked it in the Commons as 'a cruel and brutal anti-colour measure', but it was popular in polls.

100 Clarke, *Hope and Glory*, pp. 277–82.

Panic about moral decline persisted. Television was blamed for encouraging crime and sexual excess, especially the 'Americanized' programmes on commercial channels. The government appointed the Pilkington Committee to consider the future of broadcasting. In 1962, it recommended what the government did not want to hear: radical restructuring of the ITA to raise standards; the more responsible BBC should provide a second channel and remain the sole radio broadcaster, while Conservatives advocated competition from commercial radio. It proposed restricting representations of violence and crime before 9 pm when many children watched. The government conceded a second BBC TV channel, but succumbed to pressure from the commercial companies against restructuring. It refused to control programme content, arguing that parents should supervise children's viewing. Attacks on broadcasters continued, most persistently and publicly by Mrs Mary Whitehouse, who launched the 'Clean-Up TV' campaign in 1964 (the National Viewers and Listeners' Association (NVLA) from 1965) to purge the 'disbelief, doubt and dirt that the BBC projects into millions of homes through the television screen', and similar ITV evil. As a secondary school teacher teaching sex education, she claimed to know how TV harmed schoolchildren. She campaigned for thirty years, with little obvious effect on programmes or government policy,[101] another symptom of the cultural divide in what the *Daily Mirror* labelled the 'Effluent Society'.

More serious was the crisis of October 1962, over the installation of Soviet nuclear missiles on Communist Cuba, 90 miles from the United States. Fear of nuclear war was widespread in the United Kingdom. Khrushchev agreed to remove the missiles if President Kennedy withdrew his threat to invade Cuba. The United States agreed and withdrew missiles from Turkey, close to the USSR. Macmillan insisted that Britain must keep its 'independent nuclear deterrent', though it was wholly dependent on the United States for launching missiles via American Polaris submarines. This sign of the United Kingdom's close relationship with the United States destroyed hopes of acceptance into the EEC. De Gaulle, now President of France, was already dubious about Britain's commitment to Europe. He took the nuclear arrangement as proof of Britain's preference for the United States and in January 1963 vetoed UK entry.

In the Labour Party even Gaitskell disapproved of a nuclear strategy that was no longer independent, removing a major division. Opposition to nuclear arms grew. The Campaign for Nuclear Disarmament (CND) was founded in 1958 to 'Ban the Bomb' supported by well-known intellectuals of diverse views, including Bertrand Russell, J. B. Priestley, historian A. J. P. Taylor, playwright John Osborne and Bevanite MP Michael Foot. The movement became increasingly divided between unilateral and multilateral

101 Lawrence Black, 'There was Something about Mary. The National Viewers and Listeners' Association and Social Movement History', in N. Crowson, M. Hilton and J. MacKay (eds), *NGOs in Contemporary Britain. Non-State Actors in Society and Politics since 1945* (London: Palgrave, 2009), pp. 182–200.

disarmers, but for several years it held large much publicized, good humoured annual Easter marches from Trafalgar Square to the nuclear research station at Aldermaston, Berkshire.

Labour was also divided about the EEC. Gaitskell, surprisingly, announced his opposition to UK membership, which, he told the conference, would spell 'the end of Britain as an independent state … the end of a thousand years of history' and undermine the multi-racial Commonwealth. This upset some of his colleagues, but he was supported by left-wing opponents of the 'capitalist club' as they labelled the EEC. Then, in January 1963, Gaitskell suddenly died, aged 56, following an apparently minor illness. In the ensuing leadership election, his deputy, George Brown, whose drinking habits and volatile personality caused doubts, was opposed by another Gaitskellite, James Callaghan. Both were beaten by the ex-Bevanite, Harold Wilson, who was seen as less divisive.[102]

Then the government was rocked by scandal, when John Profumo, Minister of War, was seen frolicking with naked young women other than his wife in the swimming pool at Cliveden, the Astors' country house, among other antics relished by the ever less deferential press. Widely rumoured in the press and elsewhere, then leaked by *Private Eye*, it emerged that Profumo shared a girlfriend with an attaché at the Russian Embassy. This diplomatic indiscretion rather than his sexual behaviour plus, above all, his denial of the stories in the Commons (though he later admitted them), provoked his resignation and unleashed more explicit media revelations. Stories of the misdemeanours of other protagonists in the scandal, especially the young women with colourful sexual histories, Christine Keeler and Mandy Rice-Davies, including their links with Rachman, kept the scandal live for months.[103] Macmillan held aloof, but his government looked increasingly weak as it and he were attacked in the press, spiced with rumours of his wife's long affair with Conservative MP Robert Boothby (of which Macmillan was aware) and other ministerial sexual transgressions.

The scandal aroused further conflicts between moralists and advocates of freedom in private life and further evidence of cultural shifts and social divisions. *The Times* called for a reaffirmation of traditional moral values, attacking 'widespread decadence beneath the glitter of a large segment of stiff lipped society',[104] though it had less press support than before. Mervyn Stockwood, Bishop of Southwark, demanded a campaign to cleanse the 'national stables' of evil practices festering in London's 'high places'.[105] Some accepted Profumo's activities as normal behaviour among upper-class men, if indiscreet, others sought a more open, tolerant society and criticized 'puritanism'. The *Evening Standard* noted a deep-seated 'public questioning of long-established Victorian

102 Thorpe, *History of the British Labour Party*, pp. 150–4.
103 Bingham, *Family Newspapers*, pp. 148–51, 254–7.
104 'It *Is a* Moral Issue', *The Times*, 11 June 1963, p. 13.
105 'These farmyard morals can corrupt us', *People,*16 June 1963, p. 12.

moral standards'.[106] Butler tried to reassure viewers of ITV's *About Religion* programme that 'Britain is fundamentally moral at heart'.[107] Labour politicians and social critics took the opportunity to attack the 'Establishment', which Profumo and his friends represented, as impeding progress and democratization. *Daily Mirror* columnist 'Cassandra' gloated that 'High Society is dragged in the dirt and people love it', echoed by other left-of-centre media.[108]

In October 1963, Macmillan fell ill from a misdiagnosed prostate condition and resigned. The Conservative Party did not elect leaders, they emerged from negotiations among the party elite, in which Macmillan, who soon recovered, played a major role. Again, he opposed Butler, preferring the relatively obscure Earl of Home. Home benefited from two years' agitation by Labour MP Wedgwood Benn to avoid inheriting his father's title and leaving the Commons for the Lords. The Peerage Act, 1963, enabled Benn and Home to abandon their titles, without affecting the succession of their heirs. It also, at last, admitted female hereditary peers to the Lords. Home, now Sir Alec Douglas-Home, was invited by Her Majesty to serve as Prime Minister.

Douglas-Home

Douglas-Home's premiership was a one-year campaign for the election due in 1964. Harold Wilson enjoyed the contest between Conservatives led by an Old Etonian fourteenth earl and Labour by a man with a northern accent whose father was a works chemist, his mother a schoolteacher. Douglas-Home's riposte to the 'fourteenth Mr Wilson' hardly undermined the contrast. A Cabinet of twenty-four men, twenty-one privately educated, eleven at Eton, reinforced the image of a party trailing behind national social change. Douglas-Home was uneasy in the Commons, while Wilson developed a lively media-aware style with catchy quotes. He began to transform Prime Minister's Questions, held twice a week in the Commons, into entertainment, responding to and feeding the fashion for political satire.

Wilson was younger, at 46, than any previous twentieth-century party leader. When US President John Fitzgerald Kennedy (JFK) was assassinated in November 1963, and widely mourned in Britain, parallels were made with Wilson as a new, younger, transforming type of politician. He represented the Conservatives as relics of the past when Britain urgently needed change and modernization. He courted technocrats and scientists whom he believed could help to regenerate the economy if business would use their skills. He supported joining the EEC with its large market

---

106 Frank Mort, *Capital Affairs. London and the Making of the Permissive Society* (New Haven, CT: Yale University Press, 2010), p. 344.
107 Ibid., p. 333.
108 Quoted in ibid., p. 327.

for exports and competitive stimulus for producers. He drew the party together, sympathetic to the left but emphasizing continuity of policy with Gaitskell, including several Gaitskellites in the Shadow Cabinet and persuading a reluctant George Brown to remain deputy leader.

Labour's election programme, *Signposts for the Sixties*, promised the re-nationalization of steel and a Land Commission to buy building land, but focused on stimulating innovation and growth by applying the resources of modern technology available in Britain but under-used outside the defence industries.[109] Wilson presented it to the 1963 conference in phrases which resonated through the election campaign and beyond:

> We are re-defining and we are re-stating our socialism in terms of the *scientific revolution* ... the Britain that is going to be forged in *the white heat* of this revolution will be no place for restrictive practices or outdated methods on either side of industry.

He called for a 'socialist inspired scientific and technological revolution releasing energy on an enormous scale ... for enriching mankind beyond our wildest dreams', expressing concerns about Britain's industrial backwardness and poorly trained management. He criticized the 'stop–go' policies of the Conservatives as driven by short-term electoral considerations rather than by economic strategy, deterring investors from investing in British manufacturing. Labour published *Twelve Wasted Years*, 459 pages of exhaustive analysis of what they saw as the government's failings in all areas of policy. 'Thirteen wasted years' was an election slogan the following year.[110]

The Conservatives were driven to promote their version of economic modernization. Another upwardly mobile, lower middle-class Oxford graduate, Edward Heath, contemporary with Wilson, born 1916, became President of the Board of Trade, briefed to free the economy of what were perceived as antiquated restrictions on competition. Resale price maintenance, which obliged retailers to sell at prices set by the suppliers, was abolished. The Chancellor, Reginald Maudling, faced with 878,000 unemployed, took the accustomed Conservative pre-election path: lowering the bank rate and stimulating demand. Growth rose from 4 per cent in 1963 to almost 6 per cent in 1964, but higher consumption increased imports. Pensions were raised but were still (at 33.7 per cent of average earnings, compared with 30.5 per cent in 1948) inadequate to live on and many pensioners still needed means-tested NAB supplements. The Conservatives encouraged occupational and private pensions provided by commercial insurers, which mainly benefited better-paid, mainly male, workers. Other national insurance allowances remained low.[111]

---

109 Edgerton, *Warfare State*.
110 Thorpe, *History of the British Labour Party*, pp. 153–6; Ben Pimlott, *Harold Wilson* (London: HarperCollins, 1993).
111 Clarke, *Hope and Glory*, pp. 293–5.

A hopeful sign for Labour, in April 1964, was victory, sixty-four seats to thirty-six, in the first elections for the Greater London Council (GLC). Against Labour opposition, the government had combined London and Middlesex County Councils, expecting to end Labour's thirty-year control of London government through the LCC by merging central and suburban London. Labour made substantial gains in other local elections. In the General Election the Conservatives promoted the familiar message of self-congratulation about rising living standards and prophecies of doom about the return of socialism. Douglas-Home performed satisfactorily in public but Wilson rated higher in opinion polls. In October 1964, Labour won narrowly, with 317 seats to the Conservatives' 304 and Liberals' nine. Labour gained 44.1 per cent of votes to the Conservatives' 43.4 per cent on a turnout of 77.1 per cent. Twenty-nine women were elected, the largest number so far in a House of 630 MPs: eighteen Labour, eleven Conservatives. Labour gained most in its strongholds of inner London, Lancashire, Yorkshire and Scotland. After its deep divisions it had still to win the trust of many voters.

In the Midlands, the sitting MP for Smethwick since 1945, Patrick Gordon Walker, Labour's prospective Foreign Secretary, was defeated in a racist campaign featuring the slogan 'If you want a nigger neighbour, vote Labour'. The successful Conservative candidate, local councillor Peter Griffiths, exploited anxiety over housing shortages, blaming immigrants. The national swing to Labour was 3.5 per cent; Smethwick swung to the Conservatives by 7.2 per cent. In the following year, Gordon Walker ran in a by-election in the normally safe Labour seat of Leyton, east London, and was defeated in a campaign featuring opponents dressed as monkeys, brandishing the slogan 'We immigrants are voting for Gordon Walker'. He won the seat in 1966. Elsewhere, race was not a major issue in 1964. Labour did not pledge to repeal the Commonwealth Immigration Act, but committed to introducing anti-discrimination legislation.

Thirteen Wasted Years?

Economic growth, employment and living standards in the United Kingdom were all stronger between 1950 and the early 1970s than before or later, despite fluctuations. But, throughout, competitors, including the renewed economies of Germany, France and Japan, outperformed the United Kingdom as, it seemed from official statistics, did those of Eastern Europe, amid expanding international trade and finance. The United Kingdom still failed to upgrade its industry or diversify into new, modern areas of manufacturing, and its share of world manufactured exports fell from 25 per cent in 1950 to 16.5 per cent in 1960, while imports grew. As Wilson pointed out, there was little sign that the economy had modernized like its competitors or that Conservative governments had tried, except belatedly and sporadically, to encourage this. 'Stop–go' fiscal and budgetary policies, sometimes influenced more by the electoral cycle than the needs of the economy, were damaging.

Income and wealth inequality did not shrink significantly. Nor did gender inequality despite women's continuing protests, while racial inequality and tension grew with increasing immigration in an insecure society. Manual workers were still a majority while the middle-class expanded. White-collar employment increased by 500,000 between 1951 and 1957, contributing more to social mobility than the education system.[112] The welfare state survived more or less intact, with some erosion, including charges for health services and the lower quality of public housing, and it did not notably improve. When possible the Conservatives encouraged private rather than public provision. The proportion of housing built for private ownership increased and, under Macmillan, the Treasury and some Conservative backbenchers complained about the extent of state subsidies for mortgagees and mortgage providers. In 1959, Housing Minister Henry Brooke proudly opened 'the millionth' private house built since the war, in Blackheath, London. The belief that owner-occupation encouraged Conservative voting had not gone away. Aspirations to further privatization, notably in the health service, was constrained by public opinion and expert advice. State welfare remained popular though it cost taxpayers more in 1964 than in 1951.[113]

The postwar social and economic situation is often described as a 'settlement'. By 1964, present and future trajectories were far from settled. Nor was there political 'consensus'. Labour and the Conservatives differed fundamentally on key areas of social and economic policy, though extreme Conservative free marketeers were restrained by the electorate. And this was not the dull, socially conservative era often described. Much was changing in British culture, heralding future changes, to the consternation of cultural conservatives and the pleasure of their radical critics.

112 Butler and Rose, *The British General Election of 1959*, p. 14.
113 Glennerster, *British Social Policy*, p. 94.

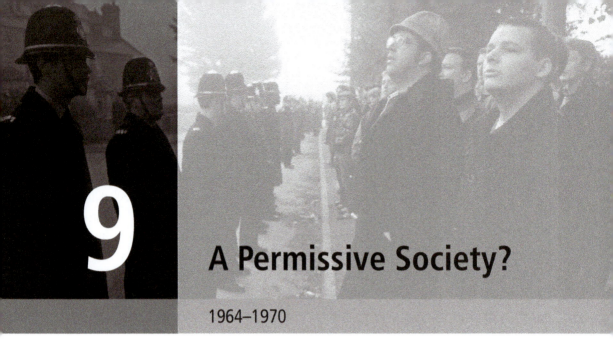

9 A Permissive Society?

1964–1970

The 'Swinging Sixties'

In 1964, the Beatles held the top five positions in the US singles charts. For the first time a British group took the world of pop music by storm, with the Rolling Stones following close behind. British youth fashion also led the world, centred on Carnaby Street in London's Soho where leading designers opened stores, pre-eminently Mary Quant inventor of the mini skirt which revolutionized female fashion. In 1966, a cover article in the mass-selling US magazine, *Time*, proclaimed: 'nothing illustrates the new swinging London better than … Carnaby St'.[1] Also in 1964, 'Rockers' fought 'Mods' at Clacton-on-Sea, alarming the UK tabloids, but this made less impact internationally than music and fashion. Popular culture was gaining the world role British manufacturing and politics appeared to be losing. Harold Wilson longed to restore both, while upholding the successes. The record industry was one of the fastest-growing British industries, using the new technology he wanted older industries to adopt. He rewarded the Beatles – they came from Liverpool, where he was an MP, hopeful products of a depressed local economy – by awarding them MBEs in 1965. It was unprecedented to honour young popular celebrities and some offended MBEs returned their medals. John Lennon returned his in 1969 in protest at Britain's support for the Nigerian government in the civil war in Biafra, the US war against communist North Vietnam, and at the thoughtless banning of his anti-drug song, 'Cold Turkey' for its references to drugs – signs of new turns in youth culture in the later 1960s.

1 *Time*, 15 August 1966.

Youth culture still provoked predictable conservative disapprobation of assumed rampant sexuality. The sexual culture continued to change, not only among young people. Between 1966 and 1970, 82 per cent of the UK population married at least once, the peak of the historically exceptional postwar marriage boom (between 1901 and 1905 only 60 per cent ever married). Divorces in Great Britain rose from 25,672 in 1960 to 62,010 in 1970, the year before major divorce reform was implemented. At this time divorce had not become easier, but perhaps more people could afford it. Also expectations of marriage appeared to be rising and women, in particular, were less willing to tolerate disappointment and readier to seek independence.[2] Outside marriage, the later conviction that premarital sex was rare before the 1960 is challenged by official statistics of births within the first eight months of marriage: 14 per cent of births in 1951, 22 per cent by 1965.[3] Births to unmarried parents rose from 5 per cent of all births in 1950–2 to 8.2 per cent in 1971.[4] In 1971, 45 per cent of 'illegitimate' births were jointly registered by the parents, suggesting that they had stable, often cohabiting, relationships.[5] The culture was changing, fuelling pressure for further change.

Labour Government, 1964–1966

The incoming Labour government faced persistent challenges by campaigners for radical reforms, but initially it focused on reviving less successful features of the UK economy and society than pop music and fashion. Wilson modelled his approach on JFK's 'first 100 days' in 1960. They had much in common. Kennedy was born a year after Wilson, also the youngest US President, and won narrowly against Richard Nixon on a programme of civil rights and social reform which he hoped to implement sooner and more completely than proved possible. He was widely admired and mourned in Britain and Wilson sought reflected glory. He was determined to unify the party, giving his leadership rivals prominent roles, Callaghan as Chancellor, while a new Department of Economic Affairs (DEA), dedicated to economic planning, was created for George Brown, horrifying the Treasury. Optimistically, they were intended to co-exist in 'creative tension', the DEA focused on long-term planning for economic development, the Treasury on short-term finance. Wilson's closest allies, Richard Crossman and Barbara Castle, the only woman in the Cabinet, took the Ministry of Housing and Local Government and the new Ministry of Overseas Development (MOD), respectively. The MOD signified the new postcolonial era and

2 Langhamer, *The English in Love.*
3 Kiernan et al., *Lone Motherhood,* p. 35.
4 Butler and Butler, *Twentieth-Century British Political Facts,* p. 350.
5 Kiernan et al., *Lone Motherhood,* p. 42.

Wilson's personal commitment to aiding poorer countries, former colonies or not, and reducing global inequality.

Economic Planning

Wilson aimed to expand Attlee's welfare state while sharing his conviction that a prosperous economy was the best means to raise workers' living standards and fund support for those unable to work. But Labour was shocked to discover that Maudling's pre-election budget concessions had created an estimated £800 million balance of payments deficit, the worst since the war.[6] Wilson was criticized for refusing to devalue in response, but this was difficult politically for a government with a slim majority and Labour had suffered from devaluations in 1931 and 1949. Also many poorer countries kept their reserves in sterling in London. Wilson, committed to overseas development, stated 'I am not prepared to cut India's savings by 10 per cent'.[7] Instead, the bank rate rose to 7 per cent, there was a temporary surcharge on imports and standard income tax rose to 41.25 per cent. Wilson sought a loan from the United States, now led by Lyndon Johnson. War between communist North Vietnam and the non-communist South in the former French colony had been building for years, with growing US support for the South becoming active military support in 1964. Vietnam became the major, seriously violent, front in the Cold War and a growing cause of international anti-war protest. Johnson wanted Wilson's support in return for a loan. Wilson refused to send British troops, which would have been unpopular and expensive, though he allowed the military to give strategic advice and expressed broad support for the war against communism, arousing left-wing criticism. Johnson agreed the loan, if only because British devaluation would have threatened the dollar and the Bretton Woods commitment to fixed exchange rates, which he was anxious to preserve. The Treasury kept a tight grip on spending. In 1965 a National Board for Prices and Incomes was appointed to establish controls; the TUC agreed a voluntary incomes policy, setting increases at 3–3.5 per cent pa. Denis Healey, Defence Minister, cut spending where possible, including three major aircraft programmes. Through 1965 the bank rate eased, the economy grew slowly, unemployment averaged only 1.5 per cent. In 1966, prices were 9 per cent higher than in 1964, but earnings were 11 per cent higher.

Modernization and development of manufacturing to match overseas competitors was Wilson's main ambition and election promise. The financial sector prospered, but

6 Alec Cairncross, *The British Economy since 1945. Economic Policy and Performance, 1945–95*, 2nd edn (Oxford: Blackwell, 1995), p. 152.

7 Roy Hattersley, 'Harold Wilson's Moral Crusade can Still be a Rallying Cry', *The Guardian*, 15 October 2014.

he and his advisers did not believe it could sustain and enhance UK prosperity and world economic prominence alone. He was determined to end 'Stop–Go' with a settled strategy. In 1965, the DEA produced a National Plan, the intended centrepiece of economic modernization, setting targets and providing advice for industries for investment, output and productivity. It aimed for annual growth of 4 per cent, compared with average growth of 2.9 per cent between 1950 and 1964. Actual growth from 1964 to 1970 averaged 2.6 per cent.[8] In 1965, London and Manchester Business Schools opened, aiming to improve the quality of management, providing the first Masters in Business Administration (MBA) courses in Britain, modelled on the Harvard Business School and successful French institutions.[9]

The essential complement to the Plan, a Ministry of Technology, was established to lead the drive for technological innovation in manufacturing.[10] It was headed by the left-wing leader of the Transport and General Workers' Union (TGWU), Frank Cousins, who had no obvious experience in this field and was not an MP. Wilson apparently hoped he could emulate his predecessor's, Ernest Bevin, success in running the wartime labour market and could encourage greater worker participation in business management. Like Bevin, Cousins was soon elected to Parliament in a by-election, but was a less effective minister. Wilson's policy on technological advance was influenced by Patrick Blackett, a Nobel prize winner who played an important role in operational research during the war and was keen to mobilize scientists to advance the economy in peacetime. He became a temporary official and adviser in the new ministry. 'Mintech', as it was known, absorbed most of the functions of the Department of Scientific and Industrial Research (DSIR) and the National Research Development Corporation (NRDC), created by Wilson in 1948 at the Board of Trade, then absorbed most of the Board of Trade's responsibilities for industry. It took over the Atomic Energy Authority and development of atomic power and gave limited funds to the private sector to develop new technologies. Research and development was encouraged in public sector enterprises, leading to technological change and increased efficiency in postal and telephone services, the mines and gas supply. It particularly sponsored development of four key industries: computers, electronics, telecommunications and machine tools.[11] Labour's economic strategy and goals were clearly established in its first year.

---

8 Cairncross, *British Economy since 1945*, pp. 154–5.

9 Jo Workman, 'Paying for Pedigree? British Business Schools and the MBA Degree', unpublished DPhil, University of Sussex, 2005.

10 H. Wilson, *Purpose in Politics* (Littlehampton Book Services, 1964), p. 3.

11 Richard Coopey, 'Industrial Policy in the White Heat of the Scientific Revolution', in R. Coopey, S. Fielding and N. Tiratsoo (eds), *The Wilson Governments, 1964-1970* (London: Pinter, 1993), pp 102–22; Edgerton, *Warfare State*, pp. 244–51.

Welfare Planning

Average incomes, living standards and consumption continued to rise and income inequality gradually to narrow, but pockets of unemployment and deprivation survived, including on Merseyside and Clydeside. For this reason and because Labour still believed that strong health, education and social security systems were essential underpinnings of a strong economy, it promised to expand state welfare and did so, as far as economic constraints allowed. Prescription charges were immediately abolished. The 1964 manifesto promised to raise all social security payments which 'have been allowed to fall below minimum levels of human need'. Pensions were immediately raised by 12s 6d per week, the largest increase since state pensions began in 1908. This was popular, given the extent of poverty among older people, but the pension remained insufficient to live on, being worth only 21 per cent of average male industrial earnings. Also the cost prevented the more ambitious reconstruction of pensions proposed in 1957,[12] to Crossman's fury.[13] At least 1 million pensioners still needed means-tested NAB supplements for survival. In 1966, the NAB was replaced by the Supplementary Benefits Commission (SBC), designed, with limited success, to eliminate the stigmatizing aura of the Poor Law still clinging to the much criticized NAB, introducing less aggressive methods of assessment, simpler administration and clarifying rights to benefits. In 1965, redundancy payments were introduced, one-off payments linked to previous earnings paid by employers to workers made involuntarily unemployed. In 1966, earnings-related supplements were introduced for sickness and unemployment benefits, funded by increased contributions, signalling a shift from the flat-rate basis of social security. These measures were designed to encourage flexibility in the labour market, essential to the economic modernization programme.[14]

Crossman was disconcerted to be appointed Minister of Housing, having previously been responsible for social security. Wilson persuaded him that housing was more important to voters, as it still was. A White Paper in 1965 promised to deliver 500,000 houses a year by 1970, half in the public sector. This was never achieved but more were built each year from 1966 to 1970 than by their predecessors, peaking at 426,000 in 1968, more than half in the public sector.[15] There was a rising crisis of homelessness, which the Protection from Eviction Act 1965 aimed to stem by increasing tenants' security, while the Rent Act 1965 reintroduced private sector rent controls,

---

12 See p. 253.

13 R. H. S. Crossman, *Diary of a Cabinet Minister, vol. 1: Minister of Housing 1964–66* (London: Hamish Hamilton, Jonathan Cape, 1975), 17 July 1965.

14 Glennerster, *British Social Policy*, pp. 103–11.

15 Butler and Butler Twentieth Century British Political Facts, p.357

extended security of tenure and made harassment of tenants illegal, ending the scandals of Rachmanism.[16] But furnished rentals were excluded, encouraging unscrupulous landlords to install minimal furnishings. Some of the worst abuses were eliminated but not all.[17]

Anthony Crosland took charge of Education, long committed to equal access to good education and critical of the socially selective tripartite system. He issued a circular requesting local authorities to submit plans to reorganize secondary education on comprehensive lines, abolishing 11+ selection. By 1970, most authorities had done so. A Public Schools Commission was appointed to enquire into a major source of educational inequality, but reached no satisfactory conclusion. In 1964, 76 per cent of Conservative MPs had attended private schools, 15 per cent of Labour MPs, 76 per cent of judges, 50 per cent of top civil servants and 60 per cent of directors of leading firms, all overwhelmingly male. Three-quarters of sixth formers attended this minority of schools. Crosland aimed to improve performance in the state sector.[18]

He also announced a 'binary policy' for higher education, funding the development of thirty degree-awarding 'polytechnics' out of local authority technical colleges, alongside the autonomous universities (thirty-eight by 1970, following the foundation of seven new universities in England and one, Stirling, in Scotland), while ten existing Colleges of Advanced Technology were granted university charters. Polytechnics focused on science and technology and, unlike most universities, provided part-time courses for people of all ages, developing the skills required in a modernizing economy and, hopefully, democratizing higher education. Part-time education, usually in the evening, after work, was the most common means by which people could compensate for an inadequate school education. Crosland declared 'parity of esteem' between universities and polytechnics, though this was easier said than done in status-conscious Britain where 'polys' could be disparaged as second-class universities. Polytechnic student numbers rose from around 33,000 in 1962 to 215,000 in 1970–1, mostly male.[19] Planning also began for a favourite Wilson project, a 'University of the Air', later named the Open University, designed to extend post-school opportunities and further democratize access to higher education by broadcasting part-time degree-level classes on radio and TV, supported by correspondence with tutors, printed materials and summer schools. It opened in 1969.[20]

---

16 See p. 232.
17 Glennerster, *British Social Policy*, pp. 141–5.
18 Ibid., pp. 139–40.
19 Halsey and Webb, *Twentieth-century British Social Trends*, pp. 224–32.
20 Phoebe Hall, 'Creating the Open University', in P. Hall, H. Land, R. Parker and A. Webb (eds), *Change, Choice and Conflict in Social Policy* (London: Heinemann, 1975), pp. 155–276.

'The Rediscovery of Poverty'

Shocking evidence soon exposed the urgent need to expand opportunities for work, education, training and welfare. On 23 December 1965, to make maximum pre-Christmas impact, Brian Abel-Smith, from LSE, and Peter Townsend, Professor of Sociology at the new University of Essex, launched their research report, *The Poor and the Poorest*,[21] revealing much more poverty than generally assumed and not confined to older people. They measured poverty not by bare subsistence, but by NAB benefit rates, set by the government as a basic minimum income related to average earnings. Townsend argued that, in the modern world, poverty should be defined relative to general living standards. Since most people now enjoyed high and rising standards, deprivation was defined by exclusion from these advantages; the major problem was no longer absolute poverty, but 'relative deprivation' compared with national norms, which limited life chances from birth. By this measure, they found that 14 per cent of the UK population (7.5 million people) were poor. A high proportion of these, as expected, were retired, 22 per cent in 1961; 62.55 per cent of all retired people. There was also extensive poverty among disabled people. But 2 million in poverty were children, mostly in larger families, 41 per cent with at least one full-time working parent. This was the greatest shock. It was labelled 'the rediscovery of poverty' and made an international impact. The world was waking up to continuing international poverty. In 1964, Lyndon Johnson launched a 'War on Poverty', following similar findings in the United States,[22] while awareness grew of much greater poverty in what was increasingly called the 'Third World' of 'underdeveloped' nations, terminology developed in the self-defined 'First' world of Europe, the United States and its allies, in contrast to the 'Second' world of communist countries.

The UK findings were presented to Wilson and publicized on television and in the press, arousing shock and sympathy.[23] Public awareness of social problems and multiple continuing inequalities was further promoted by a new generation of energetic, media-aware, voluntary organizations, drawing on growing university research and the contemporary fashion for social criticism, mobilizing a young generation anxious to improve the world, hopeful after the election of a Labour government, their campaigns publicized by television and the ever less deferential, sensation-seeking, press. One organization grew directly from Townsend's and

21 Brian Abel-Smith and Peter Townsend, *The Poor and the Poorest* (London: Bell, 1965).
22 Michael Harrington, *The Other America. Poverty in the United States* (London: Macmillan, 1962, repr. London: Penguin, 1966).
23 Sheard, *The Passionate Economist*, p. 1.

Abel-Smith's research: the Child Poverty Action Group (CPAG) was founded in 1965 by social workers working with children and experiencing family poverty, supported by the two researchers, to campaign for support for families of poor children.[24] In the same year the Disablement Income Group (DIG) was launched by Megan du Boisson. Suffering from multiple sclerosis, she discovered that married women like herself, who were not employed and had not paid sufficient National Insurance contributions, and disabled people who had not paid contributions, perhaps because their disability was severe and long term, had no right to sickness benefits but had to apply for mean-tested National Assistance. The DIG campaigned for a non-contributory disability income, special allowances for those with exceptional needs, research into disability issues and, above all, greater awareness of and respect for disabled people, exposing how they were neglected in the postwar welfare state. DIG Scotland was formed in 1966 by Margaret Blackwood, who was in a similar position to du Boisson. The two organizations were new in being formed by and for the disadvantaged group concerned rather than by charitable others, launching another new trend.[25]

Shelter was founded in 1966 to help the growing numbers of homeless people. It built on the mass audience and publicity for the 1966 TV showing of Ken Loach's film about a homeless family, *Cathy Come Home*.[26] Established voluntary organizations still campaigned about continuing social problems, identified new problems, strove to help people in need and pressed the government to take action. They had all to adapt to the new world of high-profile media publicity alongside the growing numbers of international aid organizations responding to Third World poverty. From 1963, five of them – British Red Cross, Christian Aid, Oxfam, Save the Children and War on Want – collaborated to raise funds for emergencies in poorer countries. They grew as colonialism declined, sometimes out of missionary organizations and/or staffed by former colonial administrators, experienced in relief work. The five formed the Disasters' Emergency Committee, using the new media boldness to spread stark images of human suffering, previously unseen in the media, seeking donations for victims of famine, civil war and other crises.[27] Wilson was sympathetic and their pressure contributed to the establishment of the MOD. Concern about poverty at home and abroad was another feature of the 1960s.

24 Pat Thane and Ruth Davidson, *The Child Poverty Action Group 1965–2015* (London: CPAG, 2016, online, available at: www.cpag.org.uk).

25 Hampton, *Disability and the Welfare State in Britain,* pp. 88–96.

26 See p. 244.

27 M. Hilton, N. Crowson, J-F. Mouhot and J. MacKay, *A Historical Guide to NGOs in Britain. Charity, Civil Society and the Voluntary Sector since 1945* (London: Palgrave, 2012), pp. 45–6.

Labour Liberalization

Other established and new campaigning groups demanded other reforms, fuelled by optimism that Labour would be more responsive than its predecessors. Before the 1964 election Wilson promised a free parliamentary vote on abolishing capital punishment, despite polls showing large majorities against abolition. He supported action to improve race relations and women's rights and appointed liberal Roy Jenkins to the Home Office in December 1965, partly because he was riled by criticisms that his government was not radical enough, as it held back initially from sponsoring liberal legislation due to economic crisis and other urgent preoccupations.

Campaigners found support among backbenchers. The Murder (Abolition of the Death Penalty) Bill was a Private Member's Bill introduced by Labour MP, Sydney Silverman, in late 1964. Despite the polls and an imminent election, the government supported it against Conservative opposition, but accepted an amendment, abolition for an experimental period of five years, as the price for getting it through Parliament. It passed easily through the Lords, becoming law in 1965. Soon after came the sensational trial of the 'Moors Murderers', Ian Brady and Myra Hindley, who killed several children, erotically and sadistically, burying them on Saddleworth Moor. They shared a fascination with Nazism, obscene photography and the works of the Marquis de Sade and were imprisoned for life. The case was extensively covered in the press, with some restraint given the gruesome nature of the evidence.[28] It provoked attempts to reverse abolition, but the Commons rejected them and Parliament easily passed permanent abolition in 1969, opposed by a majority of Conservative and three Labour MPs.[29]

Without backbench prompting, Labour responded to Patrick Gordon Walker's failed election bids,[30] continuing racist episodes and protest against them with the Race Relations Act (RRA) 1965, prepared by Frank Soskice at the Home Office. Again Learie Constantine contributed to the protest.[31] Retired from cricket, after qualifying as a lawyer in Britain he returned to Trinidad, then in 1961 was appointed Trinidadian High Commissioner in London and was knighted. In 1963, he was appalled and complained publicly when a Bristol bus company refused to employ black staff. The policy was reversed but authorities in Trinidad thought he had intruded excessively in British affairs and his appointment was not renewed in 1964. He remained in Britain, an active anti-racist until his death in 1971. He became the first black life peer in 1969. The RRA for the first time outlawed discrimination on grounds of race, colour, ethnic or national origin in public places or on public transport, but overlooked the important

28 Bingham, *Family Newspapers*, pp. 151–3.
29 Holden, *Makers and Manner*, pp. 122, 171–2.
30 See p. 260.
31 See p. 162.

areas of employment and housing. It established the Race Relations Board (RRB), of which Constantine was one of three members, to deal with complaints of discrimination, with local conciliation committees to consider complaints, secure conciliation or, if all failed, seek court proceedings. This was unwieldy and no successful prosecutions followed. Restrictions on immigration remained. It was an important beginning, but was criticized as inadequate by immigrant and anti-racist groups.[32]

In May 1965, Labour MP Leo Abse tabled a motion to reduce criminalization of homosexuality as proposed by Wolfenden.[33] Ministers feared the timing was unfortunate, given the small majority, the impending election and the risk they were running by supporting abolition of hanging, and refused to support it, anticipating its return at a more convenient time. It was defeated in the Commons. Two days earlier, the newly liberal Lords, with growing numbers of life peers, approved by ninety-four votes to forty-nine a Bill brought by Lord Arran to decriminalize homosexual acts between adult men in private. Arran's homosexual older brother had been driven to suicide. He faced fierce opposition from two Conservative Lords Chancellor, including Lord Kilmuir warning about 'buggery clubs', and demanding 'Are your Lordships going to pass a Bill that will make it lawful for two senior officers of police to go to bed together?' They did, including both archbishops and a majority of bishops. Polls suggested that most people, regardless of age, gender or class, now agreed, 63 per cent in an NOP poll for the *Daily Mail*. The Bill was introduced in the Commons by Conservative MP, Humphrey Berkeley, supported by Jenkins as Home Secretary and passed its second reading easily in February 1966. But the election intervened, Berkeley lost his Lancaster seat to Labour on a bigger swing – 5.25 per cent – than the national average of 2.7 per cent, it was widely believed, including by Berkeley, because of the Bill.

Homosexual law reform was not the only social advance delayed, but not destroyed, by the election. The ALRA sprang into action soon after the 1964 election. Founded in 1936,[34] it flagged after the war as its leaders aged and died, but when Madeleine Simms was appointed leader in 1961 it became another very active campaign group, commissioning polls revealing higher than expected support for legalization. The press, popular and serious, discussed abortion more openly than before and more papers supported it. The growing body of female columnists highlighted how illegal 'back-street' abortions damaged the many women unable to afford private operations: 'As having an abortion has become so much a matter of having £200 and the right address, it seems grossly unfair that it should be denied to the have-nots' wrote Anne Batt in

32 Thorpe, *History of the British Labour Party*, pp. 174–5.
33 See pp. 247–8.
34 See p. 136.

the *Daily Express* in 1965.[35] The thalidomide crisis of the early 1960s, when a drug prescribed to prevent morning sickness in pregnancy caused serious foetal abnormality, raised the issue of whether women should have legal access to abortion in such cases. In 1965, NOP found 66 per cent of doctors supported legalization, only 10 per cent opposed; in July 1966, that 75 per cent of women favoured it and only 20 per cent opposed; in 1967, that Catholic women were no less likely to have had an (illegal) abortion than others and 44 per cent supported it 'if the woman is unable to cope with any more children.'[36] But Catholic and other Christian opposition was increasingly organized and outspoken, principally in the newly formed Society for the Protection of Unborn Children (SPUC). Mary Whitehouse complained that the appearance of an ALRA representative on the BBC was contrary to the BBC's obligation to political neutrality, though she did not complain about the appearance of a SPUC representative in the same programme.[37] The Church of England was officially opposed and some Anglicans were active in SPUC. Again, attempted legislation started in the Lords. In November 1965, Labour Lord Silkin introduced a Bill which won a second reading by seventy-eight votes to eight. Simultaneously, Conservative Simon Wingfield Digby, introduced a Bill in the Commons, but the government opposed it due to the pending election and abortion reform also was delayed. Liberal reforms were held back by Labour's small majority and interruption of parliamentary business by the election, but supporters kept campaigning.

Nationalisms

Labour also faced pressure from growing UK nationalisms, potentially threatening the unity of the kingdom. Wilson responded to growing unrest in Wales by creating a Welsh Office in Whitehall, headed by James Griffiths. Nationalism had been muted since 1945, as Wales, Scotland and Northern Ireland gained from full employment and the expansion of state welfare, but revived in the 1960s, as the economy and older industries slowed. Griffiths had long supported devolution to Wales and a separate Welsh office, but failed to persuade Attlee.[38] Plaid Cymru and the SNP ran significant numbers of candidates for the first time in the 1959 and 1964 elections, but won no seats and few votes. Neither was a serious electoral threat, but Labour was dependent enough on seats in both countries to court them both. In 1964, Labour held twenty-eight seats in Wales, the Conservatives six, in Scotland forty-three and twenty-four, respectively.

35 Bingham, *Family Newspapers*, p. 87.
36 Holden, *Makers and Manners*, p. 131.
37 Ibid.
38 K. O. Morgan, *Wales*, p. 377.

Devolution of administration to Wales progressed slowly from 1907, when Welsh departments were established in the departments of Education, Health, Housing and Local Government. From the late 1950s growing protest focused on the decline of the Welsh language, assisted by the closure of village schools and the dominance of English in the popular media including the BBC. From 1963, the Welsh Language Society staged demonstrations and 'sit-ins' in government departments, post offices, libraries and other public institutions which did not provide Welsh language notices and documents. They daubed Welsh slogans on buildings and obliterated English road signs. The Conservatives established a Welsh Arts Council and funded Welsh publications.[39] A new TV service, BBC (Wales), broadcast in Welsh from February 1964, initially for just seven hours a week. Militants were not appeased by this or by the establishment of the Welsh Office with powers limited to housing and local government, road transport and aspects of local planning, later extended to health, agriculture and education.[40] In July 1966, Plaid gained Carmarthen from Labour in a by-election and in later by-elections slashed its majorities at West Rhondda and Caerphilly. Labour responded with the Welsh Language Act 1967, permitting legal proceedings in Welsh and translation of official documents, the first step to official bilingualism.

Scotland, with its distinct administrative and legal systems, had long enjoyed greater devolution, with a Secretary for Scotland in the Cabinet since 1885 and a full Secretary of State and Scottish Office since 1926, which had gradually taken on wider responsibilities.[41] Scottish like Welsh nationalism became more assertive in the 1960s. In 1967, the first SNP MP, Winifred Ewing, won a by-election at Hamilton. Since 1922 Northern Ireland had greater devolved powers, headed by a governor appointed by the crown, an elected parliament responsible for internal affairs and elected members at Westminster. Discontent and Irish nationalism were growing among Catholics in the province and was shortly to explode.[42]

General Election, 1966

Douglas-Home resigned the Conservative leadership and Edward Heath narrowly beat Maudling in the party's first leadership election, the Conservatives' first 'lower-class' leader, son of a builder and a former parlour-maid. The economy looked bright enough for Labour to risk an election in March 1966 when it won a secure majority. The Conservatives lost forty-nine seats, Labour won forty-seven and the Liberals two.

39 Ibid., p. 380.
40 Ibid., pp. 376–84.
41 Butler and Butler, *Twentieth-Century British Political Facts*, pp. 457–8.
42 See pp. 297–8.

Labour seats were now more evenly spread around England, where they won a majority of seats as in 1945. Some largely middle-class seats, including in the south, went Labour for the first time since constituency boundaries were re-drawn in 1949. They made further gains, and the Conservatives further losses, in Scotland and Wales. As in 1945, more women voted Labour than Conservative,[43] though the number of female MPs slipped to twenty-six: nineteen Labour, seven Conservative.

Economic Crises

Then, in May 1966, came a seamen's strike for higher pay, which was unusual and disastrous for trade. Settling it destroyed incomes policy, provoked speculation against the pound on the international money markets and another sterling crisis in July. Winning the Football World Cup, defeating Germany in the final, boosted English morale for a while, cheered on by Wilson. Supported by most of the Cabinet, he again refused to devalue. Taxes rose, spending was cut and a six-month incomes freeze imposed, resisted by the TUC. Wilson was again attacked for his reluctance to devalue, but he and the Treasury feared it would cause inflation, devaluations in other countries and worsening international relations, signalling Britain's weakness and decline, while harming people on the lowest incomes and poorer countries holding their balances in sterling. Labour still believed it had international responsibilities.

Following a temporary recovery, the pay freeze ended, but, as incomes, consumption and imports rose again, the deficit recurred in early 1967. In June, the Arab–Israeli Six-Day War, followed by an oil embargo and the closure of the Suez Canal caused further problems. In November, the government was forced to devalue from $2.80 to $2.40 and introduce another austerity package. The National Plan appeared ineffectual and was abandoned. George Brown threatened to resign from the government but was persuaded to move to the Foreign Office. The DEA continued, under Michael Stewart, mainly concerned with incomes policy, but with little influence. Overseas aid was cut and it was decided to withdraw British forces from east of Suez, apart from Hong Kong, a major blow to Wilson's vow in 1964 that 'We are a world power and a world influence or we are nothing.'[44] He supported the Commonwealth and had promised to retain Britain's role east of Suez as a condition of American financial support in 1965, but there seemed no alternative. In 1967, he rejected a further American offer because it would be unpopular at home and he wanted greater independence from the United States, especially as Labour was considering another approach to the European

43 I. Zweiniger-Bargielowska, 'Explaining the Gender Gap', in M. Francis and I. Zweiniger-Bargielowska (eds), *Conservatives and British Society, 1880–1990* (Cardiff: University of Wales Press, 1996), pp. 192–224.
44 Reynolds, *Britannia Overruled*, p. 227.

Community (EC), as it became in 1967. Some saw entry to the EC as a solution to the recurrent economic problems, especially as British trade with Europe's booming economy was growing while its share of Commonwealth and world trade declined, though the party continued to disagree on the issue. Britain applied again in 1967, expecting de Gaulle again to say 'Non', as he did, though other members were well disposed.

Controversially, Labour decided to decimalize the currency. A committee reported in its favour in 1963, and in 1966 Callaghan announced its introduction, probably influenced by consideration of joining the EC and the fact that major Commonwealth countries, Australia and New Zealand, were decimalizing. The Decimal Currency Act 1969 was implemented under Heath in 1971, described in the *Daily Mail* on the fortieth anniversary as 'The Day Britain Lost its Soul', imposed undemocratically by 'that impatient modernizer, Harold Wilson'.[45]

Iron and steel were re-nationalized in 1967 and the nationalized industries performed well, though the economy remained in crisis through 1968. Cousins resigned from Mintech in July 1966 in protest at wage controls. He was replaced by the energetic Wedgwood Benn in what was seen as a key role in reviving British competitiveness. Benn was an eager publicist for the ministry, labelled 'the most dangerous man in Britain' by the rather conservative *Private Eye*, as a moderniser, excessively keen to replace the old with the new. In 1969–70 a popular TV satire, *Monty Python's Flying Circus*, represented Mintech as the 'Ministry for Silly Walks', promoting pretentious, pointless activities to compete with French 'silly walks'. Satire was not always progressive. Undeterred, Mintech took over the Ministry of Aviation, including its collaboration with France to build Concorde, a supersonic jet airliner capable of flying from London to New York in under 3½ hours rather than the normal 8 hours. It operated successfully until 2003. In 1966, Mintech took over regulation of shipbuilding from the Board of Trade, and in 1969 the Ministry of Power and its responsibilities for coal, electricity, gas, steel and oil. It oversaw mergers, modelled on the success of large companies in the United States, and assisted industry in adopting new technologies through a new National Computer Centre and an Engineering Advisory Service promoting the latest techniques.[46] But there were continuing concerns about the shortage of suitably skilled people. An NEDC report in 1967 charted a 'brain drain' of qualified people from the United Kingdom especially to the United States, mainly scientists and engineers, due to higher starting salaries and better promotion prospects, urging comparable improvements in Britain. The first moon landing by US astronauts in July 1969 perhaps inspired more interest in technological advance.

45 Dominic Sandbrook, 'The Day Britain Lost its Soul', *Daily Mail*, 31 January 2011.
46 Coopey, 'Industrial Policy'.

Mintech funded research and development in industry, though not always successfully.[47] Ambitious aims to make Britain a world leader in nuclear technology were unfulfilled. Britain spent more on R&D than many of its competitors, but it was over-concentrated on defence and aerospace and private business remained conservative about new techniques[48] – the central problem Mintech existed to overcome. It became 'the biggest state-directed complex of scientific and industrial power in Europe' with a staff of 38,900, including a high proportion of scientists and engineers.[49] It controlled the largest defence procurement budget in the government, spending over £400 million annually and running seventeen government research establishments, though the nuclear weapons programme was cut back in the later 1960s.[50] It developed a regional strategy to stop the drift of industry to the south and regional inequality, with some success. In 1966, five development areas were created covering almost half of Britain where businesses were subsidized to expand. Public spending on roads increased. A Selective Employment Tax (SET) was introduced in 1966 to fund improvements in manufacturing by taxing growing service industries to encourage them to shed labour which, hopefully, would shift to manufacturing.

These policies strengthened new industries, including computer, machine tools and electronics production, but they needed time to develop and Labour was over-optimistic about short-term gains, though it deserved credit for thinking and planning long term.[51] Many of the plans came to nothing when they were abandoned by Heath's Conservative government which opposed government intervention in industry. Heath, like the satirists, thought Mintech a 'useless gimmick' and terminated a serious attempt to reverse Britain's manufacturing decline.

Ministers and their advisers believed the conservatism of civil servants bore some responsibility for UK economic failures, that, too often, they were Oxbridge graduates trained in humanities or classics, lacking the skills needed in the modern world like economics, and were often reluctant to support progressive policies such as those of DEA. To compensate, ministers increasingly recruited special advisers from universities or business. The Fulton Committee on the Civil Service examined the issues from 1966 to 1968, concluding that the civil service was too much a product of the nineteenth century, lacking desirable professional training including in management skills. Too little use was made of the skills of scientists, engineers and other professionals in policymaking. It recommended greater mobility to and from the outside world, from

47 Ibid., p. 111.
48 Edgerton, *Warfare State*, pp. 251–60.
49 Coopey, 'Industrial Policy', p. 112.
50 Edgerton, *Warfare State*, pp. 266–9.
51 N. Woodward, 'Labour's Economic Performance 1964–70', in R. Coopey, S. Fielding and N. Tiratsoo (eds), *The Wilson Governments, 1964–1970* (London: Pinter, 1993), pp. 88–9.

which civil servants were too isolated by their lifetime employment.[52] One outcome was the establishment of a Civil Service College at Sunningdale, planned under Wilson and opened under Heath, to improve civil service training.

Expanding the Welfare State

Disability Rights

Despite the economic crises, Labour continued its commitment to diminishing social inequalities and expanding and improving the welfare state. Pressure continued from the voluntary groups, inspired by the 'welfare rights' movement, originating like much 1960s radicalism, in the United States, organizing 'Claimants' Unions' to advise and assist people to claim benefits, fighting tribunal and court cases on claimants' behalf when benefits were refused, training advocates and spreading information about benefit rules. Organizations, including CPAG, DIG, NCUMC and Shelter adopted these tactics and increased the pressure on government. They were prominent in the media promoting welfare reforms, particularly in the influential weekly *New Society* (established 1962), which focused on social issues.[53]

The DIG publicized the inequalities suffered by disabled people, demonstrating how lack of state support caused family breakdown, children orphaned or taken into care, the obstacles to living normal lives, including accessing buildings or transport, and preventable incarceration in institutions. It rejected the conventional pejorative language – 'cripples', 'handicapped', 'backward' – insisting that UK culture disregarded the dignity and human rights of disabled people. Crossman took over what became the Department of Health and Social Security (DHSS) in November 1968 and announced in 1969 a National Insurance Invalidity Pension for the fully insured and a non-contributory attendance allowance for severely disabled people, £4 per week for those needing 24-hour attendance. Crossman at last had the pensions reform proposed in 1957 embodied in legislation in 1969, together with the allowances for disabled people, but it was lost to the 1970 election. The DIG persuaded the Conservative minister, Sir Keith Joseph to adopt the disability measures.

Attendance allowance was important because most disabled people lived at home, cared for by family, friends or voluntary agencies. Local authority residential care was normally only available in homes for older people, though there were growing numbers of voluntary institutions. In May 1969, Megan du Boisson died in a car accident.

---

52 *The Report of the Committee on the Civil Service*, Cmnd. 3638, 1968.
53 Thane and Davidson, *Child Poverty Action Group*, pp. 14–15; Evans, 'Stopping the Poor Getting Poorer'; Thane and Evans, *Sinners?* pp. 136–8.

The DIG continued and helped to shape the Chronically Sick and Disabled Persons Act 1970, a Private Member's Bill introduced by Labour MP Alf Morris, which the government prioritized to get it through before the election. Morris knew the impact of disability as one of eight children of a Manchester worker who was gassed and badly wounded in the First World War and died when Alf was seven. The Act required local authorities to register all disabled people in their district, inform them of the services available to them and to publicize them. The Act encouraged, but did not adequately fund, expanded services, including home helps and day centres. It was implemented by the Conservatives, making some progress towards equal rights for disabled people.[54]

Housing

More homes were built between 1965 and 1969, than in any five-year period since 1918, almost half were council houses. Council housing subsidies were increased and the higher standards of construction, space and design recommended by the Parker Morris Committee in 1961 became mandatory for public sector building in New Towns from 1967, for local authorities from 1969. In 1966, means-tested rate rebates were introduced and local authorities were encouraged to introduce rent rebates, though means-testing was criticized. Still many people on low incomes could not afford council rents and experienced poor conditions in private rentals. In 1971, one-eighth of all dwellings, overwhelmingly privately rented, lacked at least one basic amenity: bath or shower (1.6 million in England), indoor toilet (2 million); 2.4 million had no hot water supply to a kitchen sink or hand basin.[55]

A new generation of New Towns was launched as planned by the Conservatives, including Milton Keynes. Labour discouraged the high-density, often high-rise, building promoted by the Conservatives, especially after the dramatic collapse in 1968 of a poorly built tower block in east London, Ronan Point, after just two months' occupation, killing four residents. For the first time, conservation and improvement of older buildings, including by local councils, was encouraged with subsidies for renovation rather than demolition of old houses and the introduction of conservation areas where development was strictly controlled. Whereas demolition had initially focused on 'slums', increasingly housing was demolished merely because it was old and unfashionable, though much Victorian building was sounder than recent developments. The change was part of a revival of appreciation of Victorian culture after decades of

54 Hampton, *Disability and the Welfare State*. pp. 83–130; G. Millward, 'Social Security Policy and the Early Disability Movement. Expertise, Disability and the Government, 1965–77', *Twentieth Century British History* 26(2) (2015): 274–97.

55 Alan Holmans, 'Housing', in A. H. Halsey and J. Webb (eds), *Twentieth-century British Social Trends* (London: Macmillan, 2000), p. 479.

disparagement in favour of the 'modern'. In 1961, the Great Arch at the entrance to Euston Station, built 1837, was demolished and the grand Victorian building of St Pancras Station nearby was threatened. A campaign led by poet Sir John Betjeman and architectural historian Nikolaus Pevsner and publications such as those of historian Asa Briggs, celebrating Victorian cities and culture,[56] turned the tide of fashion, assisted by the Clean Air Act clearing pollution from inner cities. St Pancras was saved in 1967, then restored. The changes encouraged owner-occupation by younger and low-income buyers and the revival and 'gentrification' of older urban areas. The Option Mortgage Act 1968 subsidized low-income house purchasers, and grants were available for renovation. By 1970, more than 50 per cent of households were owner-occupiers.[57]

Other schemes also sought to revive depressed inner cities. The 1967 Plowden Report on *Children and their Primary Schools* proposed 'educational priority areas' concentrating resources in poor areas, providing nursery education from children's earliest years and compensatory education for older children, with modest success. From 1968 the 'urban programme' focused aid on 'relatively small pockets of severe social deprivation' in cities and towns, working with councils, borrowing a model from the United States. In 1969, the Community Development Project placed teams in twelve areas and subsidized citizens tackling social, including racial, problems. They sought to reassure and help disadvantaged white inner city residents who blamed immigrants for lack of jobs, poor housing and services, encouraged by sections of the popular press, though immigrants shared many of their difficulties and more, and most problems had other causes, mainly limited resources. The project had hardly started in 1970 when Labour lost power but some local initiatives continued.

Social Security

National Insurance benefits were uprated again in 1967 and 1969. Following the revelations of poverty in larger families, in 1967 family allowances rose for fourth and subsequent children by 5s per week (25p). This did not satisfy CPAG, but the Chancellor refused to take the universal benefit further in an economic crisis. In November 1967 Callaghan exchanged posts with Roy Jenkins and moved, reluctantly, to the Home Office.[58] In 1968, the economy revived and Jenkins increased family allowances for all eligible children (first children were still excluded) by 10s (50p) per week, funded by reductions in child tax allowances. The CPAG advocated the abolition of tax allowances for the better-off to fund higher universal family allowances benefiting low-income non-taxpayers. Labour was cautious, partly because more people on

56 Asa Briggs, *Victorian People* (London: Odhams, 1954, repr. Pelican 1965); *Victorian Cities* (London: Odhams, 1963; Pelican, 1968);
57 Glennerster, *British Social Policy*, pp. 141–5.
58 K. O. Morgan, *Callaghan. A Life* (Oxford University Press, 1998), p. 292.

low incomes now paid income tax as incomes rose. This caused bitter exchanges with CPAG, now directed by Frank Field, later a Labour MP, and the Chair, Peter Townsend, who claimed in a pre-election manifesto in 1970, with some exaggeration, 'the Poor get Poorer under Labour'.[59] But child poverty was rising partly due to growing numbers of families headed by single mothers following divorce or separation.[60] In 1969, Crossman appointed a committee on One-Parent Families, chaired by Sir Morris Finer QC, to investigate their needs. It reported in 1974.[61]

Health

Prescription and dental charges were reimposed in 1968, following the crisis, to meet rapidly rising NHS costs and to avoid cutting the much needed hospital building programme. Pensioners, children, supplementary benefit claimants and long-term sick and disabled people were exempted. Personal social services were reorganized following an investigation by the Seebohm Committee which reported in 1968,[62] but criticism of the uneven quality and unequal outcomes of local authority services continued. Health and social services for mentally and physically disabled people living at home remained uncoordinated: healthcare was free of charge, social care means-tested, with often uncertain boundaries between them. This became urgent following a series of scandals about the serious mistreatment of people in psychiatric hospitals, publicized in a book, *Sans Everything* (1967), by Barbara Robb, who formed Aid to the Elderly in Government Institutions (AEGIS) to demand change, including improved community services to support mentally ill people at home. When Crossman took over the DHSS in 1968 he visited hospitals, urging improvements which he worked hard to implement, de-institutionalization of patients where possible and improved services to assist them at home.[63] His proposals were partially implemented by the Conservatives.

Education

By 1970 about one-third of secondary pupils in England and Wales were in comprehensive schools, a tenfold increase from 1964. The percentage in England and Wales staying on past age 15 rose from 27.3 per cent in 1960–1 to 51 per cent in 1970–1.[64] Plans to raise the school-leaving age to 16 in 1970 were disrupted by the economic crisis

59 Thane and Davidson, *Child Poverty Action Group*, pp. 16–17; Frank Field, *Poverty and Politics. The Inside Story of the Child Poverty Action Group's Campaigns in the 1970s* (London: Heinemann, 1982), pp. 29–37.
60 Kiernan et al., *Lone Motherhood.*, p. 22.
61 See pp. 322–3.
62 Glennerster, *British Social Policy*, pp. 126–9.
63 Claire Hilton, *Improving Psychiatric Care for Older People. Barbara Robb's Campaign, 1965–75* (London: Palgrave, 2017).
64 Halsey and Webb, *British Social Trends*, p. 195.

and postponed to 1973, when the Conservatives implemented it. Among the crisis cuts, free milk for secondary schools was abolished. Nevertheless, education expenditure grew by 6–7 per cent each year between 1964 and 1970; at the same time numbers of teachers in training increased by one-third.

Living Standards

Labour expanded state welfare benefits and services between 1964 and 1970, despite economic crises and, again, planned to go further had it stayed in government. From 1964 to 1970, GDP growth slowed slightly, to an average 2.6 per cent pa, but the annual average growth of public expenditure was 5.9 per cent, much of it on health and social services. The economy continued to decline in relation to competitors but it grew. Despite continuing poverty, living standards generally improved,[65] income inequality narrowed and consumption grew. Demand for household appliances continued to climb, including colour TVs when they were introduced at the end of the decade. In 1965, 75 per cent of employees had two weeks paid holiday each year, 22 per cent had two to three weeks, and more took holidays away from home, most in Britain but increasingly abroad, as relatively cheap 'package holidays' began to emerge. Cinema, sport and other leisure activities continued to boom.[66] The number of car licences rose to 10.6 million in 1965; total vehicle licences from 4.4 million to 13 million between 1950 and 1965.[67] One unwelcome outcome was growing numbers of accidents due to drunken driving. Techniques emerged to test alcohol in the blood and the Road Safety Act 1967 introduced a blood alcohol limit for drivers; it became obligatory to provide specimens on request, using the newly invented breathalyser. Publicans protested they would be bankrupted, but they survived. Road accidents in Great Britain fell from 292,000 in 1966 to 259,000 in 1976, road deaths from 7,985 to 6,570, while the number of vehicles increased to 17.5 million in 1975.[68]

Launching the 'Permissive Society'?

'Sexual Offences'

The reforms interrupted by the election returned when it was over. David Steel, the young Liberal MP for Roxburgh, Selkirk and Peebles, won from the Conservatives in

65 A. Walker (ed.), *Public Expenditure and Social Policy* (London: Heinemann, 1982).

66 Jonathan Gershuny and Kimberly Fisher, 'Leisure', in A. H. Halsey and J. Webb (eds), *Twentieth-century British Social Trends* (London: Macmillan, 2000), pp. 720–49.

67 Butler and Butler, *Twentieth-Century British Political Facts*, p. 372.

68 Amanda Root, 'Transport and Communications', in A. H. Halsey and J. Webb (eds), *Twentieth-century British Social Trends* (London: Macmillan, 2000), p. 460.

a by-election in 1965, came high in the ballot for Private Members' Bills. Lord Arran, supported by Jenkins at the Home Office, pressed him to adopt his homosexual offences Bill, though it did not cover Scotland or Northern Ireland. Steel, uncertain of his Scottish constituents' response, announced in the *Sun* (then a left-of-centre newspaper, successor to the *Daily Herald*, cautiously supporting liberal attitudes to sexuality[69]) that he would welcome suggestions of which reform to champion.[70] ALRA's lobbying tipped him towards legalized abortion. Arran reintroduced his Bill in the Lords, who again passed it in June 1966. Abse won approval to introduce it in the Commons, assured of Jenkins' support. Leading ministers, including Wilson, resisted, partly because, as Crossman put it, 'working-class people in the north jeer at their Members at the weekend and ask them why they're looking after the buggers at Westminster instead of looking after the unemployed at home.'[71] The parliamentary party was fiercely divided on all liberal reforms, but there had been an influx of younger, more liberal Labour MPs in 1964 and 1966. The proportion of university educated Labour MPs rose from 39 per cent in 1959 to 46 per cent in 1964 and 51 per cent in 1966, and surveys showed the close association between higher education and cultural liberalism.[72] Crossman supported homosexual and abortion reform and persuaded Wilson not to risk these controversies dragging on to the next election.[73]

Abse and his supporters were prepared to compromise to get the Bill passed. The Wolfenden proposals were modified, with a tighter definition of 'in private' – a couple could be prosecuted for making love when someone else was in the same building – and exemption for the armed forces. The merchant navy was excluded after lobbying by the National Union of Seamen.[74] The maximum penalty of life imprisonment for anal sex was repealed, but the penalty for 'gross indecency' – effectively any visible act perceived as homosexual – rose from two to five years' imprisonment. The age of consent was fixed at 21, as Wolfenden had recommended, not the heterosexual age of 16, for fear that young men would be seduced by older men, as though young women would not. The Sexual Offences Act passed the Commons in a twenty-hour, all-night session, at 5.30 am, by ninety-nine votes to fourteen, with Crossman and the Chief Whip encouraging Labour MPs to vote 'Yes', despite official government neutrality. Conservative MP, Gerald Nabarro, attacked the 'depravity' of Labour MPs, prophesying that 'the long hair of Mr Wilson's intellectuals on the back benches would strangle

69 Bingham, *Family Newspapers*, p. 123.

70 Holden. *Makers and Manners*. p. 126.

71 R. H. S. Crossman, *Diaries of a Cabinet Minister, vol. 2: 1966–68* (London: Hamish Hamilton, 1976), p. 407, 3 July 1967.

72 David Butler, 'Electors and Elected', in A. H. Halsey (ed.), *Trends in British Society since 1900* (London: Macmillan, 1972), p. 318.

73 Holden, *Makers and Manners*, p. 128.

74 Ibid., p 129.

him' at the next election. It passed the Lords even more easily than before, becoming law in 1967. Given its limitations, it was far from 'legalizing homosexuality' as some claimed and campaigners were not euphoric, but they recognized it as a start and that public prejudice remained so strong that it was wise to be quiet. The Archbishop of Canterbury reassured the Lords that the law 'would still leave by far the greater number of homosexual crimes and convictions unaltered', indeed prosecutions for such 'acts of gross indecency' as men holding hands in public increased, from 420 in 1966 to 1,711 in 1974.[75] Activism for further change blossomed following the formation of the Gay Liberation Front in 1970.[76]

The Act applied only in England and Wales, but in Scotland the legal ban was no longer enforced. In 1969, the Scottish Minorities Group (later the Scottish Homosexual Reform Group, SHRG) formed to campaign to extend the law to Scotland. Bills failed until in 1979 SHRG brought a case in the European Court of Human Rights (ECtHR). Probably to avoid a long, expensive and possibly unsuccessful legal battle, in 1980 Westminster extended the law to Scotland, despite continuing opposition mainly from the Churches. The reform was more fiercely opposed in Northern Ireland, where the fundamentalist Protestant, Revd Ian Paisley, led a 'Save Ulster from Sodomy' campaign. Most Ulster politicians opposed reform. Again, gay rights groups became active and in 1980 a gay man brought a successful case in the ECtHR, arguing that the law violated his right to a private and family life. The law changed in 1982. The Isle of Man and Jersey followed only in 1992.

Abortion

In July 1966, David Steel introduced his Bill to legalize abortion, which passed its second reading by 194 votes, creating a more explosive public debate than homosexual law reform, including vicious personal attacks by SPUC.[77] An amendment allowing doctors to refuse to perform abortions on conscience grounds mollified some opposition, but it remained strong and in some surprising places. Abse opposed it in the Commons, Baroness Barbara Wootton in the Lords. She was one of the first life peeresses, a long-time Labour supporter and active supporter of most other liberal issues, including homosexual law reform and legalization of soft drugs.[78] She was perhaps influenced by her own experience of an unwilling abortion at the insistence of her husband.[79] More predictable, though quiet, was the opposition of Catholic junior minister,

75 Peter Tatchell, 'Fifty Years of Gay Liberation? In Britain it's Barely Four', *The Guardian*, 23 May 2017, p. 31.
76 See p. 334.
77 Glennerster, *British Social Policy*, pp. 133–4.
78 See p. 272.
79 Oakley, *A Critical Woman*, pp. 287–90.

Shirley Williams. The medical profession was divided, though many doctors with experience of the death and damage resulting from the large, and, it was suspected, growing, numbers of illegal abortions supported legalization. It was opposed by disabled campaigners, who feared that easier abortion would prevent the birth of disabled people capable of viable lives.

The debate focused on the grounds for legal abortion. There was no question of women being allowed to choose: a doctor must decide. The main issue was whether it should be allowed strictly on health or on broader social grounds, which arguably lay outside the competence of most doctors. Narrowly defined health grounds won: abortion was allowed if the mother was judged likely to take her own life, but not if she felt too overburdened to rear a child. The Bill was guided through Parliament by Labour members ensuring it had sufficient time and space for debate.[80] The Cabinet was divided between strong supporters, including Jenkins and Gerald Gardiner the Lord Chancellor, and opponents, including the Catholic Lord Longford, supported by those who feared legalization would lose Labour votes. The government remained officially neutral, but this became less credible as it repeatedly extended the time available for debate to counter opposition filibustering. It passed the Commons in another all-night sitting, then the Lords.[81] Abortion became legal, up to twenty-eight-weeks' gestation, with permission from two doctors. The dissension enforced compromise and the legislation was imperfect and in some respects unclear about the grounds on which abortion was permissible, but it was a breakthrough, the first legal abortion in Western Europe. It was already legal in most Communist countries.

Almost immediately opponents tried, unsuccessfully, to amend it amid rumours in the press of private nursing homes giving abortion on demand and women flocking for abortions from countries where it was illegal. Legal abortions increased from 22,100 in 1968 to 75,400 in 1970, evenly divided between married and unmarried women, most over 20.[82] It is unknown how this compared with previous illegal abortions. The law applied in Scotland but not in Northern Ireland, where Catholics and Protestants united in opposition to abortion as on little else, except resisting other liberal reforms. In the twenty-first century abortion is still only permitted when there is serious risk to the health and life of the mother, and Northern Ireland has the harshest criminal penalty for abortion in Europe: theoretically, life imprisonment for a woman convicted of undergoing an illegal abortion.

---

80 Witness Seminar, 'The Making of the Abortion Act, 1967', Institute of Contemporary British History, King's College London, 2001 (website currently being reorganized).
81 Holden, *Makers and Manners*, pp. 140–1.
82 David Coleman, 'Population and Family', in A. H. Halsey and J. Webb (eds), *Twentieth-century British Social Trends* (London: Macmillan, 2000), p. 50.

Birth Control

Crossman was responsible for administering the abortion law and for the related issue of extending birth control services. These were not available on the NHS and could be provided free of charge by local authorities only if the pregnancy put the mother's health at risk, as established in 1931.[83] Charities, notably the Family Planning Association (FPA), provided free services and demand was growing. The FPA worked hard in the 1950s and 1960s to publicize its work, improve public knowledge about birth control and increase state provision. The Church of England officially supported birth control, while the Catholic Church did not. From 1960, the press was excited, and moralists alarmed, about the revolutionary new birth control pill, apparently more effective than other methods, and about the sexual liberation of women that could follow this easy, reliable form of contraception.

Kenneth Robinson, Minister of Health in 1964–8, wanted to extend free services, but this required legislation and opposition, especially from Catholics and some fundamentalist Protestants, held the government back. Pressure for change arose partly from concern about the extent of ignorance among young people about sex, its hazards and how to prevent them – at odds with protests about moral decline among modern youth, but more credible. Labour encouraged schools to extend sex education and the FPA offered them advice, but it remained at the discretion of local authorities, limited and highly variable. Labour MP, Edwin Brooks, introduced another Private Member's Bill to extend state services, largely drafted by the Ministry of Health. It allowed, but did not require, local authorities to provide contraceptive advice and supplies free of charge to anyone regardless of age, marital status or any other limitation. The Family Planning Act passed easily through Parliament in 1967, with little fuss even about supplying birth control to unmarried people, including teenagers, while sections of the press shrieked 'Sex on the rates!' Its passage was probably helped by contemporary fears about world and national population growth and potential overpopulation. Fewer than 25 per cent of local authorities complied.[84] By 1969, the pill was readily available and Crossman believed it should be free on the NHS, but his officials opposed this on grounds of cost and some did not believe routine birth control was a health issue. The tabloids sensationalized scares about the health risks associated with the pill. Keith Joseph was reluctantly pressured in 1974 to integrate birth control within the NHS, providing free advice for all but free supplies only for those in 'special social need' or 'financial need'. Shortly after, Labour returned to

---

83 See p. 113.
84 Lesley A. Hall, *Sex, Gender and Social Change in Britain since 1880* (London: Macmillan, 2000, 2nd edn, 2012), pp. 176–7; Cook, *Long Sexual Revolution*, pp. 296–317.

government and Barbara Castle, as Minister for Health and Social Security, fulfilled Labour's election promise of free family planning.[85] It remained hardest to obtain in Northern Ireland.

Censorship

Public morality was still protected by theatre censorship, at several levels. Local councils could, and did, withhold grants from productions they judged to be unsuitable. In 1968, Waltham Forest Council in outer London, which Conservatives had captured from Labour the previous year, refused a grant to a local youth theatre to stage Edward Bond's *Saved*, which included a scene with a baby stoned to death in its pram. The Lord Chamberlain could ban any 'unsuitable' play, often conflicting with the Arts Council which encouraged experimental, innovative theatre, even when some thought it risqué. Increasingly, such plays were staged at 'private' theatre clubs to evade censorship, sometimes thinly disguised adjuncts to commercial theatres. In 1965, the Royal Court in London staged John Osborne's *A Patriot for Me* after it was refused a licence for displaying homosexual behaviour. The government law officers refused to take action, but when the Royal Court staged a 'private' performance of *Saved*, they and the Lord Chamberlain felt it went too far and prosecuted. Opponents of censorship pointed out that it applied only to the theatre: a play banned on stage could be shown to millions on television. No other non-communist country practiced censorship, except Franco's Spain, and a play banned in Britain could be seen on Broadway. Mary Whitehouse's 'Clean-up' TV' campaign demanded more censorship of all media.

Jenkins had long opposed censorship and an inquiry committee was appointed in 1966, after the successful prosecution of the Royal Court. It was packed with reformers and received little evidence supporting censorship. The Church of England supported abolition, which the committee proposed in 1967. Protracted Cabinet discussion followed, with Wilson feeling dubious after he read and censored the script of a 1967 West End musical, *Mrs Wilson's Diary* by Richard Ingrams and John Wells, originally a *Private Eye* column, later a TV sketch, which gently but unmistakeably satirized George Brown's notorious drinking and an encounter between Wilson and the queen, among other sensitive episodes.[86] Jenkins was moved to the Exchequer, but Callaghan, now Home Secretary, also supported reform. Wilson realized he was unlikely to win and supported a Bill abolishing censorship introduced by Labour MP George Strauss, which became law in 1968.[87]

85 Holden, *Makers and Manners*, pp. 185–90.
86 Holden, *Makers and Manners*, p. 155.
87 Ibid., pp. 145–57.

Prison Reform

Callaghan was less comprehensively liberal than Jenkins, as Jenkins noted and feared, but he also implemented Jenkins' Criminal Justice Act, 1967, designed to liberalize the treatment of the growing numbers of prisoners to encourage rehabilitation, including establishing a Parole Board to consider early release of short-sentence prisoners. He took a close interest in prison conditions and further initiatives to improve them and their effectiveness in reducing crime, including introducing industrial work experience modelled on factory rather than prison conditions and personally intervening to calm a riot in Durham jail. He also worked to raise prison officers' morale by increasing their promotion prospects and supervised the tightening of control of high-security prisoners following some high-profile escapes during Jenkins' time as Home Secretary, including notorious train robber Ronald Biggs who fled to Australia then Brazil, returning voluntarily to prison only in 2001, and spy George Blake escaped to Moscow where he died many years later. The reform process ended when Labour lost the 1970 election.[88]

Divorce

Then came divorce reform, promoted by Gerald Gardiner, Lord Chancellor in 1964–70, after decades of campaigning. In 1963, he proposed a permanent Law Commission, an independent body of lawyers to advise government on law reforms including divorce. This was appointed in 1965 and advised government into the twenty-first century on politically and socially sensitive areas such as family law.[89] The Archbishop of Canterbury appointed a committee on divorce reform, whose report in 1966, *Putting Asunder*, accepted that secular divorce law could no longer be dictated by religious belief. It recommended 'breakdown of marriage' rather than matrimonial offence as the test for divorce, as reformers had long advocated.[90] Gardiner persuaded the Cabinet that divorce was too important to be left to a Private Member's Bill, but it took two years to draft legislation. The Archbishop, Michael Ramsey, wanted thorough discussion to prevent opposition mobilizing in the Church. Women's groups insisted that reform must include sound financial provision for divorced partners and it was agreed that divorce would be granted only when the court was satisfied that the settlement was adequate. There were outright opponents, including Labour feminist Baroness Summerskill vigorously attacking what she believed was a 'Casanova's Charter', enabling men to exploit

88 Morgan, *Callaghan*, pp. 303–6.
89 Cretney, *Family Law*, pp. 816–17.
90 See pp. 25, 100, 208, 249.

women in short-lived marriages. Other supporters of gender equality strongly supported reform. But in 1967–8 the government was preoccupied with devaluation, violence in Northern Ireland, crises in Rhodesia and Vietnam, and divorce was side-lined.

Campaigners kept it on the political agenda. The Divorce Law Reform Union (DLRU)[91] was reinvigorated, assisted by women's groups, the Methodist Church, progressive Catholics and the Church of England, though Ramsey retreated as support grew for divorce by consent, which he believed went too far. Callaghan was now Home Secretary. He held conservative views about the family and was not a strong supporter of divorce reform, though he had supported the partial decriminalization of homosexuality.[92] Jenkins had been unhappy with a successor he perceived as less liberal than himself, but, amid mounting frustration on the Labour benches and elsewhere, a government Bill went forward in 1969. It passed easily through Parliament and came into force in 1971.[93] Applicants for divorce had to prove the marriage had broken down and give one of five reasons: adultery, unreasonable behaviour, desertion, separation for more than two years if both agreed to the divorce or for at least five years if they disagreed. Supporters of no-fault divorce were disappointed; it was another compromise. The accompanying Matrimonial Proceedings and Property Act[94] allowed each divorced partner an equal share of family assets. The laws applied only in England and Wales. Scotland retained the purely fault-based system despite attempts at reform, until a Private Member's Bill by an SNP MP brought the law into line with England and Wales in 1975. The English law was forced upon Northern Ireland in 1978 by a government Order in Council, opposed by Paisley and Enoch Powell, now a Northern Ireland MP, but divorce remained difficult to obtain and there continued to be fewer divorces in Northern Ireland than elsewhere in the United Kingdom.

In Great Britain divorces rose rapidly after the law was implemented in 1971.[95] The reform enabled some people at last to marry. In 1972, a lawyer observed in the divorce court:

> A succession of elderly persons of eminently respectable appearance ... all had lived apart from their lawful spouse for more, usually much more, than the stipulated five years. In almost every case the story was essentially the same: the youthful wartime marriage, the long separation in service ... the drift apart, the formation of a new relationship, the birth of children, the woman taking the man's name, the passionate desire to legitimize those children and so on. In each case the decree was granted: in each case the elderly couple's faces reflected happiness and quiet domestic comfort.[96]

The number of such cases is unknown.

91 See p. 25.
92 Morgan, *Callaghan*, pp. 297, 320.
93 Cretney, *Family Law*, pp. 318–91.
94 Ibid., pp. 134–6, 420–1.
95 See p. 337.
96 Cretney, *Family Law*, p. 379 n. 392.

Race

Inequalities and tensions concerning race continued and some suspected they were growing along with the immigrant population. Non-white residents of Commonwealth origin in the United Kingdom in 1961 included 173,076 West Indians, 115,982 south Asians, in 1971, 302,970 and 462,125, in a total UK population of 52.7 million and 55.5 million, respectively.[97] About 100,000 Britons emigrated to Australasia each year in the late 1960s; total emigration exceeded immigration every year between 1946 and 1980.[98] In 1966, the RRB commissioned an investigation into discrimination, especially in areas not covered by the 1965 Act, showing it to be widespread in employment, housing and services. It was strongest against West Indians, especially in clerical and professional work, and as problematic for second- as first-generation black or Asian residents. Employers claimed that employing 'coloured' people, especially in direct contact with 'white' clients, put them at a competitive disadvantage.[99] The RRB appealed for extension of the Race Relations Act.

Everyday racism continued. A West Indian woman told a Community Relations Officer in Oxford, where she lived:

> I'm just fed up and I want to go home. They don't want us here. My husband work hard, I work hard, but it's just miserable. Elizabeth's teacher, she say Elizabeth is a difficult child, always fighting. You know what happened? There's some other children always teasing Elizabeth, call her monkey from the jungle, say "Monkey go home to the jungle", so Elizabeth hit them. I tell the teacher and she say she sure it not true: there isn't any prejudice in her school. Elizabeth so miserable one day she just ran out of school and came home … I see them after school, some of them, make a line with their bicycles across the path to stop Elizabeth and the other coloured children getting by and call them names … One of the fathers came to see me, shouting at me on the doorstep here … I say you tell your son not to call my daughter coon and black bastard. He say the country's overrun with us and we all ought to get out and go where we belong. And I want to get out; I want to go home.[100]

The formation of the National Front, an anti-immigrant, nationalist party, in 1967 raised tensions. So, even more, did an explosive, much publicized, speech by Enoch Powell in Birmingham in April 1968, one of several he made about immigration. Following a reference to 'wide-eyed, grinning piccaninnies', the former professor of classics proclaimed, 'As I look ahead, I am filled with foreboding. Like the Romans I seem to see "the river Tiber foaming with much blood",' referring to a passage of Virgil's *Aeneid*, as, understandably, few realized. It was well received in his Midlands constituency,

97 Butler and Butler, *Twentieth-Century British Political Facts*, pp. 347, 353.
98 Clarke, *Hope and Glory*, p. 321; Butler and Butler, *Twentieth-Century British Political Facts*, p. 351.
99 W. W. Daniel, *Racial Discrimination in England. Based on the PEP Report* (Harmondsworth: Penguin, 1968); Nicolas Deakin, *Colour Citizenship and British Society* (London: Panther, 1970).
100 Dummett, *A Portrait of English Racism*, p. 103.

Wolverhampton, which had the highest concentration of immigrants outside London. Gallup found that three-quarters of respondents agreed with Powell[101] and London dockers marched in his support, shouting 'We want Enoch'. He was dismissed from the Shadow Cabinet. Resistance to racism also continued and grew, by people of many backgrounds, inspired by the activism of the civil rights movement in the United States, reinforced by the assassination there of Martin Luther King, also in April 1968.

The government did not raise the hopes of anti-racists when it introduced the Commonwealth Immigrants Act 1968, which further limited immigration by restricting entry of citizens who obtained their British passports overseas and had no guaranteed employment in the United Kingdom, unless they had at least one white British grandparent, and immigrant numbers were severely limited. All white Commonwealth citizens retained entry rights. It was a panic measure to limit the entry of Asians fleeing persecution in Kenya following the Africanization policy of the newly independent country, rushed through Parliament in less than a week. It was strongly criticized by civil liberties groups and other liberals. To immigrants it was racist, to their harshest opponents it did not go far enough. Immigration from Asia, Africa and the Caribbean fell by half in the next ten years.

To soften the impact, also in 1968, a second Race Relations Act covered discrimination in employment and housing and strengthened the RRB's powers to investigate complaints and initiate proceedings, though Callaghan responded to police pressure and had them exempted from the law. It established the Community Relations Commission (CRC) to promote good race relations and advise the Home Office. But sanctions remained weak and many members of minority groups were unaware of the legislation or had little faith in it. Gallup found that nine-tenths of respondents approved of the immigration restrictions, a bare majority believed that 'coloured' immigrants should compete equally for work with the rest of the population or vote in British elections. Only two in five believed it should be an offence to discriminate in employment, housing or membership of an employer or worker organization.[102] The law at least signalled government opposition to discrimination, providing a moral lead, if less far reaching than some wished. As Callaghan put it, 'It had an important educative effect, but it was no more than an interim measure'.[103] An Immigration Appeals Act 1969 created an appeals system, but imposed a new limitation, that dependants seeking to join relatives in the United Kingdom should obtain an entry permit in their home country.

---

101 Robert J. Whybrow, *Britain Speaks Out, 1937–87. A Social History as Seen Through the Gallup Data* (London: Macmillan, 1989), p. 87.
102 Whybrow, *Britain Speaks Out*, pp. 87–8.
103 J. Callaghan, *Time and Chance* (London: HarperCollins, 1987), p. 269.

Gypsies and Travellers

In 1968, for the first time, the law acknowledged the inequalities and discrimination faced by Gypsies and Travellers, after they too rebelled. Their itinerant lifestyle and irregular employment excluded them from essential services, including education, access to a GP, national insurance. If they tried to settle they faced discrimination from local authorities and landlords. If they did not, their caravan sites aroused hostility, harassment and eviction, with some local authorities declaring their districts 'no-go' areas for travellers. Pubs displayed 'No Gypsies' signs. In 1965, Crossman commissioned a national survey which recorded 15,500 Gypsies and Travellers in England, Wales and Scotland, probably an underestimate. Only twelve local authorities had established caravan sites, just one-third of families had access to on-site water and children's education was severely deficient. The findings were circulated to local authorities with 'strong and detailed advice' on providing sites, requesting reports on action taken.

In 1966, the Gypsy Council formed to campaign against eviction and for equal status and respect with the settled population, with supporters including the NCCL.[104] By 1968, 300 complaints were made against pubs under the Race Relations Act, but none went to court: Gypsies and Travellers were not recognized as a 'race' under the Act. The Caravan Sites Act 1968 was initially a Private Member's Bill from Liberal MP Eric Lubbock, which the government supported. It required local authorities from April 1970 to provide sites for Gypsies and Travellers, though with no deadline; they could evict them from unauthorized sites. By 1973, between one-fifth and one-quarter of the required sites were established. The needs of this excluded group were becoming recognized though equality remained remote.[105]

Youth and 'Counter-Culture'

The peak year for protest among young people internationally was 1968. It took diverse forms as more middle-class youth became politically active and some adopted new 'counter-cultural' lifestyles. Youth culture was class-divided like most of British life, though enthusiasm for the Beatles and Carnaby Street styles cut across classes. Again, the United States led the way in new directions. 1967 was the 'summer of love' in San Francisco when the media grew excited about the alternative 'hippie' lifestyles that had been growing in America and Europe for some years, challenging conservative values, experimenting with drugs, sex and flowing hair and clothes for males and females. A huge Human Be-In rally in Golden Gate Park, San Francisco in January 1967 was

104 See p. 128.
105 Mel Porter and Becky Taylor, 'Gypsies and Travellers', in Pat Thane (ed.), *Unequal Britain. Equalities in Britain since 1945* (London: Bloomsbury, 2010), pp. 71–104.

entertained by bands and 'beat' writers, including Jack Kerouac and Timothy Leary who coined the catch-phrase of the hippie movement there: 'Turn On, Tune In, Drop Out'. Then publicity erupted around the Monterey pop festival in 1967, the world's first such major event which attracted young people from across America, the first of many, including in Britain. Hippie ideology focused upon finding one's true identity, freed from conventional culture. The clothes, drug-taking, music, festivals and creative 'happenings' attracted young people in many countries. Many were encouraged to travel and explore new worlds – cheap travel by bus and hitchhiking was now possible with the growth of motor transport. The 'hippie trail' across Europe and the Middle East to India and beyond attracted more and more young people. Many of them were involved in political protests which peaked in 1968, less in the United Kingdom than in France, the United States and Germany, perhaps because Britain still educated fewer university students, but they demonstrated in London and elsewhere against the Vietnam War and aspects of cultural and political conservatism, including what many students saw as the antiquated, paternalist approach of universities.

These activities aroused predictable, conventional disapproval, but in 1968 the government appeared to support younger people by reducing the age of legal majority, and of voting to 18. In 1965, it appointed the Latey Committee on the Age of Majority, chaired by a judge, mainly because, with growing affluence, more people were marrying, buying property and making other contracts at earlier ages, but legally could do none of these things without parental permission until age 21, which caused problems. The Committee concluded in 1967, that, contrary to contemporary moral panics, most 18–21-year-olds appeared to be as responsible as their elders and there was little to fear from treating them as adults.[106] It was the first change in the franchise not preceded by long campaigns by the disfranchised. Indeed, there was little sign of young people demanding the vote; it was attributed to Wilson's hope that they would vote Labour. Gallup found 56 per cent of a sample of 18–20-year-olds approved the change, though 30 per cent disagreed and 30 per cent said they would not vote.[107] Turnout among younger voters remained low compared with other age groups into the twenty-first century.

Most fashionable drugs were illegal and their growing use caused concern. The Dangerous Drugs Act 1965 began to bring UK law into line with the UN Convention on Narcotic Drugs. It created a new crime of allowing premises to be used for drug-taking and gave police new powers to stop and search for cannabis and other drugs. They targeted black and long-haired people and pop stars and convictions for cannabis offences rose 79 per cent within a year, 113 per cent in 1967. The NCCL was highly critical

---

106 Holden, *Makers and Manners*, p. 160.
107 Whybrow, *Britain Speaks Out*, p. 83.

and campaigning groups demanded liberalization, especially of cannabis use. In 1967, Jenkins established the Hallucinogens Sub-Committee of the Advisory Committee on Drug Dependence, at the request of the Vice-Chancellor of Oxford University who was concerned about students' use of cannabis or 'pot'. Chaired by Barbara Wootton, it reported in 1968, recommending reduced penalties for cannabis offences, on the ground that it was less harmful than 'hard' drugs like heroin and hallucinogenic LSD, the hippies' favourite, and making a clearer distinction between hard and soft drugs. It did not propose legalization of cannabis as campaigners demanded. The report was attacked in the tabloids as a 'junkies' charter' and Wootton (aged 71) as 'a little old lady gone to pot'.[108] Callaghan opposed even the proposed compromise, accusing Wootton of being over-influenced by a 'pro-pot' lobby. He strongly disapproved of drug-taking and was concerned by what he perceived as the deteriorating behaviour of many young people.[109] In the parliamentary debates on the report he announced his wish 'to call a halt to the rising tide of permissiveness … one of the most unlikeable words that has been invented in recent years'.[110] The Home Office drafted what became the Misuse of Drugs Act 1971. This compromised with campaigners by classifying cannabis as a Class B drug, liable to less severe penalties than 'hard' heroin and LSD, but it was illegal to grow, produce, possess or supply cannabis, except for licensed medical research, and maximum penalties increased to up to fourteen years for cultivation, allowing premises to be used for supply, and new offences were created of supplying or possessing with intent to supply. Five years' imprisonment was still possible for possession, though in reality fines were more common. The Bill was passed by the Cabinet but the election intervened. It was implemented by the Conservatives.

Equal Pay

Labour's final reforming breakthrough, following another long campaign, was the Equal Pay Act 1970. It was initiated by Barbara Castle, as Minister for Employment and Productivity from April 1968. In 1968, female representation in the Cabinet doubled when Judith Hart was appointed Paymaster General, giving Labour the modest distinction of appointing more women to the Cabinet than any previous government. Women in the Labour Party, trade unions and women's organizations campaigned with increasing intensity for equal pay in the 1960s, before the Women's Liberation Movement took off from 1969. Seventy per cent of new union members between 1964 and 1970 were female and the unions took notice. There was a flurry of strikes for

108 Oakley, *A Critical Woman*, pp. 264–71.
109 Morgan, *Callaghan*, pp. 316–22.
110 Ibid., p. 320.

equal pay and equal treatment at work in the mid-1960s. During the 1966 election, an alliance of women's organizations – the Six Point Group, Status of Women Committee, Suffrage Fellowship, Association of Headmistresses, British Federation of Business and Professional Women, and National Council of Married Women – demanded equality at work, in taxation, pensions and other benefits.[111] The EC, in its founding Treaty of Rome, 1957, committed member states to 'maintain the principle of equal remuner-ation for equal work as between men and women workers', following pressure from women across Europe. Labour leaders were anxious to meet EC standards where pos-sible to increase their chances of admission. In 1967, discussions between the CBI and TUC showed that little had changed since 1946. The CBI would only commit to 'equal pay for equal work', dismissing the TUC's preference for 'equal pay for work of the same value' as being too open-ended and imprecise. The breakdown of the talks convinced the TUC to support legislation.

The cause progressed when Ray Gunter, who had no known interest in gender equal-ity, was replaced at the renamed Ministry of Employment and Productivity by Castle. Gunter, a long-time trade unionist, resigned, disgruntled with pay controls imposed by a Cabinet 'over-weighted with intellectuals',[112] as he put it. Castle faced two strikes, which, she later commented, 'fired my determination to force the macho male chauvinists in the Treasury to accept the principle of equal pay'.[113] The first was the strike of women sewing machinists at Ford's factory at Dagenham, in June 1968, much mythologized and the subject of a film, *Made in Dagenham*, in 2010. The strike was not directly about equal pay but about a job evaluation scheme which women workers believed under-valued their work and skill in relation to men. The male trade unionists at Dagenham turned the issue towards equal pay as a condition of their support because they did not want the job evaluation, which favoured them, reopened. Castle intervened and the women achieved something closer to equal pay – a rise from 85 per cent to 92 per cent of the men's rate – without revisiting the job evaluation, and men and women returned to work. The strike led to the formation of the National Joint Action Committee for Women's Equal Rights among women's groups and trade unionists. It adopted a charter calling on the TUC to campaign for equal pay and equal opportunities, launched at a big rally in Trafalgar Square in May 1969. The second dispute arose from a pay demand by male engineers. The men agreed a settlement that paid women employees less and the women protested. The men switched to supporting equal pay until it became clear that they would receive lower pay than they wanted, then they agreed the deal that dis-advantaged women. Castle 'knew then that left to themselves the unions would never do anything serious about equal pay and that the government had to legislate'.[114]

111 Meehan, *Women's Rights at Work*, pp. 43–56.
112 H. Pelling and A. Reid, *A Short History of the Labour Party*, 11th edn (London: Macmillan, 1996), p. 131.
113 Barbara Castle, *Fighting All the Way* (London: Pan, 1993), pp. 408–9.
114 Ibid., p. 412.

But her time was consumed by further tussles with the unions over prices and incomes policy,[115] and legislation came about because 'once again it was the women who made the running'.[116] In spring 1970, when the election had been called, women Labour MPs, led by Lena Jeger, tabled an amendment to the government's Prices and Incomes Bill, demanding that pay controls should not prevent moves towards equal pay. Castle pointed out that the government was likely to be defeated on the amendment unless she announced equal pay legislation. The Cabinet felt forced to agree. She rushed the Equal Pay Bill through Parliament before the election, later admitting it was prepared in a hurry: 'It was far from perfect but it established the principle on which later refinements could be built. I knew that if we lost the election our Tory successors would be forced to proceed with it'.[117] It required equal rates of pay for the same or similar work, to be assessed by job evaluation schemes. Compliance would be voluntary until 1975 to allow time for evaluation. Claims of non-compliance would be made to an employment tribunal and successful claims compensated by up to two years' back-pay. The Act overlooked women's unequal access to promotion or appointment to higher paid work.

Women remained concentrated in low-status, low-paid work. Employers still argued that they were not victims of discrimination: it was rational to withhold training or promotion when women would leave to raise a family. Some evaded the law by re-grading posts where men and women did the same work for unequal pay: a shoe store re-graded male shop assistants as 'managers', though they continued, like the lesser paid women, to sell shoes. Ancillary workers, like cleaners were dismissed, replaced by 'outsourced' workers, enabling employers to evade 'like work' issues among their own employees. By 1971, in about 20 per cent of national agreements covering manual workers, discrimination was removed, mostly by levelling up women's pay.[118] In 1970 the median earnings of adult women full-time workers were 54 per cent of males', by 1983 it was 66 per cent, following further legislation.[119] The struggle continued.

The House of Lords

A notable feature of the remarkable run of reform legislation of the late 1960s was the ease with which all the changes passed the Lords, in contrast to their conservatism under previous governments. The appointment of life peers had changed their political

115 See p. 297.

116 Castle, *Fighting All the Way*, p. 427.

117 Ibid., p. 427.

118 Helen McCarthy, 'Gender Equality', in Pat Thane (ed.), *Unequal Britain. Equalities in Britain since 1945* (London: Bloomsbury, 2010), pp. 109–13.

119 A. B. Atkinson, 'Distribution of Income and Wealth', in A. H. Halsey and J. Webb (eds), *Twentieth-century British Social Trends* (London: Macmillan, 2000), p. 354.

balance. The fact that Wilson created 152 life peers between 1964 and 1970, compared with sixty-three by his Conservative predecessors since 1958 and thirty by Heath from 1970 to 1974, may help to account for it. In 1968, Labour proposed to change the Lords more drastically by eliminating the voting rights of hereditary peers and excluding their heirs from membership, allowing all other peers to vote only until age 72, if they attended at least one-third of sittings, granting each government the right to a majority of peers and reducing the Lords' powers to delay legislation approved by the Commons from one year to six months. These reforms also were approved by the Lords but they were defeated in the Commons by an alliance of right-wing Conservatives, who wanted no change, and left-wing Labour MPs, who still wanted abolition and a democratically elected upper house. The government withdrew.

The succession of liberal reforms that became law were seen by supporters as introducing a more open, equal society where behaviour deviating from assumed norms was no longer suppressed and secret, and excluded minorities – or majorities in the case of women – had equal rights. Many of the reforms were tentative beginnings, compromises attacked by Labour's many radical critics for not going far enough, but further signs of cultural progress, building on visible changes through previous decades. The pace of change was unequal across the United Kingdom, like much else, and slowest in Northern Ireland where the influence of the Churches was greatest. The reforms encouraged demands for more by the newly formed Women's Liberation Movement and Gay Liberation Front, anti-racist groups and others. For opponents, they ushered in a 'permissive', excessively individualistic society, destroying established values, undermining 'traditional' morality. In the twenty-first century the legislation is still blamed for the growth of single parenthood, youth crime and most of society's ills. It caused the 'Abolition of Britain', according to *Daily Mail* journalist Peter Hitchens,[120] 'Broken Britain' in the rhetoric of David Cameron, Conservative Prime Minister from 2010 to 2016. All the reforms followed long campaigns by passionate advocates, in the United Kingdom and internationally, and cumulative cultural and attitudinal change, though their passage in such quick succession owed a great deal to Labour support in Parliament, especially that of Jenkins as Home Secretary, despite the doubts of some Labour voters, and to the changed, more liberal, composition of the Lords.

Trade Union Strife

Labour also faced more traditional challenges. Its desire to control incomes caused conflict with the unions, who themselves had problems with unofficial, localized strikes,

120 Peter Hitchens, *The Abolition of Britain. From Lady Chatterley to Tony Blair* (London: Continuum, 1999; 2nd edn, Bloomsbury, 2008).

though days lost in strikes were lower than under the Conservatives until 1969.[121] But uncontrolled pay rises repeatedly caused inflation and economic crisis and Labour was tempted to restrict union powers. Polls suggested shifts in public opinion: in 1964, 70 per cent approved of unions, 12 per cent did not, by 1969 the numbers were 57 per cent and 26 per cent, respectively, suggesting that controls would win support. In 1969, Barbara Castle's department published a White Paper, *In Place of Strife*, proposing government powers to order twenty-eight-day 'conciliation pauses' before strikes, to demand strike ballots and penalties for breaching these rules, while compelling employers to recognize unions and encouraging them to appoint worker-directors, as in West Germany. The unions opposed the constraints on strikes, remained suspicious of worker participation in management ('selling out') and saw little need for mandatory recognition when union membership was rising. There was strong opposition in the party and the Cabinet, led by Callaghan, who supported the unions and disliked Castle. In Parliament, almost 100 Labour MPs voted against the proposals or abstained. After months of bitter dispute, they were withdrawn. The battle made the government appear weak as an election approached. In the polls, Wilson's approval rating fell to 26 per cent, then the lowest for any premier since polls began

Northern Ireland

Another, ultimately more serious, source of tension was growing nationalism in Northern Ireland as Catholic resentment against Protestant hegemony mounted. The twelve Ulster MPs in Westminster were overwhelmingly Protestant Unionists, staunch supporters of the Conservative Party, though increasingly challenged by Catholic Nationalists. Stormont was also Protestant and Unionist dominated. Catholics had long resented this and the accompanying discrimination and inequality, including in allocation of housing and employment. Government employees, including in the paramilitary police, who bore arms as they did not elsewhere in the United Kingdom, were overwhelmingly Protestant. Catholic civil rights groups protested against discrimination and against Britain and the Union, which had done nothing to protect them. They were inspired by the civil rights movement in the United States, where many Irish people had close connections due to emigration, and spurred on by unemployment, which rose disproportionately among Catholics.

In the mid-1960s, Terence O'Neill, the moderate Unionist premier, introduced limited reforms and was prodded by Wilson's government to go further, but this only aroused Catholic demands for more and alienated fundamentalist Protestant Unionists, always suspicious of the elite landowner tradition in Unionism to which O'Neill belonged.

---

121 Butler and Butler, *Twentieth-Century British Political Facts*, pp. 400–1.

Ian Paisley, representing O'Neill's liberalism as a popish plot, led a populist Orangeism threatening to split Unionism. Catholics marched for their civil rights, like the black protesters in the United States. Their discontent revived the Irish Republican Army (IRA), with a new Provisional wing dedicated to armed struggle against Britain. In 1969, demonstrations, riots and clashes were sometimes serious; five people died in Belfast in August. O'Neill had to go, but no other Unionist could exert control and in 1970, Callaghan, as Home Secretary, decided that the only option was to agree to the Unionists' request to deploy the army to Northern Ireland to keep the peace. It was an extreme move, criticized on the left who supported equality for Catholics, and the situation stabilized for a while, but was deteriorating before the 1970 election.[122] Rising nationalisms did not yet seriously threaten to disunite the United Kingdom, but there were hints of danger.

The Commonwealth

Racial inequality was not only a problem within Britain. Labour was pledged to continue decolonization and eager to uphold the Commonwealth, but in Rhodesia the white minority still rejected black majority rule. In neighbouring South Africa, Nelson Mandela was imprisoned for life in 1964 for resisting apartheid. He and his comrades were saved from hanging by an international campaign with strong support in Britain, part of another international campaign against racism. In Rhodesia Labour and the Commonwealth opposed independence without majority rule. In 1965, Ian Smith, the Prime Minister elected by a majority white electorate, made a unilateral declaration of independence (UDI), preserving the existing constitution. Talks followed but compromise was impossible. The UN imposed economic sanctions but not rigorously and South Africa evaded them. UK military intervention (against our 'kith and kin', as some put it, since white Rhodesians were mainly of British origin, often ex-servicemen who had migrated after the war) was unpopular in Britain, including with the military, deterring action in Rhodesia as it did not in Belfast. Apparently, it was less acceptable for the army to fight on behalf of excluded black people. The problem dragged on, despite protest in Africa and on the British left.[123] Britain had no obvious way forward, a symptom of its weakened international position.

The UK Anti-Apartheid movement demanded sanctions against white-controlled South Africa and its isolation from exchange with Britain and other countries. It opposed white minority rule in Rhodesia equally bitterly, and what it saw as the

---

122 Paul Bew, *Ireland. The Politics of Enmity, 1789–2006* (Oxford University Press, 2009); P. Bew and G. Gillespie, *Northern Ireland. A Chronology of the Troubles 1968–1999* (London: Gill & Macmillan, 1999).
123 Clarke, *Hope and Glory*, pp. 297–8.

government's weak response, adding to its growing body of critics. It urged British consumers and businesses to boycott South African goods, campaigned for the release of people detained without trial, and against sporting, artistic and academic contacts with South Africa, leading big demonstrations at all twenty-four matches of the 1969–70 South African Rugby tour of Britain and Ireland and achieving cancellation of a tour by the all-white South African cricket team in 1970. Labour banned the sale of arms to South Africa, but nothing changed within South Africa or Rhodesia apart from growing internal racial tensions.

1970 General Election

By 1970, Labour could claim substantial achievements. Despite economic crises, income inequality was approaching its narrowest of the century,[124] though poverty persisted. Major inequalities of gender, race and disability and homosexual rights were confronted and modified as never before, though far from eliminated. There were substantial, if incomplete, welfare reforms and significant legal reforms, though never enough to satisfy the growing body of radical critics, especially among young people. Both major parties declined in membership as affluence and wider leisure opportunities opened other interests and alternative political movements – including anti-racism and campaigns for women's and gay liberation – emerged.[125] Labour slipped in local elections, in 1968 losing Sheffield for the first time since 1932 and losing seats in inner London. It lost sixteen by-elections between 1966 and 1969.

In 1970, the economy was recovering, with a £700 million trade surplus aided by an upturn in world trade; unemployment averaged 2.5 per cent from 1966 to 1970. By May 1970, Labour had a seven-point lead in the polls and Wilson led Heath by twenty-one points on personal popularity. He called an election. The parties were even in the polls on which could best manage the economy and four-fifths of respondents disapproved of the government's handling of the cost of living, but up to the election the polls predicted a Labour win.[126] Labour issued a cautious manifesto, but, on a lower turnout than in 1966 – 72 per cent – lost the election, narrowly on votes, 12.1 million, 43.5 per cent, to the Conservatives 13.1 million, 46.5 per cent, but convincingly on seats, losing fifty-eight on a swing of 4.7 per cent, the highest since 1945. Race probably played a part: the Conservatives targeted marginal constituencies where it was a particular issue. Labour was not helped by the announcement, two days before the election, of an unexpected balance of payments deficit, nor by the conflict with the unions and in

---

124 Gazeley, 'Income and Living Standards', p. 160.
125 Butler and Butler, *Twentieth-Century British Political Facts*, p. 141.
126 Whybrow, *Britain Speaks Out*, pp. 93–4.

Northern Ireland. The liberal reforms may have alienated some voters. Asked by Gallup why Labour had lost, one in four voters replied 'the cost of living'; no other reason came close.

Labour performed best in much of northern England and Scotland, but weakly in the south. Support among men, especially manual workers, fell more than among women, from 69 per cent in 1966 to 58 per cent. The Liberals slumped again to six seats. Mrs Ewing kept her seat for the SNP, their only victory from sixty-five candidates. Plaid Cymru fought all thirty-six Welsh seats for the first time, winning none, gaining 11.5 per cent of the Welsh vote.[127] The Northern Ireland 'Troubles', as they became known, surfaced in the election. Just eight Ulster Unionists were returned, one Protestant Unionist, Ian Paisley, a Catholic Nationalist, Gerry Fitt of the Social Democratic and Labour Party (SDLP), two independent Catholic Republicans, including Bernadette Devlin (later McAliskey), aged 21, the UK's youngest ever female and third youngest MP, first elected in a 1969 by-election. Northern Ireland was just one problem inherited by the incoming Conservatives.

127 Morgan, *Wales*, p. 393.

10 The Seventies

We have seen that historical reality does not divide neatly into decades, but in popular and media memory the 'seventies' like – but in important ways unlike – the 'sixties' has acquired a mythologized unity and notoriety: not 'permissive' or 'swinging', but a 'dismal, benighted'[1] decade of turbulent discontent, terminating the postwar 'golden age' of stable progress. It was indeed a time of recurrent economic crises, more severe than in the 1950s and 1960s, increased industrial conflict, inflation and unemployment. The United Kingdom again became divided between regions of decline and unemployment, prosperity and consumption as manufacturing and its share of world trade continued to decline relative to its competitors. Politicians, and historians, were, and are, divided about whether the main cause was excessive government intervention to increase investment, modernize production and improve management, or too little.[2] If consensus between the major parties on economic and social policy is hard to detect in the preceding decades, it vanished in the 1970s.

Yet income inequality fell to its lowest point of the century and the welfare state reached its peak. There were legal advances towards gender and racial equality. The sexual and cultural practices derided as 'permissive' – divorce, separation, cohabitation, open homosexuality – were more evident than in the 1960s. For some these were further signs of decline, for others of progress – a cultural division that did not decline.

---

1 Lawrence Black and Hugh Pemberton, 'Introduction. The Benighted Decade? Reassessing the 1970s', in L. Black, H. Pemberton and P. Thane (eds) *Reassessing 1970s Britain* (Manchester University Press, 2013), pp. 1–24.

2 Michael Kitson and Jonathan Michie, 'The De-industrialization Revolution. The Rise and Fall of UK Manufacturing', in Roderick Floud, Jane Humphries and Paul Johnson (eds), *The Cambridge Economic History of Modern Britain, vol. 2: 1870 to the Present* (Cambridge University Press, 2014), pp. 318–30.

Similarly divisive was the growth of 'new social movements', including the Women's Liberation Movement (WLM), the Gay Liberation Front (GLF) and anti-racist movements, all highly visible responses to continuing inequalities. One outcome of increasing regional inequality was growing nationalisms in Scotland and Wales, most destructively in Northern Ireland where the Troubles deepened.

Britain at last joined the European Community, though that also caused division at home and did not signify increased international power.

Heath in Power?

As 'Women's Lib' emerged, Heath appointed one woman to his small, eighteen-member, Cabinet, Margaret Thatcher. Fifteen ministers were privately educated, four at Eton.[3] Heath and Thatcher were exceptions, both upwardly mobile, via Oxford, from the borders of the working and lower middle classes, her father a shopkeeper. They had little else in common. She married a millionaire businessman, he was unmarried. His stiff manner won him few admirers in an increasingly televisual political world. He believed in firm policies and aimed for close control of the party. He excluded Powell from the Cabinet and others with whom he disagreed. Margaret Thatcher was the one minister prepared to challenge him, but in the contemporary culture he believed he needed a token woman and, in charge of the suitably female terrain of Education, she was not involved in major affairs of state. His choice as Chancellor, Iain Macleod, died a month later and was replaced by the relatively unknown Anthony Barber. Douglas-Home became Foreign Secretary and returned to the Lords, now a life peer. Heath's, decidedly unconsensual, programme, launched in March 1970, included curbing unions, making social security benefits more 'selective', ending incomes policies and liberating business from government shackles.

Economic Policy

Reversing the perceived relative weakness of the economy compared with Britain's competitors was as central for Heath as for Wilson, though their approaches were very different. Heath believed the state could assist growth in a free enterprise economy, if its institutions were suitably reformed, though state intervention should be limited, max-imizing space for free enterprise. Unlike their predecessors, the Conservatives had the advantage of inheriting a large budget surplus, with revenue exceeding expenditure by over 5 per cent of GDP. Labour's Prices and Incomes Board and income controls were abolished and subsidies to development areas phased out. The Ministry of Technology

3 Tim Bale, *The Conservatives since 1945. The Drivers of Party Change* (Oxford University Press, 2012), p. 154.

was merged into a new Ministry for Trade and Industry under John Davies, Director-General of the Confederation of British Industries (CBI), 'the bosses' trade union', and its commitment to industrial modernization terminated. Strongly committed to free enterprise, Davies announced that taxpayers' money should not assist 'lame duck' industries. He refused support when the Mersey Docks and Harbour Board faced difficulties. Then, early in 1971, a more formidable lame duck emerged: internationally prestigious Rolls-Royce, Britain's leading manufacturer of aero-engines and luxury cars, faced bankruptcy following difficulties fulfilling an overseas contract. It was too important to lose and, to Labour's glee, it was nationalized. The car manufacturing arm was privatized in 1973.

Then Upper Clyde Shipbuilders (UCS), a leading shipbuilding firm, threatened to collapse, causing heavy unemployment around Glasgow. UCS was formed by Labour in 1968 from an assortment of failing shipbuilding firms to revive a flagging industry. The government took a 48.4 per cent holding, making substantial grants and loans. By 1970, UCS was recovering well. In early 1971, without negotiation with UCS, Davies announced the sale of shares and termination of subsidy. UCS' creditors panicked, demanded repayment and refused further credit. Cheered on by Conservative back-benchers, Davies would not save it from bankruptcy. The unions responded with the unusual tactic of a 'work-in', keeping the yards going, whereas a strike could destroy the business. This much publicized move gained strong support from unions, Labour, Glasgow City Council and Roman Catholic and Church of Scotland leaders. The workers, led by the charismatic Jimmy Reid, were supported by demonstrations in Glasgow and London, and received donations including £1,000 from Beatle John Lennon and £2,700 from shipyard workers of the USSR. Scottish businessmen did not support Davies. In February 1972 he was forced to return UCS to partial government ownership with a grant of £35 million, handing over management to a US firm, Marathon, the world's largest deep-sea oil-rig construction company, whose directors were convinced of its viability. The alternative was the collapse of a major local employer with alarming political consequences. UCS then operated successfully for some years.[4] The crisis was an avoidable outcome of an ideologically driven, crudely implemented policy. Davies left the government in November 1972.

Underlying the policy retreats was concern over a rise in unemployment to 900,000 in early 1972, heading to the symbolically dangerous 1 million, while commodity prices rose internationally. By early 1973, most industrial nations experienced inflation and slower economic growth, the United Kingdom more than most. The Bretton Woods system of fixed exchange rates[5] collapsed and the pound slipped badly.

4 See at: www.gcu.ac.uk/radicalglasgow/chapters/ucs_workin.htm, last accessed 13 January 2015.
5 See p. 219.

Inflation caused union pressure for wage rises averaging 13 per cent in 1971–3. In the 1971 Budget Barber sought to encourage investment and demand by halving Labour's Selective Employment Tax on services, cutting corporation tax and increasing child tax allowances, with little effect. By summer 1971, urgent action was needed to avert a serious crisis. A large programme of public works in development areas, increased house improvement grants and capital allowances for industry were introduced, while hire purchase controls were abolished and purchase tax cut, again without great effect. The Bank of England removed the ceiling on bank lending and cut interest rates to encourage borrowing, while increasing the stock of money, stimulating further inflation. The government tried to restrain wage demands by limiting price rises. Domestic prices steadied, but import prices could not be controlled and wage demands continued. In 1972 prices rose by 7 per cent.[6] House prices rose, especially in London, due partly to continuing 'gentrification' of previously unfashionable inner districts, pioneered in Islington.[7] Meanwhile, decimalization of the currency began in 1971, calmly.[8]

Industrial Relations

To control wage demands, the Industrial Relations Act 1971 established an Industrial Relations Court empowered to enforce strike ballots and 'cooling-off periods' before strikes, similar to Labour's failed *In Place of Strife* proposals.[9] Effectively it restricted the right to strike. It was bitterly opposed by Labour, led by Barbara Castle and the TUC, now reconciled, with a large protest march in London.[10] Employers avoided the Court, fearing worsening labour relations; when it intervened in projected strikes, workers became more militant. The TUC instructed unions to restrain strike action to avoid conflict but days lost in strikes rose to 24 million in 1972, the highest since 1926. Union membership rose from 47.7 per cent to 49.6 per cent of the workforce between 1970 and 1974. When the Court ordered the arrest of five shop stewards on the London docks and fined their union, the Transport and General Workers, £5,000, a dock strike and trade paralysis loomed. The Official Solicitor secured the release of the 'Pentonville Five'. Public support for the unions rose in the polls. Again 'decisive' government action backfired. It wrongly assumed that workers were forced into strikes by over-powerful 'union barons', unaware that they were mainly driven, often reluctantly, by rising living costs.

6 Clarke, *Hope and Glory*, pp. 329–33.
7 See p. 279.
8 See p. 275.
9 See p. 297.
10 Reid, *United We Stand*, pp. 301–2.

of emergency was declared on 13 November, followed in December by another three-day week for all industries, to preserve power. The bank rate rose to 13 per cent, the highest ever, and hire purchase controls were reintroduced. The government planned to cut public spending in 1974–5 by an unprecedented £1,200 million. Oil prices doubled.[15] Efforts to settle the miners' dispute continued, but in a ballot 80 per cent voted in favour of another strike to start on 10 February.

Heath called an election for 28 February, declaring as the central issue 'Who Governs Britain?', claiming that the unions were challenging government power. The miners continued their strike but kept it lower key than the last for fear of harming Labour in the election.[16] They were not the Conservatives' biggest problem, however. The inherited budget surplus had been transformed into a deficit and tax revenue fell as a proportion of GDP by at least 7 per cent, due to the oil shock and tax cuts.[17] Amid a three-day week, power cuts and petrol shortages disrupting business and everyday life – candles, long unused, sold out, TV shut down early, at 10.30 pm to save power – polls suggested the Conservatives were widely believed to have mishandled the economy, lacking consistent policies.

Social Security and Health

Nor did their social policies win voters. They fulfilled the pledge to extend 'selectivity', that is, means-testing, to cut social security costs. Crossman's pensions reforms were abandoned because they were costly and threatened the increasingly powerful private pension sector with more generous state pensions. CPAG still campaigned for higher universal child allowances. Sir Keith Joseph at the DHSS introduced a cheaper alternative, Family Income Supplement (FIS), a means-tested benefit for low-paid working families. It was designed to tackle the problem, highlighted by CPAG, of the many full-time workers who were too low paid to support their families, but, as ever with means-tested benefits, take-up was low, only 50 per cent of eligible claimants, leaving many in poverty. Rather than solving the child poverty problem, FIS subsidized and encouraged low-paying employers and created a disincentive for low-paid workers to earn more for fear of exceeding the means limit and losing benefit, making a net loss, the 'poverty trap' as it is known.[18]

Joseph modified Crossman's plans for integrating health and social services and the severe problems continued. On another issue raised in the late 1960s, he was reluctantly

15 Cairncross, *British Economy since 1945*, pp. 182–93.

16 Reid, *United We Stand*, pp. 328–9.

17 Clarke, *Hope and Glory*, pp 338–9.

18 Thane and Davidson, *The Child Poverty Action Group*, pp. 18–19.

pressured in 1974 to integrate birth control services into the NHS, providing universal free advice, but free supplies only for those receiving means-tested benefits.[19]

Housing

The 1970 Conservative manifesto attacked Labour's failure to build as many houses as promised, despite their building more than any other government in the twentieth century.[20] It pledged to build more, especially owner-occupied, homes. Housebuilding then declined from a total of 378,000 in 1969, mostly public sector, to 280,000 in 1974, about 60 per cent private sector.[21] The major policy change was the Housing Finance Act 1972, which required council rents to rise to 'fair rent' (i.e., local market rent) levels, aiming to end government subsidies. Labour's means-tested rent rebate scheme, which was optional for councils, was extended to private tenants, supported by government funds, subsidizing landlords and extending the 'poverty trap'.[22] The Act was strongly resisted by Labour-controlled councils, but they were forced to comply. It did not apply in Scotland.

Education

Margaret Thatcher became notorious for withdrawing free milk from primary schoolchildren over age 7, lampooned by Labour as 'Margaret Thatcher, milk snatcher', despite its own record of withdrawing milk from secondary schools. She raised the cost of school meals, following Treasury pressure for further cuts. By 1970, most local authorities had adopted comprehensive secondary schooling. Thatcher withdrew Crosland's circular recommending the changeover, but authorities of all political persuasions continued to switch. More comprehensives were established during her period of office than in any other. There was little enthusiasm among voters or education professionals for returning to the inequities of grammar schools and 11+ selection. The school leaving age was raised to 16 in 1973, as planned by Labour. Education spending rose faster than in 1964–70, largely due to the implementation of Labour policies. The expansion of universities, polytechnics and teacher training colleges continued: 13 per cent of 18–21 year olds entered some form of higher education in 1972 compared with 8.5 per cent in 1962,[23] while older students had access

19 See p. 285.
20 Butler and Butler, *Twentieth-Century British Political Facts*, p. 357.
21 Ibid., p 357.
22 Michael Hill, *The Welfare State in Britain. A Political History since 1945* (Aldershot: Edward Elgar, 1993), p. 100.
23 A. H. Halsey, 'Further and Higher Education', in A. H. Halsey and J. Webb (eds), *Twentieth-century British Social Trends* (London: Macmillan, 2000), p. 226.

to the Open University as well as other higher education institutions, though expansion slowed when the Conservatives cut means-tested grants. The student population remained predominantly middle class and male, though numbers of female and lower middle-class students slowly increased.

Northern Ireland

The situation in Northern Ireland deteriorated. Four days after the election, Bernadette Devlin MP lost her appeal against a six-month sentence for her part in disturbances in Derry (as Nationalists called it, officially Londonderry) in 1969 and was imprisoned for four months. Severe rioting in Derry followed. Troops were pelted with stones and petrol bombs and responded with CS gas. Twenty-five people died in the 'Troubles' in 1970.[24] The first British soldier was killed in February 1971. Unionist divisions continued. In 1971, Ian Paisley formed the Democratic Unionist Party (DUP), closely linked to the fundamentalist Protestant, deeply anti-Catholic and conservative church he had founded in 1951 and still led, the Free Presbyterian Church of Ulster. Violence worsened when, in August 1971, the government imposed internment without trial for those accused of violence, in a doomed attempt to undermine the IRA. Instead it grew stronger, fired by brutal treatment of internees, causing more civilian and military deaths.[25] In September 1971, the Ulster Defence Association (UDA) was formed from Protestant paramilitary groups, gaining 40,000–50,000 volunteers by 1972. In 1971, 174 people died. In 1972, William Craig, a former Stormont minister, formed another Unionist breakaway closely linked to Protestant paramilitaries, the Vanguard Movement, from loyalists who believed the Stormont and Westminster governments did not challenge the IRA strongly enough.

A civil rights demonstration planned for Derry on Sunday, 30 January 1972, was banned and troops sealed off the planned route. Ten thousand people marched along a different route through a strongly Nationalist area. Following skirmishes, thirteen unarmed Catholics were shot dead by British troops. The army insisted soldiers had retaliated against demonstrators carrying bombs and guns. This was serious enough for the Home Secretary to appoint, the following day, an enquiry into 'Bloody Sunday' as it was soon called, chaired by the Lord Chief Justice, Lord Widgery. This speedily exonerated the army and cast suspicion on many of the victims, accepting army claims that they were armed and threatening. This exacerbated the conflict, causing bitter controversy for decades as relatives of the dead and the wider Nationalist community

---

24 Bew and Gillespie, *Northern Ireland*, p. 31.
25 Ibid., p. 43.

demanded a public enquiry. It was finally granted by Tony Blair in 1998. It took twelve years, at massive cost, to conclude that the victims were innocent and that the blame lay wholly with the army.

Catholics no longer trusted the neutrality of British forces, whom they initially welcomed as preferable to the Protestant police. IRA violence spread to bombings in England (not Wales or Scotland); the first, in February 1972, at the Aldershot HQ of the Parachute Regiment, whose soldiers had fired the shots on Bloody Sunday. Seven people were killed: a gardener, a Roman Catholic chaplain and five women kitchen workers, making the IRA slow its campaign. In March, Stormont was suspended and its functions transferred to a new Secretary of State for Northern Ireland, William Whitelaw, initially for one year. In June, Colonel Gaddafi, ruler of Libya, started supplying arms to 'the Irish revolutionaries who are fighting Britain', continuing until 1992.[26] Violence and strikes continued; 470 people died in 1972, with two civilians killed for each soldier.[27]

When Stormont was suspended, Heath promised a 'border poll' to determine the future constitution. Direct rule was extended for a further twelve months in March 1973, when voters were invited to choose in a referendum whether to 'remain part of the United Kingdom' or 'be joined with the Republic of Ireland outside the United Kingdom': 58.1 per cent of voters turned out, voting 591,820 to remain in the United Kingdom and 6,493 to join the Republic.[28] Nationalists boycotted the poll. Soon after, car bombs in central London killed one person and injured almost 250.

A Northern Ireland Constitution Act vested executive power in the crown, exercised by the Secretary of State, and established a new elected Assembly. For the first time, Northern Ireland departments were authorized to consult or enter agreements with authorities of the Republic of Ireland, aiming to appease Catholic Nationalists. In June 1973, the Assembly was elected with a large Unionist majority. In December, a conference in Sunningdale, Berkshire, the first since 1922 at which the governments of Britain and both parts of Ireland were represented, agreed to establish a Council of Ireland representing both Irish governments, though its role remained unclear and it threatened to increase tension by inflating Nationalist hopes and Unionist fears. Paisley joined the leaders of the UUP and Vanguard in forming the United Ulster Unionist Council (UUUC) to oppose it. In 1973, 252 people were killed and 1,418 were charged with terrorist offences.[29]

26 Bew and Gillespie, *Northern Ireland*, p. 53.
27 Ibid., p. 57.
28 Butler and Butler, *Twentieth-Century British Political Facts*, p. 465.
29 Bew and Gillespie, *Northern Ireland*, p. 76.

General Election, February 1974

The government was also preoccupied with the first major political sex scandal since Profumo. In May 1973, Lord Lambton, Minister for the RAF, resigned when Sunday newspapers threatened to expose his visits to prostitutes. Then Earl Jellicoe, leader of the Lords, resigned for the same reason. The *News of the World* and the *People* published photographs of Lambton in 'compromising situations', implying that other ministers were involved. There were no apparent security issues, the activities were not illegal and the revelations aroused less excitement than in the past, suggesting social attitudes were changing. The *People* tried to arouse readers by suggesting, 'Even in this permissive age "illicit" sex is widely condemned', though 'not as savagely as it used to be', for, it stated, many people now claimed to 'believe that sex is the private affair of the participants'. But, it insisted, 'this tolerance doesn't extend to everyone. It stops short of men and women who are in authority ... '[30] A majority of Gallup respondents believed that ministers should lead their lives as they wished.[31]

Sex was not the government's greatest problem. Heath entered the election discredited by his failures with the economy, Northern Ireland and the miners. Conservatives were divided. Enoch Powell was more hostile than ever, bitterly opposing entry to the EC and believing Heath wrong to call an election over the miners' strike instead of standing firm. He refused to run as a Conservative, advising voters to vote Labour because they questioned EC membership. He supported a referendum. Margaret Thatcher also believed Heath should stand firm on his economic policies. After the election, she and Joseph founded the Centre for Policy Studies, a free market think-tank designed to construct policies they thought suited to the current international environment. The Conservatives had been divided throughout the century between supporters of some state intervention in the economy and opponents, with a shifting balance between them. Strong support for free enterprise, increasingly described as 'neoliberalism', was becoming powerful internationally amid the crises of the 1970s and was increasingly evident, though not universal, in the Conservative Party.[32]

Labour was not optimistic about the election. The Conservatives were marginally ahead in the polls. Labour leaders feared that, as Heath hoped, they would not win an election fought over union power. There was no clear winner. Labour won 301 seats, the Conservatives 297 though they were just ahead on votes: 11.8 million to 11.6 million on a 78.7 per cent turnout. The country was closely divided, particularly over economic conditions and policy. The Liberals held the balance with fourteen seats. The

30 Bingham, *Family Newspapers*, pp. 258–9.
31 Whybrow, *Britain Speaks Out*, p. 103.
32 Daniel Stedman Jones, *Masters of the Universe. Hayek, Friedman and the Birth of Neoliberal Politics*, 2nd edn (Princeton University Press, 2012).

National Front fielded fifty-four candidates, but gained only 76,865 votes and no seats. The results expressed growing national divisions. Plaid Cymru won an unprecedented two seats, both from Labour in mainly Welsh-speaking areas with high unemployment. The SNP won a record seven seats for similar reasons. Northern Ireland had the lowest turnout, 68.9 per cent. Voters there were tired of elections, fear of violence kept many at home and fewer polling stations were open for security reasons; three were fired on during polling day. The UUUC won eleven of the twelve seats; Gerry Fitt held West Belfast for the SDLP. Heath could have retained power if he had kept the support of the Ulster Unionists, but that was lost and he had no other support. He tried to negotiate a coalition with the Liberals, but the leader, Jeremy Thorpe, and his party resisted the temptation to return to government after their long absence and refused. Twenty-three female MPs were elected: thirteen Labour, nine Conservative, one SNP.

Wilson Returns

Wilson returned to Downing Street with no overall majority. He opted for a, hopefully brief, minority administration, attempting no deals with other parties. Despite criticisms of his previous government and Labour divisions, with the left growing stronger, he remained secure as leader, still the pragmatic conciliator, reflected in the title of Labour's manifesto, *Let Us Work Together*. Labour was committed, with the approval of the party conference, to 'a fundamental and irreversible shift in the balance of power and wealth in favour of working people and their families' via a wealth tax, capital gains tax and nationalization of development land and mineral rights. It promised higher pensions and renegotiation of the terms of entry to the EC. A National Enterprise Board (NEB) would buy into and seek to improve the performance of private firms, still a central Labour aim. A 'social contract' was agreed with the TUC, exchanging pay restraint for price controls, welfare reforms and repeal of Heath's Industrial Relations Act.

Healey became Chancellor and Callaghan Foreign Secretary, while Jenkins returned to the Home Office. Other moderates in the Cabinet included Crosland and Shirley Williams at two new departments, Environment (uniting transport, local government and housing) and Prices and Consumer Protection. The left was represented by Benn at Industry, Michael Foot as Employment Secretary, Castle at Health and Social Security. Crossman was seriously ill and died in April 1974 of liver cancer, aged 67. Again, there were just two women in the Cabinet. There were more left-wingers among the new Labour MPs and more were union sponsored, 42 per cent compared with 38 per cent in 1964.[33]

---

33 Reid, *United We Stand*, p. 385.

Another election was unavoidable. Determined to win, Labour settled the miners' strike with a 29 per cent pay rise, terminated statutory pay controls and repealed the Industrial Relations Act, supported by the CBI, since business did not gain from industrial turmoil. The three-day week ended. Healey recalled, 'My predecessor left me with an economy on the brink of catastrophe.'[34] Again, developing the economy was at the heart of government policy. Value Added Tax (VAT), the EC's preferred consumption tax introduced by Barber, was reduced from 10 per cent to 8 per cent and income tax rose. Basic foods were subsidized: bread, flour, butter, cheese, milk, tea. Council rents were frozen and the Housing Finance Act was replaced by a Housing, Rents and Subsidies Act restoring local authorities' power to fix rents and increasing subsidies to stabilize rents as part of the anti-inflationary strategy. Government spending rose from 39 per cent to 46 per cent of GDP between 1973 and 1975, mostly funded by further overseas borrowing, already exceptionally high under Heath.[35] Earnings outstripped prices and unemployment remained around 500,000 in 1974. Renegotiation of Britain's relationship with the EC began.

In Northern Ireland in May 1974 a strike of Protestant workers with UUUC support paralysed the economy, as intended, causing a state of emergency and resignation of the Executive. Direct rule was reimposed. In June, the Provisional IRA exploded a bomb in Westminster Hall, injuring eleven people. In July, bombs in Manchester, Liverpool and the Tower of London killed one person and injured forty-one. In October, bombs in two Guildford pubs killed two soldiers, three civilians and injured fifty others. Three men and one woman were found guilty and sentenced to life imprisonment; they were exonerated in a retrial in 1990. It was not the last time the British justice system rushed to a mistaken judgment in such cases.[36]

Wilson judged it safe to call another election in October 1974. Polls suggested most voters believed the cost of living was their greatest problem and that Labour were best equipped to handle it. Labour won 319 seats, the Conservatives 277, the Liberals thirteen. Plaid rose to three; a sign of its growing strength was that all Labour candidates in Wales committed to an elected Welsh assembly. The SNP rose again to eleven seats and 30.4 per cent of the Scottish vote, more than the Conservatives. The UUUC won ten of the twelve Northern Ireland seats. Labour's overall majority was only three, but the minority parties were unlikely to support the Conservatives.

After losing another election, Heath had to go, reluctantly. In February 1975, Margaret Thatcher stood against him and, to everyone's surprise including her own, won decisively in the second round. For the first time a British political party was led by

34 D. Healey, *The Time of My Life* (London: Michael Joseph, 1989), p. 292.

35 Richard Roberts, *When Britain Went Bust. The 1976 IMF Crisis* (London: OMFIF, 2016), p. 33.

36 Bew and Gillespie, *Northern Ireland*, p. 77–97.

a woman. The Conservatives immediately went ahead of Labour in Gallup polls. This was the height of feminist campaigning but few feminists sympathized with Thatcher's politics or believed she was sympathetic to them, though some believed her victory signalled progress for women, a hopeful sign for the future.

EC Referendum

The referendum on EC membership came on 5 June 1975, the first referendum of the century in Great Britain, following the 1973 vote in Northern Ireland.[37] Debates about the EC centred almost wholly upon the likely economic effects of membership. Immigration from other European countries, which was a big issue in the next referendum, in 2016, about membership of a much larger European Union (with twenty-seven members compared with nine in 1975) was not an issue. Wilson and Callaghan negotiated minor concessions for Commonwealth imports and modification of Britain's budget contribution. The party remained split and a special party conference rejected the proposals by two to one. Wilson allowed ministers a free vote. Foot, Benn, Enoch Powell and the Scottish and Welsh Nationalist parties supported 'No', but differed on too much else to cooperate. The Labour left believed the EC was too free-market oriented, Powell and his allies that membership was a betrayal of the Commonwealth, while the nationalist parties thought it would diminish their prospects for independence. On the 'Yes' side, with substantial funding from business, were Heath, Jenkins, Thorpe, the Church of England and most newspapers. Supporters believed membership would enable Britain to match the EC's economic growth. Margaret Thatcher called for 'a massive "Yes" to Europe', wearing a sweater featuring the flags of all the member states, while calling referenda 'a device for dictators and demagogues' and refusing to be bound by the result.[38] Wilson seemed equally divided but was ultimately a reluctant 'Yes'. There was a lively debate, sometimes sinking to the level of disputing whether baked beans would cost more in or out of the EC, but the need for Britain to keep a world leadership position, to strengthen the economy through closer ties to a highly successful economic area and resist communism were more prominent. Heath warned, 'A vote against the Market could lead to a Soviet invasion of Europe'. Tesco issued 'Yes to Europe' carrier bags.[39] The outcome was 64.5 per cent for 'Yes', on a 64.5 per cent turnout. Support was greatest in England (68.7 per cent on a 64.6 per cent turnout), least in Northern Ireland (52.1 per cent on a 47.4 per cent turnout), where Paisley warned 'A Vote for the Common Market is a vote for Ecumenism, Rome,

37 See p. 310.
38 Robert Saunders, 'What Can We Learn from the 1975 Campaign?' *Britain and the European Union*, Mile End Institute, Queen Mary College, London, 2016, p. 17.
39 Ibid., p. 18.

Dictatorship, Anti-Christ'[40]; in Scotland it was 58.4 per cent on a 61.7 turnout, and in Wales it was 64.8 per cent on a 66.7 per cent turnout.[41]

Northern Ireland

In Northern Ireland republican prisoners burned huts in the Maze prison. In November 1974, a bomb killed one person in Woolwich, south London, and injured twenty-eight. In the same month a bomb killed twenty-one and injured 182 people in a pub in Birmingham. Six men were convicted. In 1991, after sixteen years' imprisonment, they were exonerated; the real culprits were never indicted. Northern Ireland itself experienced far more violent deaths, 220 in 1974.[42] Tougher anti-terrorist laws were introduced throughout the United Kingdom, permitting detention without charge for seven days and expulsion from Britain. Meanwhile, the Northern Ireland Office secretly negotiated with the Provisional IRA and Sinn Féin, raising their hopes of British withdrawal, achieving a temporary ceasefire by the Provisionals over Christmas and New Year, which was later extended. Official IRA violence continued in Ulster and on the mainland.

Labour proposed a Constitutional Convention to manage Northern Ireland affairs, elected on 1 May 1975 with the UUUC winning most seats. The government reduced army activity, promising a further reduction and the release of detainees if violence stopped, still negotiating secretly with paramilitaries on both sides. But official IRA violence continued and the Provisionals abandoned their truce. Both made attacks on both sides of the Irish Sea, while feuding with each other. In November, a prominent right-winger, Ross McWhirter, was shot dead in London, among other violent incidents. Intransigent Unionists, led by Paisley, refused all compromise with Nationalists. Labour kept talking to all sides and in December announced the end of detention without trial. In 1975, 247 people were killed in Northern Ireland.

Wilson thought a united Ireland impracticable, but contacts with the Provisionals continued. The Constitutional Convention was dissolved in March 1976, having achieved little, and direct rule was re-instituted. The Northern Ireland Secretary, Merlyn Rees, announced that primary responsibility for security would shift to an expanded Royal Ulster Constabulary (RUC). Violence continued. Then, in August, more than 1,000 women in Andersonstown demonstrated for peace. A second rally attracted 10,000, the first of several leading to the launch of the Women's Peace Movement (later the Peace People) on 21 August. For the first time since the Troubles

---

40 Ibid.
41 Butler and Butler, *Twentieth-Century British Political Facts*, p. 242.
42 Bew and Gillespie, *Northern Ireland*, p. 97.

began, Protestants and Catholics (women only) marched together. In November, 30,000 marched in London. In September, the ECtHR upheld charges by the Irish government that British treatment of IRA suspects in 1971 breached the European Convention on Human Rights (ECHR) 'in the form not only of inhuman and degrading treatment but also of torture'.

Economic Policy

Labour returned to the mission of reversing the decline of British manufacturing and trade relative to other expanding economies, including those in the EC. In January 1975, the NEB was established, chaired by Lord Ryder, a businessman and Labour peer. Its main function became supporting and aiming to modernize 'lame ducks', including the car manufacturer Chrysler, to save jobs. The once vibrant motor industry was failing against overseas competition and ailing British Leyland was part-nationalized in 1975. British Aerospace was nationalized in 1977. There were also successes in growth areas, including the British National Oil Corporation, nationalized in 1976 following the welcome discovery of oil in the North Sea, which came on stream through the rest of the decade. It produced a financial surplus in 1977–8 and by 1980 oil exports and imports balanced.[43] Labour also revived the attempted technological revolution, though not Mintech, revitalizing the Ferranti electronics company and funding the establishment of Inmos in Bristol, which had a major influence on the development of advanced computing technology. But it was less successful at reviving established industries than some hoped.

The apparently relentless decline of UK manufacturing continued. Compared with its main competitors, it suffered from too little long-term investment, especially in new technology and skilled workers, due to management weakness and the preference of the financial sector for short-term gains. City finance had long been criticized for its apparent lack of concern about the fate of national manufacturing when it could profit in international markets. It proved impossible to balance the rising costs of imports with declining exports at a time of international inflation. The most successful economies – notably Germany and Japan and parts of the US economy such as pharmaceuticals and biotechnology – benefited from coherent, consistent industrial policies and government support, especially for research, development, innovation and training. Arguably UK manufacturing suffered from the lack of consensus between parties and governments on industrial policy through the postwar decades and consequent absence of long-term planning.[44]

43 Clarke, *Hope and Glory*, p. 352.
44 Kitson and Michie, 'The De-industrialization Revolution', pp. 310–25.

The economy was changing. In 1975, the largest industrial sector, metals and mechanical engineering, employed 4.2 million people, compared with 1.5 million in banking, insurance and finance. Over the next fifteen years the balance shifted, and the service sector, including retail, hotels and catering, grew to dwarf them both as the consumer market continued to expand, while finance, focused on the City, flourished, less influential internationally than earlier in the century, but still a major player. White-collar jobs still grew in the public and private sectors, while manual work contracted, increasing the demand for graduates and providing opportunities for mobility into the middle-classes for some young people from working-class backgrounds, as state education improved and more gained qualifications. 'Upward' social mobility increased through the 1950s–1970s due primarily to the changing economy assisted by greater educational opportunities.

Inflation soared internationally, still propelled by the oil shock. It rose above 19 per cent in the United Kingdom in December 1974, peaking at 27 per cent in August 1975, falling to 21 per cent in early 1976 fuelled by pay demands, while averaging only 10 per cent in comparable countries.[45] Labour avoided serious industrial conflict due to the social contract and the Employment Protection Act 1975, largely drafted by the TUC. This extended employee rights to appeal against unfair dismissal and trade union rights to recognition by employers, and established an Advisory, Conciliation and Arbitration Service (ACAS) for neutral settlement of disputes. In victories for female trade union activism, demanding rights already normal in the EC, it became illegal to dismiss a woman because she was pregnant (previously commonplace, and it continued) and statutory maternity leave was introduced for full-time workers, granting eleven weeks' leave before the birth and twenty-nine weeks after, at 90 per cent of normal pay for six weeks, then statutory sick pay. Mothers were guaranteed reinstatement in similar, though not necessarily the same, work on return.[46]

But high wage settlements fuelled inflation, while public spending and the budget deficit rose. In the 1975 Budget Healey cut public expenditure severely and raised taxes, prioritizing inflation reduction over full employment, opposed by left-wing members of the Cabinet. Moderate trade union leaders also worried about inflation stimulating industrial unrest. In July 1975, the unions agreed a £6 per week ceiling on wage increases and a freeze for those earning more than £8,500 a year, for one year, though it was approved only narrowly by the TUC due to left-wing opposition, and left-wing MPs voted against it in Parliament.

Unemployment rose from 628,000 in January 1974 to 1.4 million in January 1976, passing the symbolic 1 million for the first time since 1947. Unemployment was

45 Roberts, *When Britain Went Bust*, p. 34.
46 Reid, *United We Stand*, p. 387.

concentrated in the areas of traditional manufacturing and mining as both declined: South Wales, southern Scotland, Belfast, northern England and parts of the Midlands, further increasing regional inequalities. For those in adequately paid work, spending on more comfortable lifestyles grew. Central heating spread, a welcome liberation from huddling around inefficient coal fires, oil and electrical heaters in UK winters. The first huge shopping centres opened: Brent Cross in north London in 1976, with long opening hours to encourage shopping after work, and the Arndale Centre in Manchester in 1978. There was some decline in football attendance as more was available on colour TV, a further increase in cinema-going, continued moderate participation in sport, more eating out as the number of restaurants increased and improved, and more holiday travel abroad with the growth of affordable all-in package holidays.

Wilson Retires

Then in March 1976 Wilson, aged 60, unexpectedly retired, causing shock and speculation. It emerged, much later, that he was suffering from the early stages of dementia. One of the few people he informed was Callaghan, with whom his relations had improved, allowing him to prepare for the leadership election. Callaghan was the centrist candidate, close to the unions, more experienced in high office than his rivals. Healey was also in the centre, but was seen as more combative and likely to exacerbate party splits. On the social democratic right, Crosland and Jenkins appeared rather faded. On the left, Foot had impressed with his dealings with the unions, while Benn appeared too combative and unpredictable. Callaghan defeated Foot in the final ballot by 176 votes to 137.[47]

Callaghan as Prime Minister

Callaghan was well known and respected in Whitehall, with high approval ratings in the polls. Born in 1912, the son of a Chief Petty Officer in the Navy, his family could not afford to send him to university as he hoped and he entered the civil service where he became a full-time union official, then joined the Labour Party, becoming an MP in 1945. He made few changes to the Cabinet, other than sacking his old antagonist, Barbara Castle. Crosland replaced him as Foreign Secretary. To improve relations with the left, Foot was elevated to Lord President of the Council, with an overview of policy, and Callaghan tried to establish good relations with Benn, holding the party together quite successfully. Jenkins left to become President of the European Commission and Merlyn Rees replaced him as Home Secretary, while Shirley Williams became Secretary

47 Morgan, *Callaghan*, p. 474; Thorpe, *History of the British Labour Party*, pp. 188–9.

for Education, now the only female Cabinet minister. In February 1977, Crosland died of a stroke and was replaced by his deputy, the young Dr David Owen. The right-wing was strong in the Cabinet but weaker in the wider party. The party conference in September voted for nationalization of the clearing banks and major insurance companies. There was concern about a Trotskyite group, Militant, its influence in the party's youth section and policy of 'entryism', joining and aiming to control party branches, most successfully in depressed Liverpool. In October, Michael Foot beat Shirley Williams, 166 to 128, for deputy chair of the parliamentary party.[48]

In July 1976, two Scottish Labour MPs created the Scottish Labour Party, aiming to hasten devolution of government to an elected Scottish assembly and out-manoeuvre the SNP as concern grew in Scotland over its faltering economy. They resigned the Labour whip, weakening it in Parliament. Labour declined in the polls and lost four by-elections to the Conservatives between 1975 and 1977, losing its parliamentary majority but still supported by the minority parties. In March 1977, Margaret Thatcher tried to take advantage by moving a No Confidence motion. Callaghan and Foot sought an alliance with the new Liberal leader, David Steel. Thorpe had been forced to resign in dramatic circumstances, charged with conspiracy to murder a male model who was allegedly blackmailing him over a homosexual relationship. He was later acquitted. The Liberals did not want an election in the shadow of this scandal and agreed a 'Lib-Lab pact'. In return, Labour promised progress towards devolution for Scotland and Wales and direct elections to the European parliament. The Ulster Unionists were placated by Labour's tough anti-terrorist policy and a promise to review Northern Ireland's representation at Westminster. Thatcher's motion failed. The pact weakened when Liberal demands for PR in the European elections were defeated in the Commons by Labour MPs.[49]

Northern Ireland

Roy Mason became Northern Ireland Secretary. He prioritized economic reconstruction and reducing unemployment, but was stalled by the growing economic crisis. In 1976, 297 people died in the Troubles; there were 1,908 shootings and 1,192 bombs planted.[50] Labour's attempts to withdraw the army and appease Catholic grievances while controlling the administration failed. In January 1977, seven IRA bombs exploded in London and British businessmen were attacked in Northern Ireland. Expanding the RUC and reducing the army presence continued. On 10 August, the Queen visited the province for the first time in eleven years, during her silver jubilee celebrations.

---

48 Ibid.
49 Thorpe, *History of the British Labour Party*, pp. 195–6.
50 Bew and Gillespie, *Northern Ireland*, p. 117.

The IRA threatened bombs and riots and the SDLP refused to attend a reception in her honour. Security was ultra-tight. A small bomb exploded at the University of Ulster in Coleraine shortly after her visit, but no harm was done.

In September, Callaghan and the Irish Taoiseach, Jack Lynch, met to discuss resuming devolved government. For the first month since 1968 no one died in the Troubles. In October, Betty Williams and Mairead Corrigan, founders of the Peace People, accepted the Nobel Peace Prize. Deaths in 1977 fell to 112, shootings were 1,081, bombs planted 535, explosions 366.[51] In January 1978, the ECtHR finally ruled that the interrogation techniques of British forces constituted 'inhuman and degrading treatment', but not torture. In a 'dirty protest' at the Maze prison, Nationalist prisoners, wearing only blankets, smeared walls with excrement. Accounts of the conditions brought increased donations to the IRA from the United States. The Provisionals launched a fresh bombing campaign throughout Northern Ireland and in British cities. In March 1979, Airey Neave, Conservative Party spokesman on Northern Ireland, strong pro-Unionist and friend of Margaret Thatcher, died when a bomb exploded under his car as he left Parliament. Overall, violence still declined: in 1979 there were 81 deaths, 755 shootings, 633 bombs planted, 455 explosions.[52]

Economic Crisis 1976: IMF Loan

Callaghan was more preoccupied with the weakness of the economy. He told the party conference in September 1976: 'We have been living on borrowed time … We used to think that you could spend your way out of a recession', but this stimulated inflation 'which hit hardest those least able to stand [it]'. He insisted it was essential to reduce labour costs and make Britain more competitive.[53] Labour appeared to have abandoned Keynesianism. He was unenthusiastically received by the conference, more so by the international markets. Following a brief revival, UK output was lowest since the 1930s. In September 1976, over 1.25 million were unemployed. The balance of payments deficit approached £1 billion, annual inflation was 16 per cent, the bank rate 15 per cent, sterling was worth an exceptionally low US$1.66 and falling.[54] Following cuts in the 1976 Budget, public spending (not least supporting the unemployed), government borrowing and the deficit remained high. Raising taxes was now harder for Labour politically since, as incomes rose, workers on average incomes or less now paid income tax as most previously had not.

51 Ibid., p. 126.
52 Ibid., p. 138.
53 Callaghan, *Time and Chance*, p. 426.
54 Roberts, *When Britain Went Bust*, p. 7.

Healey tried to increase international confidence in sterling with extensive further spending cuts. When this failed he acceded to pressure from the Treasury to request a loan from the International Monetary Fund (IMF), to whom he turned 'cap in hand', as hostile newspapers portrayed it. The United Kingdom was the first major industrial nation to request an IMF loan. The decision and ensuing negotiations caused a further crisis of confidence in sterling. A prolonged battle ensued in the Cabinet over the up to £1 billion expenditure cuts required in return for the loan, but it was well managed by Callaghan, who allowed all sides their say, determined to avoid a 1931-style split.[55] The loan, $39 billion, was the largest the IMF had ever made. The terms were relatively soft, following successful negotiations by Healey and Callaghan, and the IMF had no desire to undermine the UK economy. Effectively the episode increased Callaghan's and Healey's control over economic policy, as they desired. In December, Healey announced cuts mainly to housing and education, though less than the IMF requested; twenty-six Labour MPs voted against, while the deficit fell. He then sold 15 per cent of the government's majority shareholding in British Petroleum (BP) which it had held since 1914 when it was the Anglo-Persian Oil Company. BP had been the first to strike oil in the North Sea and remained highly active there. It was a wise move when oil share prices were booming and the government retained a 55 per cent majority holding.

Healey revealed much later that the Treasury had 'grossly overestimated' the deficit and the loan had been unnecessary, that the main problem when managing the economy was lack of reliable data, which perhaps helped to explain the failings of successive government policies.[56] His policies preceding completion of the loan assisted the subsequent recovery, while IMF support did much to restore international confidence in the economy.[57] Most cuts were restored the following year and public sector borrowing was much lower than forecast. Healey drew on only half the loan and it was fully repaid before Labour left office in 1979, but this was unknown at the time and Labour's reputation for financial management suffered, assisted by a hostile media. The *Sun* (since 1969 a right-wing paper owned by media baron, Rupert Murdoch) screamed '3 Million Face the Dole Queue', though just 1.3 million were unemployed and the 3 million figure was not reached until the 1980s under a Conservative government, arousing less passion in the *Sun*. Soon there were large inflows of capital to the United Kingdom. From 1977, confidence in sterling, and its exchange value, rose, assisted by increasing North Sea oil flows. By the end of 1977, the pound was worth $1.91, causing concern about export prices. But inflation rose sharply, eroding incomes policy, and consumer spending and investment declined. Healey introduced a

55 Ibid., pp. 54–94.
56 Healey, *Time of My Life*, p. 432.
57 Kathleen Burk and Alec Cairncross, '*Goodbye Great Britain'. The 1976 IMF Crisis* (New Haven, CT: Yale University Press, 1992), pp. 225–6.

reflationary budget in 1978 and the balance of payments achieved a £1 billion surplus. Inflation fell to 7.45 per cent, along with improved balances of payments and trade amid international economic revival, though GDP growth remained slow.

Despite panic at the time and negative memories, kept alive by Labour's political opponents, the IMF crisis was minor compared with other twentieth-century financial crises, with no severe economic outcomes or dramatic changes in government policy, which continued on lines established before the crisis, but perceptions of it damaged Labour politically.[58]

The Apex of the Welfare State: Pensions

Despite the economic crises, the postwar welfare state reached its zenith in the later 1970s in terms of expenditure and range of services. Healey's 1974 Budget raised taxation, social security allowances and total social spending. Labour was committed to raising pensions and other allowances regularly in line with earnings or prices, whichever was higher. Castle at the DHSS withdrew the Conservatives' pension scheme and revised that of the previous Labour government.[59] The Social Security Pensions Act, 1975, introduced State Earnings Related Pensions (SERPS) for implementation in 1978, a much modified version of Labour's 1957 national superannuation plan.[60] Pensions would accumulate over twenty years, fully funded by contributions, both earnings-related, supplementing the flat-rate basic pension which would increase annually with average earnings. Based on the best-paid twenty years of working life, SERPS would yield around half-pay for those on average earnings, comparable with pensions elsewhere in Western Europe and a massive improvement on the still inadequate basic pension. Carers for children at home or for older or disabled relatives, counted as contributors. Widows inherited their husbands' pensions. It was the most advanced state pension in the world concerning equal rights for women and carers. Workers could contract-out into occupational schemes providing equivalent benefits, if they were transferable, inflation-proofed and strictly quality controlled.[61]

Family Poverty

Labour's February 1974 manifesto promised 'a new system of CHILD CASH ALLOWANCES for every child, including the first, payable to the mother', replacing FIS. The Finer Committee on One-Parent Families, appointed by Labour in 1969,[62]

58 Roberts, *When Britain Went Bust*, pp. 105–19.
59 Castle, *Fighting All the Way*, p. 461; Sheard, *The Passionate Economist*, pp. 318–21.
60 See p. 253.
61 Glennerster, *British Social Policy*, pp. 113–14.
62 See p. 280.

produced a comprehensive survey of the incomes, social conditions, housing and employment situation of this growing population in July 1974: 8 per cent of all families in 1971, 10 per cent in 1975. It documented their relative poverty, recommending a Guaranteed Maintenance Allowance for all one-parent families, the introduction of child benefits for all children with 'the utmost priority' and expansion of day-care services, prioritizing lone parents. It criticized the discrimination which effectively excluded single mothers from council tenancies, proposing that local authorities take responsibility for those in housing need. Since single parents were overwhelmingly mothers on low incomes, it urged faster progress to equal pay and equal opportunities for women in employment, education and training, equalization of employment rights between full- and part-time workers and extended maternity leave. Unfortunately, these expensive proposals appeared when the economy was in the 'oil shock' crisis and rising unemployment, inflation and cuts to public spending, including on day care, worsened the situation of many families. Castle admitted that 'my heart sank' when she read them, since, already, 'my spending demands were making me unpopular in the Cabinet'.[63]

She focused on increased child allowances, which reappeared in the October manifesto. Child poverty remained at similar levels to the mid-1960s (around 13 per cent of all children),[64] no higher despite rising unemployment and single parenthood, but still too high. Labour preferred to help all families in hard times rather than risk unpopularity by singling out lone parents and universal Child Benefit became law in August 1975, replacing family allowances and child tax allowances with a weekly cash benefit for every child, payable to the mother, as originally proposed by CPAG. Under Treasury pressure to delay payment, Healey announced a start date of April 1977, but, to satisfy campaigners including CPAG, introduced a tax-free 'Child Interim Benefit' from 1976, granting £1.50 per week to the first child in all single-parent families. He raised the income single parents could earn without losing benefits.

Callaghan was hostile to Child Benefit, convinced that abolishing child tax allowances, mainly payable to men, and paying Child Benefit to mothers would alienate male voters, including trade unionists, though the TUC favoured the reform. When he dismissed Castle, her replacement, David Ennals, announced that Child Benefit must be sacrificed to public spending cuts. Then *New Society* published details of acrimonious Cabinet discussions, leaked to Frank Field, the Director of CPAG. CPAG, supported by other NGOs, trade unions, the Church of England, women's organizations and academics, mounted a 'Child Benefits Now' campaign, forcing a government climb-down.[65]

---

63 Castle, *Fighting All the Way*, pp. 469–70.
64 See p. 268.
65 Thane and Davidson, *Child Poverty Action Group*, pp. 21–2; Sheard, *The Passionate Economist*, pp. 325–7; Field, *Poverty and Politics*, pp. 43–9.

The full Child Benefit of £4 per week for all children was paid from 1979, with an additional 50p for children of lone parents, greatly assisting low-income families.[66]

The Housing (Homeless Persons) Act 1977 gave local authorities responsibility for housing the 'unintentionally homeless', improving single mothers' access to council housing. The tabloids quickly accused women of becoming pregnant to obtain a council home, a slur which continued though repeatedly disproved by research.[67] Throughout the 1970s, some tabloids agitated about widespread benefit fraud, though evidence showed it was minimal. Rising numbers of one-parent families and unemployed people aroused unsubstantiated attacks on an 'over-indulgent' welfare system encouraging 'shirkers' and 'scroungers'.

Health and Social Services

In February 1974, Labour pledged 'to phase out private practice from the hospital service' because it absorbed too many NHS resources. It established a Royal Commission to review the future of the NHS, which did not report while it was in power. Castle extended free NHS family planning services to all (including vasectomy, previously free only for medical reasons), overruling Joseph's decision to charge for services. Also, in her short time in office, she continued Crossman's attempts to improve and integrate health and social services for the neglected groups of physically and mentally disabled and frail older people, though they remained inadequate into the twenty-first century, despite repeated complaints and campaigns.[68] She set funding priorities for the NHS to allocate resources to neglected groups and aimed to reduce local inequalities in resources and health outcomes. A Resource Allocation Working Party (RAWP) produced a funding formula based on regional population and health needs, which for a decade prioritized deprived areas quite successfully. But inequalities in health and life expectancy were due not only to unequal services but to socio-economic differences. In April 1977, Ennals appointed a committee of medical and social scientists to analyse these inequalities, which reported after the 1979 election.[69]

Weaknesses in local social services were revealed by the death in 1973 of eight-year-old Maria Colwell from abuse by her stepfather. Neighbours reported her being beaten and she was visited by social workers, doctors and other officials, but no action followed. She was taken to hospital by her mother and stepfather and pronounced dead,

---

66 Thane and Evans, *Sinners?* pp. 161–7.
67 Ibid., pp. 166, 171–4.
68 Glennerster, *British Social Policy*, pp. 132–3; Hampton, *Disability and the Welfare State*, pp. 181–230.
69 Hill, *Welfare State*, pp. 116–18.

following severe bruising, internal injuries and brain damage. Her stomach was empty. Her stepfather was sentenced to eight years' imprisonment, halved on appeal. The case received massive publicity, bringing into public discourse abuses which were not novel but long suppressed. In 1974, Castle established firmer guidelines for local social services, but over the next twenty years, forty similar cases of child deaths by family violence came to public notice.[70]

Education and Housing

Labour was dissatisfied with the incomplete spread of comprehensive schools. The 1976 Education Act allowed the Education Secretary to compel local authorities to submit proposals for comprehensive reorganization. By 1981, about 83 per cent of children in state secondary schools in England, 96 per cent in Scotland and 96.6 per cent Wales were in comprehensives, compared with 69 per cent, 87.6 per cent and 88.5 per cent, respectively, in 1975.[71] More children stayed on to later ages, more gained qualifications than ever before, while more students entered higher education.[72]

Homelessness fell following the 1977 Act. Fewer homes were built than under the Conservatives but fewer were now needed and improvements to existing housing continued, assisted by improvement grants. Between 1971 and 1981 the number of homes lacking basic amenities fell in England from 1.6 million to 0.5 million without a bath or shower, from 2 million to 0.6 million lacking an indoor toilet and from 2.4 million to 0.7 million without hot water supply to the kitchen.[73]

Industrial Relations

Despite Foot's efforts at conciliation, inflation caused wage demands and days lost in disputes shot up in 1977–9. An unprecedented 50 per cent of the total workforce – 13 million – was unionized by 1979. Membership grew particularly among white-collar workers, especially in the public sector, who were now as militant as manual workers. The total membership of the National Association of Public Employees (NUPE) and the National Association of Local Government Officers (NALGO) at 1.4 million was more than three times the combined membership of the NUM and NUR. They were restive because public sector pay was firmly controlled while prices rose and they suffered

70 Nicolas Timmins, 'Maria Colwell's Death Led to Legislation over Two Decades', *The Independent*, 24 March 1994.
71 George Smith, 'Schools', in A. H. Halsey and J. Webb (eds), *Twentieth-century British Social Trends* (London: Macmillan, 2000), p. 199.
72 Ibid., pp. 208–16.
73 Holmans, 'Housing', p. 479.

from repeated cuts to public spending which threatened jobs and increased workloads. Female public sector workers increased to almost 4 million by 1979, largely explaining why twice as many women as men joined unions in the 1970s.

More workers from black and minority ethnic (BME) groups engaged in disputes and joined unions, and unions became more responsive to their needs. A much publicized example was the strike in 1976 of more than 130, mainly Asian, female staff at the Grunwick photo-processing firm in Willesden, north London, over pay and conditions, including forced overtime, and the owner's refusal to let them join a union. They were supported by the TUC, white workers, feminists and Labour politicians.[74] The strike lasted two years but failed, signalling the limits to union power and the strength of opposition to it. The militantly right-wing owner, supported by increasingly assertive right-wing political groups, was intransigent. Such groups were growing, by 1976 the National Federation of the Self-Employed and Ratepayers Associations among others,[75] part of a rising international neoliberal tide, signified most dramatically by the violent overthrow of the moderate socialist government of Salvador Allende in Chile in 1973, supported by the US government. In 1976, the American economist, Milton Friedman, bizarrely predicted that Britain under Labour would go the way of Chile, whose post-Allende dictatorship he advised: socialist crisis followed by military coup was 'the only outcome that is conceivable'.[76] At Grunwick 130 workers were sacked, none were reinstated, despite an official committee headed by Lord Justice Scarman recommending that they should, and no union was recognized.

Unions supported other radical movements. In 1978, the Union of Postal Workers refused to handle mail for South Africa, supporting the anti-apartheid movement. It was illegal for postal workers to refuse mail but the Attorney-General took no action, consistent with government and Commonwealth policy.[77] A meeting of Commonwealth prime ministers in 1977 agreed to ban all sporting contacts with the apartheid regime, following trade sanctions.

The 'Winter of Discontent'

In 1978, the government set a norm of 5 per cent for pay rises, below inflation, which Healey later admitted was unattainable.[78] It was rejected by the TUC and the party conference. Some private sector unions demanded and got higher settlements, including

74 Reid, *United We Stand*, pp. 354–5.

75 Roger King and Neill Nugent (eds), *Respectable Rebels. Middle Class Campaigns in Britain in 1970s* (London: Hodder & Stoughton, 1979).

76 Reynolds, *Britannia Overruled*, p. 253.

77 Morgan, *Callaghan*, pp. 582–3.

78 P. Dorey, '"Should I Stay or Should I Go?" James Callaghan's Decision Not to Call an Autumn 1978 General Election', *British Politics* (2015): 15.

17 per cent following a two-month strike by Ford car workers. The government tried to impose sanctions on Ford, but was defeated in Parliament with the help of left-wing Labour MPs. When Callaghan returned from a successful meeting with the leaders of the United States, France and Germany on issues of common interest, including agreement to renew Britain's independent nuclear deterrent, in sunny Guadeloupe in a freezing British January, journalists asked him what he would do about the 'mounting chaos' in industrial relations. He was relaxed, after a short holiday in Barbados, where the press photographed, and criticized, him swimming. He replied 'I don't think that other people in the world would share the view that there is mounting chaos', reasonably enough, given the serious world crises discussed at Guadeloupe. The *Sun* translated this into the headline 'Crisis? What Crisis?', and Callaghan was not allowed to forget it.[79]

Industrial relations deteriorated in what the irrepressible *Sun* labelled the 'Winter of Discontent'. Lorry drivers struck in January demanding a 20 per cent pay rise, high but, due to the impact on precarious incomes of the rising cost of living, followed by railwaymen and water workers. Sewage workers threatened to join them. Ports and depots were blocked by secondary picketing and there were rumoured shortages of food and medical supplies. NUPE, representing some of the lowest paid public sector workers, demanded a £60 per week minimum wage, leading to strikes and overtime bans by NHS workers, ambulance drivers, refuse collectors, local government employees, including school caretakers, which closed some schools. Militancy among these workers in essential services was rare, suggesting desperation at worsening conditions. In a harsh winter, roads were not gritted, probably causing accidents. The press carried pictures of cancer-stricken children and older people suffering hypothermia. Union leaders pointed out that essential supplies always got through: 98 per cent of establishments had no dispute in 1977–9, and more days were lost through sickness and accidents than through strikes.[80] But Conservatives and the tabloids highlighted unburied bodies in Liverpool cemeteries and the, few, places where uncollected rubbish piled up in the streets, claiming the unions were out of control.[81] Bricks were thrown through the windows of striking gravediggers in Liverpool and their children were attacked at school. On 22 January, 1.5 million workers joined a day of action.

Callaghan gave no clear lead and there was no planning for the election that was unavoidable in 1979. The Civil Contingency Unit, formed by Heath to combat strikes, worked quite effectively with unions to maintain essential supplies and services. The government was unwilling to declare a state of emergency and mobilize the army, and

79 Morgan, *Callaghan*, pp. 660–2.

80 L. Black and H. Pemberton, 'The Winter of Discontent in British Politics', *Political Quarterly* 80(4) (2000): 553–61.

81 Morgan, *Callaghan*, pp. 662–4; Colin Hay, 'Narrating Crisis. The Discursive Construction of the "Winter of Discontent"', *Sociology* 30(2) (1996): 253–77.

Callaghan, encouraged by civil servants, reluctantly surrendered. The lorry drivers gained rises of up to 20 per cent, water workers the 14 per cent they claimed. Inflation fell but unemployment rose to 1.34 million.[82] In mid-February, the government and TUC agreed a voluntary code limiting picketing and the closed shop and maintaining essential services during strikes.[83] Wage settlements in 1978–9 were higher than before, but without the disastrous consequences forecast by the hostile media; inflation fell further. The agreement helped Labour to stabilize the economy, though the long-term problems of declining manufactures and trade and poor productivity remained.

Women's Liberation?

Trade unionists were not the only people working together to reduce inequalities and improve living and working conditions for themselves and others. What is sometimes seen as a period of growing individualism saw a striking growth of collective organization by a variety of groups, mainly of younger people, cooperating to promote their own and others' interests, including concerning gender, sexual preference and race, choosing what was later called 'identity politics' over more traditional political forms, though not always wholly rejecting them.

Persistent gender inequalities were challenged by feminists in a revived women's movement, the so-called 'second wave', a label that mistakenly implied that women had been quiescent since the 'first wave' before 1918. They certainly had not, but much remained to campaign about. Indeed, the extent of women's activism since 1918 was largely unknown in the 1970s because women's history was so neglected. The UK Women's Liberation Movement (WLM) was born at an Oxford conference of the radical History Workshop movement in 1969, among women infuriated by men radical enough to attend the event who sneered at women's history. Writing women into history became one of WLM's objectives and achievements, notably the work of Sheila Rowbotham who initiated the first meeting.[84]

Like other contemporary radical movements, feminists preferred direct, public action to patient lobbying and were critical of, or hostile to, conventional party politics. Similar movements were emerging in other countries, including the United States, but the UK WLM was among the leaders and further to the left than much US feminism. Its activism grew out of home-grown discontents. In 1969, there were seventy local

82 Morgan, *Callaghan*, pp. 665–72.
83 Reid, *United We Stand*, p. 388.
84 Including Sheila Rowbotham, *Hidden from History. 300 Years of Women's Oppression and the Fight Against It* (London: Pluto, 1974); Sheila Rowbotham, *Women, Resistance and Revolution. A History of Women and Revolution in the Modern World* (London: Random House, 1973). See her account of the women's movement in *Threads Through Time. Writings on History and Autobiography* (London: Penguin, 1999), pp. 13–83.

women's liberation groups in London,[85] and the numbers grew nationally. A national conference met annually from 1970 to 1978, with attendance peaking at 3,000 in 1977. Feminism became public and flamboyant again, notably when women dramatically interrupted the televised Miss World event at the Royal Albert Hall, London, in 1970, shouting 'We're not beautiful, we're not ugly, we're angry'. This followed a similar demonstration against a Miss America contest in New York in 1968. At this event women threw bras, nylons, false eyelashes and other items into a bin, challenging the false images they believed these consumer items imposed on women. They intended to burn them but did not. This seems to have given birth to a hostile media image of feminists as 'bra-burners', ugly, dungaree-wearing man-haters, as prevalent in the UK tabloids as in the United States. Like negative stereotypes of feminism in the past, it was an image that sometimes alienated even women sympathetic to gender equality, making them reluctant to identify as feminists.

It was a movement mainly of younger women that temporarily displaced the older, more constitutional, women's organizations such as the Fawcett Society, though these survived. The international character and impact of women's activism was signalled in 1977 when the UN instituted an annual International Women's Day to promote women's rights. The movement in Britain brought hidden issues into public view and new groups of women into activism, reflecting and advancing cultural change. Black and Asian women created the Organisation of Women of Asian and African Descent (OWAAD) in 1978 and Southall Black Sisters in 1979. Brixton Black Women, Liverpool Black Sisters, Baheno Women's Organization in Leicester and groups elsewhere in Wales, Scotland and England campaigned against restrictive immigration laws, virginity tests imposed on women immigrants, domestic and sexual violence, discrimination in employment and other spheres, which these women experienced due to both race and gender. They resisted marginalization by male-dominated organizations and by the white-dominated WLM, increasing its sensitivity to race. OWAAD organized the first national black women's conference in 1979; 250 women attended.[86]

Labour's Sex Discrimination Act 1975 tackled some inequalities by outlawing discrimination in employment, education, advertising and the provision of housing, goods or services. At last married women no longer needed their husband's agreement to undertake hire purchase or other financial arrangements even when they had independent earnings. The Equal Opportunities Commission (EOC) was established to investigate complaints and support women claiming discrimination. The Act was partly a response to WLM, partly completion of unfinished business from

---

85 Eve Setch, 'The Women's Liberation Movement in Britain, 1969–1979. Organization, Creativity and Debate', unpublished PhD thesis, Royal Holloway College London, 2000.
86 Brixton Black Women's Group, 'Black Women Organizing', *Feminist Review* 17 (1984): 84–8; Natalie Thomlinson, *Race, Ethnicity and the Women's Movement in England, 1968–93* (London: Palgrave, 2016).

the 1960s resulting from previous women's campaigns, partly conformity with the expectations of the EC. In 1975 also the Equal Pay Act came fully into force. The average gender pay gap narrowed only from about 50 per cent to 40 per cent between 1970 and 1980.[87]

The Sex Discrimination Act forced medical schools to remove the quotas restricting women's entry: by the early 1990s women had grown from a small minority to over 50 per cent of students. It put pressure on other institutions. The proportion of female lawyers rose from 4 per cent in 1971 to 27 per cent in 1990.[88] Most male Oxford and Cambridge colleges at last admitted women, and the number of women students at Oxford and Cambridge increased from 15 per cent and 10 per cent, respectively, to over 50 per cent by the 1990s. More women were employed, though a high proportion, mainly mothers, still worked part-time with fewer employment rights than full-time workers. About 38 per cent of married women were employed in 1960, approximately 45 per cent in 1970 and 60 per cent in 1980. In 1977, 5 per cent of mothers of children under 5 were in full-time employment, 22 per cent part-time.[89] In 1975, the TUC adopted the Charter for Working Women, a sign of the growing numbers and influence of women in unions. It demanded equal pay, equal opportunities at work, eighteen weeks' paid maternity leave, a minimum wage, increased family allowances and an end to discrimination against women in social security and tax, some of which Labour delivered.

More women were ambitious for careers while others were driven to work by inflation, especially of housing costs, and single motherhood. Childcare remained scarce and expensive. Two-thirds of households owned a washing machine by 1972,[90] which eased housework, following the rapid spread of self-service neighbourhood launderettes in the 1950s and 1960s. But domestic standards and expectations rose and the time women, employed or not, spent on housework hardly changed between the 1930s and 1970s, indeed for most middle-class women it rose as domestic servants disappeared,[91] though many employed cleaners. Most men still contributed very little. Gender roles in marriage appeared to be shifting, but Gallup in 1973 found that only two in three women even knew their husband's take-home pay.[92]

87 Meehan, *Women's Rights at Work*, pp. 72–96; A. Zabalza and Z. Tzannatos, *Women and Equal Pay. The Effects of Legislation on Women's Employment and Wages in Britain* (Cambridge University Press, 1985).

88 Women and Equality Unit, *Key Indicators of Women's Position in Britain* (London: Department of Trade and Industry, 2001), p. 83.

89 Ina Zweiniger-Bargielowska, 'Housewifery', in Ina Zweiniger-Bargielowska (ed.), *Women in Twentieth Century Britain* (London: Pearson, 2001), p. 158.

90 Zweiniger-Bargielowska, 'Housewifery', p. 159.

91 Ibid., p. 160.

92 Whybrow, *Britain Speaks Out*, p. 102.

Feminists and other women, including in trade unions, protested that the work-force remained heavily gender-divided with unequal pay and opportunities. Women's opportunities were limited partly by their continuing under-representation in higher education. More girls than boys still left school without qualifications, though the proportion of female university students rose from 28 per cent in 1971 to 38 per cent in 1979.[93] They were concentrated in arts and social sciences, few in the natural sciences, fewer still in engineering and few in academic posts especially at the higher levels. Women remained the great majority of students in teacher training colleges.[94] It became a little easier to re-train on returning to work after childcare and more older women attended universities, but women still had fewer opportunities than men to gain further training at work.

Another cause of protest, domestic violence, had been exposed intermittently since the 1860s when Frances Power Cobbe campaigned against 'wife torture'.[95] But still in the 1970s upholders of the justice system, including the police, refused to take it seriously, insisting that 'domestic disputes' were private, beyond their powers to intervene. Public resistance was sparked by Erin Pizzey, who in 1971 started a support group for married women with children because she thought her local WLM group too unconcerned with the needs of mothers like herself. She was not a feminist, she wrote, because her affluent parents (her father was a diplomat) were both violent towards her and her siblings as children, convincing her that women could be as vicious as men. Pizzey's concern about domestic violence, especially its effects on children, grew partly from personal experience, reinforced by victims revealing their experiences at her meetings. Her home became a refuge. Soon forty women and children were crammed into four small rooms and Pizzey was threatened with prosecution for overcrowding. Publicity brought a private donation enabling them to take a larger house in Chiswick, which also became overcrowded. Publicity about 'battered wives', as they were known, and the failure of the police to support them, along with demonstrations by Pizzey and her supporters gained her a grant from the DHSS in 1974 to support the families. Shortly after, her book, *Scream Quietly or the Neighbours will Hear*, brought further publicity, and the Women's Aid Federation (WAF) was formed to promote the campaign. Volunteers founded more refuges, and Pizzey and her allies, by squatting in empty buildings, joined a wider contemporary squatting movement protesting at rising housing costs and homelessness.[96]

Pizzey showed the way, but she had a tense relationship with the WLM and increasingly with the WAF. Activists felt she wanted too much control and personal publicity.

93 Dyhouse, *Students. A Gendered History*, p. 99.
94 Butler and Butler, *Twentieth-Century British Political Facts*, p. 366.
95 Williamson, *Power and Protest*, pp. 80–4.
96 Erin Pizzey, *This Way to the Revolution. A Memoir* (London: Peter Owen, 2013).

In 1975, she stormed out of WAF's AGM and severed her connection with the Chiswick Refuge. The WAF drew close to WLM, whose supporters founded and staffed refuges throughout the country, raising funds from charities, private donors, central and local government, revealing the shocking dimensions of a long-hidden problem. By 1980, there were about 200 refuges. The WLF campaigned for legal reform. In 1974, a Private Member's Bill introduced by Labour MP Jo Richardson led the Commons to appoint a Select Committee on Violence in Marriage, which noted that the law allowed courts to grant injunctions prohibiting men from molesting their female partners (and occasionally vice versa), on pain of imprisonment, and could order them to leave the family home, but it was rarely implemented. Women did not always seek protection from the justice system, fearing reprisals from their partners. Police were reluctant to act and lacked powers to arrest perpetrators who breached injunctions. The Domestic Violence and Matrimonial Proceedings Act 1976 made domestic violence a specific offence. Courts could punish violence against a partner, married or unmarried, or child, and exclude violent partners from the family home; from 1978 magistrates' courts could issue personal protection orders and exclusion orders, though not to unmarried partners.[97] The law was imperfect but better than anything before. The 1977 Housing (Homeless Persons) Act[98] removed a barrier to victims leaving violent partners by obliging local authorities to house them if they became homeless. But still in 2008–10 one in four women in the United Kingdom were estimated to experience domestic violence at some point in their lives; on average, two women, and occasional men, were killed each week by partners or ex-partners.[99] Still the police did not always take complaints seriously and the WAF and women's refuges continued, though the latter were severely reduced following public spending cuts from 2010.

The WLM also raised awareness of rape, another long-standing form of violence rarely publicly discussed, mainly against women, though the GLF publicized attacks on gay men. There was no evidence that rape was increasing, but the incidence appeared high and victims often failed to complain, fearing reprisals from the perpetrator, feeling shame or that they would be disbelieved and denigrated. Again the police and the courts did not always treat reports seriously, but blamed the victim, for drunkenness or wearing 'provocative' clothing, rather than the perpetrator.[100] The first Rape Crisis Centre opened in north London in 1976 providing counselling, refuge and support, established by feminists, funded by charities and radical local authorities. Sixteen centres, plus rape crisis phone lines, were established by 1981. From 1977, women's

97 Cretney, *Family Law*, pp. 753–5.
98 See p. 324.
99 See at: www.amnesty.org.uk/violence-against-women#.VMTOG1, last accessed 25 January 2015.
100 Jackson, *Women Police*, pp. 185–93.

'Reclaim the Night' marches walked through streets at night asserting their right to walk unmolested. A less positive outcome of publicizing the issue was more frequent, explicit and sensational coverage of rape trials by the popular press, distressing the victims and creating further obstacles to their coming forward. The Sexual Offences (Amendment) Act 1976, introduced by Labour backbencher Robin Corbett, guaranteed anonymity for victims alleging rape, but not for the alleged perpetrator.[101] But still in the early twenty-first century 167 women are reported to suffer rape in the United Kingdom every day; only one attack in five was reported to the police because the victims were traumatized, feared reprisals or publicity, uncertain of support and fearing blame from police or the courts, all too realistically.[102]

The WLM also campaigned for men to share domestic work, for twenty-four-hour nurseries for parents required to work 'unsocial' hours, such as low-paid women night-time office cleaners, and they protested about such work conditions. Also for abortion on demand, without the obligatory agreement of two doctors, which was hard to obtain in some, especially strongly Catholic, areas. Groups formed to promote equality in specific occupations, including Women in Media, Women in Publishing. Feminist journals included *Spare Rib*, founded 1972. A publisher, Virago, was founded and run by women from 1973, reprinting as low-cost paperbacks books by neglected women authors and publishing new works by and about women past and present, an outlet for the growing body of work on women's history. The WLM liberated women's creativity in many spheres, including theatre, film and fashion. The campaigns had some, gradual, successes, though important inequalities were overlooked by this predominantly young women's movement, including poverty among older women and their inadequate pensions.

As the WLM grew so did divisions, including race and class tensions in a mainly white, middle-class movement from which many women felt excluded.[103] The final WLM conference in 1978 descended into chaos following conflict between 'revolutionary feminists' who opposed cooperation with men, and the rest, yet pressure for progress continued. There was no gender revolution in the 1970s, but there were steady if incomplete improvements in women's pay, education and work opportunities, in legal rights and protection against physical and sexual violence. Many young women grew up with higher expectations, encouraged by parents who could no longer assume that marriage was their only future as divorce increased. Aspiration to greater equality appeared increasingly realistic.

---

101 Bingham, *Family Newspapers*, pp.155–6.
102 See fn 86.
103 Thomlinson, *Race, Ethnicity and the Women's Movement*; George Stevenson, *The Women's Liberation Movement and the Politics of Class* (London: Bloomsbury, 2018).

Gay Liberation

The British GLF was formed in autumn 1970, following the Stonewall riots in New York after police raided a gay bar, though it had roots in the longer history of campaigns for homosexual rights in Britain and the somewhat greater openness following reform in 1967. Two students organized the first meeting, at LSE, attended by nine people. A few months later 400–500 attended weekly meetings. Like other 'new social movements', the GLF defined itself as a revolutionary collective organization challenging oppression, rejecting the constitutionalist caution of older groups like the Homosexual Law Reform Society.[104] It aimed to be a mass movement organizing public events: 'Gay Days' in London parks; 'zapping' gatherings of opponents, like a rally by the fundamentalist Christian Festival of Light in 1971. In 1971, lesbians invaded the WLM conference platform, believing it marginalized them.

The GLF ran the first Gay Pride march in London in 1972 involving 1,000 people. They supported campaigns by women's and anti-racist groups, marched with the TUC against Heath and supported striking miners with a 'Pits and Perverts' campaign. In Scotland and Northern Ireland campaigners fought to bring their laws into line with those of England and Wales, ultimately successfully.[105] In 1972, the weekly *Gay News* was launched. The GLF encouraged individuals to 'come out' and acknowledge their sexuality publicly. The term 'gay' (Good As You) became international. But the GLF also experienced divisions: lesbians felt their interests were ignored by male homosexuals, transgender people felt excluded, as did members of minority ethnic groups, some of whom faced particular prejudice within their communities. But the cultural 'coming out' encouraged by the GLF left a lasting legacy, while new groups formed. The Campaign for Homosexual Equality (CHE), formed 1971, became the largest gay organization in Britain by 1972, preferring orthodox lobbying and appeals to the law. It too was accused of marginalizing lesbians, who organized separately, publishing *Sappho* magazine from 1972, holding regular meetings and forming Action for Lesbian Parents in 1976, seeking rights to custody of their children, which they could lose due to their lesbianism if they left a heterosexual partnership. Local counselling and befriending services and helplines for gay men and women grew, especially in London and larger cities. The London Gay Switchboard, established 1974, received 200,000 calls in its first year. By 1976, all major political parties and professions, Jewish and Christian faith groups, theatre and cinema organizations had gay support groups.[106]

---

104 See p. 248.
105 See p. 283.
106 Holger Nehring, 'The Growth of Social Movements', in P. Addison and H. Jones (eds), *A Companion to Contemporary Britain, 1939–2000* (Oxford: Blackwell, 2005), pp. 393–5.

Transgender campaigns emerged alongside other new movements, demanding social acceptance for a condition not previously discussed in public, improved medical treatment and the abolition of legal disabilities concerning marriage and birth certificates, without great effect but providing support and publicity. They gained some respectability when, in 1974, Jan Morris, a respected author and travel writer, published an account of her male–female transition.[107] But homophobia and transphobia persisted, promoted stridently by Mary Whitehouse and the NVLA. In 1977, Whitehouse brought a successful prosecution against *Gay News* under the ancient Blasphemy Act for publishing a poem, 'The Love that dares to Speak its Name', in which a Roman centurion expressed homosexual fantasies about the crucified Christ.[108] A week later a gay man was murdered in north London and another in Liverpool the following year. An opinion poll for *Gay News* in 1975 found general support for the 1967 legislation but little for further change.

The Permissive Seventies?

Partly due to the new movements, many aspects of sex were discussed more openly, continuing trends of preceding decades. A manual *The Joy of Sex* (1970), describing practices formerly hidden from public scrutiny, was a widely discussed bestseller. In 1970, the *Sun* serialized 'the most explicit sex manual ever published', Joan Garrity's *The Sensuous Woman*, with 'sexercises' to help women become 'sexually irresistible', so successfully that it printed a succession of sequels and its rivals followed, including the *Mirror*'s more 'educational' 'Guide to Sexual Knowledge' in 1975, with explicit advice on birth control.[109] The tabloids also condemned what the shameless *Sun* described in 1973 as 'a permissive epidemic which is still growing … the cost of careless love will mean a record number of venereal disease cases and a staggering rise in abortions'.[110] 'The moral structure of two thousand years of civilization is collapsing' declared the *Daily Mail* in 1971, though Geoffrey Gorer concluded from a survey of 'Sex and Marriage in England Today', published in the *Sunday Times* also in 1971,that 'England still appears to be a very chaste society'.[111]

Uncensored theatre performances became more daring, notably *Oh! Calcutta!* featuring naked men and women in almost 4,000 performances in London from 1970. Mrs Whitehouse was predictably outraged and new organizations emerged to fight 'the rising tide of filth', including the Festival of Light and the Responsible Society.

107 Jan Morris, *Conundrum* (London: Faber & Faber, 1974).
108 Hall, *Sex, Gender and Social Change*, p. 181.
109 Bingham, *Family Newspapers*, pp. 89–94.
110 Ibid., p. 122.
111 Ibid.

Pornography flourished as businessmen found lucrative loopholes in the law, assisted, it emerged, by corrupt members of the Metropolitan Police. Erotic magazines, some originating in the United States, expanded in the 1960s and became more explicit in the 1970s: from 1970 *Penthouse* displayed the pubic hair of its famous nude women. Its monthly sales rose from 150,000 in 1966 to 429,000 in 1976, surpassed by *Mayfair* (461,000) and *Men Only* (434,000) both also promoting explicit sexual imagery.[112] Successful films portrayed nudity, swearing and violence, notably *Last Tango in Paris* (1972) and *Clockwork Orange* (1971), though the BBFC kept pornography at bay and barred under-18s from the more explicit content.

The new culture had ambiguous outcomes. Feminists argued for greater openness about the body and sex, but some feared this encouraged exploitation of women in pornography and the press, while some newspapers claimed they were celebrating the female body and valued women's sexual pleasure as highly as men's.[113] In 1970, in the very week that feminists invaded the Miss World event, the *Sun* introduced a new daily feature: the bare-breasted 'page three girl', first presented as a 'birthday suit girl' on the paper's first anniversary under Murdoch.[114] It was the latest, most explicit, example of sexualized female 'pin-ups' in the popular press, following their preoccupation with women in bikinis and skimpy skirts in the 1960s. Feminists attacked 'page three girls' as objectifying and degrading women. The *Sun* responded:

> From time to time some self-appointed critic stamps his tiny foot and declares that the *Sun* is obsessed with sex. It is not the *Sun* but the critics who are obsessed. The *Sun*, like most of its readers, likes pretty girls. And if they're pretty … who cares whether they're dressed or not?[115]

It claimed, perhaps accurately, to reflect, not influence, changes in popular culture.[116] 'Pin-ups' had long featured in male culture but were now publicly flaunted as never before. The *Sun*'s circulation rose from 1.5 million in 1970 to 3.8 million in 1980, becoming the biggest seller, overtaking the *Mirror*.[117] The images continue to appear, causing controversy, in the twenty-first century. The *Mirror* was occasionally tempted to compete with exposed nipples and, with other papers, occasionally responded to feminist criticism with pictures of 'hunky' men, but generally it chose restraint, while its circulation sank. Sunday papers, notably the *News of the World*, were more explicit. The *Daily Star* was launched in 1978 to compete with the *Sun*, introducing the first full-colour topless images, 'Starbirds'.[118]

112 Ibid., pp. 33–4.
113 Ibid., p. 223.
114 Ibid., p. 208.
115 17 November 1970; Bingham, *Family Newspapers*, p. 221.
116 Ibid.
117 Butler and Butler, *Twentieth-Century British Political Facts*, p. 538.
118 Bingham, *Family Newspapers*, p. 226.

Tabloids also probed the private lives of public figures. The collapse of Princess Margaret's marriage in 1976, following a succession of affairs by her husband Lord Snowden with women and probably also with men, as well as her own infidelities, was discussed in even more salacious detail than their previous lifestyle, presented as epitomizing the 'swinging sixties'. Divorce followed in 1978 – the first divorce in the royal family, another sign of cultural change.

Press discussion of child sexual abuse also surfaced, castigatory rather than salacious. It too was not new, but was openly recognized for the first time. By the mid-1970s, paedophiles, previously an unfamiliar word, were increasingly discussed and denounced, stimulated by their new-found openness in forming an organization, Paedophile Action for Liberation (PAL). This represented them as another unjustly stigmatized group indulging a natural inclination, deserving toleration in these liberal times. Some radicals were persuaded, but the *Sunday People* came closer to the public mood and denounced them as 'The Vilest Men in Britain'.[119] Bricks were thrown through the windows of PAL headquarters. The *Daily Mirror* later attacked a similar organization, Paedophile Information Exchange (PIE), but much sexual exploitation of children continued unpublicized and unpunished for many decades.[120]

This increasingly 'permissive' climate particularly affected metropolitan culture and the lives of minorities with modern lifestyles, those of the majority much less, or more gradually. Closer to everyday life, divorces shot up when the 1969 divorce reform was implemented in 1971, from 285,449 in England and Wales in 1966–70 to 812,403 in 1976–80, in Scotland 20,280 and 45,340, respectively, most following petitions by wives.[121] It had long been argued that easier divorce would reduce unmarried cohabitation; the opposite occurred. Numbers of cohabiting couples in England and Wales are unknown before 1979. In Scotland they were officially registered and accounted for 12 per cent of couples at the beginning of the century.[122] Three per cent of women aged 18–49 in Great Britain were officially estimated as cohabiting in 1979, rising to 5 per cent in 1985 and 9 per cent in 1991, mostly never-married.[123] Marriage rates fell from 82.3 per 1,000 men and 97.9 per 1,000 women in 1971 in England and Wales to 46.6 per 1,000 men and 64 per 1,000 women in 1981. The mean age at marriage rose in England and Wales from 24.6 for men and 22.6 for women in 1971 to 25.4 and 23.1, respectively, in 1981,[124] with similar changes in Scotland. As the rising number of divorces made marriage appear more precarious, people perhaps became more cautious, delaying or

119 25 May 1975; Bingham, *Family Newspapers*, p. 195.
120 Ibid., pp. 195–6.
121 Coleman, 'Population and Family', p. 62.
122 See p. 26.
123 Lewis, *The End of Marriage?*; Langhamer, *The English in Love*.
124 Ibid., p. 30.

choosing a trial period of cohabitation before commitment, though some consciously rejected official sanction for a committed partnership. The birth rate continued to decline from 16.9 per 1,000 population in 1966–70 in England and Wales to 12.2 per 1,000 in 1976–80; in Scotland it fell from 17.9 per 1,000 to 12.7; in Northern Ireland from 21 per 1,000 to 17.5.[125] Births to unmarried parents fell more gradually, from 21.5 per 1,000 women aged 15–44 in England and Wales in 1970 to 19.6 per 1,000 in 1980, but more were registered by both unmarried parents, 45.5 per cent in England and Wales in 1971 and 58.2 per cent in 1981, suggesting that more were in a stable relationship, often cohabiting.[126] There were more unconventional households, including gay couples and complex families of divorced and re-partnered parents, increasingly openly acknowledged and accepted.

Youth Culture

These changes in sexual and partnership patterns particularly involved people in their twenties and younger, who were also experiencing other cultural changes. Some better-off young people felt the urge in the later 1970s to display their difference from popular, hippie and Carnaby Street fashion, wearing what became known as the 'Sloane Ranger' style: costly, classically tailored tweed rather than the near-universal popular denim, women in pearls and shoes and bags from up-market French and Italian designers, men in Barbour raincoats and flat caps. They revived visible class difference in a society in which long-established differences of dress, physical fitness and language had diminished with growing affluence. They had opposing popular analogues, including the punk rock movement. This burst into public consciousness in 1976 when a recently formed, little known band, the Sex Pistols, appeared on an early evening Thames TV chat show to promote their debut single 'Anarchy in the UK'. Baited by the presenter, they brought temporary anarchy to TV, sneering, swearing and disrupting its polite conventions. The tabloids erupted, condemning 'The Filth and the Fury', 'Foul Mouthed Yobs', unleashing another moral panic about the degeneration of British youth. Promoters cancelled the Sex Pistols' concerts, the BBC banned their music and record companies shunned them. Their records soared up the UK charts and punk style became fashionable: drape jackets, drainpipe trousers, work-boots, stiletto heels, leather jackets, ripped and torn, held together with safety pins, buckles and zips. Hair was short, spiky, often dyed. The Pistols and their style were inspired, then promoted, by Malcolm McLaren and his partner fashion designer Vivienne Westwood, both famous counter-culturalists involved with international avant-garde radicalism, rock and fashion since the 1960s.

125 Coleman, 'Population and Family', p. 34.
126 Lewis, *The End of Marriage?* p. 35.

Never apologetic, the Pistols revelled in challenging established tastes and conventions even with their names: Johnny Rotten (born John Lydon) was their lead singer. Never more so than when they released their version of *God Save the Queen* in Elizabeth II's Silver Jubilee year, 1977:

> God Save the Queen, her fascist regime
> They made you a moron, potential h-bomb.
> God Save the Queen, she ain't no human being
> There's no future in England's dreaming.
> Don't be told what you want, don't be told what you need
> There's no future, no future, no future for you ...

It was, of course, banned by the BBC and the Independent Broadcasting Authority (IBA), and reached Number 1 in the UK charts. The Pistols were less successful abroad: their libertarian rudeness made their 1978 US tour a disaster and they disbanded soon after. Media commentators represented punk as 'dole-queue rock', representing a dispossessed generation from decaying council estates and high-rise blocks. It did present a disillusioned challenge to conventional cultures, but not just by marginalized working-class youth. Art students and middle-class young people from the suburbs flocked to punk concerts and festivals. There was no clear underlying philosophy, but it was one more expression of cultural dissatisfaction that further boosted the conventional capitalism of the popular music industry.[127]

Race and Youth

Punk linked with emerging subcultures among black youth. From the 1960s West Indian clubs and record labels grew in Britain along with the young Caribbean population, popularizing dance music influenced by Caribbean and US styles. In the early 1970s young black men adopted the Jamaican 'rude boy' style, particularly after release of the Jamaican film *The Harder They Come* in 1972, the style of young Caribbean men on the margins, hustling a living from gambling, drug-dealing and pimping, wearing gangster-style suits, leather jackets, dark glasses, wide-brimmed hats.

A new influence in the 1970s was Rastafarianism, a version of Christianity critical of Western culture and society as dominating, oppressing and enslaving black people. It was created by Marcus Garvey (d. 1940) founder of the Universal Negro Improvement Association in 1914, active in Jamaica and America, who appealed to the descendants of slaves to return to Africa where a black king would be their Redeemer. When Haile Selassie was crowned Emperor of Ethiopia in 1930 he was declared Ras Tafari, the Living God, and the movement grew. Beards and long 'dreadlocked' hair symbolized

---

127 Osgerby, *Youth in Britain since 1945*, pp. 107–10.

the faith, ganja (marijuana) was smoked as a holy sacrament and the red, green and gold of the Ethiopian flag became its symbolic colours. Rastafarianism grew among younger West Indians in Britain in the 1960s. The rhythmic drumming at Rasta gatherings influenced new styles of music, especially reggae which became closely identified with Rasta, particularly in the music of Bob Marley and his band, the Wailers, based in Jamaica. Marley's increasingly militant songs became popular with black young people in Britain and elsewhere in the 1970s. Second-generation immigrants, struggling to construct a cultural identity in a racist environment where they had limited opportunities and faced aggressive policing and growing unemployment, adopted dreadlocks, Rasta colours and loose-fitting army fatigues as symbols of black solidarity and resistance.

At the 1976 Notting Hill Carnival they fought running battles with the police, together with young white men. Black culture increasingly attracted white people, especially after the arrival of punk. The styles and sentiments of reggae and punk were similar, both critical of British culture, aesthetics of revolt by people identifying as outsiders. Punk bands like the Clash adopted reggae styles, punk and reggae played at the same concerts and festivals, and reggae began to attract the big record companies who had previously kept their distance. This fusion helped to mobilize a popular anti-racist movement uniting black and white youth. In 1976, activists in the Marxist Socialist Workers' Party, incensed when rock star Eric Clapton supported Enoch Powell, organized Rock against Racism (RAR), running events, linked with punk, where black and white bands played under anti-racist banners. Within a year they had arranged 200 concerts. It was necessary because throughout the 1970s as well as unity there were conflicts between white and black youths, particularly in districts with rising unemployment. Some white youths supported the National Front which tried hard to attract them, lowering its membership age to 14 and leafletting outside schools. Surveys showed considerable racism among younger, like older, white Britons.[128]

Resentment among immigrants of all ages was fuelled by the Conservative Immigration Act 1971, which restricted the right to remain to British passport-holders or people whose parents or grandparents (or those of their husband – not their wife) were native-born British subjects, effectively excluding most non-white Commonwealth citizens, increasing the sense of racial exclusion. However, in 1973, Heath's government accepted more than 20,000 Ugandan Asians fleeing President Idi Amin's Africanization drive.

Labour responded differently. Its Race Relations Act, 1976, outlawed discrimination in employment, training, education and provision of goods and services, and it became an offence to incite racial hatred. The definition of discrimination was extended to

128 Osgerby, *Youth Britain since 1945*, pp 123–33.

include indirect discrimination and victimization. The CRC and RRB were amalgamated into the Commission for Racial Equality (CRE), which gained powers of investigation and to assist individuals taking complaints to court. This followed pressure from anti-racist organizations, including the Campaign Against Racial Discrimination (CARD), the West Indian Standing Committee, and the Indian Workers Association, which increasingly cooperated, supported by backbench MPs and the influential Society of Labour Lawyers.

Still, few black or Asian people were employed in management or the professions, other than the NHS to which south Asian doctors and Caribbean nurses remained indispensable, though still rarely at the highest levels or in more prestigious specialisms. More were in skilled manual work: one-fifth of men with university degrees equivalent to British standards were manual workers in 1974, almost unimaginable for a white British graduate. Many Asians, particularly, were self-employed, often in small shops and restaurants. BME people still lived mainly in segregated areas of inner cities with poor amenities. People of black Caribbean origin were now owner-occupiers and council tenants in similar proportions to white people, but often in poorer properties. Only 4 per cent of Asian households were council tenants and 75 per cent were owner-occupiers, also often of poor quality homes. The numbers and geographical concentration of immigrants and their increasing tendency to vote made them potentially decisive in certain constituencies; polls showed they inclined strongly to Labour. The Conservatives were identified with strict controls on immigration, not least when, in 1978, Margaret Thatcher remarked in a TV interview:

> People are really rather afraid that this country might be rather swamped by people with a different culture and ... If there is any fear that it might be swamped people are going to react and be rather hostile to them coming in. So, if you want good race relations, you have got to allay people's fears on numbers.[129]

Despite continuing racism, the National Front gained no more than 3.6 per cent of votes in any constituency in the General Elections of 1970 and 1974, then declined into insignificance. Anti-racist organizations challenged them, including RAR, then the Anti-Nazi League (ANL) formed in 1977 primarily by white activists with black and Asian involvement. The ANL was a more conventional campaigning organization than the RAR, drawing wide support from writers, academics, entertainers, sports stars and others – organizing rail workers, teachers, architects, bikers, schoolchildren, football fans, skateboarders against the Nazis – producing popular magazines, badges and stickers to attract young people. The RAR and ANL organized demonstrations and carnivals. Their first joint event, in Victoria Park, east London, in April 1978, attracted

---

129 Wendy Webster, 'Immigration and Racism', in P. Addison and H. Jones (eds), *A Companion to Contemporary Britain, 1939–2000* (Oxford: Blackwell, 2005), p. 98.

80,000 people with punk and reggae bands. At the same time, BME groups became increasingly active in local politics, especially in London where the Labour-led GLC and some borough councils were active in anti-racist campaigning, working with voluntary organizations created by and for minorities.[130]

Gypsies and Travellers

The Gypsy Council kept campaigning, nationally and internationally, against exceptional inequalities, hosting the first World Romani Congress in 1971. It pioneered mobile caravan-schools: it was estimated in 1971 that of 6,000–8,000 school-age children only about 2,500 attended school and attainment was low. Labour's 1968 Act was not delivering enough sites,[131] causing problems for settled and travelling communities. In 1976, Sir John Stafford Cripps, son of the former Labour Chancellor, campaigner for improved quality of life in rural areas, was appointed to investigate. He reported that 133 local authority sites had opened in England and Wales since 1970, containing 2,131 pitches, but leaving about 6,000 caravans with no legal site and there were few temporary pitches for Travellers on the move. Many authorities created sites for enforced settlement and assimilation, often:

> excessively close to sewage plants, refuse destructors, traffic laden motorways, intersections of these and other busy highways, main railway tracks and other features contaminating the environment by odour, noise and so on. No non-Gypsy family would be expected to live in such a place.[132]

They were isolated from shops, schools and surgeries. Cripps highlighted public prejudice and sometimes violent hostility against Travellers and recommended government funding and enforcement of adequate provision.[133] Labour introduced 100 per cent grants for local authorities to build sites, which grew substantially after implementation in 1980, but other inequalities continued.[134]

Environmentalism

Environmental campaigns were long established in Britain, mainly concerning the protection of animals and birds (the RSPCA was founded 1824, RSPB in 1889) and the countryside (the National Trust was founded 1895). Animal rights campaigns

---

130 Nick Kimber, 'Race and Equality', in Pat Thane (ed.), *Unequal Britain. Equalities in Britain since 1945* (London: Bloomsbury, 2010), pp. 37–9.
131 See p. 291.
132 J. Cripps, *Accommodation for Gypsies* (London: HMSO, 1976), para. 3.17.
133 Ibid.
134 Porter and Taylor, 'Gypsies and Travellers', pp. 84–7.

grew. The Hunt Saboteurs Association, founded by RSPCA radicals in 1964, disrupted fox hunts to prevent hounds savaging foxes. The Animal Liberation Front from 1976 opposed the use of animals in research, as protesters had since the formation of the Anti-Vivisection Society in 1875, but more aggressively, invading laboratories and making arson attacks on furriers. From the 1960s new groups sought to protect the whole environment, using contemporary protest tactics, again attracting mainly younger activists, notably Friends of the Earth (FOE) founded in the United Kingdom in 1970, a branch of a US organization. It gained media attention in 1971 by dumping thousands of bottles outside the offices of Schweppes, protesting against the company's switch to non-returnable bottles. Within a year there were forty FOE groups in the United Kingdom, preoccupied especially with the (in)security of atomic energy, particularly at the Windscale processing plant in Cumbria. These were smaller than the feminist, gay and anti-racist movements, but active and lasting.[135]

Nationalisms

Northern Ireland remained tense and nationalism grew in Scotland and Wales, both suffering from the decline of coal mining and rising unemployment and demanding greater control over future development. Callaghan promised devolution in order to hold Welsh and Scottish support as Labour's majority dwindled. The Kilbrandon Commission on the Constitution, appointed by Labour in 1969, reported in October 1973, recommending elected assemblies for Scotland and Wales. Wilson's government published consultation documents, then in 1976 a Scotland and Wales Bill provided for devolution and elected assemblies, with more limited powers in Wales, financed by grants allocated by Parliament. There would be no reduction in Welsh and Scottish MPs in Westminster, which would undermine Labour's likely majorities, and the secretaries of state for both nations would remain in the Cabinet. A White Paper, *The English Dimension*, in December 1976 offered reassurance that the English would not be disadvantaged, including by Welsh and Scottish MPs voting on matters exclusively concerning England – known as the 'West Lothian question' when raised by Tam Dalyell, MP for that Scottish constituency.

The Bill passed its second reading in December 1976, but created such dissension in all parties that, after lengthy all-party talks, it was withdrawn. After further talks, separate Scotland and Wales Bills were introduced in November 1977. An amendment by a Labour backbencher made devolution in both countries subject to referenda in which a minimum 40 per cent of each electorate voted 'Yes'. In 1978, the Cabinet agreed a formula for allocating funds to Wales, Northern Ireland and Scotland devised by

135 Nehring, 'The Growth of Social Movements', pp. 295–7.

Joel Barnett, Chief Secretary to the Treasury (known thereafter as the 'Barnett formula'), which favoured Scotland, where Labour had most votes to lose, and troublesome Northern Ireland. The legislation passed in July 1978, followed by referenda on 1 March 1979, St David's Day, amid strikes and wintry weather. Scotland voted 'Yes' by 33 per cent to 31 per cent on a 64 per cent turnout, too small a majority to meet the terms of the legislation; 59 per cent of Welsh electors voted 'No' by 47 per cent to 12 per cent, overwhelmingly even in strongly Welsh-speaking areas. The 'No' campaign united Conservatives, left-wing Labour MPs and businesspeople concerned that devolution would further harm the Welsh economy.[136]

General Election, 1979

The protracted devolution issue ensured that nationalists kept Labour in office longer than might otherwise have been possible, but the outcome contributed as much to destroying the government as the industrial conflicts. Callaghan backed off the General Election expected in October 1978 because the economy was recovering, which he hoped would benefit Labour. But the following 'winter of discontent', put the Conservatives twenty points ahead in the polls by February 1979. Following the referendum, the government lost SNP support. In late March, it supported an opposition no-confidence motion which the government lost by one vote. A General Election was called for May. Thatcher's Conservatives made much of the 'winter of discontent', with a prominent poster of a lengthy dole queue captioned 'Labour Isn't Working'. She won.

Conclusion

It was a turbulent decade, but hardly 'benighted' for many, perhaps most, British people, a decade of diverse experiences, new movements and ideas, not easily expressed in a simple word or phrase. Despite international economic crises, inflation, rising unemployment and manufacturing decline, most people enjoyed improving living standards and leisure. In 2004, the New Economics Foundation think-tank devised an index of national economic, social and environmental well-being and concluded that Britain's best year since 1950 had been 1976, the year of the IMF loan.[137]

---

136 Thorpe, *History of the British Labour Party*, pp. 195–6; Christopher Harvie, 'The Politics of Devolution', in P. Addison and H. Jones (eds), *A Companion to Contemporary Britain, 1939–2000* (Oxford: Blackwell, 2005), pp. 434–5; Christopher Harvie and Peter Jones, *The Road to Home Rule* (Edinburgh University Press, 2000); T. M. Devine, *The Scottish Nation 1799–2007. A Modern History* (London: Penguin, 2012); Morgan, *Wales*, pp. 376–408; Morgan, *Callaghan*, pp. 677–9.

137 Andy Beckett, *When the Lights Went Out. What Really Happened to Britain in the Seventies* (London: Faber& Faber, 2009), p. 420.

In the first half of the decade income inequality reached its lowest point of the century. Gender inequalities continued their slow progress to elimination due partly to new feminist militancy. Equality for homosexuals progressed still more slowly, for racial minorities hardly at all, despite advances in anti-discrimination legislation and anti-racist protest. Public tolerance of unconventional lifestyles appeared to be growing, along with a greater willingness especially of younger people to embrace them, which to some signified just how 'benighted' the decade was – a cultural division that showed no sign of decline.

Shifts towards greater equalities and cultural change were promoted and expressed by an exceptional range of collectively organized groups – workers, feminists, gay activists, anti-racist campaigners, nationalists – organizing and campaigning against perceived disadvantage more actively than at any time since the beginning of the century, though not in formal political parties whose membership dwindled. It was a time of lively intellectual and cultural ferment when many new possibilities seemed to be opening, with uncertain outcomes. A generation that had grown up since 1945, mostly better educated, better off, more confident and less deferential than older generations, challenged established values in diverse ways, seeking to transform the culture, not just for themselves but for everyone.

Nevertheless some inequalities grew. Income inequality widened later in the decade, due partly to the renewed division between regions of high unemployment and continuing prosperity. Unemployment in Northern Ireland, Scotland and Wales strengthened nationalism and premonitions that the Kingdom might not remain United. It exacerbated conflict between Nationalists and Unionists in Northern Ireland, rooted in Catholic–Protestant inequalities, which became fiercer and more lethal, showing little sign of resolution. Nor did the major cause of unemployment, the decline of manufacturing, which neither successive governments with radically different policies nor the free market showed signs of reversing. Economic weakness and declining trade weakened the United Kingdom in international politics. The new government faced more challenges than the militant trade unionism that had dominated its election message.

11

The Iron Lady

1979–1990

Rolling Back the Postwar State

Margaret Thatcher's victory in 1979 produced the most radical break in postwar UK society and politics. She profoundly challenged many aspects of culture and tradition, though in very different ways from 1970s radicals. More determinedly than any previous Conservative premier, she aimed to dismantle the welfare state and collective social responsibility, minimizing state direction of the economy, maximizing private enterprise in all fields, 'rolling back' advances in state action since 1945, in practice by utilizing and often strengthening central state mechanisms.

Poverty and income and wealth inequality increased dramatically during her period as premier, until 1990. Top incomes and wealth shot to previously unimagined heights, while the highest unemployment since the war combined with low pay and benefit cuts raised poverty to levels thought to have been banished since 1945, while other inequalities, including of race and gender, did not diminish. She believed inequality was the natural and desirable state of society, incentivizing the disadvantaged to aspire and strive to do better, but she thought the word inequality unacceptably pejorative and banned it from official discourse, preferring the more ambiguous 'variations'.

Strongly individualist, she sincerely believed that poverty was caused by personal not societal failings, and that people should be incentivized to adopt the commitment to self-help and family support she thought had been destroyed by the welfare state. People should work rather than expect support from the state or the community (as, in reality, overwhelmingly they did) or, if they could not, look to their families for support. The economy, she believed, was similarly crippled by the state feather-bedding business and/or strangling it with official 'red tape'; business also should be freed to shape its own future. Such convictions shaped her increasingly hostile attitude to the EC, which she saw as attempting excessively to control the British economy and society. She was far more attracted by American hostility to 'socialist' welfare and commitment to the free market, as encouraged under Reagan's presidency. Like her predecessors she aimed to strengthen the UK's international status, mainly through alliance with the United States, not at all through Commonwealth links for which, unlike most of her predecessors, she had no use – one of many traditions she rejected.

Profound changes in society and culture, politics and the economy resulted. The increasing social divisions were challenged, not only by predictable radicals but by the Church of England among others, but the challengers could do little more than restrain her more unpopular ambitions, including privatizing the NHS. The trade union movement was undermined by legislation combined with the effects of unemployment and manufacturing decline. The first woman premier was intensely hostile to feminism and she allowed few, reluctant, moves towards gender equality, again because she believed unequal outcomes were due to lack of effort not to discrimination; nor did racial inequality diminish or gay rights significantly advance, though protest and campaigns continued.

She did not reject all traditions and cultural change did not cease. She strongly promoted her vision of the 'traditional family' based on life-long marriage and intergenerational support which she, wrongly, believed had declined. Nevertheless, divorce rose to unprecedented levels, more children than ever before were born to unmarried, cohabiting parents, more openly gay partners, female and male, lived together, increasingly with children. Much changed in the 1980s, not always in directions chosen by Margaret Thatcher.

The First Woman Premier

The UK's first female prime minister entered government with a clear majority (forty-three seats). The election results reflected the social divisions and inequalities that provoked protest through the 1970s, suggesting deep continuities in UK politics and culture. More starkly than since 1945, the Conservatives represented the prosperous south of England and Labour the declining industrial regions: the divide deepened between southern England and the North and the other countries of the United Kingdom. Welsh and Scottish Nationalists won two seats each. Despite the rise of feminism, just nineteen women were elected among 635 MPs, the fewest since 1951, eight Conservative, eleven Labour. The Conservatives won 44 per cent of votes to Labour's 37 per cent, their lowest share since 1931, with a 76 per cent turnout. The Liberals took 14 per cent and eleven seats.

Thatcher cautiously chose a Cabinet balancing relatively progressive Conservatives, including Heath supporters – 'wets' she called them – and those closer to her convictions. It was deeply split between old, 'one nation', Conservatism and newer neo-liberalism and between 'grandees' and self-made men; 91 per cent were privately educated, 27 per cent at Eton.[1] Old school Whitelaw became Home Secretary, supporting and sometimes restraining her through her first two terms in office, as loyally as he had supported Heath. She expressed her gratitude with the comment 'every Cabinet should have a Willie', a *double entendre* of which the innocent girl from Grantham was apparently unaware until the media erupted. Heath was offered the Washington Embassy in an effort to banish him, but he refused and remained glowering on the backbenches. Another of his supporters, Lord Carrington, became Foreign Secretary. Thatcher's closest allies were Sir Geoffrey Howe, Chancellor, and Sir Keith Joseph, Secretary of State for Industry, a leading neoliberal influence.

Only one other woman was appointed, briefly, to the Cabinet throughout Thatcher's three terms of office: the unelected Baroness Young was Chancellor of the Duchy of Lancaster, October 1981–April 1982, then Lord Privy Seal to June 1983 before moving to a non-Cabinet role at the Foreign Office. Women MPs slowly increased: in 1983, thirteen Conservatives and ten Labour; in 1987, more than ever before, seventeen Conservative, twenty-one Labour, two Liberals and one SNP, a modest contribution to the international rise in elected women in the 1980s. In 1991, women made up 38.5 per cent of members of the Finnish lower house, 20.4 per cent in Germany, both with PR electoral systems that assisted diversity in representation[2]; they were 9 per cent of Westminster members. By the late 1980s there was growing pressure from women in the Labour Party and the TUC for positive action to increase female MPs. Emma Nicolson, Vice-Chairman (sic) of the Conservative Party from 1983 to 1987, soon to defect to the Liberal Democrats, complained repeatedly about local parties' reluctance to select women and the leadership's lack of interest in this inequality.[3]

Margaret Thatcher was unresponsive. She was emphatically not a feminist. She told a group of children in a TV programme in 1982:

> I think most of us got to our position in life without Women's Lib and we got here, not by saying 'you've got to have more women doing so-and-so' but saying 'look we've got the qualifications, why shouldn't we have as much chance as a man?' And you'll find that so many male bastions were conquered in that way, whereas Women's Lib, I think, has been rather strident, concentrated on things that don't really matter and, dare I say it, being rather unfeminine. Don't you think that?[4]

1 Bale, *Conservatives since 1945*, p. 246.

2 Sarah Childs, Joni Lovenduski and Rosie Campbell, *Women at the Top, 2005. Changing Numbers, Changing Politics* (London: Hansard Society, 2005), 'International Comparisons', pp. 75–93.

3 Emma Nicholson, *Secret Society. Inside – and Outside – the Conservative Party* (London: Indigo, 1996), pp. 85–105.

4 Thames TV, 13 December 1982, Thatcher Foundation Website.

Women volunteered as candidates for all parties, but were still rarely selected for winnable seats,[5] like Thatcher in the past.[6] Under her premiership women voters shifted from Conservatism, dividing between the opposition parties, part of a growing international 'gender gap' in voting as men were more attracted to growing neoliberalism, while women resisted its effects, particularly welfare cuts. There were no MPs from BME backgrounds until four were elected in 1987, all Labour.[7]

Thatcher wrote later, that, from the beginning, 'I was determined to send out a clear signal of change'.[8] She became notorious for demanding that those around her, including ministers and civil servants, must be 'one of us', sharing her neoliberalism and contempt for those she regarded as clinging to outmoded attitudes. Her press secretary, ex-Labour supporter Bernard Ingham, a straight-speaking Yorkshireman, cultivated the media, especially the *Sun*, more successfully than any previous government representative. Presentation mattered with the growing influence of TV and outspoken press scrutiny, especially of an unusually prominent woman. Before the election Thatcher took elocution lessons to lower and project her voice and avoid the 'shrillness' with which female speakers were stereotyped, while presenting a stereotypically middle-class female image. She was advised on hair and clothing styles, as was not required of male politicians. She was popular with the party and played this up in conference speeches, aware of media scrutiny. The party was changing. Fewer MPs came from public schools, Oxbridge, landowning and inherited wealth, more from grammar schools and provincial universities, from business and newer professions: from estate owners to estate agents as one critic put it.

Civil Service Reform

Thatcher was more cautious in her first term, 1979–83, than later, but she made significant changes. She was determined to reduce the numbers and power of civil servants, convinced they depleted rather than created wealth, burdening the economy with regulatory 'red tape', lacked the skills essential for the modern world, had excessive job security and pensions and worked at too leisurely a pace, shielded from real life. Wilson, Heath and Callaghan had tried to reform the civil service, resenting its traditional political independence when officials challenged them, also believing it was out of touch with modern needs. Thatcher went further, with severe cuts, transfer of

5 Hansard Society, *The Report of the Hansard Society Commission on Women at the Top* (London: Hansard Society, 1990).

6 Richard Vinen, *Thatcher's Britain. The Politics and Social Upheaval of the 1980s* (London: Simon & Schuster, 2009, 2nd edn, 2009), p. 25.

7 Bernie Grant, Diane Abbott, Paul Boateng and Keith Vaz.

8 Margaret Thatcher, *The Downing St Years* (London: HarperCollins, 1993), p. 38.

services and responsibilities to the private sector, appointing Derek Rayner, from Marks and Spencer, to run an Efficiency Unit to eliminate 'the waste and ineffectiveness of government' by introducing civil servants to techniques of business management. The number of civil servants fell by 142,515 between 1980 and 1990.[9] Exceptional numbers of policy advisers were appointed from outside the service, often at higher cost, mainly businessmen or academic economists who shared her views.[10] Areas of the civil service delivering services, including vehicle licensing, publication of official documents (HMSO) and highway management, were transferred to semi-autonomous 'agencies', still under tight central budgetary controls but not responsible to ministries. It was the greatest transformation of the service since the Northcote–Trevelyan reforms of the mid-nineteenth century, which accelerated under John Major, her successor.

Industrial Relations

Another Thatcher priority was to 'reform', that is, crush, the unions.[11] Surprisingly, including to him, she placed 'wet' James Prior, at the Department of Employment, a proponent of relative industrial appeasement. The largest social group swinging to the Conservatives in 1979 were male skilled workers who believed Labour's pay controls had disadvantaged them and she did not wish to alienate them immediately.[12] Class awareness and the need for politicians to appease the substantial working class still suffused UK politics. In 1979, the miners received a 20 per cent pay rise, 9 per cent the following year and the pay of public sector workers rose significantly in 1979–80, followed by tight limits and relative decline. Thereafter, trade union demands for higher pay were regarded as 'selfish', while those of businesspeople were fair rewards for effort.

Prior's Employment Act 1980 outlawed secondary picketing and required 80 per cent support in ballots for establishing a closed shop. It provided funds for ballots for full-time officers and strike action. Then the Social Security (No. 2) Act 1980 imposed a tight £12 per week restriction on Supplementary Benefits for strikers' families. In 1981, Prior was replaced by the uncompromisingly anti-union Norman Tebbit. Another Employment Act in 1982 made unions financially liable for actions judged unlawful during strikes, narrowing the definition of 'lawful' disputes by outlawing solidarity action supporting other unions and public sector strikes judged political, that is,

9 Butler and Butler, *Twentieth-Century British Political Facts*, p. 309.

10 Andrew Blick, *People Who Live in the Dark. The History of the Special Adviser in British Politics* (London: Politico's, 2004).

11 P. Dorey, 'The Stepping Stones Programme. The Conservative Party's Struggle to Develop a Trade Union Policy 1975–9', *Historical Studies in Industrial Relations* 35 (2014): 89–116.

12 Dorey, '"Should I Stay or Should I Go?"' p. 14.

against government actions affecting the working lives of teachers etc.[13] No industrial relations legislation of the Thatcher period applied in Northern Ireland, where trade unionism was so intertwined with sectarian politics that ministers kept their distance. There was no immediate union response. Days lost in strikes declined by almost 75 per cent by 1983, partly because unemployment rose from 1.2 million in May 1979 to 3.2 million in January 1983, by far the highest since the war, highest in manufacturing and mining which weakened the unions. Union membership fell from 12.1 million in 1980 to 10 million in 1984 due to unemployment and the continued decline of manufacturing and mining.[14] Between 1979 and 1982 5,000 factories closed.[15] Apparently Conservatism was not working.

The Economy

Howe's 1979 Budget reduced the basic rate of income tax from 33 per cent to 30 per cent, the top rate from 83 per cent to 60 per cent, while VAT, which hit the lowest incomes hardest, rose from 8 per cent to 15 per cent. Prices soared. Economic policies were founded on 'monetarism', the belief that controlling the money supply was the key to economic management, though its meaning was not widely understood and interpretations differed.[16] A version was incorporated in the Medium-Term Economic Strategy revealed in Howe's 1980 Budget, drafted by Nigel Lawson, a financial journalist, now Financial Secretary to the Treasury. It aimed through control of money supply to reduce inflation and limit wage rises, while increasing employment by liberating private enterprise from state control and high taxation. It failed, partly because 'money supply' was hard to measure in a modern economy less dependent upon cash.

Howe abolished controls on currency exchange transactions in 1979, pursuing market freedom but removing one means of controlling money supply. This benefited City of London financiers who were surprised and delighted. Restrictions on bank lending were eased, though the bank rate remained 14 per cent in 1980. The Governor of the Bank of England, Gordon Richardson, did not share the City's pleasure. He agreed with a letter to *The Times* from 364 economists following the 1981 Budget, rejecting monetarism and arguing that 'present policies will deepen the depression, erode the industrial base of the economy and threaten its social and political stability'. Indeed, unemployment continued to rise and manufacturing output to fall. Thatcher thought

13 Reid, *United We Stand*, pp. 396–400.
14 Butler and Butler, *Twentieth-Century British Political Facts*, p. 401.
15 N. Crafts, 'Economic Growth', in N. Crafts and N. Woodward (eds), *The British Economy since 1945* (Oxford University Press, 1991), p. 285.
16 Stedman Jones, *Masters of the Universe*, pp. 1180–214.

Richardson another patronizing mandarin, like many of his City colleagues 'overfed, slow-moving relics of a now discredited paternalist consensus',[17] convinced the City also needed reform. She was irked when they did not initially support privatization of nationalized industries, believing their stocks would not sell. To her relief Richardson retired in 1983 and she ensured the surprise succession of the relatively inexperienced but more conciliatory Robin Leigh-Pemberton of NatWest Bank.[18]

National Insurance contributions also rose in 1979. By 1990 all state contributions to the National Insurance fund were withdrawn; for the first time since 1911 pensions and other contributory benefits were financed entirely by employer and employee contributions, reducing the redistributive element of social insurance. The government was committed to cutting total public expenditure while raising it on defence and law and order and keeping it level on the popular NHS. Police and armed services' pay rose while other defence costs were cut. Gallup found the 1979 budget 'one of the least popular budgets, proposed by one of the least popular Chancellors of the past 27 years'[19]; a majority claimed the government only helped the well off. The government and premier had consistently bad ratings.[20]

Manufacturing output fell 14 per cent in 1979–80. International oil prices shot up, including for North Sea oil, which raised the exchange value of the pound, and exports fell. By summer 1980 inflation was above 20 per cent and 2 million were unemployed, the deepest slump for fifty years. The government was driven to what looked very like U-turns: North Sea oil revenues were taxed; in 1981, a 'once and for all' levy was imposed on banks, raising £400 million, on the grounds that 'peculiar circumstances' had generated 'windfall profits' in both sectors.[21] Economic growth was only 0.6 per cent in 1980–3, well below the average 2.4 per cent pa since 1950.[22] In 1979, manufacturing contributed 26 per cent of GNP, by 1990 it was 20 per cent. Employment growth in the 1980s was concentrated in low-paid work and insecure self-employment. Women experienced less unemployment than men mainly because so many were employed in low-status, low-paid, often part-time work often in the growing service sector, selling fast food, clothing and household goods, staffing call-centres. More women now expected employment, more needed it when household budgets were under pressure, more were single parents. Demand for work grew as the 'baby boom' from the 1940s to the late 1960s brought more young people into the labour market, along with declining

17 David Kynaston, *The City of London, vol. 4: A Club No More, 1945–2000* (London: Chatto & Windus, 2001), pp. 585–8.
18 Ibid., p. 590.
19 Whybrow, *Britain Speaks Out*, p. 121.
20 Ibid., p. 121.
21 Vinen, *Thatcher's Britain*, pp. 106–7.
22 Crafts, 'Economic Growth during the Long Twentieth Century', p. 46.

numbers of immigrants. In 1979, 69,670 immigrants were accepted for settlement in the United Kingdom, in 1990, 52,400.[23]

Despite the economic problems, Thatcher stood by her policies, telling the party conference in October 1980: 'You turn if you want to. The lady's not for turning.' 'Wets' who expressed doubts about monetarism were removed from key posts. Prior was exiled to Northern Ireland, Lawson promoted to the Cabinet as Secretary for Energy. Cable and Wireless, British Petroleum, British Aerospace and the British Sugar Corporation were privatized by the end of 1981, and Mercury was licensed to compete with the state-owned monopoly British Telecom. Lawson launched the privatization of Britoil in 1982, though it was overvalued and, as many in the City predicted, made heavy losses. By 1983, Associated British Ports, British Rail hotels and National Freight had been privatized.[24]

Housing

The Housing Act 1980 introduced one of the first privatizations, giving council tenants of at least three years' standing the right to buy the freehold of their house, or a 125-year lease of a flat, at heavily discounted prices. Council house sales had always been possible, at local authority discretion, which was now withdrawn. Discounts of up to 30 per cent of the market value were introduced by Heath's government, then withdrawn by Labour. Tenants were now entitled to discounts of 33–50 per cent of the market value, depending on their length of tenancy, to a maximum of £25,000, later increased to a maximum of 70 per cent and, from 1989, up to £50,000 in some areas. Owners, like other mortgagees, received tax concessions on mortgage payments.

More houses sold than flats, especially sounder, more attractive older houses. Buyers were mainly middle-aged couples from better-paid, skilled working-class backgrounds in more prosperous parts of the country, further increasing social and regional inequality. More homes were council-owned in Scotland than in England but fewer were sold. By 1995, 1.7 million tenants in Great Britain had bought a quarter of the 1980 stock. Councils were forbidden from spending income from sales on housebuilding, so the stock shrank: council housing fell from almost one-third to one-fifth of total housing between 1979 and 1994. Housing was the area of government spending that dropped furthest, but, unlike many other Conservative policies, council house sales were popular, at least with better-off people. In 1987, 40 per cent of owners of former council houses voted Conservative, as Thatcher hoped, 25 per cent of tenants. An increasing share of government funding went to non-profit housing associations, to help cover the

23 Butler and Butler *Twentieth-Century British Political Facts*, p. 352.
24 Vinen, *Thatcher's Britain*, pp. 195–200.

growing lack of affordable housing. By the 1990s, these were the main suppliers of what was now called 'social' housing for lower-income people.[25]

Tax relief on mortgages rose from £1.6 million to £5.5 million from 1979 to 1989, stimulated by and stimulating house price inflation, while subsidies to local authority housing fell from £1,258 million to £520 million.[26] Prices rose also due to the removal in 1982 of restrictions on personal credit, facilitating larger mortgages. Previously, substantial deposits (generally 25 per cent of the price) were required and mortgages were fixed in proportion to the income of the mortgagee(s). Less responsible mortgage selling, credit and indebtedness grew. New UK housing loans increased from £6 billion to £63 billion between 1978 and 1988; non-housing loans by UK banks from £4 billion to £28 billion.[27]

The 1980 Housing Act assumed that local authorities would replace subsidies by raising rents for the remaining tenants, following new government rent guidelines. By 1986–7 only 25 per cent of English local authorities received any housing subsidy; rents rose by 50 per cent on average.[28] As real incomes fell and unemployment rose, more households could not cope. In 1982–3, a means-tested Housing Benefit was introduced to assist them, amalgamating Supplementary Benefit rent support and rate rebate, available to council and private tenants at considerable public cost. It was paid directly to landlords, creating an incentive to raise rents. Sixty per cent of council tenants received it in 1984–5.[29] As better-off council tenants became owner-occupiers, more lower-income tenants became dependent on state benefits. For the first time, council tenants were predominantly on low incomes, in contrast to the original ideal of socially mixed council housing, as a reduced stock of council housing provided only for those in greatest need.[30] Clearer divisions were emerging between those who were prospering and increasing numbers who felt 'left-behind'.

Rolling Back the Welfare State

Thatcher believed that:

> Welfare benefits, distributed with little or no consideration of their effects on behaviour, encouraged illegitimacy, facilitated the breakdown of families, and replaced incentives

25 John Hills and Beverley Mullings, 'Housing. A Decent Home for All at a Price Within their Means?' in John Hills (ed.), *The State of Welfare. The Welfare State in Britain since 1974* (Oxford University Press, 1990), pp. 135–201.

26 Vinen, *Thatcher's Britain*, p. 204.

27 Ibid., p. 205.

28 John Hills, 'Housing. A Decent Home Within the Reach of Every Family', in H. Glennerster and John Hills (eds.) *The State of Welfare. The Economics of Social Spending*, 2nd edn (Oxford University Press, 1998), p. 127.

29 Ibid., p. 132.

30 Glennerster, *British Social Policy*, pp. 187–8.

favouring work and self-reliance with perverse encouragement for idleness and cheating. The final illusion – that state intervention would promote social harmony and solidarity or, in Tory language, 'One Nation' – collapsed in the 'winter of discontent' when … the prevailing mood was one of snarling envy and motiveless hostility.[31]

Keith Joseph wrote in 1978 that, 'The pursuit of equality has done, and is doing, more harm, stunting the incentives and rewards that are essential to having a successful economy'.[32] Thatcher was encouraged by poll evidence of declining public support for social spending, from 44 per cent to 22 per cent since 1969, though support for the NHS and other universal services remained high.[33]

She proceeded to remove the 'safety net' which since the late 1940s had protected those on the lowest incomes from falling too far behind the rest as affluence increased. The first target for cuts was social security, the largest, fastest growing social spending programme, mainly due to unemployment. Income-related, short-term unemployment and sickness benefits were axed, justified by assertions that they encouraged idleness. Where possible payments were privatized. From 1983, sickness pay was no longer paid from public funds but by employers for the first eight weeks, later extended to twenty-eight weeks. Employers were expected to police and discourage sickness leave, potentially deterring them from hiring workers with health problems. From 1982 benefits were uprated in line with prices not earnings, ensuring lower rises. Pensions fell from over 23 per cent of average male earnings in 1981 to 15 per cent in 1993, cutting the cost by one-third but increasing the numbers of pensioners needing means-tested supplements, while the value of Supplementary Benefits fell from 61 per cent of median earnings in 1978 to 53 per cent in 1987.[34]

Labour's legislation compelling local authorities to abolish selective secondary education was repealed. It had almost disappeared in Wales and Scotland. A few English authorities, including Kent and Lincolnshire County Councils, never abandoned it. Very few reintroduced it. By 1995–6 only 5 per cent of pupils in UK secondary schools attended grammar schools, the highest proportion being in Northern Ireland where selection prevailed in schools strictly divided by religion.[35] The 1980 Education Act introduced 'Assisted Places', funding initially 5,300, later 35,000, places at independent schools on a means-tested basis. By 1992, 7 per cent of all pupils attended private schools, 5 per cent of these with free places.[36]

31 Thatcher, *Downing St Years*, p. 8.
32 Keith Joseph, 'Proclaim the Message. Keynes is Dead!', in P. Hutber (ed.), *What's Wrong with Britain* (London: Sphere, 1978), pp. 105–6.
33 Glennerster, *British Social Policy*, pp. 171–3.
34 P. Dorey, 'A Farewell to Alms. Thatcherism's Legacy of Inequality', *British Politics* 10 (2015): 87.
35 H. Glennerster, 'Education. Reaping the Harvest?' in H. Glennerster and John Hills (eds), *The State of Welfare. The Economics of Social Spending*, 2nd edn (Oxford University Press, 1998), p. 33.
36 Ibid., pp. 27–74.

Thatcher and Howe aimed for more cuts and the privatization of social services in the first term, but were restrained by resistance in Cabinet and among voters.[37]

Foreign and Commonwealth Policy

An achievement of Thatcher's first year was settlement in Rhodesia.[38] This owed most to Carrington's, and most Commonwealth leaders', determination to end the long, bitter guerrilla war. Carrington persuaded Thatcher to agree to attempted settlement. Ian Smith, the Rhodesian Prime Minister and initiator of UDI, was weakened by the collapse of the Portuguese empire in Angola and Mozambique, his main ally. At a London meeting, Commonwealth leaders led successful negotiations for a settlement with majority rule. An election in 1980 brought the first black Prime Minister, Robert Mugabe, leader of the armed struggle, a landslide victory in what was now Zimbabwe, cheered by those in Britain and elsewhere who had campaigned for majority rule throughout southern Africa. It was not quite the settlement Mrs Thatcher was expected to support, but she had little choice and few British politicians believed UDI should drag on.[39]

It was a blow for nostalgic imperialists, but Thatcher appeared uninterested in Britain's imperial past or in the Commonwealth. Imperialism was not the main motive for the great adventure of her first term, the Falklands War. She entered 1982 with the lowest approval ratings of any Prime Minister since opinion polls began.[40] Then the economy started to revive and she was rescued by something less expected: the invasion by Argentina, led by the right-wing dictator, General Leopoldo Galtieri, of the Falkland Islands, the Malvinas as they were known in nearby Argentina which had long claimed them. The 1,850 islanders made clear they preferred distant, benign British rule to absorption by a nearby dictatorship whose opponents met terrible ends, including ejection from aircraft over the Atlantic. Since the mid-1960s, British governments, including Thatcher's, had tried unsuccessfully to negotiate a settlement acceptable to the islanders and the Argentinians. In 1981, the Falklands' already minimal defences were reduced as part of wider defence cuts and the Argentinians took advantage, believing Britain would not resist, while UK intelligence underestimated their intentions. Thatcher seized an opportunity to show her determination and patriotism and to distract voters from economic problems. The navy was dispatched. Carrington nobly took the blame for not averting the crisis and resigned, though he had warned of the danger of reducing the Falklands' defences.

37 *The Guardian*, 25 November 2016, 'Thatcher pushed for breakup of welfare state despite NHS pledge', based on newly released Treasury papers from Howe's private office.
38 See p. 298.
39 Vinen, *Thatcher's Britain*, pp. 221–4.
40 Butler and Butler, *Twentieth-Century British Political Facts*, p. 208.

The war lasted two months from April 1982 until Argentina surrendered[41]: 255 British servicemen were killed and 777 injured; six British ships were sunk. After some hesitation, President Reagan's Republican administration, otherwise close allies of Mrs Thatcher, with similar views, but supporters of Galtieri until he became too openly oppressive, provided crucial supplies and intelligence support. 'We're friends of both sides' claimed Reagan. Thatcher revelled in the role of Churchillian war leader, declaiming, 'Great Britain is Great again'. When the war ended, the Conservatives had 51 per cent support in polls to Labour's 29 per cent. Labour supported the war, since Foot, now party leader,[42] believed in self-determination for the Falklanders and opposed Galtieri's regime, though some left-wingers had doubts. Others rejected her triumphalism, including the Archbishop of Canterbury, Robert Runcie, a former soldier with an impressive war record. His sermon at the Thanksgiving Service in St Paul's Cathedral insisted on commemorating Argentinian as well as British deaths, regarding neither as reasons to 'Rejoice! Rejoice!' as she had cried. He further infuriated Thatcher by warning against the international arms trade and nuclear rearmament: 'War is a sign of human failure' he declared. Many churchmen opposed the service. Thatcher had alienated another established institution. Runcie was attacked by Conservative backbencher Julian Amery as one of the 'pacifist, liberal, wet establishment'.[43]

Thatcher was determined to cement ties with America, especially when Reagan replaced Democrat Jimmy Carter in 1980. She had more in common with Reagan than with most European leaders, particularly valuing the alliance against the 'Communist menace', which she attacked with a Cold War zeal uncommon at this time even among Conservatives. In return, Soviet propaganda labelled her 'the Iron Lady', to her immense pleasure. Polls in the mid-1980s showed that most respondents feared a third, nuclear world war and were as dubious about the United States as about the USSR. In 1984, 61 per cent agreed with the statement, 'they take a superior attitude towards the British and they have no grounds for this'.[44]

Thatcher's lack of interest in the Commonwealth disturbed Queen Elizabeth. To the queen's fury, she hardly protested in 1983, when, without consulting Britain, the United States invaded Grenada, a Commonwealth country, when left-wingers took power.[45] She was less neglectful of prosperous Hong Kong. This was due to revert to Chinese control in 1997 under the Treaty of Nanking of 1842. She visited Beijing in 1982 hoping Britain could concede sovereignty to China but retain control. China refused and in 1984 she reluctantly agreed to recognize 'one country, two systems', as China phrased it,

41 Vinen, *Thatcher's Britain*, pp. 134–53.
42 See p. 360.
43 Eliza Filby, *God and Mrs Thatcher. The Battle for Britain's Soul* (London: Biteback, 2015), pp. 158–9.
44 Whybrow, *Britain Speaks Out*, pp. 130, 134.
45 Eric J. Evans, *Thatcher and Thatcherism* (London: Routledge, 1997), p. 95.

that different economic systems could co-exist in a single (Chinese) state. China made no commitment to preserve capitalism, still less to promote democracy (not conspicuous under British rule) in Hong Kong, which transferred to Chinese sovereignty in 1997. Beijing's vicious repression of the pro-democracy movement in China in 1989 removed hopes of social and economic freedom in Hong Kong and emigration from the colony accelerated.[46]

Europe

In July 1979, the first elections for the European parliament brought just a 32.7 per cent turnout in the United Kingdom.[47] Tensions with the EC were another theme of Thatcher's premiership. At first Thatcher's attitudes to Europe were unclear even to some of her close advisers. She appeared to support entry under Heath's government, for most of her time as party leader she insisted she was pro-European and favoured economic union and she promoted pro-European ministers, including Douglas Hurd and Kenneth Clarke, though she often disagreed with them. Many EC leaders were certainly too socialistic for her taste. It was in Conservative interests to appear united on Europe when Labour remained split, but it was another issue on which they were increasingly divided.

In its favour, from Thatcher's perspective, the EC was closely allied with the United States and opposed communism, even more important as the Cold War froze deeper when the USSR invaded Afghanistan in 1979. But there were tensions when the EC, including Britain, opposed Reagan's Strategic Defence Initiative, a planned network of space stations and lasers to protect America from nuclear attack in place of long-range nuclear missiles. They feared this would weaken Europe's defences. Thatcher switched sides when British firms gained from supplying the project. In 1980, she bought expensive Trident nuclear missiles from the United States and US Cruise missiles were stationed in Britain, part of a NATO-led deployment of US missiles across Western Europe, not debated in Parliament, arousing fears that the United States planned to fight a nuclear war in Europe, protecting itself.[48] The missiles had destructive power four times greater than the bomb that destroyed Hiroshima. Labour opposed both decisions. CND, which had been dormant since the mid-1960s, leapt from 5,000 members in 1979 to 100,000 in 1985. A vigorous, increasingly publicized women's peace camp was established in 1981 outside the US airbase where the missiles were placed, at Greenham Common in Berkshire. Growing numbers of women (only, potential male

---

46 Ibid., pp. 102–3.
47 Butler and Butler, *Twentieth-Century British Political Facts*, p. 514.
48 Evans, *Thatcher and Thatcherism*, p. 93.

campers were rejected, infuriating some) camped in miserable conditions, repeatedly evicted, suffering violence from police and bailiffs, but carrying on. They chained themselves to fences, invaded the base; in 1982 35,000 women surrounded it. They brought legal cases challenging the legality of the base located on what had been common land until it was appropriated. Supporters came from abroad, including celebrities, including men: Labour politicians Michael Foot and Neil Kinnock as well as John Lennon's widow Yoko Ono, following his murder in 1980. Conservative politicians were less sympathetic. Michael Heseltine, at the Ministry of Defence (MoD), warned that the women might be shot if they invaded the base; he was angrily mobbed when he tried to visit. It was the largest, longest women's demonstration then known, while the women's movement flagged, faced with Thatcher's intransigence. It closed in 1991 when the missiles were removed as the Cold War and relations between East and West began to defrost.

European leaders criticized Britain's relationship with the United States, increasing Thatcher's antagonism. She had no close personal links with Europe, spoke no other languages and was regarded by her foreign secretaries as ignorant of foreign affairs. As in domestic policy she preferred her own way. She mistrusted senior foreign office officials, as civil servants with outmoded ideas, exerting too much power over foreign secretaries and out of touch with Britain's best interests concerning Europe and the rest of the world. Her open resistance began with objections to Britain's contribution to the EC budget, which she believed was disproportionate, especially now that Britain was economically weaker than Germany and France. She negotiated for a rebate, winning support in the tabloid press and with many voters, and in 1980 a reluctant EC agreed rebates of £1,570 million over three years. She wanted more but was persuaded to accept by Carrington who feared harming Britain's relations with other countries.[49]

Labour Divided

The Labour Party did not gain from the government's problems, despite being well ahead in the polls through 1980 and 1981. It was even more divided than before over how to revive the economy and reduce unemployment, about nuclear arms and relations with Europe. The 1980 conference voted to withdraw from the EC and for unilateral nuclear disarmament, but also for multilateral disarmament and against leaving NATO. Many trade unionists, whose block vote dominated conference decisions, opposed the party leadership for their policies in office, but their margins of victory were narrow, suggesting a deeply divided party rather than an ascendant

49 Evans, *Thatcher and Thatcherism*, pp. 79–89; Vinen, *Thatcher's Britain*, pp. 230–48.

left. Callaghan resigned following the conference. In November 1980, Foot defeated Healey for the leadership by just 139 votes to 129, again suggesting a close balance of opinion in the party. Foot was to the left of Healey but not the wild revolutionary portrayed in the right-wing press and was seen in the party as conciliatory, willing to negotiate with all sections, unlike Healey who was not. Benn was a more outspoken supporter of unilateralism, withdrawal from the EC and socialization of the economy, and in 1981 was narrowly beaten by Healey for the deputy leadership. He failed to gain election to the Shadow Cabinet. In both cases the electorate was just MPs; left-wingers campaigned to give votes in these contests to unions and constituency parties. In January 1981, a special conference agreed on an electoral college, allocating votes 40:30:30 to MPs, unions, local parties.

Roy Jenkins had floated the idea of a new centre party in a televised lecture in 1979, to a cool reaction. His term in Brussels ended in January 1981. Within twenty-four hours he, Shirley Williams, David Owen and William Rodgers (the 'Gang of Four' as the media dubbed them) issued the 'Limehouse Declaration' (from Owen's home in Limehouse, east London) declaring the conference decision 'calamitous', demanding 'a new start in British politics'. In March they formed the breakaway Social Democratic Party (SDP). Just ten Labour MPs defected to the SDP, thirty by 1983, out of 269, including George Brown. Leading figures on the parliamentary right wing, including Healey, did not defect. Most did not share the defectors' view that the party had swung far-left with policies inappropriate for the modern world. Rather, they recognized that Labour had always represented a range of views from far-left to centre-left, had regularly experienced left–right tensions when out of office, as in the 1930s and 1950s, but had reconciled and could do so again, as it did. They valued the 'broad church', representative nature of the party, its capacity to adjust to social change and the needs of voters and questioned narrowing its appeal, though party tensions continued. They still believed Labour alone sought to protect working-class interests, still the largest social class,[50] currently seriously threatened, and division would not help them. They also recognized how rarely new parties prospered in the first-past-the-post system.

It is unclear how many party members defected. Individual party membership had fallen from 666,000 in 1979 to 277,000 in 1981, following a steady decline in membership of all parties since the 1950s, but rose to 313,000 in 1985.[51] The SDP allied with the Liberals, agreeing not to oppose each other in elections. In July 1981, Jenkins performed well enough in a by-election in the normally safe Labour seat of Warrington to shock Labour but not to win. In a November by-election, Shirley Williams won

---

50 Geoffrey Evans and James Tilley, *The New Politics of Class. The Political Exclusion of the British Working Class* (Oxford University Press, 2017), p. 7.
51 Butler and Butler, *Twentieth-Century British Political Facts*, p. 159.

the previously safe Conservative seat of Crosby in the Liverpool suburbs.[52] Polls put the Alliance ahead of Conservatives and Labour for some months, assisted by media dramatization of the malign influence of the Labour left, especially Militant, which still sought to radicalize local parties but was small, influential in very few parties and proscribed by the Labour Party in 1982.[53]

The Second Term

Economic growth headed towards a more normal 4 per cent, but unemployment rose to 3.2 million in January 1983. The government preferred to stress falling prices, which affected more people and more potential Conservative voters. They removed mortgage interest payments from official price indices, reducing the apparent inflation level, one of their many manipulations of official statistics. Howe's 1983 Budget increased the mortgage tax relief limit to £30,000 and increased Child Benefit. Following the Falklands victory and the Labour split, Thatcher judged it safe to hold an election in May 1983.

She was helped by Labour's split. Its lengthy manifesto – described as 'the longest suicide note in history' by a shadow minister – was rushed out with too little preparation. It promised to reduce unemployment by increasing public spending, introduce a five-year economic plan, restore trade union powers and promote industrial democracy, re-nationalize privatized industries, increase spending on education and welfare, end gender and race discrimination and withdraw from the EC.[54] Its statement on defence policy, like the conference votes, was confused. The Conservatives were so convinced it would damage Labour that party officials bought and distributed 1,000 copies.[55] Foot did not present a strong leadership image, looking uncomfortable on TV, rambling when interviewed.

Labour slumped to under 28 per cent of votes and 209 seats to the Conservatives' 42.4 per cent and 397 seats. The Alliance gained 25 per cent, the Liberals seventeen seats, Social Democrats six. The Conservatives benefited from the Falklands victory and economic growth, probably still more from the SDP breakaway. Following the split it is unlikely that Labour could have won even with a more effective leader and different manifesto. The Conservative vote fell slightly from 1979, from 13.6 million to 13 million, while the combined Labour/Social Democrat vote rose slightly, but it was split in 311 constituencies, helping the Conservatives win many marginals. Labour lost

52 Thorpe, *History of the British Labour Party*, pp. 206–8.
53 See p. 319.
54 Thorpe, *History of the British Labour Party*, pp 210–13.
55 Vinen, *Thatcher's Britain*, p. 128.

particularly heavily in the southeast while holding on to its heartlands, though winning only 38 per cent of skilled workers, to the Conservatives' 35 per cent.[56] The Scottish and Welsh Nationalists held two seats each. Benn lost his seat in Bristol. Foot and Healey resigned and the electoral college chose Neil Kinnock and Roy Hattersley to replace them, a 'dream ticket' balancing Kinnock's left-wing credentials with Hattersley on the right, their decisive majorities again suggesting a party seeking compromise and unity. Thatcher's self-confidence was reinforced. She eliminated more 'wets' from the Cabinet. Howe moved to the Foreign Office and Lawson to the Treasury.

The 'Enemy Within'

Then came a battle with the miners. Following the 1974 strike, employment relations stabilized around the NCB's Plan for Coal, negotiated with the NUM, committing it to long-term expansion of mining while oil prices soared, including large government subsidies for deep mining and new mines in Yorkshire. By 1980, oil prices had fallen and the Coal Industry Act cut subsidies to force mining to pay its way; pit closures were proposed. Strikes in the areas most affected, especially South Wales, forced the government to back down and maintain subsidies. Thatcher ordered the build-up of coal stocks against future strikes and chose tougher negotiators.

In 1983, Ian McGregor was appointed to chair the NCB. He had halved the British Steel Corporation workforce and was briefed to deal similarly with coal. The NUM had a new, uncompromising, president, Arthur Scargill. In April 1984, he called a strike over pit closures but failed to call a national ballot, relying on each district to do so. Nottinghamshire miners, who were least at risk, continued working. Many other miners were dubious but supported the strike. Other unions were too concerned about their members in precarious times to support them. The government was prepared: substantial coal stocks prevented serious shortages and three-day weeks, and past successful union tactics, especially secondary picketing, were now illegal. Thatcher chaired a Cabinet committee overseeing the strike. £200 million was invested in a mobile police force drawn from forty-three forces. During the strike they made 11,000 arrests while maintaining access to the collieries and were accused of excessive violence, especially when police horses charged pickets at Orgreave, Yorkshire, coking plant in June 1984, where more than 120 pickets and police were injured. Controversy long raged about police culpability. Polls indicated less public support than in 1974 but substantial sympathy. The Labour Party kept its distance. The strike lasted a year until privation drove many miners back to work. The NUM was bankrupted by court rulings against mass picketing. There was no prospect of a negotiated settlement since neither Thatcher nor

56 Thorpe, *History of the British Labour Party*, p. 213.

Scargill would back down. She won. Pit closures accelerated and NUM membership fell from 200,000 in 1984 to 105,000 in 1986, and 53,000 in 1990. By 1994, there were only seventeen deep mines in the county and 11,000 miners.[57]

Another strike followed by another powerful union facing modernization, newspaper printers. It was provoked by Australian newspaper mogul, Rupert Murdoch, who in 1981 added the ailing *Times* to his empire. In 1985, he moved his papers from the traditional home of the national press, Fleet Street, to Wapping in what had been London docklands before their decline, installing computerized printing equipment and threatening to sack all 5,000 employees if they did not adopt the new technology on his terms. The union was heavily fined and capitulated in February 1987, against total intransigence. Faced with such antagonism, plus unemployment, trade union membership fell from its all-time peak of 13.5 million in 1979 to under 9.5 million in 1991, at 34.4 per cent of the labour force the lowest since 1940.[58] Thatcher successfully crippled the 'enemy within', as she called the unions.

Unemployment rose to 3.4 million in 1986, possibly over 4 million following changes to government policies and statistics. It became more difficult to qualify for unemployment benefit and older unemployed people were, when possible, transferred to disability benefit, while official statistics included only those 'unemployed and claiming benefit', as not all unemployed people did. From 1979 to 1996 the basis for calculating unemployment was adjusted thirty-one times, always in a downward direction.[59] The official numbers fell to 1.5 million in June 1990.[60] For those in work, job insecurity grew as protection of less organized workers was dismantled. EC Directives increasing workers' protection were not implemented.

Northern Ireland

The government had more lethal enemies than unions. In October 1984, the IRA bombed the Grand Hotel, Brighton, where Thatcher and her colleagues were staying for the party conference. Five people were killed, including one MP, Sir Anthony Berry, and the wife of another. More than thirty people were injured, including Norman Tebbitt's wife seriously, himself less so. Thatcher narrowly escaped injury. She insisted the conference continue as usual and gave an undaunted speech next day. Five people were found guilty of the bombing and received long sentences. Northern Ireland was still ruled directly from London. Thatcher aspired to stop terrorism, especially following

57 Reid, *United We Stand*, pp. 402–6; Evans, *Thatcher and Thatcherism*, pp. 38–9; Vinen, *Thatcher's Britain*, pp. 154–77.
58 Thorpe, *History of the British Labour Party*, p. 215.
59 Evans, *Thatcher and Thatcherism*, p. 30.
60 Butler and Butler, *Twentieth-Century British Political Facts*, p. 401.

the assassination of her close adviser, Airey Neave, in 1979, then the Brighton bombing, but she proposed no clear way forward and showed little understanding of the province and its problems, while her mainland policies damaged its flagging economy.

The Brighton bombing followed a succession of targeted attacks. In August 1979, the queen's cousin, the last Viceroy of India, 79-year-old Earl Mountbatten, was killed by a bomb on his boat at his holiday home in Co. Sligo, with his daughter, grandson and a young boatman; 113 others died in the Troubles in 1979.[61] Government-initiated talks with political representatives proved fruitless. Unemployment grew as businesses closed. The IRA prisoners' 'dirty protest'[62] transmuted into a hunger strike, ending after fifty-three days when one hunger striker was near death. No concessions followed and it was renewed the following year. In April 1981, the most prominent hunger striker, Bobby Sands, won a Westminster by-election in Fermanagh-South Tyrone, then died on the sixty-sixth day of his strike. This caused Nationalist rioting, intensified when more hunger strikers died. Bombs, shootings and killing of soldiers continued. Prisoners were banned from standing in elections; a Provisional Sinn Féin candidate won the by-election caused by Sands' death. Prior, as Northern Ireland Secretary, allowed prisoners to wear their own clothes, with other improvements. In October, the hunger strikers gave up, under pressure from their families and the Church. Support for the strikes, combined with unemployment, greatest among Catholics, increased Nationalist unity and militancy. Also in October, bombs in London killed three people and injured forty-one others; 101 people died in 1981.[63]

The government then introduced a Bill for another devolved Assembly, arousing little enthusiasm in Northern Ireland or Westminster. In July 1982, eight soldiers were killed and forty-one others injured by IRA bombs in London. Unemployment in Northern Ireland climbed to 22 per cent. The election for the Assembly was held in October, the first contested by Sinn Féin, who won five seats. Its leaders, Gerry Adams and Martin McGuinness, were elected, causing the government some panic. Shootings, bombing and deaths continued.[64] Gerry Adams increased the panic by defeating Gerry Fitt in the Westminster seat of West Belfast in 1983, but would not take his seat in a parliament he refused to recognize. In December a bomb outside Harrods in London killed six people, including three policemen, and injured over ninety.[65]

In September 1984, Douglas Hurd replaced Prior as Northern Ireland Secretary, his punishment for excessive pro-Europeanism. Violence mounted. Following the Brighton bomb, Mrs Thatcher publicly refused all compromise, but negotiations

---

61 Bew and Gillespie, *Northern Ireland*, p. 138.
62 See p. 320.
63 Bew and Gillespie, *Northern Ireland*, p. 161.
64 Ibid., p. 169.
65 Ibid., p. 176.

were in progress with the Irish government, since only compromise with nationalism seemed likely to end the violence. In November 1984, she and the Taoiseach, Garret Fitzgerald, signed an Anglo-Irish Agreement affirming that 'any change in the status of Northern Ireland would only come about with the consent of the majority of the people in Northern Ireland'. For the first time the Irish government was involved in deciding the future of the north. The Unionists thought it a betrayal and in December 1984 all fifteen Unionist MPs resigned to fight by-elections on the issue, including Enoch Powell. As Ulster Unionist MP for South Down since 1974 he wanted permanent rule from Westminster and full integration with the rest of the United Kingdom, opposing any role for the Republic in Northern Ireland affairs.

The by-elections were held in January 1986, under the slogan 'Ulster says No', led by Paisley. The SDLP won one seat, the Unionists held the other fourteen. The Agreement was opposed by Belfast City Council and most councils in Northern Ireland. On 3 March 1986, a Unionist Day of Action, a general strike, closed most businesses and there was rioting in loyalist areas of Belfast. A week later, the US House of Representatives approved a $250 million aid package to Northern Ireland to assist the Agreement. In June, the Assembly was dissolved having achieved little. Violence continued.[66] With unemployment at 23 per cent in September, twice as high among Catholics as Protestants, the British and Irish governments established a fund of £35 million to promote social and economic development. Ninety-five people died in 1987;[67] ninety-four in 1988.[68] So it continued for the remainder of Thatcher's premiership, costly in human life and funds, with no solution in sight.

Closing the GLC

In Great Britain local authorities faced still greater central control. Like the unions, many of them were perceived as socialist enemies of government principles. None more so than the GLC, the largest council in the country, headed from 1981 by Labour's Ken Livingstone. In 1986, it was wound up, with the other seven metropolitan counties, all Labour controlled. Thatcher opposed Livingstone's use of GLC income to regenerate the London economy, reduce transport costs and aid radical groups, including feminist and BME campaigners in the increasingly culturally diverse capital. Livingstone did not help to save the GLC by posting London's rising unemployment figures on large signs outside County Hall, across the river from Parliament, with defiant political slogans. Many GLC powers were taken over by central government, others, including

66 Ibid., p. 204.
67 Ibid., p. 211.
68 Ibid., p. 223.

housing and education, by the London boroughs, others by new semi-independent 'agencies', including the London Regional Transport Authority. All local transport was deregulated by the Transport Act 1985, enabling private companies for the first time to run bus and other public transport routes.[69]

Social Security

The second term also brought more fundamental reforms of social security. Norman Fowler, Minister for Social Security, aspired to what he called its most profound overhaul since Beveridge, aiming to cut costs and simplify a system that had become increasingly complex. Simplification was difficult. Benefits were complex due, not just to bureaucracy as he implied, but to the complexity of many people's lives and incomes, increased by the extension of means-testing. The United Kingdom had one of the most 'targeted', complex social security systems in the world. Fowler's recommendations were embodied in the Social Security Act, 1986. Income Support replaced Supplementary Benefit, introducing new benefit scales applied to all means-tested provision, categorizing claimants into broad types rather than assessing individual needs. The universal Child Benefit was frozen and supplemented by a means-tested Family Credit for low-income families with a parent working up to twenty-four hours per week. Most discretionary Supplementary Benefit payments – for example, for furniture or special dietary needs – were replaced by cash loans from a new, limited Social Fund. The 'poverty trap' became still more severe and more people were excluded due to failure to apply. The numbers in poverty rose also due to unemployment and growing numbers of single-parent families, from about 5 million living below the official poverty line of 60 per cent of average household income in 1980 to over 11 million in 1990[70]; as did social security spending, from £49.9 billion pa to £61.4 billion in real terms from 1979–80 to 1990–1.[71]

The Fowler Review also proposed cutting costs by abolishing Labour's SERPs pension reform[72] and shifting responsibility for pensions to individuals, employers and the private market. This was opposed by the CBI and the pensions industry, which did not want to provide for low-paid people with poor job prospects, while actuaries were rightly concerned that most people lacked the financial skills to choose private pensions and risked unscrupulous mis-selling. Instead SERPS was amended, becoming less generous especially to those with low earnings and interrupted work histories, mostly

---

69 Evans, *Thatcher and Thatcherism*, pp. 58–62; Vinen. *Thatcher's Britain*, p. 125.
70 Martin Evans, 'Social Security. Dismantling the Pyramids?', in H. Glennerster and John Hills (eds), *The State of Welfare. The Economics of Social Spending*, 2nd edn (Oxford University Press, 1998), p. 299.
71 Ibid., p. 270.
72 See p. 322.

women, increasing inequalities in later life. Despite the actuaries' warnings, workers were encouraged with increased tax relief to take out private pensions which were deregulated.[73] At least 400,000 people were sold disadvantageous pensions, often persuaded to leave better public sector schemes, creating a mis-selling scandal reversed, at considerable cost in compensation, by the next Labour government.

Health

In 1982 Thatcher assured the party conference that, 'The National Health Service is safe with us ... The principle that adequate health care should be provided for all regardless of the ability to pay must be the function of any arrangements for financing the NHS. We stand by that'.[74] This followed press reports of her plans to privatize and charge for health and social services, and negative responses. The NHS survived the first term relatively unscathed, but severe inequalities in services and outcomes continued. The committee of medical and social scientists appointed by Labour to investigate these inequalities reported in 1980.[75] The government circulated 260 duplicated (not printed) copies of this very thorough, damning, report, over the August Bank Holiday weekend, with limited press access. It concluded that people on low incomes had poorer health throughout their lives and lower life expectancy than better-off people for reasons connected more with social and economic conditions than with the NHS. The health and life expectancy of men and women in classes I and II had improved in the previous twenty years, while those in classes IV and V had changed little or deteriorated, a difference probably greater than in comparable countries.[76] BME groups had worse health outcomes than British-born white people.[77] Journalists made a furore, but the government refused to act, claiming that the recommendations, for improved health services targeted at deprived people, were too costly.[78]

The 1983 manifesto 'welcome[d] the growth in private health insurance in recent years'. Lawson aspired to privatization of the NHS, but Treasury officials correctly argued that it was cost-effective, comparing well with other countries. Sir Roy Griffiths was imported from Sainsbury's to advise and proposed professional managers to replace medical professionals to increase efficiency. Thatcher was as critical of medical as of all public sector professionals. The Griffiths reforms were introduced from 1983, greatly increasing central supervision and management costs with no obvious increase

---

73 Glennerster, *British Social Policy*, pp. 183–5.

74 Peter Riddell, *The Thatcher Government* (Oxford: Blackwell, 1985), p. 137.

75 See p. 324; Peter Townsend and Nick Davidson (eds), *The Black Report* (London: Pelican, 1982).

76 Ibid., p. 2.

77 Ibid., p. 51.

78 Ibid., pp. 3–4.

in efficiency or quality of services. Prescription, dental and ophthalmic charges rose. Hospital catering and cleaning services were 'outsourced' to private providers and private medical services were encouraged and deregulated; consultants' opportunities for private practice increased and tax exemptions were introduced for employer-provided medical insurance.[79]

The effects of unemployment and the erosion of health and welfare services aroused much concern, including among Anglican clergy encountering poverty in their parishes. In 1981, Robert Runcie appointed a commission which visited more than thirty towns and in 1985 published a highly critical report, *Faith in the City*. It exposed the 'two nations' they found of 'shabby streets, neglected houses, sordid demolition sites of the inner city ... [and the]... busy shopping precincts of mass consumption'. It urged the government to act and the Church established a fund to help the inner cities, improved training for urban clergy and support for Afro-Caribbean Anglicans who were especially deprived. An unknown Cabinet member leaked the report to the press, labelling it 'pure Marxist theology',[80] greatly increasing its public impact. A shortened version sold over 60,000 copies. Runcie had it debated in all parishes. In 1986, the Church's Board for Public Responsibility published *Not Just for the Poor: Christian Perspectives on the Welfare State*, a vindication of Beveridge's principles as fair, humane and closer to Christian ideals than those behind current government policy. The Church forcefully opposed Fowler's Social Security Act, arguing that it reintroduced Victorian notions of 'deserving' and 'undeserving' poor.[81] Thatcher had grown up a Methodist and was now a church-going Anglican, but she believed the clergy shared the narrow-minded traditionalism of all professionals and ignored them.

Secularization?

The archbishop was unusually outspoken as a critic both of the Falklands War and of government social policy. Apart from his personal commitment on these matters, he was perhaps anxious to demonstrate the relevance of the Church to everyday life and its concern about matters of importance to many people in a society that appeared to be increasingly secular. Levels of serious religious belief are always hard to measure, but formal membership of all Christian churches fell in Great Britain – of the Church of England from 2,862,000 in 1960 to 1,540,000 in 1990, the numbers baptised from 631 to 557 per 1,000 population, with similar falls in church attendance – more slowly

---

79 Julian Le Grand and Polly Vizard, 'The National Health Service. Crisis, Change or Continuity?' in H. Glennerster and John Hills (eds.) *The State of Welfare. The Economics of Social Spending*, 2nd edn (Oxford University Press, 1998), pp 78–9.
80 Filby, *God and Mrs Thatcher*, pp. 171–3.
81 Ibid., pp. 174–6.

in Scotland than in England, much more gradually in Northern Ireland where religion dominated politics and culture.[82] Even in Great Britain more people still attended church than took part in most other non-work activities, more women than men: in 1980 women were 55 per cent of churchgoers in England, 62 per cent in Scotland and 63 per cent in Wales.[83] Numbers of observant Jews also fell; numbers of Muslims, Hindus, Sikhs and Buddhists increased with immigration but were modest. Immigrants from Africa and the Caribbean were often Christians, generally more evangelical and fundamentalist than the British. Religious conventions were challenged like all others ever more openly from the 1960s, when the Churches' opposition to legalized abortion and increased tolerance for homosexuals failed. When the NVLA declared, in the name of Christianity, abhorrence of 'the propaganda of disbelief, doubt and dirt … promiscuity, infidelity and drinking' broadcast on the BBC and called on the BBC to 'encourage and sustain faith in God and bring Him back to the heart of our family and national life', they, with other moralists, alienated particularly younger people. Religion was not a powerful force in British life, unlike in Northern Ireland, yet, as Runcie showed, the Churches believed they had a role in modern life and were prepared to speak up and act – including through extensive voluntary humanitarian work at home and abroad – where they thought necessary.

Freeing the Economy

The government pursued privatization ever more determinedly. Until 1983 annual receipts from privatization never exceeded half a billion pounds. After 1983 they were never less than £1 billion pa and peaked in 1988–9 at £7.1 billion.[84] The sale of British Telecom (BT) in 1984 was the turning point. It was a national institution with a place in most British homes in a sector undergoing major technological change, likely to yield substantial future profits. BT shares were sold at a fixed price, set artificially low to yield quick profits for investors who sold on quickly, as many did. These and other privatized stocks were widely publicized to build a market of small capitalists, grateful to the government. In particular, shares in British Gas in 1986 were promoted in a major advertising campaign featuring 'ordinary' people urging others to buy the bargain shares and 'Tell Sid' to do likewise. More than 4 million small investors applied for the shares which were over-subscribed five times. British Airways and the airports were sold in 1987, the electricity companies in 1990. By 1990, forty companies, employing 600,000 people, had been sold. City financiers gained from arranging the sales and buying and

82 Butler and Butler, *Twentieth-Century British Political Facts*, pp. 558–64.
83 John Wolffe, 'Religion and "Secularization"'; Paul Johnson (ed.), *Twentieth-Century Britain. Economic, Social and Cultural Change* (London: Longman, 1994),p. 428.
84 Vinen,*Thatcher's Britain*, p. 197.

selling shares. Seven per cent of British people held shares in 1980, 29 per cent in 1990, though the proportion held by individuals rather than institutions remained lower than in 1950.[85] Many small shareholders sold quickly at a profit; the greatest beneficiaries and biggest shareholders were pension funds.

Privatized companies did not obviously become more efficient to the benefit of consumers. Most became private rather than public monopolies, cutting workforces and raising the salaries of senior management, increasing inequality within the business. The 'rolled back' state did not entirely cast them off. They were subject to new 'arm's length' regulatory offices with modish names – 'Ofgas', 'Oftel' – empowered to regulate prices to reassure consumers.

Finance

The financial sector, above all its apex, the City of London, was increasingly successful and internationalized as regulation declined. Abolition of exchange controls stimulated City investment overseas and the UK investment market became more closely integrated with other countries. Banks and brokers expanded through mergers and takeovers. More foreign banks bought into the City, in particular from the United States, fleeing stricter regulation at home. The established gentleman's club atmosphere of the City changed to a more competitive, profit-seeking culture, with fewer leisurely lunches and longer working hours. Salaries – 'compensation' in less vulgar City terminology – rose fast enough to shock even Thatcher. She told BBC TV in 1985, 'Top salaries in the City fair make one gasp, they are so large'.[86] The average income of directors of Morgan Grenfell investment bank rose from £45,000 in 1979 to £225,000 in 1986, salaries of bankers and brokers in their twenties and thirties from £25,000 to £100,000 pa, while profits boomed.[87] In 1982, it made headlines that a leading Lloyd's underwriter earned over £320,000. The governor of the Bank of England earned £85,000.[88] The beneficiaries were overwhelmingly male in higher status occupations. There were few women above the level of secretary and, despite gradual change, the City was notorious into the twenty-first century for sexual harassment and extreme gender differences in employment and pay.

Financial reform affected the wider population. Hire purchase controls were abolished in 1982, regulation of bank charges for loans was relaxed, leading to increased use of credit cards, first issued in 1962. The number of credit card holders grew between 1980 and 1990 from 11.6 million to 29.8 million.[89] Personal debt rocketed from £7 million

85 Ibid., p. 199; Evans, *Thatcher and Thatcherism*, pp. 34–7.
86 Kynaston, *The City of London*, p. 713.
87 Vinen, *Thatcher's Britain*, p. 183.
88 Kynaston, *The City of London*, p. 713.
89 Filby, *God and Mrs Thatcher*, p. 340.

in 1979 to £52.5 million in 1990,[90] a growing proportion owed by low-income families to new payday loan companies at high interest rates, another sign of growing poverty and inequality.[91] Debt also fuelled consumption among the better off: from 1978–88 households with telephones increased from 62 per cent to 85 per cent, those with central heating from 54 per cent to 77 per cent, more people took package holidays abroad, bought clothes, leisure and household goods. Pension funds profited from high interest rates, encouraging some businesses to raid them to restructure the business, raise salaries or pay shareholders, instead of building the fund for future rainier days. A champagne-quaffing branch of celebrity culture emerged from the huge salaries, cars, yachts and (multiple) homes of financiers and other high-paid businessmen, often primarily resident in low-tax havens like Monaco, to the disadvantage of the UK Treasury. In Britain, deregulation enabled unprecedented tax evasion; partly in consequence one of the fastest growing occupations of the 1980s was accountancy.

The clergy were not the only critics of growing inequality encouraged by financial deregulation. From 1983, 'Stop the City' demonstrations protested at financiers' profits amid unemployment, gained from investing abroad while British industry declined. A merchant banker asked by a journalist why he did not invest in a high unemployment area like Liverpool, replied 'Would you invest there? In a lot of bloody-minded Liverpudlians?'[92] Thatcher commented in 1986, 'On salaries in the City, I am the first to say this does cause me great concern. I understand the resentment …' She failed to understand that 'freeing' the economy could encourage selfish greed as well as the stimulus to hard work to which she aspired. A measure of change was that the real value of the wealth held by the top 1 per cent of wealth-holders in the United Kingdom and the gap between their wealth-holding and that of the remaining 99 per cent narrowed from the Second World War to the late-1970s, then both grew to the end of the century and beyond.[93]

The City revolution culminated in the 'Big Bang' of 1986, a rather over-hyped event that mainly extended changes already in progress. In a court case in 1983, the Office of Fair Trading claimed that Stock Exchange rules embodied unfair restrictive practices. In return for the case being dropped, the Chairman of the Stock Exchange agreed reforms which came into force on 'Big Bang Day', 27 October 1986. The Stock Exchange became a private limited company and share-trading and banking were no longer separated. Trading by the traditional method of shouting out prices on the floor of the Stock Exchange was replaced by computer and telephone dealing, suited

90 Butler and Butler, *Twentieth-Century British Political Facts*, p. 427.
91 Filby, *God and Mrs Thatcher*, p. 342.
92 Kynaston, *The City of London*, p. 718.
93 Anthony B. Atkinson, *Inequality. What Can Be Done?* (Cambridge, MA: Harvard University Press, 2015), pp. 156–7.

to the modern world of globalized trading and technology, essential if London was to remain at the heart of international finance. The change was doubtfully received by the *Financial Times* among others, and their fears were realized as corruption and fraud were revealed. The government reverted to tighter regulation in the Financial Services Act 1987, increasing controls over takeovers among other transactions. But the City remained far less regulated than before; its culture had changed fundamentally, while it boomed. Despite the scandals, the government talked of the UK's economic future based on services, especially financial services, rather than manufacturing.

A feature of the City revolution was profit-seeking company takeovers, one of which shook the government. In 1985, an American company, Sikorsky, bid for the relatively small British firm, Westland Helicopters. Michael Heseltine, Defence Secretary, an independent-minded, pro-European, businessman, the richest man in the Cabinet, who never got on well with Thatcher, opposed American control of a company which did most business with the British government. To Thatcher's displeasure, he organized an alternative bid by a European consortium with British members. What should have been just a business matter divided the government and forced Heseltine's resignation in January 1986, following a leak of confidential material designed to discredit him, with clear collusion from No. 10.[94]

The Third Term

When Lawson replaced Howe at the Treasury in June 1983 he effectively abandoned monetarism, indicators of money supply having proved unreliable. He pursued a largely independent policy, achieving the 'Lawson boom' before the 1987 election. With unemployment declining, Thatcher called an election in June 1987. The Conservatives won twenty fewer seats than in 1983 but gained an overall majority of 101, benefiting again from Labour's split and from a recent redrawing of constituency boundaries. Labour won twenty more seats. The Conservative vote remained 42 per cent, Labour rose to 31 per cent, the Alliance fell to 23 per cent, of which the Social Democrats gained just 9.7 per cent and five seats. Shortly after the election, SDP members voted narrowly to merge with the Liberals, becoming the Liberal Democrat Party in 1989. Again, the Conservatives swept southern England, but in Scotland, still suffering from unemployment and industrial decline, they fell from twenty-one to ten seats, while Labour gained fifty, its highest ever. Thatcher assured the Scottish Conservatives' conference in 1988 that Scotland, in the person of Adam Smith, had 'invented Thatcherism',[95] but this did not turn the tide. In Wales, also suffering high unemployment, the Conservatives

94 Vinen, *Thatcher's Britain*, pp. 183–5, 265–6.
95 Ibid., p. 212.

fell from fourteen seats to eight, the Alliance rose from eight to nine, Labour from twenty to twenty-four. Plaid and the SNP each won three seats. Among skilled workers only 36 per cent voted Labour, 40 per cent Conservative.[96] Some doubted whether Labour would ever be elected again as the manufacturing working class dwindled and Conservatism attracted many survivors.

Before and after the election, Thatcher faced opposition to privatization and cuts to the public sector from her secretaries of state for Scotland, Wales and Northern Ireland due to the negative impact on these countries, all with high proportions of public sector jobs and high unemployment. Another 'wet', Peter Walker, was exiled to Wales. Subsidies to Northern Ireland rose from £100 million in 1972 to £1.6 billion in 1988–9, not including the costs of the army, seeking to soften economic decline and resulting conflict.

Lawson's 1988 Budget cut interest rates to 7.5 per cent, the lowest since 1978, to secure the value of the pound and boost confidence. He announced that the public sector deficit would be repaid for the first time since 1968, due largely to revenue from privatization.[97] He cut income tax again, the basic rate from 27 per cent to 25 per cent and top rate from 60 per cent to 40 per cent, below 50 per cent for the first time since 1945. Those earning median annual male incomes (£12,750) now paid a slightly higher proportion of their income in taxes, rates and National Insurance; those earning five times the average paid 15 per cent less. The budget was criticized for encouraging spending and increasing inflation, which reached 8.3 per cent in January 1989. It stimulated imports, creating a massive balance of payments deficit. Interest rates rose again to 15 per cent in October 1988.[98] House prices fell while mortgage costs rose, causing some to lose their homes.

Europe

Thatcher was increasingly impatient and imperious, more distant from the world beyond her security guards and trusted advisers since the Brighton bombing, with less support in the Cabinet, having alienated Howe and Hurd over Europe. Tebbit withdrew from frontline politics after the bombing, Whitelaw was ageing and sick and left the Cabinet in 1988. Younger men (still no women) were promoted but did not always toe the line, causing much reshuffling. Her attitude to Europe caused growing dissension. In 1988, she successfully negotiated reform of the Common Agricultural Policy; subsidies to over-production were reduced and Britain gained substantial rebates. She

96 David Butler, *British General Elections since 1945* (Oxford: Blackwell, 1989), p. 64.

97 Butler and Butler, *Twentieth-Century British Political Facts*, p. 431.

98 Charmley, *Conservative Politics*, p. 225.

increasingly represented the EC as imposing too much control on sovereign states. This poured out in a speech in Bruges in 1988: 'We have not successfully rolled back the frontiers of the state in Britain, only to see them reimposed at a European level, with a European super-state exercising a new dominance from Brussels'. She attacked attempts to create 'some sort of identikit European personality', but made no clear proposals for change. She agreed to the Single European Act in 1986 because she believed it helped to free the market, but perhaps did not understand its implications, including a range of unpalatable European 'directives' covering reduced working hours, holiday pay, health and safety safeguards, gender and race equality, from some of which Britain negotiated opt-outs. The Bruges speech isolated her further within Europe and intensified division in the party, including the formation of an anti-EC 'Bruges Group', which later became the UK Independence Party (UKIP).[99]

Changes in communist Europe influenced her attitude to Western Europe. In 1984 her aides connected her with Mikhail Gorbachev, one of the younger generation of soviet leaders, to soften tensions. Thatcher decided they 'could do business together', shortly before he became general secretary of the Soviet Communist Party, far more conciliatory than his predecessors. West European unity mattered to her while it helped to contain the threat from the East, less as the threat diminished. She visited Hungary and Poland to build bridges and encourage liberal reform, convinced that something as unnatural as communism could not survive, keen to encourage its opponents. In Poland, she visited the dissidents known as Solidarity in the Gdansk shipyard, trade unionists though they were, and was cheered by the workers. Her Bruges speech stressed that the eastern countries were part of Europe, while insisting on the importance of NATO and nuclear weapons and the association of the EC with the United States.[100]

The fall of the Berlin wall in 1989 heralded the end of communism in Europe. Thatcher wanted to be seen as helping to bring it about, but there were limits to the changes she supported. She strongly opposed German reunification, regarding Germans as innately aggressive and territorial.[101] There was change also in the United States: in 1988 Reagan was replaced by George H. W. Bush, another Republican but less congenial especially when he supported German reunification. She wanted the former communist countries admitted to the EC to counter Germany, which upset the Foreign Office. She disagreed with Howe and Lawson who wanted Britain to join the new EC Exchange Rate Mechanism (ERM), designed to stabilize exchange and interest rates. She reluctantly agreed in October 1990, but too late: Britain joined at too high an

99 Evans, *Thatcher and Thatcherism*, pp. 79–89; Vinen, *Thatcher's Britain*, pp. 238–47.
100 Ibid., pp. 105–7.
101 Ibid., pp. 104–5.

exchange rate and was forced out two years later following a sterling crisis. Howe was removed from the Foreign Office in July 1989 for excessive Europeanism, appointed deputy Prime Minister and replaced by John Major, who had little experience of foreign affairs. In October 1989, Lawson resigned over the ERM and was also replaced by Major; Douglas Hurd took over the Foreign Office. Some suspected she was grooming Major as her successor. Howe resigned in November 1990. He and Lawson made resignation speeches in Parliament calculated to damage Thatcher, Howe uncharacteristically withering in denouncing monetarism and her attitude to Europe, blaming her dithering over the ERM for the high inflation.[102]

Social Policy

In her third term Thatcher was even more determined to shrink the public sector and 'dependence' on the state, sparking opposition including in her party. She told *Woman's Own*, 'I think we've been through a period where too many people have been given to understand that if they have a problem, it's the government's job to cope with it … they're casting their problem on society. And, as you know, *there is no such thing as society*. There are individual men and women, and there are families, and no government can do anything except through people, and people must look to themselves first'.[103] A view that curiously contradicted her determination to encourage voluntary organizations – which above all represented a commitment to help others – to replace state welfare. But the idea soon permeated all areas of social policy.

Education

The government described the Education Reform Act 1988 as 'the most important change in the administration of schools since 1944'.[104] It followed minimal consultation with education professionals, like most of Thatcher's policy initiatives. Again, it increased central control over the professionals, imposing managerial orthodoxies, increasing financial accountability to central government while theoretically extending 'consumer choice' in a 'quasi-free market'.

Schools could opt out of local authority control, with central government funding, if most parents approved. The remaining local authority secondary and larger primary schools would control their own budgets, managed by school governors, now required to include parents, local community representatives and teachers, further reducing

---

102 Vinen, *Thatcher's Britain*, pp. 241–2; Clarke, *Hope and Glory*, pp. 394–5, 398.

103 *Woman's Own*, 31 October 1987.

104 Glennerster, 'Education. Reaping the Harvest?, p. 33.

local authority control. The notoriously progressive Inner London Education Authority (ILEA) was abolished and its powers devolved to London boroughs. The Act introduced Britain's first 'National Curriculum' for 'core' subjects (English, Maths and Science) and 'foundation' subjects (History, Geography, Technology, Music, Art, PE and Modern Languages), specifying curriculum content and attainment targets and tests for children aged 7, 11, 14 and 16. Schools were required to provide religious education 'reflecting Britain's Christian character', while religious diversity grew and church attendance fell. The curriculum was compulsory for state schools, discretionary for private schools, limiting teachers' freedom to shape course content. But it could be drafted only by subject specialists, academic professionals, with whose proposals the premier often disagreed. She complained that those for History 'put an emphasis on interpretation and enquiry as against content and knowledge': insufficient emphasis was given to British history or to history as 'chronological study' providing 'an account of what happened in the past' based on 'knowing dates'.[105] Teachers criticized the constraints, confirming Thatcher's conviction of their inflexible traditionalism. There was more support for a single General Certificate of Secondary Education (GCSE) for 16 year olds, replacing the socially divisive O levels and CSEs. Exam results were published in league tables of school attainment, designed to stimulate school performance through competition, though they did not take account of intake and tended to increase social selection, as better-off parents used them to determine where to live. House prices rose fastest close to schools high in league tables.[106]

As shown in Table 11.1, such dramatic changes were not justified by declining school performance since numbers of well-qualified school-leavers had grown with comprehensivization, nor did they bring a sustained reduction in numbers leaving school without qualifications. Scotland, where the 1988 Act largely did not apply, retained its distinctive educational structure, the national curriculum was not introduced, local authorities retained most of their powers over state education and outcomes continued to improve.[107]

Girls had long shown greater ability than their exam results and employment patterns suggested.[108] Table 11.1 illustrates that, as their opportunities for work and further education expanded, they had incentives to match ability with performance and increasingly outperformed boys. The shift was widely interpreted as a 'problem

105 Thatcher, *Downing St Years*, pp. 595–6, n. 5.

106 Glennerster, 'Education. Reaping the Harvest? pp. 27–74; Evans, *Thatcher and Thatcherism*, pp. 70–4.

107 Smith, 'Schools', pp. 210–11.

108 J. W. B. Douglas, J. M. Ross and H, R, Simpson, *All Our Future. A Longitudinal Study of Secondary Education* (London: Panther, 1971), pp. 42–7; Michele Cohen, 'Knowledge and the Gendered Curriculum. The Problematisation of Girls Achievement', 2004, available at: www.historyandpolicy.org/policy-papers/category/michele-cohen.

Table 11.1 School Leavers Leaving With/Without Qualifications

With at least 5 O levels/GCSEs, England and Wales
1961–2: 10.5%
1970–1: 18.1%
1980–1: 21.8%
1990–1: 32.7%
Without qualifications, England
1980–1: 15% boys, 10% girls
1989–90: 11% boys, 8% girls
1995–6: 11% boys, 8% girls.
Leaving without qualifications, Scotland
1980–1: boys 31%, girls 26%
1988–9: boys 16%, girls 10%
1996–7: boys 7%, girls 5%
17 year olds in full-time education, UK
1965–6: 14.8%
1980–1: 17.8%
1990–1: 25.5%
1996–7: 28.2%

SOURCE : Halsey and Webb, *Twentieth-century British Social Trends*, pp. 212, 211, 210, 195.

of underperformance' by boys, as the previous lesser performance of girls was not. Children from BME backgrounds also performed better than 'white' children, on average, with differences among and within minority groups: girls of black Caribbean origin outperformed boys, children of Pakistani and Bangladeshi origin included some of the best and worst performers, while those of Indian and Chinese origin outperformed all others.[109] There was a certain narrowing of class differences, though poverty was still seriously disadvantageous.[110] Pessimists attributed improved school performance to falling exam standards, without convincing evidence. Comprehensive education had generally improved outcomes,[111] though independent schools, with smaller classes and greater funding outperformed most state schools in exams and university entrance.

Public spending on education fell from 5.2 per cent of GDP in 1979–80 to 4.8 per cent in 1989–90, after rising for three decades, the biggest cut of the century.[112] By 1990, concern had grown about large class sizes, shortages of books and equipment, the declining

---

109 B. Parekh, *The Future of Multi-ethnic Britain* (London: Runnymede Trust, 2000).
110 Glennerster, 'Education. Reaping the Harvest?' pp. 57–63.
111 Ibid., pp. 65–6.
112 Ibid., pp. 36–7. Charmley, *Conservative Politics*, p. 225.

real pay and increased workload of teachers, whose morale sank, like other professionals disparaged by the premier. The annual, independent British Social Attitudes Survey (started 1983) revealed demand to 'increase taxes and spend more on health, education and social benefits' rising from 32 per cent of respondents in 1983 to 58 per cent in 1994, with particular concern about education. Nevertheless, more young people stayed longer at school (rather fewer in England than in Wales and Scotland), probably because the introduction of GCSEs enabled more to gain qualifications, while higher education expanded and the job market contracted especially for the less qualified. The percentage of 18–21 year olds in higher education rose from 12.7 per cent to 20.3 per cent between 1977–8 and 1990–1.[113] Female students increased from 28 per cent to 38 per cent from 1970 to 1980 and were above 50 per cent by the mid-1990s, though courses remained gender segregated, with females still concentrated in the Arts and Social Sciences. The higher social classes were over-represented among male and female students, while BME groups were under-represented. But higher education was also squeezed financially. In 1981, university funding was cut by 18 per cent over three years despite rising student numbers. Class sizes grew and investment in libraries and other facilities fell. Overseas students' fees rose. In 1984, Joseph proposed fees for home students, but withdrew following opposition from Conservative backbenchers, alarmed at the likely reaction of their constituents. In 1988, student grants were reduced and loans introduced, repayable when the graduate's income surpassed 85 per cent of median earnings, further reducing incentives for working-class students to attend university, particularly universities away from home which would increase their costs. The 1988 Education Act transferred university funding to a Universities Funding Council, replacing their previous financial near-autonomy with government control, and shifted polytechnic funding from local authorities to central government. It also abolished secure tenure of university posts from appointment to retirement, another blow to professional security.[114]

Housing

Council housing continued to shrink. The Housing Act 1988 further reduced the role of local authorities, allowing non-profit housing associations and profit-making landlords to take over council housing. Tenants and councils resisted and estates of poorer tenants were unattractive to both sectors, but by 1995 more than fifty councils had transferred their entire housing stock to housing associations, whose share of 'social' housing rose from 5 per cent in 1978 to 19 per cent in 1995,[115] while their government grants

---

113 Halsey, 'Further and Higher Education', p. 239.
114 Glennerster, *British Social Policy*, pp. 47–8.
115 Hill, *The Welfare State*, p. 153.

were cut, leading to higher rents and increased Housing Benefit claims. Supplementary Benefit rent payments of £2.8 billion in 1980–1 rose to £12.2 billion Housing Benefit costs in 1995–6.[116] The 1988 Act abolished rent controls for new private tenants, while landlords received generous tax incentives to expand the private market. The social housing sector was increasingly residualized and stigmatized. Council tenants in the bottom two income quintiles increased from 51 per cent in 1979 to 76 per cent in 1994, with similar proportions among housing association tenants.[117]

Homelessness grew. From 1979 to 1992 households statutorily homeless under the 1977 Act increased from 70,000 to 180,000.[118] Homeless families placed in bed and breakfast accommodation due to lack of council housing grew to 12,000 in 1991, a costly, inadequate solution.[119] Desperate people sleeping on streets were not included in the official homeless figures, which excluded single people. A survey of sleepers on the streets and railway stations of London on a cold night in April 1989 found 789, three times the number detected in December 1965 and a probable underestimate. The April 1991 Census recorded 1,197 rough sleepers in Greater London, 2,852 throughout Great Britain. Shelter estimated over 8,000 in 1993. Thatcher failed to persuade the Charity Commission to withdraw Shelter's charitable status due to its 'political' attacks accusing her housing policies of increasing homelessness.[120] An independent survey in 1981 concluded that rough sleepers were rarely criminals or wasters as was often claimed, but mostly homeless for medical or other reasons beyond their control, such as lack of support after leaving local authority care.[121] Thatcher dismissed the report, but the situation became so desperate that in 1990 the DoE funded the 'Rough Sleepers Initiative' providing hostel places and attempting to improve access for single people to permanent housing, initially only in London, from 1996 in other cities and towns.

Housing suffered most from cuts to social spending, from 3 per cent to 1.8 per cent of GDP between 1980 and 1990,[122] despite the rising cost of Housing Benefit. Council house building in Great Britain collapsed from 146,000 in 1975 to under 2,000 in 1995. Total housing completions were about 200,000 pa from 1980 to 1995, mostly for owner-occupation, while renovation of older properties continued in all sectors and there were fewer severely substandard homes.[123] Between 1971 and 1991, dwellings in the

116 Hills, 'Housing. A Decent Home', p. 134.

117 Ibid., pp. 153–5.

118 Ibid., p. 149.

119 Ibid., p. 151.

120 M. Hilton, J. McKay, N. Crowson and J-F. Mouhot, *The Politics of Expertise. How NGOs Shaped Modern Britain* (Oxford University Press, 2013), p. 199.

121 M. Drake, M. O'Brien and T. Biebuyck, *Single and Homeless* (London: HMSO, 1981), Department of the Environment; Hilton et al., *Politics of Expertise*, pp. 237–8.

122 Hills, 'Housing. A Decent Home', p. 134.

123 Ibid., p. 142.

United Kingdom lacking one or more standard amenities (bath or shower, kitchen sink or washbasin with hot and cold water, indoor WC) fell from 17.4 per cent to 1 per cent. The worst conditions were still in the private rental sector.[124]

Social Services

Labour's guidelines for improved local services were abandoned, council budgets cut, the rate cap restricted spending and central government sought to shift services to the private or non-profit sectors or to families. The Local Government Act, 1988, required local authorities to put most services out to competitive tender, theoretically to increase efficiency and cost-effectiveness, although too often it led to deteriorating services and rising costs.[125] Disabled activists campaigned all the more for improved support. In 1981 Disabled Peoples International was formed, then in 1985 Voluntary Organizations for Anti-Discrimination, coordinating UK disability charities, later renamed Rights Now! The Disabled Persons (Services, Consultation and Representation) Act, 1986, required councils to assess the needs of all disabled people requesting services and to provide help in accessing telephone, TV, radio, libraries, holidays, recreation, education, transport to and from services and occupational, cultural and social facilities. It defined as disabled, people who were 'blind, deaf or dumb or who suffer from a mental disorder of any description or who are substantially and permanently handicapped by their illness, injury or congenital deformity'. Cuts hampered implementation, while demand grew as the population aged and higher living standards and improved medical care enabled disabled people to live longer.[126]

Voluntary organizations still provided essential services, under growing pressure from government and subsidized to replace public services. Aware of their limited resources and fearing dependence on government funds and the controls attached, they often felt they had little alternative in the interests of people in need. In reality, most care was provided by families and neighbours. The Office of Population Census and Surveys (OPCS) reported in 1992 that 16 per cent of British adults had caring responsibilities for disabled or frail people, often at considerable personal cost. Few could do more without expert support, which dwindled, but it was widely, mistakenly, believed, including by some government representatives, that families neglected needy relatives, compared with some mythical past time, and that family care should be enforced.[127]

---

124 Ibid. pp. 147–9; Holmans, 'Housing', p. 479.
125 Maria Evandrou and Jane Falkingham, 'The Personal Social Services', in H. Glennerster and John Hills (eds), *The State of Welfare. The Economics of Social Spending*, 2nd edn (Oxford University Press, 1998), pp. 189–256.
126 Gareth Millward, 'Invalid Definitions, Invalid Responses. Disability and the Welfare State, 1965–1995', PhD thesis, London School of Hygiene and Tropical Medicine, 2013.
127 Evandrou and Falkingham, 'Personal Social Services', pp. 200, 242–5; Thane, *Old Age in English Society*, pp. 428–35.

Public spending on social services rose, while service users paid more.[128] From 1948 local authorities could charge for residential care at their discretion. From 1983 they were obliged to do so, according to ability to pay, also for home-care, including home helps and meals-on-wheels, at discretionary, highly variable, rates. In 1995, a meal cost £1.65 in Kent, 35p in Derbyshire.[129] The uncertain boundary between free healthcare and chargeable social care remained deeply problematic. The extent and standard of residential and community services declined. Numbers of older and disabled people in local authority institutions fell following cuts to local funding, while those in voluntary and, especially, profit-making institutions grew. Fees rose in the latter and the cost of social security funding for residential care for those unable to pay rose from £10 million to £2,072 million pa between 1979 and 1991.[130] In 1990, responsibility for funding was largely shifted from Income Support to local authorities to reduce central costs, another charge on their shrinking budgets, causing further cuts to home services. There was growing concern at the low pay of home care providers, affecting the quality and skills of recruits.

Health

The 1987 manifesto promised to 'improve' the NHS. The third term began with protests by NHS staff about cuts. Waiting times for treatment grew, with outcomes highlighted by the press and arousing complaints in the Commons. Thatcher established and chaired a ministerial committee to review NHS finances. She believed, she wrote later, that 'the NHS had become a bottomless financial pit',[131] but had no clear solutions other than, as ever, to extend business practices and discipline the professionals. She leaned strongly towards private health insurance, but the Treasury still believed that it created costlier healthcare, citing the US example. Private medical insurance policies in the United Kingdom rose from 1.3 million in 1979 to 3.3 million in 1990, encouraged by tax incentives, but still arousing little interest.

Thatcher introduced the White Paper, *Working for Patients* (1989), pledging the NHS to 'continue to be available to all, regardless of income … financed out of general taxation'.[132] It proposed radical changes, modified after strong opposition from the BMA, then incorporated in the Health Service and Community Care Act, 1990. Under a new 'internal market', hospitals became independent 'trusts', non-profit organizations, within the NHS but with greater freedom over pay and service delivery. They could

---

128 Ibid., pp. 203–4.
129 Ibid., p. 208.
130 Glennerster, *British Social Policy*, p. 209.
131 Thatcher, *Downing St Years*, p. 608.
132 Le Grand and Vizard, 'The National Health Service', p. 80.

contract with district health authorities, GP practices or private providers to deliver services. They were encouraged to seek 'efficiency savings', as cuts were described. GPs received spending limits, forcing them to prescribe cheaper drugs when possible. More managers and administrators were required; their salaries cost £158.8 million in 1990, £609.6 million by 1994.[133]

Greater local inequalities in treatment, outcomes and funds followed. By 1996, thirty-four NHS trusts were in deficit and there were fewer NHS beds.[134] Hospital-acquired infections, previously rare, became a serious problem as hygiene deteriorated when cleaning and other services were 'outsourced' to private companies. Opposition grew. Ambulance crews struck for higher pay, the first strike for years to win wide popular support, especially when the new Minister of Health, Kenneth Clarke, described them as 'glorified taxi drivers'. Spending on older patients and mental illness fell, while life expectancy rose and mental illness did not decline.[135] Dental charges rose to a point where fewer dentists thought NHS practice worthwhile and NHS provision shrank. Prescription charges rose from 20p per item in 1979 to £5.65 in 1997, though the proportion of free prescriptions for pensioners, children and people on benefits rose from 65 per cent to 84 per cent, so they raised little revenue.[136] Social Attitudes Survey respondents giving health as the highest priority for government spending rose from 36.7 per cent in 1983 to 60.7 per cent in 1989, surpassing any other item, reinforcing evidence of the strong popular commitment to the NHS since its foundation.[137]

An Ageing Population

The birth rate remained historically low. More people lived longer and the over-60s increased from 17 per cent of the UK population in 1960 to 20.7 per cent in 1990. In 1981, average male life expectancy at birth was 71, at age 65 it was 78. Women could still expect longer lives, at birth to 77, at 65 to 82. More people remained healthy longer: men aged 65 to age 75, on average, women to age 77.[138] The averages, as ever, masked major inequalities: the poorest died on average 10–15 years earlier than the richest and experienced poorer health. Through the 1980s inequality between rich and poor increased among older and younger people, with women in all age groups still more at

133 Glennerster, *British Social Policy*, pp. 203–8.

134 Evans, *Thatcher and Thatcherism*, pp. 68–9.

135 Le Grand and Vizard, 'The National Health Service', p. 91.

136 Ibid.

137 Social and Community Planning Research (SCPR), *British Social Attitudes. Cumulative Sourcebook: The First Six Surveys* (London: Gower, 1992), F11.

138 ONS, p. 3, *Statistical Bulletin. Older People's Day*, 30 September 2010, available on-line at: www.ons.gov.uk/ons/rel/mortality-ageing/focus-on-older-people/older-people-s-day-2011/index.html, last accessed 22 November 2017.

risk of poverty than men. Older workers were especially vulnerable to unemployment. Employment among men aged 50–64 fell from 88 per cent in 1973 to 63 per cent in 1995. They suffered especially from the decline of manufacturing; once unemployed they were unlikely to work again. Also, more senior managers retired early with generous pensions as businesses cut their costs, taking advantage of surpluses in their pension funds due to high interest rates.

The international improvement in life expectancy and health in higher income countries followed unprecedented improvements in living standards, diet and health care. But, as in the 1930s,[139] the dominant response was panic about the growing 'burden' of ageing populations requiring healthcare and pensions funded by a shrinking younger generation. The fears were, again, reinforced, by assumptions that low birth rates and lengthening lives were now permanent features of modern societies. In reality, the healthcare costs of older people were relatively high mainly because younger people suffered serious illness or death much less than ever before, and the rising costs of healthcare owed more to the costs of drugs, technology and salaries than to the ageing population.[140] As older people stayed fit to later ages they made major contributions to the care of family, friends, neighbours and others, much needed as services declined, at substantial savings to the public purse, while contributing more to the economy through taxes and spending than they received.[141] This was rarely noticed and the 'burden' of ageing was invoked by government to justify cutting the real value of pensions and the costs of healthcare. In response, older people, like other excluded groups, became more assertive, campaigning against inequality, inadequate pensions and discrimination, including the formation in 1988 of the Campaign against Age Discrimination in Employment.

Changing Families

Thatcher was convinced that 'the family' was declining, undermined by the welfare state, 'permissiveness' and general moral deterioration. In 1982, a Cabinet Family Policy Group was appointed 'to identify characteristics of behaviour and attitude which the government might legitimately hope to see adults possess, or, conversely, avoid'.[142] A leaked paper suggested that this might include 'what more could be done to encourage families, in the widest sense, to assume responsibilities taken on by the state, for example responsibility for the disabled, the elderly, unemployed 16 year olds'. It asked 'Do

139 See pp. 136–7.
140 J. Gill and D. Taylor, *Active Ageing. Live Longer and Prosper* (London: UCL School of Pharmacy, 2012).
141 Women's Royal Voluntary Service, 'Gold Age Pensioners. Contribution Outweighs Cost by £40 billion', 2011, available at: www.goldagepensioners.com.
142 Holden, *Makers and Manners*, p. 227.

present policies for supporting single parents strike the right balance between insuring adequate child support to prevent poverty and encouraging sensible and self-reliant behaviour by adults'.[143] Thatcher later recalled:

> There was great pressure, which I had to fight hard to resist, to provide tax reliefs or subsidies for child care. This would, of course, have swung the emphasis further towards discouraging women from staying at home. I believed that it was possible – as I had – to bring up a family while working, as long as one was willing to make a great effort to organize one's time properly and with some extra help. But I did not believe that it was fair to those mothers who chose to stay at home and bring up their families on the one income to give tax reliefs to those who went out to work and had two incomes.[144]

Of course, her husband was a millionaire, better able to afford 'some extra help' than most families.

Support for families declined. From 1980 councils were no longer required to provide school meals. In 1986, benefits were reduced for 18–25 year olds, on the assumption, often mistaken especially about the poorest, that they had families able to support them. In 1988, Income Support was withdrawn from 16–18 year olds and Child Benefit from those not in full-time education or training. Student loans and withdrawal of students' right to claim benefits during vacations increased their dependence on their families or part-time work. Many families could not afford to support their children unaided, and young people in care, without family support, ceased to be the responsibility of local authorities at age 16. Yet Thatcher became:

> Increasingly concerned ... that ... we could only get to the roots of crime and much else besides by concentrating on strengthening the traditional family. All the evidence – statistical and anecdotal – pointed to the breakdown of families as the starting point for a range of social ills ... The most important, and most difficult, aspect of what needed to be done was to reduce the positive incentives to irresponsible conduct.[145]

There was no such evidence. Research indicated that the major cause of problems among younger, and older, people, including 'family breakdown', was poverty. She blamed Labour, the 'prophets of the permissive society ... who robbed a generation of their birth-right ... where did the hooligans, the louts and the yobs on the late night trains learn their contempt for the security of the law-abiding citizen?'[146] As though 'hooligans' etc. were unknown before the 1960s.

Polls suggested that most British people were more optimistic. In 1984, Gallup repeated questions from 1948 to assess how society had changed. The responses challenged narratives of past more cohesive communities and social decline. Eighty-four per cent thought their neighbours 'mainly pleasant', compared with 68 per cent in 1948.

143 Ibid., p. 227.
144 Thatcher, *Downing St Years*, pp. 630–1.
145 Ibid., p. 628.
146 Holden, *Makers and Manners*, p. 264.

They were more likely to invite neighbours to their homes, lend them things, look after their children.[147] Only 21 per cent ascribed poverty to lack of effort, compared with 33 per cent in 1977. Thirty-two per cent thought unemployment benefits were too high, discouraging work, but 41 per cent thought them too low, causing hardship.[148] The British Social Attitudes survey found high levels of contact and mutual support within families and changing expectations of gender roles. In 1984, 43 per cent of respondents agreed that 'A husband's job is to earn the money; a wife's job is to look after the home and family'. By 1989 only 25 per cent agreed.[149]

Despite much government rhetoric about 'preserving' the family, never had families changed so much, so fast or so many unconventional families lived openly together, including gay couples, some with children.[150] Births outside marriage rose from 11.5 per cent of all UK births in 1980 to 28 per cent in 1990 and 33.6 per cent in 1995. In 1995, 78 per cent were registered by both parents, often living together. In 1980 there were 940,000 single-parent families, one in eight families with 1.5 million children, rising to 1.3 million single-parent families, one in five families with 2.1 million children in 1992, overwhelmingly headed by mothers, 60 per cent divorced or separated, 33 per cent never married, 7 per cent widowed. Sixty-six per cent received Income Support. They clustered in poorer districts.

In 1983, leaked government papers described supporting one-parent families as 'subsidizing illegitimacy and immorality'. In 1988, Nigel Lawson claimed that the benefit system encouraged family break-up and Thatcher referred to the 'growing problem of young girls who deliberately become pregnant in order to jump the housing queue and gain welfare payments'.[151] This accusation was beloved of the tabloids, though all research dismissed it.[152] More single mothers indeed now had council homes, but only because this had been almost impossible before the 1977 Housing Act which obliged local authorities to house them if they were otherwise homeless.[153] Few were teenagers. Teenage pregnancy fell slightly through the 1980s, though it was higher in the United Kingdom than elsewhere in Western Europe. Any woman convinced by the rhetoric and desperate enough to become pregnant to get a council home was likely to be disappointed. As the council housing stock shrank she would be allocated, at best, a

---

147 Whybrow, *Britain Speaks Out*, pp. 135–7.
148 Ibid., p. 138.
149 SCPR, *British Social Attitudes. Cumulative Sourcebook*, tables N1-16–25, N2-2.
150 Jeffrey Weeks, Brian Heaphy and Catherine Donovan, 'Families of Choice. Autonomy and Mutuality in Non-heterosexual Relationships', in S McRae (ed.), *Changing Britain. Families and Households in the 1990s* (Oxford University Press, 1999), pp. 297–316.
151 Quoted in Hilary Macaskill, *From the Workhouse to the Workplace. 75 Years of One-parent Family Life, 1918–1939* (London: NCOPF, 1993), p. 45.
152 Thane and Evans, *Sinners?* p. 172.
153 See p. 324.

substandard dwelling, sometimes a bed and breakfast room, with some sad outcomes, including

> Fatima Ali [who] cares for her seven year-old child on her own. She lived in a ground floor council flat, and was subjected to severe racial harassment. The flat was burgled six times, windows were broken and excrement and rubbish were pushed through her letter-box.[154]

Disadvantage deepened by racism. Shortage of affordable childcare made it hard for many single mothers to work. If they did, they were often low-paid, while social security reforms reduced their incomes.

Thatcher was convinced that 'feckless fathers' caused the poverty of many single-parent families, contrary to the common tendency to blame the mother. She later wrote that she 'was appalled by the way in which men fathered a child and then absconded, leaving the single mothers – and the taxpayer – to foot the bill for their irresponsibility'.[155] In the late 1980s only one in three lone mothers received regular maintenance from the fathers. Not all non-payers were 'feckless' but were unemployed, very young, low-paid or had a second family. Social security policy had long assumed that a father's primary responsibility was to the family with whom he lived. Thatcher vowed to make fathers responsible for all their children, partly in the improbable hope of dissuading them from forming new families they could not afford. The outcome was the Child Support Act 1991, drafted in a hurry with little research or consultation and rushed through Parliament under pressure from Thatcher before she lost office in 1990, assisted by Treasury officials keen to cut the benefits bill.[156]

It established the new principle that the needs of first families took priority over second even when the father lived with the latter. Officials could initiate maintenance procedures even if claimants wanted no contact with the father, often due to domestic violence. Refusal to name the father 'without good cause' could lead to benefit reduction of up to 40 per cent. 'Good cause' was initially defined as the child having been conceived due to rape or incest, despite evidence that one in six divorced and one in ten single or separated women gave domestic violence as the cause of separation. This was rejected in the Lords then amended in the Commons to allow that 'risk to her or any child living with her suffering harm or undue distress' must be considered. The Act was implemented in 1993, after Thatcher left office. It proved costly and inefficient.[157]

154 Thane and Evans, *Sinners?* p. 173.
155 Thatcher, *Downing St Years*, p. 630.
156 Mavis MacLean, with Jacek Kurzewski, *Making Family Law. A Socio-legal Account of Legislative Process in England and Wales* (Oxford: Hart, 2011).
157 See p. 408.

In a rare piece of good news for some one-parent families, the Family Law Reform Act 1987 at last removed the historic distinction between 'legitimate' and 'illegitimate' children, eliminating the words from legal language. The separate affiliation procedure for unmarried parents was abolished; unmarried fathers gained rights to custody, after court scrutiny for fear of advantaging violent fathers. Children of unmarried parents gained rights of inheritance from both parents, though the Lords drew the line at their inheriting peerages. The Law Commission recommended the changes partly because UK law was out of line with European conventions.[158]

Crime

Recorded crime grew in the 1980s, though there was no evidence that 'broken' families were a cause. In 1979, Thatcher promised more funds for 'law and order'.[159] Public spending rose, almost 10,000 more police were appointed and their pay rose. 'Short, sharp shock treatment' was introduced for young offenders in detention centres and a major prison-building programme begun. Recorded offences in Great Britain rose from about 2.5 million to 4.5 million from 1979 to 1990, particularly vehicle theft, vandalism and burglary. As ever it was difficult to assess to what extent this was due to changes in the law or in police practices, but criminologists stressed the impact of deteriorating social conditions, including youth unemployment, and the temptingly larger numbers of cars and consumer goods.[160] Thatcher was unconvinced by such professional judgements, especially from what she assumed were left-wing sources, believing crime to be a moral not a social issue, blaming declining authority in homes, schools and churches.

Social Movements

In addition to Greenham Common, activists continued to demand more equalities in new, often less public, ways. Refuges and helplines continued, often supported by Labour-controlled councils. Gay activism revived as HIV-AIDS emerged as a serious crisis. The first death in Britain occurred in July 1982 – the Terence Higgins Trust was founded in his name to support other victims. Three more were known to have died by 1983, and what the tabloids described as a 'gay plague' unleashed panic-stricken homophobia. Gay men were portrayed not as innocent victims of a new disease but as deviants spreading fatal illness through their disgusting practices. A *Times* editorial claimed:

---

158 Cretney, *Family Law*, pp. 563–5.
159 Evans, *Thatcher and Thatcherism*, p. 75.
160 Ibid., p. 76.

> The infection's origins and means of propagation excites repugnance, moral and physical, at promiscuous male homosexuality – conduct which, tolerable in private circumstances, has with the advent of 'gay liberation' become advertised, even glorified as acceptable public conduct, even a proud badge for public men to wear. Many members of the public are tempted to see in Aids some sort of retribution for a questionable style of life but Aids of course is a danger not only to the promiscuous nor only to homosexuals.[161]

AIDS unified a renewed movement. More self-help and support groups were established. Deaths rose to around 1,000 per year by the early 1990s. Partners of victims suffered the additional trauma of lacking legal rights even to visit the sick person in hospital, stimulating calls for formal partnership rights for gay couples.

The DHSS and Chief Medical Officer recommended leaflets and advertisements advising on safe sex, but Thatcher was reluctant. By late 1986, heterosexuals were diagnosed and panic multiplied. An unprecedented £20-million health education campaign followed. Press, radio and TV advertising proclaimed 'Don't Die of Ignorance' and leaflets were delivered to 23 million homes. Thatcher cut the campaign when no heterosexual AIDS epidemic materialized. Nevertheless, it dispelled misapprehensions, encouraged safe sex and minimized harm to drug users.[162] Gay organizations, including the Higgins Trust, played a major role in promoting safe sex, urging gay men not to donate blood and dispelling false rumours, including that AIDS could be spread via public lavatory seats.

Homophobia was rampant when gay activist Peter Tatchell stood as Labour candidate in a by-election in Bermondsey, central London, in 1983. The normally safe Labour seat was won by Liberal Simon Hughes, another unmarried man who was, *The Times* reported, 'mercifully' free of homosexual smears,[163] though some blamed Tatchell's left-wing views rather than his sexuality for the outcome.[164] To combat prejudice and discrimination, some Labour-controlled London boroughs and the ILEA promoted positive images of gays through sex education in schools, which were publicized and often caricatured in the media and opposed by morality groups (Mrs Whitehouse was still active). Sex education was not compulsory and pressure grew in the Conservative Party to allow parents to withdraw their children.

The 1987 Conservative manifesto announced it would 'clamp down' on 'sexual propaganda' in schools.[165] In her post-election conference speech, Thatcher attacked 'positive images', claiming that 'children who need to be taught traditional moral values are being taught that they have an inalienable right to be gay'.[166] Section 28 of the Local

---

161 *The Times*, 21 November 1984.

162 V. Berridge, 'Crisis? What Crisis?' *Health Service Journal*, 8 August 1996, pp. 20–1.

163 'Unlikely Local Boy Makes Good', *The Times*, 23 February 1983.

164 Thorpe, *History of the British Labour Party*, p. 210.

165 Holden, *Makers and Manners*, p. 252.

166 Ibid.

Government Act 1988 forbade local authorities to 'intentionally promote homosexuality or publish material with the intention of promoting homosexuality' or 'promote the teaching in any maintained school of the acceptability of homosexuality as a pretended family relationship'. As it went through Parliament opposition mobilized: three women abseiled into the Lords, then invaded the BBC newsroom in protest, 15,000 people demonstrated in Manchester and 40,000 joined a Gay Pride march.[167] Section 28, like AIDS, stimulated gay and lesbian organization. Stonewall was founded in 1988 to lobby against it, for equalizing the age of consent, gay adoption and parenting, and partnership recognition. In January 1989 the AIDs Coalition to Unleash Power (ACT-UP) was formed to protest against health authorities denying treatment to infected people.[168] OutRage, was formed in May 1990 by Peter Tatchell and others, following the homophobic murder of actor Michael Boothe, specializing in public events designed to arouse the tabloids, including a kiss-in in Piccadilly Circus.

Section 28 was never enforced, but councils and schools became cautious about library holdings and sex education. Gay rights campaigners believed it intensified police activity which had grown since the advent of AIDS: arrests of gay men for offences such as cottaging and procuring reached record levels in the late 1980s.[169] Yet the Social Attitudes Survey found homophobia was slowly declining. In 1983, 41 per cent of respondents thought homosexual schoolteachers were acceptable and 53.3 per cent would allow gays 'to hold a responsible position in public life'; in 1989, the numbers had risen to 45.1 per cent and 58.1 per cent, respectively. In 1985, 13.2 per cent thought lesbians should be allowed to adopt children, 5.6 per cent that gay men should, by 1989 this had risen to 17.9 per cent and 9.7 per cent, respectively. In 1987, 57.2 per cent 'agreed or agreed strongly' that 'most people with AIDs have only themselves to blame'; in 1989, 55.1 per cent. But in 1983, 49.6 per cent thought 'sexual relations between two adults of the same sex' was 'always wrong'; in 1990 it was 55.5 per cent.[170]

Women

Gender equality also progressed slowly. The EOC, firmly led, with closer relations with trade unions and support from the EC, became more effective. Thatcher's enthusiasm for the EC was not enhanced when in 1983 she was forced by a decision in the ECtHR to revise the Equal Pay Act to replace equal pay for 'like work' with 'work of comparable value'. It followed a successful case brought by women cooks at a Merseyside

167 Mel Porter, 'Gender Identity and Sexual Orientation', in Pat Thane (ed.), *Unequal Britain. Equalities in Britain since 1945* (London: Bloomsbury, 2010), pp. 153–4.
168 Nehring, 'The Growth of Social Movements', p. 394.
169 Holden, *Makers and Manners*, p. 256.
170 SCPR, *British Social Attitudes*, tables M-1, 3–7.

shipbuilding firm, aided by the EOC, arguing that their work was comparable with that of male painters, joiners and engineers employed by the company and should be paid equally. Another ECtHR ruling in 1983 judged unlawful Britain's exemption from the Equal Treatment Directive of people employed in private households and businesses with fewer than five employees. The Sex Discrimination Act 1986 outlawed discrimination in collective bargaining agreements and extended anti-discrimination law to small businesses.

Since the 1970s the EOC had queried the gendered nature of the tax system. The incomes of married couples were aggregated for tax purposes even if both were earning. Husbands (only) received marriage allowances, hence more net pay per pound earned than wives, undermining the principle of equal pay. After long discussion and pressure from the EC, in 1989 a 'married couple's allowance' was introduced which either partner might claim,or they could opt for separate assessment. This later became automatic and husbands and wives were treated as separate individuals for tax purposes. The change also enabled better-off couples to place unearned income, for example from investments, in the name of the lower earner, normally the wife, reducing tax liability.

Feminist activists engaged more in formal politics, local and national, and in unions, as potentially more effective than public campaigns for challenging a hostile government. In Scotland nationalism revived in opposition especially to welfare cuts and privatization and the erosion of local government, and Scottish feminists campaigned for gender equality in local government employment, for consultation with women about housing, education, childcare and leisure services, and support for women's organizations. Women became active in the growing movement for devolution, determined to be fully represented in any elected Scottish government.[171] More slowly, similar movements emerged in Wales where the 1970s women's movement was weaker.[172]

Environmentalism continued to grow as knowledge increased about damage to the environment from pollution and climate change and its potential impact upon health, poverty in disadvantaged countries due to drought, and famine and economic damage in richer ones. Concern about pollution from all energy sources, particularly nuclear energy which was increasingly promoted, multiplied in 1986 following an explosion in a nuclear reactor in Chernobyl, Ukraine. It released 400 times more radioactive material than the Hiroshima bomb, made 100,000 km of land uninhabitable and spread

171 E. Breitenbach and F. Mackay, 'Feminist Politics in Scotland from the 1970s–2000s. Engaging with the Changing State', in Esther Breitenbach and Pat Thane (eds). *Women and Citizenship in Britain and Ireland in the Twentieth Century* (London: Bloomsbury, 2010), pp. 157–9.

172 P. Chaney. 'Devolution, Citizenship and Women's Political Representation in Wales'. Esther Breitenbach and Pat Thane (eds). *Women and Citizenship in Britain and Ireland in the Twentieth Century* (London: Bloomsbury, 2010), pp. 189–208.

detectable contamination through much of Europe, affecting the health of at least 1 million people. Membership of Friends of the Earth increased from about 18, 000 in 1981 to 190,000 in 1990, and that of the RSPB from 441,000 in 1981 to 852,000 in 1991. Meanwhile, denial of climate change as a left-wing fantasy emerged, encouraged by the Reagan Administration and the oil industry.

Race

1981 brought riots in deprived inner city areas, Toxteth in Liverpool, Brixton in London, later in parts of Bristol and Birmingham, partly responses to racism and aggressive policing, including increasingly stopping and searching young black men, disproportionately, under the 'Sus' law, police power under the Vagrancy Act 1824 to stop and search people suspected of intending to commit crime. The riots were also provoked by unemployment and poverty; members of BME groups were twice as likely to be unemployed as white people. Police forces were overstretched and unable to cope. An investigation by Lord Justice Scarman recommended action to alleviate inner-city crime and racial disadvantage. His report acknowledged widespread discrimination and inequality, but denied accusations that 'institutional racism' pervaded the police, recommending recruiting more police from ethnic minorities. Partial implementation of the report did not prevent further outbreaks challenging police behaviour, most seriously in Tottenham, north London, in 1985, where a policeman was killed. This led to substantial investment in the area and improved relations between police and the community.

Immigration declined. The British Nationality Act 1981 further restricted the rights of Commonwealth citizens to British nationality, which was effectively restricted to those with a British-born grandparent, while high unemployment made the United Kingdom less attractive. Anti-racist groups remained active. BME activism in formal politics increased, mainly for Labour. By the mid-1980s Bernie Grant (Tottenham), Linda Bellos (Lambeth) and Merle Amory (Brent), all of Afro-Caribbean origin, led Labour-controlled London councils. Four black MPs were elected for Labour in 1987, including Bernie Grant. In 1992, the first Asian Conservative MP was elected.[173]

Gypsies and Travellers were still profoundly excluded, though they gained from Labour's reforms.[174] Settled sites grew, but mainly for permanent settlement which not all Travellers wanted. They improved access to education, health and welfare services, but there was no security of tenure and there were tensions with local

173 Kimber, 'Race and Equality', pp. 38–40.
174 See p. 342.

residents and police harassment continued. By 1985, of the estimated 9,900 Gypsy and Traveller caravans in England, 4,600 were on local authority sites, 1,900 on private sites and 3,400 on unauthorized sites. Gypsies and Travellers challenged inequalities and evictions in court. In 1986, West Glamorgan County Council's eviction of an illegally camped group was quashed in court because the council provided no sites. The 1989 Local Government and Housing Act ring-fenced grants for sites but problems continued.[175]

Downfall

Cuts to public services, especially the NHS, and continuing economic problems increased opposition to Thatcher in the country and her party. Then came the 'poll tax', a fundamental reform of local taxation, another blow to local government. A persistent source of frustration for a government seeking to control local authorities was their capacity to raise local rates to spend as they wished. For centuries rates had been fixed according to the valuation of each property. Thatcher first capped rate income, then determined to abolish the councils' remaining income-raising powers. Supporters argued that it was unfair that a stereotypical old lady living alone in a property paid the same rates as a family in a similar property with two or more earners. Rates were abolished and replaced by a 'community charge', a regressive, flat-rate tax on all individuals living in a local authority area regardless of income or assets. It was dubbed a 'poll tax' by its many opponents, causing riots and large demonstrations.

It passed through Parliament, with significant Conservative as well as Labour opposition, in 1987. It was not implemented in Northern Ireland, where there were troubles enough. In Scotland, it was introduced in April 1989, a year earlier than in England and Wales, and was strongly opposed. When Thatcher attended the Scottish Cup final in Glasgow in 1988 – surely more a sign of her need to woo the Scots than of passion for football – fans waved red cards, to 'send her off'. It was evaded throughout Britain as rates had rarely been. People who refused to pay were imprisoned, though often released on appeal. It was opposed by many Conservative voters, complaining, among other things, about varying tax levels in different areas and because, for many people, it increased their tax liability at a time of rising prices and financial pressure.[176]

Thatcher sank in the polls: Gallup recorded 43.8 per cent approval ratings in January 1989, 21.6 per cent in March 1990.[177] Further Irish bombing made things

175 Porter and Taylor, 'Gypsies and Travellers', pp. 85–8.
176 Evans, *Thatcher and Thatcherism*, pp. 62–4; Vinen, *Thatcher's Britain*, pp. 261–3.
177 Butler and Butler, *Twentieth-Century British Political Facts*, pp. 276–7.

worse, including the murder in July 1990 of another trusted adviser, Ian Gow, by a bomb planted under his car. So did the resignation of Lawson, then Howe, from the Cabinet and their obvious disaffection. Michael Heseltine challenged her for the leadership in November 1990. Thatcher did not stoop to campaign and attended a European summit in Paris, while her supporters did a poor job. There was no great enthusiasm for Heseltine, but her support ebbed among Conservative MPs, pressured by their constituents and disliking her increasingly arrogant tone and lack of consultation. In the first round she failed to win outright, insisted she would fight on, but was dissuaded by ministers, fearing that her evident weakness and the divisions in the party would lose them the next election. She resigned in style with a high-spirited speech in the Commons.

John Major won the vote to succeed her, against Heseltine and Hurd, probably because he was less divisive, more emollient amid party tensions. Another sign of changing times was that Hurd's Old Etonian background was regarded as a disadvantage which he sought unsuccessfully to play down. Major was the son of a former music hall performer who ran a small garden ornaments business. He left grammar school at 16, did not attend university and trained in banking, working his way up from the cashiers' desk, also becoming a councillor in Lambeth, south London. He was hailed as the Conservatives' third leader in succession to 'represent the new Tory generation' as *The Telegraph* put it.[178]. He insisted he was not running as 'son of Thatcher' but most of her supporters backed him. It was the only occasion in peacetime in the twentieth century that a governing party with a secure majority withdrew support from its leader. The immediate reason was the poll tax, but others included party divisions over Europe and fears that she would be defeated by a Labour Party in recovery since Neil Kinnock replaced Foot as leader and fiercely attacked the left.

Conclusion: 'Thatcherism'

Margaret Thatcher's name became a slogan, an 'ism', because her thinking and actions so challenged her party's and other traditions, as well as less traditional features of British culture, and remained influential after her demise, creating long-term changes in politics, the economy and society. As Nigel Lawson put it, 'more than any other prime minister, [she] was unafraid of controversy and generally devoid of the instincts and thought processes of the establishment'.[179] The shopkeeper's daughter rejected the *noblesse oblige* sentiments of the old Conservative elite, invoked by Churchill, Eden

178 Charmley, *Conservative Politics*, p. 237.
179 Nigel Lawson, *The View from Number 11* (London: Bantam, 1992), p. 249.

and Macmillan, which expressed a certain responsibility for less privileged people. She espoused other 'Victorian values', as she put it, the 'traditional' family, as younger people steadily rejected it, and self-help, reviving the language of blaming the poor while encouraging popular ownership of property and shares. As she wrote in her memoirs:

> The Victorians ... distinguished between the 'deserving' and the 'undeserving' poor. Both groups should be given help: but it must be help of very different kinds if public spending is not just going to reinforce dependency culture ... The purpose of help must not be to allow people merely to live a half-life, but rather to restore their self-discipline and their self-esteem.[180]

The 'outsider' challenged institutions she believed protected established structures and practices at the public expense: civil servants, doctors, teachers, universities, including her own university, Oxford, whose academic staff refused her an honorary degree in 1985 because her policies were doing 'deep and systematic damage to the whole public educational system in Britain'.[181] She could not see the point of the Commonwealth. She constantly challenged the EC and was the strongest supporter of the transatlantic alliance since Churchill.

She was Prime Minister for eleven and a half years, the longest of the twentieth century, longest since Lord Liverpool retired in 1827. In her memoirs she summed up her view of the state of Britain in 1990:

> There was still too much socialism in Britain ... Socialism was still built into the institutions and mentality of Britain. We had sold thousands of council homes; but 29% of the housing stock remained in the public sector. We had increased parents' rights in the education system; but the ethos in the classrooms and teachers' training colleges remained stubbornly Left wing. We had grappled with the problem of bringing more efficiency into local government; but the Left's redoubts in the great cities still went virtually unchallenged. We had cut back union power; but still almost 50 per cent of the workforce was unionized.[182]

She aimed to reduce direct taxation and by 1990 income tax cuts had increased incomes of £10,000 by £320 pa, those of £70,000 by £36,310.[183] Poverty increased,[184] among children from 8 per cent in 1979 to 28 per cent in 1992[185] by the official measure of incomes below 60 per cent of the median. Average real incomes rose 37 per cent between 1979 and 1992, but those of the poorest 10 per cent fell 18 per cent while the

180 Thatcher, *Downing St Years*, p. 627, n 2.
181 Evans, *Thatcher and Thatcherism*, p. 119.
182 Thatcher, *Downing St Years*, quoted in Vinen, *Thatcher's Britain*, pp. 299–300.
183 House of Commons, *Debates*, 6th series, vol. 170, col. 525, 3 April 1990.
184 See p. 450.
185 J. Cribb, R. Joyce and D. Philip, *Living Standards, Poverty and Inequality in the UK* (London: Institute for Fiscal Studies, 2012).

richest 10 per cent were 61 per cent richer.[186] Unemployment reached its highest level since 1940, manufacturing dwindled while the City of London boomed. This deepened social divisions and the sense of exclusion of unemployed people in northern England, Wales, Scotland and Northern Ireland, often, though not always, expressed in the language of class. Urban areas, including council estates, became more socially divided following rising house prices and council house sales. Thatcher herself was strongly class conscious, determined to win over employed workers particularly with sales of council houses and shares, with some success. Though she banned use of the word 'inequality', under her rule inequalities – economic and cultural – grew spectacularly after narrowing since 1945.

186 Evans, *Thatcher and Thatcherism*, p. 118.

12 Son of Thatcher?

John Major, 1990–1997

John Major's supporters included Conservatives who expected him to modify Thatcher's more extreme and unpopular policies, in particular the poll tax, but not to break with her broad trajectory of economic and social liberalization. Initially, he appeared more liberal, but over time his actions seemed hardly distinguishable from hers and there was little sign of an alternative vision, while income inequality continued to widen, poverty to grow, unemployment and personal debt rose, and living standards stalled. Expressions of discontent multiplied until Labour's resounding victory in 1997.

Major was the youngest, least experienced premier of the century so far, born in 1943, far from privileged. He entered Parliament in 1979 and the Cabinet in 1987 as Chief Secretary to the Treasury.[1] He and his family appeared unassuming and uncharismatic. He was portrayed by cartoonists and satirists, including the BBC's popular *Spitting Image*, which lampooned politicians including an aggressive Thatcher from 1984 to 1996, as dull and grey. 'This doesn't happen to people like us' commented his wife, Norma.[2] He displayed no obvious contact with contemporary cultural change: his first Cabinet was the first since the Conservative governments of 1951–64 to include no women. Unlike Thatcher, he was a calm presence, a reason for his election. He was aware of his predecessor on the backbenches, but she did not obviously seek to undermine him as she had experienced with Heath. His first challenge was to unite the party and the country, aiming to create 'a country that is at ease with itself'. He appointed Heseltine as Secretary of State for the Environment, charged with calming tensions by revising the poll tax. Initially, he led the Cabinet collaboratively, not driving

1 See p. 375.
2 Charmley, *Conservative Politics*, p. 238.

proceedings like his two predecessors. He risked appearing a stop-gap with little power until he gained the legitimacy of winning an election, though his Gallup approval rating was soon 50 per cent compared with Thatcher's 30 per cent when she resigned.[3]

Reaching Out?

He tried at first to distance himself from Thatcher's unpopular policies and appeal to disaffected groups. Curbs on social spending were relaxed. He ordered Lamont (still Chancellor) to unfreeze Child Benefit, then in 1991 it was increased and index-linked, as CPAG proposed. Compensation was awarded to haemophiliacs infected with HIV during blood transfusions. He met gay rights campaigners and in 1991 launched Opportunity 2000, initiated by businesspeople to achieve gender balance at all levels of employment by 2000. With scant support from most employers little changed. Equalities for women and homosexuals did not advance significantly by 1997.

In March 1991, Heseltine introduced the Council Tax for implementation in 1993, replacing the Poll Tax on individuals with a local tax levied on the value of broad 'bands' of properties, with discounts for residents living alone, but it did not revive the independence of local authorities. Under Major – the first premier since Attlee to have been a local councillor – central control of local government increased further. The spending cap was extended to smaller councils and all councils faced intensified pressure to privatize remaining services. The Conservatives continued to lose heavily in local elections, especially in Scotland.

Major's big idea to establish his distinctive identity was the 'Citizen's Charter', launched in July 1991. He called it 'the centrepiece of our policies for the 1990s', designed to improve the quality of the increasingly privatized public services while supporting the 'ordinary person' against 'faceless bureaucrats', a response to growing criticisms of privatized and 'outsourced' services. Charters listed standards for services; independent inspectorates monitored performance, league tables were published, complaints and redress procedures were established though without enforcement processes. Major's administration continued, while theoretically humanizing, privatization, contracting-out and competitive tendering, like Thatcher notionally 'rolling back' the state while increasing central control in many respects. By 1996, forty-two charters had been published, including for patients, taxpayers and jobseekers; a Parents' Charter went to every household stressing parental responsibility for children's behaviour and well-being, to the bafflement, or annoyance, of many parents. 'Ordinary people' did not seem to notice improved services.[4]

---

3 Butler and Butler, *Twentieth-Century British Political Facts*, p. 277.
4 Glennerster, *British Social Policy*, p. 213.

Civil Service Reform

Civil service powers continued to shrink. Following the Rayner recommendations to improve civil service efficiency by introducing business management techniques,[5] by 1991, fifty semi-autonomous 'Next Steps' agencies were established, employing 50 per cent of all civil servants. Whitehall's role was to be restricted to formulating policies, while the agencies provided the services implementing them. By 1997, there were 137, including the Benefits Agency created in 1991 to administer social security payments, Customs and Excise, the Inland Revenue (now Her Majesty's Revenue and Customs, HMRC), the Crown Prosecution Service and the Serious Fraud Office, together employing almost 384,000 staff. Their CEOs were mostly appointed by open competition, 35 per cent from outside the civil service; agencies employed their own staff and were responsible for their own budgets. They were overseen by ministers who were accountable to Parliament, but agencies' relationship with civil service departments was often unclear and ministers could now avoid traditional collective responsibility for failed outcomes of poor policies, displacing blame onto the CEOs.[6] Performance did not obviously improve.[7] The Child Support Agency (CSA)[8] descended into a costly shambles due to poorly designed legislation, and the Prison Service Agency (PSA) faced riots and break-outs by prisoners, including IRA convicts. The CEO of the CSA resigned and the CEO of the PSA was sacked by the Home Secretary. The Benefits Agency was criticized for inefficiency by the National Audit Office, and it lost a number of costly appeals by claimants against its decisions, including to the European Court of Justice. In 1991, this ruled UK social security law guilty of discrimination because, since 1984, married or cohabiting women, but not men, claiming disability allowances were required to prove they were incapable of performing both paid work and 'normal household duties'. Almost 300,000 had been disqualified in consequence.

Catering, cleaning, estates management, security, financial, legal and IT support continued to be 'outsourced' from civil service departments as elsewhere in the public sector, generally worsening the pay, benefits, security and working conditions, especially of lower-level staff. From 1995–7, under Heseltine, now Deputy Prime Minister with responsibility for public service reform, more agencies were wholly privatized, including Her Majesty's Stationery Office (HMSO), the long-established government publishing arm, and the Recruitment and Assessment Service, responsible for recruiting

---

5 See p. 350.
6 N. Panchamia and P. Thomas, *The Next Steps Initiatives* (London: Institute for Government, n.d., available at: www.InstituteforGovernment.org.uk).
7 Kevin Theakston, 'A Permanent Revolution. The Major Governments and the Civil Service', in P. Dorey (ed.), *The Major Premiership. Politics and Policy under John Major, 1990–97* (London: Palgrave, 1999), p. 28.
8 See pp. 385–6.

to the civil service elite fast-stream, generally regarded as highly efficient. This was strongly, unsuccessfully, opposed by senior civil servants and politicians. Civil servants' morale declined and resignations grew as they perceived few efficiency gains, but felt serious concern about the decline of accountability and commitment to public service. Increasingly, senior appointments, including permanent secretaries, were filled by external advertisement rather than by traditional internal promotion, and budgets and staff were cut. There was growing criticism of politicization of the service and of ministerial preference for advice from the growing numbers of Special Advisers appointed from outside the service.[9]

International Relations

The defence budget was cut more sharply than at any time since 1945 while the armed forces became more active. Nuclear weapons were eliminated, other than the submarine-based Trident missile which entered service in 1994. The government was determined that the United Kingdom should remain at the centre of international politics, retaining its place as the smallest of the five permanent members of the UN Security Council.[10] Apart from the 20,000 troops still in Northern Ireland, in January and February 1991, 45,000 serving men and women were engaged in 'Desert Storm', the UN mission to liberate Kuwait from invasion by Iraq. From 1992, Britain joined the UN intervention in the deepening post-communist civil war in the Balkans. The Cabinet was divided on all these issues, but Major consulted it less over international than domestic matters.

In the leadership election Major gained more votes from Eurosceptics than from Europhiles, who supported Heseltine, but he announced in Germany in March 1991 that he wished Britain to be 'at the very heart of Europe'. He wrote in his memoirs, 'I was keen to rebuild shattered fences, to prevent Britain from being seen forever as the odd man out to be excluded from the private consultation that so often foreshadowed new policy in Europe'.[11] Yet, he continued, 'I shared many of [Thatcher's] concerns. I recoiled at the prospect of a "federal" Europe. I was deeply suspicious of political union. I did not wish to ditch sterling. I believed the conditions the Social Chapter sought to impose would add to employers' costs and push up unemployment. I did not wish to see a more powerful Commission. I did believe it was right to enlarge the Community and bring in the nation states of Central Europe...'[12] He tried to satisfy both sides.

9 Blick, *People Who Live in the Dark*.
10 With Russia, China, France and the United States.
11 John Major, *John Major. The Autobiography* (London: HarperCollins, 1999), p. 265.
12 Ibid., p. 266.

Negotiations over what became the Maastricht Treaty (officially the Treaty of European Union) began in December 1991. Major took his accustomed conciliatory approach, making Britain's reservations clear to the other nations, but less aggressively than his predecessor. They too were conciliatory, letting Britain defer a decision on joining the projected common currency (the future euro) and opt out of the Social Chapter (later the Social Charter) introducing EU-wide employment standards, including a minimum wage, which were anathema to neoliberals.[13] Labour increasingly saw the EU as a bulwark against neoliberalism and opposition declined.

General Election, 1992

In an unpromising environment, Major left it almost to the last minute to call the election for April 1992. Inflation fell to 4 per cent, but unemployment rose close to 3 million again, GDP shrank and interest rates remained above 10 per cent. Labour stayed ahead in the polls by between 3 and 7 per cent, though they proved to be exceptionally inaccurate in this election.[14] Major adopted a 'man of the people' image, mounting a (fabricated) soap-box to speak in the streets. In contrast, a glittering, noisy, televised Labour rally a week before the election, 'to celebrate the next Prime Minister', was widely regarded as a mistake by media advisers, a gift to right-wing tabloids, which undermined Kinnock's reputation. Labour was also still damaged by its recent internal conflicts. Thatcher retired from the Commons, becoming a life peeress.

Major spoke a different language from Thatcher, of creating a 'classless society', while upholding popular features of her policies. He attacked the 'Socialists' (a label Kinnock resisted), appealing to voters who had bought their council houses and shares in privatized industries not to 'let Labour ruin it'. He criticized 'Labour's Tax Bombshell' when John Smith, the shadow Chancellor, outlined a prospective Labour budget including higher direct taxation to fund improved services, labelling Labour the 'tax and spend party'.[15] Major won a clear but reduced majority: 336 seats (42.3 per cent of the vote) to Labour's 271 (35.2 per cent), the Liberal Democrats' twenty (18.3 per cent), Plaid four, SNP three, on a 77.7 per cent turnout. There were minor changes in Scotland and Wales, while in England the North–South divide and that between metropolitan areas, including mainly Labour-controlled inner London which also had high levels of unemployment and deprivation, and the suburbs remained. Kinnock resigned and Smith won the leadership easily. Margaret Beckett was elected deputy leader, the most senior woman in Labour's history. Women MPs increased to sixty, twenty Conservatives, thirty-seven Labour, two Liberal Democrats and one SNP.

---

13 Clarke, *Hope and Glory*, pp. 404–5.
14 Butler and Butler, *Twentieth-Century British Political Facts*, p. 280.
15 Charmley, *Conservative Politics*, pp. 242–4.

The smaller overall majority left Major vulnerable to divisions in his party, including over Europe. The fifty-four new Conservative MPs were more Eurosceptic than their predecessors, probably for the first time forming a majority.[16] He appointed two female Cabinet ministers: Gillian Shephard at Employment and Virginia Bottomley at Health, having gained a higher proportion of female votes than Thatcher. He supported the establishment of a Sex Equality branch at the Department of Employment and Shephard appointed an investigation into the difficulties of working women. But these were exacerbated by continuing labour market deregulation, including the abolition in 1993 of Wages Councils (established by Churchill in 1909) which minimally safeguarded mainly female pay, and there were few obvious improvements. Heseltine moved to the Board of Trade, where he caused protest by trying to close thirty-one coal mines, causing 30,000 redundancies. Enough Conservative MPs threatened rebellion for the decision to be reversed.

'Black Wednesday'

Major favoured joining the ERM in 1990, but the UK joined this system of controlled exchange rates, designed to create international financial stability, at too high an exchange rate, around $1.90 against the US dollar, increasing trading costs and inflation. This increased pressure on the pound which threatened to sink in value below the minimum level set by the ERM, causing large sales of sterling on international markets on 16 September 1992 – 'Black Wednesday' as it became known. Despite the Bank of England selling over £15 billion of its reserves, the largest sale in its history, while interest rates rose to 15 per cent, Britain left the ERM that evening in an atmosphere of serious crisis. The pound was then devalued by 10 per cent, which assisted exporters and balanced the balance of payments, but the deficit of government revenue over spending (the public sector deficit) was over 10 per cent of GDP in 1993–4, the highest figure recorded in peacetime.[17] Lamont was sacked as Chancellor the following May and replaced by Kenneth Clarke who cut public spending and increased indirect taxes, hitting the lowest-paid hardest, while reducing income tax by 1 per cent in 1995 and again in 1996. Interest rates fell to around 6 per cent, inflation was checked and economic growth rose to 4.7 per cent in 1994,[18] but the government never recovered from what were seen as misjudgments leading to Black Wednesday. Labour established a lasting lead in opinion polls.

---

16 Philip Cowley, 'Chaos or Cohesion? Major and the Parliamentary Conservative Party', in P. Dorey (ed.), *The Major Premiership. Politics and Policy under John Major, 1990–97* (London: Palgrave, 1999), p. 6.
17 Clarke, *Hope and Glory*, p. 408.
18 Ibid., p. 409.

When the Maastricht Treaty was rejected in a Danish referendum in 1992, back-benchers forced Major to defer British ratification. Black Wednesday caused further delay and deepened Europhobia. The government made ratification a confidence issue. Opponents knew that if the government fell and Labour ruled they would get the full treaty, including the Social Chapter. Major survived and ratified the treaty, opting out of the Social Chapter. Commons rebellions were frequent through the 1970s, 1980s and 1990s, whichever party was in power, and they constrained Major's government as they had others.

Back to Basics

If 1992 was a bad year for the Conservatives, for the royal family it was an *annus hor-ribilis*, as the Queen described it in her annual TV Christmas message. Apart from a serious fire at Windsor Castle in November, all three of her children joined the tide of cultural change. In March, her second son, Andrew, Duke of York, separated from his wife, Sarah. In April, her daughter, Anne, divorced her husband, Captain Mark Phillips. Then, in December, exciting the tabloids most of all, Charles, Prince of Wales, announced his separation from his far more popular wife, Princess Diana.

The royal family was not alone with its sexual problems. David Mellor, Chief Secretary to the Treasury, was revealed to have had an affair with an actress. He only made it worse by parading his 'traditional' family, including parents-in-law, wife and children, before the cameras.[19] Major himself was indignant at media rumours, which he denied, of an affair with a society caterer. Only in 2002 was it was revealed that in the 1980s he had an affair with a parliamentary colleague, Edwina Currie. At the 1993 party conference he appealed to the nation to 'get Back to Basics' and unite behind 'common sense British values'. Echoing Thatcher, he pledged to end 'permissiveness' and promote 'accepting responsibility for yourself and your family and not shuffling it off on the state … It is time to return to those old core values'. These included emphasizing the '3Rs' in education, which he believed were being neglected by 'trendy teachers': 'the Conservative Party will lead the country back to these basics right across the board: sound money; free trade; traditional teaching; respect for the family and the law. And above all lead a new campaign to defeat the cancer that is crime'.[20]

This was enthusiastically received but in the next seven months one minister was revealed to have fathered an illegitimate child, two to have had secret gay relationships, another resigned when his wife committed suicide over his affair with another women and another, Thatcher's successor in Finchley, a Methodist lay preacher and father

19 Holden, *Makers and Manners*, p. 276.
20 Ibid., pp. 278–9.

of three, over his 'friendship' with a House of Commons researcher. Then, Stephen Milligan, Conservative MP, died pursuing the obscure sexual practice of autoerotic asphyxiation.[21] Financial scandals followed. In 1994, Neil Hamilton resigned when he and another junior minister, Tim Smith, were accused by *The Guardian* of accepting cash from Mohamed al-Fayed, owner of Harrods, for asking questions on his behalf in Parliament: 'Cash for Questions' screamed the press. Smith resigned. Hamilton claimed innocence, but failed to clear his name and was eventually forced to resign. Then Jonathan Aitken, Junior Minister at Defence 1992–4, was accused in the media of allowing the Saudi royal family to pay his expenses at the Ritz Hotel, Paris, when he was engaged in arms sales negotiations with Saudi Arabia. He resigned and tried to sue the media, claiming, untruthfully, that his wife paid his bill. In 1999, he was jailed for perjury. The scandals sparked lively debate about standards in public life. A House of Commons Standards and Privileges Committee was established, requiring MPs to register their financial interests.[22]

A different crisis followed an epidemic of Bovine Spongiform Encephalopathy (BSE), known as 'mad cow disease', which from the 1980s caused the slaughter of millions of cattle. By 1996, it had emerged that it could transmit a severe neurological, degenerative disease in humans, Creuzfeldt-Jacob disease (CJD). There were alarming, overstated, projections of the numbers expected to suffer, though about 117 people in Britain died of the disease over the next twenty-five years. In 1996, panic reduced beef consumption and an international ban on British beef, including by the EU, hurt farmers. The origin of the crisis was deregulation in the 1980s of procedures for feeding and slaughtering animals. Stricter regulation returned.

There were growing tensions in the Cabinet, revealed when Major was caught on tape referring to 'three bastards' among his colleagues, assumed to be arch-Thatcherites, Michael Portillo, Peter Lilley and John Redwood. He sank in the polls: by May 1994 only 18.6 per cent of Gallup respondents approved of him as premier.[23] Local election results were poor. The introduction of a National Lottery in 1994 proved to be a popular and novel way of raising funds to replace public spending, mainly on the arts and national heritage, administered by a private company. But a leadership challenge loomed. Major announced he would stand for re-election, to make his critics 'put up or shut up'. His only opponent in June 1995 was Redwood, Welsh Secretary, neoliberal and Eurosceptic. Major won easily, despite growing Europhobia, but was weakened and increasingly isolated. In 1995, the financier Sir James Goldsmith founded the Referendum Party, supporting a referendum on membership of the EU, which he opposed. Polls showed strong opposition to Britain joining the euro. Clarke supported

21 Ibid., pp. 276–8.
22 Clarke, *Hope and Glory*. pp. 413–15.
23 Butler and Butler, *Twentieth-Century British Political Facts*, pp. 277–8.

the euro but reluctantly agreed to a referendum before adoption. Labour agreed. Plans to privatise the Royal Mail were shelved in 1994 due to backbench, and popular, opposition. One of the few other publicly owned undertakings remaining to be privatised was British Rail, for which there was also little obvious public enthusiasm, but sales of rail services to a series of regional companies and the track to another company, were rushed through before the 1997 election.[24]

Northern Ireland

Throughout Major's premiership, bombing continued in Northern Ireland and on the mainland. In February 1991, mortar bombs were fired at the garden of 10 Downing Street but no one was injured. Soon after, one person was killed and forty-three injured by a bomb at Victoria Station. More bombs followed later in the year. In March, the 'Birmingham Six' were freed amid suggestions that the police had given false evidence.[25] In June, the 'Maguire Seven' were also exonerated of the 1974 Guildford bombings after spending between four and fourteen years in jail. Neither event calmed feelings in Northern Ireland, while the British and Irish governments continued inconclusive talks, businesses closed and unemployment climbed.

There were more bombings in 1992, injuring twenty-eight people at London Bridge Station in February, killing three in the City of London in April, injuring sixty in a Manchester shopping centre and eleven shopping in Wood Green, London, in December. In July, representatives of the British and Irish governments and the Northern Ireland parties started talks, but in November the unionists withdrew. The differences still seemed irreconcilable. Through 1993 bombings, violence, deaths and injuries continued in both countries. The *Observer* revealed that the government had been secretly communicating with Sinn Féin for three years, attempting a peace deal; the government denied it. In December, Major and the Taoiseach, Albert Reynolds, delivered what became known as the Downing St Declaration, committing both governments to work for a new political framework founded on the consent and cooperation of all parties, but they did not suggest a timetable or how to overcome the differences. Then in August 1994, the IRA announced 'complete cessation of military operations', believed to have originated in a secret deal with the UK government, though Major still denied it. A month later, Combined Loyalist Military Command (the combined unionist paramilitaries) announced that they, too, would cease 'all operational hostilities' while the IRA ceasefire held, following reassurance that Northern Ireland's position in the United

24 Clarke, *Hope and Glory*, pp. 413–16.
25 See p. 315.

Kingdom was guaranteed, though this was irreconcilable with the central nation-alist aim of independence from the United Kingdom and unity with Ireland. In December, Major announced a £73 million government investment in the Northern Ireland economy.

Unofficial bombings and shootings continued but declined: nine people were killed in 1995. Negotiations continued, public and private, and more prisoners were released but, despite efforts by both governments, there was no progress and in February 1996 the IRA ceasefire ended. A bomb in London, at the new docklands financial centre, Canary Wharf, killed two people, injured 100 and caused £100 million damage. In one more attempt to achieve compromise between apparently irreconcilable opponents, purportedly all-party negotiations opened in June, chaired by the neutral American, George Mitchell, lawyer, businessman and recently retired leader of the Democratic majority in the US Senate. Sinn Féin stayed away and unionists objected to Mitchell, who was a Catholic, so assumed to be biased towards the Nationalists. Bombing con-tinued: 335 died, with many injured in 1996 in both countries. The talks became dead-locked and adjourned until after the UK election.[26]

Social Policy

Education

Major's social policies also largely continued those of Thatcher. The 1992 Education (Schools) Act followed on from that of 1988.[27] It required schools to publish exam results, including National Curriculum tests, arousing such hostility from teachers, including threatened boycotts, that the tests and the curriculum were simplified. The Act established a new Funding Agency for Schools, allowed to remove state schools from local authority control and fund private schools opting into the state sector. Sex education became voluntary: schools were advised not to emphasize sex but 'the value of family life'. Polytechnics were removed from local authority control and re-designated as universities. All university funding was now channelled through new Higher Education Funding Councils in each country of the United Kingdom, further increasing government control over once autonomous institutions. Unprecedented regular national assessment of the quality of university teaching and research was introduced and league tables were encouraged. Universities could now admit as many students as they wished, with little additional funding, but could boost income by charging overseas students what fees they chose. The government still dared not risk

---

26 Bew and Gillespie, *Northern Ireland.*
27 See pp. 375–6.

alienating voters by charging fees for home students, despite rising numbers and costs. It announced a target of one-third of the age group to enter universities by the end of the century. This was reached by 1994–5, when numbers were again capped. As student numbers grew faster than funding, class sizes grew.

Further education colleges were also removed from ever dwindling local authority control. Teacher training colleges were amalgamated with universities or became independent universities and training extended from two to three years, leading to a degree, though ministers periodically proposed that teachers should primarily be trained in schools, gaining practical skills rather than theoretical knowledge which, they argued, encouraged left-leaning teaching fashions. Thatcher's suspicion of public sector professionals and increased central control of all levels of education continued, while salaries were curbed as elsewhere in the public sector.[28]

Housing

Housebuilding fell to 190,000 in 1995, overwhelmingly in the private sector. Council house construction shrank further, to 10,200 in 1991, 1,900 in 1995.[29] Tax relief on mortgage payments was progressively reduced from 1991, mainly to offset rises in other housing costs, especially Housing Benefit, the costly outcome of Thatcher's determination that the market must rule rents even of council housing.[30] One result of encouraging owner-occupation among the lower-paid when unemployment was rising was the growing cost of mortgage interest payments for those on Income Support. From October 1995 mortgagees became ineligible for this relief for their first nine months on IS; some lost their homes. High interest rates caused mortgage arrears, repossessions and the newly prevalent phenomenon of negative equity: houses valued at less than the owners' mortgage.

The Housing Benefit bill soared due to unemployment and low pay combined with rising private rents and the shortage of local authority housing. To limit costs, rents eligible for Benefit were required not to rise above local market rents, and from 1996 single people under-25 could receive it only for a single room in shared accommodation. More positively, homeless people requiring local authority rehousing declined 172,000–135,000, 1990–5, after the sharp rise in the 1980s,[31] while households placed in bed and breakfasts fell, from 12,200 to 4,500, as councils provided more hostels, including refuges for women homeless after fleeing

28 Glennerster, 'Education. Reaping the Harvest?' pp. 27–74.
29 Hills, 'Housing. A Decent Home', p. 142.
30 See pp. 354, 379.
31 See p. 379.

domestic violence, and leased private accommodation, all cheaper than costly bed and breakfasts.[32]

Health

In 1991, the Patients' Charter included three new 'rights': to information on local health services, including on quality and waiting times; guaranteed treatment within the hardly reassuring period of two years from joining a waiting list; complaints about the NHS would be properly investigated. Seven national standards were listed, including that ambulances should arrive within fourteen minutes in urban areas, nineteen in rural; patients in outpatient clinics would receive specific appointment times and be seen within thirty minutes; those in hospital accident and emergency departments would be seen immediately. All were desirable and in many areas much needed, but not enforceable or fully complied with by health authorities under increasing financial pressure. The Conservatives' regular device to achieve improvement through competition, as with schools and universities, annual Performance Tables, was employed from June 1994, without obvious effects.

From 1992, specific health conditions were targeted for improved treatment: cancer, heart disease, stroke, mental illness, HIV/AIDS, sexual health and accidents. Targets were set for reducing death rates and behaviours known to increase risk, such as smoking, strategies recommended by the WHO for some years. Still, some serious health, especially mental health, problems were overlooked and it was not clear how, or whether, targets could be achieved, or the source of funds to pursue them. Inequalities in NHS expenditure and the availability and numbers of GPs across English regions grew,[33] and there were continuing inequalities between rich and poor in expected years of life and good health.[34] In 1995, a departmental committee urged health authorities and GP practices to identify and tackle health 'variations', as they described inequalities echoing Thatcher,[35] and target resources appropriately. In 1993, Thatcher's 'care in the community' initiative was implemented, giving local authorities responsibility for chronically sick, aged and disabled people living at home, obliging authorities, without further funding, to purchase 'care packages' from private or voluntary providers rather than providing their own services. Fragmented, less publicly accountable, services resulted.[36]

---

32 Hills, 'Housing. A Decent Home', pp. 122–88.
33 Le Grand and Vizard, 'The National Health Service', pp. 104–5.
34 See pp. 382–3.
35 See p. 346.
36 Evandrou and Falkingham, 'The Personal Social Services', pp. 196–9.

Single Parents

Thatcher's Child Support Act 1990 was implemented by the CSA from 1993.[37] The regulations, like the legislation, were drafted in a hurry and administered by inexperienced officials. The CSA took over the courts' powers to assess, collect and enforce maintenance payments to all single parents receiving benefits (527,000) and new claimants, on the assumption that many were claiming benefits from the state because 'feckless fathers' failed to pay due maintenance. Income Support was reduced by the full amount of maintenance payments. A large backlog quickly developed, mainly because most cases were more complex than anticipated. The system was intended to cut benefit costs but, remarkably, it was not foreseen that prioritizing fathers' responsibility for first families disadvantaged many second families, who then needed benefits, also that many fathers were not evading maintenance but were unable to afford it. Fathers who believed they were doing their best for both families were infuriated and some fathers, not always the most deserving, staged dramatic, much publicized protests in prominent London spaces. Most single mothers struggled rather than protested. The Inland Revenue was expected to pursue fathers who failed to pay maintenance, but grew tired of hounding them, sometimes fruitlessly, for small sums and the CSA added this to the tasks for which it was unprepared. It was ordered to cut £530 million from the benefits bill in the first year, undershooting by £112 million, while arranging maintenance in fewer than one-third of eligible applications. It was a widely criticized fiasco. The CEO resigned after a year. The system was modified in the Child Support Act, 1995, but was little improved.[38]

Major revealed that his sister and mother-in-law had raised children alone, to convey his understanding of single mothers, but he and ministers attacked them to justify cutting benefits, like Thatcher blaming state welfare for encouraging partnership breakdown and unmarried motherhood. At the party conference in October 1992, Peter Lilley, Secretary of State for Social Security, intoned a widely publicized pastiche of Gilbert and Sullivan, announcing he 'had a little list' of:

> Benefit offenders who I'll soon be rooting out …
> Young ladies who get pregnant just to jump the housing list.
> And dads who won't support the kids of ladies they have kissed.
> And I haven't even mentioned all those sponging socialists …

He later argued in the *News of the World*, without evidence, that the rise in violent crime was due to growing numbers of fatherless families. Then John Redwood, Secretary of State for Wales, visited an estate in Cardiff which, he claimed, was 50 per

---

37 See pp. 385–6, 398.
38 Thane and Evans, *Sinners?* pp. 184–6.

cent populated by one-parent families, including many young, never-married mothers. In fact only 17 per cent of the 3,500 families were headed by single mothers, 60 per cent of them over 24, most previously married or in long-term relationships. Redwood later proposed withholding benefits from single mothers until the father moved back, to provide 'the normal love and support that fathers have offered down the ages', presumably abandoning any second families. He complained of a worrying trend 'for young women to have babies with no apparent intention of even trying marriage or a stable relationship with the father', also offering no evidence. The vice-chair of Cardiff Social Services Committee, a social worker, commented that in an area of high unemployment the main problem for the families was poverty; most mothers were loving and supportive and wanted to work if they could. A senior police officer commented: 'as the police had exclusion orders for violence against half the men involved, the last thing they wanted was to see women and children forced to allow the fathers to return'.[39]

But Redwood's pronouncements were enthusiastically received by sections of the press. *Daily Mail* columnist, Keith Waterhouse, attacked the:

> Single Parent State … the single mum can rake in over £100 a week in state benefits … she can jump the housing queue and raise her family in one of those lovely tower blocks … Then there is the Unmarried Mothers' Union – the single parents' militant wing where having a baby is not so much a happy event as a political statement. You cradle the little mite in your boiler suit and carry a placard demanding crèche facilities at the bingo hall.[40]

An outpouring of stereotypes unrecognizable in real life.

Single mothers did not receive priority for council housing. Department of the Environment researchers discovered that over 40 per cent of unmarried mothers under 20 lived with their parents. The liberal *Independent* pointed out how many single-parent families were in bed and breakfast accommodation, while *The Guardian* commented that it was indeed desirable to cut the number of teenage single pregnancies, so it was unfortunate that one in four family planning clinics had closed following government cuts. Government representatives sounded uncomfortable. A Department of Social Security (DSS) source stated that Redwood's comments did not represent government policy. Lilley stated that single mothers would continue to receive benefits, adding 'we can give money but we cannot give love and commitment'.[41]

Amid media denigration of 'scroungers' on benefits, the 1996 Budget announced the freezing of One Parent Benefit and its abolition for new claimants. As the 1997 election approached, John Redwood proposed, in the name of 'family values', that single mothers should give their children up for adoption. Single mothers faced the most sustained attack from the government and the media of the twentieth century, but denigration

39 Thane and Evans, *Sinners?* pp. 187–8.
40 *Daily Mail*, 5 July 1993.
41 Thane and Evans, *Sinners?* pp. 189–93.

was not universal: 53 per cent of poll respondents believed women capable of bringing up children alone. Never before had so many children been born outside marriage or so many unmarried couples openly lived together, facing little evident disapproval from family, friends and neighbours. Cutting benefits did not get more mothers into work, but made families poorer amid high levels of child poverty.[42] Many mothers desired to work but were hampered by lack of childcare and high unemployment.[43]

The government tried to deal with one major cause of partnership breakdown. The Family Homes and Domestic Violence Bill 1995 strengthened and simplified the law, treating married and unmarried couples equally, but 'pro-marriage' Conservative MPs were strongly opposed and it was withdrawn. An amended version returned in the Family Law Act 1996, which also made legal aid available for mediation preceding, hopefully averting, divorce. Legal aid was now available for divorce only following mediation; £2 million was granted to the voluntary marriage guidance service, Relate.[44] In the Lords, Baroness Patricia Hollis (Labour) successfully inserted an amendment allowing partners, normally wives, to claim 50 per cent of the other's pension rights as part of the divorce settlement.

Social Security

The shift from universal contributory social security benefits, proposed by Beveridge and introduced by Labour in 1946,[45] to selective, means-tested payments targeted on the poorest but relatively costly and inefficient, started under Heath, continued.[46] In 1996, contributory, universal unemployment benefit and means-tested Income Support were merged into 'Job-Seekers' Allowance' (JSA). The right to the contributory benefit was halved to the first six, rather than twelve, months' unemployment, then means-tested and reduced by 20 per cent for 18–25 year olds. Claimants had to sign a 'job-seekers' agreement' to seek work and risked penalties if they failed to find it, even in areas of high unemployment. The Social Security (Incapacity for Work) Act 1994 replaced long-term Invalidity Benefit with Incapacity Benefit. Previously claimants had to prove unfitness for any available work for which they had appropriate skills and aptitude. They must now prove unfitness for *any* work, as assessed by a doctor appointed by the Benefits Agency rather than, as before, their own GP, beginning a lasting process of severely tightening conditions for payment, causing severe hardship for many claimants and many successful appeals, which were costly to the government.

42 See Figure 12.1, below.
43 Thane and Evans, *Sinners?* pp. 193–4.
44 Cretney, *Family Law*, pp. 761–3.
45 See pp. 198–9.
46 See pp. 307–8.

Peter Lilley explained that 'The number of people receiving Invalidity Benefit has doubled in the past ten years, although the nation's health has been improving', implying extensive, unproven, fraud.[47] Through the previous ten years, older unemployed people in particular had been encouraged to claim Invalidity Benefit in order to lower the unemployment statistics, moving them from then relatively generous insurance-based allowances onto lower, means-tested, payments, under pressure to seek work, though older people could rarely hope to succeed.

The social policy changes started under Heath, taken further under Thatcher and continued under Major seriously increased hardship for many disadvantaged people, replacing their right to support when in need for no fault of their own, which Beveridge and Labour had established, with dependence on the state which Beveridge sought to remove. The postwar welfare state was continuously eroded. Where possible also responsibility for social welfare was transferred from the state to profit-making private providers and non-profit voluntary organizations at no significant saving to the taxpayer. Voluntary organizations, including CPAG, Citizen's Advice Bureaux and One-Parent Families, campaigned against the changes, with little effect though perhaps preventing further cuts, while supporting claimants' legal appeals against harsh decisions.

Figure 12.1

Source: A. B. Atkinson and S. Morelli, *The New Chartbook of Economic Inequality* (2014). www.chartbookof economicinequality.

47 M. Hill, 'Rolling Back the (Welfare) State. The Major Governments and Social Security Reform', in P. Dorey (ed.), *The Major Premiership. Politics and Policy under John Major, 1990–97* (London: Palgrave, 1999), p. 171.

Income and Wealth Inequality

Income inequality continued to increase, though more slowly than in the 1980s.[48] This was true of most OECD countries, but from the late 1970s was greatest in the United Kingdom; by 2000 only the United States, Portugal and Mexico experienced greater income inequality.[49] By 2001–1 approximately 10.4 million individuals were receiving below 60 per cent of median income (the official poverty measure), mostly adults of working age, many in work.[50] Single-parent families were most likely to suffer poverty, together with 40 per cent of pensioners. Top incomes continued to soar, with businesspeople increasingly joined by sports stars. The rewards of successful male footballers, tennis players, golfers, motor-racing drivers, etc. rose to previously unimaginable heights as sports became increasingly commercialized and the target of foreign takeovers and ambitious investors seeking short-term gains, like many areas of British business. Household debt continued to grow. From 1960 to 1980, individuals declared insolvent in England and Wales averaged under 4,600 pa; by 1990 this had risen to almost 14,000, in 2000 to 30,000.[51]

Crime

Crime, including violent crime, indeed increased, including the shooting of sixteen children and a teacher in a schoolyard in Dunblane, Scotland, in 1996 by a gunman who then killed himself. Such crimes aroused particular publicity and shock because they were unusual in Britain, far less common than the rarely publicized murders of women by violent partners (averaging two each week). The media fuelled panic about rising crime. Government representatives blamed 'soft' judges, the police or 'do-gooders', when not blaming fatherless families, and increased central control over the justice system. Michael Howard, Home Secretary in 1996, introduced mandatory prison terms for certain offences, intended as a deterrent, infuriating the judiciary with this unprecedented limitation of their freedom to determine sentences. In 1996, long-established local authority control of police forces was shifted to new local police authorities with appointed members less accountable to communities.

Another government intervention, the Criminal Justice and Public Order Act 1994 was a strange ragbag aiming to reduce crime and solve multiple problems but

---

48 Gazeley, 'Income and Living Standards', pp. 160 ff.

49 Ibid., p. 163.

50 Ibid., pp. 169–72.

51 Peter Scott, 'The Household Economy since 1870'. in Roderick Floud, Jane Humphries and Paul Johnson (eds), *The Cambridge Economic History of Modern Britain, vol. 2: 1870 to the Present* (Cambridge University Press, 2014), p. 382.

exacerbating others. Rape in marriage became a crime, following demands since the nineteenth century and a series of court judgments. Edwina Currie successfully introduced an amendment to lower the homosexual age of consent to 18, after three teenagers, backed by the gay rights organization Stonewall, brought a case to the ECtHR claiming that British law breached their rights to privacy and family life. Stonewall then lobbied for equality with heterosexuals, at age 16. Crowds gathered outside Parliament, erupting in protest when this was rejected. The Act introduced restrictions on 'raves', newly fashionable, large, generally noisy, sometimes days-long, all-night music festivals in otherwise peaceful urban parks and country places. It enabled police to shut down events featuring music 'characterized by the emission of a succession of repetitive beats', arousing more angry protests organized by a new activist group, Reclaim the Streets. Controls were also introduced on newly developed human stem-cell and fertility treatment, the first designed to help and hopefully cure sufferers of a range of degenerative diseases, the second to assist infertile couples give birth, but opponents believed both interfered unacceptably with nature. Penalties were increased for pornography, obscenity, rape, buggery, obscene telephone calls and racially motivated offences. Conservative backbenchers unsuccessfully moved an amendment to reintroduce hanging. Certain Conservatives again blamed the 'permissive' changes of the 1960s for rising crime and disorder, vigorously denied by Tony Blair, Labour Shadow Home Secretary, arguing that the government and its immediate predecessors should bear responsibility due to deteriorating socio-economic conditions.[52]

Race

In 1993, a black teenager, aspiring architect Stephen Lawrence, standing harmlessly at a bus stop in south London, was murdered in a clearly racist attack. The failure of the police to conduct serious investigations caused outrage among the black Caribbean community and more widely and was much covered in the media. Five young white men were arrested and acquitted, though two were re-tried and convicted in 2012. Public anger and persistent campaigning by Stephen Lawrence's parents and their supporters led eventually to an investigation by former High Court judge, Sir William Macpherson, which reported in 1999.

Immigrants became increasingly diverse, including political refugees and economic migrants from more countries, fewer from former colonies. Organization within and across BME groups grew. The 1990 Trust grew out of black community and lobby groups formed in the 1970s and 1980s, a research and networking organization coordinating campaigns on local and national issues and for individuals experiencing

52 Holden, *Makers and Manners*, pp. 269–70.

discrimination or other forms of mistreatment. In 1996, it established Operation Black Vote to urge BME people to campaign, register and vote on equality issues.[53]

By the 1990s the small Chinese and African-Asian populations had, on average, similar incomes and employment opportunities to the white population and higher educational attainment. At the other extreme, more than four in five Pakistani and Bangladeshi households had incomes below half the median, four times as many as white households.[54] By 1999, unemployment among all BME groups was double that of white people, reinforcing disadvantages in health, education and housing.[55] In the 1980s the government refused to grant Muslim schools voluntary-aided status equally with Jewish, Catholic, Methodist and Anglican schools, despite the growth of the Muslim population in the United Kingdom (600,000 in 1980, 1 million in 1990, 1.2 million in 1995[56]). Increasingly Muslims and other faith groups formed national organizations. The Hindu Council was formed in 1994; the Muslim Council of Britain in 1997, when Britain's first Muslim MP was elected, Mohammed Sarwar, Labour, in Glasgow, Govan.[57] They provided services and support for their communities, aiming to improve understanding of their faiths and the living conditions of their followers.

Gypsies and Travellers

Gypsies and Travellers remained the most excluded minority group. They were further disadvantaged following the panic about 'rave' culture. The tabloids decried hordes of anarchic 'nomads', camping and travelling from rave to rave, they and the government conflating Gypsies and Travellers with these new travellers. The Criminal Justice and Public Order Act removed local authorities' duty to provide permanent caravan sites, introduced under Labour,[58] cancelling their grant aid, to encourage Gypsies and Travellers to move into permanent housing, while introducing tougher measures to remove them from unauthorized sites and prohibiting sites on Green Belt land. The Housing Minister, Sir George Young, described existing legislation as 'a drain on the taxpayer's money' and a disincentive for Gypsies 'to provide for themselves'. The proposals received at least 1,000, mainly critical, responses, including from organizations not known as radical – the Country Landowners Association, the Council for the Preservation of Rural England and the National Farmers' Union – and from

53 Kimber, 'Race and Equality', p. 41.
54 Ibid., pp. 41–2.
55 Butler and Butler, *Twentieth-Century British Political Facts*, p. 564.
56 Peter Brierley, 'Religion', in A. H. Halsey and J. Webb (eds), *Twentieth-century British Social Trends* (London: Macmillan, 2000), p. 662.
57 E. Filby, 'Religion and Belief', in Pat Thane (ed.), *Unequal Britain. Equalities in Britain since 1945* (London: Bloomsbury, 2010), p. 62.
58 See p. 342.

local councils, which were ignored. Some described them as 'ethnic cleansing'. Save the Children was concerned about the impact of insecurity and evictions on children's health and welfare, and there was strong opposition in Parliament, mainly from Labour, but from 1994 travelling or stopping in groups of more than six vehicles became a criminal offence and harassment and eviction of Gypsies and Travellers grew rapidly. They had difficulty getting planning permission for sites, even on land they owned; about 90 per cent of planning applications were rejected. Anger and organization grew. Friends, Families and Travellers was formed, initially as an informal support group which developed into an advice, information and training organization providing a wide range of services to all Gypsies and Travellers, aiming for equal rights. The Traveller Law Research Unit at Cardiff University provided research, lobbying and advice, including a telephone legal advice service,[59] but the tentative moves towards greater equality for Gypsies and Travellers since the 1960s[60] went into reverse in the 1990s.

Women

Women's employment and educational opportunities gradually improved, partly due to EU influence, but gender equality remained distant. In 1991, 67.6 per cent of working-age women were employed, by 2001 this had increased to 70.3 per cent,[61] many still in low paid, often part-time, work. The government resisted the EOC's calls for stronger legislation on equal pay and sex discrimination, believing that regulation hampered the free market. As we have seen, single mothers had an especially hard time. The 1992 manifesto promised to 'encourage the development of child-care arrangements in the voluntary and independent sectors' and some funding was provided for pre-school and after-school care. From 1990, employers could offset against tax the cost of workplace nurseries, which increased, while local authority nursery places declined following funding cuts.[62] In 1993, Major declared that he wanted 'over time to move to universal nursery education', but John Patten, Education Secretary, opposed this and nothing happened. A childcare allowance of up to £28 per week was introduced to help single parents and other low-income mothers work full-time.[63] The EU recommended accessible childcare services and flexible leave arrangements to help parents, including fathers, fulfil their family and work obligations, and extending employment rights to part-time workers,

59 Porter and Taylor, 'Gypsies and Travellers', pp. 88–92.

60 See pp. 291, 342.

61 Timothy J. Hatton, 'Population, Migration and Labour Supply. Great Britain, 1871–2011', in Roderick Floud, Jane Humphries and Paul Johnson (eds), *The Cambridge Economic History of Modern Britain, vol. 2: 1870 to the Present* (Cambridge University Press, 2014), p. 108.

62 Evandrou and Falkingham, 'Personal Social Services'. p. 217.

63 Ruth Lister, 'The Family and Women', in A. Seldon and D. Kavanagh (eds), *The Major Effect* (London: Macmillan, 1994), pp. 357–9.

who were overwhelmingly female. In 1994, responding reluctantly to an EU directive, the government ruled that fourteen weeks' maternity leave should be available immediately a woman took a job, rather than after two years, and extended to part-timers. After two years in the same employment it was extended to twenty-eight weeks. Portillo, Employment Secretary, refused to introduce paternity leave. Britain had the worst provision for working parents in the EU and trailed in most areas of gender equality.

One hint of progress was that women were admitted to combat roles in all the armed services, though not yet on the frontline, partly due to a shortage of male recruits and later than several other countries including the United States. The women's and men's services were amalgamated. From 1990, women in the Royal Navy were at last allowed to go to sea with men, despite the trepidation of some sailors' wives; not until 2014 could they serve in the intimacy of submarines. Only in 2016 were army women admitted to frontline combat; opponents still questioned their physical capability.[64]

Transgender Activism

Transgender people increasingly demanded legal recognition of their acquired gender and the right to NHS gender reassignment treatment, led by Press for Change, founded in 1992, mobilizing its highly educated membership. A founder member, Stephen Whittle, a law lecturer, in 1990 founded the Female to Male support group. He and his long-term partner – wife when it became possible in 2005 – achieved change and inspired others through successful litigation. In the early 1990s they established their right to artificial insemination, then, through the European Court, their children's right to have Whittle legally recognized as their father, assisted by EU equality initiatives. In 1994, a British transsexual woman successfully appealed to the European Court of Justice against an employment tribunal's rejection of her discrimination case against her employer. In 1999, gender reassignment was incorporated in the discrimination regulations, but trans people still faced conflicts over which toilets to use, assignment to male or female hospital wards or prison cells. Male to female transsexuals were forbidden to draw their pension at the female age of 60. The struggle continued.[65]

Gay Rights

The fight for gay equality also continued. Former service personnel fought court cases against the MoD following dismissal under the ban on homosexuals in the services. Judges felt they had no alternative but to uphold the legal ban, though some urged

64 Kathleen Sherit, 'The Integration of Women into the Royal Navy and the Royal Air Force post-World War II to the mid-1990s', PhD dissertation, King's College London, 2013.
65 Porter, 'Gender Identity and Sexual Orientation', pp. 159–61.

the MoD to review it. An appeal to the ECtHR was likely when, in October 1995, a parliamentary review was announced. Service leaders defended the ban. Nicolas Soames, Armed Services Minister, insisted it should remain, 'not based on any moral judgement but on the impracticality of homosexual behaviour, which is clearly not compatible with service life'.[66] MPs heard the experiences of service-people discharged under the ban. A lesbian former Wren described how she was frightened to report rape by a male colleague for fear her sexuality would be revealed. She was discharged when it became known. The ban was lifted in 2000 following a ruling in the European Court of Justice.[67]

Stonewall and other campaigners fought to promote gay rights in a climate where acceptance was slowly growing, especially in London, but was far from universal. In 1996, Glenda Jackson, formerly a well-known actor now a London Labour MP, tabled an amendment to the Housing Bill extending succession rights to secure tenancies, including of council houses, to same-sex couples. It was supported by a Conservative, David Ashby, who faced allegations of an adulterous affair with a man. His constituency association deselected him. The Commons rejected the amendment.[68]

Disability

In 1992, Nicolas Scott, minister responsible for disabled people, admitted they experienced discrimination at work, breaking with the Conservative stress through the 1980s on the burden on employers of ensuring equal treatment of disabled workers. From 1982 to 1993, fifteen unsuccessful Private Members' Bills sought equal rights, while EU pressure to resolve this and other forms of discrimination grew.[69] In 1992, Labour MP Roger Berry introduced a Civil Rights (Disabled Persons) Bill, supported by an unprecedented thirty-three Conservative MPs. During the debate, 2,000 demonstrators descended on Parliament, a building exceptionally poorly adapted to the needs of disabled people. Two hundred and fifty thousand postcards were sent to MPs urging support for the Bill. Scott's disabled daughter was a leading campaigner, but the government sent out anonymous press briefings suggesting that reform would cost employers at least £17 billion. Ministers did not openly oppose the Bill, but worked to destroy it. They fixed the final stage for the day that Labour MPs were attending the funeral of their leader, John Smith, who had died suddenly. The Bill fell when there were too

---

66 Holden, *Makers and Manners*, p. 300.
67 Ibid., pp. 300–1.
68 Ibid., p. 301.
69 Simon Millar, 'Disability', in Pat Thane (ed.), *Unequal Britain. Equalities in Britain since 1945* (London: Bloomsbury, 2010), p. 170.

few votes to be quorate. Disabled activists, invited by Labour MP Denis Skinner, were refused access to Parliament for five hours, causing further protests, including attempts by disabled people to haul themselves over the threshold.[70]

After a media furore, with images of wheelchair protesters, Scott was replaced by the emollient William Hague. A compromise Disability Discrimination Act 1995 in principle increased protection against direct discrimination in employment, provision of services and sale of land, though not in education. It established the National Disability Council to advise government on disability issues, but without powers to act against discrimination. It defined as 'disabled' 'someone who has a physical or mental impairment that has a substantial and long-term adverse effect on his or her ability to carry out normal day-to-day activities', and defined impairment more precisely than before, though still imperfectly – some people with learning difficulties were excluded, among others – but the official definition was now substantially broader.[71] Applicants for disability benefits continued to be harshly treated. The 1996 Community Care (Direct Payments) Act allowed local authorities to fund essential services for disabled people. This followed growing criticism of community services for sick and disabled people released from institutions, especially following the murder in 1992 of Jonathan Zito by a paranoid schizophrenic man who had been released but unsupported in the community. But depleted local authority funding was not increased and services remained poor. Zito's friends, family and others campaigned for better services.[72]

Age Discrimination

Discrimination against older people had never been openly acknowledged. It was taken for granted, like other forms of discrimination, until victims protested. Life expectancy continued to rise, and by 1995 at age 65 a man could, on average, expect to live a further 15 years, a woman 18 years, though severe socio-economic inequalities continued. People over 65 were now 15.7 per cent of the UK population. More people were healthy and active to later ages, which partly explains their growing assertiveness against discrimination in healthcare, employment and much else. The international panic continued about the growth of 'dependent' older age groups while younger workforces shrank along with the birth rate. Yet, though more people were fit to work later in life, in the early 1990s one-third of workers in Britain and elsewhere in Western Europe retired, often reluctantly, earlier than had long been normal, before age 60. The fortunate minority were on comfortable company pensions, as employers 'downsized' by

---

70 House of Commons, *Debates*, vol. 244, cols 759–60, 16 June 1994.
71 Millar, 'Disability', pp. 171–2.
72 Ibid., p. 178.

pensioning off expensive senior workers, but others were forcibly retired due to the decline of manufacturing, facing survival on deteriorating state pensions.[73] About 40 per cent of UK pensioners lived in poverty by the official measure.[74] Earlier retirement was often represented as unavoidable due to technological change and the presumed incapacity of older workers to adapt and re-train. Hence, workers even in their forties might not receive training, despite decades of research demonstrating that smart 60 year olds could outperform average 25 year olds at most mental activities, helped by their greater experience, and most older people could learn new skills, including use of modern technology. Older workers had fewer absences for sickness or other reasons and could be more highly motivated and productive than younger workers.[75] Older people protested, the Campaign Against Age Discrimination in Employment formed in 1988, then in 1992 the Scottish Pensioners' Forum was created by the Scottish TUC, 'to allow pensioners to speak on behalf of pensioners'.[76]

Pensioners faced new problems. After the body of media tycoon, Robert Maxwell, was found floating in the Atlantic in 1991, it emerged that £400 million had been diverted from the pension funds of Maxwell's Mirror Group to support his failing companies. Employees, past and present, lost their pensions, highlighting the insecurity of the occupational pensions successive Conservative governments had encouraged, while it became clear how many suffered because the Thatcher government's deregulation enabled private finance companies to persuade people with secure public sector pensions to transfer to more expensive, less advantageous, private schemes. Also, in 1990 the European Court upheld a man's contention that the lower UK pension age for women, 60, discriminated against men. The government then announced the gradual raising of the female age to 65 from 2010 to 2020, though it failed to warn women adequately and many were shocked when the change came. There was no evident public protest at the time, including from women's organizations, who continued, like the rest of society, to marginalize older women.[77]

'New Labour'

John Smith, as party leader after Kinnock, was keen to reshape Labour and prevent further divisive battles. 'Modernizers', including two emerging stars, Tony Blair and Gordon Brown, urged him to reduce the unions' power in the party. Smith introduced

---

73 Pat Thane, 'Demographic Futures. Addressing Inequality and Diversity Among Older People', in P. Taylor-Gooby (ed.), *New Paradigms in Public Policy* (Oxford University Press/British Academy, 2013), pp. 150–1.
74 Gazeley, 'Income and Living Standards', p. 170.
75 Thane, 'The Debate on the Declining Birth Rate'.
76 Thane, 'Older People and Equality', pp. 16–19.
77 Ibid. pp. 17–18.

one member one vote (OMOV) for conference votes and elections, including for parliamentary candidates, though not for the party leadership, in place of the traditional 'block vote' of union members, which gave unions considerable power due to their large, if shrinking, size. This was agreed by the party conference in September 1993. At the same time, Smith proposed and conference approved all-women shortlists (AWS) in candidate selections for half of all seats deemed winnable on a 6 per cent swing and half of all vacant Labour-held seats. Labour women, including feminists who joined Labour as the best means to advance their cause against Thatcher's government, demanded female quotas from the 1980s as the only means to overcome the reluctance of local parties to select women for winnable seats. Similar positive discrimination measures had increased female representation in other legislatures, notably Norway.

But within eight months of these reforms, Smith was suddenly dead, aged 55, from a heart attack. The likely battle for the succession was between the Shadow Chancellor, Gordon Brown, like Smith a Scot, son of a minister in the Church of Scotland, aged 43, and the Shadow Home Secretary, Tony Blair, aged 41, born in Edinburgh, where he attended the independent Fettes College, though he grew up in Durham. His father was a lawyer, once a Conservative parliamentary candidate. Blair graduated from Oxford, also becoming a lawyer. Brown entered Edinburgh University at the early age of 16, gained an outstanding first class degree in History, became a lecturer, then a journalist and gained a PhD at Edinburgh for a biography of the Scottish left-winger, James Maxton. Both entered Parliament in 1983, becoming good friends. After Smith's death, they agreed, on grounds that remain uncertain, that Blair would stand for the leadership. His only opponent was working-class former trade unionist, John Prescott.

Blair won a clear majority, among MPs and party members and, more surprisingly, the unions. He emphasized his youth and distance from traditional 'Old Labour'. He spoke respectfully of Thatcher, but called for a 'modern' (a key word in his political vocabulary), post-Thatcher agenda, appealing to the left and centre against pure neoliberalism. He appointed Prescott deputy leader to help unite the party. His public presentation owed much to Peter Mandelson, Oxford graduate grandson of Herbert Morrison, former TV producer, appointed Labour's Director of Communications by Kinnock, elected to Parliament in 1992. Media presentation was central to Blair's project. He presented his middle-class background as an asset, shifting Labour from identification with a dwindling working-class towards promoting the aspirations of 'middle England', the now dominant middle-class. At Blair's first party conference as leader in October 1994, he launched the concept of 'New Labour', calling successfully for rewriting clause 4 of the party's 1918 constitution, eliminating its commitment to nationalization. Party membership grew.[78]

78 Clarke, *Hope and Glory*, pp. 409–12.

General Election, 1997

Major failed to unite the Conservatives on Europe or on much else, but held on for the full five years of the Parliament. By 1997, unemployment remained close to 2 million, the economy was not flourishing, middle-class people were suffering particularly from rising prices, public sector workers from pay restraint and cuts, and the party from the successive scandals. The election was fixed for 1 May 1997. Blair's campaign stressed the contrast between 'New' and 'Old' Labour. Brown underlined this by abandoning 'tax and spend', promising to adhere to Clarke's stringent public spending guidelines for the first two years in office, without increasing direct taxation. Polls predicted a Labour landslide. Blair courted Rupert Murdoch and even the *Sun*, with the rest of Murdoch's media empire, supported Labour. The unpopular Conservatives could rely only on the *Daily Mail*, the *Telegraph* and their Sunday equivalents.[79]

Labour won 419 seats (44.5 per cent of voters) in the biggest electoral swing against the Conservatives since 1945, though the turnout, at 71.5 per cent, was the lowest since 1935. The Conservatives won only 165 seats, their fewest since 1906, with none in Scotland or Wales. Labour won most seats in England as it had in 1945 and 1966, but turnout was low in some of its traditional heartlands where unemployment was high and New Labour's appeal to 'Middle England' made working-class voters feel that their considerable problems were neglected by the party which had always spoken for them. The Liberal Democrats won an unprecedented forty-six seats, Plaid Cymru four, the SNP six. Goldsmith's Referendum Party fielded 547 candidates, won 3.1 per cent of votes and no seats. Following a series of bombs and scares in England in the run-up to the election, Sinn Féin won a record 16.1 per cent of Northern Ireland votes and two seats, which they again refused to take up. Remarkably, 120 women MPs were elected (of 659). Of these 102 were Labour, 'Blair's Babes' as the *Daily Mail* could not resist captioning a picture of most of them clustered around the leader, to their intense irritation. Thirteen were Conservatives, three Liberal Democrats, two SNP. The transformation followed the endorsement by the 1993 Labour conference of AWSs. It was not popular with some male party members who resented their exclusion from selection, but in this respect the incoming Labour government was certainly 'new'.[80] It had an exceptional majority following the weak Major administration and Labour's own recovery and exceptional opportunities to achieve change.

79 Ibid., pp. 415–16.
80 Breitenbach and Thane, *Women and Citizenship*, passim.

13 Things Can Only Get Better?

New Labour, 1997–2010

Labour's theme tune in the victorious election campaign in 1997 was 'Things Can Only Get Better' by D:Ream, a group from Northern Ireland, where hopes for better times had particular urgency. Blair was very conscious of change since 1979, determined to overcome Labour's troubles in the 1980s and work with the changes wrought by Thatcher, accepting that private had replaced public ownership and government must have good relations with business, that the decline of manufacturing, trade unionism and the public sector had eroded Labour's traditional voting base and it must appeal to a more diverse population and culture where old class boundaries were blurred and questioned. But he recognized the need to challenge certain legacies of Thatcher: that inequality between richest and poorest had grown unacceptably and must be reduced, especially the extent of poverty and insecurity, and that services, particularly the NHS and education, which mattered to most voters, had declined too far. He did not aim for an equal society. Like Thatcher, he believed inequality was unavoidable and, up to a point, desirable because it encouraged aspiration to a better life, which he wanted to facilitate. This was the 'New' Labour vision that drove him.

Blair was, at 44, the youngest ever UK premier until matched by Conservative David Cameron in 2010. From more middle-class origins than the three recent Conservative leaders, he lived in gentrified Islington, the first premier with a working wife, Cherie, a successful lawyer. Her father was a well-known TV soap actor who left the family when Cherie was young. Their mother raised Cherie and her sister in modest circumstances in Liverpool. She was the first in her family to attend university, LSE, gaining a First in Law. Tony achieved a Second in Law at Oxford, but beat her to a first post as a trainee barrister, benefiting from the male public school ethos of the Bar.[1] Cherie had been an unsuccessful Labour candidate and was a working mother of three young children. A fourth, Leo, in 2000 was the first child born to a serving Prime Minister for 150 years. Both Blairs were committed Christians, she Roman Catholic, he an Anglican who converted to Catholicism after his premiership. As MP for Sedgefield, County Durham, from 1983, close to where he grew up, he encountered working-class people, many of them initially not working following the decline of the major local industry, mining.

Major resigned as Conservative leader. Kenneth Clarke was beaten by 36-year-old William Hague, the youngest party leader since Pitt the Younger, whose biography he later wrote, best known for a much publicized teenage party conference speech twenty years before, and his Yorkshire accent, treasured by satirists. Educated at state school and Oxford, but from a more prosperous background than his three predecessors (his parents ran a soft drinks business), he was the first of a succession of short-lived Conservative leaders and resigned after another decisive election defeat in 2001. Iain Duncan Smith, Roman Catholic, former army officer, replaced him but soon lost the party's confidence. Michael Howard QC took over in 2003 until the next defeat in 2005, when David Cameron succeeded.

The Blair Regime

Polls recorded Blair as the most popular premier since 1945 and expectations of the new government were high, but it made no extravagant promises. It was inexperienced after eighteen years out of government; only three ministers had previous junior ministerial experience, none at Cabinet level. Blair was as determined as Thatcher to subvert established institutions, but different institutions in different ways. He wanted to control policy, though he met resistance particularly from Brown, with whom relations were now tense, arousing media gossip. Cabinet meetings were short and relatively infrequent. In Parliament he participated in just 8 per cent of votes in his time in office, 1997–2007, a record low for any premier. He quickly, without consultation, changed Prime Minister's Questions from two fifteen-minute sessions weekly to one of thirty minutes, which took less of his time and provided lengthier entertainment for the media.[2] He preferred 'sofa government', informal discussion with chosen advisers. Six Special Advisers worked in the Prime Minister's office in 1997, twenty-five by 1999, with growing numbers in other departments they were increasingly influential.[3]

1 Michael Beloff, 'Law and the Judiciary', in Anthony Seldon (ed.), *Blair's Britain, 1997–2007* (Cambridge University Press, 2007), p. 291.

2 Philip Cowley, 'Parliament', in Anthony Seldon (ed.), *Blair's Britain, 1997–2007* (Cambridge University Press, 2007), p. 16.

3 Paul Fawcett and R. A. W. Rhodes, 'Central Government', in Anthony Seldon (ed.), *Blair's Britain, 1997–2007* (Cambridge University Press, 2007), pp. 80–1; Blick, *People Who Live in the Dark*.

Media presentation was ever more important and Blair was acutely responsive to the new twenty-four-hour news cycle and proliferating media outlets, as the internet expanded and newspaper circulation declined. He held regular, televised press conferences. 'Spin' (news management) became a word indissociable from political presentation. It was controlled by Labour's Director of Communications and Strategy, former *Mirror* journalist, Alastair Campbell. Campbell's skills became evident following the sudden death of Princess Diana in August 1997. Blair took maximum advantage of the widespread grief and the queen's public reticence about the death of her heir's estranged wife. He led public mourning for the 'People's Princess', a Campbell-invented 'sound-bite' (another new key word). But public scepticism and impatience with spin mounted, above all concerning the Iraq War in 2003.[4] Campbell became so unpopular that he resigned after the war, though remained Blair's close adviser. His reputation inspired the popular TV satire, *The Thick of It*, which ran from 2005 to 2012, doing nothing to reverse Labour's declining popularity. It portrayed civil servants, PR team and ministers in a fictional department with the appropriately New Labour title, Social Affairs and Citizenship, presented as blundering, directionless, dominated by spin and by the PM's Director of Communications, 'Malcolm Tucker', who bullied, intimidated and swore at staff, including ministers, focused above all on the department's media image. Insiders claimed it was highly accurate.

Blair sought to centralize policymaking, 'modernize' and 'join up' (more New Labour key terms) different areas of central and local government, but, rightly, never believed he achieved it. Too often policies were impatiently changed before they had time to work through, with no consistent vision behind the restless innovation.[5] Blair was increasingly criticized for his isolation from public opinion (except as represented in the media), including in the Labour Party, from which he was distant. Individual party membership rose from 265,000 in 1994 to 405,000 in 1997, then sank to 248,294 in 2002 and 198,026 in 2005, the lowest since 1918. Membership of the other main parties also declined.

Falling election turnouts also suggested popular disillusion with formal politics. That of 1997 was the lowest since 1935. The next election, in 2001, produced the lowest turnout, at 59.4 per cent, since the 58.9 per cent in the unusual circumstances of 1918[6]; it fell below 1997 in every constituency in Great Britain. Labour won more middle-class and southern English votes, as it had striven to do, but there were signs that this alienated working-class voters. New Labour perhaps overestimated the decline in working-class identification and made little obvious effort to appeal to them. Turnouts were especially low in some traditionally working-class Labour constituencies, especially in northwest

4 See p. 435.

5 Fawcett and Rhodes, 'Central Government', p. 93.

6 See p. 65.

England and Glasgow. Lowest was impoverished Liverpool Riverside at just 34.1 per cent. The divided Conservatives offered them no alternative and many working-class people appear to have chosen not to vote.[7]

Economic and Social Policy

In 2001 and later, the government perhaps received less credit than it deserved for real improvements to public services, higher employment, low inflation and sustained GDP growth, because it was surprisingly reticent about these successes at elections, perhaps fearing accusations of high spending. Gordon Brown built his own empire in the Treasury, highly influential in domestic policy, rarely 'joining up' with Blair's units. Brown was the first Labour Chancellor to inherit a relatively sound economy, by the standards of recent years. Unemployment fell to what now seemed a moderate 1.5 million in mid-1997. He was determined to end the recent boom and bust cycle, achieve stability and practice what he called financial 'prudence'. One of his first, unexpected, moves was transferring control of interest rates to the Bank of England, which established an independent monetary committee, of bank officials and external members (normally economists), to set interest rates, aiming to control inflation to a target of 2.5 per cent. This was popular in the City, designed to stop the previously all too frequent manipulation of interest rates for short-term political motives. He established the Financial Services Authority (FSA) for closer control of financial institutions excessively deregulated by the Conservatives. Prudent Brown paid off the inherited deficit by 1998 and, more gradually, much of the national debt, helped by buoyant tax revenues and £22 billion from the sale of digital channels in 2000.[8]

He pledged to dispel Labour's 'tax and spend' image by accepting the spending and income tax limits set by Clarke for 1997–9. But no limits were set for indirect taxes, which increased, including fuel taxes, to protect the environment by discouraging motoring as well as raising revenue. Environmental protection was a serious Labour commitment as it became more salient internationally. With EU encouragement they promoted recycling, which increased significantly by 2010. But the fuel tax caused public protests. In 2000, farmers and lorry drivers barricaded supply depots and petrol stations ran dry as prices rose, due also to international price rises.

Tax rises funded some redistribution, though the word was largely banned from the New Labour lexicon lest it disturb 'Middle England'. It was rumoured that part of the arrangement between Blair and Brown in 1994, when they agreed that Blair would run

---

7 David Butler and Dennis Kavanagh (eds), *The British General Election of 2001* (London: Palgrave, 2002), pp. 235–7, 256–8, 299, 304 ff; Evans and Tilley, *The New Politics of Class*, pp. 170–7.
8 Ibid., p. 2.

as leader and Brown succeed him,[9] was that Brown would lead on social policy, in which Blair had less interest. Policies originating in the Treasury included a major innovation in 1999, the Working Families Tax Credit (WFTC), a means-tested supplement to low pay paid through the tax system, designed to eliminate the serious problem of poverty in families where one or more full-time workers received inadequate pay. It helped many, but had the usual problem of means-tested payments that about a half a million eligible workers had not applied by 2000–1; it also subsidized low-paying employers.

Inflation remained low, while unemployment fell to under 1 million in 2001. Reducing it was another of Brown's commitments, and a manifesto pledge, especially to reduce youth unemployment, described as an employment New Deal. 'Work is the best welfare' was another New Labour mantra – as Labour had argued from its foundation, though its current leaders seemed unaware of this.[10] It was also a Conservative belief, but this government provided positive assistance to find work, rather than 'incentivizing' by the punitive withdrawal of benefits under the Thatcher and Major governments. Brown imposed a windfall tax on the privatized utilities, which were accused of exploiting their monopoly positions to maintain excessive prices. It yielded £5 billion which was dedicated to advice and training for 18–25 year olds. By 2005, 500,000 long-term unemployed young people had work. Official unemployment figures had never fallen below 5 per cent of the workforce in eighteen years of Conservative rule; by 2001 they were 2.5 per cent.[11]

Labour introduced the first universal minimum wage in UK history in 1999 (following New Zealand in 1894, the United States in 1938, then most other developed countries). Previously Trade Boards, from 1909, then Wages Councils had set them for some occupations but these had been abolished in 1993.[12] It was set at a cautiously low level: £3.60 per hour for workers aged 22+, £3 for those aged 18–22, who were assumed to have fewer expenses; 1.9 million workers were expected to benefit. An independent Low Pay Commission was appointed, of academics and trade union and employer representatives, to recommend annual upgrading. Business leaders forecast catastrophic effects on their competitiveness, which proved unfounded.

Blair believed strongly in social responsibility, that there was such a thing as society and an obligation on all its members to contribute to social stability, cohesion and well-being. He rejected the social injustices of the previous period while embracing the market. For his moderation, some labelled him 'son of Thatcher', but his 1998 conference speech was a robust defence, listing the improvements already announced:

9 See p. 420.

10 Thane, 'Labour and Welfare', pp. 80–2.

11 Abigail McKnight, 'Employment. Tackling Poverty through 'Work for Those Who Can', in J. Hills and K. Stewart (eds), *A More Equal Society? New Labour, Poverty, Inequality and Exclusion* (Bristol: Policy Press, 2004), pp. 23–46.

12 See p. 401

Don't give me this nonsense that we're just a more moderate or competent Tory government … What Tory government ever put £800 million into our poorest estates in order to give them a future of hope? What Tory government would have raised child benefit by over 20 per cent? Or given free eye tests to pensioners? Or four weeks' minimum holiday entitlement to Britain's workers? And what Tory government would have been prepared to increase by 25 per cent our spending on art and museums, not just for what the sneer squad call luvvies, but because we believe that art and culture are a liberating, wonderful addition to human experience and an integral part of the country we are creating?

Then you tell me what Tory government would have introduced as we have from 1 April 1999, the first British statutory minimum wage? A pay rise for two million people. And backed it up with a Working Families Tax Credit that means that no family earning less than £220 a week pays a penny in income tax. Or for the first time given people the right to be represented by a trade union where the majority of the workforce want it? Campaigned for during more than a century. Promised by every Labour government there has ever been. It will be delivered by this one.

And you tell me what Tory government would have given the peoples of Africa and Asia a 25 per cent increase in aid and development?[13]

It was all true. Among other changes, Labour did indeed increase arts funding and in 2001 abolished admission charges for museums and art galleries introduced under Thatcher, resulting in 30 million extra visits in the next five years, including a wider social range of visitors. But he failed to mention that Labour was planning to introduce tuition fees for university students, and that it had cut the Lone Parent Premium and One Parent Benefit following Brown's pledge to preserve stringent Conservative spending plans. This was opposed by Labour backbenchers. Single parents were recompensed when the straitjacket was abandoned in 1999.

Constitutional Change

Labour also moved fast to introduce significant constitutional reforms, mostly inherited from John Smith, the most radical reforms since those of Attlee's government, with the same aim of promoting democracy. Smith's legacy was promoted by his friend and fellow Scot, Lord Derry Irvine, Tony and Cherie Blair's former pupil master at the Bar, a former Labour candidate and Lord Chancellor from 1997.

Devolution

Nationalism continued to grow in Scotland and Wales under the Conservative governments, which showed no interest in devolution. Smith and Irvine were committed to devolution and referenda were held again in Scotland and Wales in September 1997. The Scots

13 Quoted in John Rentoul, 'Tony Blair 1994–' in Kevin Jeffreys (ed.), *Leading Labour. From Keir Hardie to Tony Blair* (London: I. B. Tauris, 1999), p. 221.

voted 74.3 per cent for a devolved parliament and 63.5 per cent, on a separate vote, to grant it tax-raising powers. The Welsh voted by 50.3 per cent to 49.7 per cent, on a 50 per cent turnout, for a devolved assembly with more limited powers than the Scots but controlling taxes. The first elections were held in both countries in May 1999 under the additional member PR system. This was partly due to intense involvement of women activists in the negotiations for the devolved constitutions, determined to gain fair female representation which international experience showed was promoted by PR.[14] In both countries Labour and the nationalist parties, and in Scotland the Liberal Democrats, committed to equal numbers of male and female candidates. In Wales, 41.7 per cent of representatives elected to the first Assembly were female, in Scotland 37.2 per cent, both far ahead of Westminster's 18.2 per cent. The second election, in 2002, returned 51.7 per cent female representatives in Wales, the first elected assembly in the world to achieve gender equality, remarkably since no women were elected for Welsh constituencies between 1970 and 1984; before 1997 only four women had been elected in the country's history.[15] In both countries elected women pressed with some success for progressive social policies, including in Scotland for improved childcare, support for carers of older and disabled people, and measures to pre-vent domestic violence.[16] The Welsh government also improved childcare and support for carers and increased pressure on employers to provide equal pay. By 2016, in Scotland the three major parties (SNP, Labour, Conservative) had female leaders, as had Plaid in Wales.

Coalition government was probable in the devolved assemblies under PR. The first and second Scottish governments were Labour–Liberal Democrat coalitions. In 2007, the SNP gained one seat more than Labour and formed a minority administration with the Greens. Labour governed in Wales, usually in a minority. The Scots asserted their independence of New Labour policies particularly by introducing free social care for disabled and older people from 2002 and abolishing the new university tuition fees for Scots students at UK universities. Wales lacked powers to abolish fees, but in 2002 reintroduced means-tested maintenance grants for Welsh students in UK universities. Both rejected league tables for schools, hospitals or local authority performance and Blair's quasi-market reforms of the NHS.[17]

Parliamentary Reform

Labour's 1997 manifesto proclaimed 'Our system of government is centralized, ineffi-cient and bureaucratic', promising to reform the House of Lords and 'modernize' the Commons. In November 1998, a Bill sought to end the voting rights of hereditary peers. To appease the Lords, it was amended to retain ninety-two voters, elected by their fellow

14 Childs et al., *Women at the Top*, pp. 80–2.
15 Breitenbach and Thane, *Women and Citizenship*, pp. 171–3, 190–2.
16 Ibid., p. 164.
17 See pp. 453–6.

hereditaries, plus the bishops and law lords, while further reform was discussed. A Royal Commission recommended a partially elected Chamber. Several options were put to Parliament, but the Lords would go no further. They defeated the government 120 times between 1997 and 2001, during the second term 245 times – by no means always resisting progress – despite Blair creating 380 peers, more than any previous premier. No party had a Lords majority and less than one-third supported Labour.

The Constitutional Reform Act 2005 removed the Lords' ancient powers as the highest court of appeal. A Supreme Court was established from 2009, composed of twelve judges, no longer chaired by the Lord Chancellor, the presiding officer of the House of Lords, but by the Lord Chief Justice, head of the judiciary. In 2006, the Lords elected its first Speaker, Labour Baroness Helene Hayman. Political responsibility for the new justice system moved from the Home Office to a Secretary of State for Constitutional Affairs (from 2007, Secretary of State for Justice) who had the title of Lord Chancellor but need not be legally qualified. The 2005 Act also created a Judicial Appointments Commission, with a lay majority and chair, initially Baroness Usha Prashar, to achieve greater transparency in appointments. A separate body appointed Queen's Counsel. Both sets of appointments had previously been made by the Lord Chancellor, long perceived as a branch of the old boys' network. The first female Law 'Lord', Baroness Brenda Hale, was appointed in 2004. In 2005, ten High Court judges of 107 were female; sixty-seven circuit judges of 626; eighty-five district judges of 433. There was one BME representative above the circuit level, Justice Linda Dobbs; about 10 per cent of circuit judges had BME backgrounds.[18] Qualified barristers increased by 50 per cent between 1994 and 2004, to 121,165, 39,199 of them female, an increase of 120 per cent; BME representatives rose to 8,031, from 2.2 per cent to 9 per cent. Among 1,078 QCs, eighty-seven were female, including Cherie Blair from 1994.[19]

Proposals by a cross-party Select Committee on the Modernization of the House of Commons, 1997–2001, were mostly implemented, including bringing the timetable closer to a normal working week, in particular ending all-night sittings. Select Committees were granted increased resources and payment of chairs, to attract able MPs. MPs were no longer required to wear top hats when making points of order during divisions. From 2006, the age of eligibility to stand for Parliament and other public offices was reduced from 21 to 18. Proposals to introduce a PR voting system for Westminster elections were opposed in the Labour Party, which feared losing its majority, and Blair was unenthusiastic. The Political Parties, Elections and Referendums Act 2000 restricted party spending in elections and donations to parties, requiring that they be reported to a new Electoral Commission and prohibited from anonymous donors or residents outside the EU.

18 Beloff, 'Law and the Judiciary', p 297, n. 23.
19 Ibid., p. 311.

Local Government

Labour promised to restore elected government to Greater London if approved by a London referendum. In May 1998, a 34 per cent turnout voted 72 per cent in favour. The first election, in May 2000, returned Ken Livingstone, now Labour MP for Brent East, to his former role as Mayor of London, as an Independent since he was opposed by Blair and Brown as excessively Old Labour. He comprehensively defeated their candidate, a reluctant Frank Dobson, Secretary of State for Health and MP for an inner London constituency. A twenty-five-member Assembly was elected, like the mayor, by the single transferable vote PR system. Livingstone proved moderate – his limited powers left him little choice – and at the next election, in 2004, Blair, also with little choice, given Livingstone's popularity, let him stand for Labour. The mayor had most control over roads and transport and Livingstone introduced Britain's first Congestion Charge, limiting traffic in central London by charging for entry during working hours. He improved bus services and held transport fares steady and relatively low for regular users, but he could not prevent Brown insisting upon a complex and ultimately costly Private Finance Initiative (PFI) arrangement for much needed improvements to the underground. PFI had been introduced by the Major administration in 1993, but was relatively little used. It enabled public institutions to contract-out construction work to private firms, since Treasury concern about public spending prevented much necessary construction. It was extensively used under Brown's Chancellorship, often proving highly profitable to private business at public cost.[20]

Labour also promised elected mayors in other cities and revival of local authority powers lost since the 1980s. The Local Government Act 2000 recommended that larger council areas elect executive mayors and cabinets of councillors, paid, for the first time, for their greater responsibilities; fewer than twenty councils chose elected mayors. But central control persisted, sometimes in new forms. Labour aimed to shift from the Tory emphasis on cost of services to quality and effectiveness, which they believed could be achieved by targets and performance indicators. From 2000, each authority had to produce a performance plan and a ceiling was placed on the level of Council Tax they could raise. Competitive tendering for service provision was no longer compulsory and councils gained greater control over capital spending but not significantly greater funding.

Many authorities, including those that were Labour-controlled, disliked the targets and indicators and wanted more devolution. But, increasingly, education funding was nationally determined.[21] More 'social' housing was transferred to housing associations

20 See p. 452.
21 See pp. 453, 456.

and local authorities were granted no housebuilding funds despite a growing shortage of low-cost homes. Private builders were required to provide a proportion of 'affordable' housing as a condition of planning permission, but the definition of 'affordable' was uncertain and it was not enforced. The supply of 'social' housing slipped further behind demand and need. Housebuilding fell to one of its lowest points since 1947 with 179,160 units completed in 2000–1, of which 25,527 were publicly owned. House prices still rose. The number of statutorily homeless people in England grew from 44,000 in 1997 to 75,000 in 2002, 12,000 in bed and breakfast accommodation.[22] Response to housing need was the greatest failure of the three Labour governments.

Freedom of Information

The Freedom of Information Act, 2000, which came into force in 2005 with the Freedom of Information (Scotland) Act, 2002, entitled members of the public to request previously restricted information from all public authorities. The complementary Data Protection Act, 1998, allowed individuals to access their personal data and protect it from disclosure to unauthorized people. The aim, in principle, was more open, accountable government, increasing public trust. The 1997 White Paper, *Your Right to Know* explained:

> Openness is fundamental to the political health of a modern state ... At last there is a government ready to trust the people with a legal right to information ... unnecessary secrecy in government leads to arrogance in governance and defective decision-making.

Such openness was long familiar in other countries, in Sweden since 1766. In Britain, fears arose that officials would become reluctant to record sensitive information. Journalists, particularly, took advantage, often to the embarrassment of the government, though it sometimes required persistence. *The Guardian* spent ten years demanding letters written by Prince Charles to government ministers, seeking to influence policy. An illuminating batch was finally released in 2015, while the government banned access to more.

The Human Rights Act 1998

Another important innovation was the Human Rights Act (HRA), 1998, embedding the ECHR into UK law from 2000, outlawing public authorities acting in any way incompatible with the Convention. This led to legal changes, including the Gender Recognition Act 2004, enabling transgender people to be legally recognized in their new gender. Some hopes were dashed. In 2001, Diane Pretty, dying of Motor Neurone Disease, applied to the courts under the HRA to let her husband assist her to die,

22 Lowe, *The Welfare State in Britain since 1945*, pp. 429–30.

invoking her right to respect for private and family life. The courts refused because only Parliament could change the law prohibiting assisted suicide, which it failed to do. This was the first case to go to the ECtHR after the HRA. It also ruled against Pretty, since it was required to take account of national traditions and culture. She died soon after.

There were fewer applications under the HRA than supporters hoped or opponents feared. One outcome was the Equality and Human Rights Commission (EHRC), established 2007 to protect and promote all equality issues. It merged the EOC, CRE and Disabilities Rights Commission and took responsibility to protect and promote equalities for gay, transgender and older people, since more comprehensive action was needed and many individuals experienced multiple inequalities. In Northern Ireland, the statutory Human Rights Commission, established in 1998 with similar responsibilities, continued. Scotland moved quickly to appoint a commission for equality issues, which were among its devolved powers.

Women in Parliament

From 1997, the changed composition of the Commons reflected the gradual, wider shift towards greater equalities, with more women than ever before and an unprecedented nine black and Asian MPs, though still distant from representing the demographic structure of the population. Blair's first Cabinet included five women (among twenty-three), more than ever before. But there were limits to progress: before the election, but too late to influence most candidate selections, disappointed men made a successful court challenge to AWS under sex discrimination legislation. The leadership did not challenge it – Blair was not strongly committed to AWS – and shifted to 50:50 male–female shortlists. Forty male Labour MPs who retired before the 2001 election were replaced by four women and 36 men. Labour had six fewer female MPs in 2001 (ninety-five, 23 per cent of the parliamentary party), while Conservative women increased to fourteen, the Liberal Democrats to five. The Sexual Discrimination (Election Candidates) Act 2002 freed all parties to take positive action to increase female representation, enabling Labour to revive AWS, with little obvious response from other parties.

The 2005 election returned 128 women (ninety-eight Labour, seventeen Conservative, ten Liberal Democrats, UUP and Sinn Féin one each), a record 20 per cent of MPs. They still reported discrimination in Parliament, but successfully pushed issues up the agenda, including flexible working to assist combining employment with other, especially caring, responsibilities.[23] Under John Smith, Labour promised a Ministry for Women to conduct gender audits of government legislation, responding to the commitment to 'gender mainstreaming' promoted by the EU since

23 See p. 439.

the 1980s. Gender equality was to be integrated within all policies and programmes. Blair was less enthusiastic than Smith and no ministry emerged. A junior minister, Joan Ruddock, was appointed Under-Secretary for Women in the DSS. A Women's Unit was established in the Cabinet Office, to pursue gender mainstreaming, as were the Equality Units established by the devolved Scottish and Welsh governments. The Women's Unit conducted useful research but its remit was ill-defined and its influence limited.[24]

Resolution in Northern Ireland

In Northern Ireland Blair aimed to continue, more successfully, Major's attempts at negotiated settlement. He appointed an unconventional woman, Mo Mowlem, as Northern Ireland Secretary. She proved to be popular and skilful at negotiating with conflicting groups, despite being diagnosed with cancer in 1997. She immediately proposed to resume all-party talks, conditional on ceasefires. In July, the IRA declared a ceasefire and in September Sinn Féin joined the talks, chaired by Mowlem, supported by George Mitchell. Mowlem announced the end of internment, but bombings continued, including by an intransigent splinter group, the Continuity IRA. In 1997, twenty-two people died, with 228 casualties.[25]

The talks, tensions and killings continued into 1998, though in January the UUF resumed its ceasefire. Mowlem visited the Maze Prison to persuade convicted paramilitaries to support the peace process. Their political representatives joined the talks. By April agreement seemed possible, supported by US President Clinton, with whom Blair was on good terms, the Irish government, Unionist leader David Trimble, Gerry Adams and Martin McGuinness for Sinn Féin, all relatively flexible compared with their predecessors, with Mowlem's skilful chairing. Blair visited Belfast, announcing 'I feel the hand of history on my shoulders'. The outcome was the 'Good Friday Agreement', signed on that day by all the significant parties. It proposed a power-sharing administration, to be ratified by referenda north and south of the border, an assembly elected by PR, with a North–South Ministerial Council to direct cooperation on key issues. The UK and Irish governments agreed to early release of prisoners and the political parties to aim for decommissioning within two years after referenda endorsed the agreement. A police service would be established representing Catholics and Protestants.

Nationalists overwhelmingly supported the agreement. Nelson Mandela, Clinton and other international figures praised it. Unionists remained divided. Blair and

24 McCarthy, 'Gender Equality', pp. 120–2.
25 Bew and Gillespie, *Northern Ireland*, p. 352.

Mowlem worked to reassure them. In May, with an 81 per cent turnout, the north voted 71.1 per cent in favour. In the south, 56 per cent voted, with 94.45 per cent in favour. In the Assembly elections in June the UUP narrowly gained more votes than the SDLP and Trimble became leader of the power-sharing executive, though he refused the role until a lasting peace was assured. Killings continued, mainly but not only by dissident republicans, most tragically in July when a bomb planted by the 'Real IRA' killed twenty-eight and injured 360 in a shopping street in Omagh. It was universally condemned, including by McGuinness, and the Real IRA suspended military operations, followed by the Irish National Liberation Army (INLA).

In September, Adams and Trimble held unprecedented talks, opposed by some unionists, and the Assembly opened. Disagreements continued and Blair worked for reconciliation. In November, he met local politicians in Belfast, then next day became the first UK Prime Minister to address the Dáil and Seanad in Dublin: 'We have come too far to go back now' he declaimed. British soldiers were gradually withdrawn. Still, in 1998, fifty-five people were killed, 211 shot and 243 bombs planted. The UUP demanded Mowlem's dismissal, believing she favoured the IRA, and she became Chancellor of the Duchy of Lancaster in October 1999. She was disillusioned with Blair and did not stand in 2001. She died, aged 55, from the cancer in 2005. She was replaced by loyal New Labour Peter Mandelson, returning from ten months' resignation from the Cabinet following his failure to declare a large loan from a colleague in the parliamentary Register of Business Interests. It was not reassuring when, in his first speech in the post, he described himself as 'Secretary of State for Ireland'. He lasted until January 2001 when he was forced to resign again, accused of using his influence to gain a passport for a relative of an Indian businessman who contributed £1 million towards the Millennium Dome, for which Mandelson was responsible. He wanted to emulate his grandfather, Herbert Morrison's, success with the Festival of Britain[26] with a celebration of the millennium on the Thames. It was less successful, drawing only half the number of visitors expected amid complaints of excessive cost.

In November 1999, the power-sharing executive was functioning and devolved powers followed. The peace was uneasy but the IRA did not resume violence and negotiation continued. In March 2007, Sinn Féin and the DUP, now the dominant unionist party, led by Ian Paisley, agreed Paisley's nomination as First Minister and Martin McGuinness as Deputy. They appeared to get on surprisingly well. It was a major achievement, perhaps the greatest of Blair's premiership. With patience, commitment and indispensable help from Mowlem, he brought Northern Ireland closer to peace than for almost forty years.[27]

---

26 See pp. 215–18.

27 Bew and Gillespie, *Northern Ireland*; Clarke, *Hope and Glory*, pp. 435–7.

Foreign Affairs

Robin Cook, as Foreign Secretary, was overshadowed by Blair's determination to be a major figure in world politics, based, as he put it, on the principle of humanitarian 'liberal interventionism', opposing oppression and autocracy, with military power when all else failed.[28] The first major crisis came in Kosovo, a mainly Muslim province of the former Yugoslavia, which since the fall of Communism had faced aggressive domination by Serbia. A Kosovan independence movement led to intense fighting from 1998. Blair with Clinton persuaded NATO to intervene and air strikes began in March 1999. The Serbs capitulated after eleven weeks' bombing.[29] In 1998, the United Kingdom joined inconclusive air strikes against Iraq, following its leader, Saddam Hussein's, refusal to let UN inspectors examine suspected nuclear weapons sites.

Britain acted alone in the former colony of Sierra Leone in 2000 in a limited, effective military operation to restore the authority of the legitimate government against rebellion and provided aid to assist recovery.[30] Then came the attack on the World Trade Centre in New York on 11th September 2001 – 9/11 as it became known. Britain supported the United States in waging war in Afghanistan, where the perpetrators, the fundamentalist Muslim group, El Qaida, were based. There was little opposition in the United Kingdom amid revulsion at the attack. Republican George W. Bush, US President since 2000, then attacked Iraq in 2003, though there was no evidence of its involvement in 9/11. Blair supported him, believing this was humane intervention to bring peace to the Middle East and the world, convinced, mistakenly, that Saddam Hussein had, and would use, 'weapons of mass destruction'. This war was widely believed to be unjustified and was strongly opposed, including an exceptionally large, wholly ineffective, demonstration in London, of at least 2 million people. One hundred and thirty-nine Labour MPs voted against the war, the largest rebellion against a party whip since 1846. The Cabinet was not adequately consulted or briefed about the decision to go to war and four ministers resigned, including Robin Cook, now Leader of the Commons. Party membership, already falling, shrank to its lowest level ever. Blair's already declining poll ratings plummeted and never recovered. Labour crashed in local and European elections in 2004, winning just 23 per cent of the European vote and 26 per cent of local votes.

In the General Election of May 2005 it faced growing media hostility as more newspapers supported the Conservatives, though it gained from the weakness of successive

28 Michael Clarke, 'Foreign Policy', in Anthony Seldon (ed.), *Blair's Britain, 1997–2007* (Cambridge University Press, 2007), pp. 597–605.
29 Clarke, *Hope and Glory*, pp. 438–9.
30 Clarke, 'Foreign Policy', p. 604.

Conservative leaders. Blair fought the election on a New Labour programme, empha-sizing 'diversity and choice' for providers and consumers of public services, which mar-ket research suggested appealed to Middle England, while wooing female and trade union support by pledging to extend maternity pay and protect the rights of workers transferred from public to private employment. The turnout rose to a still low 61.2 per cent, while Labour slipped to 356 seats and 35.2 per cent of votes compared with the Conservatives' 198 and 32.4 per cent, an overall majority of sixty-five. Turnout in work-ing-class constituencies remained low and hostility to the Iraq War was widespread. Blair was the first Labour leader to win three successive elections but celebrations were muted. 'Blair limps back' headlined *The Times*, which had returned to the Tory fold with all the Murdoch media. 'Ouch!' exclaimed the *Financial Times*, which approved Labour's (mainly Gordon Brown's) management of the economy. 'Hold your nose and vote Labour' advised *The Guardian* columnist Polly Toynbee, echoing many voters who were critical of Labour, especially after Iraq, but opposed the Conservatives more.[31] In 1997, 6 per cent of poll respondents thought Blair out of touch with ordinary people, by 2007 it was 51 per cent. In 2000, 46 per cent thought him 'trustworthy', in 2006, only 29 per cent, largely due to his arguments for war in Iraq.[32]

Following the election, the Conservatives again changed their leader for the rela-tively inexperienced, 39-year-old David Cameron, the first Old Etonian leader since Douglas-Home, and distantly related to the queen. He claimed privately to aspire to be 'heir to Blair' and to support many Labour policies, promoting a moderate, 'compas-sionate Conservative' image, also seeking as wide an appeal as possible.

The war soured relations with other European powers and throughout the world, especially when apparent victory did not lead to stable government in Iraq and other Middle Eastern countries slid into political crisis, while the war in Afghanistan dragged on. Then on 7 July 2005, while London celebrated being chosen to host the 2012 Olympic Games, the international crisis came home, not for the last time, when five British Muslim suicide bombers exploded three bombs on London transport killing fifty-two people and injuring over 700.

Until his resignation two years later, Blair sought world leadership on the more peaceable issues of international aid and climate change, supported by Brown. They had some success, notably in June–July 2005 when Blair chaired the summit in Edinburgh of the G8, the forum of the eight largest economies, formed, as six (G6, Group of Six), in 1974 following the oil shock,[33] to discuss issues of common concern. Interrupted by the London bombings and amid large demonstrations for international aid, world peace

31 D. Butler and D. Kavanagh (eds), *The British General Election of 2005* (London: Palgrave Macmillan, 2006).
32 Ben Page, 'Culture and Attitudes', in Anthony Seldon (ed.), *Blair's Britain, 1997–2007* (Cambridge University Press, 2007), pp. 436–67.
33 See pp. 306–7.

and action against global warming, it agreed to increase aid to developing countries by $50 billion and cancel the debt of the eighteen poorest countries in Africa, aiming to reduce international inequalities.[34] Blair and Brown were under pressure from UK NGOs united in a lively 'Make Poverty History' coalition, and hoped to revive popular support by courting celebrities active in the campaign, including pop stars Bono and Bob Geldof, who with other stars raised huge sums, at concerts live and on TV.[35]

Europe

Blair aimed to play a leading role in Europe while remaining close to the United States, indeed to strengthen relations between the two. In 1997, Labour was committed to the Social Chapter and rapid completion of the single market, EU enlargement to include the former communist countries and greater openness and democracy in EU institutions, while retaining a veto on matters of national interest. The euro was not mentioned in the manifesto, though Blair favoured joining and Labour promised a referendum on entry. Brown's strong opposition prevailed. He opposed UK interest rates being set in Frankfurt and, with the UK economy now out-performing most of the Eurozone, saw no economic case for entry, a view there was no pressure, or good reason, to reverse thereafter.

The failure to join the euro weakened Blair's hope of leadership in Europe, though less than his later intervention in Iraq, but the United Kingdom appeared a less awkward member of the EU than for many years. Blair spoke French and carried some weight. The EU was not an important electoral issue in 2001 or 2005, though opposition continued. In the 2004 European elections, when many voters were alienated by the Iraq War, the PR voting system gained the new, anti-EU, United Kingdom Independence Party (UKIP) 28 per cent of votes and twelve of the UK's seventy-eight seats, on a 34.19 per cent turnout.[36] Enlargement of the EU from 2005 included Cyprus, Malta and Central and Eastern European states, granting their citizens the right of free movement within the EU, stimulating some UK opposition, especially when the government imposed fewer controls on migration than some other countries.[37] UKIP, with its slogan 'Take Back Control of our Country' gained much of its support from critics of immigration, not only from Europe. It spread panic about impoverished East Europeans invading Britain, taking welfare and work. It attracted some working-class

34 Page, 'Culture and Attitudes', pp. 608–9.

35 Richard Manning, 'Development', in Anthony Seldon (ed.), *Blair's Britain, 1997–2007* (Cambridge University Press, 2007), pp. 551–71.

36 Ian Bache and Neill Nugent, 'Europe', in Anthony Seldon (ed.), *Blair's Britain, 1997–2007* (Cambridge University Press, 2007), p. 541.

37 See p. 440.

voters who felt abandoned by the Labour party. UKIP's main appeal was to the dispossessed, mainly in England, despite its name. It won few votes and no seats elsewhere in the United Kingdom.

Business and Unions

Blair and Brown believed the state could stimulate economic growth and social improvement not through 'Old Labour' nationalization, but by constructive cooperation with business and investment in education and training to improve skills. In April 1997, Brown declared: 'It is business not government that creates lasting prosperity … The job of government is not to tell people how to run their businesses but to do what it can to create the conditions in which business can thrive and opportunities for all can flourish'. They built close links with finance and the City continued to boom, attracting more foreign businesses and investors from Russia, the Middle East and increasingly from China. Incomers bought London property for investment or, at most occasional, residence, inflating prices further. Pay and bonuses continued to soar. The *Sunday Times* described 1997–2007 as a 'golden' age for the very rich, estimating that in 1997 the wealth of the UK's wealthiest 1,000 totalled £98.99 billion; by 2007 it was £359,943 billion. Blair, who amassed a considerable fortune after resigning as premier, never criticized this burgeoning of wealth. He wrote in the 1997 manifesto 'I want a country in which people get on, make a success of their lives. I have no time for the politics of envy', and later, 'We favour true equality; equal worth and equal opportunity, not an equality of outcome focused on incomes alone',[38] telling BBC TV *Newsnight* in 2001 'It's not a burning ambition of mine to make sure David Beckham earns less money'.[39] Peter Mandelson notoriously remarked in 1998 that the government was 'intensely relaxed about people getting filthy rich', specifically by forming productive new companies, adding hastily, within earshot of a journalist, 'as long as they pay their taxes'.

Blair pledged to re-establish trade union rights, within limits, stating in 1997 that he would not wholly repeal Thatcher's anti-union laws: 'there will be no return to flying pickets, secondary action, strikes with no ballots or the trade union laws of the 1970s'. Union membership declined to 16 per cent of the workforce by 2006, lower than at any time since 1945, overwhelmingly in the public sector, where they were constant irritants to Blair and Brown, opposing their adoption of Thatcher-style managerialism and targets. To many younger workers, and to Blair, unionism now appeared unfamiliar and its purpose unclear. He regarded them as 'Old Labour' relics and refused to

---

38 Tony Blair, Fabian Society pamphlet, 2002.
39 Kitty Stewart, 'Equality and Social Justice', in Anthony Seldon (ed.), *Blair's Britain, 1997–2007* (Cambridge University Press, 2007), p. 430.

meet the TUC in his first six months in office. John Monks, the TUC general secretary, described their relationship as like 'embarrassing elderly relatives at a family reunion'.[40]

However, Blair promised and delivered an exceptional new framework of workers' rights and sought to persuade business that a more secure workforce would benefit not disadvantage production. Britain remained opted-out of the EU's preferred maximum forty-eight-hour working week but, in addition to the minimum wage, implemented other EU improvements to employee rights, especially benefiting women: equal rights for part-time with full-time workers including to holiday and sickness pay; for all workers, increased protection against, and compensation for, unfair dismissal; universal paid maternity leave extended from fourteen to twenty-six weeks; unpaid paternity leave after one year's service; women gained the right to return to their previous job, or a suitable equivalent, after maternity leave and could not be dismissed for any reason connected with pregnancy and maternity, as was still all too common; parents could request flexible working hours to match their childcare responsibilities, though employers could refuse; 'reasonable' unpaid leave for deaths or accidents among close family or friends became a right; all workers gained four weeks annual paid leave, excluding public holidays; night working was restricted to eight hours; minimum rest periods were established; discrimination at work on grounds of gender, age, race, disability, sexual orientation, union membership or part-time working was prohibited; processes for trade union recognition in a workplace were established and strengthened.[41]

Blair and Brown shared 'Old' Labour's commitment to full employment and entered government with a programme of 'Employment Opportunities for All', Brown's 'New Deal', which increased employment at all ages, assisted by economic revival.[42] It was harder to improve skills and productivity and business did little to help. In 2006, it was estimated that one-third of working-age adults were low-skilled, despite Labour funding workplace training schemes and other initiatives; productivity still trailed behind Germany, France and the United States. In 2005, 20 per cent of young people aged 16–24, almost 1 million, were still not in education, employment or training – NEETS, as they became known. The skilled working-class continued to shrink despite high unmet demand for labour and the economy suffered from sluggish research and development in the private sector.[43] This led the government to open the labour market to well-educated and trained immigrants from poorer countries of Central and Eastern Europe, welcoming free movement within the EU on easier terms than some other countries, while immigration continued from elsewhere.

40 Robert Taylor, 'New Labour, New Capitalism', in Anthony Seldon (ed.), *Blair's Britain, 1997–2007* (Cambridge University Press, 2007), p. 220.
41 Ibid., pp. 232–3.
42 McKnight, 'Employment', pp. 23–46.
43 Taylor, 'New Labour', pp. 235–7.

Immigration

Immigration was not a major issue in the 1997 or 2001 elections. Polls showed only 3 per cent of voters rated it among their top three concerns. Labour believed Conservative immigration controls were too harsh, but feared losing votes by appearing too soft. The 1997 manifesto promised 'firm control' but offered no clear vision. In fact, the Conservatives had quietly increased work permits for immigrants to meet skill shortages in the NHS, which still depended heavily upon immigrants at all levels, and parts of the private sector, though business was critical of the slow, unpredictable permit system. Labour eased the controls further, enabling highly skilled people to enter the United Kingdom without a job offer. Labour shortages in hospitality, food processing and seasonal agricultural work (all unattractive to British workers because they were low paid, but important to the economy) led to an entry scheme for low-wage work. Visa restrictions were eased for international university students and they were allowed to work while studying. By 2004, the United Kingdom had captured 24 per cent of the world English-speaking student market and income from overseas student fees grew from £622 million in 1997–8 to £1,275 million in 2003–4.

When entry to Britain opened to citizens of new EU countries on 1 May 2004 the tabloids and UKIP warned of Roma and other undesirables flocking to claim welfare benefits. Between May 2004 and March 2007, 630,000 entrants registered; there was no record of numbers leaving. There was an unknown amount of illegal immigration, arranged by highly exploitative, profit-making syndicates. A Worker Registration Scheme recorded EU immigrants' employment and monitored their, highly restricted, access to benefits. Most were young and migrated to find work: their work and tax payments contributed substantially more to the economy than they took in benefits, health and social services, though they often experienced poor pay, working and living conditions.[44] Local authorities receiving large numbers of immigrants had no help to expand services to meet the increased demand; immigrants were unfairly blamed for inadequate, over-stretched education and health services and housing shortages and hostility grew. Media-driven panics ensured that when Bulgaria and Romania joined the EU in 2007 their nationals were not allowed free access to the United Kingdom. The poor treatment and low pay of migrant workers, legal and illegal, led to a trade union campaign for improvement, partly from a realistic fear that it would drive down standards for all workers. This was reinforced by the tragedy in Morecambe Bay in 2004, when at least twenty-one illegal Chinese workers were drowned by an unexpected sea surge while collecting cockles for sale, for which they were unlawfully employed below the minimum wage. The Gang Masters (Licensing) Act 2004 attempted, without total success, to regulate employment agencies in agriculture and fisheries to prevent exploitation of migrant workers.

44 Sarah Spencer, 'Immigration', in Anthony Seldon (ed.), *Blair's Britain, 1997–2007* (Cambridge University Press, 2007), p. 352.

Immigration was swelled by growing numbers of refugees seeking asylum. In 1997, 'swift and fair' action was promised to reduce a backlog of 52,000 asylum applications and crack down on the 'bogus' applications trumpeted by the tabloids. The asylum queue grew to 125,000 by 1999 as refugees fled the growing number of crisis-hit countries: Kosovo, Sierra Leone, later Iraq and civil war in Sri Lanka. The backlog was worsened by Conservative staff cuts in the Immigration and Nationality Directorate (IND), which were not reversed. The Immigration and Asylum Act, 1999, continued Conservative restrictions on asylum-seekers' access to the United Kingdom. It increased penalties on people transporting incomers with no right of entry and the number of countries from which a visa was required for entry grew from nineteen in 1991 to 108 in 2005.[45] Persistent media assertions that asylum-seekers were undeserving economic migrants masquerading as refugees, fleeing poverty not war, attracted by Britain's health and welfare benefits, ignored the heart-breaking stories of many of them, the ungenerous level of British benefits compared with many other west European countries and evidence that these were not significant motives for undergoing the stress and dangers of travelling for asylum; also that they were forbidden to work to support themselves and their families for at least six months after arrival. The Act replaced cash payments to often destitute refugees with vouchers for essential supplies, lest cash be spent on drink and drugs as some alleged. The black TGWU leader, Bill Morris, led protest against this 'cruel' system, which 'deepened the misery of those in need', leaving them without cash for essentials like public transport.[46] Refugees were then allowed cash payments equalling 70 per cent of regular Income Support.

The 1999 Act established a National Asylum Support System to manage the dispersal of asylum-seekers from crowded southeast England. Refugees were often placed in areas where housing was vacant because there were many disadvantages and few jobs, receiving minimal support in unfamiliar environments, though churches and voluntary agencies did a lot. Still, local authorities received little help to meet the resulting pressure on services, causing resentment. Under pressure from minority groups, the Act removed the requirement for those seeking entry in order to marry to prove that the marriage was not a phoney pretext for entry – not always easy – and cut waiting times for families to join close relatives in the United Kingdom. Due to the difficulty of entering the United Kingdom legally, by 2001 there were nightly TV images of residents of the Sangatte refugee camp at Calais scaling fences, attempting to board trains for Dover. In December 2002, the French government closed the overcrowded camp and refugees camped even more miserably elsewhere. From 2002, those seeking UK citizenship had to take the 'Life in the United Kingdom' test to demonstrate their

---

45 Spencer, 'Immigration', p. 343, n. 6.
46 Ibid., p 344.

understanding of UK language and culture, often requiring greater knowledge than many British-born people possessed.[47]

Labour hopes that its measures would satisfy public opinion failed: by 2002, polls showed that 39 per cent rated immigration and race among their top three issues of concern, by 2006 40 per cent placed it top. IND remained seriously understaffed and overworked officials made mistakes in processing applications, leading to costly appeals. The Asylum and Immigration (Treatment of Claimants etc.) Act, 2004, limited access to appeals and excluded failed asylum-seekers from hospital care. Asylum seekers declined to 49,000 in 2003, 23,500 in 2006, partly due to increased controls, though probably more to the end of the Balkan war and peace in Sri Lanka. Some rejected asylum-seekers vanished and could not be traced and removed despite intensified efforts. Some employers readily employed illegal workers willing to work hard for low pay.

Fears of terrorism increased tension around immigration. 9/11 in New York was followed in Britain by the Anti-Terrorism, Crime and Security Act, introducing indefinite detention of foreigners suspected of involvement in terrorism. After a legal challenge it was replaced in 2005 by Control Orders, enabling suspects to remain under restricted conditions in their own homes. Then the London bombings in July 2005 led Blair to promise that any asylum-seeker involved in terrorism would be denied refugee status, though the bombers were all British citizens. This was enacted in 2006, with tighter checks on foreign nationals entering and leaving the United Kingdom.[48]

Race

The increasingly diverse UK population of immigrant origin often experienced the same hostility as refugees, among other difficulties (Table 13.1).

The enquiry into the death of Stephen Lawrence in 1993 chaired by the former High Court judge, Sir William Macpherson, reported in 1999.[49] It was a damning indictment of what Macpherson described as 'institutional racism' among the police, causing their failure to investigate the killing adequately. Still, no one was convicted of the crime.[50] The Race Relations (Amendment) Act 2000 placed a new, enforceable duty on public authorities, including the police, to promote equal opportunities and eliminate discrimination. Police forces appointed more BME officers; some complained of their colleagues' racism.

---

47 Tania Burchardt, 'Selective Inclusion. Asylum Seekers and Other Marginalized Groups', in J. Hills and K. Stewart (eds), *A More Equal Society? New Labour, Poverty, Inequality and Exclusion* (Bristol: Policy Press, 2004), pp. 219–27.

48 Spencer, 'Immigration', pp. 354–5.

49 See p. 413.

50 See p. 413; Kimber, 'Race and Equality', p. 41.

Table 13.1 Identities Recorded in the 2001 Census, % UK Population

Indian	1.8%
Pakistani	1.3%
Bangladeshi	0.5%
Black Caribbean	1%
Black African	0.8%
Chinese	0.4%
Total minority ethnic population	7.9%
660,000 people in England and Wales identified as mixed race, the first time this question was asked in a census.	

SOURCE: Census, April 2001, Office for National Statistics. Available at: www.statistics.gov.uk

In 1999, unemployment among BME groups was double that of white people, deepening inequalities of income, health, education and housing. Disadvantage was greatest among Bangladeshis and the small Somali population, mostly recent refugees from conflict in their home country. A report in 2000, *The Future of Multi-Ethnic Britain*, by Bhikhu Parekh, a distinguished political scientist of Asian origin, commissioned by the Runnymede Trust (an NGO devoted to promoting racial harmony, founded in 1968) illustrated cultural diversity. Five-year-olds of black Caribbean origin started school performing at national average standards, but by age 10 had fallen behind; attainment of GCSEs at A*–C grades, was 50 per cent below the national average, boys performing worse than girls. Indians achieved above the national average throughout their school careers. Pakistani and Bangladeshi children started below average but steadily closed the gap: they were well represented among university entrants but over-represented among pupils with the poorest qualifications; more girls took A-levels than white females. National attainment levels on entry to university were exceeded by Indian, Pakistani and black Caribbean women and Indian, Pakistani and Bangladeshi men, despite the relative disadvantages many of them experienced.[51]

Occasional conflicts erupted. In May 2001, in Oldham, Lancashire, hundreds of young Pakistani and Bangladeshi men rioted for three nights and eighty-six policemen were injured. Soon after, clashes between white and Asian youths in Burnley, Lancashire, caused extensive damage. Then in Bradford, Yorkshire, with a large Pakistani population, in July an Anti-Nazi League march was attacked by National Front supporters, with prolonged clashes. Discontents caused by unemployment and police treatment of BME youths sparked riots. Professor Ted Cantle, a specialist in community cohesion, was appointed to investigate. He criticized the separation of people of different ethnic

51 Kimber, 'Race and Equality', p. 42; Y Li, F. Devine and A. Heath, *Equality Group Inequalities in Education, Employment and Earnings. Research Review and Analysis of Trends over Time*, Research Report No.10, Equality and Human Rights Commission, available at: www.equalityhumanrightscommission.com.

backgrounds at home, school, work, worship, leisure and cultural activities, proposing an 'open and honest' debate on how to increase cohesion and equalize opportunities. Among other things, he recommended that no school should have more than 75 per cent pupils of one ethnicity and proposed more training of local officials and citizens in the realities of a diverse society and ways of fostering cohesion. The government then required local authorities to consult minority groups about local plans, but change was slow and more clashes followed in Birmingham in 2005 between black Caribbean and Pakistani residents. London, with the most culturally diverse population, experienced no serious conflicts. BME groups were poorly represented on the staff of media organizations, including the BBC and national newspapers, which perhaps influenced their representation in the media. They were similarly under-represented in all high-profile occupations, including Parliament and senior business management.[52]

Following 9/11 and 7/7 Muslims faced attacks and heightened discrimination and concern grew about religious discrimination. For the first time, a question on religious identity was included in the 2001 Census (Table 13.2).

Despite talk of 'secularization', 85 per cent identified with a religion. Existing faith-based support groups continued and new ones formed, including Sikhs in England in 2000. Polish immigrants helped to revive the Catholic Church in some areas. The Church of England encouraged contact and understanding among faith groups, as it had for some time. The government encouraged closer communication between faith communities and the state, partly influenced by Blair's own faith. More were represented at official functions, including the annual Remembrance Day ceremony in Whitehall. In 2006, the Faith Communities Consultative Council was established to succeed the Inner Cities Religious Council, founded 1992, to communicate with government, provide services and encourage social cohesion. It received £5 million government funding in 2006–7, but was closed by the Coalition government in 2011.[53]

Table 13.2 Religious Identity, 2001 Census, % UK Population

Christian	71.8%
Muslim	2.8%
Hindu	1%
Sikh	0.6%
Jewish	0.5%
Buddhist	0.3%
No religion	15%

SOURCE: Census, April 2001, Office for National Statistics, available at: www.statistics.gov.uk.

52 Kimber, 'Race and Equality', pp. 43–5.
53 Filby, 'Religion and Belief', pp. 66–7.

In 2001 a Home Office report, *Religious Discrimination in England and Wales*, revealed that 30 per cent of Muslims, 25 per cent of Jews and 16 per cent of Christians reported discrimination at work. The Employment (Religion and Belief) Regulations Act, 2003, outlawed discrimination on grounds of religion or belief in the workplace. The Race and Religious Hatred Act, 2006, created the offence of 'inciting religious hatred', covering a gap in the law which in 2004 prevented police action against a BNP pamphlet *The Truth about Islam*, which was far from the truth. Also in 2006, Part 2 of the Equality Act extended protection against religious discrimination to education, provision of goods and services, management of premises and the exercise of public functions. The HRA for the first time gave all faith groups legal recognition, freedom and rights to practice their beliefs. In 2004, a Muslim schoolgirl won, on appeal under the HRA, the right to wear the ankle-length jilbab to her school where it was previously forbidden by school uniform policy. The refusal by Heathrow Airport in 2006 to allow a Christian employee to wear a small crucifix at work caused a media furore. Some Christians protested at what they perceived as growing denigration and discrimination. When in 2005 BBC TV screened *Jerry Springer the Opera*, they received 55,000 complaints about its irreverent representation of Jesus. The Christian Voice organization tried, unsuccessfully, to sue it under the Blasphemy Act. Religious belief, including Christianity, could itself embody intolerance of minorities, including the refusal to accept equal rights for homosexuals or to allow women equal rights with men. The HRA tried to stipulate that individuals could exercise their religious beliefs only in ways that did not infringe the rights of others.[54]

A high-profile issue was forced marriage within communities from the Indian subcontinent. The Forced Marriages (Civil Protection) Act 2007, introduced in the Lords as a Private Member's Bill, supported by the government, enabled individuals to apply to the civil courts to prevent a forced marriage or protect them from the outcome of one. Women were often too frightened of family intimidation to apply. The problem continued until forcing a woman into marriage became a criminal offence in 2014. Another problematic practice was female genital mutilation (FGM), said to have been undergone by 74,000 first-generation African women in the United Kingdom. It was forbidden by the Prohibition of Female Circumcision Act 1984, with enhanced protection for children under the Children Act 1989. But, like forced marriage, it was cloaked in secrecy and could be evaded by taking young females abroad for the procedure. Since 1985 just two doctors in the United Kingdom have been struck off for performing FGM. The Female Genital Mutilation Act, 2003 (2005 in Scotland) made FGM illegal whether carried out in the United Kingdom or abroad, criminalizing parents responsible and extending the maximum penalty from five to fourteen years, but few cases followed.

54 Ibid., pp. 63–7.

Yet, despite the tensions, even after July 2005, polls suggested that most people – 68 per cent, 74 per cent of Muslims – supported a society that valued all cultures. The number of BME MPs crept up: twelve in 2001, all Labour. In 2002, Paul Boateng became the first black Cabinet Minister, as Chief Secretary to the Treasury. He left Parliament in 2005 to become UK High Commissioner in Mandela's South Africa. In 2005, thirteen Labour and two Conservative BME candidates were elected, in 2010, sixteen Labour (including the first three Muslim women MPs) and eleven Conservatives, as parties strove to increase their diversity and appeal to BME voters.

Gypsies and Travellers

Gypsies and Travellers gained further advances, as under previous Labour governments, though far from full cultural acceptance and equality. They benefited from the HRA and subsequent race relations legislation, while campaigning for further reform. Helped by sympathetic MPs, who formed the All Party Parliamentary Group for Traveller Law Reform, they achieved greater toleration of unauthorized encampments, improved access to healthcare and voting rights. Growing numbers battled for permission to stay on unauthorized sites they had bought and settled, often against bitter opposition. Human rights law helped some defend their right to live on land they owned, but others failed. In theory they had equal rights and equal access to public services with other citizens, but not always in practice. In 1998, the CRE brought a successful case under the RRA against Cheltenham Borough Council for imposing exceptionally stringent conditions on two Gypsy women wishing to hire a hall for a wedding reception. But in 2003 the Firle Bonfire Society in East Sussex was not prosecuted, despite police efforts, when it burned an effigy of a caravan with a Gypsy family painted on the side and the registration plate 'P1KEY', claiming the village had experienced problems with Travellers camping on local land. In the same year, 15-year-old Irish Traveller, Johnny Delaney, was kicked and stamped to death at Ellesmere Port, Merseyside. Several witnesses testified that the killers had shouted racist abuse, but the judge dismissed the police case for racially motivated murder, found the killers guilty of the lesser offence of manslaughter and sentenced them to just four-and-a-half years in prison.

The 2004 Housing and Planning Acts required local authorities to identify and provide for the needs of local Gypsies and Travellers and a Select Committee recommended the reintroduction of the statutory duty on local authorities to provide sites. A tabloid furore erupted over 'problem' sites, whose residents were accused of noise, fly-tipping and environmental damage. A *Sunday Express* poll found that 75 per cent of householders believed they should pay lower council tax if Gypsies camped nearby. Sixty-three per cent thought 'Labour's stance on Gypsies' was 'ruled by political correctness and fear of accusations of racism'. A 2005 poll for Stonewall showed 35 per cent of respondents feeling 'less positive' towards Gypsies and Travellers, 34 per cent to refugees/asylum-seekers, 18 per cent to ethnic minorities, including black and Asian people and 17 per cent to gays and lesbians.

In 2005, the Conservative leader, Michael Howard, made an election issue of the 'Gypsy problem', pledging to prevent their using the HRA to stall eviction proceedings and toughen enforcement powers against unauthorized sites. The *Sun* launched a 'War on Gipsy free-for-all', headlined 'Stamp on the Camps', labelling the HRA 'the villain of the piece'. An appeal to the Press Complaints Commission failed, despite the CRE recording increased incidents of discrimination against Gypsies and Travellers following the article. Similar abuse followed in other tabloids. No action was taken, despite complaints by the broadsheets and some broadcast media, the CRE and MPs. In 2007 Gypsies and Travellers were included in the remit of the EHRC. They continued to experience the greatest inequalities of any social group.[55]

'Tough on Crime'?

Margaret Thatcher attacked Labour for being 'soft on crime'. In polls in the 1980s it was the issue on which Labour was furthest behind the Conservatives. When Blair became Shadow Home Secretary in 1992, he made another of his resounding pledges, to be 'tough on crime, tough on the causes of crime'.[56] The two key measures of crime, police-recorded crime (PRC) and the British Crime Survey (BCS) of household experiences of crime, increased explosively during the Thatcher and early Major years.[57] From 1997, crime fell according to the BCS, while the PRC measure rose to 2004, partly due to inclusion of reported but unproven offences and legal changes creating more offences.

Labour believed the main cause of crime was economic deprivation and sought remedies through welfare, education and employment reforms. It introduced preventive and punitive measures. The Crime and Disorder Act 1998 established local Youth Offending Teams, run by councils to help young offenders avoid further crime, while police and the courts acquired new powers, including Anti-Social Behaviour Orders (ASBOs) banning people from neighbourhoods where they committed offences, child curfew schemes, detention and training orders. Police pay rose substantially. More CCTV cameras were installed than in any other country to deter offences in public

55 Porter and Taylor, 'Gypsies and Travellers', pp. 92–102.
56 Tony Blair, 'Why Crime is a Socialist Issue', *New Statesman*, 25 January 1993; T. Newburn and R. Reiner, 'Crime and Penal Policy', in Anthony Seldon (ed.), *Blair's Britain, 1997–2007* (Cambridge University Press, 2007), pp. 318–19.
57 Newburn and Reiner, 'Crime and Penal Policy', pp. 321–2.

places. Over forty significant Acts of Parliament on criminal justice and penal policy between 1997 and 2006 created more than 3,000 criminal offences and increased police powers to intercept communications, conduct covert operations, stop, search and arrest.[58] One motive was prevention of terrorism following 9/11 then 7/7. Prisoners increased from about 62,000 in 1997 to 80,000 by 2006, due mainly to more and longer sentences, risking over-crowding since prisons did not expand. More offenders received community sentences.[59]

Greater police powers led to more complaints of abuse, in particular that police stopped and searched black and Asian men far more than white men on suspicion of crime. An Independent Police Complaints Commission (IPCC) operated from 2004. Yet the picture was not wholly bleak: by the end of 2008 the BCS reported fewer murders than for twenty years. It assessed the risk of being a victim of any crime at 40 per cent in 1995, 22 per cent by the end of 2008, probably due to greater prosperity and increased policing. But polls showed that 75 per cent of respondents were convinced that crime was rising and out of control, perhaps influenced by the media.[60]

Poverty and Inequality

From 1997 to 2007 low incomes rose but the top 1 per cent rose faster. Income inequality increased though more gradually than in the 1980s. Wealth inequality grew rapidly: the share of the richest 10 per cent (excluding housing) rose from 57 per cent to 63 per cent in the two decades to 1996, to 71 per cent by 2003. Tax and social security changes under New Labour were more redistributive than any since 1979,[61] but Britain was now one of the most unequal societies in the developed world. Among the thirty-one richest countries, UK income inequality was outstripped only by Chile, the United States, Israel and Portugal; Iceland was the most equal.[62]

The manifestoes for Blair's three elections all pledged not to raise income tax. Consistent with New Labour's 'relaxed' attitude to the very wealthy, it focused on improving opportunities at the bottom and reducing the income gap between the bottom and the middle, not on the growing gap between the middle and the top. Redistribution and poverty reduction owed most to Brown. From 1997 to 2008, poverty fell among pensioners and families with children, but rose among childless unemployed and working age people. In 1997, 20 per cent of pensioners were poor by the

58 Ibid., p. 330.
59 Ibid., p. 336.
60 Ibid.
61 Stewart, 'Equality and Social Justice', p. 433.
62 John Hills, *Good Times, Bad Times. The Welfare Myth of Them and Us* (Bristol: Policy Press, 2015), pp. 28–31; see Figure 13.1, below.

official measure (income below 60 per cent of median income), 14 per cent in 2005–8. Long-term poverty diminished, from 12 per cent of the UK population and 16 per cent of all children in 1998, to 8 per cent and 10 per cent, respectively, in 2003, though following the financial crisis from 2008 it returned to 2000 levels.[63]

Labour's 1997 campaign made little direct reference to poverty, inequality or social justice, though it promised to reduce educational disadvantage, introduce the minimum wage and get 250,000 under-25s off benefits and into work. After the election, Blair gave his first major speech outside Parliament on a Peckham (south London) housing estate, promising there would be 'no forgotten people and no no-hope areas'. The employment New Deal, WFTC and minimum wage followed. But 500,000 eligible people did not take up means-tested tax credits and the minimum wage was low.

In March 1999, in a lecture to commemorate William Beveridge at Toynbee Hall (where the Child Poverty Action Group formed in 1965[64]), Blair unexpectedly announced: 'Our historic aim [is] that ours is the first generation to end child poverty forever … it is a twenty-year mission, but I believe it can be done'.[65] He promised to end child poverty by 2020. There was no sign of a strategy to fulfil the pledge, though Brown – as surprised as anyone by the announcement – was working on it. In September 1999, the DSS issued the first of a series of annual audits of poverty and exclusion, *Opportunity for All*, much influenced by Brown. It promised an 'integrated and radical policy response' to childhood deprivation, worklessness, health inequalities, crime, poor areas, poor housing, pensioner poverty, ill-health and isolation, and discrimination on grounds of age, ethnicity, gender or disability. A list of policies followed, including a comprehensive 'Sure Start' programme for children under 4 in deprived areas; more generous maternity leave; substantial increases to health and education funding, especially favouring poorer areas; targets for employment, crime, education, health and housing in the most disadvantaged areas, with another ambitious aim that 'within 10–20 years, no one should be seriously disadvantaged by where they live'. It also announced Educational Maintenance Allowances to enable young people from low-income families to stay in education to 18; improved benefits for disabled adults and children; a Pension Credit, increasing the means-tested supplement to the inadequate state pension, free TV licences from age 75, free eye tests and increased income tax allowances for pensioners; action to reduce inequalities in income between ethnic groups, including grants to local authorities to improve and equalize educational attainment. All were implemented.

63 Hills, *Good Times, Bad Times*, p. 132; Stewart, 'Equality and Social Justice', pp. 434–5.
64 Thane and Davidson, *Child Poverty Action Group*, pp. 6–10.
65 Tony Blair, 'Beveridge Revisited. A Welfare State for the 21st Century', in Robert Walker (ed.), *Ending Child Poverty. Popular Welfare for the 21st Century* (Bristol: Policy Press, 1999), p. 7; Stewart, 'Equality and Social Justice', p. 441.

By 2010 about 1.1 million children had been removed from poverty, not meeting Blair's target of halving child poverty since 2000, but a substantial improvement (Figure 13.1).

This was partly due to the strong underlying economy, which owed much to Labour's management. WFTC, the minimum wage, increased Child Benefit and the increased length and generosity of maternity pay increased family incomes, while the employment New Deals, including mothers gaining work through the New Deal for Lone Parents which provided childcare and training opportunities, reduced workless families. Children under-16 in workless households fell from 2.4 million in 1996 to 1.7 million in 2006. Forty-five per cent of single parents were in work in 1997, fifty-seven per cent in 2008, though concerns arose that mothers of young children were now forced into work without the choice to care for their children at home, as the benefits system had previously allowed.[66]

For older people, annual winter fuel payments of £100 to everyone over 60 were introduced in 1997, raised by 2008 to £250, £400 from age 80, to protect their health. In 1999, means-tested Income Support for poorer pensioners was rebranded as Minimum Income Guarantee (MIG), with an above-inflation rise and future increases linked to the more generous measure of earnings rather than prices. The universal state pension increased by less, remaining linked to prices and still inadequate for survival without

Figure 13.1 Relative UK Child Poverty Rates since 1961

Note: Poverty line is 60% of median income. Years up to and including 1992 are calendar years; thereafter years refer to financial years. Incomes are measured before housing costs have been deducted and equivalized using the modified OECD equivalence scale. Author's calculations based on Family Expenditure Survey and Family Resources Survey, various years.

Source: Cribb et al., *Living Standards, Poverty and Inequality in the UK*, p. 84. Updated from recent IFS data available at: www.ifs.org.uk/tools_and_resources/incomes_in_uk.

66 Thane and Evans, *Sinners?* p. 196.

a supplement. Anti-poverty groups complained that Labour, like the Conservatives, focused on raising means-tested rather than universal benefits, though the increases were greater. In 2003, the MIG was renamed Pension Credit (PC). The maximum means-tested PC plus pension rose to the highest level ever, though still only just above the official poverty line. In 2008, Brown introduced free travel on public transport buses for over-60s throughout England. This was already available in Scotland, Wales and some English towns, including Greater London where Livingstone introduced it also for 11–15-year-olds on buses. Universal free travel and winter fuel allowances were criticized for benefiting rich as well as poor pensioners, but means-testing was costly and inefficient while universal benefits were sure to reach the poorest: up to 30 per cent of eligible pensioners, often the neediest and most isolated, failed to claim PC, unaware they were eligible or deterred by the complexity of the process.[67]

In 2003, WFTC was extended to low-wage households without children and renamed Working Tax Credit (WTC), while a new Child Tax Credit (CTC) amalgamated means-tested Income Support and tax credits for children, particularly benefiting low-income families and significantly reducing child poverty. Take-up increased. The Welfare Reform Act, 2007, provided greater support for Incapacity Benefit claimants who joined work-related activity and training, but it rose only in line with retail prices, as did Jobseekers Allowance and Income Support, and they declined in real value.[68] Benefits for disabled people increased, but so did means- and fitness-testing and sanctions for those failing the tests; disabled campaigners criticized poor information, more severe conditionality and difficulty in accessing benefits. Unemployed and disabled people of working age – both unpopular with the tabloids and, polls suggested, with many voters – were less favourably treated than pensioners, children and workers.

Support for the youngest children improved dramatically. By 2002, 93 per cent of 3- and 4-year-olds from social classes IV and V received nursery education compared with 17 per cent in 1997. In 500 most disadvantaged districts Sure Start centres provided parenting support, childcare, play and learning opportunities, healthcare and advice, and support for children with 'special needs', as the various forms of childhood disability were now known. Outcomes were positive and Sure Start was popular with parents. In 2006, it came under local authority control and centres spread through England and Wales, beyond deprived areas. There were 1,000 by 2006[69]; they were severely cut by the Coalition government after 2010. In 2003, Labour introduced two weeks' paternity leave, but it was so brief and low paid that few fathers took it up, often preferring to take better-paid holiday leave for childcare purposes.

---

67 Stewart, 'Equality and Social Justice', pp. 419–21.
68 Ibid., pp. 421–4.
69 Ibid., pp. 425–6.

The share of education funding for deprived areas grew from 1999. Initiatives included Excellence in Cities, funding learning mentors and other provision for talented pupils in the most deprived third of LEAs, and grants to schools with high concentrations of BME students, both successfully improving outcomes, especially in London. School performance targets were adjusted to take account of socio-economic intake. By 2006, the performance at GCSE of black, Pakistani and Bangladeshi compared with white pupils improved as did the relative performance of children receiving free school meals in every ethnic group, though the gap remained substantial especially among older pupils.[70]

'Education, Education, Education'

While means-testing or restricting some cash benefits, Labour substantially increased spending on universal services, mainly education and health. Another Blair rallying call on entering office was 'Education, Education, Education!' A Standards and Effectiveness Unit was established in what became the Department of Education and Employment, to stress the government's determination to raise skill levels. Ambitious targets were set for literacy and numeracy at age 11, measured by national tests, supported by David Blunkett, Secretary of State for Education, 1997–2001, who was blind, the first minister ever with such a disability. Targets were introduced for the percentage of pupils per secondary school gaining five or more GCSEs, as a measure of success.

Labour continued the city technology colleges and 'specialist' secondary schools introduced by the Conservatives, partially funded by private sponsorship in the (dubious) belief that this raised standards. A special adviser to Blair, former journalist Andrew Adonis, elevated to the House of Lords and appointed Minister for Education, 2005–8, branded them 'academies', effectively state-funded independent schools, free from local authority control, with 10 per cent capital funding from private sponsors who controlled boards of governors and owned the land and buildings. Local authorities lost more education powers. The schools employed their own staff and set their own admission requirements. Blair was enthusiastic about them and admired independent schools, like the one he had attended, encouraging their cooperation with state schools. From 2000, schools with fewer than 15 per cent of pupils gaining five A*–C grades at GCSE three years running were considered for closure or conversion to academies. There were fifteen academies in 1997, forty-six in 2006–7.

To promote equality, many disabled children were moved from special to mainstream schools, where mentors, learning support units and pupil referral units were established to improve performance among all disadvantaged children, reduce truancy

70 Ibid., pp. 426–8.

and keep pupils in school to age 18.[71] In 2003, following the brutal neglect and murder of 8-year-old Victoria Climbie by the aunt to whose care she had been entrusted by her parents in Africa, the government established the 'Every Child Matters' strategy, ideally providing integrated support for everyone from birth to age 19. The Children's Act, 2004, required schools, hospitals, local social services, police and voluntary groups to cooperate for this purpose. To help disadvantaged children, tests were introduced for 5-year-olds, to identify needs, also extended schooling from 8 am to 6 pm year-round, after-school and school holiday clubs, help with study and referral to specialist services such as speech therapy. Schools were encouraged to open centres combining early years care, education and healthcare. Healthy Eating guidelines were devised for school meals by popular TV chef Jamie Oliver. The changed expectation of schools was expressed in another name-change, in 2007, for the responsible Department to Children, Schools and Families.

A problem was shortage of teachers, especially as class sizes fell. Successful students from elite universities rarely entered school-teaching as they commonly had until the 1950s, as opportunities widened. Pay rises had little effect. Unqualified teaching assistants were recruited to support teachers.[72] It was harder to recruit heads, despite substantial pay rises, as the pressure of targets, league tables and other demands grew. Changes to the curriculum had uneven effects. At secondary level, compulsory citizenship, social, health and careers education were introduced. Some established subjects, including foreign languages, became optional after age 14 and take-up fell. The focus on exams and testing arguably narrowed education. Vocational diplomas were introduced alongside A-levels, but were under-funded and it was hard to attract suitable staff. In 1999–2002, £19 billion more was spent on schools, a further 60 per cent by 2005–6, much of it on 'initiatives' and consultants.[73] Many school buildings badly needed expansion and renovation. Government spending on building rose from £1.26 billion in 1997–8 to £3.02 billion in 2005–6. To restrain it, Labour adopted PFI, also for NHS and transport developments.[74] Private firms owned and operated the buildings and works, leasing the buildings back to the taxpayer at considerable profit. As critics commented at the time, PFI saved the public purse in the short run at significant long-term cost, generally twice that of direct public funding, causing the services concerned major future financial problems.

Blair's main contribution to higher education was the introduction of tuition fees. He recalled this in his resignation speech as a 'deeply controversial and hellish hard to do',

71 Alan Smithers, 'Schools', in Anthony Seldon (ed.), *Blair's Britain, 1997–2007* (Cambridge University Press, 2007), p. 372, n. 28.
72 Ibid., p. 381.
73 Ibid., pp. 378–9.
74 See p. 430.

but believed he had been 'moving with the grain of change around the world',[75] though not elsewhere in the EU, including Scotland, where tuition remained free. In 1997, Labour committed to ensuring 'the costs of student maintenance should be repaid by graduates on an income-related basis', to meet the costs of the growing university population. In 1997–8 there were 5,853,000 students in full-time higher education in the United Kingdom, compared with 2,165,000 in 1981–2, as it moved belatedly from an elite to a mass system.[76] The Major government appointed an enquiry into university funding, chaired by former civil servant Lord Dearing, which reported in 1997, after the election, that the system was over-stretched but maintaining standards. It proposed that students should pay 25 per cent of their tuition costs, but that maintenance grants should continue. But Blunkett, under Treasury pressure, announced their abolition and the introduction of fees of £1,000 pa, with means-tested loans for lower-income students to pacify opposition, expressed in the biggest backbench revolt of Blair's first term. Students demonstrated and some occupied university and Department of Education offices. Following costly means-testing, one-third of students did not pay fees. Universities received £40 million for hardship funds for students who exhausted their loan entitlement. Blunkett fought hard to prevent fees rising further and the 2001 manifesto promised they would not, but after the election and Blunkett's departure from Education, universities were allowed to charge up to £3,000 pa from 2006.[77] More student demonstrations followed. Charles Clarke, Education Secretary from 2001, modified the policy: payment of fees was deferred until graduates earned £15,000 pa and a more generous package of grants and bursaries was introduced. This scraped through the Commons by only five votes, opposed by Liberal Democrats and some Conservatives with many Labour backbenchers.

The government was concerned about unequal social access to universities, especially Oxbridge. The gender balance improved, but 50 per cent of places at Oxford and Cambridge went to independent school pupils, female and male. Universities became subject to 'performance indicators', including proportions of entrants from state schools, lower socio-economic classes and districts with low higher education participation. Those meeting the targets received 5 per cent additional funding, laggards were named and shamed. Critics feared that fees and loans would deter low-income candidates. Their numbers did not rise and mature student numbers fell, often unable to support both themselves and their children through university, especially damaging the Open University.[78] Blair did not help with another public promise, in 1999, that

75 John O'Leary, 'Higher Education', in Anthony Seldon (ed.), *Blair's Britain, 1997–2007* (Cambridge University Press, 2007), p. 468.
76 Halsey, 'Higher and Further Education', p. 229.
77 O'Leary, 'Higher Education', p. 475.
78 See p. 267.

50 per cent of the population by 2010 would receive higher education by age 30. The current figure was 43 per cent. There was controversy about whether university education really was best for 50 per cent of people or for the economy, given the shortage of skilled tradespeople. The tabloids attacked universities for filling their places with 'mickey mouse' courses like golf course management (rare) and, most derided despite growing work opportunities, media studies. But, overall, universities were in a better state by 2007 than in 1997.

Health and Welfare

'There are twenty-four hours to save the NHS' was yet another Blair soundbite on entering office. Problems included long waiting times for operations, under-funding and poor outcomes by international standards, including for cancer and heart disease. Targets were introduced for waiting times and a national framework for treatment of heart disease. Prevention was emphasized, a Minister for Public Health appointed and cutting smoking prioritized. It was banned in enclosed public spaces in England, including pubs and restaurants, from July 2007, following bans in Scotland in 2006, Wales and Northern Ireland in April 2007, all successful and remarkably calm. The National Institute for Health and Clinical Excellence (NICE) was established in 1999, an independent regulator of NHS standards. All the early changes were positive, but Frank Dobson, Minister of Health, not among the Blair inner circle, demanded more funds to improve services, supported by media criticism of the NHS.

Blairite Alan Milburn replaced Dobson in 1999. During the 2001 election campaign, Blair had difficult exchanges with patients in Birmingham, then took a greater interest in health, convinced that NHS performance would improve through competition, internally and from the private sector. There were several reorganizations, including transformation of hospitals into Foundation Trusts, comparable with academy schools, managing their own budgets and services, competing with each other in an 'internal market'. The cost was criticized by the Audit Commission and the Commons Public Accounts Committee.[79] NHS funding grew from £30 billion to £90 billion between 1997 and 2007, raising NHS investment to the EU average, and more went to deprived areas. It was not always well managed when there were so many competing agencies that lines of responsibility and accountability were blurred, but outcomes and patient satisfaction improved, staffing levels rose by 25 per cent, especially at senior levels, waiting times fell. Hospitals became cleaner and fewer patients suffered hospital-acquired infections. Medical students increased by 50 per cent,

---

79 Dennis Kavanagh, 'The Blair Premiership', in Anthony Seldon (ed.), *Blair's Britain, 1997–2007* (Cambridge University Press, 2007), p. 11.

nursing students by 30 per cent, GPs by 9 per cent.[80] Buildings improved, but mainly through PFI, bringing long-term costs. Mental health was still relatively neglected and socio-economic inequalities continued. In 2005, 66 per cent of the most deprived areas had over 10 per cent fewer GPs than the average.

Life expectancy continued to rise, but unequally: in 2010, men born in wealthy Kensington and Chelsea, London, averaged 88 years, in poorer, mixed-race Tottenham, 71.[81] It was lowest in poorer parts of Glasgow: 70 for males, 77 for females. Sixteen per cent of the UK population was aged 65 or over, the highest proportion ever.[82] The ageing population created new challenges for healthcare, though more people were active and healthy to later ages and the difficulties were sometimes over-stated. Less positively, obesity was a growing problem and cause of ill-health partly because American-inspired cheap fast food was widely available, despite campaigns to improve diet from school onwards. The widespread ill-effects of alcohol was another concern.

The extension of health advice and services in schools, with additional clinics and nursing services, and increased emphasis on sex education, probably contributed to a 10 per cent fall in pregnancy among under-18s from 1998 to 2003. From 2000, the morning-after pill was available from pharmacies without prescription, amid accusations of government-sponsored promiscuity and failed court challenges by anti-abortionists.[83] They tried again to limit the law on abortion, but the government's Sexual Health and HIV Strategy from 2001 prioritized improved abortion services and equalizing and speeding access for women.[84] Abortion remained illegal in Northern Ireland; around 1,500 women each year travelled to Britain for private abortions, though they were not eligible for NHS care.[85]

An Ageing Society

Many pensioners gained from New Labour reforms, especially PC, and pensioner poverty fell, but did not disappear.[86] Some were wealthy, benefiting from high pay while working, good private pensions and the unprecedented rise in the value of homes bought before prices boomed. Some commentators constructed from this minority good fortune a narrative of generational conflict, with a wealthy 'baby boomer'

80 N. Bosanquet, 'The Health and Welfare Legacy', in Anthony Seldon (ed.), *Blair's Britain, 1997–2007* (Cambridge University Press, 2007), pp. 393–4.

81 M. Marmot, *Fair Society, Healthy Lives. Strategic Review of Health Inequalities in England*, 2010, available at: www.marmotreview.org.

82 Office of National Statistics, available at: www.ons.gov.uk.

83 Holden, *Makers and Manners*, pp. 368–9.

84 Ibid., p. 372.

85 Ibid., p. 373.

86 See pp. 448–9; Hills, *Good Times, Bad Times*, p. 57.

generation, born *c.* 1945–1960s, living in luxury while younger people suffered rising housing costs, declining pensions and paying through taxes the healthcare and pensions costs of their selfish elders.[87] This overlooked continuing pensioner poverty and the considerable financial and personal support provided by older for younger people.[88] Inequalities within the older and younger generations were at least as great as those between generations.

A Commission chaired by financial expert Adair Turner pointed out in reports in 2004 and 2005 that UK state pensions remained among the least generous in the developed world. It recommended uprating the pension in line with earnings, raising the pension age in line with average life expectancy and requiring workers to join occupational pension schemes or a state-provided alternative, to supplement the state pension.[89] This was unlikely to help many women (still a majority of pensioners) and older members of minority ethnic groups, including Gypsies and Travellers, who had lower incomes than average white males after, as before, retirement, receiving lower state pensions if they had not been in insurable employment for at least forty years, less likely to receive occupational pensions or, at best, they were low, due to low earnings and/ or fewer working years which determined most occupational pensions. Hence, much pensioner poverty. The Pensions Act, 2007, helped by reducing the qualifying period for state pensions to thirty years and introducing credits for long-term disabled people, their carers and carers of children. It proposed gradually raising the state pension age to 68 between 2024 and 2046. The timing was distant to stem protest, though the TUC, and an official report in 2010, pointed out that about 20 per cent of workers – generally the poorest – were already forced to retire before state pension age due to ill-health and would suffer from the change.[90]

Increasing numbers of older people already worked to later ages, because they wanted to or needed the income, though if they became unemployed it was hard to get another job and employers still discriminated against them. But some employers regretted the loss to their businesses following over-enthusiastic dismissal of higher paid, experienced older workers since the 1980s, and the government encouraged later retirement to cut the cost of pensions and compensate for the declining number of younger workers due to the low birth rate. This was expected to continue but, unexpectedly, it rose from 2001, continuing into the twenty-first century, though it took

87 David Willetts, *The Pinch. How the Baby Boomers Took their Children's Future: and Why They Should Give It Back* (London: Atlantic Books, 2010); E. Howker and S. Malik, *Jilted Generation. How Britain has Bankrupted its Youth* (London: Icon Books, 2010).
88 Thane, 'Demographic Futures', pp. 151–4.
89 Pensions Commission, First Report, *Pensions: Challenges and Choices* (London: The Stationery Office, 2004); Second Report, *A New Pension Settlement for the Twenty-first Century* (2005); Final Report, *Implementing an Integrated Package of Pension Reforms* (2006).
90 Marmot, *Fair Society, Healthy Lives*.

some time to be recognized and for policies to adjust. Immigration of younger workers helped balance the age structure, though this was rarely recognized as a benefit of immigration.

Contrary to caricatures of 'baby boomers' as selfish, dependent burdens, they contributed significantly to society and the economy. From 2001 to 2011 (when it was discontinued by the Coalition government) a biennial Home Office Citizenship Survey revealed the regular community and voluntary action of people over 65: in 2001, 27 per cent volunteered regularly with NGOs or helped sick and frail family, friends and neighbours, the pattern in all the surveys.[91] In 2008, 28 per cent of volunteers with Voluntary Service Overseas (VSO), established in 1958 to encourage young people to volunteer in poorer countries, were aged over 50 compared with about 3 per cent twenty years earlier. Older people offered more useful skills and experience – of medicine, teaching, engineering and much else – than younger volunteers. By 2010, one in three working mothers relied on grandparents for childcare, some giving up their own employment to help their daughters work. Thirty-one per cent of grandparents helped their grandchildren buy a home; far from selfishly hoarding their assets, 'baby boomers' who could shared them with younger relatives.[92]

Older people increasingly resisted inequalities and discrimination, no longer accepting this as a normal fact of later life. They were more educated, confident and active than previous generations and more willing and able to assert themselves – the rebellious '1968ers' were ageing. In 1998, the voluntary Third Age Employment Network was founded to advise on finding work and training and to lobby for more.[93] The government responded with an Age Positive Campaign and New Deal 50+, introduced in 2000 to help over-50s find work; 120,000 succeeded by 2004. In 2000, an EU Directive on Equal Treatment in Employment specified age as a dimension of inequality for the first time. As ever, the United Kingdom implemented it slowly and incompletely. From 2006, workers could request to work past fixed retirement ages, but employers could refuse without explanation. Following protest, Labour abolished fixed retirement ages, implemented in 2011. Employers could then insist on retirement only by workers demonstrably unable to work efficiently.[94] But discrimination at work continued, experienced by women at earlier ages than men, including in high-profile occupations. In 2011, Miriam O'Reilly successfully brought a much publicized case for age discrimination against the BBC

91 Available at: www.ukdataservice.ac.uk.
92 Thane, 'Demographic Futures', pp. 152–4.
93 Thane, 'Older People and Equality', pp. 17–21.
94 Ibid.

when she was sacked as presenter of a TV show, aged 53, on grounds of age, while her visibly older, male co-presenter continued. She then campaigned on behalf of other victims.

Discrimination in healthcare was also nothing new, but older people and their families were less willing to tolerate it. Women were routinely called for screening for breast cancer only to age 70, although breast cancer is most common past 70. There was still insufficient coordination of health and social care for frail older and disabled people. Discrimination in health and social care became illegal under the Equality Act 2010, one of New Labour's last measures, implemented by the Coalition in 2012; few cases followed. Casual ageism continued in many areas of life. A national survey for Age Concern in 2005 found more people (29 per cent) reporting discrimination on grounds of age than any other cause. Almost 30 per cent of respondents believed it was growing; one-third thought people over 70 'incompetent and incapable'.[95] In 2007, the EHRC took responsibility for researching and monitoring age discrimination at all ages. Old age was at last recognized as a significant dimension of inequality, though the EHRC was accused of giving it low priority.

Women and Inequality

Women continued to experience discrimination and inequality at all ages. On average, they still outlived men, though the gap was narrowing, and they still tended to be poorer than men at all ages. Poverty among younger women increased with the numbers of single mothers. In 2006, there were 1.8 million single-parent families, overwhelmingly headed by mothers, caring for almost 3 million children, though lone parenthood was often transient, lasting for five years on average before forming a new partnership. Forty-two per cent of children in poverty were in single-parent households. Only 3 per cent of single mothers were teenagers; 12 per cent were from BME groups, with major differences particularly between households of black Caribbean origin where single parenthood was widespread and Muslims for whom it was unacceptable.[96]

Inflation, including of housing costs, combined with the relative poverty of single mothers, contributed to shorter career breaks for most working mothers: by 2000, most mothers of children under 5 were employed, often part-time, despite the continued inadequacy of childcare, hence the need for grandparents. The need increased from 2001 when the birth rate reversed its long decline and rose from the exceptionally low level of 1.63 births to each pair of parents to 1.94 in 2010, still not replacement rate but

95 Thane, 'Older People and Equality', p. 19.
96 McCarthy, 'Gender Equality', p. 116.

closer than since the early 1970s. This was partly due to births to immigrant women, most of whom were young, but more to higher fertility among native-born women in their later thirties and forties. More women delayed childbirth until they were established in a career and/or found a stable partner and felt they could afford the costs of a family, then had more than one child.[97] The parents did not necessarily marry; still about one-third of babies were born to unmarried parents. In 2001, marriages in the United Kingdom fell to an all-time low of 286,000, of which 114,200 were remarriages,[98] a trend continuing into the next decade.

Girls in all ethnic and socio-economic groups out-performed boys at all levels of education. By the mid-1990s more than half the university intake was female, though courses remained heavily gender-segregated: still few women studied sciences and engineering.[99] Despite out-performing them in education, women, young and old, married and unmarried, with and without children, still trailed men in employment opportunities and pay. In 2007–8 just 11 per cent of directors of the top FTSE 100 companies were female, up from 8.3 per cent in 2003. Female editors of national newspapers rose from 9.1 per cent to 13.6 per cent (Table 13.3).[100]

The average gender pay gap was 27.5 per cent in 1997, 16.4 per cent in 2010 and 19 per cent in 2014, with variations across occupations. It remained especially stark in finance, where women still reported particular discrimination.[101] Women were still concentrated in low-paid, low-status work.

Table 13.3 Employment, Women, 2003 / 2007–8

13.1/19.5% local authority chief executives
0.6/0.9% senior officers in the armed services
7.5/11.9% senior police officers
6.8/9.6% senior judges
22.9/26.6% civil service top management
30.1%, 2003 secondary school heads
34.1%, 2006 secondary school heads

SOURCE: Equality and Human Rights Commission, *Sex and Power: Who Runs Britain, 2008* (London: EHRC, 2008), pp. 5–7.

97 ONS, 'Fertility. UK Fertility Remains High', 24 June 2011, available at: www.ons.gov.uk/index.html.
98 ONS, *Social Trends*, 40, p. 20.
99 Halsey and Webb, *Twentieth-century British Social Trends*, pp. 210–12, 226, 234; McCarthy, 'Gender Equality', pp. 117–18.
100 Equality and Human Rights Commission *Sex and Power: Who Runs Britain, 2008?* (London: EHRC, 2008) pp. 5–7
101 *Stop Gap*, the Fawcett Society Magazine, London, autumn 2008, pp. 10–11.

Gay Rights

In 1997, Chris Smith became Minister for National Heritage, the first openly gay Cabinet minister. Angela Eagle, soon to be a junior minister, became Labour's second backbencher, following Maureen Colquhoun in 1978, to come out as lesbian, exciting the media less than in the 1970s. In the election the 'out' gay Labour candidate, Ben Bradshaw, fought Exeter against the Director of the Conservative Family Campaign, Adrian Rodgers, who warned of the danger to children of electing a gay MP. A sign of change was that, unlike Tatchell in 1983,[102] Bradshaw won with a swing of 12 per cent.

Also in 1997, the Equality Network was founded in Scotland to fight for lesbian, gay, bisexual and transgender rights, and foreign partners of lesbians and gay men were granted immigration rights to the United Kingdom on the same terms as straight couples. Labour promised free votes on equalizing the age of consent at 16 and repealing section 28.[103] Then the European Commission on Human Rights (succeeded in 1998 by the ECtHR) accepted the plea of a British man that the unequal age breached the Convention. Some tabloids, echoed in Parliament, warned of teenagers being seduced by predatory gay men, as though young women faced no risk from straight men, and that change would encourage homosexuality. Labour MP Ann Kean introduced an amendment to the Crime and Disorder Bill 1998, equalizing the ages, which passed the Commons but was defeated in the Lords. It was reintroduced in the government's Sexual Offences (Amendment) Act 1998, using the Parliament Act to overrule the Lords. It was adopted in Scotland and Northern Ireland, where equality existed but at age 17. Public opinion was shifting. In 1994, NOP found only 13 per cent of respondents supporting equality, by 1999 it was 66 per cent.[104]

Less positively, in 1999 a nail bomb exploded in a well-known gay pub in Soho, the Admiral Duncan, killing three people. The prejudices expressed over the age of consent recurred in debates about repeal of section 28 and gay adoption. The Scottish parliament easily repealed section 28 in 2000, despite vigorous opposition from religious groups and the tabloids. At Westminster, the Lords were again opposed but it was forced through in 2003.[105] It was repealed also in Northern Ireland. Equal rights for same sex couples to adopt children caused protest from the Anglican and Roman Catholic Churches, invoking the HRA, arguing that requiring their adoption organizations to assist gay and lesbian couples infringed their members' right to practice their faith. Faith-based adoption agencies were granted a twenty-one-month exemption.[106]

---

102 See p. 388.
103 See p. 388–9.
104 Porter, 'Gender Identity and Sexual Orientation', pp. 156–9; Holden, *Makers and Manners*, pp. 336–43.
105 Holden, *Makers and Manners*, pp. 346–8.
106 Porter, 'Gender Identity and Sexual Orientation', p. 158.

When this expired, in January 2009, many observed the law. It was introduced in Northern Ireland in 2013.

In 2003, Employment Equality (Sexual Orientation) Regulations made workplace discrimination illegal.[107] In 2004, the Sexual Offences Act abolished the crimes of buggery and gross indecency between men and the Civil Partnership Act granted registered same sex couples the same rights and responsibilities as married, heterosexual couples.[108] Some unmarried heterosexual couples complained that they had no such rights, but nothing changed for them while gay couples celebrated real progress. In 2005, the first gay civil partnerships were registered. The 2006 Equality Act outlawed discrimination on grounds of sexuality in provision of goods and services. Some boarding-house keepers argued in court, unsuccessfully, that the requirement to let shared rooms to gay couples contravened their religious beliefs. In 2008, incitement to homophobic hatred became an offence, for which Stonewall had campaigned. Polls indicated high levels of public support for the reforms, from 68 per cent for civil partnership to 93 per cent for protection of gay people from discrimination and harassment at work.[109] This liberalizing legislation was adopted, with variations, throughout the United Kingdom.

In 1999, the ban was lifted on lesbians, gays and transgender people (LGBT – lesbian, gay, bisexual, transgender – as they became known) serving in the armed forces, following an ECHR ruling.[110] In the same year, Channel 4 broadcast the first high-profile drama about gay life, *Queer as Folk*. From the first scene, featuring a 30-year-old man seducing a 15-year-old schoolboy, it tested public attitudes and those of the Broadcasting Standards Commission, but it survived and was popular. Sensationalized sex became more common on TV.[111] Images of all kinds, harder to police, were emerged on the increasingly pervasive internet. Fears of paedophilia grew. The problem was real, but sometimes whipped into unhelpful panic by tabloid representations causing public demonstrations against suspected paedophiles, often innocent people, including an attack by a confused mob on the house of a paediatrician.[112]

Trans campaigners continued to lobby politicians and make effective use of the courts. In 1999, Sex Discrimination (Gender Reassignment) Regulations established that employment rights gained in European courts applied to those intending to undergo gender reassignment as well as to those who had completed or were undergoing it,

107 Ibid., p. 128.
108 Holden, *Makers and Manners*, pp. 356–7.
109 Porter 'Gender Identity and Sexual Orientation', p. 158.
110 Holden, *Makers and Manners*, pp. 336, 343–5.
111 Ibid., pp. 380–1.
112 Ibid., pp 381–2.

following (tardily) a decision by the European Court of Justice in 1994 concerning a British transsexual woman. Also in 1999, the Court of Appeal held that the NHS could not refuse gender reassignment treatment, on the grounds that gender dysphoria (the feeling of being trapped in a body of the wrong sex) was an illness under the terms of the NHS legislation. But trans people continued to face conflicts over which hospital wards or prisons they were assigned to, which public and workplace toilets they used and pension rights.

In 2002, the ECtHR found Britain in breach of the right of trans people to marry and receive respect for their private lives. In 2004, the Gender Recognition Act gave people the legal right to live in their acquired gender, enabling trans people to apply for gender recognition certificates. Applicants had to establish that that they had lived in their acquired gender for at least two years and intended to do so until death, backed by a medical diagnosis of gender dysphoria. Successful applicants gained all the rights of their lived gender, including to pensions and other benefits, and protection under anti-discrimination and equality legislation. In 2005, the first certificates were awarded and the first transsexual marriages celebrated, but trans people still experienced discrimination.[113]

The Conservatives officially opposed most reforms concerning gay and trans-gender equalities, though they were divided and there were hints of change.[114] In 2002, Theresa May, the first female Chairman (sic) of the party, from 2016 its second female leader and premier, berated the conference for appearing to be a 'nasty party'. In the same year, the first Tory MP, Alan Duncan, came out as gay and, as a respected MP, was widely supported including by Iain Duncan Smith, then leader, a commit-ted Catholic. In 2015, a review by the Brussels-based International Lesbian, Gay, Bisexual, Trans and Intersex Association, founded in 1996 and recognized by the UN, gave the United Kingdom the highest score in Europe for 86 per cent progress towards 'respect of human rights and full equality for LGBT'. Scotland was awarded 92 per cent.[115]

Campaigns for the environment and animal protection continued. One Labour response was the successful encouragement of recycling. Another, in 2004, was ban-ning fox hunting with dogs in England and Wales, following Scotland in 2002. It had to be forced through the Lords with the Parliament Act, amid marches and demonstra-tions by opponents.

---

113 Porter, 'Gender Identity and Sexual Orientation', pp. 159–61.
114 Holden, *Makers and Manners*, pp. 311–12, 315–18, 336–58.
115 International Lesbian, Gay, Bisexual, Trans and Intersex Association, *State-sponsored Homophobia. A World Survey of Sexual Orientation, Criminalization, Protection and Recognition*, 11th edn, 2016, available at: www.ilga .org/worldwide-legislation.

From Blair to Brown: Financial Crisis

In June 2007, Blair resigned and was replaced by Brown, the first time Labour had changed leaders without a contest since 1932, apparently as agreed when Blair became leader.[116] There was no evident opposition in the party, though potential challengers were discouraged and subtly undermined in the press by New Labour's spin-masters. Before resigning, Blair rushed through a series of measures designed to secure his 'legacy', including expansion of academy schools and renewal of Trident, which both passed the Commons only with Conservative votes. Blair's second term was the most rebellious Parliament since 1945, due not least to Blair's unwillingness to discuss policies with the party and build up goodwill. Labour MPs rebelled in 21 per cent of divisions, most against the Iraq War in 2003, followed by opposition to university fees and foundation hospitals. In the first session of the 2005 Parliament they rebelled twenty-eight times, defeating the government twice, on anti-terrorism legislation and schools reform.

On taking power, Brown proclaimed outside No. 10, 'Let the work of change begin'. But soon his plans were derailed by attempted terrorist attacks in London, then Glasgow, which fortunately were averted with just one death, of a terrorist. Then came major floods, followed by a serious epidemic of foot-and-mouth disease among cattle. Brown handled the crises calmly and effectively. Even the *Daily Mail* conceded that 'Brown could be a great Prime Minister'.[117] In the polls he was well ahead of the Conservatives on managing the economy, and as party leader ahead of David Cameron. Then, in September 2007, a serious financial crisis emerged in the United States, where banks had granted too many insecure mortgages. Confidence collapsed and banks stopped lending to one another. The British bank, Northern Rock, experienced a run on its deposits until the government guaranteed all bank and building society savings up to £35,000, later raised to £50,000, then nationalized Northern Rock to prevent its collapse and resulting chaos.

Over the following year things worsened. By autumn 2008, after a succession of US bank collapses, British bank shares plummeted and the government nationalized the Bradford & Bingley Building Society to save it, while the crisis hit other European countries, especially Ireland and Iceland. In October, the Treasury, now headed by Alastair Darling, outlined a £500 billion international bank rescue plan which Brown persuaded EU leaders, then G7 finance ministers, to accept. In Britain it entailed costly part-nationalization of three big, failing banks: Royal Bank of Scotland (RBS), Halifax and Lloyds. The Bank of England cut interest rates to 3 per cent then to an unprecedented

116 See p. 420.
117 Dennis Kavanagh and Philip Cowley, *The British General Election of 2010* (London: Palgrave, 2010), p. 3.

0.5 per cent in 2009 and announced £75 billion of 'quantitative easing', printing money to subsidize the still collapsing banks. Darling temporarily reduced VAT to encourage consumer demand and raised the top rate of income tax from 40 per cent to 45 per cent on incomes over £150,000.

Brown again took the lead, persuading a meeting of the G20 (representing the governments and central banks of the twenty major economies, formed in 1999 to discuss promotion of international financial stability) in London in April 2009 to pledge £1.1 trillion to the IMF to prevent another collapse, while declaring a crack-down on tax havens and hedge funds (which did not evidently occur). Economic meltdown was averted, but the effects on the British economy were acute because it was exceptionally dependent on financial services for employment and tax revenue and many households were in debt. Banks tightened lending to businesses and consumers. Unemployment rose past 2 million in early 2009 for the first time since 1997 and retailers were hard-hit. Woolworths went out of business in the United Kingdom, after trading for almost 100 years, shocking the nation. Brown deserved credit for averting the international crisis but got less than he merited and was blamed, especially by the opposition, for the national economic problems, which would have been worse had he and Darling not acted. The government failed to defend itself effectively, especially when popular sympathy for the bail-out declined as executives who had led their banks into chaos received big pay-offs which the government seemed powerless to prevent, especially the £693,000 pension package for Sir Fred Goodwin as he departed as CEO of RBS; his successor received a £9.6 million pay package, starkly illustrating income inequality. The banks seemed to have learned nothing and repented not at all.

Then, in March 2009, the *Daily Telegraph* discovered from an FOI request that some MPs were inflating their, relatively modest, incomes (they had not shared top salary inflation since the 1980s; their pay was low compared with other EU countries) with dubious expenses claims. The public were entertained by reports of claims for such essentials as dog food and horse manure and, by two Tory MPs, for dredging a moat and equipping a pond with a floating duck island, but they were shocked. Some claims were clearly mistakes because the system was disorganized, and a number made repayments, including David Cameron who repaid £680 claimed for removal of wisteria from his constituency home in Oxfordshire. But, apart from the absurd claims, some appeared fraudulent or dubious and some MPs were eventually jailed. The main outcome was further public disillusion with politicians, encouraged by a media frenzy.

Brown, after his successes in the first weeks, appeared ineffectual at handling such difficulties. He was understandably distracted by the severity of the financial crisis, where his greatest competence lay. He lacked lightness of touch in public, and indeed in private, where he was notoriously short-tempered, as the media revealed. Eventually, he proposed a Parliamentary Standards Act, establishing an Independent Parliamentary

Standards Authority (IPSA) to oversee MPs' expenses. He faced criticism about immigration and its assumed ill-effects on jobs and services, which grew with unemployment numbers. Faced with complaints that EU immigrants took jobs from British workers by taking lower pay, he pledged to secure 'British jobs for British workers', but did little about it. Nor did the government promote the substantial evidence that EU migrants boosted economic growth and tax revenues.

Labour performed worse in local elections. It lost control of the Scottish parliament to the SNP and overall control of the Welsh Assembly in May 2007. In May 2008, Livingstone lost the London mayoral election to Conservative journalist, Boris Johnson. Number 10 was increasingly perceived as conflict-ridden and leaderless. Brown faced pressure to resign as the Tory lead in the polls grew. In 2008, he tried to lay Labour's biggest ghost by appointing an independent committee chaired by retired civil servant, Sir John Chilcot, to investigate the decision to go to war in Iraq. It took years to report (in 2016) amid growing impatience.

An election was unavoidable in 2010 and came in May. It would have been hard for any government to survive the financial crisis, however deftly handled. The Conservatives relentlessly, often unfairly, attacked Labour's responses, including the bank bail-out, while encouraging voters' concerns about immigration, crime and the EU. Brown entered the campaign under the slogan 'A Future Fair for All', stressing Labour's successful handling of the recovery, pledging to support jobs, not to increase income taxes or VAT, to protect services, work for economic recovery and halve the deficit, though he underplayed many real achievements of Labour's years in power, especially in reducing inequalities. The campaign focused upon him rather than other Labour figures, probably mistakenly given his poor public image, 'toxic on the doorstep' said some Labour MPs. In the first ever TV party leaders' debates his dour, pedantic style came over poorly, while Nick Clegg, Liberal Democrat leader since 2007, was a surprising triumph. Labour was short of funds and ran a poor campaign. The Conservatives spent four times as much. Labour's only supporters in the press were the declining *Mirror* papers, while six out of ten national dailies supported the Conservatives. Women were barely visible in any party's campaign, though there were more women, and more BME, candidates than ever before for all main parties.

Brown was attacked by the *Sun* as 'Prime Sinister', waster of taxpayers' money, 'deceitful', a 'ditherer'. Polls, however, suggested that, unpopular as Labour was, voters were unconvinced by the Conservatives and a close result was likely. The turnout rose, though still low by the standards of 1922–97 at 65 per cent. The Conservatives gained 36 per cent of votes and 307 seats, Labour 29 per cent and 258; Labour suffered in areas of highest unemployment, though it remained strong in Scotland, northern England and inner London and among BME voters, including Muslims, despite Iraq. The first female Muslim MPs were elected for Labour, in Bethnal Green and Bow, Bolton and

Birmingham. After five days' deliberation the Conservatives agreed to form a Coalition government with the Liberal Democrats, whose leaders resisted Labour overtures.

Conclusion

New Labour did much to reduce inequalities, though some gains were eroded by the crisis from 2008. Poverty declined and lower incomes rose, but income inequalities grew, though more slowly than in the 1980s, as top incomes grew faster, peaking in 2009–10 following the financial crisis.[118] The quality of the major universal public services, education and health, improved; effective measures got more people into work and improved the life chances of children in low-income families, though the social security system became more selective and punitive particularly of long-term unemployed and some disabled people.[119] Regional inequalities persisted, with highest incomes concentrated in London and southeast England, the lowest in Northern Ireland, northeastern England and parts of Scotland and Wales,[120] though Northern Ireland had other reasons to be grateful to Blair. Conditions for some low-income families deteriorated due to Labour's greatest failure: to reverse the decline since the 1980s in the supply of decent housing they could afford. Productivity remained poorer than in comparable countries. Other inequalities – of gender, race, age, sexuality – continued gradually to narrow, assisted by government action, but success in lessening inequalities did not loom large in New Labour's public campaigns, for fear of alienating 'Middle England'. Historically low election turnouts suggest they may instead have alienated some of Labour's more traditional support among working-class people, feeling it no longer spoke for or to them. The numbers who identified as working class dwindled with the decline of manufacturing, but by less than New Labour appeared to believe. They had not disappeared and their resentment at being 'left-behind' continued to harm Labour electorally.[121] Also another, smaller, traditional source of support, radical intellectuals, had been alienated by the Iraq War in particular. Blair's 'legacy' was, at best mixed, Brown's rather better, but unjustly scarred by the international financial crisis which he received little credit for helping to alleviate.

---

118 The Equality Trust, *How Has Inequality Changed* (London: Equality Trust, 2016), available at: www .equalitytrust.org.uk; Tom Sefton and Holly Sutherland, 'Inequality and Poverty under New Labour', in John Hills and Kitty Stewart (eds), *A More Equal Society? New Labour, Poverty, Inequality and Exclusion* (Bristol: Policy Press, 2005), pp. 231–50.
119 Hills and Stewart, A More Equal Society?; Polly Toynbee and David Walker, *The Verdict. Did Labour Change Britain?* (London: Granta, 2010).
120 Equality Trust, *The Scale of Economic Inequality in the UK*, 2016, available at: www.equalitytrust.org.uk.
121 Evans and Tilley, *The New Politics of Class*, pp. 170 ff.

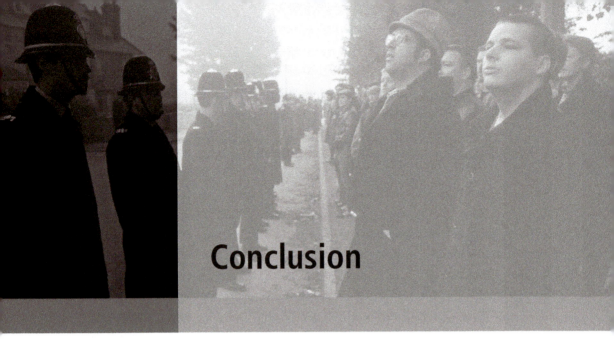

Conclusion

How united is the United Kingdom in the early twenty-first century? What had changed since 1900 and what had not? Constitutionally it was more divided. Most of Ireland was independent and the remainder, in the north, had greater devolved powers, intermittently after its internal religious division became explosive from 1968. Mounting demands for independence in Wales and Scotland led to devolution from 1999. Demands for full independence did not go away, especially in Scotland where nationalism survived losing an independence referendum in 2014; 55.3 per cent voted 'No', 44.7 per cent 'Yes' from a 84.6 per cent turnout, the largest for any UK election under universal suffrage, suggesting how much the issue mattered to Scots. The growth of nationalism elsewhere in the United Kingdom spurred its development in England. This book has tried to trace and highlight differences and similarities across the nations of the United Kingdom and their importance, though space has not always allowed for sufficient detail. Nor of the regional and local diversity within the nations, though we have seen, broadly, how this shifted particularly with economic change, especially the decline of mining and manufacturing – central to the UK economy in 1900 – while the expanding financial sector increased the gap between prosperous southeast England and the rest.

However, London, the capital, is deeply divided between the very richest and the poorest, with average incomes below the GB average in 2015 and the highest rate of child poverty in the United Kingdom, alongside owners of massive wealth and income. London is also the most culturally diverse region of a country whose diversity steadily grew. It was a cosmopolitan city in 1900, with many residents originally from other European countries or from colonies, though the numbers are unknown. According to the 2011 Census, 107 languages were spoken in Greater London; a minority, 45 per cent, of the 8.8 million population identified as white Britons, 37 per cent were foreign born, 10 per cent of children were mixed race. From 2016, it has had a Muslim mayor, Sadiq Khan, born in London to Pakistani immigrant parents, an upwardly mobile lawyer, the first graduate in his family, representing Labour, succeeding a white, Eton-educated, Conservative, Boris Johnson. Meanwhile, Bristol, built on the slave trade, elected a mayor with a Jamaican father and white British mother. People of different origins and cultures lived scattered through the capital, not in exclusive ghettoes, generally peaceably, though with periodic tensions through the century. Racial attacks mounted throughout the United Kingdom following the 2016 referendum on EU membership, then lethal attacks by terrorists from an unrepresentative minority of militant Muslims, both of which stimulated anti-immigrant nationalism. The hostility of a nationalist minority to immigrants and residents of other cultures was comparable in content and intensity with the antisemitism of the early 1900s, partly fuelled by similar fears of competition for work and housing which successive governments did little to allay. Rather, they responded by making immigration and naturalization increasingly difficult. The millions who could claim full British citizenship rights in 1900 due to birth within the Empire dwindled with decolonization and legislation from the 1960s restricting those rights. It was ever more difficult to become British.

The decline of Empire was both a symptom and a cause of the United Kingdom's changing world role from its prominence in 1900, marginalized in particular by the growing dominance of the United States. But still in the twenty-first century the United Kingdom retains a prominence disproportionate to its size, including in the UN, partly due to its significance in international finance, partly to alliance, some say subservience, to the United States. After the Second World War it slowly, rather reluctantly, built closer links with other European countries formally united in what became the EU, though there was recurrent tension with other EU countries and within the United Kingdom about the relationship. In 2016, the United Kingdom voted narrowly to leave the EU, by 52 per cent to 48 per cent on a 72 per cent turnout, though a majority of voters in Scotland (62 per cent), Northern Ireland (55.8 per cent), London (59.9 per cent) and some other English conurbations voted to remain. Wales, suffering high unemployment and deprivation, especially in the south once dominated by now defunct coal mining, voted 52.5 per cent to leave. The largest vote to remain was in Gibraltar (95.5 per cent) by virtue of its status (mysterious to most UK residents) as a 'British Overseas Territory'. Fourteen of these remnants of Empire survive, all islands which have not become independent, generally because they were uninhabited, or had voted, like Gibraltar, to remain under British jurisdiction and sovereignty, internally self-governing while the United Kingdom controls defence and foreign relations. They include the Falkland Islands and a cluster of tax havens, including Bermuda and the Cayman Islands. Unlike France, which took all its remaining colonies into the EU, the United Kingdom did not. Gibraltar is the only Overseas Territory in Europe. It chose control by the distant United Kingdom over the claims of nearby Spain, still under Franco's right-wing dictatorship until his death in 1975, and it voted to join the EU with the United Kingdom in 1973. The Channel Isles and the Isle of Man, with their subtly different status as Crown Dependencies, are not in the EU and did not vote in 2016.

Apart from such postcolonial oddities, the referendum result exposed divisions and inequalities within the United Kingdom, not always predictably. Overall, polls suggested, men and women divided equally between 'Remain' and 'Leave'. Prosperous southeast England (where incomes averaged 25 per cent above the poorest region, the West Midlands), apart from London, voted 51.8 per cent to leave, along with the deprived regions of the Midlands and north of England. Culturally diverse, relatively poor, districts of London had the second highest remain votes after Gibraltar: Lambeth, 78.6 per cent and Hackney 78.5 per cent. Since the future outside the EU is quite unclear, some prosperous people seem to have voted to leave out of optimism and/or narrow nationalism, the less prosperous as a desperate protest.

The vote exposed another division more evident in the early twenty-first than the early twentieth century, between age groups. Seventy-three per cent of voters aged 18–24 supported remaining in the EU, 62 per cent aged 25–34 and 52 per cent, 35–44. All older age groups voted in progressively higher proportions to leave, peaking at 60 per cent among voters aged 65 and over. The differences are hard to explain, although younger people were perhaps more cosmopolitan than older, and many more were graduates, who also mostly voted to remain, though turnout was lower among younger voters. The difference exposed age consciousness and age divisions which had emerged with distinctive youth cultures from the 1950s, followed from the 1990s by increasingly assertive, positive, age identity among older people, no longer willing to tolerate deeply embedded discrimination as more of them lived and were fit and active to later ages. This was another dimension of social and cultural change that affected how everyone could imagine their life course. Many younger people felt embittered because rising living, especially housing, costs, limited their opportunities and lifestyles compared with other young people from more privileged backgrounds, and with what were, mistakenly, assumed to have been the superior opportunities of most of the older, 'baby boomer' generation. In reality very many of this generation had left inferior secondary modern schools without qualifications to enter manual work and few had opportunities to attend universities. Another change over the century was improvement in educational opportunities and rising occupational and lifestyle expectations. Some 'baby boomers' had prospered, including from rising house prices, many others had not. Inequalities within all generations are as acute in the early twenty-first century as those between generations, but are often underestimated.

Older people were slow to protest against inequalities, which were not new but taken for granted in the early twentieth century. Earliest to protest were workers challenging insecurity and disadvantage from the nineteenth century. Then, women demanded equality, continuing into the twenty-first century because it was still necessary. These and other forms of inequality diminished following protest but did not disappear, indeed, the insecurity of many workers increased in the twenty-first century. Campaigns for race equality, and against it, also survived the century, increasingly active from the 1950s as immigration, cultural diversity and racism grew. Homosexuals protested quietly against the extreme discrimination that criminalized their practices until change began in the more liberal atmosphere of the 1960s. Greater social acceptability, and livelier activism, gradually followed, though homophobia never disappeared. Trans people and disabled people also gained somewhat greater recognition and equality through protest.

Such movements revealed divisions largely hidden in 1900 and, as they emerged, encouraged more complex imaginings of social identity. In the early twentieth century the dominant social identity and social and cultural division focused on social class, though national identity was always strong. Later in the century class identities shifted, largely due to economic change, particularly the decline of classic manual work, while other identities strengthened and intersected. To a black, disabled, middle-class woman all her identities could matter, among very many people conscious of multiple identities. Class divisions and consciousness of them survived, especially evident at times of political crisis. When in 2017 a disastrous fire in a twenty-four-storey housing block in Kensington, Grenfell Tower, killed many inhabitants due, it seems, to financial savings by the richest borough in London, indeed in the United Kingdom, on renovations to a block inhabited by predominantly low-income, immigrant-origin residents, it provoked a sustained, widespread outburst by and on behalf of the residents, uniting different cultures, expressed in the language of class, insisting that working-class people had been lethally neglected by the very rich. The episode starkly illustrated extreme inequality in London and dramatically supported contemporary sociological evidence that the unmistakeable economic divisions persisting in the United Kingdom were widely experienced as class divisions, though occupational definitions of class had changed over time and they intersected with race, gender, national and other divisions and identities.[1] The strong support given to victims of this and other crises also demonstrated that the commitment to communal, collective responsibility had not been displaced by neoliberal individualism, much as the latter had grown.

Socio-economic inequality continued through the century, though its dimensions shifted back and forth. At the beginning of the twentieth century, Booth and Rowntree

---

1 Savage, *Social Class in the Twenty-first Century*.

caused profound shock by revealing the extent of poverty in London and York, especially that it was greatest not among the idle and feckless, as traditionally supposed, but among full-time workers on low pay, especially in larger families. In the early twenty-first century the United Kingdom is vastly wealthier; most people live at a standard unimaginable in 1900. The absolute, miserable lack of food, adequate clothing and shelter visible in 1900 had dwindled, but it has not disappeared. In 2015, 69,140 families were officially homeless in England, many living in temporary shelter.[2] In 2010, 1,768 single people were found sleeping on the streets on one night (1,353 in London), 4,134 (3,170) in 2016, almost certainly underestimates, while others slept temporarily in shelters or hostels.[3] In 2017, at least 500,000 people each week need free food from burgeoning voluntary food banks, unimaginable a few decades earlier, including large numbers of children during school holidays when they no longer receive free school meals. The definition of poverty had changed, taking account of social change, but the reality had changed rather less. An official, internationally recognized, poverty measure now allowed for the fact that many people had sufficient incomes for survival, but life chances so limited compared with the average that they could reasonably be described as experiencing 'relative poverty'. By this measure, of incomes below 60 per cent of the median, about 16.5 per cent of the UK population (10 million people) were poor in 2009–10 compared with Rowntree's 15.46 per cent in the 'typical' city of York in 1899 by a measure appropriate for that time.[4] Those in poverty in 2009–10 included 19.7 per cent of all children, 17 per cent of working-age parents, including many full-time workers on low pay and single mothers, whose growing numbers from the 1970s were another sign of cultural change. The numbers in poverty continued to rise thereafter.[5]

This was the level of poverty in what was still, despite past forebodings, the fifth largest economy in the world, vastly lower than in many other countries especially in Africa. Inequality across the world was much greater than within the United Kingdom, and concern in wealthier countries to find remedies and give aid was more widespread than at the beginning of the century, though not universal. In the United Kingdom, wealth and incomes and wealth and income inequality grew over the century, though not consistently. The share of income held by the top 0.1 per cent of the UK population narrowed from about 11 per cent in 1914 to barely 1 per cent in 1979, when food banks

2 Available at: gov.uk/government/statistics/statutory-homelessness-in-England-october-to-december-2015.

3 Department of Communities and Local Government, *Rough Sleeping Statistics, Autumn 2016, England,* January 2017, available at: www.gov.uk/government/organizations/department-for-communities-and-local-government/about/statistics.

4 Gazeley, 'Income and Living Standards', pp. 166–71.

5 M. Brewer, J. Browne and R. Joyce, *Child and Working Age Poverty from 2010–2020* (London: Institute for Fiscal Studies, 2011).

were unheard of and unnecessary, then rose to almost 10 per cent by 2010. The top 1 per cent held over 40 per cent of total wealth in 1923, falling to around 20 per cent in 1980, rising again to 25 per cent in 2000, though the super-rich grew skilled at concealment as taxation increased from the low levels of 1900 and accurate estimates of their assets became difficult. Ethnic inequalities persisted. In 2017, median Bangladeshi household incomes were 35 per cent below those of white Britons, Pakistanis were 34 per cent below, black African households 22 per cent.[6]

The Second World War and the 1960s and 1970s were periods of sustained decline in overall inequality. In the 1960s and 1970s social mobility peaked, due more to the expansion of white-collar employment than to educational opportunities. Falling inequalities followed the redistributive policies of Labour governments, including taxation of high incomes.[7] But Labour could not sustain mass support for equality and redistribution against the international growth of neoliberal commitment to unfettered free enterprise and a minimal state, promoted vigorously by the Thatcher governments from 1979 to 1990. Their policies increased inequality, benefiting enough people to keep Conservatism in power, while abandoning others to unemployment and insecurity. They removed the welfare safety-net that had stopped the poorest falling too far behind growing affluence since the late 1940s, and facilitated a massive rise in top incomes, creating a steady expansion of inequality into the next century. When New Labour returned to power in 1997, it rescued many of the poorest without constraining the wealthiest and inequality between individuals and regions continued to grow, though more slowly.

In the twentieth century, UK politics underwent three major shifts: to New Liberalism from 1906, which, as the Labour Party emerged, increased state action to improve social conditions and economic performance. This was promoted further by the First World War and sustained, unevenly, through the interwar years, particularly to prevent popular revolt against high unemployment, though constrained by resistance from sections of the Conservative Party who always preferred a minimal state and a free (privately owned) economy. Another war, again requiring strong state action, increased popular support for sustaining it in peacetime, producing the first majority Labour government. This from 1945 to 1951 created a 'welfare state' and revived the economy, achieving full employment for the first time in peacetime.

But if UK society was briefly more united by the 'People's War', divisions revived after 1945 along with middle-class resentment at the high taxes and continued rationing which assisted Labour improving the economy and social conditions. The deep,

---

6 Adam Corlett, *Diverse Outcomes. Living Standards by Ethnicity* (London: Resolution Foundation, 2017).

7 A. B. Atkinson and S. Morelli, *Are We 'All In It Together'? The New Chartbook of Economic Inequality*, 2014, available at: www.chartbookofeconomicinequality.com/inequality-by-country/united-kingdom.

near-equal, social division was revealed in the 1951 election, which Labour narrowly lost while gaining a majority of votes from an exceptionally high turnout. It lost the opportunity to fully develop its economic and social strategies, unlike the more fortunate Swedish Social Democrats who were in power from 1932 to 1976, with time to create the most equal welfare state in Europe to the envy of radicals in Britain and elsewhere. Labour gained enough popular support for its universal welfare reforms, which especially benefited the middle classes, for its Conservative successors not to risk dismantling them, but they did not develop them, preferring, wherever possible, to encourage self-help and free enterprise.

This deep socio/political divide continued, indeed deepened, into the twenty-first century, contrary to notions of a postwar political 'consensus'. For this reason most post-1945 chapters of this book survey distinct periods of party government because the dominant Labour and Conservative parties, which alternated in power, differed sufficiently in their social and economic policies to have distinct impacts upon society and culture. Social and cultural change was not, of course, wholly dependent upon politics – profound changes in attitudes to the family and sexuality, for example, developed largely independently of, sometimes in opposition to, the aims of politicians. But the social structure shifted as manual work declined, especially in the 1980s, aspirations changed with growing 'affluence', and the middle class grew to outnumber the working class, creating particular challenges for Labour, traditionally the party of the working class, to develop and sustain majority support. In the 1960s and 1970s governments shifted between Labour seeking to direct economic modernization and extend state welfare and social equality and Conservatives who did not, until from 1979 Margaret Thatcher decisively abandoned compromise with state action, and with older Conservative 'one nation' values which had constrained her predecessors, promoting a return to the extreme inequalities of the earlier twentieth century, and before. She challenged sentiments of collective social responsibility, inherent in the idea of a 'welfare state', by asserting 'There is no such thing as society … people must look to themselves first'. Beveridge, in the 1940s, presciently feared that if the welfare services he proposed were not universal, better-off taxpayers would reject support for poorer people, returning to the nineteenth-century culture of blaming the 'undeserving poor' for their plight, as indeed many did as welfare benefits for the unemployed and sick were severely cut, while continuing to support universal services, especially the NHS which benefited everyone. They were encouraged to reject social responsibility by the government and by an increasingly right-wing, strident popular press – another significant change of the later twentieth century.

Margaret Thatcher went too far with the poll tax and lost office, but the spirit of neoliberalism lived on, including through the New Labour governments of 1997–2010, despite their reversing cuts to state welfare and increasing employment. It was fully

Further Reading

There are footnotes throughout to enable readers to follow up specific points in greater detail and to provide sources. This is intended as a guide to the most helpful wider reading.

General

An indispensable source of political facts for the twentieth century is David Butler and Gareth Butler *Twentieth-century Political Facts, 1900–2000* (London: Macmillan, 2000), updated to 2017 in Roger Mortimore and Andrew Blick (eds), *Butler's Political Facts* (London: Macmillan, 2018).

Similarly valuable for facts about social conditions, policies and social change, incorporated in expert surveys, is A. H. Halsey and Josephine Webb (eds), *Twentieth-century British Social Trends* (London: Macmillan, 2000).

The Oxford Dictionary of National Biography is invaluable for biographies of key figures, available online at: www.oxforddnb.com.

B. R. Mitchell and Phyllis Deane, *Abstract of British Historical Statistics* (Cambridge University Press, 1962), is valuable for a wide range of economic statistics to 1939 and demographic statistics to 1951.

B. R. Mitchell and H. D. Jones, *Second Abstract of British Historical Statistics* (Cambridge University Press, 1971), carries on to *c.* 1965.

For the later period, chapters in Roderick Floud, Jane Humphries and Paul Johnson (eds), *The Cambridge Economic History of Modern Britain, vol. 2: 1870 to the Present* (Cambridge University Press, 2014), are quite comprehensive, providing surveys and analysis as well as statistics up to the early twenty-first century.

For wide-ranging, authoritative surveys relevant to most chapters of this book, a valuable overview of twentieth-century British history is Peter Clarke, *Hope and Glory. Britain, 1900–2000*, 2nd edn (London: Penguin, 2004), and, for the early part of the century, John Davis, *A History of Britain, 1885–1939* (London: Macmillan 1999).

On international relations, 1899–1999:David Reynolds, *Britannia Overruled. British Policy and World Power in the Twentieth Century*, 2nd edn (London: Routledge, 2000).

On the British Empire: Bernard Porter, *The Lion's Share. A Short History of British Imperialism, 1850–2004*, 4th edn (Harlow: Pearson Longman, 2004), provides a helpful overview. For detailed studies: Judith M. Brown and William Roger Louis (eds), *The Oxford History of the British Empire, vol. IV: The Twentieth Century* (Oxford University Press, 1999).

On the nations of the United Kingdom: Kenneth O. Morgan, *Wales. Rebirth of a Nation, 1880–1980* (Oxford University Press, 1987); Kenneth O. Morgan, *Revolution to Devolution. Reflections on Welsh Democracy* (University of Wales Press, 2015); Christopher Harvie (historian and former Member of the Scottish Parliament), *Scotland and Nationalism. Scottish Society and Politics, 1707 to the Present*, 4th edn (London: Routledge, 2004); T. M. Devine, *The Scottish Nation, 1799–2007. A Modern History* (London: Penguin, 2012); Roy Foster, *Modern Ireland 1600–1972* (London: Penguin, repr. 1990); Paul Bew, *Ireland. The Politics of Enmity, 1789–2000* (Oxford University Press, 2009).

On the main political parties through the twentieth century: Andrew Thorpe, *A History of the British Labour Party* (London: Palgrave Macmillan: 1997, 4th edn, 2014). John Charmley, *A History of Conservative Politics since 1830*, 2nd edn (London: Palgrave, 2008). Anthony Seldon and Stuart Ball (eds), *Conservative Century. The Conservative Party since 1900* (Oxford University Press, 1994), essays on Conservatism up to the end of Thatcher's premiership.

On the history of trade unions and industrial relations, Alastair J. Reid, *United We Stand. A History of Britain's Trade Unions* (London: Allen Lane, 2004).

On sexual, including homosexual, cultures, social attitudes and political responses: Jeffrey Weeks, *Sex, Politics and Society. The Regulation of Sexuality since 1800*, 3rd edn (London: Longman, 2012); Lesley Hall, *Sex, Gender and Social Change in Britain since 1880* (London: Palgrave Macmillan, 2000, 2nd edn 2012). Andrew Holden, *Makers and Manners. Politics and Morality in Post-War Britain* (London: Politico's, 2004), provides a valuable survey for the post-1945 period. Deborah Cohen, *Family Secrets. Living with Shame from the Victorians to the Present Day* (Penguin Viking, 2013), is a readable account of changing attitudes to 'deviant' sexual behaviour. Claire Langhamer, *The English in Love. The Intimate Story of an Emotional Revolution* (Oxford University Press, 2013), challenges common assumptions about love and marriage in Britain between the First World War and the 1970s.

Pat Thane (ed.), *Unequal Britain. Equalities in Britain since 1945* (London: Continuum 2005), includes surveys of inequalities concerning age, race (including Gypsies and Travellers), gender, sexuality, religion, disability, campaigns to redress them and related legal and cultural changes from 1945 to the early twenty-first century.

On aspects of family law which run through the book Stephen Cretney, *Family Law in the Twentieth Century* (Oxford University Press, 2003).

Further Reading for Specific Chapters

1 United Kingdom? 1900–1914

An excellent overview combining social, economic and political history, including discussion of wealth and income distribution: Jose Harris, *Private Lives, Public Spirit. Britain 1870–1914* (London: Penguin, repr. 1994). Also Geoffrey Searle, *A New England? Peace and War, 1886–1918*, The New Oxford History of England (Oxford University Press, 2004).

On nationality and the rights of immigrants, Anne Dummett and Andrew Nicol, *Subjects, Citizens, Aliens and Others: Nationality and Immigration Law* (Chicago, IL: Northwestern University Press, 1990).

Perceptive studies of immigrants and their reception in United Kingdom: David Feldman, *Englishmen and Jews: Social Relations and Political Culture, 1840–1914* (New Haven, CT: Yale University Press, 1994); Laura Tabili, *Global Migrants, Local Culture. Natives and Newcomers in Provincial England, 1841–1939* (London: Palgrave Macmillan, 2011).

On key figures in the early Labour Party: David Marquand, *Ramsay MacDonald* (London: Jonathan Cape, 1977); Kenneth O. Morgan, *Keir Hardie: Radical and Socialist* (London: Faber & Faber, [1975] 2011).

Ian Gazeley, *Poverty in Britain, 1900–1965* (London: Palgrave, Macmillan, 2003), provides a clear survey of poverty studies and their findings relevant to several chapters.

On social policies in the emerging welfare state: Pat Thane, *Foundations of the Welfare State*, 2nd edn (London: Longmans, 1996); Pat Thane, *Old Age in English History. Past Experiences, Present Issues* (Oxford University Press, 2000); Jose Harris, *Unemployment and Politics, 1886–1914* (Oxford University Press, 1977); Jose Harris, *William Beveridge. A Biography*, 2nd edn (Oxford University Press, 1997); Deborah Dwork, *War is Good for Babies and Other Young Children. A History of the Infant and Child Welfare Movement in England, 1898–1918* (London: Routledge, 1987). On the Poor Law: M. E. Rose, *The Relief of Poverty, 1834–1914* (London: Macmillan, 1982); M. A. Crowther, *The Workhouse System 1834–1929* (London: Batsford, 1981).

On taxation: Martin Daunton, *Trusting Leviathan. The Politics of Taxation in Britain, 1799–1914* (Cambridge University Press, 2001).

Among the best studies of the women's movement are: Jill Liddington and Jill Norris, *One Hand Tied Behind Us. The Rise of the Women's Suffrage Movement* (London: Virago, 1978), especially on the roles of northern working-class women; Sandra Stanley Holton, *Feminism and Democracy. Women's Suffrage and Reform Politics in Britain, 1900–1918* (Cambridge University Press, 1986) on the NUWSS; June Purvis, *Emmeline Pankhurst a Biography* (London: Routledge, 2002) on the WSPU; June Purvis and Sandra Stanley Holton (eds), *Votes for Women* (London: Routledge, 2000).

2 First World War

On international politics leading up and during the war, see Reynolds, *Britannia Overruled*, above.

On national politics, Searle, *A New England?* above. John Turner (ed.), *Britain and the First World War* (London: Unwin Hyman, 1988; rev. edn London: Routledge, 2016), is a comprehensive collection of specialist essays.

J. M. Winter, *The Great War and the British People* (latest edn, London: Palgrave Macmillan, 2003), is an excellent study of the social impact of the war.

On the economic impact: Alan S. Milward, *The Economic Effects of the Two World Wars in Britain* (London: Macmillan, 1970, 2nd edn 1984).

Martin Daunton, *Just Taxes. The Politics of Taxation in Britain, 1914–79* (Cambridge University Press, 2002), carries forward his study of taxation.On the role of the Empire in the war: Robert Holland, 'The British Empire and the Great War', in Brown and Louis (eds), *Oxford History of the British Empire*, above.

On women's roles: Gail Braybon, *Women Workers in the First World War* (London: Routledge, 1989); Holton, *Feminism and Democracy*, above, discusses feminism during the war and women's enfranchisement.

3 Reconstruction? 1918–1922

On the United Kingdom and international politics after the war: David Reynolds, *The Long Shadow. The Great War and the Twentieth Century* (London: Simon & Schuster, 2013). Also Reynolds, *Britannia Overruled*, above; Susan Pedersen, *The Guardians. The League of Nations and the Crisis of Empire* (Oxford University Press, 2015); Helen McCarthy, *The British People and the League of Nations. Democracy, Citizenship and Internationalism c. 1918–45* (Manchester University Press, 2011).

Davis, *History of Britain*, above, provides a clear survey of domestic politics; on the conflict in Ireland and independence, Foster, *Modern Ireland*, above. On the emerging Indian independence movement, Judith M. Brown, 'India', in Brown and Louis (eds), *Oxford History of the British Empire*, above.

On social conditions and social reforms: Winter, *Great War*; Thane, *Foundations of the Welfare State*; Harris, *Beveridge*; Gazeley, *Poverty in Britain*; W. R. Garside, *British Unemployment, 1919–1939* (Cambridge University Press, 1990).

On the women's movement: Cheryl Law, *Suffrage and Power. The Women's Movement, 1918–28* (London: I. B. Tauris, 1997), provides a well-informed overview; Pat Thane, 'What Difference did the Vote Make?' in Amanda Vickery (ed.), *Women, Privilege and Power. British Politics, 1750 to the Present* (Stanford University Press, 2001), pp. 253–88, assesses enfranchised women's campaigns for legal equalities. Adrian Bingham, *Gender, Modernity and the Popular Press in Inter-War Britain* (Oxford University Press, 2004), explores the role of the press in shaping attitudes to gender; his *Family Newspapers. Sex, Private Life and the Popular Press, 1918–78* (Oxford University Press, 2009), examines the cultural role of the expanding press more broadly.

J. M. Winter, *Sites of Memory, Sites of Mourning* (Cambridge University Press, 1998), examines memorialization of the war

4 Democratic Britain? 1922–1931

On domestic politics: Davis, *History of Britain*; Clarke, *Hope and Glory*; Marquand, *Ramsay MacDonald*; Thorpe, *History of the British Labour Party*, above; Stuart Ball, *Portrait of a Party. The Conservative Party in Britain, 1918–45* (Oxford University Press, 2013).

Ross McKibbin, *Classes and Cultures. England 1918–51* (Oxford University Press, 1998), surveys in depth social class and cultural change between the wars.

On the General Strike: H. A. Clegg, *A History of British Trade Unions since 1889, vol. 2: 1911–1933* (Oxford University Press, 1985); Reid, *United We Stand*, above.

Morgan, *Wales*; Harvie, *Scotland and Nationalism*; Devine, *Scottish Nation*, are valuable on nationalism; and Gazeley, *Poverty in Britain*, on poverty and social research, as above.

On the women's movement: Law, *Suffrage and Power*; Thane, 'What Difference did the Vote Make?'; Caitriona Beaumont, *Housewives and Citizens. Domesticity and the Women's Movement in England, 1928–64* (Manchester University Press, 2013), and Bingham, *Gender, Modernity and the Popular Press*, both cover the whole interwar period, as does Tabili, *Global Migrants*.

5 The Thirties, 1931–1939

Philip Williamson, *National Crisis and National Government. British Politics, the Economy and Empire, 1926–1932* (Cambridge University Press, 2003); Philip Williamson *Stanley Baldwin. Conservative Leadership and National Values* (Cambridge University Press, 2007), contribute to understanding the politics of the period.

John Stevenson and Chris Cook, *The Slump. Britain in the Great Depression* (London: Routledge, 2009), is a useful inclusive survey. McKibbin, *Classes and Cultures*, above, continues his analysis of social class and social change.

On social policy: Anne Crowther, *British Social Policy, 1914–1939* (London: Macmillan, 1988); Thane, *Foundations of the Welfare State*; Garside, *British Unemployment*.

On sex, marriage and the declining birth rate: Hera Cook, *The Long Sexual Revolution. English Women, Sex and Contraception, 1800–1975* (Oxford University Press, 2004); S. Szreter and K. Fisher, *Sex Before the Sexual Revolution: Intimate Life in England, 1918–1963* (Cambridge University Press, 2010).

6 The People's War

R. A. C. Parker, *Chamberlain and Appeasement. British Policy and the Coming of the Second World War* (London: Palgrave, Macmillan, 1993), a fair assessment of a contentious topic. Keith Robbins, *Churchill* (London: Routledge, 2000), is an accessible, judicious study.

International relations and the war: Reynolds, *Britannia Overruled*, above; David Reynolds, *From World War to Cold War. Churchill, Roosevelt and the International History of the 1940s* (Oxford University Press, 2007); David Reynolds, *The American Occupation of Britain, 1942–45* (London: Phoenix, 2000).

War and the Empire: Keith Jeffrey, 'The Second World War', and Brown, 'India', in Brown and Louis (eds), *Oxford History of the British Empire*, above.

On the war in Britain: Angus Calder, *The People's War. Britain, 1938–1945* (London: Panther [1969] 1971; repr. London: Pimlico, 1996); Sonya O. Rose, *Which People's War? National Identity and Citizenship in Wartime Britain, 1938–1945* (Oxford University Press, 2003); Harris, *William Beveridge*, above; Paul Addison, *The Road to 1945. British Politics and the Second World War*, rev.

edn (London: Pimlico, 1994). Milward, *The Economic Effects of the Two World Wars on Britain*, above.

On women's wartime experience: Gail Braybon and Penny Summerfield, *Out of the Cage. Women's Experiences in Two World Wars* (London: Pandora, 1987); Penny Summerfield, *Reconstructing Women's Wartime Lives* (Manchester University Press, 1998), oral histories of women's experiences; Penny Summerfield, *Women Workers in the Second World War*, latest edn (London: Routledge, 2012); Beaumont, *Housewives and Citizens*, above.

On moral panics and realities about wartime sexuality: Pat Thane and Tanya Evans, *Sinners? Scroungers? Saints? Unmarried Motherhood in Twentieth Century England* (Oxford University Press, 2012).

David Edgerton, *Warfare State. Britain 1920–1970* (Cambridge University Press, 2006), examines the development of British science and technology in the war and after.

7 Facing the Future: Labour Britain, 1945–1951

Politics: K. O. Morgan, *Labour in Power, 1945–51* (Oxford University Press, 1985), gives a clear, balanced overview; S. Fielding, P. Thompson and N. Tiratsoo, *England Arise! The Labour Party and Popular Politics in 1940s Britain* (Manchester University Press, 1995), is a collection of well-informed essays; Thorpe, *History of the Labour Party*, above; Charmley, *History of Conservative Politics*, above; Tim Bale, *The Conservatives since 1945. The Drivers of Party Change* (Oxford University Press, 2012), is helpful for this and later chapters.

Political biographies: Kenneth Harris, *Attlee* (London: Weidenfeld & Nicolson, 1984); John Bew, *Citizen Clem. A Biography of Attlee* (London: riverrun, 2016), places Attlee in the context of twentieth-century history; Alan Bullock, *Ernest Bevin. Foreign Secretary, 1945–51* (Oxford University Press, 1985); John Campbell, *Nye Bevan. A Biography* (London: Hodder & Stoughton, 1987); Ben Pimlott, *Hugh Dalton: A Life* (London: Macmillan, 1985).

International relations: Reynolds, *Britannia Overruled*, above.

Empire and the beginnings of decolonization: Brown, 'India', William Roger Louis, 'The Dissolution of the British Empire', both in Brown and Louis (eds), *Oxford History of the British Empire*, above; Porter, *The Lion's Share*, above.David Kynaston, *Austerity Britain, 1945–51* (London: Bloomsbury, 2007), the first of a series of studies of Britain from 1945 to 1979 by Kynaston, brings to life, comprehensively, accurately and readably, the social, cultural, political and economic history of the period.

On social policy and the creation of the welfare state: Nicolas Timmins, *The Five Giants. A Biography of the Welfare State* (London: Fontana, 1996; rev. edn London: HarperCollins, 2001; new edition, William Collins, 2017), is an accessible survey. Best read alongside Jose Harris, *William Beveridge*, above, and Charles Webster, *The National Health Service: A Political History* (Oxford University Press, 2002).

On the economy: Alec Cairncross, *Years of Recovery. British Economic Policy, 1945–51* (London: Routledge, 1985, repr. 2013), is a well-informed survey by a member of the Treasury at the time.

Ina Zweiniger-Bargielowska, *Austerity Britain. Rationing, Controls and Consumption, 1939–55* (Oxford University Press, 2000), is a thorough study of a key feature of the period.

8 An Affluent Society? 1951–1964

Kevin Jeffreys, *Retreat from New Jerusalem. British Politics, 1951–64* (London: Macmillan, 1997), is a good overview.

David Kynaston, *Family Britain, 1951–7* (London: Bloomsbury, 2009); David Kynaston, *Modernity Britain, 1957–62* (London: Bloomsbury, 2014), continues his wide-ranging and readable survey.

Alec Cairncross, *The British Economy since 1945. Economic Policy and Performance, 1945–95*, 2nd edn (Oxford: Blackwell, 1995), carried forward his earlier well-informed study.

On decolonization: Porter, *The Lion's Share*, above; William Roger Louis, 'The Dissolution of the British Empire', and Shula Marks, 'Southern Africa', both in Brown and Louis (eds), *Oxford History of the British Empire*, above.

Reynolds, *Britannia Overruled*, is again helpful on international relations.

Linda McDowell, *Migrant Women's Voices. Talking about Life and Work in the UK since 1945* (London: Bloomsbury, 2016); Linda McDowell, *Working Lives. Gender, Migration and Employment in Britain, 1945–2007* (Oxford: Wiley Blackwell, 2013), both are insightful on immigration generally and, unusually, study female immigration.

Howard Glennerster, *British Social Policy since 1945*, 3rd edn (Oxford: Blackwell, 2007), is a reliable survey of postwar welfare relevant to this and later chapters, with Timmins, *The Five Giants*, above.

Bill Osgerby, *Youth in Britain since 1945* (Oxford: Blackwell, 1998), on emerging youth culture.

On sexual, including homosexual, cultures, social attitudes and political responses: Holden, *Makers and Manners*, above, is comprehensive; also Frank Mort, *Capital Affairs. London and the Making of the Permissive Society* (New Haven, CT: Yale University Press, 2010); see also Bingham, *Family Newspapers*, above.

Ben Pimlott, *Queen. Elizabeth II and the Monarchy* (London: HarperCollins, 2012), on the Coronation and the role of the monarchy.

9 A Permissive Society? 1964–1970

On politics: R. Coopey, S. Fielding and N. Tiratsoo (eds), *The Wilson Governments, 1964–70* (London: Pinter, 1993), is a thoughtful collection of essays; Ben Pimlott, *Harold Wilson* (London: HarperCollins, 1993).

The economy: Cairncross, *The British Economy since 1945*, above.

Reynolds, *Britannia Overruled*, above, on foreign affairs.

Edgerton, *Warfare State*, above, stresses the underestimated extent of scientific and technological research and development in the United Kingdom, especially for defence purposes. For detailed analysis of Labour's policies to extend it in manufacturing, see R. Coopey, 'Industrial Policy in the White Heat of the Technological Revolution', in Coopey et al. (eds), *The Wilson Governments*, above.

On the 'permissive' legislation, Holden, *Makers and Manners*, above.

Bew, *Ireland*, above; Paul Bew and G. Gillespie, *Northern Ireland. A Chronology of the Troubles, 1968–1999* (Dublin: Gill & Macmillan, 1999), provide background and detail concerning the Northern Ireland 'Troubles' for this and later chapters.

Nicolas Deakin, *Colour, Citizenship and British Society* (London: Panther, 1970), is a well-informed contemporary account of race relations.

10 The Seventies

Political biographies of key figures: John Campbell, *Edward Heath. A Biography* (London: Jonathan Cape, 1993); K. O. Morgan, *Callaghan. A Life* (Oxford University Press, 1998); Ben Pimlott, *Harold Wilson*, above.

Andy Beckett, *When the Lights Went Out. What Really Happened to Britain in the Seventies* (London: Faber & Faber, 2009), is a thought-provoking, readable survey of politics and culture based on wide-ranging sources, including interviews.

Reynolds, *Britannia Overruled*, again, on foreign affairs

On the economy: Cairncross, *The British Economy since 1954*; Richard Roberts, *When Britain Went Bust. The 1976 IMF Crisis* (London: OMFIF, 2016), is up to date and reliable on an important episode.

Daniel Stedman Jones, *Masters of the Universe. Hayek, Friedman and the Birth of Neoliberal Politics*, 2nd edn (Princeton University Press, 2012), is an excellent study of the emergence of neoliberalism.

On industrial relations, Reid, *United We Stand*, above. See Holden, *Makers and Manners*, and Bingham, *Family Newspapers*, on 'permissiveness' and social movements; Osgerby, *Youth in Britain since 1945* on youth culture, black and white.

Morgan, *Wales*; Devine, *Scottish Nation*; Harvie, *Scotland and Nationalism*, are all informative on the referenda and the background.

11 The Iron Lady, 1979–1990

Two helpful overviews are: Eric J. Evans, *Thatcher and Thatcherism*, 3rd edn (London: Routledge, 2013); Richard Vinen, *Thatcher's Britain. The Politics and Social Upheaval of the 1980s*, 2nd edn (London: Simon & Schuster, 2010).

David Kynaston, *The City of London, vol. 4: A Club No More, 1945–2000* (London: Chatto & Windus, 2001), is comprehensive and well informed about the Big Bang and other changes in the City.

On social policies and their impact: John Hills (ed.), *The State of Welfare. The Welfare State in Britain since 1974* (Oxford University Press, 1990), a collection of well-informed essays. As is Howard Glennerster and John Hills (eds), *The State of Welfare. The Economics of Social Spending*, 2nd edn (Oxford University Press, 1998).

On the economy: Cairncross, *The British Economy since 1945*; relevant chapters of Floud et al., *Cambridge Economic History of Modern Britain*.

Stedman Jones, *Masters of the Universe*, remains highly relevant on neoliberalism.

On changes to the family, marriage, cohabitation, attitudes to sexuality: Susan McCrae (ed.), *Changing Britain. Families and Households in the 1990s* (Oxford University Press, 1999), also discusses change before the 1990s; Kathleen Kiernan, Hilary Land and Jane Lewis, *Lone Motherhood in Twentieth-century Britain* (Oxford University Press, 1998); Thane and Evans, *Sinners? Scroungers? Saints?*; Holden, *Makers and Manners*, especially on gay campaigns and experiences including concerning AIDs.

Reid, *United We Stand*, on trade unionism.

12 Son of Thatcher? John Major, 1990–1997

Peter Dorey (ed.), *The Major Premiership. Politics and Policy under John Major, 1990–97* (London: Palgrave, 1990), expert essays on the central themes; Anthony Seldon, *Major. A Political Life* (London: Phoenix, 1998), a well-informed survey.

Chapters in Floud et al., *Cambridge Economic History of Modern Britain*, survey the economic context.

Holden, *Makers and Manners*, is good and readable, again, on continuing campaigns for liberalization, and opposition to them, and on the political scandals of the period.

On attitudes to and experiences of single mothers: Thane and Evans, *Sinners? Scroungers? Saints?*

Glennerster and Hills, *The State of Welfare*, again provides valuable essays on most aspects of social policy.

13 Things Can Only Get Better? New Labour, 1997–2010

Anthony Seldon (ed.), *Blair's Britain, 1997–2007* (Cambridge University Press, 2007), a collection of expert essays; Anthony Seldon, with Peter Snowdon, *Blair Unbound, 1997–2007* (London: Pocket Books 2009), is a clear overview; Anthony Seldon and Guy Lodge, *Brown at 10* (London:Biteback, 2011), on George Brown's premiership.

John Hills, Tom Sefton and Kitty Stewart (eds), *Towards a More Equal Society? Poverty, Inequality and Policy since 1997* (Bristol: Policy Press, 2009), a comprehensive collection of expert essays. Usefully supplemented by Polly Toynbee and David Walker, *The Verdict. Did Labour Change Britain?* (London: Granta, 2010), a good analysis especially of the positive features of New Labour's social policies and their impact.

On devolution and independence movements: Morgan, *Revolution to Devolution. Reflections on Welsh Democracy*; Devine, *Scottish Nation*; Harvie, *Scotland and Nationalism*.

Geoffrey Evans and James Tilley, *The Political Exclusion of the British Working Class* (Oxford University Press, 2017), explores the role of class in politics from the 1960s to the present, while Michael Savage, *Social Class in the Twenty-first Century. A Pelican Introduction* (London: Penguin, 2015), reveals the importance of class identities and perceptions in the early twenty-first century.

Index